AMERICAN POLITICAL WRITING DURING THE FOUNDING ERA

1760–1805

LIBERTY FUND
LIBRARY OF THE AMERICAN REPUBLIC

Works of Fisher Ames
W.B. Allen, ed.

Union and Liberty
John C. Calhoun

In Defense of the Constitution
George W. Carey

American Political Writing During the Founding Era: 1760-1805
Charles S. Hyneman and Donald S. Lutz, eds.

Political Sermons of the American Founding Era: 1730-1805
Ellis Sandoz, ed.

George Washington: A Collection
W.B. Allen, ed.

AMERICAN
Political Writing
during the
Founding Era

1760–1805

Volume I

CHARLES S. HYNEMAN

DONALD S. LUTZ

Liberty Fund

INDIANAPOLIS
1983

This book is published by Liberty Fund, Inc., a foundation established to encourage study of the ideal of a society of free and responsible individuals.

The cuneiform inscription that serves as our logo and as the design motif for our endpapers is the earliest-known written appearance of the word "freedom" (amagi), or "liberty." It is taken from a clay document written about 2300 B.C. in the Sumerian city-state of Lagash.

Library of Congress Cataloging-in-Publication Data
Main entry under title:

American political writing during the founding era,
    1760–1805.

    Includes bibliographies and index.
    1. United States—Politics and government—Colonial period, ca. 1600–1775—Sources. 2. United States—Politics and government—Revolution, 1775–1783—Sources. 3. United States—Politics and government—1783–1809—Sources. I. Hyneman, Charles S., 1900– . II. Lutz, Donald S., 1943– .
JK113.A716 1983   973.3.   82-24884
ISBN 0-86597-038-6 (set)
ISBN 0-86597-039-4 (v. 1)
ISBN 0-86597-040-8 (v. 2)
ISBN 0-86597-041-6 (pbk. : set)
ISBN 0-86597-042-4 (pbk. : v. 1)
ISBN 0-86597-043-2 (pbk. : v. 2)

94 93 92 91 90 C 6 5 4 3 2
01 00 99 98 97 P 7 6 5 4 3A

TABLE OF CONTENTS

Preface, xi

Acknowledgments, xvii

VOLUME I

[v]

CONTENTS

[vii]

CONTENTS

CONTENTS

CONTENTS

CONTENTS

PREFACE

The political writing of the founding era is tremendous in volume. The books, pamphlets, and letters to newspapers written in the last quarter of the eighteenth century that would repay careful reading by students and teachers of American political thought would fill a few dozen volumes the size of the two that this comment introduces. And even appraisals of amount, and worth take no account of the personal letters printed in the collected writings of men and women who achieved prominence and of the correspondence in manuscript preserved in archives and libraries. At least one collection of essays, *The Federalist,* has long been a classic of western literature. In the light of such an impressive literature, the appearance of a score, if not a half a hundred, brief essays hitherto unknown except to scholars ought to be high priority reading for political leaders and for those who make analysis and criticism of government a prime concern.

The second volume of this collection closes with the editors' choice of five-hundred-odd items thought to represent the best analytic and polemic writing put into print in the English colonies that converted into states during the forty-five years following 1760; if printed in the type-size of this collection, they would overflow at least fifteen, and possibly eighteen, volumes the size of these two. The editors are convinced that in compiling a selected list of political writings by Americans between 1760 and 1805, they have rejected an equal amount of wordage that met tests of relevance but seemed to be less satisfying on some test of merit.

It is quite clear that a vast amount of wordage went into print during this era and that only a modest proportion of that wordage is in places where readers can get to it today. With few exceptions, what the compilers of this collection examined and considered for inclusion is confined to items available in major university libraries, the less accessible holdings of a few rare book libraries, and the newspapers of that early period which have been preserved. Catalogs of American imprints cite many items which are not to be found in the libraries that were visited, and it must be supposed that much that is in print has not yet been transferred to microcards and microfilm.

Much more important than speculation about the enormous volume of writing from this era are questions about the tests applied and the judgment invoked by the editors in deciding which item to reprint, which to cite in a selected list of political writings by Americans between 1760 and 1805, and which to exclude in either case for lack of interest or merit or because of present accessibility. How the selections were made is best disclosed by giving a brief account of how the enterprise originated and how it was executed. The probe into the early writing was initiated by the senior editor, and the story will be told in fewest words if related by him in the first person.

Three years before my retirement from teaching I was asked to provide a seminar for selected freshmen. The initial specification was that attention would be restricted to "the founding of the American political system and getting it under way." I had a fair acquaintance with the books of readings to be found in the university library and I was aware that, whether compiled by a historian or political scientist, those that touched on early experience tended to feature government documents over analytic and argumentative writing. I was totally unprepared, however, for the dearth of expository and polemical essays defining and describing republican government, setting forth its ideals and goals, and offering advice on surest ways of making popular self-government operative in North America. The thought that went into the design of the state constitutions turned out to be a valley of unexplored terrain all but concealed from sight by towering preoccupation with the case for independence from Britain and the strategies for forming a federal union. Students could read in print John Adams' *Thoughts on Government* and *The Essex Result* if I would risk their tearing to shreds a volume of the Works of John Adams and the Handlins's *Popular Sources of Political Authority*. It turned out when my syllabus was completed that, save for what was in *The Federalist* or a less illustrious later publication, *A Second Federalist,* compiled by Hyneman and Carey, almost everything the students were asked to read was supplied to them in mimeographed copy.

So provoked, I swore a mighty oath that as soon as I could find time for it I would put into print a collection of the best writings of the founding era on the conception and establishment of republican government in America.

Proceeding beyond Indiana University and its Lilly Library I settled down in The Huntington Library. The first thing I learned on arrival in San Marino was that Huntington maintained an up-to-date file of all American imprints in its possession arranged by year of publication and alphabetically by author. This chronological file became my primary guide for identifying the books, pamphlets, and broadsides that I was to examine. For newspapers I would have to look elsewhere. The titles that I had noted from footnotes and bibliographies of other writers and from the aids provided by professional bibliographers would tip me off to items that the Huntington Library did not have. My first resort was to examine every printed piece in the Huntington Library that carried a title suggesting it might have something interesting to say. If the title page identified an election day sermon, or a sermon delivered before the local militia or at the funeral of a former public official, I read it; if it celebrated the ordination of a minister or promised to weigh the pros and cons of baptizing infants in cold weather, I did not read it. Discourses, dissertations, and orations on comets and pleas for kindness to dumb animals I did not look at. But if the title was simply *A Discourse; A Dissertation; An Oration; A Sermon*—in that case I had the piece before me and turned enough pages to make a decision to reproduce or to reject on the basis of judgment rather than presumption. David Daggett's Oration: *Sunbeams May Be Extracted from Cucumbers, But the Process Is Tedious* I would have sent for even if it had carried a subtitle: *A Repository of Advice Recommended for Morons Only.*

Assuming the Huntington chronological file was as complete as the Library's staff supposed it to be, the probability of overlooking anything relevant to the subjects I kept at the front of my mind is slight indeed. Far more critical are these two questions: (1) What did I conceive to be relevant to the founding experience? And (2) What considerations ought to control a decision that a piece of writing would repay reading by polished scholars and aspiring students in our own time? Lacking foreknowledge of what bounds a prospective publisher might set for range of subject matter, and unwilling to guess how many pages of print I might have to settle for, I resolved all doubts in favor of inclusion. My personal interest was fixed on the character of republican government and whatever might hinder or support it but I examined pamphlets that promised attention to the placement of America in the British empire, sentiments of localism and union, satisfaction and dissatisfaction with political institutions, policies, and practices; and on to disputes and strategies relating to independence, formation of new governments, union, and nationhood. Visions of the virtuous individual and the good society, exposition of ideals, analysis of conditions affecting the achievement of goals—anything commonly conceived to be theoretic or philosophic in constrast to the descriptive and narrational was prospective content for the compilation I had in mind.

Cut-off points for quality were settled in an arbitrary if not perfunctory manner. It seemed to me that when the time came to choose the items to be reprinted, I ought to have before me for comparative scrutiny three to five pieces for every one that would finally claim a place in the collection. And so, if I saw a chance that for one reason or another a piece might ultimately be selected for appearance in a collection of 2,000 pages, I placed an order for its reproduction by Xerox or photo-film. Subsequent experience justified the decision. The repository of political thought now before you contains forty pamphlets which were located in the Huntington Library or Library of Congress by the process just described; they were final choices from more than five times that number of pamphlets which were copied for comparative evaluation.

It is now time to introduce the other half of the team, Donald Lutz. When I was deep enough into the search to sense the size of the lion whose tail I had latched onto, apprehensions of geriatric origin prompted an appeal for help. Lutz assumed the responsibility of searching out the content of newspapers available on microcards or to be found in original print in the Library of Congress, pursuing essentially the policies for selection described above. Beyond this, he checked out the two volumes of Shipton and Mooney, *National Index of American Imprints* (NIAI) for items not located at the Huntington Library or the Library of Congress, and guided by the abbreviated titles supplied in NIAI read microcards for promising items that had so far been missed. Finally, titles found in the footnotes and bibliographic listings of prominent writers—Bernard Bailyn, Trevor Colburn, Jack Greene, Jack Pole, Gordon Wood, etc.—were brought under scrutiny if they had not already been encountered.

PREFACE

This account of procedure should assure readers that the items reprinted here were selected with care. In addition to the purposeful exclusion of personal correspondence, many important writings are missing here because they are already readily accessible in university and major college libraries. More regrettable are the items missed because considerations of time and resources set limits to this search.

Within the restrictions just noted, no piece was denied a place in this collection if the editors viewed it as among the best of the best. But for most of the candidates for inclusion there were rival contenders. In some instances where aptness and force of argument seemed near equal we made the choice that favored a wider distribution of authorship or extended the range of topics discussed. Also, we sacrificed two or three pieces of unusual length whose primary value was reinforcement of points made in other essays, and so made room for several short statements that addressed basic principles, assumptions, or beliefs widely held but rarely discussed in the public press. A good example is Essay 49, the 1788 piece by "An Elector" which lays out the case against electioneering, a practice commonly viewed with apprehension at the time.

With only a very few exceptions, every piece is reproduced in its entirety. The literature of the founding period included a number of essays running to a hundred pages or more, some that were of book length, and a few multi-volume histories. Such lengthy texts could not be reprinted in full, yet to exclude some of them altogether would not only have repressed some extremely good writing but have denied notable and influential authors a rightful claim to stand with their peers in public memory. We chose in those instances to reproduce selected portions of the lengthy work.

Care has been taken to preserve the original text, with certain exceptions. The letters "f" and "s" are scarcely distinguishable in much of the original print. To ease readability we have made the letter "f" look the way it ought to. Aside from this consistent alteration, such other changes as were made are mentioned in the notes introducing the items where the revisions occur. These exceptions are rare. In general we have retained the original grammar and spelling whether correct or not. If a word could not be deciphered from the original a bracketed space is inserted in its place. If there is more than one version of a text available and some later editor has inserted the supposed word, we have placed this word in brackets. When more

PREFACE

than one version of the text was available we chose the earliest version for reproduction. This usually meant choosing the newspaper version over the pamphlet form where both were available. In a few instances the newspaper version was so blurred that we felt more secure reproducing the later pamphlet form. If the newspaper version is being reprinted we have identified the title and date of the newspaper. If it is a pamphlet that is being reproduced, only the date and place of publication are noted. The original pagination of each essay is indicated by bracketed page numbers embedded in the text—the only other emendation made in the original.

Finally, the reader unfamiliar with the literature of the period should be warned that there is one important respect in which these essays are not representative of the massive outpouring of printed material during the era. Political writing then was often quite colorful as a result of being vituperative, self-serving, prone to name-calling, full of high-flown rhetoric, or just plain nasty. The anonymity of authors was as likely to be used so as to avoid action for libel as to avoid prosecution by authorities. The essays reproduced here retain a certain colorful quality, but the reasoned analysis they contain is exceptional, not necessarily typical.

CHARLES S. HYNEMAN
DONALD S. LUTZ

Charles S. Hyneman is Professor Emeritus of Political Science at Indiana University. He is a past President of the American Political Science Association and author of many books and articles, including Popular Government in America *and* The Supreme Court on Trial.

Donald S. Lutz, a former student of Professor Hyneman, is Associate Professor of Political Science at the University of Houston. He is book review editor of Publius, The Journal of Federalism, *and the author of* Popular Consent and Popular Control.

ACKNOWLEDGMENTS

This compilation of the best writing of the founding fathers received the warm support of William J. Baroody, Sr., from its inception until his death, and that relationship continued when William J. Baroody, Jr., succeeded his father as President of American Enterprise Institute for Public Policy Research. From the beginning AEI picked up the tab for travel and living costs incurred by either of the editors in visiting libraries and meeting occasionally in conference, and for reproduction of pamphlets and newspaper articles from which final selection of items was made. Howard R. Penniman was a skillful negotiator of the terms and conditions of this collaboration, later joined by Austin Ranney, who came to share with Penniman some of the responsibility for AEI's projects relating to American politics. To all these men everyone who finds these two volumes useful is indebted. For two years the Woodrow Wilson International Center for Scholars provided the senior editor a living and a room for work and accumulation of litter, all of which necessities for scholarship contributed substantially to this project. Finally, Richard Ware and the Earhart Foundation once more exhibited a disposition to come to the relief of the editors when commendable ambition of either of them rubbed too abrasively against limited resources.

There is no chance of saying too much in favor of the Huntington Library as a place to explore the holdings they have accumulated. For the literature of the founding period their collection is voluminous. Without miss, in several visits, the service staff was genial, courteous, diligent, and knowledgeable, words especially applicable to those we mainly did business with: Virginia J. Renner, Noelle Jackson, and Mary Wright in Readers' Services; Barbara Quinn of Photographic Reproduction; and Senior Research Scholar Ray A. Billington. Staff of the Rare Book Room of the Library of Congress were consistently courteous and concerned to meet every request. Anne C. Palumbo at the Woodrow Wilson Center and Raymond L. Faust at Indiana University helped in the early stages of the search for elusive material and have earned our appreciation.

ACKNOWLEDGMENTS

Jack P. Greene of the Johns Hopkins University, Ronald M. Peters of the University of Oklahoma, Gordon S. Wood of Brown University, and James M. Banner, Jr., Director of the American Association for the Advancement of the Humanities, each made suggestions for inclusion in this collection which were heeded. Although we appreciate their interest and efforts, their approval for what has finally appeared in these two volumes was neither sought nor given. Responsibility for what was finally included for publication rests solely with the editors.

Dean Charles F. Bonser, Professor Charles Moffatt, and Judy Deckard threw the doors of Indiana University wide open for the comfort and convenience of the senior member of the team. The junior member did much of the culling and assembly of the manuscript while on a leave granted by the Faculty Development Leave Committee of the University of Houston. Professor David Brady, Professor Richard Hofstetter, and Provost George Magner at the University of Houston each made administrative decisions which eased the work or made available resources for work on the manuscript. Final preparation of the manuscript by the junior editor was done as part of the program of Liberty Fund, Inc. Last but not least Sharon McCormick, Martha Knutson, Lucy Redding, and Denise Reddick ably assisted in the final manuscript preparation.

VOLUME I

[1]

ABRAHAM WILLIAMS 1727–1784

An Election Sermon

BOSTON, 1762

Independent and audacious enough while a student at Harvard to be known in some ministerial groups as "the Grand Heretick Williams," Abraham chose to pursue a course of caution and reasonableness after his selection for a Congregationalist pulpit in Sandwich, near Boston. "Doctrines and opinions that have been long and generally received," he proclaimed, "have at least such a presumption in their favor as to demand a fair and impartial examination." Examine them he did, but the limited amount we know about him affords no reason to suppose that his determination to be fair and impartial ever enticed the Reverend Williams to testify to something he did not believe or to find much to praise in the teachings of John Calvin. The sermon delivered before the Governor and General Court of Massachusetts at the age of thirty-five appears to mark his closest approach to an intrusion into political affairs. In this sermon he rather efficiently lays out almost all the basic assumptions underlying American political thinking on the eve of the Stamp Act—principles that would inform theoretical discourse during the Revolution until challenged by Federalist theory in the 1780s.

I Cor. XII. 25.

That there should be no Schism in the Body, but that the Members should have the same Care one for another.

The natural Body consists of various Members, connected and subservient one to the other, each serving some valuable purpose and the most perfect and happy State of the Body results from all the Members regularly performing their natural Offices; so collective Bodies, or Societies, are composed of various Individuals connected together, related and subservient to each other. Every Person has his proper Sphere, and is of Importance [2] to the whole; and the public Peace and Welfare is best secured and promoted, by every Member attending to the proper Business of his particular Station. This Resemblance between the natural Body and Societies, being so obvious, affords a striking Argument from *Analogy* from one to the other, and was improved, with good Effect, by the ancient Sages, to appease Commotions, perswade to Contentment, and a faithful Discharge of all relative Duties.

The Apostle Paul has applied this Argument to Christian Societies, and from hence strongly inforced *Unity, Peace* and *Harmony, Justice* and *Truth, Fidelity* and *Kindness.* By a beautiful Allusion to the natural Body, he reproves the improper Behaviour of the Corinthians, in their Use of the spiritual Gifts, bestowed for the Edification of the Church, as well as their own Benefit; and directs them to such an Improvement, as would render them all harmonious, and highly advantageous to themselves, to the Church, and to the World.

As the natural Body is *one*,—though it have many Members, yet they are all so adjusted and fitted one to the other, as never to interfere,—none is superfluous,—each contributes it's Part to the Perfection and Happiness of the Body:—So the Body of Christ is *one*,—all it's Members are related to one another—tho' their Gifts and Stations are different, [3] yet they are all consistent, and ought to be so used, as to promote the Peace and Edification of the Church; that there be no *Schism,* Discord or Division in the Body; but that all the Members consider their mutual Relations and Dependencies, and duly perform the Duties of their respective Stations, and thus express their *Care one for another.*—The Christian Church would be happy, if a due Regard was paid to the Apostle's Argument.

The same Reasoning is evidently applicable to civil Societies; and were their Members of all Ranks influenced thereby, it would greatly promote their Peace and Happiness.

In this View, I shall take the Liberty to improve my Text as an Introduction to some Observations, concerning the—Origin—Nature—and End of civil Societies and Government;—the various Orders and Ranks necessary to answer the Purposes of Society;—and

the Obligations the different Orders are under faithfully to discharge
the Duties of their Stations, to answer the general Ends of Government,
*that the Members have the same Care one for another, and there be no Schism
in the Body.*

As to the origin of civil Societies or Governments; the Author of
our Being, has given Man a Nature fitted for, and disposed to Society.
It was not good for Man at first to be *alone;* his Nature is social,
having [4] various Affections, Propensities and Passions, which respect
Society, and cannot be indulged without a social Intercourse: The
natural Principles of Benevolence, Compassion, Justice, and indeed
most of our natural Affections, powerfully incite to, and plainly
indicate, that Man was formed for Society. To a Man detached from
all Society, many essential Parts of his Frame are useless—are
troublesome: He is unable to supply himself with many Materials of
Happiness, which require the Assistance and Concurrence of others:
Most of the *Conveniencies* of Life require the *Concurrence* of *several.* If we
suppose a Man without exterior Assistance, able to procure what is
barely necessary to his *Being,*—at best it would be with Difficulty,—
but in Sickness and the Decline of Life, would be impossible: yet
allowing it possible, all the Elegancies and Comforts, of Life would
be wanting. If we examine the Materials of our temporal Happiness,
we shall find they chiefly result from Society: from hence proceed the
Pleasures,—of books,—Conversation,—Friends,—Relations, and all
the social and relative Virtues. So that the social Nature of Man, and
his natural Desire of Happiness, strongly urge him to Society as
eligible;—to which, if we add, the natural Principle of Self-Preservation, the Dangers Mens Lives and Properties are exposed to, when
considered as unconnected with others, Society will appear necessary.

[5] All Men being naturally equal, as descended from a common
Parent, enbued with like Faculties and Propensities, having originally
equal Rights and Properties, *the Earth being given to the Children of Men*
in general, without any *difference, distinction, natural Preheminence,* or
Dominion of one over another, yet Men not being equally industrious
and frugal, their Properties and Enjoyments would be unequal. This
would tempt the idle and imprudent to seize what they had not
laboured for; which must put the industrious and honest upon Methods
of Self-defence, and dispose them to unite in Societies for mutual
Security, against the Assaults of rapacious Men, as well as voracious
Animals. The social Affections of human Nature, and the Desire of

the many Conveniencies, not to be obtained or enjoyed, without the concurrence of others, probably, first induced Men to associate together: the *Envy, Ambition, Covetousness,* and *Sensuality,* so much prevailing in the *Depraved* Nature of Man, since the *Apostacy,* obliged them to enter into closer Connections, Combinations and Compacts, for mutual Protection and Assistance. Thus civil Societies and Governments would be formed which in this View appear to be natural. Some Societies being formed, interfering Interests, and Men's unruly *Lusts,* would cause *Wars.*—The same Principle of Self-Preservation, upon which they at first associated would induce several [6] of these small Societies to unite and form greater Bodies; from which Coalition, with the natural Increase of Mankind, all Civil Societies and governments, probably arose. In this Way; *Government comes from God,* and is his *Ordinance. The Kingdom is the Lords, and he is Governor among the Nations;* (Psal. 22.28.) *By him Kings reign, and Princes decree Justice, even all the Judges of the Earth,* (Prov. 8, 15, 16) *He has made the Earth, and given it to whom it seemeth meet to him;* (Dan. 2. 20.) *He changes Times and Seasons, and ruleth in the Kingdoms of Men,* (Dan. 4. 17.) *There is no Power but of God—The Powers that be, are ordained by God* etc. (Rom. 13. ch.) The Meaning is, That God is the *Supreme Governor* and *Disposer* of all Things.—His *alwise Providence* super-intends all Events, particularly those relating to Mankind: And Government is a divine Constitution, founded in the Nature and Relations of Things,— agreeable to the Will of God,—what the Circumstances of his Creatures require:—And when Men enter into civil Societies, and agree upon rational Forms of Government, they act right, conformable to the Will of God, by the Concurrence of whose Providence, Rulers are appointed. Thus the origin of Government if from God, tho' it be an *human Ordinance* or *Creature,* (1 Pet. 2, 13) and immediately proceeds from Men; as all other Blessings and Things advantageous to Mankind, proceed from him, tho' visibly effected by second Causes.

[7] The End and Design of civil Society and Government, from this View of it's Origin, must be to secure the Rights and Properties of it's Members, and promote their Welfare; or in the Apostle's words, *that Men may lead quiet and peaceable Lives in Godliness and Honesty,* (I Tim. 2.1.) i.e. that they may be secure in the Enjoyment of all their Rights and Properties righteously acquired, and their honest Industry quietly proffess it's proper Rewards, and they enjoy all the Conveniencies of a social Life, to which Uprightness entitles them; and that

Men may peaceably practice Godliness,—may worship & serve the Supreme Being, in the Way they believe most acceptable to him, provided they behave peaceably, and transgress not the Rules of Righteousness in their Behaviour towards others.

In all Governments, *Magistrates* are *God's Ministers,* designed *for Good to the People.* The End of their Institution, is to be Instruments of Divine Providence, to secure and promote the Happiness of Society; to *be Terrors to the doers of Evil,*—to prevent and punish Unrighteousness, and remedy the Evils occasioned thereby; and *to be a Praise,* a Security and Reward *to them that do well,* (Rom. 13. ch.) The End and Design of Government, is to secure Men from all Injustice, Violence and Rapine, that they may enjoy their Rights and Properties; all the Advantages of Society, and peaceably practice [8] Godliness:—that the Unjust and Rapacious may be restrained, the ill Effects of their Wickedness be prevented, the secular Welfare of all be secured and promoted.

The Nature of civil Society or Governments is a temporal worldly Constitution, formed upon worldly Motives, to answer valuable worldly Purposes. The Constitution, Laws and Sanctions of civil Society respect this World, and are therefore essentially distinct and different from the *Kingdom of Christ,* which is *not of this World.* (Joh. 18.36.) The Notion of a civil Society, includes a Number of Persons combined together for civil Purposes.

As in a *State of Nature prior to Govenment,* every Man has a Right to the Fruits of his own Labour, to defend it from others, to recover it when unjustly taken away, or an Equivalent, and to a Recompence for the Damage and Trouble caused by this unrighteous Seizure; and to take reasonable Precautions for Security against future Rapine; So when civil Societies are formed, the *Community is naturally possessed of all the civil Rights of its Members.* Men reasonably surrender to the Society the Right they before had of judging in their own Case, and of executing those righteous Judgments: It is therefore the Right, and is the Business of the Society, to defend it's Members, to secure [9] their Properties from foreign Invasions, and to preserve Order and Peace, and execute Justice between it's own Members. The Law of Nature (or, those Rules of Behaviour, which the Nature God has given Men, the Relations they bear to one another, and the Circumstances they are placed in, render fit and necessary to the Welfare of Mankind) is the *Law* and *Will* of the *God of Nature,* which all Men are obliged to obey. Almighty God, as Head of the System, and Supreme Governor of the Universe, will suitably animadvert upon every Violation. And every Man, prior to Government, is authorized by the universal King, so far as his Happiness is interrupted, his Property disturbed or injured, by any Violation of these immutable Laws of Equity, to vindicate his own Right, and inflict adequate Punishment on the Invader; not from a Spirit of Revenge,—or to cause Misery for it's own Sake;—but to inflict such Penalties, as will probably prevent future Injuries, and render Mens Right and Properties, as secure as they were before this dangerous Example of Injustice. In civil Society this Right is in general, transfer'd to the Body, or Government, who have a Right, and it is their Duty, to punish those Violations of the Laws of Nature, whereby the People's Properties are injured. Every Society has a Right to publish, and execute equitable Laws and Rules, for the civil Order, Peace and Welfare [10] of the People;—for ascertaining and securing their Rights and Properties, with suitable Penalties to the Transgressors: Which Laws are, or ever ought to be, only the Laws of Nature explained and applied, both Laws and Sanctions being founded in Reason and Equity. Things unreasonable, or absolutely indifferent (if such there be) ought not to be imposed by Law. A Law without a Penalty is of no Force; and to subject a Man to suffer, for *doing* or *forbearing* what in the Nature of things is *indifferent*, is wrong and unreasonable. Men's outward Behaviour only affects, or may injure the Properties and Enjoyments of others; this therefore is all the Society ought, 'tis indeed all it can command. Human Laws can't controul the Mind.—The Rights of Conscience, are unalienable; inseparable from our Nature;—they ought not—they cannot possibly be given up to Society. Therefore *Religion, as it consists* in *right Sentiments, Affections,* and *Behaviour* towards God,—as it is chiefly *internal* and *private,* can be regulated only by God himself:— Yet civil Societies have a Right, it is their Duty, to encourage and maintain social public Worship of the Deity, and Instructions in Righteousness; for without *social Virtues, Societies can't subsist;* and *these Vertues can't be expected, or depended on,* without a belief in, and regard to, the Supreme Being, and a future World: Consequently, a religious *Fear* and Regard to God, ought to be encouraged in every Society, [11] and with this View, publick social Worship and Instructions in social Virtues, maintained. This is consistent with an entire *Liberty of Conscience* as to *Forms* and *additional Principles, and Duties,* which however important with Respect to *another* World; it is possible Men may think and act *differently* about, and yet practice that Piety and Virtue, which the Nature and Ends of civil Society require.

Upon the whole, the general Idea of a civil Society or Government, is a Number of Persons united by Agreement, for mutual Defence and Convenience in this World, with a Power of Making and executing Laws, or of publishing those Laws of Nature, which respect Mens civil Rights and Properties, and inflicting reasonable Punishment upon Transgressors.

As to the various Orders and Ranks necessary to answer the Purposes of civil Society,—A Society without different Orders and Offices, like a Body without Eyes, Hands and other Members, would be uncapable of acting, either to secure its internal Order and Well-being, or defend itself from external Injuries. Whatever Power is in the Society, unless it be united, under one Direction, will be useless, or hurt instead of serving the Community. The natural Laws of Reason and Equity, Carelessness may over-look, or Prejudice and Vice misunderstand or pervert. In many Cases more Attention [12] and Care is required to discover them than most will allow: And the general Security and Happiness of Mankind depending on the Knowledge and Observation of these Rules of Equity,—Persons of Penetration, Attention and Uprightness, ought to be employed for this Purpose; and when thus discovered, the Reasonableness and Obligation of them, may immediately appear to Persons that of themselves would never have investigated them. The Transgression of these natural Laws of Equity must be punished, to compensate the Injured, and prevent future Offences: Unless proper Persons are appointed for this Purpose in Societies, it will probably be omitted, or unduly multiplied, and *Schism* and Confusion be in the Body. Therefore as a Society has a Right to defend it self, and regulate its own Members; to secure their Rights and Properties from the Violence of one another, as well as from foreign Enemies,—it is expedient, and even necessary, to have established Forms of civil Government;—Some to guide and direct their publick Affairs, and secure their Rights with Relation to other Societies, some to search into and publish the natural Laws of Equity, with proper Sanctions, which relate to Society in general, and to that Society in particular under it's peculiar Circumstances;—And some to execute these Laws, punish Evil-doers, adjust Differences, and determine Men's Rights and Properties according [13] to them. These

Considerations show the Necessity of different Orders, with various Subordinations, to answer the Ends of Society.—The Forms of Government are various, every Society having a Right to chuse that which appears best, and if upon Trial it prove inconvenient, to alter it for a better. Persons that manage the Affairs of Government, may be considered as distinct from the *Governed*, but in Reality, they are closely united in one Body,—have a common Interest—and are appointed for their *Benefit*.—All these *Orders* and *Ranks*, in the *Body Politic*, however distinct one from the other, having *different Provinces* and *Duties*, designed for *different Purposes*, and immediately answering *different Ends*, are in themselves *Harmonious*, and when *properly conducted*, *coincide* and *center in one grand End*,—the Security and Happiness of the whole, and of *every Member*.

This leads me to consider,

The Obligations of the different Orders and Ranks in civil Society, to attend to their respective Duties, that they may answer the important Ends of Society;—*that the Members have the Care one for another, and there be no Schism in the Body*.

As in the natural Body, the several Members have their distinct Offices, for which they are adapted, and when in their proper Order, they perform [14] their natural Functions, the Body is in it's most perfect State; so in the politic Body, when it's several Orders attend to their respective Duties, proper to their Rank; the Welfare of the whole Community, and of every Individual, is secured and promoted. In the natural Body, if the Eye would do the Office of the Ear, or the Ear of of the Eye; Discord and Confusion would ensue, and the usurped Office not be performed: the same holds proportionably in the civil Body. 'Tis the Concern of every Person, in every Station, to attend to his proper Duty, and mind his own Business, if he would be a good Member of Society and promote the public Weal. Schisms will rend the Body, if the Members forsake their proper Sphere, and act out of Character.

The great Ends of Society,—the secure Enjoyment of our Rights and Properties, can't ordinarily be obtained, unless the various Ranks and Offices, carefully perform their respective Duties—Whatever Precedency, some may claim above others, and whatever Subordinations in Rank, there may be, yet the *Dignity* and *Authority*, of *each*,—of *all*, is *derived* from the *whole Society*, for whose Good they are ordained by HIM, from whom originally all Power proceeds. As in a natural, so in the civil Body, all the Parts are harmonious; there is no superfluous Order, none whose real Interest is detached from, or inconsistent with the public Good. The Peace and [15] Prosperity of the Community depends upon the regular Discharge of the relative Duties incumbent on the various Members: To a faithful and honest Performance of which Duties, the Nature and Relations of Things indispensably oblige them.

If we consider some of the principal Orders in civil Society, it will be very evident that the public Security and Happiness greatly depends on their Fidelity to their Trusts, which proves their Obligation.

The Business of *Legislation* is very important, and the Capacity, Fidelity, and public Spirit, of those concerned in it, are closely connected with the public Welfare. They are to investigate and publish the Rules of Equity, as the Circumstances of Things require, and to annex such Sanctions as Reason directs, to secure the Rights and Properties of the Society, and of every Individual: The due Performance whereof requires a penetrating and calm Mind, and upright and benevolent Heart: Whereas Carelessness, selfish Passions, and private Interest, acting in this Sphere, will produce the greatest Disorders and Injuries.—Rules by which the Lives and Properties of Men are to be determined, ought to be demonstrably good and righteous.

As it is of the greatest Importance to Society, therefore those to whom this great Trust is committed, of making Laws, are from the Ends of Society, and the [16] Nature of the Office, under the strongest Obligations, rationally and faithfully to discharge the Duties of their exalted Station. A *Fault here* will produce the greatest *Schism*, and may *ruin* the Body; but *Wisdom* and *Uprightness* will most effectually secure and promote the public Good, the Order, Harmony, Peace and Prosperity of the whole, and engage the Members to a due Care of *one for another.*

The *Application* and *Execution* of *Laws* made for the *public Good*, is another *great Trust* in civil Society. The Peace and Welfare of the Community, the Security and Enjoyment of every Individual, much depend upon the *Skill* and *Uprightness* of those to whom it is committed. The End of their Institution, is to be a Terror to evil Doers, and a Praise to those that do well. Laws are published to be observed: The Fitness of them is the Reason and Ground of their Obligation:—The Security and Happiness of Society depend upon their Observation. As it is fit that Persons be appointed to execute these Laws, the Society must greatly suffer, and the Ends of it be frustrated, if they neglect their Business:—Communities may be ruined, if they pervert those Laws, design'd for general Security, to the Prejudice of it's Members— But a faithful Execution of these Rules of Equity, and a due Punishment of Transgressors, will secure the innocent and honest; and answer the great Purposes of civil Society. They [17] that execute equitable Laws, establish Peace and Righteousness, make others, and are themselves good Members of the Body, and express a proper Care for the other Members.

The Persons whose Business it is to secure the Society against foreign Enemies, are obliged to exert themselves with Courage, Prudence and Fidelity, to defend the Public, because the Security and Continuance of civil Societies, under God, greatly depends on their Wisdom, Virtue and Fortitude.

The public Good is promoted, and therefore the People in general who constitute the Body, are obliged in their private Stations and Occupations, to mind their own Business, with Industry, Frugality and Uprightness,—treating others, as they would reasonably desire to be treated by them—observing the equitable Laws of the Community, rendering Obedience, Honour and Tribute to those that are employed in the important Affairs of the Public, and are *God's Ministers to them for Good.*

I might proceed to other Orders of the Common-Wealth, and shew their Obligation to a proper Discharge of their relative Duties, from the Nature and Ends of civil Society, as well as from the plain Precepts of our holy Religion; but the Point seems to require no further Illustration. I shall therefore endeavour to offer some pertinent Reflections.

[18] And,

1. Let us gratefully acknowledge the Goodness of divine Providence, in favouring us with so wise and good a civil Government: A Constitution the best proportioned and adapted to answer the Ends of civil Society, to secure the Enjoyment of our private Properties, and every Satisfaction and Advantage of social Life. By a happy Mixture and Union of the several Forms of Government; most of the Inconveniencies of each are avoided, and the peculiar Advantages of each secured.—A Government, so prudently and righteously administered, that most of our Laws are just and reasonable; and in general, equitably executed. If we take a Survey of other Nations—their Forms of

ABRAHAM WILLIAMS 1727–1784

Government—the Menaces of their Rulers—the Poverty and Slavery of the common People,—we shall find abundant Reason for Gratitude to God, *who maketh us to differ: He hath not dealt so with other Nations— Praise ye the Lord.* The great Governor of the World, imperceptibly, yet effectually influences the Minds of Men, in Ways adapted to their rational Nature, to execute his own divine Schemes, with Relation to this World and the next, to our temporal and everlasting Interest. His wise and good Providence is to be acknowledged in all Revolutions of Government; and we ought sincerely to praise him, for placing us under a Government, so wise and good in its Constitution and Administration.

[19] 2. Let us humbly adore and praise the Supreme Lord of the Universe, that he has so remarkably interposed, for the Preservation of our civil Constitution, and that he gives us so reasonably Hopes of it's Continuance to the latest Generations. We still enjoy our Liberties and Properties, and the same free and good Government, notwith-standing the Attempts of domestic Traitors, arbitrary bigotted Tyrants, and foreign unrighteous Enemies, in former and later Times; *He that sitteth on High, to whom Victory belongs, has confounded the Devices of the Crafty and scattered* those that *delight in*, and prompted by the *Lusts* of Ambition and Covetousness, injuriously began *War.* Whatever new Enemies join the unrighteous Cause, yet from the Justice of our Cause, the Deliverances and Successes already afforded us by the Lord of Host, the almightly Judge, that will do Right, we have Reason to hope and trust, he will still favour us, and bring to nought the Combinations of unreasonable Men, and that the Cause of Truth and Right shall finally prevail.

3. Let all concerned in the Administration of Government, be excited to Unanimity and Fidelity in their respective Trusts; to prevent as much as possible any *Schism* in the *Body.* And by expressing their Care for the Members, promote public Harmony and Prosperity. However different their Ranks, Offices and Duties, they are all connected, and tend when properly [20] conducted, to one End. There is no Discord or interfering in the *Constitution*; and if there be among those that administer public Affairs, it indicates a *Defect* in *Capacity* or *Integrity*—it arises from unruly Lusts or turbulent Passions, and not from the Nature of their Offices. As in the Body, every Member ought to perform it's proper Office, and not that of others; so in Government, since there must be various Orders and Subordinations, every Person's

Concern is to *act his own Part well*, not envying or usurping what belongs to others. As the natural Body is more frequently destroyed by internal Disorders, than external Violence; so Factions, Divisions, and Parties in the State, (fomented by those whose Business it is to preserve Order and Peace,) are more dangerous, and have more frequently proved fatal than foreign Enemies. It is a great,—a scandalous Immorality,—a crying Sin against God,—an insufferable Injury to Men—to accept a Trust—an important Trust,—and *even* to *neglect* it,—much *more* to *abuse* it,—to improve it to different Purposes from what was intended, to Purposes inconsistent with, or subversive of the good Ends proposed by their Employers:—This is an Iniquity deserving the Indignation of Mankind, and may expect the Wrath and Curse of God in this and the future World.

In a wise civil Constitution, all the Orders and Offices, tend by different Ways to the same Point, [21] the public Good; the Way to this, in general, is *plain* and *easy*, to those that will *attend*, and are disposed to walk in it. Private Views, selfish Lusts, and haughty Passions, lead another Way; and when these are cloaked over with specious Pretences to public Good, we may naturally expect, Tergiversations, Intrigues, and all the artful Labyrinths of Machiavellian Politicks.

The Nature and End of Government is not so mysterious, but a Person of *common Sense,* with *tolerable Application,* may attain a competent Knowledge thereof, and with an *upright* Heart, *Honourably perform any Part* Providence may assign him. Therefore, since the Happiness of Society, so much depends upon the faithful Discharge of the Duties of the various Offices, and all who are well disposed, can so easily perform them; this shows the Obligation, and should be a powerful Motive to Fidelity, as they well answer it at the Tribunal of the great Judge, when he calls them to account for their Talents

4. This Subject may suggest suitable Reflections, to those at the Head of our political Body, by reminding them, of what I ought to suppose they already know,—the Nature and Importance of their Trust, and the Obligations they are under to Uprightness, Fidelity and Unanimity.

[22] We may esteem it a Happiness, that the Gentleman, who fills the most exalted Station in our Government, whose Consent is necessary to our Laws, is so well acquainted with the Laws of our Nation (in general so agreeable to the Law of Nature)—born and

educated in the Land of Liberty, under the best civil Government;—whose *Interest* it is—to whom it must be natural to *defend* and *secure* the *Rights and Liberties of British Subjects*:—who is particularly acquainted with the Importance of Understanding and Knowledge, Uprightness and Fidelity, in the executive Part of Government—Under whose Administration, therefore we may reasonably expect, no arbitrary, illegal Measures, no unreasonable, trifling, or unrighteous Laws—that all Officers of his Nomination and Appointment, will be Persons of known Capacity and Integrity, and in all Respects the fittest for their respective Posts;—that so far as his Influence extends, Piety and Virtue, Peace and Union, Order and Fidelity in every Trust, will generally prevail among all Ranks:—that his Administration, will be wise and equitable, and happy to himself and to us;—that when all secular Honours shall cease, He may receive a Crown of Glory, that fadeth not away.

In the political Body, by the *Voice of the People,* which in this Case is the *Voice of God,* the honourable his Majesty's Council, and House of [23] Representatives, are raised to the most important Trust,—They are as Eyes to the Body, to direct the Way: *If the Eye be single,* be sincere, *the Body is full of Light,* will be properly directed, but if the Eye be depraved, the Body is exposed to numberless Inconveniences and Disasters. Tis their Business to discover and publish the Rules of Equity, and inforce them with proper Sanctions. The *Law of Nature,* which is the *Constitution of the God of Nature,* is universally obliging,—it varies not with Men's Humours or Interest, but is immutable as the Relations of Things: Human Laws bind the Conscience only by their Conformity hereto.—Laws ought to be plain and intelligible, consistent with themselves,—with Reason—with Religion.—Government ought to be supported by it's Members, in exact Proportion to the Benefits they enjoy, and the Protection they receive from it. Those therefore who conduct these Affairs, we have Reason to expect will pay a due Regard to them.—As a public Spirit, a rational Desire and Endeavour to promote the publick Welfare, ought to animate all the Members of the Community; so it should be more conspicuously the Character of those intrusted with public Affairs. 'Tis their proper Business, to which they should continually attend, to preserve the public from Damage,—to promote social Virtue, Peace and Happiness: To this End they ought to encourage social Worship,—Instructions in Righteousness,—well regulated Schools [24] and Means of Education.—The civil and religious Liberties of the Community ought to be held inviolable, by all the Members, especially by those at the Head of Government.

As the Community has originally the Right to chuse it's Magistrates, so it seems prudent to retain so much of this Right, as is consistent with Order and Peace; which may require other Methods for continuing some Officers than was expedient, or practicable for their first Appointment.—There appears a peculiar Propriety in, many Advantages result from, a considerable Part of the Legislature being frequently chosen, from all Parts of the Society: Hereby it's true State is better known; and those arbitrary Principles and Practices too apt to prevail where Power is hereditary or long continued, are check'd, and their fatal Influence prevented.—As the apparent Danger of natural Death often restrains many Extravagances, and causes Men to practice many Duties, which are not regarded when this Danger is removed; so probably there may be something analogous to this in elective Offices. Therefore the annual Choice of two Branches of our Legislature, is *generally tho't* a valuable Priviledge, that properly improved greatly conduces to the publick Safety and Welfare.—By Virtue of this Privilege one Branch of the Legislature is this Day to be chosen, for the ensuing Year.—The honourable *Gentlemen,* intrusted with this important [25] Affair, as the *public Good* was the *End,* they ought, and professed to have in View, in *seeking* and *accepting* this Trust; with *Reason we expect,*—and *have good Right to expect,* that in the Choice of Councellors, the public Welfare will be their sole Aim:—that sinister Views will not be allowed in the *least Degree* to biass their Minds;—that partial Affections, natural Relations, private Piques, and Passions, will not be permitted in *any Measure* to influence their Choice.—The supreme Legislator of Mankind, has graciously condescended to describe the Character suited to this Trust—(Exod. 18. 21.) *Provide out of all the people, able men.* Persons of *Wisdom* and *Capacity* to *discern between Good and Evil; that fear God,* have a Sense of his Perfections, that reverance his Authority, fear his Displeasure, believe themselves accountable to him, and pay a due Regard to his Approbation: *Men of Truth,* Sincerity, Uprightness and Faithfulness in every Trust; hating *Covetousness,* not govern'd by private Interests, but truly regarding the public Good.—The Ruler in Israel, was obliged to *write a Copy of the Law, and read therein all the Days of his Life,* (Deut. 17. 18.). Proportionably, in other Governments, the Care of the Public should be committed only to such Persons as pay a suitable Regard to the Laws established by the great Governor of the World.—Societies of Christians act an imprudent Part, to trust their public [26] Affairs to those who pay no Regard to their holy Religion,—who disbelieve it,—whose Tempers and Lives are manifestly inconsistent with it. Christianity fairly proposed, has sufficient Evidence, to engage the assent of upright, impartial Minds; and there is reason to distrust the Capacity or Integrity of the Person that rejects it:—While he behaves well, and lives honestly, he ought peaceably to enjoy the Protection of Government; yet it is a Reflection upon Christians, if they are obliged to chuse Persons of this Character into places of great Trust. Once more, Rulers should be *Men known among their Tribes,* (Deut. 1. 13.) Persons whose good Characters are known and established, who will probably behave well in whatever Station they are placed. These Qualifications must be regarded by the Electors, as they will answer it to God, to the Community, or to their own Consciences.

Those who are called *Gods,*—who by divine Providence, are raised to important Stations; particularly, who conduct the weighty Affairs of this Day; ought to remember, that there is *One higher than They;*— *who judgeth among the Gods;* (and tho' they may not in legal Form be accountable to their Constituents, yet) to Him they are accountable for all their Talents. *He Fitteth upon the Circle of the Earth, and views all the Children of Men; and with Him is no respect of Persons:* He has said, that [27] the *Gods,* those raised to the highest Authority over their Fellows, *shall die like other Men;* and after *Death, is the Judgment;* when they that have been *faithful in little,* and rightly improved their temporal Trust, shall be crowned with everlasting Honours; but the unfaithful, however great and dignified —shall in vain try to hide themselves in Caves of the Earth *from the Face of him that sitteth on the Throne, and from the Wrath of the Lamb.—He that is wise will consider these Things.*

Finally, let us all of every Rank and Order, consider our selves as Members of the civil Body, who have our proper Sphere of Action; and whatever Part Providence has assign'd us, let us perform it well. It is not our Concern, who fills this or that Station provided the Duties of it are faithfully performed, and *there be no Schism in the Body.* If the public Good be promoted, we ought to be content, tho' we may imagine *our selves,* or some of our Friends, better qualified for some Posts, than the present Possessors. *Our* proper *Concern* is to be *faithful* to *our own Trusts,* not making a Schism in the Body, but expressing a real Care and good Will for the other Members: Thus we shall preserve Harmony, and promote general Happiness.

Government is a natural and a divine Ordinance, and when tolerably answering the good Ends of it, [28] ought quietly to be submitted to, for Conscience sake. Did we more cultivate Love to God, and to Mankind, this mutual Care for one another, would more prevail, and fewer Schisms be in the Body: Public Vertue would diffuse public Peace, Tranquility and Happiness. Did we consider and improve the Text in the view the Apostle used it as a Motive and Reason for Peace and Faithfulness as Members of the Body of Christ, it would render us *good Members of civil Society.* Let this then be our Endeavour, to be true and living Members of Christ's Body; in the Ways of his Appointment, let us seek an Union to and Interest in him, and pray that his Spirit, as a vital Principle may animate us, that we may be sincerely pious toward God, universally righteous toward Men, strictly sober with Regard to ourselves; then we shall be at Peace with God, and with one another. We shall be true Members of his Church here, peaceable and useful Members of the Body politic; and when all civil Societies shall be disbanded,—all secular Honours laid in the Dust,—and civil Distinctions be no more,—we shall be Members of the General Assembly and Church of the First-born in Heaven, where universal Love, Order and Virtue, shall reign with uninterrupted and everlasting Peace, Harmony and Felicity. *Amen.*

FINIS.

[2]

T. Q. AND J.

[*Untitled*]

BOSTON, 1763

Contrary to our broader understanding today, the doctrine of "separation of powers" was originally understood essentially as a prohibition on multiple office holding. These three letters nicely illustrate this and discuss the reasons for the prohibition as well as the possible limits to the prohibition. The lower chamber of the legislature under the Massachusetts Charter of 1691 was elected by the freemen of the colony, while the upper legislative chamber, the Council, was elected at a joint session of the lower house and last year's Council. The Council was a full partner in the lawmaking process and served also to advise and assist the governor. In 1763 the possibility arose of the lieutenant governor and one or more judges being elected councillors, and the three letters reproduced here discuss the propriety of such multiple office holding. All but a few paragraphs are reproduced, some modernization of spelling and punctuation occurs, and words in brackets have been added to ease the understanding of the text.

* * *

1. Letter by T.Q. in *The Boston Gazette and Country Journal* for April 18, 1763.

Political liberty, as it is defined by a great writer [Baron de Montesquieu] is "a tranquility of mind arising from the opinion each man has of his own safety." When this liberty is once destroyed it is to very little purpose to enquire how it was brought about; but before that is done, it is wisdom to guard against whatever has a tendency to it, in order to prevent it. Among many other things of this nature and tendency, the entrusting the same gentlemen with legislative and judiciary power, or the power of *making* laws and *judging* of them after they are made, has been warmly objected against in this paper. Such an objection we conceive may be made without breaking upon the rules of strict decency. It cannot however be a reflection upon a single gentleman because there are and have been for more than two years past, more instances than one of these different powers being invested in the same persons. Some of the arguments that have been used for this purpose, were taken from the admired writer of *The Spirit of the Laws* [Montesquieu]. We should be glad to see them fully answered, the doing of which before the ensuing elections would tend much more to the conciliating the minds of the good people of this province than many such pieces as we have seen published of late. Those who think the reasoning of the aforementioned writer conclusive are humbly of opinion that though "we are in the enjoyment of as great civil and religious liberties as any people under heaven," we are at present in a way "most effectually to destroy them." "There is no liberty," says this writer, "if the power of *judging* be not separated from the *legislative* power; for the judge being the maker of the law, the life and liberty of the subject would be exposed to arbitrary control." Consequently no subject how honest soever could be sure of his safety, and this uncertainty is inconsistent with political liberty.

It has also been questioned whether a Lieutenant-Governor can with any propriety be chosen a counsellor. If the question had been of a commander-in-chief no one perhaps would hesitate a moment to determine the impropriety of it, for this would be evidently to unite the legislative and executive powers in one person—a thing equally destructive to liberty as the other because "apprehensions may arise lest he should make tyrannical laws [in order] to execute them in a tyrannical manner." Let it then be considered that in the absence of a commander-in-chief, a Lieutenant Governor fills his place, becomes invested with his *executive* powers, and acts in his stead. This has been the case and may be again. Have we not seen the time when the province must have been deprived of one of its able counsellors, [because otherwise] the same gentleman must have acted as governor and councellor, or in the *executive* and *legislative* trusts at the same time. The expediency of the one or the congruity of the other with the constitution, we should be glad to have explained to us. Besides,

T . Q . AND J .

a gentleman must have an uncommon steadiness of mind to act with impartiality in the one of these truths while he is so nearly connected as to be continually almost within the sphere of the other. Many inconveniencies might be mentioned which ought by no means to be imputed to disaffection to, much less construed as an *injurious* reflection on, the present Lieutenant Governor who in our opinion fills up his different places with as much reputation as any other gentleman in the province could. At the same time it will give him no offence, however some others may take it, to suppose that some gentleman may be found in the province as well qualified, at least for a seat at the council board, as he. The objection we are now considering is not a new one; it was made many years ago. Lieutenant Governor Dummer was a gentleman of a most amiable character, and deserved as well from his country as perhaps any man ever did. Yet some of the best and most sensible men in the province, who had the highest personal regard for that excellent man, strenuously opposed his election for a counsellor upon the principles now urged. And their reasons were so prevalent in that day as at length to prevent his being chosen, after which he never had a seat at the board though he lived many years. What situation must the poor subjects be in under those republics where [the body of magistrates who execute the laws are able to utilize a whole body of powers] which they have given themselves in another capacity as legislators. They may plunder the state by their general determinations; and as they have likewise the judiciary power in their hands, every private citizen may be ruined by their particular decisions.

All men will allow that it is possible for one gentleman to be possessed of more power than is consistent with the safety of a community. The enquiry ought not to be how much he may possess with safety, but with prudence. The greater good any man hath done to his country, the more danger there is of his being entrusted with exorbitant power. Power, if we may be allowed the expression, naturally intoxicates the mind. It even alters men's dispositions and inclines them to be masters instead of benefactors of their country. It affords them opportunity and prompts them to the exercise of a sort of tyranny by art, as fatal as if exercised by the sword. The Greeks found out an expedient to prevent these mischiefs, that is to keep their good men from growing formidably great. The *Greeks* were a wise people, and all governments would do well in this particular to imitate their example. It may be said, there can be no danger at present. But let it be considered that history affords us instances of men who had done great good to their country, for which they were even adored; and afterwards, having too much power in their hands, they betrayed their country! As long therefore as human nature is the same, as long as there is the same ambition in the minds of men, exorbitant power will have the same operations, and the same causes will produce the same effects. Julius Caesar, says a fine writer, was employed by the commonwealth to conquer for it, and he succeeded in his commission. Thus he was a benefactor to his country. But as a reward he took the commonwealth for his pains. Julius Caesar was a man of art and address. He distinguished himself by a courtesy and politeness of behavior as well as by his learning and his arms. He knew very well how to ingratiate himself with his countrymen. He gained their confidence by flattery and intrigue. And as soon as he had got power enough he made himself their master and ruined their liberties. If we have not a Caesar among us, and we would be far from insinuating that we have, it is wisdom for us to take care not to introduce one. If Gentlemen are now armed with so much fortitude and possessed of so much moderation, wisdom, and public virtue as to be aware of and withstand those temptations by which men in power are always encountered, and which have bore down even good as well as great men in former times, it ought to be remembered that great men are not always wise and good. The time may come when an ill use may be made of the precedents which are now establishing; when others—by being invested with the same offices with which it is said Gentlemen may be *now* entrusted with safety—may have an inclination as well as power not barely to disturb the peace, but to destroy the liberties of a province. This, then, may be as happy a reason to put a stop to such precedents as we may ever expect to have, since the only reason assigned for lessening the powers of any gentlemen at present is: that they possess rather too much.

* * *

2. Letter by J. in *The Boston Evening Post* for May 23, 1763. Supplement.

I am led into these reflections, by the alarms which have, of late, been industriously sounded upon all occasions, in public assemblies and in more private meetings, of the imminent dangers which threaten the liberties and constitution of this province [resulting from the circum-

T. Q. AND J.

stance of] his Honour the Lieut. Governor and the honourable justices
of the Superior Court having a seat at the council board. . . .

I have before me the Boston Gazette of the 18th of April last,
wherein is a piece upon this subject, signed T.Q.—a piece which, if
compared with some other productions of the Gazette, may be called
a moderate piece. It is the first I remember to have read in the Gazette
in which sound argument and sober reasoning has not seemed to have
been industriously avoided; all the others, upon this subject, having
consisted wholly in bold assertions and personal reflections—and how
far the reasoning in this is conclusive shalt now be considered. . . .

The Gentleman has given us a definition of political liberty, from
the very justly celebrated author of *The Spirit of the Laws*: "The political
liberty of the subject," says this great writer, "is tranquility of mind,
arising from the opinion each person has of his safety." To which I
beg leave to add what the same inimitable author says, a little before,
upon this subject: "Political liberty does not consist in an unrestrained
freedom. In governments, that is in societies directed by laws, liberty
can consist only in the power of doing what we ought to will, and in
not being constrained to do what we ought not to will. We must
have continually present to our minds the difference between independence and liberty. Liberty is a right of doing whatever the laws
permit." The whole of this taken together forms, in my opinion, the
just idea of *political liberty* as it regards the constitution and as it has
relation to the subject—any other, than this complex idea of *political
liberty*, is partial and will lead to endless error.

The question then to be considered is, whether it be inconsistent
with, or dangerous to, our political liberty (taken in this complex
sense) to have the Lieut. Governor, or the Justices of the Superior
Court, members of His Majesty's Council for this Province? T.Q. has
taken the affirmative side of the question; and, if I rightly understand
him, his main argument is grounded upon this single maxim of the
same penetrating Montesquieu, viz: That, "in order to the preservation
of liberty, it is necessary that the three powers—the legislative,
executive, and judiciary—be not united, but be kept separate"—a
maxim which, T.Q. and I shall agree, is perfectly consonant to right
reason, sound policy, and common sense. But I believe we shall not
so readily agree upon the sense in which it is to be understood. In
my apprehension, Montesquieu no where says or would be understood
to mean that liberty is in danger, or is lost, whenever any *one member*

of that body which exerciseth the judiciary power is a *member* also of that body which exerciseth the legislative power—or in other words, when the same person is a *judge* and [at the same time] a *member* of one branch of the *legislative body*. [Montesquieu's] meaning, I conceive, is no more than this: that the body which exerciseth the legislative power should be composed of members, a *majority* (or if it be more agreeable to T.Q., a *large* majority) of whom should have no share in the exercise of the judiciary power. I confine myself at present to the legislative and judiciary powers; the executive will be considered presently.

The sense in which T.Q. does, and must, understand this maxim, if he would avail his argument of it, is this (viz.): "There is no liberty where the legislative and judiciary powers are not kept so entirely separate, that the same person is not a judge and [at the same time] a member of the legislative body." Now if my construction be right, it is evident, I think, that all arguments against the judge's being of His Majesty's Council, founded upon the foregoing maxim of Baron Montesquieu, are sophistical and inconclusive. To the easy task of proving my construction to be right, I proceed therefore in very few words.

Let it be observed then, and kept in mind, that the chapter of *The Spirit of the Laws* from which this maxim, and most of T.Q.'s other quotations, are taken is that wherein the Baron is professedly treating of the constitution of England. Let it also be observed that by the constitution of England the Lords Temporal, who sit in Parliament by reason of their dignities held by descent or creation, are not deprived of their seats or voices in Parliament by being made Chancellors or Judges of any other courts in the kingdom; but continue to sit and vote there notwithstanding such commissions. Let it be farther observed that from the first institution of the courts of Westminster-Hall to this day, it has been no uncommon thing for the Chancellors and Lord Chief Justices of the courts of Kings-Bench and Common Pleas to be created Peers of the Realm by patent or summons, *at* or *after* the time of their appointment to their respective offices. These are facts so well known to all who have the least acquaintance with the constitution of England that it would be needless to produce authorities in support of them. However, if any one doubts the truth of them, let him consult the 4th Institute and Rapin's, or any other good history of England. It may not be amiss here just to mention, as a recent instance of this last kind, that the present Lord Chief Justice of the Kings-Bench in England was created a Peer, Anno 1756, by the title of Lord Mansfield of Mansfield; and has now a *seat* and *voice* in the House of Lords, and is, to all intents and purposes as completely a member of that branch of the legislative body, as any one member of that august house. Once more, let it be observed that the House of Lords is the supreme court of judicature in the nation, to whom appeals lie from decrees given in chancery, and before whom writs of error are brought upon judgments given in the court of King's-Bench. Now can it be supposed that the great Montesquieu, who had but just before observed that the English nation "has for the direct end of its constitution political liberty," and was now professedly describing the constitution of England, should yet lay it down as a maxim that: "there is no liberty where the legislative and judiciary powers are not *entirely* separated," in T.Q.'s sense? Or can it be supposed that the Baron was unacquainted with facts so notorious and so essentially incompatible with his grand maxim (as T. understands it) as the foregoing are? Or will it be said that the legislative and judiciary powers are not separate, and consequently that there is no political liberty in England? No man, I think, who has read *The Spirit of the Laws* will suppose the former; and no Englishman in his senses, I am sure, will say the latter. Therefore I conclude, and I think very fairly, that T.Q. has essentially misapprehended the Baron's meaning— i.e., that Judges may be members of the legislative body in perfect consistency with the constitution of England and with Montesquieu's maxim. I will only add here that if my argument is conclusive with respect to England, which I presume cannot be denied, it is so *a fortiori* in regard to this Province because our Board of Councellors is not the Supreme Court of Judicature here, as the House of Lords is there.

I come now to consider "whether a Lieut. Governor can with any propriety be chosen a Councellor." I must here first premise that to assert: "There can be no liberty where he who exerciseth the executive power, has any share in the legislative"—is such a mistake as I cannot suppose the great Montesquieu to be guilty of; because it is well known, that by the constitution of England, of which (it must be remembered) he is speaking, the King, who has the sole exercise of the executive power and is therefore by our English lawyers called "the universal judge of property"—"the fountain of justice"—"the supreme magistrate of the kingdom, intrusted with the whole executive power of the law," and the like,—has also an essential share in the exercise of the legislative power; namely, the power of rejecting. Therefore when this great writer says: "the executive and legislative powers ought not to be *united*," he must be understood to mean, as he often expresseth himself, "the *whole* executive, and the *whole* legislative powers ought not to be united" as they are in the republics of Italy—or in other words, a *majority* of the *body* which exerciseth the legislative power should have no share in the executive. Understood in this sense, and in no other, the Baron speaks like himself—a man of superior genius, and extensive knowledge. And so long as the legislative and executive powers are kept thus separate, they are an effectual check upon each other; which is the reason assigned by this great writer, why they ought not to be united.

I readily agree with T.Q. that "there would be an impropriety in choosing the commander-in-chief a Councellor," though not for the reason which he assigns, namely, that "this would be evidently to unite the legislative and executive powers in one person." For I deny that the *whole* or the *major* part of the legislative power would in this case be in the commander-in-chief. And consequently [I deny] that the two powers would in reality, or could with any propriety of language, be said to be united in him any more than they are now because he exerciseth the executive power and hath also the power of rejecting or negativing in the legislative—which, as has been shown, is precisely conformable to the constitution of England.

The same answer may be given to this objection applied to the Lieut. Governor upon the supposition of his becoming Commander-in-Chief by the absence of the Governor. And so long as his Excellency is resident in the province, I can conceive no objection to the Lieut. Governor's being of the Council, unless a bare title without power, disqualifies him—which, as it has not been, so I presume it will not be pretended.

But it is objected that "in case of the absence of the commander-in-chief, the Lieut. Governor fills his place, and then the province must either lose one of its Councellors or else the same Gentleman must act as Governor and Councellor." To this I answer: (1) This is a contingent event which may or may not happen—and to deprive

T. Q. AND J.

ourselves of an able councellor forever for fear we should some time or other be deprived of him for a short space of time, would be as if we should starve ourselves this year for fear we should not have an abundance twenty years hence. (2) Considering Councellors as councellors or advisers to the commander-in-chief, the objection is grounded on a wrong supposition for, in the case put, we should not in fact be deprived of one of our able councellors unless it be said that because he is commander-in-chief, therefore he must not consult his own understanding. (3) Considering them as legislators, the most that can be said is that in this case we should have but twenty-seven of twenty-eight members in one branch of the legislative body, a case which often happens without any apprehensions of danger to our political liberty. Whether this mere possibility be a sufficient reason for our depriving ourselves of an able counsellor, I leave to all reasonable men to judge. The objection, as it supposeth an unconstitutional union of the legislative and executive powers, is answered by adding to what is said above: that if the chief command should devolve upon the Lieut. Governor, in such case his Honour would not act as a Councellor, considering them as legislators.

Thus I have endeavored, in compliance with T.Q.'s desire, "to conciliate the minds of the good people of this province" by showing that his Honour the Lieut. Governor, and the honourable justices of the Superior Court, may be of His Majesty's Council in perfect harmony with the great Montesquieu's eternal maxim of truth: "there is no liberty where the legislative, executive and judiciary powers are not kept separate."

Some other positions in T.Q.'s piece should be considered; but that I perceive this would carry me to too great a length. I shall only add that the pretended danger of arbitrary power must appear a mere phantom, a bugbear, to any one who only considers that we are a dependent state, under the control and protection of Great-Britain. If we could be weak enough to suspect his Honour the Lieut. Governor of having the wicked design to enslave his country (though I can't make the supposition, even for the sake of the argument, without pausing to ask his Honour's pardon) yet we must be weak indeed to *fear* him, unless we can also suppose the King, Lords, and Commons of Great-Britain to be in combination with him.

Upon the whole, I submit it to all sober men to examine and judge for themselves whether the late indecent clamor and uproar about liberty and the constitution has not had it's true source in something essentially different from or diametrically opposite to a sincere concern for the public good.

* * *

3. Letter by T.Q. in *The Boston Gazette and Country Journal* for June 6, 1763.

I think myself particularly obliged to the author of the piece in the last Monday's *Evening Post* that he hath not treated me in such high terms of reproach with which several performances in that paper, distinguished by the same capital letter J, have so much abounded. On the contrary, he condescends to say that I am, comparatively, a moderate writer, and thinks it is the only *Gazette* he has read in which sound arguments and sober reasoning has not seemed to have been industriously avoided. . . .

Political liberty is a tranquility of mind arising from the opinion each person has of his own safety. This is an independent proposition in *The Spirit of the Laws* and needs not any thing that goes before or follows after it to give us a just idea of what the author would define by it, it being itself a full definition of political liberty. And I desire Mr. J would observe it is the only one contained in the chapter on the constitution of England. It needs no great stretch of understanding to conclude that whatsoever has a tendency to destroy the opinion which each man has of his own safety, and the tranquility of mind arising therefrom, is inconsistent with political liberty. The aforesaid author tells us that when the judge is the maker of the law, the life and liberty of the subject is exposed to arbitrary control. Now this arbitrary control destroys the subject's opinion of his own safety and the tranquility of mind arising therefrom; and is consequently inconsistent with political liberty according to the above definition of it. I should then have concluded, had not the wisdom of the Government determined it otherwise, that it is inconsistent with our political liberty for the justices of the Superior Court to be members of His Majesty's Council, considered as legislators, [or to be members] of the House of Representatives in the province, which is the question in dispute. I have nothing against Mr. J's taking into his idea of liberty what the author of *The Spirit of the Laws* says of it in another distinct chapter: that it does not consist in an unrestrained freedom—that it

T . Q . AND J .

can consist only in a power of doing what we ought to will—that we must have continually present to our mind the difference between independence and liberty—and that it is a right of doing what the laws permit. But I cannot see why he need to insist upon it, for it does not appear to me to be necessary [in order] to form an adequate idea of liberty.

"In order to the preservation of liberty, it is necessary that the three powers—the legislative, executive, and judiciary—be not united, but be kept separate." This Mr. J says is perfectly consonant to right reason, sound policy, and common sense. And yet he very soon after tells us that it is not to be understood that liberty is in danger when [an executive officer is] *one member* of that body which exerciseth the legislative power. But I should think, and I believe it is obvious to any man, that according to the aforesaid maxim, liberty must be in danger in proportion to the degree of influence which a single member of one body may have in the other. Mr. J's argument admits of this— though he does not seem to be aware of it or intend it—when he allows that it is necessary that a large majority of the members of the legislative body should have *no share* in the judiciary power. Pray from when should this necessity arise but from its being incompatible and dangerous to liberty? And if for this reason it is necessary that a large majority of the legislative should have no share in the judiciary powers, for the same reason it is necessary that not a single man who has a share in the judiciary power should be a member of the legislative body. If a single member of the one body may also be a member of the other, why may not more? Why not five as is contended for? I must own Mr. J seems to have *one* more particularly in his view. The more addition is made of the members of the one body to the other, the nearer it approaches to a large majority, and so in Mr. J's own opinion to such a degree of influence as is destructive to liberty. If every addition of one man tends to the destruction of liberty, it is dangerous to liberty. If every such addition weakens the subject's opinion of his safety and the tranquility of mind arising therefrom, it is a breach upon liberty. Mr. J may easily see that it is the weight of influence we are all along speaking of as alarming. And he himself is aware, when he speaks of a large majority, of the certain destruction of liberty if the weight of influence in the legislative should be in those members of it who are also members of the judiciary body. It is then worth his consideration how much greater the influence of a judge may be supposed to be than that of any other gentleman is presumed to be. [A judge] generally is of the first character for natural endowments and acquired abilities. The authority involved upon him is great. His dependents, whether he chuses it or not, are many— that is, there are many who are constantly expectant upon his *decisions*. Hence his connections must be very strong and his influence very powerful, too powerful perhaps for one man, even to a degree of danger to common liberty.

Chancellors and other judges, Mr. J says, have their seats and voices in parliament; it is no uncommon thing for them to be created peers of the realm, at or after the time of their appointment to their respective offices. Be it so. The author of *The Spirit of the Laws* no where that I know of says that it is not inconsistent with liberty that it should be so or that it is reconcileable with his maxim—which Mr. J allows is perfectly consonant with right reason, sound policy, and good sense. But it is not so very common a thing, as he would insinuate, for Lord Chief Justices to be created peers of the realm. It is however confessed there are such instances, and the present Lord Chief Justice of the King's Bench is one. A Peer of the Realm and a Councellor of this province are created by two very distinct powers. The one is the Sovereign's act; the other the election of the people. A Sovereign may exercise his legal prerogative as he pleases. But will it follow that because the Sovereign is pleased to create a Lord Chief Justice a Peer of the Realm, it is expedient for the people of this province to make a judge a Councellor? This is the force of Mr. J's reasoning here. Or will it necessarily follow that it is perfectly consistent with liberty, according to his own complex idea of it? Or lastly, will it follow that it is agreeable to *Montesquieu's* sentiments of liberty, after he has expresly said: there can be no liberty if the power of judging be not separated from the legislative power? "The nation has for the direct end of its constitution, political liberty"; this is *Montesquieu's* opinion. Yet it may so happen that a practice may sometimes take place, which may interfere with and obstruct the direct end of the constitution. Mr. J's inference that it is constitutional because it has sometimes been a fact, I take to be inconclusive. His argument, therefore, *a fortiori;* with regard to this province, upon which he builds so much, must fall to the ground.

This writer [J] says that to assert that "there can be no liberty where he who exerciseth the executive power has any share in the legislation" is a mistake because [says J] the King, who has the sole exercise of the executive power, has also an essential share in the exercise of the legislative power, normally that of rejecting. By the power of rejecting, the author of *The Spirit of the Laws* tells us, he means not the right of ordaining by their own authority or of mending what has been ordained by others, for this is the power of resolving. If a prince says he should have a share in legislation by the power of resolving, liberty would be at an end. Mr. J then should take away from a Councellor his *essential* power which he partakes in—of ordaining and amending what has been ordained by others—or his argument fails. [It is not enough for J to say] "as the executive power has no other part in legislation than the power of rejecting, it can have no share in the public debates." A commander-in-chief, if he is a Councellor, has *another* part in legislation besides the power of rejection and a share in the public debates. The whole share which the executive power has in legislation is barely legislative; it may or may not annul the resolutions of the legislative body as it pleases. But a Councellor has a positive share in those resolutions.

The legislative body is composed of two parts. Each one checks the other by the mutual privilege of rejection. They are both checked by the executive power, as the executive by the legislative. There is and should be a sufficient weight in each of these powers to keep an *even balance*. . . .

If the commander-in-chief should be a Councellor at the same time, the two powers being invested in the same person (though with respect to the legislative, in part only), unavoidably, in certain degree, there would fall in the scale of executive power too much weight of influence. In other words the person possessed of the whole executive power would have an undue weight in the legislative body, and the balance would be *disadjusted*. Mr. J seems to allow that this should be an *unconstitutional* union, and says that in such a case a Lieutenant-Governor would not act as a Councellor, considering them as legislators. But can he assure the public of this? Power is enchanting. All men are fond of it. There are few men, if any, who would refuse at least as much as is offered to them. And if a Lieutenant Governor, in the case supposed, should choose to think that it was not an unconstitutional choice, and to act in both capacities, who could hinder him? Mr. J says: "It is a *contingent* event, and it may not happen." But it has happened, and how soon it may happen again can only be conjectured.

BOSTON, 1763

"To deprive ourselves," says he, "of an able Councellor forever for fear we should some time or other be deprived of him for a short space of time, would be as if we should starve ourselves this year for fear we should not have an abundance twenty years hence." Whether, if his honor the Lieutenant Governor should be left out of the Council, some other gentleman might not possibly be found qualified to fill his seat or whether we should be totally deprived of an able Councellor forever without any hopes of ever repairing the loss, is a question quite new. I choose for prudent reasons to waive it, at least till I hear further from my friend Mr. J.

[3]

U.

[*Untitled*]

BOSTON, 1763

The author of this letter to the editor, writing only under the name of U., is apparently responding to an altercation in the Massachusetts legislature. Despite the obvious depth of feeling, the author places the incident in a broad theoretical context that reveals much about the grounds of political discourse at the time. The essay appeared in the *Boston Gazette* on August 1, 1763.

TO THE PRINTERS.

Man is distinguished from other Animals, his Fellow-Inhabitants of this Planet, by a Capacity of acquiring Knowledge and Civility more than by any Excellency, corporeal, or mental, with which mere Nature has furnished his Species.—His erect Figure, and sublime Countenance, would give him but little Elevation above the Bear, or the Tyger: nay, notwithstanding those Advantages, he would hold an inferior Rank in the Scale of Being, and would have a worse Prospect of Happiness than those Creatures; were it not for the Capacity of uniting with others and availing himself of Arts and Inventions in social Life. As he comes originally from the Hands of his Creator, Self Love, or Self-Preservation, is the only Spring that moves within him.—He might crop the Leaves, or Berries, with which his Creator had surrounded him to satisfy his Hunger—He might sip at the Lake or Rivulet to slake his Thirst—He might screen himself behind a Rock or Mountain from the bleakest of the Winds—or he might fly from the Jaws of voracious Beasts to preserve himself from immediate Destruction.—But would such an Existence be worth preserving?

Would not the first Precipice, or the first Beast of Prey, that could put a Period to the Wants, the Frights and Horrors, of such a wretched Being, be a friendly Object, and a real Blessing?

When we take one Remove from this forlorn Condition, and find the Species propagated, the Banks of Clams and Oysters discovered, the Bow and Arrow invented, and the Skins of Beasts or the Bark of Trees employed for Covering: altho' the human Creature has a little less Anxiety and Misery than before; yet each Individual is independent of all others: There is no Intercourse of Friendship: no Communication of Food or Cloathing: no Conversation or Connection, unless the Conjunction of Sexes, prompted by Instinct, like that of Hares and Foxes, may be called so: The Ties of Parent, Son, and Brother are of little Obligation: The Relations of Master and Servant, the Distinction of Magistrate and Subject, are totally unknown: Each Individual in his own Sovereign, accountable to no other upon Earth, and punishable by none.—In this Savage State, Courage, Hardiness, Activity and Strength, the Virtues of their Brother Brutes, are the only Excellencies to which Men can aspire. The Man who can run with the most Celerity, or send the Arrow with the greatest Force, is the best qualified to procure a Subsistence. Hence to chase a Deer over the most rugged Mountain; or to pierce him at the greatest Distance will be held, of all Accomplishments, in the highest Estimation. Emulations and Competitions for Superiority, in such Qualities, will soon commence: and any Action which may be taken for an Insult will be considered as a Pretension to such Superiority; it will raise Resentment in Proportion, and Shame and Grief will prompt the Savage to claim Satisfaction, or to take Revenge. To request the Interposition of a third Person to arbitrate, between the contending Parties would be considered as an implicit Acknowledgment of Deficiency in those Qualifications, without which none in such a barbarous Condition would choose to live. Each one then, must be his own Avenger. The offended Parties must fall to fighting. Their Teeth, their Nails, their Feet or Fists, or perhaps the first Clubb or Stone that can be grasped, must decide the Contest by finishing the Life of one. The Father, the Brother, or the Friend begins then to espouse the Cause of the deceased; not indeed so much from any Love he bore him living, or from any Grief he suffers for him, dead, as from a Principle of Bravery and Honour, to shew himself able and willing to encounter the Man who had just before vanquished another.—Hence arises the Idea of an

U.

Avenger of Blood: and thus the Notions of Revenge, and the Appetite for it, grow apace. Every one must avenge his own Wrongs, when living, or else lose his Reputation: and his near Relation must avenge them for him, after he is dead, or forfeit his.——Indeed Nature has implanted in the human Heart a Disposition to resent an Injury when offered. And this Disposition is so strong, that even the Horse, treading by Accident on a gouty Toe, or a Brick-batt falling on the Shoulders, in the first Twinges of Pain seem to excite the angry Passions, and we feel an Inclination to kill the Horse and to break the Brick-batt. Consideration, however, that the Horse & Brick were without Design, will cool us; whereas the Thought that any Mischief has been done on Purpose to abuse raises Revenge in all its Strength and Terrors: and the Man feels the sweetest, highest Gratification when he inflicts the Punishment himself.—From this Source arises the ardent Desire in Men to judge for themselves when and to what Degree they are injured, and to carve out their own Remedies, for themselves.—From the same Source arises that obstinate Disposition in barbarous Nations to continue barbarous; and the extreme Difficulty of introducing Civility and Christianity among them. For the great Distinction between Savage Nations and polite ones lies in this, that among the former, every Individual is his own Judge and his own Executioner; but among the latter, all Pretensions to Judgment and Punishment are resigned to Tribunals erected by the Public: a Resignation which Savages are not without infinite Difficulty persuaded to make, as it is of a Right and Priviledge extremely dear and tender to uncultivated Nature.

To exterminate from among Mankind such revengeful Sentiments and Tempers is one of the highest and most important Strains of civil & humane Policy: Yet the Qualities which contribute most to inspire and support them may, under certain Regulations, be indulged and encouraged. Wrestling, Running, Leaping, Lifting, and other Exercises of Strength, Hardiness, Courage and Activity may be promoted among private Soldiers, common Sailors, Labourers, Manufacturers and Husbandmen, among whom they are most wanted, provided sufficient Precautions are taken that no romantic cavalier-like Principles of Honor intermix with them, and render a Resignation of the Right of judging and the Power of executing, to the Public, shameful. But whenever such Notions spread, so inimical to the Peace of Society, that Boxing, Clubbs, Swords or Fire-Arms, are resorted to for deciding every Quarrel, about a Girl, a Game at Cards, or any little Accident, that Wine, or Folly, or Jealousy, may suspect to be an Affront; the whole Power of the Government should be exerted to suppress them.—

If a Time should ever come when such Notions shall prevail in this Province to a Degree that no Priviledges shall be able to exempt Men from Indignities and personal Attacks; not the Priviledge of a Councellor, not the Priviledge of an House of Representatives of "speaking freely in that Assembly, without Impeachment or Question in any Court, or Place," out of the General Court; when whole armed Mobs shall assault a Member of the House—when violent Attacks shall be made upon Counsellors—when no Place shall be sacred, not the very Walls of Legislation—when no Personages shall over awe, not the whole General Court, added to all the other Gentlemen on Change—when the broad Noon-Day shall be chosen to display before the World such high, heroic sentiments of Gallantry and Spirit,— when such Assailants shall live unexpelled from the Legislature—when slight Censures and no Punishments shall be inflicted—there will really be Danger of our becoming universally ferocious, barbarous and brutal, worse than our Gothic Ancestors before the Christian Æra.

The Doctrine that the Person assaulted "should act with Spirit," "should defend himself, by drawing his Sword, and killing, or by wringing Noses and Boxing it out, with the Offender," is the Tenet of a Coxcomb, and the Sentiment of a Brute.—The Fowl upon the Dung-Hill, to be sure, feels a most gallant and heroic Spirit at the Crowing of another and instantly spreads his Cloak and prepares for Combat.—The Bulls Wrath inkindles into a noble Rage, and the Stallions immortal Spirit can never forgive the Pawings, Neighings, and Defiances of his Rival. But are Cocks, and Bulls and Horses, the proper Exemplars for the Imitation of Men, especially of Men of Sense, and even the highest Personages in the Government!

Such Ideas of Gallantry have been said to be derived from the Army. But it was injuriously said, because not truly. For every Gentleman, every Man of Sense and Breeding in the Army has a more delicate and manly Way of thinking; and from his Heart despises all such little, narrow, sordid Notions. It is true that a Competition, and a mutual Affectation of Contempt, is apt to arise among the lower, more ignorant and despicable of every Rank and Order in Society. This Sort of Men, (and some few such there are in every Profession) among Divines, Lawyers, Physicians, as well as Husbandmen, Man-

U.

ufacturers and Labourers, are prone from a certain Littleness of Mind to imagine that their Labours alone are of any Consequence in the World, and to affect a Contempt for all others. It is not unlikely then, that the lowest and most despised Sort of Soldiers may have expressed a Contempt for all other Orders of Mankind, may have indulged a Disrespect to every Personage in a Civil Character, and have acted upon such Principles of Revenge, Rusticity, Barbarity and Brutality, as have been above described. And indeed it has been observed by the great Montesquieu, that "From a Manner of Thinking that prevails among Mankind (the most ignorant and despicable of Mankind, he means) they set an higher Value upon Courage than Timourousness, on Activity than Prudence, on Strength than Counsel. Hence the Army will ever despise a Senate, and respect their own Officers; they will naturally slight the Orders sent them by a Body of Men, whom they look upon as Cowards; and therefore unworthy to command them."—This Respect to their own Officers, which produces a Contempt of Senates and Counsels, and of all Laws, Orders, and Constitutions, but those of the Army and their Superiour Officers; tho' it may have prevailed among some Soldiers of the illiberal Character above described, is far from being universal. It is not found in one Gentleman of Sense and Breeding in the whole Service. All of this Character know that the Common Law of England is Superiour to all other Laws Martial or Common, in every English Government; and has often asserted triumphantly its own Preheminence against the insults and Encroachments of a giddy and unruly Soldiery. They know too that Civil Officers in England hold a great Superiority to Military Officers; and that a frightful Despotism would be the speedy Consequence of the least Alteration in these Particulars.—And knowing this, these Gentlemen who have so often exposed their Lives in Defence of the Religion, the Liberties and Rights of Men and Englishmen, would feel the utmost Indignation at the Doctrine which should make the Civil Power give Place to the Military; which should make a Respect to their superior Officers destroy or diminish their Obedience to Civil Magistrates, or which should give any Man a Right, in Conscience, Honor, or even in Punctilio and Delicacy, to neglect the Institutions of the Public, and seek their own Remedy for Wrongs and Injuries of any Kind.

U.

[4]

[ANONYMOUS]

[*Untitled*]

BOSTON, 1764

The importance of public virtue for a self-governing people, and the importance of religion for public virtue, were constant themes during the founding era. This short piece, published in the September 17, 1764 issue of the *Boston Gazette,* is representative of many similar essays to be found in newspapers throughout the founding era.

To the PUBLISHERS, &c.

There is an inseparable connection between publick virtue and publick happiness: *Individuals,* we are assured, must render an account *hereafter* of every part of their moral conduct in this state; but communities, as *their* existence will cease with this world, can neither be rewarded or punish'd as such in the next: It therefore appears rational to conclude, that *present* rewards and punishments are distributed to them, according to their *present* moral behaviour. Hence we see the importance of *morality* to a community: It should engage the serious attention of every individual, and his endeavor, to do all that lies in his power in his own sphere to encourage and promote it; and I think it is worth consideration, whether the decay of morality, which is too visible among us, is not very much owing to too much laxness in *family government:* I am far from being *austere* in my principles of the government of a family: I believe that too *rigid* a restraint upon young folks is usually attended with bad effects in the end; yet I will venture to ask whether we are not in general in the opposite extreme, and whether there are not *already* some instances of the fatal consequences of it?

ANONYMOUS

I believe it will be allowed by all christians, that a due observation of the Lord's Day is one material branch of *moral* duty: The legislature of Great-Britain, and every subordinate legislature in her dominions, and to be sure the civil authority of *this* province, have always consider'd the first day of the week as wholly set apart for the purposes of devout religion: If then the supreme civil power; & if by far the greater part, if not every private individual, who is a *serious christian,* are not all mistaken in this matter, it must be very affecting to see the contempt that is cast, and the opposition that is made by some of our youth, to the good and wholesome laws of the province for the strict observation of that day. It is evident I think, that it is not only the particular law *lately* made that gives offence to these young people: let any one recollect four or five years ago, before this law was pass'd, what opposition was made to the Sabbath laws then in being: this his Honor the chief justice was pleas'd to observe upon in open court, the last Week: As much contempt was cast upon the justices of the peace who executed those laws then, as is now cast upon the gentlemen appointed to execute this: so that it rather seems to be an *impatience* in these thoughtless giddy youth under the restraint of any law at all: such restraint they cry out against as an attack upon their *liberty:* and so it is, upon a liberty to prophane a part of time which GOD ALMIGHTY at the creation of the world was pleas'd to pronounce *holy:* corrupt minds are apt to mistake all laws for reformation as an attack upon *liberty:* these young people it is to be fear'd are countenanced by some others, from whom as *citizens* at least, better things might be expected: but tis hoped their parents or masters will instruct them otherwise.

A good deal depends upon the youth of a country being train'd up to virtue and good manners: *They* are to act upon the stage of life, when the *present* generation is gone: It ought therefore to be the common concern of all—magistrates—ministers of the gospel & heads of families—all who have a regard for the future happiness of their country—and may I not say, all who wish that the Supreme Being, (who hath shown so much favor to New England in former and later times) may be honer'd by its posterity, to use all possible means to destroy vice & immorality of every kind, and to cultivate & promote the fear of God and a love to religion in the minds of our young people—I cannot help thinking that this chiefly depends upon the *good government and instruction of families:* public laws are made for the punishment and terror of evil doers: now, if every family was duly instructed and governed; if the youth were restrained by those who have the care of them at *home,* from acting in public, contrary to the declared mind of the public, there would be less occasion to put the laws in severe execution: but when the laws of God and man are openly violated, and those who are entrusted with the execution of them, are abused and insulted, it is high time for all orderly citizens to unite in a proper defence of them, and *as openly* to countenance them in bringing such notorious offenders to punishment—otherwise, what mischief may we not expect! The contagion will spread like the leprosy and infect the whole land! I should pity the father whose son should be bro't to shame and the punishment of the law: but as I am a Father, and an *aged* father, I should in such a case willingly sacrifice *my* son, though it should bring my grey hairs with sorrow to the grave.—Have not all civilized nations of the world regarded their morals, and made provision for the reformation of their manners? But what are all laws, if not animated by a laudable execution of them? The most solemn enacting clauses are but the image of authority while they remain in parchment.—Is there any one amongst us, who can look upon spreading vice, and think of the train of evils which must attend it, and not be inspired with [a] degree of zeal for a reformation? At this particular juncture especially, when we feel the just punishment of Heaven for our sins, and have reason to dread more? Are not our poor multiplied, and still multiplying and the charges upon others increasing? Are not our taxes heavy, and is not our trade labouring under new and intollerable burthens? Have we not trembled under severe judgments—fire, earthquake, sword and pestilence! and ought not these things to awaken our attention? When we shall be restored to virtue and sobriety, we may hope by the kind interposition of providence, to be eas'd of our present burthens, and have all our fears remov'd: but 'till then, what thoughtful man will expect it?——

I did not intend to have said so much upon a subject which seems to be more adapted to the pulpit, than a weekly newspaper: I shall conclude with a quotation from an author of great repute in England—

> Think, what will become of us, if we suffer the laws for the reformation of manners to be broken, or born down: Think, if the wretches that debauch your children or servants, can find money, friends and advocates, to entangle the prosecutions, by

ANONYMOUS

increasing the difficulties and charge, and thereby make the law a terror to them that do well: Think, if those laws that fence about your property, and guard your peace, are so often violated now; if religion is not only neglected, but insulted, the Sabbath prophaned, and GOD blasphemed! If dissoluteness and debauchery now face the sun, and often out-brave both Heaven and the laws at once: Good GOD! What would it be if there were none to call for justice? if there were none to make the laws heard and felt, or sinners afraid by the due execution of them, which is their only significancy. The Devil would return upon us with *seven spirits worse than the former.* All future attempts for a reformation would be laughed out of countenance; and a flood of iniquity that has been long swelling on its dam, would at length bear down all before it. Vice would be triumphant: The very laws against immorality would become obsolete, or be voted a *public nuisance, and an abridgement of the people's liberty:* Can any one profess a love to virtue and good manners, and not dread things coming to such a pass? or rather is it not of the last importance to prevent them?—

[5]

PHILO PUBLICUS

[*Untitled*]

BOSTON, 1764

Frugality was a central virtue for the Puritans, and it was esteemed throughout New England as one of the pristine American virtues setting them apart from the corrupt, venal, and extravagent English in the mother country. The anonymous author of this short essay stakes out a position frequently reiterated in American newspapers during the founding era. Frugality was a virtue with political implications for two reasons. First, a people hoping to be self-governing, it was felt, needed to be frugal if they were to restrain themselves in their demands on the public wealth. Money saved rather than spent could be invested to increase the common wealth. Also, the colonies, and later the young republic, produced few of the luxuries of life. These had to be imported from England and elsewhere, which not only used up scarce sterling but also tended to undercut American independence from foreign influence. *Messrs.* Edes and Gill were the editors of the *Boston Gazette* when this letter appeared on October 1, 1764.

Messieurs EDES & GILL,

As I am a hearty Well-wisher to every Attempt towards a public Reformation, it gives me peculiar Pleasure to hear that Numbers of the Inhabitants of Boston have entered into an Agreement to suppress Extravagance and promote Frugality; as Friends to Society they deserve the Thanks of every Individual; thro' the Channel of your Paper I return them mine.

We have taken wide Steps to Ruin, and as we have grown more

Luxurious every Year, so we run deeper and deeper in Debt to our
Mother Country; and 'tis hard to say where the growing Evil will
stop, if some vigorous Endeavours are not speedily us'd to retrieve our
Affairs. Industry and Frugality are Virtues which have been buried
out of Sight; 'tis Time, high time to revive them. He that Leads in
this Cause, and is himself the Example, is a Patriot. I hope the present
Appearances will not issue in a bare Flourish, but be exhibited in real
Life; and that not only the Extravagancies of Dress, but of the House
and the Table, will come under proper Regulations. When I enter the
Doors of a Gentleman in Trade, and observe the Decorations of the
Parlour, the shining Side Boards of Plate, the costly Piles of China;
when he asks me to take a friendly Meal, and I behold a Variety of
Meats and other Elegancies on his Table, and his Side Board enrich'd
with a Collection of different Wines; and see the Mistress of it dress'd
in Apparel which can be worn by none with Propriety but those who
live on their Income; I say when I observe all this, I wonder not when
I hear of frequent Bankruptcies.—I therefore beg Leave humbly to
propose, that some Addition be made to the Articles agreed to by
those Gentlemen who aim to give a helping Hand to their sinking
Country, and wou'd ask. Why we may not limit the Number of
Dishes at our Tables to Two?—Why we can't sleep as well after
supping on an Oyster, or a Bowl of Milk, as if we had feasted on a
Patridge or a Rabbit?—And why the Cyder and the Beer of our own
Manufacture will not agree as well with our Constitutions, as the
Wines of Madeira, Bordeaux or Lisbon?—or at least may not the latter
be us'd with Caution; and rather presented as a Cordial is to the Sick,
when Nature really requires its Aid? and while our Gardens and our
Fields afford us so many excellent Plants and Roots which our merciful
Creator has provided for our Use, why need we on ev'ry slight Mallady
run to the Physician to prescribe, and the Apothecary to supply us
with foreign and very expensive Drugs? In this Article only great
Sums are annually expended, and to my Knowledge in many Cases
very needlessly—Here I am aware some Gentlemen of the Faculty will
think me their declared Enemy, but not so the more judicious. I
esteem the Profession, and am for supporting a sufficient Number of
them in an honourable Manner; but I appeal to the most sensible of
them, whether they are not often causelessly applied to, and even
forced against their Judgments to prescribe Medicines where there is

scarce any real Disease, at least none but Temperance, Exercise and Simples wou'd soon remove?

And on this Occasion, my fair Country-women will allow me to wish a general Reformation among them.—May they lay aside their Fondness for Dress and Fashions, for Trinkets and Diversions, and apply themselves to manage with Prudence the Affairs of the Family within, while their Husbands are busied in providing them the Means. May none think themselves above looking into every Article of Expence,—nor exempt from performing any Part of Family Business, when properly called to it—And especially do I wish they would bear on their Minds the Importance of educating their Children in the Principles of Virtue and Oeconomy, and assiduously apply themselves to cultivate the Minds, and form the Manners of those who in future Times will be either the Glory or the Disgrace of NEW ENGLAND.

PHILO PUBLICUS.
Cambridge, Sept. 26, 1764

[6]

STEPHEN HOPKINS 1701–1785

The Rights of Colonies Examined

PROVIDENCE, 1764

S tephen Hopkins wrote this pamphlet, with the approval of the Rhode Island legislature, while he was governor of the state. Hopkins later served in the First and Second Continental Congresses, signed the Declaration of Independence, and helped write the Articles of Confederation. While not a brilliant theorist, Hopkins was a superb writer and here captures as well as anyone the central convictions held by most thoughtful Americans during the Stamp Act crisis.

---

*Mid the low murmurs of submissive fear
And mingled rage, my* Hampden *rasi'd his voice,
And to the laws appeal'd . . .*
THOMPSON'S *Liberty*

Liberty is the greatest blessing that men enjoy, and slavery the heaviest curse that human nature is capable of. This being so makes it a matter of the utmost importance to men which of the two shall be their portion. Absolute liberty is, perhaps, incompatible with any kind of government. The safety resulting from society, and the advantage of just and equal laws, hath caused men to forego some part of their natural liberty, and submit to government. This appears to be the most rational account of its beginning, although, it must be confessed, mankind have by no means been agreed about it. Some have found its origin in the divine appointment; others have thought it took its rise from power; enthusiasts have dreamed that dominion was founded in grace. [4] Leaving these points to be settled by the descendants of Filmer, Cromwell, and Venner, we will consider the British constitution as it at present stands, on Revolution principles, and from thence endeavor to find the measure of the magistrate's power and the people's obedience.

This glorious constitution, the best that ever existed among men, will be confessed by all to be founded by compact and established by consent of the people. By this most beneficent compact British subjects are to be governed only agreeable to laws to which themselves have some way consented, and are not to be compelled to part with their property but as it is called for by the authority of such laws. The former is truly liberty; the latter is really to be possessed of property and to have something that may be called one's own.

On the contrary, those who are governed at the will of another, or of others, and whose property may be taken from them by taxes or otherwise without their own consent and against their will, are in the miserable condition of slaves. "For liberty solely consists in an independency upon the will of another; and by the name of slave we understand a man who can neither dispose of his person or goods, but enjoys all at the will of his master," says Sidney on government. These things premised, whether the British American colonies on the continent are justly entitled to like privileges and freedom as their fellow subjects in Great Britain are, shall be the chief point examined. In discussing this question we shall make the colonies in New England, with whose rights we are best acquainted, the rule of our reasoning, not in the least doubting but all the others are justly entitled to like rights with them.

New England was first planted by adventurers who left England, their native country, by permission of King CHARLES I, and at their own expense transported themselves to America, with great risk and difficulty settled among [5] savages, and in a very surprising manner formed new colonies in the wilderness. Before their departure the terms of their freedom and the relation they should stand in to the mother country in their emigrant state were fully settled: they were to remain subject to the King and dependent on the kingdom of Great Britain. In return they were to receive protection and enjoy all the rights and privileges of freeborn Englishmen.

This is abundantly proved by the charter given to the Massachusetts colony while they were still in England, and which they received and brought over with them as the authentic evidence of the conditions they removed upon. The colonies of Connecticut and Rhode Island also afterwards obtained charters from the crown, granting them the like ample privileges. By all these charters, it is in the most express and solemn manner granted that these adventurers, and their children after them forever, should have and enjoy all the freedom and liberty that the subjects in England enjoy; that they might make laws for their own government suitable to their circumstances, not repugnant to, but as near as might be agreeable to the laws of England; that they might purchase lands, acquire goods, and use trade for their advantage, and have an absolute property in whatever they justly acquired. These, with many other gracious privileges, were granted them by several kings; and they were to pay as an acknowledgment to the crown only one-fifth part of the ore of gold and silver that should at any time be found in the said colonies, in lieu of, and full satisfaction for, all dues and demands of the crown and kingdom of England upon them.

There is not anything new or extraordinary in these rights granted to the British colonies. The colonies from all countries, at all times, have enjoyed equal freedom with the mother state. Indeed, there would be found very few people in the world willing to leave their native country [6] and go through the fatigue and hardship of planting in a new uncultivated one for the sake of losing their freedom. They who settle new countries must be poor and, in course, ought to be free. Advantages, pecuniary or agreeable, are not on the side of emigrants, and surely they must have something in their stead.

To illustrate this, permit us to examine what hath generally been the condition of colonies with respect to their freedom. We will begin with those who went out from the ancient commonwealths of Greece, which are the first, perhaps, we have any good account of. Thucydides, that grave and judicious historian, says of one of them, "they were not sent out to be slaves, but to be the equals of those who remain behind"; and again, the Corinthians gave public notice "that a new colony was going to Epidamnus, into which all that would enter, should have equal and like privileges with those who stayed at home." This was uniformly the condition of all the Grecian colonies; they went out and settled new countries, they took such forms of government as themselves chose, though it generally nearly resembled that of the mother state, whether democratical or oligarchical. 'Tis true, they were fond to acknowledge their original, and always confessed themselves under obligation to pay a kind of honorary respect to, and show a filial dependence on, the commonwealth from whence they sprung. Thucydides again tells us that the Corinthians complained of the Corcyreans, "from whom, though a colony of their own, they had received some contemptuous treatment, for they neither payed them the usual honor on their public solemnities, nor began with a Corinthian in the distribution of the sacrifices, which is always done by other colonies." From hence it is plain what kind of dependence the Greek colonies were under, and what sort of acknowledgment they owed to the mother state.

[7] If we pass from the Grecian to the Roman colonies, we shall find them not less free. But this difference may be observed between them, that the Roman colonies did not, like the Grecian, become separate states governed by different laws, but always remained a part of the mother state; and all that were free of the colonies were also free of Rome, and had right to an equal suffrage in making all laws and appointing all officers for the government of the whole commonwealth. For the truth of this we have the testimony of St. Paul, who though born at Tarsus, yet assures us he was born free of Rome. And Grotius gives us the opinion of a Roman king concerning the freedom of colonies: King Tallus says, "for our part, we look upon it to be neither truth nor justice that mother cities ought of necessity and by the law of nature to rule over their colonies."

When we come down to the latter ages of the world and consider the colonies planted in the three last centuries in America from several kingdoms in Europe, we shall find them, says Pufendorf, very different from the ancient colonies, and gives us an instance in those of the Spaniards. Although it be confessed these fall greatly short of enjoying equal freedom with the ancient Greek and Roman ones, yet it will be said truly, they enjoy equal freedom with their countrymen in Spain: but as they are all under the government of an absolute monarch, they have no reason to complain that one enjoys the liberty the other is deprived of. The French colonies will be found nearly in the same condition, and for the same reason, because their fellow subjects in France have also lost their liberty. And the question here is not whether all colonies, as compared one with another, enjoy equal liberty, but whether all enjoy as much freedom as the inhabitants of the mother state; and this will hardly be denied in the case of the Spanish, French, or other modern foreign colonies.

[8] By this it fully appears that colonies in general, both ancient

and modern, have always enjoyed as much freedom as the mother state from which they went out. And will anyone suppose the British colonies in America are an exception to this general rule? Colonies that came out from a kingdom renowned for liberty, from a constitution founded on compact, from a people of all the sons of men the most tenacious of freedom; who left the delights of their native country, parted from their homes and all their conveniences, searched out and subdued a foreign country with the most amazing travail and fortitude, to the infinite advantage and emolument of the mother state; that removed on a firm reliance of a solemn compact and royal promise and grant that they and their successors forever should be free, should be partakers and sharers in all the privileges and advantages of the then English, now British constitution.

If it were possible a doubt could yet remain, in the most unbelieving mind, that these British colonies are not every way justly and fully entitled to equal liberty and freedom with their fellow subjects in Europe, we might show that the Parliament of Great Britain have always understood their rights in the same light.

By an act passed in the thirteenth year of the reign of his late Majesty, King GEORGE II, entitled An Act For Naturalizing Foreign Protestants, etc., and by another act, passed in the twentieth year of the same reign, for nearly the same purposes, by both which it is enacted and ordained "that all foreign Protestants who had inhabited and resided for the space of seven years or more in any of His Majesty's colonies in America" might, on the conditions therein mentioned, be naturalized, and thereupon should "be deemed, adjudged, and taken to be His Majesty's natural-born subjects of the kingdom of Great Britain to all intents, constructions, and purposes, as if they, and every one of them, had been or were born [9] within the same." No reasonable man will here suppose the Parliament intended by these acts to put foreigners who had been in the colonies only seven years in a better condition than those who had been born in them or had removed from Britain thither, but only to put these foreigners on an equality with them; and to do this, they are obliged to give them all the rights of natural-born subjects of Great Britain.

From what hath been shown, it will appear beyond a doubt that the British subjects in America have equal rights with those in Britain; that they do not hold those rights as a privilege granted them, nor enjoy them as a grace and favor bestowed, but possess them as an inherent, indefeasible right, as they and their ancestors were freeborn subjects, justly and naturally entitled to all the rights and advantages of the British constitution.

And the British legislative and executive powers have considered the colonies as possessed of these rights, and have always heretofore, in the most tender and parental manner, treated them as their dependent, though free, condition required. The protection promised on the part of the crown, with cheerfulness and great gratitude we acknowledge, hath at all times been given to the colonies. The dependence of the colonies to Great Britain hath been fully testified by a constant and ready obedience to all the commands of his present Majesty and his royal predecessors, both men and money having been raised in them at all times when called for with as much alacrity and in as large proportions as hath been done in Great Britain, the ability of each considered. It must also be confessed with thankfulness that the first adventurers and their successors, for one hundred and thirty years, have fully enjoyed all the freedoms and immunities promised on their first removal from England. But here the scene seems to be unhappily changing: the British ministry, whether induced by a jealousy of the colonies by false informations, or by some alteration in the system of political [10] government, we have no information; whatever hath been the motive, this we are sure of: the Parliament in their last session passed an act limiting, restricting, and burdening the trade of these colonies much more than had ever been done before, as also for greatly enlarging the power and jurisdiction of the courts of admiralty in the colonies; and also came to a resolution that it might be necessary to establish stamp duties and other internal taxes to be collected within them. This act and this resolution have caused great uneasiness and consternation among the British subjects on the continent of America: how much reason there is for it we will endeavor, in the most modest and plain manner we can, to lay before our readers.

In the first place, let it be considered that although each of the colonies hath a legislature within itself to take care of its interests and provide for its peace and internal government, yet there are many things of a more general nature, quite out of the reach of these particular legislatures, which it is necessary should be regulated, ordered, and governed. One of this kind is the commerce of the whole British empire, taken collectively, and that of each kingdom and colony in it as it makes a part of that whole. Indeed, everything that concerns the proper interest and fit government of the whole commonwealth, of keeping the peace, and subordination of all the parts towards the whole and one among another, must be considered in this light. Amongst these general concerns, perhaps, money and paper credit, those grand instruments of all commerce, will be found also to have a place. These, with all other matters of a general nature, it is absolutely necessary should have a general power to direct them, some supreme and overruling authority with power to make laws and form regulations for the good of all, and to compel their execution and observation. It being necessary some such general power should exist somewhere, every man of the least knowledge of the British [11] constitution will be naturally led to look for and find it in the Parliament of Great Britain. That grand and august legislative body must from the nature of their authority and the necessity of the thing be justly vested with this power. Hence it becomes the indispensable duty of every good and loyal subject cheerfully to obey and patiently submit to all the acts, laws, orders, and regulations that may be made and passed by Parliament for directing and governing all these general matters.

Here it may be urged by many, and indeed with great appearance of reason, that the equity, justice, and beneficence of the British constitution will require that the separate kingdoms and distant colonies who are to obey and be governed by these general laws and regulations ought to be represented, some way or other, in Parliament, at least whilst these general matters are under consideration. Whether the colonies will ever be admitted to have representatives in Parliament, whether it be consistent with their distant and dependent state, and whether if it were admitted it would be to their advantage, are questions we will pass by, and observe that these colonies ought in justice and for the very evident good of the whole commonwealth to have notice of every new measure about to be pursued and new act that is about to be passed, by which their rights, liberties, or interests will be affected. They ought to have such notice, that they may appear and be heard by their agents, by counsel, or written representation, or by some other equitable and effectual way.

The colonies are at so great a distance from England that the members of Parliament can generally have but little knowledge of their business, connections, and interest but what is gained from people who have been there; the most of these have so slight a knowledge themselves that the informations they can give are very little to be depended on, though they may pretend to determine with confidence [12] on matters far above their reach. All such kind of informations are too uncertain to be depended on in the transacting business of so much consequence and in which the interests of two millions of free people are so deeply concerned. There is no kind of inconveniency or mischief can arise from the colonies having such notice and being heard in the manner above mentioned; but, on the contrary, very great mischiefs have already happened to the colonies, and always must be expected, if they are not heard before things of such importance are determined concerning them.

Had the colonies been fully heard before the late act had been passed, no reasonable man can suppose it ever would have passed at all in the manner it now stands; for what good reason can possibly be given for making a law to cramp the trade and ruin the interests of many of the colonies, and at the same time lessen in a prodigious manner the consumption of the British manufactures in them? These are certainly the effects this act must produce; a duty of three pence per gallon on foreign molasses is well known to every man in the least acquainted with it to be much higher than that article can possibly bear, and therefore must operate as an absolute prohibition. This will put a total stop to our exportation of lumber, horses, flour, and fish to the French and Dutch sugar colonies; and if anyone supposes we may find a sufficient vent for these articles in the English islands in the West Indies, he only verifies what was just now observed, that he wants truer information. Putting an end to the importation of foreign molasses at the same time puts an end to all the costly distilleries in these colonies, and to the rum trade to the coast of Africa, and throws it into the hands of the French. With the loss of the foreign molasses trade, the cod fishery of the English in America must also be lost and thrown also into the hands of the French. That this is the real state of the whole business is not fancy; this, nor any part of it, is not exaggeration but a sober and most melancholy truth.

[13] View this duty of three pence per gallon on foreign molasses not in the light of a prohibition but supposing the trade to continue and the duty to be paid. Heretofore there hath been imported into the colony of Rhode Island only, about one million one hundred and fifty thousand gallons annually; the duty on this quantity is fourteen thousand three hundred and seventy-five pounds sterling to be paid

yearly by this little colony, a larger sum than was ever in it at any one time. This money is to be sent away, and never to return; yet the payment is to be repeated every year. Can this possibly be done? Can a new colony, compelled by necessity to purchase all its clothing, furniture, and utensils from England, to support the expenses of its own internal government, obliged by its duty to comply with every call from the crown to raise money on emergencies; after all this, can every man in it pay twenty-four shillings sterling a year for the duties of a single article only? There is surely no man in his right mind believes this possible. The charging foreign molasses with this high duty will not affect all the colonies equally, nor any other near so much as this of Rhode Island, whose trade depended much more on foreign molasses and on distilleries than that of any others; this must show that raising money for the general service of the crown or of the colonies by such a duty will be extremely unequal and therefore unjust. And now taking either alternative, by supposing, on one hand, the foreign molasses trade is stopped and with it the opportunity or ability of the colonies to get money, or, on the other, that this trade is continued and that the colonies get money by it but all their money is taken from them by paying the duty, can Britain be gainer by either? Is it not the chiefest interest of Britain to dispose of and to be paid for her own manufactures? And doth she not find the greatest and best market for them in her own colonies? Will she find an advantage in disabling the colonies to [14] continue their trade with her? Or can she possibly grow rich by their being made poor?

Ministers have great influence, and Parliaments have great power—can either of them change the nature of things, stop all our means of getting money, and yet expect us to purchase and pay for British manufactures? The genius of the people in these colonies is as little turned to manufacturing goods for their own use as is possible to suppose in any people whatsoever; yet necessity will compel them either to go naked in this cold country or to make themselves some sort of clothing, if it be only the skins of beasts.

By the same act of Parliament, the exportation of all kinds of timber or lumber, the most natural produce of these new colonies, is greatly encumbered and uselessly embarrassed, and the shipping it to any part of Europe except Great Britain prohibited. This must greatly affect the linen manufactory in Ireland, as that kingdom used to receive great quantities of flaxseed from America; many cargoes, being made of that and of barrel staves, were sent thither every year; but as the staves can no longer be exported thither, the ships carrying only flaxseed casks, without the staves which used to be intermixed among them, must lose one half of their freight, which will prevent their continuing this trade, to the great injury of Ireland and of the plantations. And what advantage is to accrue to Great Britain by it must be told by those who can perceive the utility of this measure.

Enlarging the power and jurisdiction of the courts of vice-admiralty in the colonies is another part of the same act, greatly and justly complained of. Courts of admiralty have long been established in most of the colonies, whose authority were circumscribed within moderate territorial jurisdictions; and these courts have always done the business necessary to be brought before such courts for trial in [15] the manner it ought to be done and in a way only moderately expensive to the subjects; and if seizures were made or informations exhibited without reason or contrary to law, the informer or seizor was left to the justice of the common law, there to pay for his folly or suffer for his temerity. But now this course is quite altered, and a customhouse officer may make a seizure in Georgia of goods ever so legally imported, and carry the trial to Halifax at fifteen hundred miles distance; and thither the owner must follow him to defend his property; and when he comes there, quite beyond the circle of his friends, acquaintance, and correspondents, among total strangers, he must there give bond and must find sureties to be bound with him in a large sum before he shall be admitted to claim his own goods; when this is complied with, he hath a trial and his goods acquitted. If the judge can be prevailed on (which it is very well known may too easily be done) to certify there was *only* probable cause for making the seizure, the unhappy owner shall not maintain any action against the illegal seizor for damages or obtain any other satisfaction, but he may return to Georgia quite ruined and undone in conformity to an act of Parliament. Such unbounded encouragement and protection given to informers must call to everyone's remembrance Tacitus' account of the miserable condition of the Romans in the reign of Tiberius their emperor, who let loose and encouraged the informers of that age. Surely if the colonies had been fully heard before this has been done, the liberties and properties of the Americans would not have been so much disregarded.

The resolution of the House of Commons, come into during the

same session of Parliament, asserting their rights to establish stamp
duties and internal taxes to be collected in the colonies without their
own consent, hath much more, and for much more reason, alarmed
the British subjects in America than anything that had ever been done
before. [16] These resolutions, carried into execution, the colonies
cannot help but consider as a manifest violation of their just and long-
enjoyed rights. For it must be confessed by all men that they who are
taxed at pleasure by others cannot possibly have any property, can
have nothing to be called their own. They who have no property can
have no freedom, but are indeed reduced to the most abject slavery,
are in a condition far worse than countries conquered and made
tributary, for these have only a fixed sum to pay, which they are left
to raise among themselves in the way that they may think most equal
and easy, and having paid the stipulated sum the debt is discharged,
and what is left is their own. This is much more tolerable than to be
taxed at the mere will of others, without any bounds, without any
stipulation and agreement, contrary to their consent and against their
will. If we are told that those who lay these taxes upon the colonies
are men of the highest character for their wisdom, justice, and
integrity, and therefore cannot be supposed to deal hardly, unjustly,
or unequally by any; admitting and really believing that all this is
true, it will make no alteration in the nature of the case. For one who
is bound to obey the will of another is as really a slave though he may
have a good master as if he had a bad one; and this is stronger in
politic bodies than in natural ones, as the former have perpetual
succession and remain the same; and although they may have a very
good master at one time, they may have a very bad one at another.
And indeed, if the people in America are to be taxed by the
representatives of the people in Britain, their malady is an increasing
evil that must always grow greater by time. Whatever burdens are
laid upon the Americans will be so much taken off the Britons; and
the doing this will soon be extremely popular, and those who put up
to be members of the House of Commons must obtain the votes of
the people by promising to [17] take more and more of the taxes off
them by putting it on the Americans. This must most assuredly be
the case, and it will not be in the power even of the Parliament to
prevent it; the people's private interest will be concerned and will
govern them; they will have such, and only such, representatives as
will act agreeable to this their interest; and these taxes laid on

Americans will be always a part of the supply bill, in which the other branches of the legislature can make no alteration. And in truth, the subjects in the colonies will be taxed at the will and pleasure of their fellow subjects in Britain. How equitable and how just this may be must be left to every impartial man to determine.

But it will be said that the monies drawn from the colonies by duties and by taxes will be laid up and set apart to be used for their future defense. This will not at all alleviate the hardship, but serves only more strongly to mark the servile state of the people. Free people have ever thought, and always will think, that the money necessary for their defense lies safest in their own hands, until it be wanted immediately for that purpose. To take the money of the Americans, which they want continually to use in their trade, and lay it up for their defense at a thousand leagues distance from them when the enemies they have to fear are in their own neighborhood, hath not the greatest probability of friendship or of prudence.

It is not the judgment of free people only that money for defending them is safest in their own keeping, but it hath also been the opinion of the best and wisest kings and governors of mankind, in every age of the world, that the wealth of a state was most securely as well as most profitably deposited in the hands of their faithful subjects. Constantine, emperor of the Romans, though an absolute prince, both practiced and praised this method. "Diocletian sent persons on purpose to reproach him with his neglect of the public, and the poverty to which he was [18] reduced by his own fault. Constantine heard these reproaches with patience; and having persuaded those who made them in Diocletian's name, to stay a few days with him, he sent word to the most wealthy persons in the provinces that he wanted money and that they had now an opportunity of showing whether or no they truly loved their prince. Upon this notice everyone strove who should be foremost in carrying to the exchequer all their gold, silver, and valuable effects; so that in a short time Constantine from being the poorest became by far the most wealthy of all the four princes. He then invited the deputies of Diocletian to visit his treasury, desiring them to make a faithful report to their master of the state in which they should find it. They obeyed; and, while they stood gazing on the mighty heaps of gold and silver, Constantine told them that the wealth which they beheld with astonishment had long since belonged to him, but that he had left it by way of depositum in the hands of his people, adding, the richest and surest treasure of the prince was the love of his subjects. The deputies were no sooner gone than the generous prince sent for those who had assisted him in his exigency, commended their zeal, and returned to everyone what they had so readily brought into his treasury." *Universal Hist., vol. XV, p. 523.*

We are not insensible that when liberty is in danger, the liberty of complaining is dangerous; yet a man on a wreck was never denied the liberty of roaring as loud as he could, says Dean Swift. And we believe no good reason can be given why the colonies should not modestly and soberly inquire what right the Parliament of Great Britain have to tax them. We know such inquiries by a late letter writer have been branded with the little epithet of *mushroom policy*; and he insinuates that for the colonies to pretend to claim any privileges will draw down the [19] resentment of the Parliament on them. Is the defense of liberty become so contemptible, and pleading for just rights so dangerous? Can the guardians of liberty be thus ludicrous? Can the patrons of freedom be so jealous and so severe? If the British House of Commons are rightfully possessed of a power to tax the colonies in America, this power must be vested in them by the British constitution, as they are one branch of the great legislative body of the nation. As they are the representatives of all the people in Britain, they have beyond doubt all the power such a representation can possibly give; yet great as this power is, surely it cannot exceed that of their constituents. And can it possibly be shown that the people in Britain have a sovereign authority over their fellow subjects in America? Yet such is the authority that must be exercised in taking people's estates from them by taxes, or otherwise without their consent. In all aids granted to the crown by the Parliament, it is said with the greatest propriety, "We freely give unto Your Majesty"; for they give their own money and the money of those who have entrusted them with a proper power for that purpose. But can they with the same propriety give away the money of the Americans, who have never given any such power? Before a thing can be justly given away, the giver must certainly have acquired a property in it; and have the people in Britain justly acquired such a property in the goods and estates of the people in these colonies that they may give them away at pleasure?

In an imperial state, which consists of many separate governments each of which hath peculiar privileges and of which kind it is evident the empire of Great Britain is, no single part, though greater than another part, is by that superiority entitled to make laws for or to tax such lesser part; but all laws and all taxations which bind the whole must be made by the whole. This may be fully verified by the empire of Germany, which consists of many states, some [20] powerful and others weak, yet the powerful never make laws to govern or to tax the little and weak ones, neither is it done by the emperor, but only by the diet, consisting of the representatives of the whole body. Indeed, it must be absurd to suppose that the common people of Great Britain have a sovereign and absolute authority over their fellow subjects in America, or even any sort of power whatsoever over them; but it will be still more absurd to suppose they can give a power to their representatives which they have not themselves. If the House of Commons do not receive this authority from their constituents it will be difficult to tell by what means they obtained it, except it be vested in them by mere superiority and power.

Should it be urged that the money expended by the mother country for the defense and protection of America, and especially during the late war, must justly entitle her to some retaliation from the colonies, and that the stamp duties and taxes intended to be raised in them are only designed for that equitable purpose; if we are permitted to examine how far this may rightfully vest the Parliament with the power of taxing the colonies we shall find this claim to have no sort of equitable foundation. In many of the colonies, especially those in New England, who were planted, as before observed, not at the charge of the crown or kingdom of England, but at the expense of the planters themselves, and were not only planted but also defended against the savages and other enemies in long and cruel wars which continued for an hundred years almost without intermission, solely at their own charge; and in the year 1746, when the Duke D'Anville came out from France with the most formidable French fleet that ever was in the American seas, enraged at these colonies for the loss of Louisbourg the year before and with orders to make an attack on them; even in this greatest exigence, these colonies were left to the protection of Heaven and their own efforts. These colonies [21] having thus planted and defended themselves and removed all enemies from their borders, were in hopes to enjoy peace and recruit their state, much exhausted by these long struggles; but they were soon called upon to raise men and send out to the defense of other colonies, and to make

STEPHEN HOPKINS 1701–1785

conquests for the crown. They dutifully obeyed the requisition, and with ardor entered into those services and continued in them until all encroachments were removed, and all Canada, and even the Havana, conquered. They most cheerfully complied with every call of the crown; they rejoiced, yea even exulted, in the prosperity and exaltation of the British empire. But these colonies, whose bounds were fixed and whose borders were before cleared from enemies by their own fortitude and at their own expense, reaped no sort of advantage by these conquests: they are not enlarged, have not gained a single acre of land, have no part in the Indian or interior trade. The immense tracts of land subdued and no less immense and profitable commerce acquired all belong to Great Britain, and not the least share or portion to these colonies, though thousands of their men have lost their lives and millions of their money have been expended in the purchase of them, for great part of which we are yet in debt, and from which we shall not in many years be able to extricate ourselves. Hard will be the fate, yea cruel the destiny, of these unhappy colonies if the reward they are to receive for all this is the loss of their freedom; better for them Canada still remained French, yea far more eligible that it ever should remain so than that the price of its reduction should be their slavery.

If the colonies are not taxed by Parliament, are they therefore exempted from bearing their proper share in the necessary burdens of government? This by no means follows. Do they not support a regular internal government in each colony as expensive to the people here as the internal government of Britain is to the people there? Have not [22] the colonies here, at all times when called upon by the crown, raised money for the public service, done it as cheerfully as the Parliament have done on like occasions? Is not this the most easy, the most natural, and most constitutional way of raising money in the colonies? What occasion then to distrust the colonies—what necessity to fall on an invidious and unconstitutional method to compel them to do what they have ever done freely? Are not the people in the colonies as loyal and dutiful subjects as any age or nation ever produced; and are they not as useful to the kingdom, in this remote quarter of the world, as their fellow subjects are who dwell in Britain? The Parliament, it is confessed, have power to regulate the trade of the whole empire; and hath it not full power, by this means, to draw all the money and all the wealth of the colonies into the mother country at pleasure? What motive, after all this, can remain to induce the Parliament to abridge the privileges and lessen the rights of the most loyal and dutiful subjects, subjects justly entitled to ample freedom, who have long enjoyed and not abused or forfeited their liberties, who have used them to their own advantage in dutiful subserviency to the orders and interests of Great Britain? Why should the gentle current of tranquillity that has so long run with peace through all the British states, and flowed with joy and happiness in all her countries, be at last obstructed, be turned out of its true course into unusual and winding channels by which many of those states must be ruined, but none of them can possibly be made more rich or more happy?

Before we conclude, it may be necessary to take notice of the vast difference there is between the raising money in a country by duties, taxes, or otherwise, and employing and laying out the money again in the same country, and raising the like sums of money by the like means and sending it away quite out of the country where it is raised. Where the former of these is the case, although the sums raised may be [23] very great, yet that country may support itself under them; for as fast as the money is collected together, it is again scattered abroad, to be used in commerce and every kind of business; and money is not made scarcer by this means, but rather the contrary, as this continual circulation must have a tendency to prevent, in some degree, its being hoarded. But where the latter method is pursued, the effect will be extremely different; for here, as fast as the money can be collected, 'tis immediately sent out of the country, never to return but by a tedious round of commerce, which at best must take up much time. Here all trade, and every kind of business depending on it, will grow dull, and must languish more and more until it comes to a final stop at last. If the money raised in Great Britain in the three last years of the late war, and which exceeded forty millions sterling, had been sent out of the kingdom, would not this have nearly ruined the trade of the nation in three years only? Think, then, what must be the condition of these miserable colonies when all the money proposed to be raised in them by high duties on the importation of divers kinds of goods, by the post office, by stamp duties, and other taxes, is sent quite away, as fast as it can be collected, and this to be repeated continually and last forever! Is it possible for colonies under these circumstances to support themselves, to have any money, any trade, or other business, carried on in them? Certainly it is not; nor is there at present, or ever was, any country under Heaven that did, or possibly could, support itself under such burdens.

We finally beg leave to assert that the first planters of these colonies were pious Christians, were faithful subjects who, with a fortitude and perseverance little known and less considered, settled these wild countries, by GOD's goodness and their own amazing labors, thereby added a most valuable dependence to the crown of Great Britain; were ever dutifully subservient to her interests; so taught their children [24] that not one has been disaffected to this day, but all have honestly obeyed every royal command and cheerfully submitted to every constitutional law; have as little inclination as they have ability to throw off their dependency; have carefully avoided every offensive measure and every interdicted manufacture; have risked their lives as they have been ordered, and furnished their money when it has been called for; have never been troublesome or expensive to the mother country; have kept due order and supported a regular government; have maintained peace and practiced Christianity; and in all conditions, and in every relation, have demeaned themselves as loyal, as dutiful, and as faithful subjects ought; and that no kingdom or state hath, or ever had, colonies more quiet, more obedient, or more profitable than these have ever been.

May the same divine goodness that guided the first planters, protected the settlements, inspired Kings to be gracious, Parliaments to be tender, ever preserve, ever support our present gracious King; give great wisdom to his ministers and much understanding to his Parliaments; perpetuate the sovereignty of the British constitution, and the filial dependency and happiness of all the colonies.

P—.

[7]

AEQUUS

From the Craftsman

BOSTON, 1766

This piece appeared in the *Massachusetts Gazette and Boston Newsletter* on March 6, 1766. Supposedly reprinted from a London newspaper, it was either written by an American living in London, or else the attribution to an anonymous London author was made for propaganda purposes, and it was really written by someone in Boston. The reasoning is concise, and the conclusion is pro-colonist. As with the next piece in this volume, written by Richard Bland the same week this appeared, the present essay illustrates advanced thinking on the matter of England's relationship with her colonies and clearly foreshadows the arguments to be used ten years later. The careful exposition lifts this piece beyond mere rhetoric and nicely summarizes colonial attitudes toward their mother country.

An *ex post facto* question, soon expected to be advisedly discussed, is "whether the mother-country has a right of imposing local taxes on *all* her American colonies?" The *precedent fact* is supposed to have been ministerially pre-resolved, and influentially established. This necessary previous question, *as to the right,* remains still to be put; and it is hoped the wisdom and equity of Both Houses will not suffer it to be craftily slurred over, and much less precipitately carried—as it were by a *Coup de Main.*

    The proper arguments, stript of all political refinements and expediences, must turn on the two political points, viz. the *constitutional power* of the British Parliament, respecting the aforementioned fact; and the *actual exertions* of Royal Prerogative, in the point of right;

under which it is admitted that the colonies lay claim to and avow their respective legislative privileges.

English Liberty is a propriety attached to the individuals of the community, founded on the original frame or constitution of our government, and might be defined, "the primitive right that every freeholder had of *consenting* to those laws by which the community was to be obliged." Time and a change of circumstances extended this circle of comprehension, and made every subject in some respect or other a member of the legislature; his consent, at first personally denoted, was afterward allowed to be given by a proxy or representative. Usage and conveniency transformed that indulgence into a right; and a general presence in parliament being only judicially supposed, is thus rendered something more than a legal fiction; hence the maxim prevailed,—"that every one was a party to all acts of parliament." This privilege of becoming a *party to the laws,* or being in effect his own governor, was as it were the consideration or price of individual subjection: and from the express or implied exercise of it, the duty of our *legal obedience* is inferred. But an Englishman in America has no means of being present or represented in the British Legislature quasi a *colonist;* where then is to be found his consent to parliamentary acts operative there; and by what construction can he be said to give his voice? being thus in neither sense a party, as wanting the fundamental privilege above-mentioned; and not having been subjected to any obligation of this kind by original patent or charter; but on the contrary, an express power being thereby granted to the colonies of *enacting their own laws,* provided the same be not repugnant to those of Great-Britain. It is hard to conceive from what constitutional principle applicable to a colony, not a conquered country, his obedience to a statute-law can be deduced. I say, to statute-law or a mere act of parliament, independently of any auxiliary jurisdiction derived from the blended exertion of prerogative in cases of that legal *repugnancy,* which in terminis are excepted by their said charters; and wherein prerogative singly, or conjunctively with both Houses, has and may acknowledgedly interpose, pursuantly to the same. This obedience would certainly be, with respect to him a naked duty; an *ex parte* obligation obtruded upon him, which is repugnant to the nature of all legalities and destructive of that principle wherein English Liberty essentially consists. But farther, were the English Americans not only to be bound there by the acts of the British parliament in all cases,

but also by those of their own assemblies:—here would be a subjection
within a subjection, which might subordinate their actions to alternate
contrarities and cross penalties! a duplicity of jurisdiction over the
same objects, and equally in the first instance, unknown to the law!
a supersaetation in the legislative system, which seems monstrous and
unnatural! The delegation therefore of a legislative power to the
colonies must, one would think, from its necessary efficacy, be
considered not only as uncurrent with, but as exclusive of all
parliamentary participation in the *proper subjects* of their legislation,
that is to say, in cases not repugnant to the laws of Great-Britain.
And in all such cases may not the maxim be fitly applied;—"Designatio
unius est exclusto alterius, et expressum facit cessare tacitum?"

That such a question should be occasioned at this time of day,
seems altogether surprizing; after our very parliaments have taken
occasional notices of and impliedly confirmed the acts of the American
assemblies, in local levies and assessments; and the *administration* itself
having had frequent resources to them for supplies in such pressing
seasons, when, if the mother country had a right of imposing taxes,
the importance of the occasion would have worthily becomed her to
have done so, and, on the supposition of that right, should have done
it,—for the sake of certainty and dispatch.

But it has been asserted with more justice and consistency that
the King's Scepter is the instrument of power over the colonies, and
Prerogative the rule by which their obedience must be regulated. In
this case, however, have not the *royal charters* been granted, establishing
a constitution, and delegating to them the before-mentioned qualified
power of legislation? To which the crown, even for the necessary
provision and maintenance of their government, has frequently referred
itself, as to an essential principal, concurring party; thereby recognizing
that vested right in the colonies, the establishment whereof *itself* had
originally prescribed and chartered. Moreover, is not the King a
perpetual constituent branch of their legislatures representedly present
in every assembly, and an actual party to all their laws? And this
being the case, prerogative must indeed be owned to have *herein*
tempered its operations agreeable to the spirit of the English constitution, and to have thus generously bound and limited itself. Nor
could it well have happened otherwise: for if, as has been said, the
common-law followed the subject to America, it is presumed that
prerogative could have only acted there consistently with, and in

conformity to it. Further with particular respect to the point in question, numerous are the instances of money-levies and assessments enacted by the American assemblies, that have travelled through occasional examinations, of the several boards and cognizances here, and nevertheless been confirmed, or received the royal approbation: and no instance that I can find has occurred, where any such act has been disallowed merely on account of its particular tendency, or of those legislatures having exercised a power which did not appertain to them. And the royal confirmation of the actual exercise of this power proceeded, no doubt, from a respect to and consideration of the statute, *De tallagio non concedendo;* or, "The prohibition of imposing any taxes or aids without the universal consent of the freemen," &c. An exemption, founded on common law and ancient English liberty! which it seems the colonists do conceive themselves intitled to, as their *birthright:* that birthright by which they are themselves tied in interest to the mother country, and bound to a correllative loyalty, which thus requires not any military force to be secured or vindicated. So that whether this question, of a substituting right to impose œconomical taxes on the colonies, be applied to the British parliament, independently as before-noticed; or to the royal prerogative, exclusive of the American assemblies; in both cases it would be a *lost point.* On the other hand, should this right, so delegated to the colonies, be now considered by any after-thought as a reversible error; be it remembered, that at first it was so delegated by *solemn acts* of government; that it proved the means of their vast increase and cultivation, and by consequence of those immense profits and advantages which have thence accrued to us; that it is sanctified by successive usage, grounded upon a generous reliance on English Faith and Compact, and that usage—ratified by repeated authoritative acquies-cence: and lastly, that any violation of their constitutions, by what means soever executed, might unhinge the principles of their natural and civil attachment to the mother-country; thereby opening to our *foreign enemies* a direct passage to our Palladium itself.

Nor, this privilege being left them, let it be thought that the colonies will of course be independent. No! numerous are the residuary ties which the Crown and Parliament have upon them:—the *Navigation Act,* by which they are directly excluded from all foreign markets;—the power of laying duties on their *exports*—transmitted to Britain;—the right of port entry and clearance;—the command of their castles, fortifications and militia;—the appointment of their several officers, civil as well as military;—the executive power of government;—the right of convening, proroguing, and dissolving their assemblies;—the Governor's negative to any bill;—the determination of appeals from their courts of judicature;—and, as a clincher, the absolute jurisdiction of annulling their acts, when their before-mentioned legislative power appears to have been exceeded. This is a general sketch of the nature of that *supremacy,* which, with some partial exceptions, the mother-country has retained over her colonies—By it, it will appear, how little has been left them; and, were that little now to be taken away, how soon, at the best, they might probably be deserted. To conclude: were it not for this privilege, the condition of our Americans would be worse than that of our other English subjects: a condition, that would argue the most intemperate folly and perverseness to reduce them to; a folly and perverseness, which must not be imputed to the policy of the *English nation.*

AEQUUS.

[8]

RICHARD BLAND 1710–1776

An Inquiry into the Rights
of the British Colonies

WILLIAMSBURG, 1766

Born in Virginia, Richard Bland graduated from William and Mary College and served in the Virginia House of Burgesses from 1742 until 1775. Always a cautious politician, and somewhat conservative in bent, Bland was nevertheless consistently sent by his constituents to represent them in any revolutionary convention. Their trust in his ability to pursue American interests had to stem, at least in part, from the contents of this pamphlet, and from the fact that when it was published during the week of March 7, 1766, it was unique for the period in having the author's name boldly listed on the title page— "By Richard Bland, of Virginia." A collector of old documents, many of which survive to this day only because of his efforts, Bland's careful study of such documents led to his being considered the best authority of his time on colonial legal history. His expertise is reflected throughout the pamphlet. Reprinted in the *Virginia Gazette* on May 30, 1766, and then in London in 1769, Bland's essay seems to have generated surprisingly little interest elsewhere in the colonies, at least it was never reprinted again. The pamphlet was, however, the earliest published defense of the colonial attitude toward taxation and laid out the argument to be adopted during the revolutionary era. Indeed, the final outcome of the pamphlet is to be found in the Declaration of Independence.

SIR,

I take the Liberty to address you, as the Author of "The Regulations lately made concerning the Colonies, and the Taxes imposed upon them considered." It is not to the Man, whoever you are, that I address myself; but it is to the Author of a Pamphlet which, according to the Light I view it in, endeavours to fix Shackles upon the American Colonies: Shackles which, however nicely polished, can by no Means sit easy upon Men who have just Sentiments of their own Rights and Liberties.

You have indeed brought this Trouble upon yourself, for you say that

> many Steps have been lately taken by the Ministry to cement and perfect the necessary Connexion between the Colonies and the Mother Kingdom, which every Man who is sincerely interested in what is interesting to his Country will [4] anxiously consider the Propriety of, will inquire into the Information, and canvas the Principles upon which they have been adopted; and will be ready to applaud what has been well done, condemn what has been done amiss, and suggest any Emendations, Improvements, or Additions which may be within his Knowledge, and occur to his Reflexion.

Encouraged therefore by so candid an Invitation, I have undertaken to examine, with an honest Plainness and Freedom, whether the Ministry, by imposing Taxes upon the Colonies by Authority of Parliament, have pursued a wise and salutary Plan of Government, or whether they have exerted pernicious and destructive Acts of Power.

I pretend not to concern myself with the Regulations lately made to encourage Population in the new Acquisitions: Time can only determine whether the Reasons upon which they have been founded are agreeable to the Maxims of Trade and sound Policy, or not. However, I will venture to observe that if the most powerful inducement towards peopling those Acquisitions is to arise from the Expectation of a Constitution to be established in them similar to the other Royal Governments in America, it must be a strong Circumstance, in my Opinion, against their being settled by Englishmen, or even by Foreigners, who do not live under the most despotick Government; since, upon your Principles of Colony Government, such a Constitution will not be worth their Acceptance.

The Question is whether the Colonies are represented in the British Parliament or not? You affirm it to be an indubitable Fact that they are represented, and from thence you infer a Right in the Parliament to impose Taxes of every Kind upon them. You do not insist [5] upon the Power, but upon the Right of Parliament to impose

Taxes upon the Colonies. This is certainly a very proper Distinction, as Right and Power have very different Meanings, and convey very different Ideas; For had you told us that the Parliament of Great Britain have Power, by the Fleets and Armies of the Kingdom, to impose Taxes and to raise Contributions upon the Colonies, I should ot have presumed to dispute the Point with you; but as you insist upon the Right only, I must beg Leave to differ from you in Opinion, and shall give my Reasons for it.

But I must first recapitulate your Arguments in Support of this Right in the Parliament. You say

the Inhabitants of the Colonies do not indeed choose Members of Parliament, neither are nine Tenths of the People of Britain Electors; for the Right of Election is annexed to certain Species of Property, to peculiar Franchises, and to Inhabitancy in some particular Places. But these Descriptions comprehend only a very small Part of the Lands, the Property and People of Britain; all Copy-Hold, all Leave-Hold Estates under the Crown, under the Church, or under private Persons, though for Terms ever so long; all landed Property in short that is not Freehold, and all monied Property whatsoever, are excluded. The Possessors of these have no Votes in the Election of Members of Parliament; Women and Persons under Age, be their Property ever so large, and all of it Freehold, have none: The Merchants of London, a numerous and respectable Body of Men, whose Opulence exceeds all that America can collect; the Proprietors of that vast Accumulation of Wealth, the Publick Funds; the Inhabitants of Leeds, of Halifax, of Birmingham, [6] and of Manchester, Towns that are each of them larger than the largest in the Plantations; many of lesser Note, that are incorporated; and that great Corporation the East India Company, whose Rights over the Countries they possess fall very little short of Sovereignty, and whose Trade and whose Fleets are sufficient to constitute them a maritime Power, are all in the same Circumstances: And yet are they not represented in Parliament? Is their vast Property subject to Taxation without their Consent? Are they all arbitrarily bound by Laws to which they have not agreed? The Colonies are exactly in the same Situation; all British Subjects are really in the same; none are actually, all are virtually, represented in Parliament: For every Member of

Parliament sits in the House not as a Representative of his own Constituents, but as one of that august Assembly by which all the Commons of Great Britain are represented.

This is the Sum of what you advance, in all the Pomp of Parliamentary Declamation, to prove that the Colonies are represented in Parliament, and therefore subject to their Taxation; but notwithstanding this Way of reasoning, I cannot comprehend how Men who are excluded from voting at the Election of Members of Parliament can be represented in that Assembly, or how those who are elected do not sit in the House as Representatives of their Constituents. These Assertions appear to me not only paradoxical, but contrary to the fundamental Principles of the English Constitution.

To illustrate this important Disquisition, I conceive we must recur to the civil Constitution of England, and from thence deduce and ascertain the Rights and Privileges [7] of the People at the first Establishment of the Government, and discover the Alterations that have been made in them from Time to Time; and it is from the Laws of the Kingdom, founded upon the Principles of the Law of Nature, that we are to show the Obligation every Member of the State is under to pay Obedience to its Institutions. From these Principles I shall endeavour to prove that the Inhabitants of Britain, who have no Vote in the Election of Members of Parliament, are not represented in that Assembly, and yet that they owe Obedience to the Laws of Parliament; which, as to them, are constitutional, and not arbitrary. As to the Colonies, I shall consider them afterwards.

Now it is a Fact, as certain as History can make it, that the present civil Constitution of England derives its Original from those Saxons who, coming over to the Assistance of the Britons in the Time of their King Vortigein, made themselves Masters of the Kingdom, and established a Form of Government in it similar to that they had been accustomed to live under in their native Country[1]; as similar, at least, as the Difference of their Situation and Circumstances would permit. This Government, like that from whence they came, was founded upon Principles of the most perfect Liberty: The conquered Lands were divided among the Individuals in Proportion to the Rank they held in the Nation[2]; and every Freeman, that is, every Freeholder,

[1] *Petyt's Rights of the Com. Brady's Comp. Hist. Rapin. Squire's Inquiry.*
[2] *Caesar de Bell. Gall. Tacitus de Germ. C 28. Temple's Mise.*

was a member of their Wittenagemot, of Parliament[3]. The other part of the Nation, or the Non-Proprietors of Land, were of little Estimation[4]. [8] They, as in Germany, were either slaves, were Hewers of Wood and Drawers of Water, or Freedmen; who, being of foreign Extraction, had been manumitted by their Masters, and were excluded from the high Privilege of having a Share in the Administration of the Commonwealth, unless they became Proprietors of Land (which they might obtain by Purchase or Donation) and in that Case they had a Right to sit with the Freemen, in the Parliament or sovereign Legislature of the State.

How long this Right of being personally present in the Parliament continued, or when the Custom of sending Representatives to this great Council of the Nation, was first introduced, cannot be determined with Precision; but let the Custom of Representation be introduced when it will, it is certain that every Freeman, or, which was the same Thing in the Eye of the Constitution, every Freeholder,[5] had a Right to vote at the Election of Members of Parliament, and therefore might be said, with great Propriety, to be present in that Assembly, either in his own Person or by Representation. This Right of Election in the Freeholders is evident from the Statute 1st *Hen.* 5. Ch. 1st, which limits the Right of Election to those Freeholders only who are resident in the Counties the Day of the Date of the Writ of Election; but yet every resident Freeholder indiscriminately, let his Freehold be ever so small, had a Right to vote at the Election of Knights for his County so that they were actually represented; And this Right of Election continued until it was taken away by the Statute 8th *Hen.* 6. Ch. 7. from those Freeholders who had not a clear Freehold Estate of forty Shillings by the year at the least.

[9] Now this statute was deprivative of the Right of those Freeholders who came within the Description of it; but of what did it deprive them, if they were represented notwithstanding their Right of Election was taken from them? The mere Act of voting was nothing, of no Value, if they were represented as constitutionally without it as with it: But when by the fundamental Principles of the Constitution

---

[3] *Tacitus de Germ. C. 11.*
[4] *Ibid. C. 25.*
[5] 2 *Inst.* 27. 4 *Inst.* 2.

they were to be considered as Members of the Legislature, and as such had a Right to be present in Person, or to send their Procurators or Attornies, and by them to give their Suffrage in the supreme Council of the Nation, this Statute deprived them of an essential Right; a Right without which by the ancient Constitution of the State, all other Liberties were but a Species of Bondage.

As these Freeholders then were deprived of their Rights to substitute Delegates to Parliament, they could not be represented, but were placed in the same Condition with the Non-Proprietors of Land, who were excluded by the original Constitution from having any Share in the Legislature, but who, notwithstanding such Exclusion, are bound to pay Obedience to the Laws of Parliament, even if they should consist of nine Tenths of the People of Britain; but then the Obligation of these Laws does not arise from their being virtually represented in Parliament, but from a quite different Reason.

Men in a State of Nature are absolutely free and independent of one another as to sovereign Jurisdiction,[6] but when they enter into a Society, and by their own [10] Consent become Members of it, they must submit to the Laws of the Society according to which they agree to be governed; for it is evident, by the very Act of Association, that each Member subjects himself to the Authority of that Body in whom, by common Consent, the legislative Power of the State is placed: But though they must submit to the Laws, so long as they remain Members of the Society, yet they retain so much of their natural Freedom as to have a Right to retire from the Society, to renounce the Benefits of it, to enter into another Society, and to settle in another Country; for their Engagements to the Society, and their Submission to the publick Authority of the State, do not oblige them to continue in it longer than they find it will conduce to their Happiness, which they have a natural Right to promote. This natural Right remains with every Man, and he cannot justly be deprived of it by any civil Authority. Every Person therefore who is denied his Share in the Legislature of the State to which he had an original Right, and every Person who from his particular Circumstances is excluded from this great Privilege, and refuses to exercise his natural Right of quitting the Country, but remains in it, and continues to exercise the Rights of a Citizen in all other Respects, must be subject to the Laws which by these Acts he

[6] *Vattel's Law of Nature. Locke on Civil Govern. Wollaston's Rel. of Nat.*

implicitly, or to use your own Phrase, *virtually* consents to: For Men
may subject themselves to Laws, by consenting to them *implicitly;* that
is, by conforming to them, by adhering to the Society, and accepting
the Benefits of its Constitution, as well, as *explicitly* and directly, in
their own Persons, or by their Representatives substituted in their
Room.[7] Thus, if a Man whose Property does not [11] entitle him to
be an Elector of Members of Parliament, and therefore cannot be
represented, or have any Share in the Legislature,

> inherits or takes any Thing by the Laws of the Country to
> which he has no indubitable Right in Nature, or which, if he
> has a Right to it, he cannot tell how to get or keep without
> the Aid of the Laws and the Advantage of Society, then, when
> he takes this Inheritance, or whatever it is, *with* it he takes and
> owns the Laws that gave it him. And since the Security he has
> from the Laws of the Country, in Respect of his Person and
> Rights, is the *Equivalent* for his Submission to them, he cannot
> accept *that* Security without being obliged, in Equity, to pay
> *this* Submission: Nay his very continuing in the Country shows
> that he either likes the Constitution, or likes it better,
> notwithstanding the Alteration made in it to his Disadvantage,
> than any other; or at least thinks it better, in his Circumstances,
> to conform to it, than to seek any other; that is, he is content
> to be comprehended in it.

From hence it is evident that the Obligation of the Laws of
Parliament upon the People of Britain who have no Right to be
Electors does not arise from their being *virtually* represented, but from
a quite different Principle; a Principle of the Law of Nature, true,
certain, and universal, applicable to every Sort of Government, and
not contrary to the common Understandings of Mankind.

If what you say is a real Fact, that nine Tenths of the People of
Britain are deprived of the high Privilege of being Electors, it shows
a great Defect in the present Constitution, which has departed so
much from its original Purity; but never can prove that those People
are even *virtually* represented in Parliament. [12] And here give me
Leave to observe that it would be a Work worthy of the best patriotick
Spirits in the Nation to effectuate an Alteration in this putrid Part of
the Constitution; and, by restoring it to its pristine Perfection, prevent

[7] *Wollaston's Rel. of Nat.*

any "Order or Rank of the Subjects from imposing upon or binding the rest without their Consent." But, I fear, the Gangrene has taken too deep Hold to be eradicated in these Days of Venality.

But if those People of Britain who are excluded from being Electors are not represented in Parliament, the Conclusion is much stronger against the People of the Colonies being represented; who are considered by the British Government itself, in every Instance of Parliamentary Legislation, as a distinct People. It has been determined by the Lords of the Privy Council that "Acts of Parliament made in England without naming the foreign Plantations will not bind them[8]." Now, what can be the Reason of this Determination, but that the Lords of the Privy Council are of Opinion the Colonies are a distinct People from the Inhabitants of Britain, and are not represented in Parliament. If, as you contend, the Colonies are *exactly in the same Situation* with the Subjects in Britain, the Laws will in every Instance be equally binding upon them, as upon those Subjects, unless you can discover two Species of *virtual* Representation; the one to respect the Subjects in Britain, and always existing in Time of Parliament; the other to respect the Colonies, a mere Non-Entity, if I may be allowed the Term, and never existing but when the Parliament thinks proper to produce it into Being by any particular Act in which the Colonies [13] happen to be named. But I must examine the Case of the Colonies more distinctly.

It is in vain to search into the civil Constitution of England for Directions in fixing the proper Connexion between the Colonies and the Mother Kingdom; I mean what their reciprocal Duties to each other are, and what Obedience is due from Children to the general Parent. The planting Colonies from Britain is but of recent Date, and nothing relative to such Plantation can be collected from the ancient Laws of the Kingdom; neither can we receive any better Information by extending our Inquiry into the History of the Colonies established by the several Nations in the more early Ages of the World. All the Colonies (except those of Georgia and Nova Scotia) formed from the English Nation, in North America, were planted in a Manner, and under a Dependence, of which there is not an Instance in all the Colonies of the Ancients; and therefore, I conceive, it must afford a

[8] 2 *Peer Williams.*

good Degree of Surprise to find an English Civilian[9] giving it as his Sentiment that the English Colonies ought to be governed by the Roman Laws, and for no better Reason than because the Spanish Colonies, as he says, are governed by those Laws. The Romans established their Colonies in the Midst of vanquished Nations, upon Principles which best secured their Conquests; the Privileges granted to them were not always the same; their Policy in the Government of their Colonies and the conquered Nations being always directed by arbitrary Principles to the End they aimed at, the subjecting the whole Earth to their Empire. But the Colonies in North America, except those planted within the present Century, were founded by Englishmen; who, becoming [14] private Adventurers, established themselves, without any Expense to the Nation, in this uncultivated and almost uninhabited Country; so that their Case is plainly distinguishable from that of the Roman, or any other Colonies of the ancient World.

As then we can receive no Light from the Laws of the Kingdom, or from ancient History, to direct us in our Inquiry, we must have Recourse to the Law of Nature, and those Rights of Mankind which flow from it.

I have observed before that when Subjects are deprived of their civil Rights, or are dissatisfied with the Place they hold in the Community, they have a natural Right to quit the Society of which they are Members, and to retire into another Country. Now when Men exercise this Right, and withdraw themselves from their Country, they recover their natural Freedom and Independence: The Jurisdiction and Sovereignty of the State they have quitted ceases; and if they unite, and by common Consent take Possession of a new Country, and form themselves into a political Society, they become a sovereign State, independent of the State from which they separated. If then the Subjects of England have a natural Right to relinquish their Country, and by retiring from it, and associating together, to form a new political Society and independent State, they must have a Right, by Compact with the Sovereign of the Nation, to remove into a new Country, and to form a civil Establishment upon the Terms of the Compact. In such a Case, the Terms of the Compact must be obligatory and binding upon the Parties; they must be the Magna Charta, the fundamental Principles of Government, to this new Society; and every

---

[9] *Strahan in his Preface to Domat.*

Infringement of them must be wrong, and [15] may be opposed. It will be necessary then to examine whether any such Compact was entered into between the Sovereign and those English Subjects who established themselves in America.

You have told us that "before the first and great Act of Navigation the Inhabitants of North America were but a few unhappy Fugitives, who had wandered thither to enjoy their civil and religious Liberties, which they were deprived of at Home." If this was true, it is evident, from what has been said upon the Law of Nature, that they have a Right to a civil independent Establishment of their own, and that Great Britain has no *Right* to interfere in it. But you have been guilty of a gross Anachronism in your Chronology, and a great Errour in your Account of the first Settlement of the Colonies in North America; for it is a notorious Fact that they were not settled by Fugitives from their native Country, but by Men who came over voluntarily, at their own Expense, and under Charters from the Crown, obtained for that Purpose, long before the first and great Act of Navigation.

The first of these Charters was granted to Sir Walter Raleigh by Queen Elizabeth under the great Seal, and was confirmed by the Parliament of England in the year 1684[10]. By this Charter the whole Country to be possessed by Sir Walter Raleigh was granted to him, his Heirs and Assigns, in perpetual Sovereignty, in as extensive a Manner as the Crown could grant, or had ever granted before to any Person, or Persons, with full Power of Legislation, and to establish a civil Government in it as near as conveniently might be agreeable to [16] the Form of the English Government and policy thereof. The Country was to be united to the Realm of England in perfect LEAGUE and AMITY, was to be within the Allegiance of the Crown of England, and to be held by Homage, and the Payment of one Fifth of all Gold and Silver Ore, which was reserved for all Service, Duties, and Demands.

Sir Walter Raleigh, under this Charter, took Possession of North America, upon that Part of the Continent which gave him a Right to the Tract of Country which was between the twenty-fifth Degree of Latitude and the Gulf of St. Laurence; but a variety of Accidents happening in the Course of his Exertions to establish a Colony, and

---

[10] *This Charter is printed at large in Hakluyt's Voyages, p. 725, Folio Edition, Anno 1589; and the Substance of it is in the 3d Vol. of Salmon's Mod. Hist. p. 424.*

perhaps being overborn by the Expense of so great a Work, he made an Assignment to diverse Gentlemen and Merchants of London, in the 31st Year of the Queen's Reign, for continuing his Plantations in America. These Assignees were not more successful in their Attempts than the Proprietor himself had been; but being animated with the expectation of mighty Advantages from the Accomplishment of their Undertaking, they, with others, who associated with them, obtained new Charters from King James the First, in whom all Sir Walter Raleigh's Rights became vested upon his Attainder, containing the same extensive Jurisdictions, Royalties, Privileges, Franchises, and Pre-eminences, and the same Powers to establish a civil Government in the Colony, as had been granted to Sir W. Raleigh; with an express Clause of Exemption for ever from all Taxes or Impositions upon their Import and Export Trade.

Under these Charters the Proprietors effectually prosecuted, and happily succeeded, in planting a Colony upon that Part of the Continent which is now called [17] Virginia. This Colony, after struggling through immense Difficulties, without receiving the least Assistance from the English Government, attained to such a Degree of Perfection that in the Year 1621 a General Assembly, or legislative Authority, was established in the Governour, Council, and House of Burgesses, who were elected by the Freeholders as their Representatives; and they have continued from that Time to exercise the Power of Legislation over the Colony.

But upon the 15th of July, 1624, King James dissolved the Company by proclamation, and took the Colony under his immediate Dependence; which occassioned much Confusion, and created mighty Apprehensions in the Colony lest they should be deprived of the Rights and Privileges granted them by the Company, according to the Powers contained in the Charters.

To put an end to this Confusion, and to conciliate the Colony to the new System of Government the Crown intended to establish among them, K. Charles the First, upon the Demise of his Father, by Proclamation the 13th of May, 1625, declared "Virginia should be immediately dependent upon the Crown; that the Affairs of the Colony should be vested in a Council, consisting of a few Persons of Understanding and Quality, to be subordinate and attendant to the Privy Council in England; that he was resolved to establish another Council in Virginia, to be subordinate to the Council in England for the Colony; and that he would maintain the necessary Officers, Ministers, Forces, Ammunition, and Fortifications thereof, at his own Charge." But this Proclamation had an Effect quite different from what was intended; [18] instead of allaying, it increased the Confusion of the Colony; they now thought their regular Constitution was to be destroyed, and a Prerogative Government established over them: or, as they express themselves in their Remonstrance, that "then Rights and Privileges were to be assaulted." This general Disquietude and Dissatisfaction continued until they received a Letter from the Lords of the Privy Council, dated July the 22nd, 1634, containing the Royal Assurance and Confirmation that "all their Estates, Trade, Freedom, and Privileges, should be enjoyed by them in as extensive a Manner as they enjoyed before the recalling the Company's Patent;" whereupon they became reconciled, and began again to exert themselves in the Improvement of the Colony.

Being now in full Possession of the Rights and Privileges of Englishmen, which they esteemed more than their Lives, their Affection for the Royal Government grew almost to Enthusiasm; for upon an Attempt to restore the Company's Charter by Authority of Parliament, the general assembly, upon the 1st of April, 1642, drew up a Declaration of Protestation, in the Form of an Act, by which they declared "they never would submit to the Government of any Company or Proprietor, or to so unnatural a Distance as a Company or other Person to interpose between the Crown and the Subjects; that they were born under Monarchy, and would never degenerate from the Condition of their Births by being subject to any other Government; and every Person who should attempt to reduce them under any other Government was declared an Enemy to the Country, and his Estate was to be forfeited." This Act, being presented to the King at his Court at York, July 5th, 1644, [19] drew from him a most gracious answer, under his Royal Signet, in which he gave them the fullest Assurances that they would be always immediately dependent upon the Crown, and that the Form of Government should never be changed. But after the King's Death they gave a more eminent Instance of their Attachment to Royal Government, in their Opposition to the Parliament, and forcing the Parliament Commissioners, who were sent over with a Squadron of Ships of War to take Possession of the Country, into Articles of Surrender, before they would submit to their Obedience. As these Articles reflect no small Honour upon this Infant Colony, and as they are not commonly known, I will give an Abstract of such of them as relate to the present Subject.

1. The Plantation of Virginia, and all the inhabitants thereof, shall be and remain in due Subjection to the Commonwealth of England, not as a conquered Country, but as a Country submitting by their own voluntary Act, and shall enjoy such Freedoms and Privileges as belong to the People of England.

2. The General Assembly as formerly shall convene, and transact the Affairs of the Colony.

3. The People of Virginia shall have a free Trade, as the People of England, to all, Places, and with all Nations.

4. Virginia shall be free from all Taxes, Customs, and Impositions whatsoever; and none shall be imposed on them without consent of the General Assembly; and that neither Forts nor Castles be erected, or Garrisons maintained, without their Consent.

Upon this Surrender of the Colony to the Parliament, Sir W. Berkley, the Royal Governour, was removed, [20] and three other Governours were successively elected by the House of Burgesses; but in January 1659 Sir William Berkley was replaced at the Head of the Government by the People, who unanimously renounced their Obedience to the Parliament, and restored the Royal Authority by proclaiming Charles the 2d King of England, Scotland, France, Ireland, and Virginia; so that he was King in Virginia some Time before he had any certain Assurance of being restored to his throne in England.

From this Detail of the Charters, and other Acts of the Crown, under which the first Colony in North America was established, it is evident that "the Colonists were not a few unhappy Fugitives who had wandered into a distant Part of the World to enjoy their civil and religious Liberties, which they were deprived of at home," but had a regular Government long before the first Act of Navigation, and were respected as a distinct State, independent, as to their *internal* Government, of the original Kingdom, but united with her, as to their *external* Polity, in the closest and most intimate LEAGUE AND AMITY, under the same Allegiance, and enjoying the Benefits of a reciprocal Intercourse.

But allow me to make a Reflection or two upon the preceding Account of the first Settlement of an English Colony in North America.

America was no Part of the Kingdom of England; it was possessed by a savage People, scattered through the Country, who were not subject to the English Dominion, nor owed Obedience to its Laws. This independent Country was settled by Englishmen at their own Expense, under particular Stipulations with the Crown: These Stipulations then must be the sacred Band of [21] Union between England and her Colonies, and cannot be infringed without Injustice. But you Object that "no Power can abridge the Authority of Parliament, which has never exempted any from the Submission they owe to it; and no other Power can grant such an Exemption."

I will not dispute the Authority of the Parliament, which is without Doubt supreme within the Body of the Kingdom, and cannot be abridged by any other Power; but may not the King have Prerogatives which he has a Right to exercise without the Consent of Parliament? If he has, perhaps that of granting License to his Subjects to remove into a *new* Country, and to settle therein upon particular Conditions, may be one. If he has no such Prerogative, I cannot discover how the Royal Engagements can be made good, that "the Freedom and other Benefits of the British Constitution" shall be secured to those People who shall settle in a new Country under such Engagements; the Freedom, and other Benefits of the British Constitution, cannot be secured to a People without they are exempted from being taxed by any Authority but that of their Representatives, chosen by themselves. This is an essential Part of British Freedom; but if the King cannot grant such an Exemption, in Right of his Prerogative, the Royal Promises cannot be fulfilled; and all Charters which have been granted by our former Kings, for this Purpose, must be Deceptions upon the Subjects who accepted them, which to say would be a high Reflection upon the Honour of the Crown. But there was a Time when some Parts of England itself were exempt from the Laws of Parliament: The Inhabitants of the County Palatine of Chester were not [22] subject to such Laws[11] *ab antiquo,* because they did not send Representatives to Parliament, but had their own *Commune Concilium;* by whose Authority, with the Consent of their Earl, their Laws were made. If this Exemption was not derived originally from the Crown, it must have arisen from that great Principle in the British Constitution by which the Freemen in the Nation are not subject to any Laws but

[11] *Petyt's Rights of the Commons. King's Vale Royal of England.*

such as are made by Representatives elected by themselves to Parliament; so that, in either Case, it is an Instance extremely applicable to the Colonies, who contend for no other Right but that of directing their *internal* Government by Laws made with their own Consent, which has been preserved to them by repeated Acts and Declarations of the Crown.

The Constitution of the Colonies, being established upon the Principles of British Liberty, has never been infringed by the immediate Act of the Crown; but the Powers of Government, agreeably to this Constitution, have been constantly declared in the King's Commissions to their Governours, which, as often as they pass the Great Seal, are *new* Declarations and Confirmations of the Rights of the Colonies. Even in the Reign of Charles the Second, a Time by no Means favourable to Liberty, these Rights of the Colonies were maintained inviolate; for when it was thought necessary to establish a permanent Revenue for the Support of Government in Virginia, the King did not apply to the English Parliament, but to the General Assembly, and sent over an Act, under the Great Seal of England, by which it was enacted "by the King's Most Excellent Majesty, by and with the Consent of the General Assembly," that two Shillings per [23] Hogshead upon all Tobacco exported, one Shilling and Threepence per Tun upon Shipping, and Sixpence per Poll for every Person imported, not being actually a Mariner in Pay, were to be paid for ever as a Revenue for the Support of the Government in the Colony.

I have taken Notice of this Act, not only because it shows the proper Fountain from whence all Supplies to be raised in the Colonies ought to flow, but also as it affords an Instance that Royalty itself did not disdain formerly to be named as a Part of the Legislature of the Colony; though now, to serve a Purpose destructive of their Rights, and to introduce Principles of Despotism unknown to a free Constitution, the Legislature of the Colonies are degraded even below the Corporation of a petty Borough in England.

It must be admitted that after the Restoration the Colonies lost that Liberty of Commerce with foreign Nations they had enjoyed before that Time.

As it became a fundamental Law of the other States of Europe to prohibit all foreign Trade with the Colonies, England demanded such an exclusive Trade with her Colonies. This was effected by the Act of 25th Charles 2d, and some other subsequent Acts; which not only circumscribed the Trade of the Colonies with foreign Nations within very narrow Limits, but imposed Duties upon several Articles of their own Manufactory exported from one Colony to another. These Acts, which imposed severer Restrictions upon the Trade of the Colonies than were imposed upon the Trade of England, deprived the Colonies, so far as these Restrictions extended, of the Privileges of English Subjects, and constituted an unnatural Difference between Men under the same Allegiance, born equally free, and entitled to the same civil Rights. In this [24] Light did the People of Virginia view the Act of 25th Charles 2d, when they sent Agents to the English Court to represent against "Taxes and Impositions being laid on the Colony by any Authority but that of their General Assembly." The Right of imposing *internal* Duties upon their Trade by Authority of Parliament was then disputed, though you say it was never called into Question; and the Agents sent from Virginia upon this Occasion obtained a Declaration from Charles 2d the 19th of April 1676, under his Privy Seal, that Impositions or "Taxes ought not be laid upon the Inhabitants and Proprietors of the Colony but by the common Consent of the General Assembly, except such Impositions as the Parliament should lay on the Commodities imported into England from the Colony:" And he ordered a Charter to be made out, and to pass the Great Seal, for securing this Right, among others, to the Colony.

But whether the Act of 25th Charles 2d, or any of the other Acts, have been complained of as Infringements of the Rights of the Colonies or not, is immaterial; for if a Man of superiour Strength takes my Coat from me, that cannot give him a Right to my Cloak, nor am I obliged to submit to be deprived of all my Estate because I may have given up some Part of it without Complaint. Besides, I have proved irrefragably that the Colonies are not represented in Parliament, and consequently, upon your own Position, that no new Law can bind them that is made without the Concurrence of their Representatives; and if so, then every Act of Parliament that imposes *internal* Taxes upon the Colonies is an Act of *Power,* and not of *Right.* I must speak freely, I am considering a Question which affects the *Rights* of above two Millions of as [25] loyal Subjects as belong to the British Crown, and must use Terms adequate to the Importance of it; I say that *Power* abstracted from *Right* cannot give a just Title to Dominion. If a Man invades my Property, he becomes an Aggressor, and puts himself into a State of War with me: I have a Right to oppose this Invader; If I have not Strength to repel him, I must submit, but he acquires no Right to my Estate which he has usurped. Whenever I recover Strength I may renew my Claim, and attempt to regain my Possession; if I am never strong enough, my Son, or his Son, may, when able, recover the natural Right of his Ancestor which has been unjustly taken from him.

I hope I shall not be charged with Insolence, in delivering the Sentiments of an honest Mind with Freedom: I am speaking of the *Rights* of a People; *Rights* imply *Equality* in the Instances to which they belong, and must be treated without Respect to the Dignity of the Persons concerned in them. If "the British Empire in Europe and in America is the same *Power*," if the "Subjects in both are the same People, and all equally participate in the Adversity and Prosperity of the Whole," what Distinctions can the Difference of their Situations make, and why is this Distinction made between them? Why is the Trade of the Colonies more circumscribed than the Trade of Britain? And why are Impositions laid upon the one which are not laid upon the other? If the Parliament "have a *Right* to impose Taxes of *every Kind* upon the Colonies," they ought in Justice, as the same People, to have the same Sources to raise them from: Their Commerce ought to be equally free with the Commerce of Britain, otherwise it will be loading them with Burthens at the [26] same Time that they are deprived of Strength to sustain them; it will be forcing them to make Bricks without Straw. I acknowledge the Parliament is the sovereign legislative Power of the British Nation, and that by a full Exertion of their Power they can deprive the Colonists of the Freedom and other Benefits of the British Constitution which have been secured to them by our Kings; they can abrogate all their civil Rights and Liberties; but by what *Right* is it that the Parliament can exercise such a Power over the Colonists, who have as natural a Right to the Liberties and Privileges of Englishmen as if they were actually resident within the Kingdom? The Colonies are subordinate to the Authority of Parliament; subordinate I mean in Degree, but not absolutely so: For if by a Vote of the British Senate the Colonists were to be delivered up to the Rule of a French or Turkish Tyranny, they may refuse Obedience to such a Vote, and may oppose the Execution of it by Force. Great is the Power of Parliament, but, great as it is, it cannot, constitutionally, deprive the People of their *natural* Rights; nor, in Virtue of the same Principle, can it deprive them of their *civil* Rights, which are founded in Compact, without their own Consent. There is, I confess, a considerable Difference between these two Cases as to the Right of Resistance: In the first, if the Colonists should be dismembered from the Nation by Act of Parliament, and abandoned to another Power, they have a natural Right to defend their Liberties by open Force, and may lawfully resist; and, if they are able, repel the Power to whose Authority they are abandoned. But in the other, if they are deprived of their civil Rights, if great and manifest Oppressions are imposed upon them by the State on which they are dependent, their Remedy is to [27] lay their Complaints at the Foot of the Throne, and to suffer patiently rather than disturb the publick Peace, which nothing but a Denial of Justice can excuse them in breaking. But if this Justice should be denied, if the most humble and dutiful Representations should be rejected, nay not even deigned to be received, what is to be done? To such a Question Thucydides would make the Corinthians reply, that if "a decent and condescending Behaviour is shown on the Part of the Colonies, it would be base in the Mother State to press too far on such Moderation:" And he would make the Corcyreans answer, that "every Colony, whilst used in a proper Manner, ought to pay Honour and Regard to its Mother State; but, when treated with Injury and Violence, is become an Alien. They were not sent out to be the Slaves, but to be the Equals of those that remain behind."

But, according to your Scheme, the Colonies are to be prohibited from uniting in a Representation of their general Grievances to the common Sovereign. This Moment "the British Empire in Europe and in America is the same Power; its Subjects in both are the same People; each is equally important to the other, and mutual Benefits, mutual Necessities, cement their Connexion." The next Moment "the Colonies are unconnected with each other, different in their Manners, opposite in their Principles, and clash in their Interests and in their Views, from Rivalry in Trade, and the Jealousy of Neighbourhood. This happy Division, which was effected by Accident, is to be continued throughout by Design; and all Bond of Union between them" is excluded from your vast System. *Divide et impera* is your Maxim in Colony Administration, lest "an Alliance should be [28] formed dangerous to the Mother Country." Ungenerous Insinuation! detestable Thought! abhorrent to every Native of the Colonies! who, by an Uniformity of Conduct, have ever demonstrated the deepest

Loyalty to their King, as the Father of his People, and an unshaken Attachment to the Interest of Great Britain. But you must entertain a most despicable Opinion of the Understandings of the Colonists to imagine that they will allow Divisions to be fomented between them about inconsiderable Things, when the closest Union becomes necessary to maintain in a constitutional Way their dearest Interests.

Another Writer,[12] fond of his new System of placing Great Britain as the Centre of Attraction to the Colonies, says that

> they must be guarded against having or forming any Principle of Coherence with each other above that whereby they cohere in the Centre; having no other Principle of Intercommunication between each other than that by which they are in joint Communication with Great Britain, as the common Centre of all. At the same Time that they are each, in their respective Parts and Subordinations, so framed as to be acted by this first Mover, they should always remain incapable of any Coherence, or of so conspiring amongst themselves as to create any other equal Force which might recoil back on this first Mover; nor is it more necessary to preserve the several Governments subordinate within their respective Orbs than it is essential to the Preservation of the Empire to keep them disconnected and independent of each other.

But how is this "Principle of Coherence," as this elegant Writer calls it, between the Colonies, to be prevented? The Colonies [29] upon the Continent of North America lie united to each other in one Tract of Country, and are equally concerned to maintain their common Liberty. If he will attend then to the Laws of Attraction in natural as well as political Philosophy, he will find that Bodies in Contact, and cemented by mutual Interests, cohere more strongly than those which are at a Distance, and have no common Interests to preserve. But this natural Law is to be destroyed; and the Colonies, whose real Interests are the same, and therefore ought to be united in the closest Communication, are to be disjoined, and all intercommunication between them prevented. But how is this System of Administration to be established? Is it to be done by a military Force, quartered upon private Families? Is it to be done by extending the Jurisdiction of Courts of Admiralty, and thereby depriving the Colonists of legal

---

[12] *The Administration of the Colonies by Governour Pownall.*

Trials in the Courts of common Law? Or is it to be done by harassing the Colonists, and giving overbearing Taxgatherers an Opportunity of ruining Men, perhaps better Subjects than themselves by dragging them from one Colony to another, before Prerogative Judges, exercising a despotick Sway in Inquisitorial Courts? Oppression has produced very great and unexpected Events: The Helvetick Confederacy, the States of the United Netherlands, are Instances in the Annals of Europe of the glorious Actions a petty People, in Comparison, can perform when united in the Cause of Liberty. May the Colonies ever remain under a constitutional Subordination to Great Britain! It is their Interest to live under such a Subordination; and it is their Duty, by an Exertion of all their Strength and Abilities, when called upon by their common Sovereign, to advance the Grandeur and the Glory of the Nation. May the [30] Interests of Great Britain and her Colonies be ever united, so as that whilst they are retained in a legal and just Dependence no unnatural or unlimited Rule may be exercised over them; but that they may enjoy the Freedom, and other Benefits of the British Constitution, to the latest Page in History!

I flatter myself, by what has been said, your Position of a *virtual* Representation is sufficiently refuted; and that there is really no such Representation known in the British Constitution, and consequently that the Colonies are not subject to an *internal* Taxation by Authority of Parliament.

I could extend this Inquiry to a much greater Length, by examining into the Policy of the late Acts of Parliament, which impose heavy and severe Taxes, Duties, and Prohibitions, upon the Colonies; I could point out some very disagreeable Consequences, respecting the Trade and Manufacturers of Britain, which must necessarily result from these Acts; I could prove that the Revenues arising from the Trade of the Colonies, and the Advantage of their Exports to Great Britain in the Balance of her Trade with foreign Nations, exceed infinitely all the Expense she has been at, all the Expense she can be at, in their Protection; and perhaps I could show that the Bounties given upon some Articles exported from the Colonies were not intended, primarily, as Instances of Attention to their Interest, but arose as well from the Consideration of the disadvantageous Dependence of Great Britain upon other Nations for the principal Articles of her naval Stores, as from her losing Trade for those Articles; I could demonstrate that these Bounties are by no Means adequate to her Savings in such foreign Trade, if the Articles upon which they are given can be procured from the Colonies [31] in Quantities sufficient to answer her Consumption; and that the Excess of these Savings is so much clear Profit to the Nation, upon the Supposition that these Bounties are drawn from it; but, as they will remain in it, and be laid out in its Manufactures and Exports, that the whole Sum which used to be paid to Foreigners for the Purchase of these Articles will be saved to the Nation. I say I could extend my Inquiry, by examining these several Matters; but as the Subject is delicate, and would carry me to a great Length, I shall leave them to the Reader's own Reflection.

[9]

BRITANNUS AMERICANUS

[*Untitled*]

BOSTON, 1766

Published only a week after that by Richard Bland in Virginia, this brief essay captures almost all of the same essential points in a position that was to become full-blown ten years later and enshrined in the Declaration of Independence as part of the justification for breaking with England. The anonymous author who wrote this for the March 17, 1766 issue of the *Boston Gazette* deserves to be counted among the founders of our country even though he is here responding directly only to the Stamp Act.

———

When the first settlers of this country had transplanted themselves here, they were to be considered, either as in the state of nature, or else as subjects of that kingdom from whence they had migrated: If they were in the state of nature, they were then entitled to all the rights of nature; no power on earth having any *just* authority, to molest them in the enjoyment of the least of these rights, unless they either had or should forfeit them by an invasion of the rights of other: If the Crown and people of England had at that time, no right, property or claim to that part of the earth, which they had fix'd upon to settle and inhabit, it follows, that in the suppos'd state of nature, neither the crown nor people of England had any *lawful* and *equitable* authority or controul over them more than the inhabitants of the moon: they had a right to erect a government upon what form they thought best; or to connect themselves, for the sake of their own advantage and security, either with the natives, or any other people upon the globe, who were willing to be connected with them: It is a fact, that they chose to erect a government of their own, much under the same form, as that was, which they had formerly been under in Europe; and chose the King of England for *their* King, whose subjects they had been in their state of society before their emigration.—Thus upon the foregoing supposition, the King of *Old* England became connected with the settlers of *New* England, and *their* King: But the people of England could have no more political connection with them or power of jurisdiction over them, than they now have with or over the people of Hanover, who are also subjects of the same King: And if they have since obtain'd no power of jurisdiction, by virtue of any treaty, compact agreement or consent, in which *alone,* all *legal* jurisdiction has its establishment, the people here still remain under the most sacred tie, the subject of the *King* of Great-Britain; but utterly unaccountable to, and uncontroulable by the *people* of Great-Britain, or any body of them whatever; their compact being with the King only, to him alone they submitted, to be govern'd by him, agreable to the terms of that compact, contain'd in their charter.

But on the other supposition, if after their arrival here they remained, as undoubtedly they did, the subjects of the Kingdom of England, they then remain'd without the necessity of charter declarations to confirm it justly entitled to all and every the rights, liberties, privileges and immunities of such; for to talk of English subjects who are free, and of other English subjects, not *so* free, provided they have not legally forfeited *any part* of their freedom, appears to be absurd.— Of all the rights of Englishmen, those of consenting to their own laws, and being tried by juries, are the most material and important: Upon the present supposition, the parliament of England has no more lawful power to make an act which shall deprive the people of *New* England of those rights, than they have to make an act to deprive the people of *Old* England of the same rights: If these are the indefeasible rights of the one, so they must be of the other; they being *fellow subjects,* and standing upon *equal* footing: The people of *Old* England would think it very unjust, to have an act of parliament made, which should deprive them of the unalienable rights of the constitution; just so would the people of *New* England think, and for the same reason; and human nature being the same and both being animated with the same love of freedom and equally attached to the same happy constitution, such a law in either case would probably produce the same effects: it is hoped the people of England will never think it necessary for them to make such laws for the Colonies, for it might prove a *fatal* necessity: It might at least be *detrimental* to Great Britain in *proportion* as the Colonies are *important* to her: Would not such laws, in a *moral* view, cut the thread of political connection and obligation? Does not allegiance infer protection? Has not the latter the strongest claim? Would men ever have had the idea of allegiance to an earthly Prince, had they not first found it necessary to form a government on earth, under God, to protect their natural rights? Is not therefore the Subject's allegiance first due to the constitution of government, which secures the natural rights of the governed; and as a necessary means thereof circumscribes and limits the power of those, whom they have or shall constitute to be their legislators and governors, whether Kings, or Parliaments, or both?

To ascertain the rights of the New-England subjects, the King early gave them a Charter, in which it was declared, what those rights were; and to show his royal mind, that by their attempting at their own cost and pains, to settle a new world, they could by no means be thought to have forfeited their rights as Englishmen: He expressly declares them and their posterity entitled to all those rights, as fully as if they had remained in England. Indeed, if they could possibly have been suppos'd to have lost their rights, by means of their emigration, being yet *innocent* people, and subject to *no other* power on earth, they must have been reduced to a state of nature and independence; for to talk of English subjects without any of the rights of the constitution, is a solicism.

It was not possible for them to enjoy these Rights without erecting a legislative and other powers of government among them-selves: For it was not possible for them at such a distance, to have that *weight* and *importance* in the legislative power in England, which every *individual* there has a right to by the constitution, and by act of parliament is declared actually to have: The granting them show the power of government was not mere *favor,* but that which was *right, fit, equitable;* for without it they must have been depriv'd of that right, which others enjoy'd who were no more than their *equals;* and which were some of them the essential rights of nature, as well as the constitution, and therefore inseparable from them either as men or subjects.—By virtue of these powers of government they now stand (as in all respects they ought in justice) upon a footing with their *fellow subjects* in England. Their laws are now made, with the consent of representatives of *their* own free election; which laws like those made by the two houses of the British parliament, are laid before the Sovereign, who has the same power of rejection, *upon both:* Would it not then be just as equitable, and just as consistent with the British constitution, which extends to all his Majesty's *British* subjects throughout his dominions, for the representatives of the people of New-England, or any other colony, to make a law to tax their *fellow subjects* in England, as for their representatives to make a law to tax *their* fellow subjects in the colonies?

BRITANNUS AMERICANUS.

[10]

THE TRIBUNE

No. xvii

Few Americans today realize that the revolutionary war was fought as much to preserve American virtue as it was to secure economic independence. Americans, as well as Europeans, tended to view Americans as embodying the sturdy traits of the traditional English yeomen—frugality, industriousness, temperance, simplicity, openness, and virility. They viewed England, on the other hand, as the prototype of a corrupt society characterized by luxury, venality, effete cowardice, and a love of refinement and distinction. Excessive wealth and inequality were the cause of English corruption, and a moderate wealth more or less equally distributed in America was the source of virtue. Breaking with English control thus preserved the basis of American liberty, its pristine virtues, and provided immediate political liberty. This piece appeared in the October 6, 1766 issue of the *South Carolina Gazette* (Charleston). Its theme runs throughout the literature of the founding era, although in the late 1780s and 1790s a counter argument in favor of economic growth becomes more prominent.

As the stability and prosperity of this kingdom must primarily depend on freedom, and the security of freedom can only be in public virtue, it must of course follow to be pronounced, that whatever tends to undermine public virtue should be most carefully guarded against. This hydra mischief is pictured with great life, by a late Poet in the following lines.

> He pride, he pomp, he luxury diffus'd;
> He taught them wants beyond their private means;

And strait in bounty's pleasing chains involv'd,
They grew his slaves—*Who cannot live on little,
Or, as his various fortune shall permit,*
STANDS IN THE MARKET TO BE SOLD.

That luxury naturally creates want, and that want, whether artificial or real, has a tendency to make men venal, are truths that are too evident to be disputed. Luxury therefore leads to Corruption; and whoever encourages great luxury in a free state must be a bad citizen; so, of course, whatever government does the same must be a bad government, because it therein acts against the interest of the community.

That we had ministers [   ] enough to avow and glory in such a system, there can be no intelligent man who will be so hardy as to deny; and their motives to such practice have been these, an unworthy compliance with the will of the sovereign, in un-national engagements, and unconstitutional gratifications to themselves and their adherents. The fatal effects of this wicked system are what we are now groaning under, an insupportable load of debts, taxes, pensions, sine-cures, and employments, with an universal spirit of Rapine and Combination, to supply the cravings of avarice, luxury, and prostitution; while the waste of the drones of the hive exceeds all the means of industry to furnish, with but a reserve of what is needful for its own support. And the wicked plea having long been, we must make necessity impel the utmost exercions of labour to the utmost, for public good, so it seems at least to have become the mad aim of partiallity, even to add starving to toil, upon a similar wise plan to that of the [   ] who undertook to make his horse live without eating; which he had no sooner brought him to do than the horse unfortunately died.

But surely a large body of men of eminence, who should have thought themselves free, and to have had an honour to support, must have abandoned all principles, or been made of an odd kind of stuff, to ever suffer themselves to be told openly, *that every man had his price,* and that *a minister would be a pitiful fellow, who did not turn out every one that would not implicitly obey his orders,* even in their discharge of a most sacred trust from others; and by way of countenancing the profligacy he encouraged, dared boldly to alledge; *that the man was a fool, who pretended to be a* whit honester *than the times in which he lived.* Surely, while such were open doctrines, we ought not to wonder at the wickedness of any practice, or at what we have been made since to suffer by them. All that we should wonder at is, that any man could be so daringly wicked with impunity, and yet that there should remain even a phantom of liberty.

But when ministers dare not only to talk but also to act arbitrarily in a free state, and, no matter in what mode, so as even to invert the very nature of constitutional institutions, in defiance of an inherent right in the people to call him to a strict account for so doing, and to procure punishment being inflicted on him adequate to his offense, then must public virtue have lost all its elastic powers, and not only liberty, but also right, and even justice, be alike considered to be no better than *phantoms;* for when men, from the prevalence of corruption can be flagitious with impunity, the most constitutional remedies against the worst of evils to a people may truly be said to have got out of their reach; and what then do they become, but slaves to the will of a prince, or a minister, though in a mode that perhaps may be peculiar? But surely, the mere varying of forms cannot be said to alter the essences of things.

Machiavel [Machiavelli] places all the constitutional strength of a people in a free state, in their facility of means for bringing great offenders to condign punishment; and indeed, without such sure and facile means in their hands, there may be expected a ceaseless invasion of their most sacred rights and privileges. But this right, like all others that are substantial, will be tendered of no effect, whenever their greatest right of all, their legislative right, which comprehends the former, becomes exercised, not for the good and advantage of those who are represented, but of those who represent; and how far such was the real case in the times of which I am writing, is left to the reader's determination. But this may be said, that if it ever hereafter should become the case, that sacred right will be then found so effectually inverted, that agents will become principals; and instead of acting for the service of the people, the popular rights will only be considered as their merchandize; so that the people will be made the mere instruments for aggrandizing their agents, at their own great expence and injury both in property and security; or, in other words, they will be made to invest their representatives with a power to dispose of their rights and properties to a purchaser who will pay them for so doing with their own money.

Whenever such becomes the case, the abuses will be made glaring by their mischievous effects. The system of governing policy will then be apparently corruption. Ministers will make it their chief study and care to seduce the representatives of the people and guardians of their rights into a combination or conspiracy to betray and plunder them, for their own benefit. The very necessity will be urges of executive government's being secure of a majority of tractable representatives of the people, and therefrom not only the public purse will be at their command, but ministers will also, in effect, have an uncontroulable power to do whatever they list without hazard to themselves; as they will by such wicked means, be sure of protectors in those who, in cases of iniquity, should be their accusers and prosecutors; so that the people will be left without the means of obtaining remedy or redress for any kind of injury, or the power to procure justice to be done on those by whom they are made to suffer the greatest violences and oppressions.

Without great public virtue, such a system of corruption must naturally take place, and whenever it does take place, the constitution will then become unhinged, and all liberty and right in the people indeed but a mere *phantom*. Nor can public virtue exist but by a refusance of luxury, for that is sure to create artificial wants that will be boundless, and at [   ] time be productive of more miseries than enjoyments to those who indulge it. To men who are superior to the baits of luxury there can be no temptations to become corrupt, either as electors or representatives; and therefore it must be on the virtues of such men only that public freedom, justice and security can ever rest; so that whenever there ceases to be a sufficient number of such men, then all those blessings must become in danger of being forever lost.

By these criterions, therefore, we can only frame right judgments of either administrations or individuals, and of course they may be considered as the barometers of times, for pointing to the degrees in which public virtue and security at any time exist; for if administrations are seen to encourage luxury and profusion, it may certainly be concluded, that they do it on the view of creating a necessity in men to become servile and corrupt; and if individuals by their own profusion, do reduce themselves to want and perplexity, we may be assured that their necessities will make them become corrupt; so that such ministers, or men, cannot with safety be relied on; and, of course, as undeserving of public confidence, they should ever be opposed.

Let individuals then be but true to their common interests, and it will always be secure. But if they have not virtue or sense enough to do so, they will suffer themselves first to be made fools, and then deservedly slaves and wretches; for where power, on one side, has no bounds, their misery on the other, will be sure soon to have no limits, as we may be convinced by a candid survey of the conditions of many nations, and at no great distance from our own country.

[11]

A SON OF LIBERTY

[SILAS DOWNER 1729–1785]

A Discourse at the Dedication of the Tree of Liberty

PROVIDENCE, 1768

After graduating from Harvard, Downer settled in Providence, Rhode Island, where he united minor political appointments with small business ventures to launch a career that eventually won him considerable repute as a lawyer. Politics seems to have been too attractive, however, to permit any great success in accumulating wealth. He was a rebel in the cause of resistance that steadily developed into a demand for independence, involving himself from their first appearance in the activities of the Providence Committee of Correspondence and several other local organizations devoted to information and arousal of the Rhode Island citizenry. The passionate plea for liberty printed here was delivered to a Providence audience eight years before the fateful Declaration of Independence. The tradition of dedicating a tree of liberty probably goes back to the ancient practice of Saxon clans' assembling to hold their *tungemoot* (town meeting) under some large tree. Under Norman rule since the eleventh century, the Saxons would dedicate a tree of liberty to symbolize their former liberty. In any case, the practice was common in the American colonies well before the struggle for independence. Silas Downer here uses the occasion to rehearse the American position developed during the recently concluded Stamp Act crisis. He clearly states the basic formula that the American people are equal to the British people in the mother country. This formula, implicit in one or two of the earlier pieces reproduced here, would be reiterated hundreds of times in colonial and, later, revolutionary newspaper articles and pamphlets. In this context, the words by Jefferson that "all men are created equal," despite any individualistic meaning he may have had, were certainly read by the average reader as meaning just what Downer says here: the American people are equal to the people in England, and not in any sense subordinate.

Dearly beloved Countrymen,

We His Majesty's subjects, who live remote from the throne, and are inhabitants of a new world, are here met together to dedicate the *Tree of Liberty*. On this occasion we chearfully recognize our allegiance to our sovereign Lord, *George* the third, King of *Great-Britain,* and supreme Lord of these dominions, but utterly deny any other dependence on the inhabitants of that island, than what is mutual and reciprocal between all mankind.—It is good for us to be here, to confirm one another in the principles of liberty, and to renew our obligations to contend earnestly therefor.

Our forefathers, with the permission of their sovereign, emigrated from *England,* to avoid the unnatural oppressions which then took place in that country. They endured all sorts of miseries and hardships, before they could establish any tolerable footing in the new world. It was then hoped and expected that the blessing of freedom would be the inheritance of their posterity, which they preferred to every other temporal consideration. With the extremest toil, difficulty, and danger, our great and noble ancestors founded in *America* a number of colonies [4] under the allegiance of the crown of *England.* They forfeited not the privileges of *Englishmen* by removing themselves hither, but brought with them every right, which they could or ought to have enjoyed had they abided in *England.*—They had fierce and dreadful wars with savages, who often poured their whole force on the infant plantations, but under every difficulty and discouragement, by the good providence of God they multiplied exceedingly and flourished, without receiving any protection or assistance from *England.* They were free from impositions. Their kings were well disposed to them, and their fellow subjects in *Great Britain* had not then gaped after *Naboth's* vineyard. Never were people so happy as our forefathers, after they had brought the land to a state of inhabitancy, and procured peace with the natives. They sat every man under his own vine, and under his own fig tree. They had but few wants; and luxury, extravagance, and debauchery, were known only by the names, as the things signified thereby, had not then arrived from the old world. The public worship of God, and the education of children and youth, were never more encouraged in any part of the globe. The laws which they made for the general advantage were exactly carried into execution. In fine, no country ever experienced more perfect felicity. Religion, learning, and a pure administration of justice were exceeding conspicuous, and kept even pace with the population of the country.

When we view this country in its extent and variety of climates, soils, and produce, we ought to be exceeding thankful to divine goodness in bestowing it upon our forefathers, and giving it as an heritage for their children.—We may call it the promised land, a good land and a large—a land of hills and vallies, of rivers, brooks, and springs of water—a land of milk and honey, and wherein we may eat bread to the full. A land whose stones are iron, the most useful material in all nature, and of other choice mines and minerals; and a land whose rivers and adjacent seas are stored with the best of fish. In a word, no part of the habitable world can boast of so many natural [5] advantages as this northern part of *America*.

But what will all these things avail us, if we be deprived of that liberty which the GOD of nature hath given us. View the miserable condition of the poor wretches, who inhabit countries once the most fertile and happy in the world, where the blessings of liberty have been removed by the hand of arbitrary power. Religion, learning, arts, and industry, vanished at the deformed appearance of tyranny. Those countries are depopulated, and the scarce and thin inhabitants are fast fixed in chains and slavery. They have nothing which they can call their own; even their lives are at the absolute disposal of the monsters who have usurped dominion over them.

The dreadful scenes of massacre and bloodshed, the cruel tortures and brutal barbarities, which have been committed on the image of GOD, with all the horrible miseries which have overflowed a great part of the globe, have proceeded from wicked and ambitious men, who usurped an absolute dominion over their fellows. If this country should experience such a shocking change in their affairs, or if despotic sway should succeed the fair enjoyment of liberty, I should prefer a life of freedom in *Nova-Zembla, Greenland,* or in the most frozen regions in the world, even where the use of fire is unknown, rather than to live here to be tyrannized over by any of the human race.

PROVIDENCE, 1768

Government is necessary. It was instituted to secure to individuals that natural liberty, which no human creature hath a right to deprive them of. For which end the people have given power unto the rulers to use as there may be occasion for the good of whole community, and not that the civil magistrate, who is only the peoples trustee, should make use of it for the hurt of the governed. If a commander of a fortress, appointed to make defence against the approaches of an enemy, should breech about his guns and fire upon his own town, he would commence tyrant and ought to be treated as an enemy to mankind.

The ends of civil government have been well answered [6] in *America,* and justice duly administred in general, while we were governed by laws of our own make, and consented to by the Crown. It is of the very essence of the *British* constitution, that the people shall not be governed by laws, in the making of which they had no hand, or have their monies taken away without their own consent. This privilege is *inherent,* and cannot be *granted* by any but the Almighty. It is a natural right which no creature can *give,* or hath a right to take away. The great charter of liberties, commonly called *Magna Charta,* doth not *give* the privileges therein mentioned, nor doth our *Charters,* but must be considered as only declaratory of our rights, and in affirmance of them. The formation of legislatures was the first object of attention in the colonies. They all recognized the King of *Great-Britain,* and a government of each was erected, as like to that in *England,* as the nature of the country, and local circumstances, would admit. Assemblies or parliaments were instituted, wherein were present the King by his substitutes, with a council of great men, and the people, by their representatives. Our distant situation from *Great-Britain,* and other attendant circumstances, make it impossible for us to be represented in the parliament of that country, or to be governed from thence. The exigencies of state often require the immediate hand of governments and confusion and misrule would ensue if government was not topical. From hence it will follow that our legislatures were *compleat,* and that the parliamentary authority of *Great-Britain* cannot be extended over us without involving the greatest contradiction: For if we are to be controuled by their parliament, our own will be useless. In short, I cannot be perswaded that the parliament of *Great-Britain* have any lawful right to make *any laws whatsoever* to bind us, because there can be no fountain from whence such right can flow. It is

universally agreed amongst us that they cannot tax us, because we are
not represented there. Many other acts of legislation may affect us as
nearly as taking away our monies. There are many kinds of property
as dear to us as our [7] money, and in which we may be greatly
injured by allowing them a power in, or to direct about. Suppose the
parliament of *Great-Britain* should undertake to prohibit us from
walking in the streets and highways on certain saints days, or from
being abroad after a certain time in the evening, or (to come nearer
to the matter) to restrain us from working up and manufacturing
materials of our own growth, would not our liberty and property be
as much affected by such regulations as by a tax act? It is the very
spirit of the constitution that the King's subjects shall not be governed
by laws, in the making of which they had no share; and this principle
is the greater barrier against tyranny and oppression. If this bulwark
be thrown down, nothing will remain to us but a dreadful expectation
of certain slavery. If any acts of the *British* parliament are found
suitable and commensurate to the nature of the country, they may be
introduced, or adopted, by special acts of our own parliaments, which
would be equivalent to making them anew; and without such
introduction or adoption, our allowance of the validity or force of *any*
act of the *English* or *British* parliament in these dominions of the King,
must and will operate as a concession on our part, that our fellow
subjects in another country can choose a set of men among themselves,
and impower them to make laws to bind us, as well in the matter of
taxes as in every other case. It hath been fully proved, and is a point
not to be controverted, that in our constitution the having of property,
especially a landed estate, entitles the subject to a share in government
and framing of laws. The *Americans* have such property and estate,
but are not, and never can be represented in the *British* parliament.
It is therefore clear that that assembly cannot pass *any* laws to bind
us, but that we must be governed by our own parliaments, in which
we can be in person, or by representation.

But of late a new system of politics hath been adopted in *Great-
Britain,* and the *common people* there claim a sovereignty over us although
they be only fellow subjects. The more I consider the nature and
tendency of this [8] claim, the more I tremble for the liberties of my
country: For although it hath been unanswerably proved that they
have no more power over us than we have over them, yet relying on
the powerful logic of guns and cutlery ware, they cease not to make

laws injurious to us; and whenever we expostulate with them for so doing, all the return is a discharge of threats and menaces.

It is now an established principle in *Great-Britain,* that we are subject to the *people* of that country, in the same manner as they are subject to the Crown. They expressly call us their subjects. The language of every paultry scribler, even of those who pretend friendship for us in some things, is after this lordly stile, *our colonies—our western dominions—our plantations—our islands—our subjects in America—our authority—our government*—with many more of the like imperious expressions. Strange doctrine that we should be the subjects of subjects, and liable to be controuled at their will! It is enough to break every measure of patience, that fellow subjects should assume such power over us. They are so possessed with the vision of the plenitude of their power, that they call us rebels and traitors for denying their authority. If the King was an absolute monarch and ruled us according to his absolute will and pleasure, as some kings in *Europe* do their subjects, it would not be in any degree so humiliating and debasing, as to be governed by one part of the Kings subjects who are but equals. From every part of the conduct of the administration, from the acts, votes, and resolutions of the parliament, and from all the political writings in that country, and libels on *America,* this appears to be their claim, which I think may be said to be an invasion of the rights of the King, and an unwarrantable combination against the liberties of his subjects in *America.*

Let us now attend a little to the conduct of that country towards us, and see if it be possible to doubt of their principles. In the 9th. of *Anne,* the post-office act was made, which is a tax act, and which annually draws great sums of money from us. It is true that such an establishment would have been a great use, but then the [9] regulation ought to have been made among ourselves. And it is a clear point to me that let it be ever so much to the advantage of this country, the parliament had no more right to interfere, than they have to form such an establishment in the electorate of *Hanover,* the King's *German* dominions.

They have prohibited us from purchasing any kind of goods or manufactures of *Europe* except from *Great-Britain,* and from selling any of our own goods or manufactures to foreigners, a few inconsiderable articles excepted, under pain of confiscation of vessel and cargo, and other heavy penalties. If they were indeed our sovereign lords and masters, as they pretend to be, such regulations would be in open violation of the laws of nature. But what adds to this grievance is, that in the trade between us they can set their own prices both on our and their commodities, which is in effect a tax and of which they have availed themselves: And moreover, duties are laid on divers enumerated articles on their import, for the express purpose of a revenue. They freely give and grant away our monies without our consent, under the specious pretence of defending, protecting, and securing *America,* and for the charges of the administration of justice here, when in fact, we are not indebted to them one farthing for any defence or protection from the first planting the country to this moment, but on the contrary, a balance is due to us for our exertion in the general cause; and besides, the advantages which have accrued to them in their trade with us hath put millions in their pockets. As to the administration of justice, no country in the world can boast of a purer one than this, the charges of which have been always chearfully provided for and paid without their interposition. There is reason to fear that if the *British* people undertake the business of the administration of justice amongst us it will be worse for us, as it may cause an introduction of their fashionable corruptions, whereby our pure streams of justice will be tainted and polluted. But in truth, by the administration of justice is meant the keeping up an outfit [10] of officers to rob us of our money, to keep us down and humble, and to frighten us out of our undoubted rights.

And here it may be proper to mention the grievances of the custom house. Trade is the natural right of all men, but it is so restrained, perplexed and fettered that the officers of the customs, where there happens a judge of admiralty to their purpose, can seize and get condemned any vessel or goods they see fit. They will seize a vessel without shewing any other cause than their arbitrary will, and keep her a long time without exhibiting any libel, during all which time the owner knows not on what account she is seized, and when the trial comes on, he is utterly deprived of one by a jury, contrary to the usages among our fellow subjects in *Britain,* and perhaps all his fortune is determinable by a single, base, and infamous tool of a violent, corrupt, and wicked administration. Besides, these officers, who seem to be born with long claws, like eagles, exact most exorbitant fees, even from small coasting vessels, who pass along shore, and carry from plantation to plantation, bread, meat, firewood, and other necessaries, and without the intervention of which the country would labour under great inconveniencies, directly contrary to the true intent and meaning of one of the acts of trade, by which they pretend to govern themselves, such vessels by that act not being obliged to have so much as a register. It is well known that their design in getting into office is to enrich themselves by fleecing the merchants, and it is thought that very few have any regard to the interest of the Crown, which is only a pretence they make in order to accomplish their avaricious purposes.

The *common people* of *Great-Britain* very liberally give and grant away the property of the *Americans* without their consent, which if yielded to by us must fix us in the lowest bottom of slavery: For if they can take away one penny from us against our wills, they can take all. If they have such power over our properties they must have a proportionable power over our persons; and from hence it will follow, that they can demand and take away our [11] lives, whensoever it shall be agreeable to their sovereign wills and pleasure.

This claim of the commons to a sovereignty over us, is founded by them on their being the *Mother Country*. It is true that the first emigrations were from *England;* but upon the whole, more settlers have come from *Ireland, Germany,* and other parts of *Europe,* than from *England.* But if every soul came from *England,* it would not give them any title to sovereignty or even to superiority. One spot of ground will not be sufficient for all. As places fill up, mankind must disperse, and go where they can find a settlement; and being born free, must carry with them their freedom and independence on their fellows, go where they will. Would it not be thought strange if the commonalty of the *Massachusetts Bay* should require our obedience, because this colony was first settled from that dominion? By the best accounts, *Britain* was peopled from *Gaul,* now called *France,* wherefore according to their principles the parliaments of *France* have a right to govern them. If this doctrine of the maternal authority of one country over another be a little examined, it will be found to be the greatest absurdity that ever entered into the head of a politician.—In the time of *Nimrod,* all mankind lived together on the plains of *Shinar,* from whence they were dispersed at the building of *Babel.* From that dispersion all the empires, kingdoms, and states in the world are derived. That this doctrine may be fully exposed, let us suppose a few *Turks* or *Arabs* to be the present inhabitants of the plains of *Shinar,* and that they should demand the obedience of every kingdom, state, and country in the world, on account of their being the *Mother Country,* would it be one jot more ridiculous than the claim made by the parliament of *Great-Britain* to rule and reign over us? It is to be hoped that in future the words *Mother Country* will not be so frequently in our mouths, as they are only sounds without meaning.

Another grievance to be considered, is the alarming attempt of the people of *Old England* to restrain our manufactures. This country abounds in iron, yet there is [12] an act of parliament, passed in the late King's reign to restrain us from manufacturing it into plates and rods by mill work, the last of which forms are absolutely necessary for the making of nails, the most useful article in a new country that can be conceived.—Be astonished all the world, that the people of a country who call themselves Christians and a civilized nation, should imagine that any principles of policy will be a sufficient excuse, for their permitting their fellow subjects on a distant part of the earth from making use of the blessings of the GOD of nature. There would be just as much reason to prohibit us from spinning our wool and flax, or making up our cloaths. Such prohibitions are infractions on the natural rights of men and are utterly void.

They have undertook, at the distance of three thousand miles, to regulate and limit our trade with the natives round about us, and from whom our lands were purchased—a trade which we opened ourselves, and which we ought to enjoy unrestricted. Further, we are prohibited by a people, who never set foot here from making any more purchases from the *Indians,* and even of settling those which we have made. The truth is, they intend to take into their own hands the whole of the back lands, witness the patents of immense tracts continually solicited and making out to their own people. The consequence will be shocking, and we ought to be greatly alarmed at such a procedure. All new countries ought to be free to settlers, but instead thereof every settler on these patent lands, and their descendants forever will be as compleat slaves to their landlords, as the common people of *Poland* are to their lords.

A standing army in time of profound peace is cantoned and quartered about the country to awe and intimidate the people.—Men of war and cutters are in every port, to the great distress of trade. In time of war we had no station ships, but were obliged to protect our trade, but now in time of full peace, when there are none to make us afraid we are visited with the plague of men of war, who commit all manner of disorders and irregularities; [13] and behave in as hostile a manner as if they were open and declared enemies. In open defiance of civility, and the laws of *Great-Britain*, which they protest to be governed by, they violently seize and forcibly carry on board their ships the persons of the King's loving subjects. What think ye my brethren, of a military government in each town?—Unless we exert ourselves in opposition to their plan of subjecting us, we shall all have soldiers quartered about upon us, who will take the absolute command of our families. Centry boxes will be set up in all the streets and passages, and none of us will be able to pass without being brought too by a soldier with his fixed bayonet, and giving him a satisfactory account of ourselves and business. Perhaps it will be ordered that we shall put out fire and candle at eight of the clock at night, for fear of conspiracy. From which tearful calamities may the GOD of our fathers deliver us!

But after all, nothing which has yet happened ought to alarm us more than their suspending government here, because our parliaments or assemblies (who ought to be free) do not in their votes and resolutions please the populace of *Great Britain.* Suppose a parcel of mercenary troops in *England* should go to the parliament house, and order the members to vote as they directed under pain of dissolution, how much liberty would be left to them? In short, this dissolving of government upon such pretences as are formed, leaves not the semblance of liberty to the people.—We all ought to resent the treatment which the *Massachusetts Bay* hath had, as their case may soon come to be our own.

We are constantly belied and misrepresented in our gracious sovereign, by the officers who are sent hither, and others who are in the cabal of ruining this country. They are the persons who ought to be called rebels and traitors, as their conduct is superlatively injurious to the King and his faithful subjects.

Many other grievances might be enumerated, but the time would fail.—Upon the whole, the conduct of *Great-Britain* shews that they have formed a plan to subject us [14] so effectually to their absolute commands, that even the freedom of speech will be taken from us. This plan they are executing as fast as they can; and almost every day produces some effect of it. We are insulted and menaced only for petitioning. Our prayers are prevented from reaching the royal ear, and our humble supplications to the throne are wickedly and maliciously represented as so many marks of faction and disloyalty. If they can once make us afraid to speak or write, their purpose will be finished.— Then farewel liberty.—Then those who were crouded in narrow limits in *England* will take possession of our extended and fertile fields, and set us to work for them.

Wherefore, dearly beloved, let us with unconquerable resolution maintain and defend that liberty wherewith GOD hath made us free. As the total subjection of a people arises generally from gradual encroachments, it will be our indispensible duty manfully to oppose every invasion of our rights in the beginning. Let nothing discourage us from this duty to ourselves and our posterity. Our fathers fought and found freedom in the wilderness; they cloathed themselves with the skins of wild beasts, and lodged under trees and among bushes; but in that state they were happy because they were free.—Should these our noble ancestors arise from the dead, and find their posterity trucking away that liberty, which they purchased at so dear a rate, for the mean trifles and frivolous merchandize of *Great Britain,* they would return to the grave with a holy indignation against us. In this day of danger let us exert every talent, and try every lawful mean, for the preservation of our liberties. It is thought that nothing will be of more avail, in our present distressed situation, than to stop our imports from *Britain.* By such a measure this little colony would save more than 173,000 pounds, lawful money, in one year, besides the advantages which would arise from the industry of the inhabitants being directed to the raising of wool and flax, and the establishment of manufactures. Such a measure might distress the manufacturers and poor people [15] in *England,* but that would be their misfortune. Charity begins at home, and we ought primarily to consult our own interest; and besides, a little distress might bring the people of that country to a better temper, and a sense of their injustice towards us. No nation or people in the world ever made any figure, who were dependent on any other country for their food or cloathing. Let us then in justice to ourselves and our children, break off a trade so pernicious to our interest, and which is likely to swallow up both our estates and liberties.—A trade which hath nourished the people, in idleness and dissipation.—We cannot, we will not, betray the trust reposed in us by our ancestors, by giving up the least of our liberties.—We will be freemen, or we will die—we cannot endure the thought of being governed by subjects, and we make no doubt but the Almighty will look down upon our righteous contest with gracious approbation. We cannot bear the reflection that this country should be yielded to them who never had any hand in subduing it. Let our whole conduct shew that we know what is due to ourselves. Let us act prudently, peaceably, firmly, and jointly. Let us break off all trade and commerce with a people who would enslave us, as the only means to prevent our ruin. May we strengthen the hands of the civil government here, and have all our exertions tempered with the principles of peace and order, and may we by precept and example encourage the practice of virtue and morality, without which no people can be happy.

It only remains now, that we dedicate the *Tree of Liberty*.

We do therefore, in the name and behalf of all the true SONS *of* LIBERTY *in* America, Great-Britain, Ireland, Corsica, *or wheresoever they are dispersed throughout the world,* dedicate *and* solemnly devote *this tree, to be a* TREE *of* LIBERTY—*May all our councils and deliberations under it's venerable branches be guided by wisdom, and directed to the support and maintenance of that liberty, which our renowned forefathers sought out and found under trees and in the wilderness.* [16]—*May it long flourish, and may the* SONS *of* LIBERTY *often repair hither, to confirm and strengthen each other.*—*When they look towards this sacred* ELM, *may they be penetrated with a sense of their duty to themselves, their country, and their posterity:*— *And may they, like the house of* David, *grow stronger and stronger, while their enemies, like the house of* Saul, *grow weaker and weaker.* AMEN.

[12]

DANIEL SHUTE 1722–1802

An Election Sermon

BOSTON, 1768

Harvard graduate and Congregationalist minister in Hingham on the east coast of Massachusetts, Daniel Shute took an active interest in colonial grievances against British policy but appears on the whole to have been a moderate in his views on the necessity for independence. He is said to have "stood aside and watched the Revolution run its course," but the little we know of him today does not suggest that his parishoners classified him as a Loyalist. In any event, after independence had been won and government under the Articles of Confederation had proved ineffective, Shute stood well enough in the eyes of his neighbors for the town of Hingham to name him a delegate to the Massachusetts Convention called to approve or reject the new federal constitution drawn up in Philadelphia. He supported adoption and spoke strongly in favor of its provision forbidding the application of religious tests in choosing persons for public office. Shute in this sermon is addressing the Governor, Council, and House of Representatives in the annual Election Day Sermon. As is typical for such efforts, he rehearses the values and commitments of the community through the explication of a biblical text so as to edify and instruct the decision makers of the community. Shute's effort is a good example of the breadth of concern and consistency in quality of these sermons.

Province of MASSACHUSETTS-BAY.

In COUNCIL, 26th May, 1768.

Ordered, That ISAAC ROYALL, BENJAMIN LINCOLN, and ROYALL TYLER, Esquires, be a Committee to wait on the Rev'd Mr. DANIEL SHUTE, and return him the Thanks of the Board for his Sermon preached Yesterday, before the Great and General Court, being the Day appointed by the ROYAL CHARTER for the Election of Councellors for the Province; and that they desire a Copy of the same for the Press.

A. OLIVER, Sec'y.

AN ELECTION SERMON

EZRA X. 4

> ARISE; for this matter belongeth unto thee; we also will be with thee; be of good courage, and do it.

He whose happiness can admit no accession, and whose perfect rectitude excludes every degree of malevolence, must design the happiness of those creatures he calls out of nothing into existence; to suppose the contrary is inconsistent with absolute perfection, and implies the worst of characters.

[6] The communication of happiness being the end of creation, it will follow, from the perfections of the creator, that the whole plan of things is so adjusted as to promote the benevolent purpose; to which the immense diversity in his works; the gradation in the species of beings that we know of, and many more perhaps than we know of, and the somewhat similar gradation in the same species, arising from their make, their connections, and the circumstances they are placed in, are happily subservient. And every creature in the universe, according to its rank in the scale of being, is so constituted, as that acting agreeably to the laws of its nature, will promote its own happiness, and of consequence the grand design of the creator.

Agreeably hereto, all beings in the class of moral agents are so formed, that happiness will result to them from acting according to certain rules prescribed by the creator, and made known to them by reason or revelation. The rules of action, conformity to which will be productive [7] of happiness to *such* beings, must be agreeable to moral fitness in the relation of things; in perfect conformity to which the rectitude, and happiness of the creator himself consists. And such is the connection and dependency of things, that happiness will result from conformity to these rules, not only to individuals, but likewise to the whole; for the beneficial effects of such conformity are reciprocal.—It naturally tends to promote the order and harmony of the moral system, and so the general good.

The plan of the creator being thus manifestly adapted to promote the happiness of his creation, his conduct herein becomes a pattern to his creatures that are rational moral agents, and the rule of their duty, according to their measure; for all moral obligation on such, indubitably, arises from the will of God, as there is so exact a coincidence between his will, and the relative fitness of things; so that the nearer they resemble him, the nearer they will come to the perfect standard of right action, and the nearer they come [8] to *this* the more happiness will be produced.

It being so evidently the will of God, from the general constitution of things, that the happiness of his rational creatures should be promoted, all such are under moral obligation in conformity thereto, according to their ability, to promote their own, and the happiness of others.

The nature of the human species, therefore, being so adapted to society as that society will afford vastly more happiness to them, than solitary existence could do, indicates the will of their creator, and makes it morally fit that they should associate. From the make of man, the disadvantages of a solitary, and the advantages of a social state, evidently appear. A state of separation from the rest of the species will not admit the exercise of those *affections and virtues,* in which, from his natural constitution, his happiness very much consists; but in connection with others there will be opportunity for the exercise of them. As [9] each individual living in a separate state would be preventive of the happiness for which men were evidently formed; and as this happiness can be obtained only in a social state, to form into society must be not only their interest, but their duty.

The instinct, or propensity, implanted in the human species leading them, as it were mechanically, to *that* to which they are morally obliged, is an instance of the creator's goodness as it facilitates the performance; and in the same proportion it does so, must make their neglect the more inexcusable.

Mankind being formed into society, the moral obligation they are under to civil government will appear from the same principle, as being necessary to secure to them those natural rights and privileges which are essential to their happiness. Life, liberty, and property, are the gifts of the creator, on the unmolested enjoyment of which their happiness chiefly depends: yet they are such an imperfect set of beings that they are liable to have [10] these invaded by one another: But the preservation of them in every fit method is evidently their duty. The entering into society lays the foundation of a plan for securing them; but this plan will be incomplete without the exertion of the united power of the *whole* for their mutual safety. The exertion of this power for that purpose, correspondent to the everlasting rules of right, is what is, here, intended by civil government; and as this is a method the best adapted, in their power, to secure the rights and privileges necessary to their happiness, to go into it is morally fit, and evidently the will of their creator.

Whatever mankind are obliged to perform must be within the verge of their power: The impracticability of the human species continuing to be one society for the purpose before mentioned, makes it necessary and fit they should form into distinct and separate societies, and erect civil government in them for that end.

Upon the same principle, still, the natural [11] rights of one society being invaded by the superior power of another, so long as the former are unable to assert their freedom, it is morally fit they should receive laws from the latter tending to their happiness, as being the best means in their power to promote it, rather than admit a state of anarchy, big with *confusion and every evil work:* But from these circumstances it is morally fit they should rescue themselves whenever it is in their power, only it may be as fit to use caution, that by such attempts they do not plunge themselves the deeper into distress.

The obligation mankind are under to civil government, in some form, as essential to their happiness in the present state, and perhaps not without its influence upon their happiness in a future, is not only deducible from the natural constitution of things, but also supported by written revelation; in which it is represented as greatly tending to their *good*, and therefore an ordinance of the great benefactor of the world, whose *tender mercies are over all his works.* In the epistle to the [12] Romans, the civil power is expressly said to be *of God,* to be *ordained* of him, and the civil ruler to be *the minister of God for good.*

The line, indeed, between one society, and another, is not drawn by heaven; nor is the particular form of civil government; as whether it shall be conducted immediately by the whole society, or by a few of their number, or if by a few, who they shall be, expressly pointed out; but, as mankind are rational and free agents, these are left to their determination and choice; only herein they are restricted by those rules which arise from the moral fitness of things productive of the general good, which they are ever bound invariably to observe.

Nor does the sacred story of the *Hebrew* polity militate against the established order of things relative to civil government among men. The theocracy of the Jews, was an extraordinary vouchsafement of God to that particular nation, but not counter to, or designed to alter, the general constitution of mankind.

[13] The right the supreme ruler of the world has to bestow favours upon *some* out of the common course of things, while *others* are left in the enjoyment of their natural privileges, can, in reason, no more be doubted, than his right to create one being superior to another; for, though unknown to us, *that,* as well as *this,* may be in the original plan for the communication of happiness.

The ecclesiastic, and civil polity of the *Jewish* nation, being under the immediate direction of God himself, was not only a signal favor to them, but also designed to answer very important purposes in his government of mankind.

Their civil polity coincided with the fitness of society, and civil government among men, in all their salutary effects; but the extraordinary manner, in which it was conducted, was never exhibited as a pattern to the other nations of the earth; but they were still left to judge for themselves, as to the form of civil government, within their power, that [14] might be most subservient to the public good.

That this peculiar form among the Jews was not designed to be perpetual appears probable, from the particular directions early given, by *Moses* the servant of the Lord, to regulate the administration of a king that should, from among themselves, in future time, be set over them; and also by the revolution that in process of time ensued by more than the divine permission. After which the civil state of the Jews symbolized with the civil state of other nations.

The Deity's condescending to be, in a political sense, king in Israel, being a signal favor to them, as hereby they had a civil government better adapted to their circumstances, and better contrived to promote their welfare, than they could have had by all the wisdom of man, it must have been impiously ungrateful to reject him in that character, and desire that one of the imperfect sons of men should be their supreme ruler; and therefore deserving [15] the severe reprehension given them, by the prophet, under the direction of God himself.

But though their inadvertent and rash desire was such an ungrateful resignation, and just forfeiture of the special favor they enjoyed, that God saw meet to discontinue it, and to chastize them for their wickedness therein, yet he did not withdraw the protection and blessing of his providence from them in the exercise and enjoyment of the rights and privileges common to human nature. And if the alteration made at their desire, the extraordinary vouchsafement of the Deity apart had not been agreable to the natural constitution of mankind, and fit in the relation of things, it is not easy to conceive how he should so far countenance the thing as to be active in setting kings over them: And not only direct them on their choice, but also prescribe rules for the regulation of such an office, and express his approbation of, and afford his blessing to those who formed their administration according to them.

[16] The difference between them, now, and the other nations seems chiefly to have arisen from their religious state; which indeed had still some kindly influence upon their civil. In the exercise of their natural constitutional rights relative to civil government, it was no doubt fit to seek direction from him by whose providence kings reign. Their expectation of immediate direction from heaven was founded on the peculiar gracious dispensation they were under; and therefore the like could not be expected by any other nation.

No set of beings can, in reason, suppose themselves wiser than their maker; but must think *that* to which he directs to be wisest and best; and, therefore, when they have certain notice of his pleasure respecting any transaction of theirs, both duty and interest urge them to a compliance. And what nation of men on earth, in the exercise of this natural right, unalienable to any mortal, would not be glad of immediate indubitable direction from heaven? But when [17] these special directions are not obtainable, as according to the natural constitution of mankind they are not, the affair being so important to society, and the happiness of the whole so intimately connected with it, it is fit that they should first implore the influence of providence, which may be real, though not immediate and sensible; and then transact it in the exercise of that liberty wherewith the creator has made them free.

DANIEL SHUTE 1722–1802

Ezra's advancement to the government over the Jews did not, indeed, originate from their election, but from the civil power of that nation to which they were then in subjection; but yet, as their circumstances would not admit of their exercising all the rights of a free state, it became fit that they should chearfully acquiesce in that appointment to promote their happiness, as it was the best method in their power.

They were now emerging from the lowest state of depression; for seventy years they had been unable to break the [18] iron yoke of captivity, and to assert their national freedom. But under the favor of *Cyrus* part of the nation had returned to their own land, and were laying anew the foundations of *the commonwealth of Israel.* Their dependence on a foreign power, not only for permission to return to the land of *Palestine,* but also for protection in the re-settlement of it, made it evidently their duty to submit to a deputation from that power, with a view to promote their welfare.

And *Ezra*'s being sent from the *Persian* Court, with ample commission to settle affairs among them, ecclesiastic, and civil, according to their pristine form, was no doubt highly agreable to them, as he was of their own nation, and his qualifications were so adequate to the important trust, for he was a ready scribe in the law of *Moses,* and well understood the magna charta of their constitution; and also as he was a man of great piety, and virtue, and ardently disposed to advance the interest of his nation: Who therefore could be more welcome, [19] who more likely to put things into a proper situation, and to promote the welfare of the community; the only worthy end of government?

The kind reception he met with appears, in part, from the early application made to him respecting illegal marriages in vogue among them, to which, the words I have read immediately refer.—, The story shows how ready he was to exert himself for their good; his known character points out his qualifications for the purpose; and the united efforts of the people with him, to this end, with an acknowledgement of his authority, are expressed in the text: *Arise, for this matter belongeth unto thee, and we will be with thee; be of good courage, and do it.* And if we may be indulged to take this instance as a specimen of *Ezra*'s general administration, and of the people's friendly spirited assistance through the whole; and as we go along to notice his distinguished character; the way will be open to turn our attention—

to the part of civil rulers—to the qualifications of such— [20] and to the necessity of the united exertions of the people with their rulers, to answer the salutary purposes of civil government.

And FIRST, The part of civil rulers, in general is to keep in view the end of civil government, and of their own particular advancement, and to act accordingly.

Though in the constitution of things it does not belong to man to live alone, or without government in society; yet he is invested with certain rights and privileges, by the bounty of the creator, so adapted to his nature that the enjoyment of them is the source of his happiness in this world, and without which existence here would not be desirable. And mankind have no right voluntarily to give up to others those natural privileges, essential to their happiness, with which they are invested by the Lord of all: for the improvement of *these* they are accountable to him. Nor is it fit, that [21] any of the sons of men should take from others *that* which they have no right to give, nor by their misconduct have forfeited; though in this case there should be mutual consent, the compact would be illegal, and both parties indictable at the bar of heaven.

Civil government among mankind is not a resignation of their natural privileges, but that method of securing them, to which they are morally obliged as conducive to their happiness: In the constitution of things, they can naturally have no rights incompatible with this; and therefore none to resign. For each individual to live in a separate state, and of consequence without civil government, is so pregnant with evil, and greatly preventive of that happiness of which human nature is made capable, that it could never be designed as a privilege to man by the munificent creator: And, perhaps, is not a privilege to other orders of rational creatures, as much superior to man, in virtue, as in rank of being.

[22] Mankind may naturally have a liberty to live without civil government in the same sense that they have a liberty, *i.e.* a power to neglect any moral duty: But they are evidently made dependent on one another for happiness; and that method of action, which in the constitution of things, will prevent misery, and procure happiness to the species, on supposition of their being acquainted with it, and in a capacity of going into it, is not only wrong in them to neglect, but even duty indispensible to pursue. From hence arises their obligation to civil government as mentioned before; and when the same reason

urges the lodging this government in the hands of a few of the number associated, the same obligation lies on them to do so.

A Community having determined that to commit the power of government to some few of their number is best, the right the some few can have to it, must arise from the choice of the whole; for in this state the government belongs to the whole, and one has no more right [23] to govern than another; the right therefore that individuals can have to this must be delegated. This delegation is not indeed the giving away of the right the whole have to govern, but providing for the exercise of their power in the most effectual manner.

It is by virtue of the previous consent of society as being best, that government may devolve on some by succession, and that others may be appointed to rule by those already in authority.

A compact for civil government in any community implies the stipulation of certain rules of government. These rules or laws more properly make the civil constitution. How various these rules are in different nations is not the present enquiry; but that they ought in every nation to coincide with the moral fitness of things, by which alone the natural rights of mankind can be secured, and their happiness promoted, is very certain. And such are the laws of the constitution of civil government that we, and all [24] *British* subjects are so happy as to live under.

The rectitude of the laws of a civil constitution are of more importance to the well-being of society than the particular form of administration, but that form which is best adapted to secure the uninterrupted course of such laws is most eligible, and herein also we outvie other nations.

Those laws which prescribe the rights of prerogative, and the rights of the people, should be founded on such principles as tend to promote the great end of civil institution; and as they are to be held sacred by both, it may be supposed, ought to be as plain as the nature of the thing will admit: Mysteries in civil government relative to the rights of the people, like mysteries in the laws of religion, may be pretended, and to the like purpose of slavery, *this* of the souls, and *that* of the bodies of men.

[25] The design of mankind in forming a civil constitution being to secure their natural rights and privileges, and to promote their happiness, it is necessary that the special end of the electors in chusing some to govern the whole, should be assented to by the elected to

vest them with a right to govern, so far at least as to direct the administration, without which they are indeed vested with no authority; for the being chosen to a particular purpose by those in whom the right of choice is, can give no rightful power to act beside or counter to this purpose. And therefore to the proper investiture of any in the office of civil rulers to which they are chosen by the people, it is necessary they should consent to act the part for which they are chosen; and this sets them in the high office of government, and gives them authority to regulate the whole.

Their consent to take the office to which they are chosen by the community lays rulers under a moral obligation to discharge the duties of it with fidelity. [26] And if for the greater security of society, they who are thus introduced into office are bound to the faithful discharge of it by the solemnity of an oath, their obligation hereto is the greater.

What is right in the relation of things, and which has the general consent of mankind, being the rule of civil government in a well constituted state, civil rulers are to be so far from invading, that they ought to be the guardians of the natural and constitutional rights of their subjects; which are here supposed to be so nearly the same that there is no interfering between them. To form a civil constitution otherwise would be to establish iniquity by law.

The various duties of their office then centre in one point, the end of their election, and that is to promote the public welfare.

Minutely to enumerate these duties is not indeed pretended, not only as it would take up too much time, but [27] also as the wisdom of the politician can better apply general rules to particular cases as circumstances vary; I therefore shall take the liberty only in a more general way to observe: That whatever is injurious to the community, whether foreign or intestine, is theirs to endeavor to prevent. In this state of imperfection and sin, particular societies are liable to injuries from one another, hence vigilance becomes one part of the duty of civil rulers; to this they are more obliged than other men: In office they are as eyes to the political body, the proper use of which is necessary to its safety. It is no small part of their care to descry danger, to penetrate the designs formed abroad to the detriment of the community. And as they are set for the public defence, when such dangers are discovered by them, it is their part to provide against them at the public expense; which must be in their power at all times, or at some times it may not be in their power to act in the character of guardians to the public. Individuals of the same society are likewise liable to unequal treatment from one [28] another, which also claims their attention. They are to rescue the weak and helpless, the widow and fatherless, from the cruel hands of oppression, and equally secure to all, high and low, their rights.

And whatever is for the advantage and emolument of society, is also their part to promote, not only barely to secure to their subjects the cardinal privileges of human nature, but also kindly endeavour to heighten their happiness in the enjoyment of them. Those methods which will be most conducive to the preservation and prosperity of the *whole* are to be studiously devised, and faithfully urged by them; hence agriculture and commerce, liberal and mechanical arts should be encouraged, as pointed out in providence for the benefit of mankind; in proportion to improvement in which will be the benefit resulting from them, by which a supply may be obtained not only for necessity, but also for delight; and hereby their political strength will be increased, and they become more able to support the common cause. The wealth [29] of the people is the strength of the state; and therefore, as *the diligent hand maketh rich,* they should reduce the vagrant, and call the idle to labor, and all to industry in their respective callings, so essential to the public utility.

But *wisdom is a defence* as well as *money,* and necessary to the well being of a community. The education of the youth is therefore carefully to be provided for; that hereby such improvements may be made, as happily tend to abate the ferocity of uncultivated nature, to soften the temper, and give a high relish to the sweets of social life; and such geniuses may be formed as public offices require; that the *people,* in church or state, may not be *destroyed for lack of knowledge;* but *wisdom and knowledge* may *be the stability of the times.*

The civil power also should be exerted to suppress vice as pregnant with mischief to society; and to support virtue as the foundation of social happiness.

[30] That public homage which the community owe to the great Lord of all; and which is equally their interest as their duty to pay, should be earnestly promoted by their rulers. The fitness of which, reason dictates and revelation confirms, as a proper expression of the dependence of mankind on him, and of their grateful sentiments towards him, *who giveth to all life and breath and all things;* and also as the way more deeply to impress on their minds a sense of their

obligations to conform to his will; conformity to which will produce order and harmony, and, qualify for the blessings of his providence.

The great advantages acruing from the public social worship of the Deity may be a laudable motive to civil rulers to exert themselves to promote it; and will have an influence on them who have the public good at heart, as well as a proper sense of duty to him, who *is higher than the highest:* In this way, while the ministers of religion are under the patronage of the civil power, the people will be instructed in those principles, and urged to [31] those practices, which will greatly subserve the interest of the community, and facilitate the end of government.

Ezra's commission extended to church as well as state; and there is indeed such a connection between them, and their interest is so dependent upon each other, that the welfare of the community arises from things going *well* in both; and therefore both, though with such restrictions as their respective nature requires, claim the attention and care of the civil rulers of a people, whose duty it is to protect, and foster their subjects in the enjoyment of their religious rights and privileges, as well as civil, and upon the same principle of promoting their happiness.

It is therefore the part of civil rulers to make, and as occasion shall offer, to execute such laws as tend to promote the public welfare. *These* indeed are in some measure to be varied, according to the temper and circumstances of the subjects, by the wisdom of the legislators; but yet it is necessary there should be in them [32] a conformity to the immutable laws of nature, to answer the true design of civil institution.

To these laws it is fit they should add such sanctions as will give them energy if they are suitably applied by those in civil office whose part it is to put the laws into execution.

Provided always, that no laws be made invasive of the natural rights of conscience, and no penalties inflicted by the civil power in things purely religious, and which do not affect the well being of the state: In *these,* every man has an unalienable right, in the constitution of things, to judge for himself: No man, and no number of men therefore have a right to assume jurisdiction here.

On the free exercise of their natural religious rights the present as well as future happiness of mankind greatly depends; the abridgement of which by penal laws is evidently incongruous to the eternal rules

DANIEL SHUTE 1722–1802

of equity; but these rules [33] are never to be violated in the exercise of civil power. Civil laws, of right, can relate only to those actions which have influence on the welfare of the state; and to all *such* the subject may be urged by the civil authority consistently with that freedom of mind, in judging of points of speculation, and that liberty of conscience relative to modes of worship, which he has a natural right unmolested to enjoy.

Obligation on civil rulers to secure the rights and promote the happiness of the people, most certainly implies a power in them to that purpose,—to make laws and execute them; without which, ruler is but an empty name: To this purpose they are indeed cloathed with authority, and armed with the united power of the community; only in the exercise of this power they are under the same moral restrictions with those by whom it was delegated to them.

As in a well constituted civil state there is a subordination among rulers, and each has his respective part to act [34] with a view to the public good; so to carry the grand design into execution it is necessary that each should keep the line of his own particular department; every excentric motion will introduce disorder and be productive of mischief: But each keeping a steady and regular course in his own sphere, will dispense a benign influence upon the community, and harmoniously conspire to promote the general good: As in the solar system, every planet revolving in its own orbit round the sun produces that order and harmony which secures the conservation of the whole.

The part that civil rulers have to act supposes qualifications for that purpose, and accordingly we have begged leave in the SECOND place, from the distinguished character of *Ezra* to suggest some of them.

Religion, learning, and firmness of mind in the discharge of the duties of his office, were conspicuous parts of his character, and comprehend perhaps most of the qualifications requisite in civil rulers.

[35] Religion includes piety and virtue, and is acting agreeably to the will of God according to the capacity of the moral agent. To *this* all men are under obligation as they would answer the end of their creation, and qualify themselves for the happiness for which they were formed: And to *this* they are obliged in their social connections, that the happy effects of it may be felt not only by themselves but also by others. Nor is there any station among mankind so elevated as to free from this obligation.

BOSTON, 1768

The public good is in proportion to right action in every individual.—But as in the civil subordination among men *some* have it in their power to do more *good* or *mischief* to the *whole* than others, so it is of more importance to society that *such* should be more virtuous than others. There is an essential difference between virtue and vice, and their different consequences to society will be sensibly felt: nor is it in the power of earth, or hell, to alter the natural constitution of things.

Vice is detrimental to society in some [36] degree in *any* of its members, but is more so in *those* who manage the public affairs of it. It disqualifies for public services at the same rate, as it debases the mind, weakens the generous movements of the soul, and centres it's views in the contracted circle of self-interest.

But virtue qualifies for public offices as it dilates the mind with liberal sentiments, inspires with principles of beneficent actions, and disposes to a ready compliance with the apostolic injuction, *look not every man on his own things, but every man also on the things of another.*

The religion of Jesus is designed to *destroy the works of the devil,* to bring men *from darkness to light,* from error to the truth, *and from the power of Satan unto God*—It inspires the mind with a sacred regard to God, and with benevolence to men,—it is an imitation of his example, *who came down from heaven* and *went about doing good,*—of *his, who is good to all,* and *whose mercy endures forever*—and it also more powerfully inforces all moral obligations, as it illucidates a future state of rewards and punishments.

[37] That character therefore which is formed from those principles, which are abhorrent to sinister views, and indirect measures to promote a man's own private interest, and lead to generous godlike actions diffusive of goodness to mankind, and which afford the strongest motives to such actions, evidently corresponds to a public station, and is most likely *ceteris paribus,* to discharge with fidelity the duties of a civil post.

Nor is the influence, the example of rulers will, in high probility, have upon others, unimportant to society: Facts demonstrate examples to be very forcible on human nature. Inferiours especially are apt to copy the pattern set them by superiours, and too often even to servile imitation. In some proportion then as the example of those who are in exalted stations is virtuous or vicious it may naturally be expected the character of the *whole* will be: Nor is sacred history silent as to the influence public characters have had upon the morals of a people; in this view therefore it is the wisdom and interest of a community to prefer [38] the virtuous to the vicious for their rulers.

But the goodness of the heart influential on the life, without discernment in the head, will yet leave civil rulers short of a qualification necessary to discharge the duties of their office. Men may be pious and virtuous and yet not capable of penetrating very far into the nature and connection of things, and therefore unequal to transactions which require more than common abilities.

The natural and acquired accomplishments of mankind are various, all answering good purposes in their respective situations, and subservient to the general good; and in proportion to *these* they are qualified for different employments. Of *Ezra's learning* particular notice is taken in his commission for *government,* as qualifying him for the important post. And something corresponding hereto in all civil rulers is undoubtedly requisite in their several departments; I mean a capacity of discerning the nature and duties of their office, and how to perform them. [39] It is not indeed of so much importance how they come by this qualification, whether by *less* or *greater* application, as that they are really possessed of it; on *this* in no small degree the welfare of society depends. Those posts, to perform the duties of which distinguishing abilities, clearness of understanding and soundness of judgement are required, cannot be filled to advantage by *those* in whom *these* are wanting; *if the blind lead the blind both will fall into the ditch.* In this fluctuating uncertain state, the community will, at particular seasons more especially, need *wise men* for *pilots,* to save the threatned bark from surrounding gaping ruin. The weighty and multifarious concerns of state require *great* and *extensive* abilities to stear the *whole* in that channel which will terminate in the public security and emolument.

Capacity for posts of public trust without virtuous principles is indeed precarious, and not safely to be depended on; but when probity and wisdom unite in the same person they form a character that tends greatly to support the confidence, [40] and secure the happiness of the people.

But to *these* we may yet add firmness of mind in the execution of their office as a very necessary qualification in civil rulers, without *which* an habitual disposition to do their duty, and the good sense to understand it, may not in all circumstances answer the end. The necessity of *this* is supposed by *Shechaniah* when he says to *Ezra* in the text, *be of good courage, and do it.* And was exemplified by *that ruler* in his administration.

The present state of things will afford frequent occasions of trying the virtue as well as the wisdom of rulers.—Like other men they are exposed to temptations, and perhaps to more and greater than others; and human nature at best is very imperfect. The temper of domination so strongly interwoven in the make of man may induce them to a wanton exercise of the power reposed in them. Flattery by its soothing addresses and artful insinuations may insensibly divert them from a right course, and lead [41] them to dispense the blessings of government with a partial hand. Calumny and cruel censure may provoke in them too great resentment, or subject them to that *fear of man* which *bringeth a snare:* Firmness of mind is therefore necessary to repel *these* and a thousand other temptations—to supress every undue sally of the soul, and to urge the spring of action, that they may pursue with steadiness and vigor the great end of their office.

Those noble exertions of mind which a due administration requires clearly evinces the necessity of this temper in civil rulers: As in order hereto the art of self-denial must be learned and frequently practised by them;—a prevailing attachment to their own private interests and gratifications be given up to the public—angry resentments be tempered down to the standard of right action,—their ease superseded by incessant labors, and sacrificed to the benefit of others.

Softness and timidity of mind indulged into habit will weaken resolution, and relax the nerves of effort in the most [42] trying seasons, and perhaps betray the cause their office calls, and their virtue inclines them to support. But firmness and fortitude of soul arising from principle, and cultivated with care, will not easily admit those sordid views that lead *supinely* to neglect, or *tamely* to surrender the interest of society, but enable them to comport with personal inconveniences, and stand firm amidst the severest trials, in executing the duties of their office.

Good may indeed be done by him, who is *distinguished* by one of these qualifications alone, and more especially in his connections with others employed in the same office; their different qualities may operate in subserviency to each other, and by their mutual aid lead into measures conducive to the general safety; and happy to mankind that in this imperfect state it is so! But without determining which of

DANIEL SHUTE 1722–1802

them being wanting in civil rulers would be of most dangerous consequence to society, it is very certain their meeting in the same person forms a character that will best answer the design of such promotion; and the more there [43] are of this character among them, the more likely it is that the public welfare will be promoted.

But, if every good quality should meet in civil rulers yet THIRDLY, the united exertions of the people with them are necessary to answer the salutary purposes of civil government.

A community having delegated to some of their number the power of civil government as a method of exercising that power the best adapted to secure their natural rights and promote their happiness are not at liberty to counteract the method, but under obligation, in every fit way, to support it; and indeed without their exerting themselves to this purpose, their rulers, however well qualified, will be unable to answer the end of their advancement.

The cause in which rulers and ruled are engaged is the same, though the parts they have to act are different; *these* all tend to one grand point, the welfare of [44] the community; and people are as much, obliged to fidelity and ardor in the discharge of their duty, as rulers to theirs, in supporting the common cause.

The discharge of the duties of civil office merits an adequate reward from them whose business is done thereby; and the community are unquestionably obliged to see that business performed. Rulers devoting their time and their talents to the service of the public entitles them to an easy and honourable support: For real service and great benefit done them, it is the duty of the *people to render to all their dues, tribute to whom tribute is due,* and *custom to whom custom.* If *this* should not be afforded *them* by the public, they could not attend *continually* upon the duties of their station; and of consequence civil government, on which so much depends, could not be upheld to advantage.

A respectful treatment of their rulers is also due from the people, and greatly conducive to the end of civil institution. *They* are raised to exalted station by the *people,* under the governance [45] of his providence, who wills the happiness of *all men,* and in promoting which they are to be considered as his vicegerents executing his will, and therefore worthy of esteem and veneration. Their success in administration also very much depends upon this respectful deportment toward them: To pour contempt upon rulers is to weaken government itself, and to weaken government is to sow the seeds of libertinism, which in a soil so prolific as human nature, will soon spring up into a luxuriant growth; nor will it be in the power of rulers to stop the growing mischief, or, to keep things in a proper situation, without, the concurring aid of the people.

A sacred regard to civil authority, according to the true design of it, is to be cultivated in all; and as a means naturally tending to this, including the necessity of divine influence in their arduous and benevolent work, it is directed by the supreme law-giver, *that supplications; and prayers, intercessions, and giving of thanks be made—for kings, and for all that are in authority, that we may lead a* [46] *quiet and peaceable life in all godliness and honesty.*

To keep up a veneration for rulers, is to keep up a regard to government itself in the community, and to open the way for its happier influence. Honor therefore should be rendered to them to whom it is due for the good services they have already done, and as being the way to give them opportunity of doing more, and to stimulate them to improve the opportunity by the vigorous exertions of their abilities to that purpose.

But still and more especially, the united efforts of the people with their rulers are necessary to the putting those laws into execution that are made for the good of the community.

It is here supposed, that the laws made by civil rulers coincide with moral fitness, and are calculated to answer the end for which only they are impowered to make laws; if otherwise, the subject can be under no obligation to observe them; but may be morally obliged to resist [47] them, as it must ever be right *to obey God rather than men.* The doctrine of *passive obedience* and *non-resistance* in the unlimited sense it has been urged by some, came not down from above, as it can be supported neither by reason nor revelation; and therefore if any where, may be urged with a better grace by *the rulers of darkness,* in the regions below, upon those who by the righteous decree of heaven, are excluded the common benefits of creation, than by those *powers that are ordained of God* for the *good* of mankind. But though with the highest propriety this doctrine may be exploded, it does not at all lessen the moral obligation of obedience in the people to an equitable administration; and to use their endeavours that the laws made by their rulers to promote the good of the community should take place to that purpose: This is only the continued exertion of that power which is necessary to carry into effect the plan of civil government laid by themselves, and without which the best laws will fall short of it. There may be *good* laws, and *faithful* executors of them, and yet such a practical combination of the subjects as in [48] some measure to frustrate the happy effects of them: The violation of *these* laws may be so connived at in one another, as to prevent the executors having the opportunity to suppress them. The laws of the supreme legislator of the world are unquestionably *just and good,* and yet are transgressed by daring mortals every day: And though under his all-discerning eye the impenitent shall not finally escape with impunity, yet the transgressors of human laws founded on the same principles as the divine, may illude the inspection of man and the force of his laws: And when this practice shall become general in civil society, the energy of government will of course be relaxed. Nor can it be in the power of rulers the best qualified and the most sedulously attentive to the duties of their office to prevent it, unless they were gods in a higher sense than the scripture intends by giving them that title, and were able not only to make *good* laws, but also to inspire their subjects with a principle of obedience to them.

[49] It is therefore plain, that the united efforts of the people are necessary to support civil government, and make it efficacious to the great and happy end for which it was instituted: And as rulers are holden by the strongest ties to consult and endeavour the welfare of the people; the *people* are equally bound to aid and assist them in these endeavours.

What has been imperfectly suggested in this discourse may lead to some reflections on the goodness of the supreme ruler of the world, to mankind in general and to ourselves in particular, in the present state, more especially as expressed in the institution of civil government: And give occasion to urge the attention of rulers and people to the duties of their respective stations.

The goodness of the Creator appears through all his works, but more illustriously to man than to any other creature on this earth; him he hath set at the head of this part of his creation: The place of his present abode is accomodated [50] to his necessity and pleasure; and his mind is endowed with reason and understanding to guide and regulate him in the enjoyment. With a view to secure him in the possession of the munificence of his creator, he is directed by instinct and reason to associate, and amicably unite the strength of individuals for the defence and safety of the whole.

And this method is peculiarly adapted to the present depraved state of mankind, in which by leaping the mounds of right man is the greatest enemy to man. If there was no such thing as civil government among them, what ravages! and what depredations would there be! This earth would be the habitation of cruelty, and a field of blood. The consequences of perfect anarchy among mankind would be more unhappy and mischievous to them, than if *the foundations of the earth* were *out of course, the sun* should *be darkened, and the moon not give her light, and the stars fall from heaven;* And the natural order of this system should be interrupted by a general and most ruinous confusion.

[51] But the plan of civil government, as included in the constitution of things, and obvious to the common sense of mankind, well executed by them, gives such a check to *evil doers,* and support to *them that do well,* that the nearer mankind pursue it, in its true intention, the more this earth will become a habitation of peace, of security and happiness. This privilege is put into their hands by the Lord of all, as the great security and completion of their earthly felicity; to him therefore their united acknowledgements should like incense, with fervor ascend.

We ourselves have reason, not only to join in the universal tribute, as partaking of the blessings of the creator in common with mankind, but also in particular to express our warmest gratitude to him whose providence determines *the bounds* of *the habitations of all the nations of men that dwell on the face of the earth;* that we live under a constitution of civil government the best adapted to secure the rights and liberties of the subject: The fundamental laws of which are agreeable to the laws of nature resulting from the relation [52] of things, worthy of men and christians; and the form of administration the best contrived to secure a steady adherence to those laws in the exercise of civil power. Our King sways the sceptre in righteousness, *and his throne is upholden by mercy:* The legislative and executive powers are guided by the same laws.

The beneficial effects of the happy constitution extend to the remotest parts of the *British* empire: *Britons* exult in the enjoyment of their natural rights under its auspicious influence, nor less the colonists in *North-America* while they participate with grateful and loyal hearts the like blessings from the same source.

DANIEL SHUTE 1722–1802

The colonists indeed on account of local circumstances, have been indulged to form into little distinct states under the same head, and to make laws and execute them, restricted at the same time by the laws and dependent on the supreme power of the nation as far as it is consistent with the essential rights of *British* subjects and necessary to the well-being of the whole. And this is so far from being [53] the ground of their complaint that it is in their opinion the very foundation of their happiness; from the antient stock they delight to draw nutrition as hereby they flourish, and in their turn bear to *that* proportionable fruit. Nor could any thing more sensibly affect them, or be thought of with more regret, than to be rescinded from the body of the empire, and their present connections with *Great-Britain*.

In their little dependent states they have long enjoyed her parental smiles, which has greatly increased their attachment to her: The relief she has kindly afforded them in times of danger and distress will always invigorate the addresses, and support the confidence of her children towards her, under the like circumstances, till they shall find themselves discarded by her. Which sad catastrophe may all-gracious Heaven prevent! But the same patronage is still to be hoped for by the colonists while they do nothing to forfeit it. Nor is it to be thought that *Great-Britain* would designedly enslave any of her free-born sons, and thereby break in [54] upon that constitution so friendly to liberty, and on which her own safety depends.

This Province has not the least share in privileges derived from the civil constitution of her parent country, and which are amply secured to us by royal charter.

Our Governor is by deputation from our most gracious Sovereign as the representative of his sacred person in our provincial model of civil government. His Majesty's paternal care in this respect is most readily acknowledged by us, as the Gentleman who has this honor at present is well acquainted with the laws and formalities of our civil constitution, and has abilities equal to the important post. Whose presence forbids every thing that looks like adulation, but may admit of the warmest wishes for his happiness in this world and the next.

The other two branches of the legislature are chosen by the people, either immediately by themselves or mediately by their representatives, which coincides with the freedom of the *British* constitution, [55] and we shall always esteem as a pledge of the Royal favor.

The return of *this day* is auspicious to our civil liberties, and fills every honest heart with joy. The liberty of chusing men from among ourselves, whose interest is inseparably connected with the *whole,* for his Majesty's Council in the province, whose part is not only to aid the power of legislation, but also "freely to give advice at all times to the Governor for the good management of the public affairs of government," will always be considered as a privilege *dear* and *sacred* by all who are not, by blind prejudice or sordid views, lost to a sense of the inestimable value of their natural and constitutional freedom.

The election of so important a branch of the legislature will naturally gain the attention of those who are concerned in it. Fidelity in the discharge of the trust reposed in them, and a regard to the welfare of the province will determine their choice. All personal piques, and personal friendships, and private interests will be laid aside upon this interesting occasion. And [56] while the public good is kept in view, qualifications for a place of so much weight and influence in government will be chiefly regarded.

We rest assured in the good opinion we have of the Electors, that they will divest their minds of every wrong *byass,* and will not *take* those who neither *fear God, nor regard man;* who have no steady principles of action to be depended upon, unless those that lead them to break through the highest moral obligation, and to live as *without God in the world,* and in whose minds private interest evidently turns the balance against the public. Not those who are unfriendly to learning, who at the most have only taken the intoxicating draught at the *pierian* spring, but have not drank so deep as to open their eyes and give them a just discernment of things, who in their patriotic phrenzy would deprive church and state of the means greatly conducive to the well-being of *both.* Nor yet the pusillanimous who would not dare to speak their minds in their Country's cause in trying seasons, and are only fit for a private station.

[57] *Their* virtue and wisdom will fortify them against artful addresses and wily intreagues in this important transaction. A just concern for the interest of their country will lead them to prefer those qualities and accomplishments which are most likely to promote it, and to give their suffrages for men evidently possessed of them to sit at the Council-Board the ensuing year.

And may all, who by the people under God are advanced to posts of civil power and trust, attend to the true design of their advancement, and with fidelity and incessant ardor pursue it.

The *matter* which *belongeth* unto them being altogether interesting to us, as every thing dear in this world is connected with it, we surely may be allowed to hope for an *upright* and *wise* management of it, and as the task is arduous, and attended with various and great trials, to press them by every consideration to *be of good courage, and do it.*

And no motives to urge them to patriotic [58] efforts are wanting.—The neglect of their duty, or that which is worse the counteracting the grand design of their office, by indirect methods, they will be able to answer, neither to their country, to their own conscience, nor *to God the judge of all*; for not only the present, but future generations also, will feel the unhappy consequences, and execrate the authors of what they feel. Their consciences will give them trouble at certain periods, but: especially at the near approach of the decisive day, when all their dignity will forsake them, and they will appear in their real worthless character, and creep *into the holes of the rocks, and caves of the earth for fear of the Lord,* to shelter themselves from that vengeance which yet will inevitably light on their devoted heads. On the other hand, the diligent, the faithful and intrepid execution of the duties of their office, will make them benefactors to the people at present, and transmit their names with honor to posterity, who, in futurity, will participate in the blessings. And *such* conduct will afford to their mind a satisfaction that nothing can equal short of [59] the plaudit of their judge; who will not forget their *labor of love,* but amply reward their services for mankind, and as they have *been faithful over a few things* he *will make them rulers over many things.*

The happiness of THIS PEOPLE in the enjoyment of their natural rights and privileges under providence is provided for by their being a part of the *British* empire, by which they are intitled to all the privileges of that happy constitution; and also by the full and ample recognition of these privileges to them by character.

Their civil constitution as the basis of all their temporal felicity is their dearest stake. Every privation of their natural rights is subversive of their happiness, and every infringement of the form of their constitution has a tendency to such privation: The preservation of their constitutional rights, in every fit method, will therefore ever forceably claim their attention; and to this purpose, while they are awake to a sense of their interest, the vigilance and care of their rulers [60] will, of right, be earnestly expected by them.

Their being dependent on the supreme power of the nation as a part of the *whole,* is so far from making it unfit to remonstrate under grievances of this nature, that it is a reason why they should do so; when by the constitution every subject has an equal claim to protection and security in the exercise of that very power.

Their being loyal subjects to the best of Kings, whom may God long preserve! and disposed to cultivate, and if possible to increase their loyalty, will always incline his gracious ear; and give weight to their petitions with his parliament.

With indifference to surrender constitutional rights, or with rashness to oppose constitutional measures, is equally to *rebel* against the state. Anarchy and slavery are both diametrically opposite to the genius of the *British* constitution, and indeed to the constitution of the God of nature; and equal care at least is to be [61] taken to avoid the former as the latter. A ready compliance with constitutional measures will always justify a tenacious claim to constitutional privileges, and support the hope of their continuance.

The wellfare of the province, at all times, demands the attention of the guardians of our natural and civil rights; to this purpose the legislative and executive powers are to be exercised. But laws are useless in a state, unless they are obeyed; nor will putting the executive power into the best hands avail to the designed purpose, if there is not proper application made to it upon those occasions that require the exercise of it; for in proportion to the want of this application the most excellent *code* of laws will be a dead letter. It is necessary in the nature of the thing, and indispensably obligatory upon the people to unite their endeavours with their rulers to give life and energy to the laws in producing the designed happy effects.

We have good laws; and magistrates appointed to put *those* laws into execution, [62] whose fidelity may not be impeached: What therefore seems to remain to complete our political happiness is the exerting ourselves to aid the civil power, in surpressing every thing that may be detrimental, and in promoting that which may be of advantage to the *whole.*

Though *some* are appointed and bound by oath to give information of breaches of the law which come within their knowledge, yet *all* are under certain obligation to assist in conveying such information through the proper channels to the executive power, as it is the *ordinance of God* for the good of the community. But from the want of a due regard to the public—or from a misguided fondness for ourselves, we are too apt to be criminally indulgent to one another, and of consequence to desert the magistrate, and in some degree frustrate the design of his office. We have laws *wisely* provided against the evils of *idleness* and *intemperance*—and whatever has appeared to the wisdom of the legislature to be hurtful to society; to whom then may the increase of such disorders be attributed? [63] to *those* whose business it is to execute the law upon offenders, on due information, or *those* who rather than give, such information chuse to have *fellowship* with iniquity:—But not only they who are specially appointed for the purpose, but *all* should attend to the moral obligation they are under to exert themselves, in their respective stations, to prevent the interruption of the happiness of society, and instead of leaving the magistrates unaided, should voluntarily *rise up for* them *against the evil doers,* and lend their assistance to bring *the workers of iniquity* to condign punishment.

By this general exertion the most happy effects would be produced;—transgressors would soon be taught a greater reverence for the law, and all be more secure in the enjoyment of their rights: Hereby obstructions would be removed, and the executive power have free course; and *judgment* would *run down as waters and righteousness as a mighty stream.*

Instead therefore of speaking *evil of dignities,* and cruelly charging them with [64] the blame of prevailing disorders, we should recriminate on ourselves, and do our part to aid the magistrates in putting the laws *already* made into execution, and confide in the wisdom and fidelity of the legislators to make such *new ones* as the circumstances of the community may require.

And while the guardians of THIS PEOPLE are intent upon securing their rights and promoting their happiness, in every wise and laudable method, liberal support should be granted, great honors done, and cheerful obedience yielded to them.

Our safety and happiness must always arise from the united exertions of rulers and ruled to the same salutary purposes. The security of our liberty and property by the fundamental laws of our civil constitution is the strongest motive to maintain an inviolable attachment to it; and to exert ourselves to promote the interest of the nation to which we belong. Every well-directed effort to support the constitution on which the happiness [65] of the *whole* depends, and to augment the wealth and strength of the *British* empire, as our duty and interest, should be readily made by us. To multiply settlements on the uncultivated lands, and reduce the *wilderness* to *a fruitful field,* by emigration from our older towns, and especially by the introduction of foreigners not unfriendly to our constitution—to make greater improvements in agriculture and in every useful art evidently tends to the general welfare.

Arbitrary and oppressive measures in the state would indeed dispirit the people and weaken the nerves of industry, and in their consequences lead to poverty and ruin; but a mild and equitable administration, will encourage their hearts and strengthen their hands to execute with vigor those measures which promote the strength and safety of the whole.

To lay a foundation of greater security to *ourselves* is indeed a laudable motive [66] to such efforts; and may be justified by the principle of self-preservation: But the advantages of such improvements will not be confined to ourselves—the more populous and opulent we grow, the more able we shall be to defend this important part of the *British* dominions—the more our nation will be a terror to her enemies—and the better able shall we be to make remittance for what we shall necessarily want of her manufactures.

By a proper attention to the general interest, and vigorous pursuits of measures that tend to promote it, things may be put into such a situation as to be of mutual advantage. The growth and prosperity of her colonies must be of real advantage to *Great-Britain.*—The means for exportation being increased in them, will be so to the colonies, by which they may sink their present heavy debts, and more easily defray necessary public charges.

The same attention, with a little prudence, would lead us to retrench extravagant [67] expences, and to promote frugality, good order, and industry, that we might give a seasonable check to increasing debility, enjoy what we possess to more advantage and widen the foundation of future felicity. Under greater advantages we may receive monitory and directive hints, by turning our eye to the provident ant, *which having no guide, overseer or ruler provides her meat in the summer and gathereth her food in the harvest.*

DANIEL SHUTE 1722–1802

We are now reaping the happy fruits of our Fathers *hard* labor and *ineffable* sufferings; and shall not a concern for future generations warm our hearts—produce some acts of self denial, and closer application for their sakes? or shall we do nothing for our *posterity* when the first renowned settlers, here, did so much for *theirs?* Could *they* look down—or rather be permitted in flesh to visit their dear-bought country, with what astonishment would they behold the ungrateful neglect—with what severity reprove the prostitution of patrimonial [68] privileges, and chide the criminal want of philanthropy, in their degenerate offspring: and with what ardor would they urge them to perfect the work they had nobly begun, and thereby make room for millions yet unborn quietly to enjoy their natural, their civil, and religious liberties.

In fine. To secure his own, and to promote the happiness of others, is the part of every one in this great assembly. *To this end* were we *born, and for this cause came* we *into the world.* We were placed in that rank of being, and under those circumstances, which the infinitely wise and good Creator saw proper. And as we are moral agents, and accountable; it is of great importance to us in every station, to keep in view the *end* of our being called into existence.

This is but the bud of being—we are candidates for a succeeding state; into which, we are assured by the *gospel* of the Son of God, the consequences of our actions in *this,* will follow us. Nor in [69] the constitution of things have we long to continue here, but mortality will soon translate us to the state of retribution. With what care then should we avoid every action debasing to the mind, and with what assiduity pursue those that tend to raise it to nobler heights.

By inattention and vice we may forfeit the blessings of *creation* and *redemption,* and by a continued course of sordid and unworthy actions, dishonorary to God and unfriendly to mankind, we may finish the ruins of our nature; and put ourselves into such a state, that it would have been *good* for us if we *had never been born.* But by a diligent improvement of the talents committed to our trust in exercises of piety towards God, and charity to men, we may enoble the mind, and qualify it for the sublime happiness for which it was originally designed. Having therefore acted our part with fidelity in the service of God and our generation, we shall quit this imperfect state with dignity and honor, and rise superior to the highest grandeur and felicity in these [70] regions of mortality; and by the immerited munificence of the Creator

——————————walk—

High in Salvation, and the Climes of Bliss.*

* MILTON.

THE END

[13]

A WELL-WISHER TO MANKIND

[JOHN PERKINS 1698–1781]

*Theory of Agency: Or, An Essay on the
Nature, Source and Extent of Moral Freedom*

BOSTON, 1771

Perkins was a physician of Lynn, Massachusetts, who authored a number of pamphlets on earthquakes, comets, and other natural phenomena. This present essay is the only instance where he is known to have taken on political matters in print. Americans during the founding era frequently had a deeper philosophical or theological basis for their understanding of concepts like freedom and equality than is apparent from their political writing. Such theoretical assumptions and underpinnings were frequently taken for granted. Perkins here lays out the basis for consent—a concept central to American politics but rarely analyzed philosophically.

PREFACE

The consideration of the subject of Liberty has been, not only an agreeable amusement to the Author, but really interesting; he having formerly been carried away by the metaphysical, and very specious reasonings of the Necessitarians, into a favourable opinion of their notion.

What gave him lately an occasion of considering the matter, was, the reading an Essay entitled PRINCIPLES OF MORALITY, *written as it seems, to establish the doctrine of Fatalism. In that piece, the author represents the strong sense, or feeling, as he calls it, of Liberty, so universal in mankind, as a deceitful idea. That in want of power to confer liberty, the Divinity was oblig'd to impress our minds with this fallacious perception, to dispose us to perform the part assigned us. This was too striking to pass without attention:*

It had the effect; and but for this, the Author of the following pages had probably remain'd quiet, and secure, in the Necessitarian tenets. In examining the matter, he put down his thoughts in writing, as they occurr'd [4] not indeed as any answer to that piece, but for his own information, and in the most impartial manner he was capable of; if possible to find on which side of the question the truth lay. In this way he became assured of the reality of Liberty, particularly by a discovery of what it consisted in, and how it originated in the operations of the mind. This is what he has in the following pages endeavour'd to explain. Upon the whole, he thinks a Theory of Liberty practicable, and accordingly leaves the consideration of it, together with the materials he has collected, to the candor of the publick: Not without a pleasing hope that some better hand may undertake and perfect the idea.

[5]   THEORY OF AGENCY, &c.

Considering the design'd brevity of the following Essay, any particular examination of what others have written upon the subject, may not be expected: neither that much notice should be taken of the terms they have used, to express their meanings and explain the thing. A few words concerning absolute liberty, and moral freedom, may suffice to introduce the Author's private way of thinking.

By absolute liberty, a person has been supposed capable of determining differently, all circumstances remaining the same. Coactive necessity is its reverse; and both equally destructive of true liberty: One being absolute will, without any reason for action; the other being acted from without, as a mere machine.

On both sides of the question, it has been firmly believed, that some degree of a self-determining power was necessary to the existence of liberty; on neither side, however, has any one been able to find it; and probably many may have become Fatalists for no other [6] reason, than because they could not conceive of Liberty without it.

By Moral Freedom, has been meant a power of determining according to apprehended good and evil; opposed to a state of moral necessity, either natural, or induced by long custom, habit, passion, or some special depravity; which may be further taken notice of in the sequel: For the present, we may observe, that the question of Liberty turns upon this, viz.

A WELL-WISHER TO MANKIND

Whether there be any moral power or faculty in the mind, whereby it can occasionally change a prior determination? Wherein this consists? and by what operation of the mind effected?

Preparatory to a solution of this question, we may consider some of the differences between the rational and the sensitive world; together with the nature of what is called the will.

The powers of all creatures are suited to their wants and intentions; and their liberty is of the same nature, and proper to their powers. The brute, with only sensitive powers, and what are called instincts, acts according to these, and without constraint; or as he lists; but cannot have moral freedom; this being the exclusive property of the rational nature. Man has the inherent power of controuling the animal affections, which is denominated moral. So that he is not, as may by [7] and by appear, in all things necessitated. I say in all, because in many things he is so; thus by the constitution of his nature, as a corporeal being; in what life consists; and in some appetites, desires and aversions; but wholly so, till arrived to the use of reason, as in childhood, and at any time of life when reason fails; or the subject criminally neglects the proper use of it.

All appearances evidence that man was form'd for self-direction; since by his intellectual powers he can govern the sensitive clues in the use of proper means; rectify errors in judgment; disengage himself from prejudices; foresee events, and conduct accordingly: All which, by consideration; not by any thing of an absolute intention; the appearances of which are deceitful. The same may be said of the choice of two exactly similar objects, wherein there is no preference. I mention this, because the pitching upon one, instead of the other, has been objected as a proof of free-will: Tho' the person takes one instead of the other, only to get rid of the difficulty, which is all the motive he has in the case.

But suppose a person could chuse without a motive, (i.e.) with absolute liberty, what would be the wisdom of such a power? To what purpose an unmeaning determination more likely to produce ill than good effects? It is [8] time enough for willing and determination, when some cause, some reason for it appears.

The notion of absolute liberty leads us to enquire into the nature of what is call'd the Will: A thing which, as it seems, has not been rightly understood by the writers in morals. Much has been said of it in the affair of liberty; some have imagined it the first mover in the mind; and long use has associated a notion of something arbitrary in the mental economy, which has occasioned great confusion and obscurity.

The common expression is, that man has a Will; his faults are charg'd on the Will; and his Liberty called Freedom of the Will. Now in these expressions, we have strong intimations of some certain subsistence, faculty, or distinct power in the mind, by which it chuses and refuses, wills and nills, as the terms have been, and which have, as it were, given a sanction to the notion, and prejudiced people against an examination of the thing; whereas by a little observation of what passes in their own minds, almost any one might perceive the mistake.

By looking inwards with respect to will, nothing appears but desire and aversion; and by these, we constantly observe the mind determined; and by no other means. By these, we pursue apprehended good, and avoid evil; our determination wills, or choices, which are [9] * synonimous, are as our desires and aversions; and these, as our perceptions, and the ideas we have of things; or as our external and internal senses are affected. By all which it is evident, that will is no other than the mind determined by motive.

These affections of the mind, determining to action and conduct, are what have been invariably express'd by the term will. And indeed a proper name was necessary, as well as convenient, to prevent tedious and irksome descriptions of the complex idea. The fault has been, that in the name, we have lost the true nature of the thing; we have insensibly taken that for a cause, which was only an effect. Thus much may suffice in a preliminary way. We come now to the enquiry what our Liberty is, and how it originates.

The great Mr. Lock placed it in suspension of the mind, (i.e.) as I suppose, a being duly disposed to determine as evidence should appear. Suspension implies impartiality, and a freedom from byas and prejudice; but it does not solve the difficulty of motive; so that none

---

* Will and choice may indeed be distinguished, but the difference does not affect our present subject. Will properly respects action; Choice the manner and references of it. Or otherwise; Will determines a thing shall be done; Choice the manner how, or by what agent; this or another. Or conversely, Choice determines to the greater apparent good; Will to act accordingly; but in general there is such a sameness, that to say we may change our motives, is to say we may change our Wills or Choices.

have receiv'd any real information from [10] it. But it appears that the author himself was not satisfy'd of the existence of Liberty; for in a letter to his friend Molineux, he owns that he could not conceive of Liberty being compatible to the omniscience of the Deity. This no doubt was from a notion of something absolute being necessary to the idea of Liberty; the universal mistake of all the writers in the controversy, on one side as well as on the other, while the thing is so far otherwise, that the mind is evidently passive in every thing it gives attention to, at least it is so in a state of vigilance, since the spirit here strictly observes the laws of its union with the body, though it may be otherwise in sleep. And probably from this effect of the laws of union, the Necessitarians have been induced to rest their cause on the power of motive, and latterly have persuaded themselves that this alone is an effectual bar to liberty.

If, say they, we do nothing without a motive, we cannot by any means have liberty. And they add, that a moral determination no more admits of freedom, than a natural or physical one; in which they plainly make no distinction between the sensitive, and the rational nature. Nor do they better, when they would confirm their doctrine of Fatality, by the sophistical whim of motive depending on motive, *in infinitum,* (i. e.) that there is no first [11] mover. A notion too puerile to admit of a grave answer, were it not that many sober writers have adopted it, as if it was really to their purpose. But so it is, that in attempting a system of absurdities, one must give an answer to such stuff as this as well as the rest; therefore *quo ineptia trahunt, retrahuntque sequamur.*

This notion of a boundless series of motives, must have been the offspring of contracted views, as well as the impossibility of tracing them back to a first mover, viz. the external senses in their first affecting the mind; before this, it is to be observed there could be no motive. What chiefly gave occasion to the whim, seems to have been the impossibility of tracing them back to their source. The case is such, that long before we are capable of looking back, our first perceptions in childhood have escaped us. The memory of childhood is not retentive. In infancy the perceptions are seldom retain'd to the next day; tho' in a short time they may remain two or three risings and settings of the sun; but were it otherwise, in the course of a few years our faculties pass through such a variety of action, associations, improvements, and interweavements of ideas; and too often such actual depravities of our moral powers, that the hundredth part of these may be well thought more than enough to prevent our pursuing the thread of motive back to its original.

[12] But there is yet a way by which we may satisfy ourselves; and that is, by beginning at the first perceptions of the human mind: What these are, we may be assured by considering our frame; the order of our ideas; and what must, in the nature of things, have been our first perceptions: And indeed the impossibility of their having been any other than what originated in external sense. The first of these senses in use, are feeling and tasting; we feel first, then taste, loath, or else suffer hunger. Our use of the other senses appear to follow, but no mental ones are perceptible, till the bodily ones have been exercised. Anger is the first of the passions, and grief known by shedding tears, (i. e. weeping); for in the first days, the child cries without tears. After some experience, imagination begins; and in length of time reason, and the moral sense unfolds. All these, in their uses supply a vast number of images, ideas, and correspondent motives, forming a wilderness effectually preventive of any other way of inquiry; while in this it will evidently appear, that our first motives originated in external sense. For we have no innate ideas; nor have we the least appearance of mental powers, before perception by our senses. We must have perception before we can have motive; and sensation before we can have perception: So that here is the beginning of all motive. Motive then is not such an infinite [13] thing as the Necessitarians would have us believe; they make it like space, unbounded; for which this was once deify'd: As for the same reason, according to them, motive might be too.

By the way, I have taken for granted that others have the same idea of motive that I have, (i. e.) any perception exciting to action; or determining the judgments we make of things. It may be considered of two kinds, natural and moral; the former immediately from our various senses; the latter the offspring of our understandings, in reasoning; on which account I take the liberty of distinguishing them by the terms primary and secondary.

At the first view, man appears constituted of two natures, the animal and the intellectual. Motive necessitates all mere animals without a remedy; and it does the same by every human creature; as far as he is governed by his animal affections, so far he is necessitated. But experience shows he can controul these. Socrates and others in all ages have done so, by considering things, and their circumstances; and further by disciplines and use, facilitating the capacity, and improving the habit of reflection. We can consider the bodily claims, and submit to, or reject them.

In considering the power of Motive, I readily grant the Necessitarians all the facts they build upon; but not the assumed principles, [14] and hypothesis. I own we are in all things determined by Motive; that we never act without and never contrary to the present one. These concessions no ways interfere with our Liberties. What this consists in, is a particular prior to secondary Motives. Our Liberty consists in the procuring this sort of Motive. By consideration we determine concerning the propriety of our Motives, and confirm or reject them, in lieu of such as we approve: (i. e.) We reject the primary ones occasionally, and adopt others, which I call secondary, as more eligible: In the same manner as a servant who has leave for it, upon consideration of two persons, chuses which shall be his master.

In fact, we find our Motives do often change, and why? but by seeing things in different lights. It is true that they frequently change, as it were, by chance; but this is far from being always the case. New Ideas, and of consequence, new Motives arise in a way of reasoning and reflection; and this difference of origination alters the quality of the Motives, with respect to Liberty; in the latter case, we are active in their production: It is in this way we controul our inferior affections, according to the natural order, that the nobler powers should rule the ignobler. The thing is, that upon examination, finding the reasons intended action, conduct, judgment or opinion faulty, a [15] change of Motive naturally ensues, for other, or contrary ones. Any one may recollect that he has often done so, and satisfy himself that he can on like occasions, do the same again; viz. as reasons occur in reflection.

Here the Necessitarians may probably ask, Where shall we find the Motives for consideration? since they hold it not at our command.

The question indeed is proper to the occasion; but in putting it, they virtually own a fault they have always been reprehensible for, viz. a negligence in their enquiries into the frame of the human mind, and the operations of it; or they might have answer'd this question by themselves.

We freely grant that we have no immediate power of commanding consideration: But we have an equivalent, for all human purposes, implanted in the mind; a naturally strong disposition to it, which nothing but culpable self neglects, and rejections of its use, destroy: So that we have only to submit to our native promptings, to its use, on all occasions; and we shall sufficiently consider. Where there is reason, consideration and reflection constantly and readily offer. A much wiser provision for us, than any absolute power of commanding it; we can let the disposition take place; or we can shut the eyes of the mind against it; we can use or refute it as free creatures.

[16] We may with an agreeable propriety, call consideration the eye of the mind; since we make discoveries by it. And in comparing it with the bodily organ of sight, we may find we have a like power over both. The bodily eye is automatically, and naturally kept open by a proper muscle for that purpose; while yet we have a voluntary power of shutting it by another prepar'd for that office. The power of consideration is as really and as much under our command, in its design'd use, as the bodily eye is to view, or not, any external object. And we are in the general as much promted to the use of it, with this advantage, besides others, that the new motives obtain'd by the use of it, are our own property; redound to our praise and benefit; as the neglect of it does to our guilt and injury.

But the Necessitarians object, that desires and aversions are not in our power, and therefore we have no Liberty.

The reader will easily perceive the sameness of these and Motive, in so many respects, that the same answer might have served for both: But as particular expressions and sounds have very great influence on some minds; and considering that a separate discussion may give occasion to the mentioning some things which more or less affect the argument, I was determined to give it a place by itself.

[17] It is then readily own'd, that desires and aversions are not immediately at our command, as has been observ'd of Motive; but we have a remote power of obtaining new ones; or altering them, which is sufficient for our purpose. Experience teaches that we can procure very different, and even contrary ones, by industry and application of mind.

The body and the mind are both improveable, and by improving their faculties, likings and dislikings, are generated: Custom and use have great influence in altering our likings and dislikings; so applications of mind in the use of the understandings, as in arts and sciences, we become delighted with them in proportion as we increase in understanding them: The mind is like the palate, to which many things by use become agreeable which before were irksome, as oyl, olives, tobacco, &c.

Observation and attention make some things agreeable, by giving us right notions of them; thus we see the rustic, who at first despis'd the gentle manner and obliging behavior of the well-bred and polite, esteeming them incompatible with a manly fortitude and resolution, upon further acquaintance, becoming delighted with them.

Would we rectify our tastes concerning buildings, sculpture, paintings, &c. we may do it by frequent observations on them; and thus alter our erroneous likings and aversions. And [18] it is the same with our moral likings and aversions which we rectify, or change, by obtaining better notions of the things themselves, with their tendencies and benefits.

By consideration we become reconciled to various disagreeable self-denials; as with respect to the means for recovery from sickness; for the preservation of life and health: For these we deny ourselves many, otherwise desireable gratifications; the contrary becoming desirable by reflection.

Here I cannot pass some notice of what happened in the hot weather, while I was revising these pages for the press; particularly the death of divers by drinking freely cold water, or other cold small liquors, to quench thirst, when they were overheated by the sun, or exercise; now although accounts of such accidents are well known to every one, yet they are not attended to for want of consideration, and a resolution to consider and to take their drink leisurely, and by mouthfuls, at intervals, swallowing it slowly, 'till cool enough to make free with it. One would think the past and striking instances of mortality, by indulging in such circumstances, should render every one attentive and considerate; whereas we see them soon forgot; and why? but because no astonishing sound like thunder attends them. Altho' for one that dies by lightnight, there are many that die by such inconsideration. The least [19] thought might prevent many of these accidents. If no more than this remark is remembered, of this essay, I shall think all the rest, which gave occasion to it, well rewarded; and have the satisfaction of having been useful to the world.

But to proceed,—

I have observed elsewhere, that we can consider, or we can reject consideration; and that in both these we have liberty; altho' by the latter, in the use of liberty, we act against the continuance of it, so as gradually to lose the capacity for it, by depravities which always take place in the neglect of it. Both the learned, and the unlearned, are faulty in consideration. In their inquiries, they have too many resting places; they are too apt to take up with the first appearances of truth, by which they frequently come short of it. On a cursory view, we should be at a loss to say which of these classes of men are most faulty. We have therefore to consider, that among the learned, as among the vulgar, there are the knowing, and the unknowing. That man, alone, is knowing, who has not only acquired a proper stock of ideas, but well digested his notions of things. Not the mere scholars, that have scamper'd through the fields of science for the vanity of a title, and university diploma, without any becoming improvement of mind, or substantial principles of knowledge; these are generally more disposed to avoid consideration, [20] than the illiterate; those they despise under the term of the *prophanum vulgus.* They have more important and injurious prejudices, with an additional obstinacy, and arrogant assurance, from the pride of vain and imaginary knowledge. The plain, the simple, and honestly well-meaning, are, if I may be allowed the expression, infinitely more free, than those whose self-affections are exalted by a mere formal education. Practical knowledge only is valuable; literature is but a mean for obtaining it, but often falls short of the end. Right knowledge is a moral principle, which, besides other things, qualifies for self-government, and so the enlargement of moral liberty; as literature without it tends to its destruction: We see the pride of literature and contempt of the sense of mankind in a *Bolingbroke, Morgan, Coventry, Hume, Wolston,* and others; who have made the most violent attacks upon all religion, both natural and revealed: These however suit only the grosser palates, who can swallow absurdity without any seasoning, besides a little elegance of language to recommend it; they are therefore much less dangerous to religion than another sort of writers who are little suspected; and of which there is a great number: These in a covert and insinuating way, with the specious cloak of moral principles, and refined notions of things, are unsuspectedly poisoning the minds of the people. Nothing [21] shows the depravity of mankind more than the zeal with which these writers endeavour to root out of the minds of their readers, those principles which have the best tendency for the happiness of mankind. They are prejudiced, and voluntarily continue so: They avoid a manly reflection and consideration, being apprehensive it would prove an interruption to their love of licence: Their fondness for this, has an effect upon them similar to that of the serpent's enchantment of small animals, which is said to be done by a bewitching appearance round the serpent's head, when his eyes are fixed on the creature; drawing it, by admiration, to still nearer views of the thing, till it is brought within his reach, so weaken'd that he becomes an easy prey.

It is not pretended that the most considerate can in all things find truth; but then they will be generally cautious of misleading others: And yet a strong ruling passion may without a steady watch, betray them into gross enormities. Thus ambition and an over-fondness for honor, as by high offices in church or state, or the being esteemed as persons of superiour talents, knowledge and abilities: Such persons if not sufficiently attach'd, and zealous for a particular party, will be apt to list on the side of a controversy where their most flattering hopes of distinction attract them. In this class [22] perhaps, we might place the Author of an Essay on the *Principles of Morality*. An Author, who had he written in favor of Liberty, with the same genius and capacity he has done against it, would have done himself honor; and sav'd one, unus'd to the pen, from attempting such an abstruse subject.

[23]   PART II

Containing a few presumptive Proofs of Liberty.

The Author imagined it might not be amiss to subjoin to the foregoing theoretic thoughts, some moral probabilities of the reality of our freedom; which perhaps may prove more agreeable to some readers than the other more philosophic treatment. To these may be premised a few words concerning the ancient Fatalists, and the general belief of Liberty in the first ages.

It is acknowledged that universal consent is no infallible criterion of the truth. And yet it seems worth observing, that in all ages mankind have been invariable persuaded of the reality of Liberty; and this assurance continued till the Grecian Philosophers, by their blind way of inquiry, overlook'd and deny'd it: [24] However it was several ages before the doctrine of Necessity spread farther than themselves, even to the days of Epicurus. Epicurus erected an academy, and taught it to his disciples, and these propagated it: But what manner of reasoners he and they were, may be seen in Lucretius, who handed down his imaginations to posterity. After Epicurus, Liberty became more disputed; but was still believ'd by all that were not more or less taught to disbelieve their senses. Our modern Fatalists would reduce us to this, by confusing our minds with their abstract reasonings, which if they prove any thing, imply a great deal too much; particularly by the lengths they carry their power of motive. If we would have liberty, in their way of talk, we must be void of passions, appetites, desires and aversions; and be capable of willing differently, all circumstances the same. Unless our liberty be absolute, they will not allow it to be liberty. So that according to them, if a man's property is limited, it is no property; if he is confin'd to his own house, or parcel of land, he has no liberty within his own walls; if he has not the strength of a giant, he has no strength at all: But besides this, their notion ends in ridiculous nonsense; as that only inanimate things can have liberty: A stone then, a stock, or the posts in the streets have it. A man certainly cannot, unless he is fast asleep, and does not so much as dream. [25] But enough of this; the particulars here intended follow.

The faculty of reason strongly implies Liberty. In the foregoing part, it was considered as the faculty in which it inher'd, as it was evidenced in the article of consideration. Here I take it in a different light, as a proof of its reality.

Reason in man is in lieu of instinctive direction. Man has but few instincts; and these only such as are for purposes prior to, or rather out of the province of reason; while more had been superfluous for a creature furnished with rational powers. Our frame is contriv'd, as every thing through universal nature is, with nothing wanting, nothing redundant. And our being endow'd with reason and understanding, instead of more instinctive powers, shows that we were ordain'd for self-direction, in conducting by the former: And in fact, we find that we determine frequently on action and conduct by consideration and reflection, without any instinctive impulse, further than self-love, which without the other, is blind in the human species.

Man is plainly form'd not only to provide as the sensitive hoarding species do, the necessaries of life, but to procure both them and the conveniences of life, to look beyond what sense and instinct can direct him, for this and other purposes; to take in by his understanding [26] large prospects; consider the effects and events of prosecuting excursions into them; and determining on the suitable conduct for his intentions. His understanding is accordingly analogous to a prospective glass, which furnishes views beyond what the eye unassisted could afford him; and which he is upon innumerable occasions, in wisdom and prudence oblig'd to make use of, or suffer for the neglect. This glass we may use, or refuse in supplying the mind with materials for conduct so peculiarly needful in the system of man, and no other ways provided for him: It is the mean, as before observed, by which he can occasionally change his mere animal motives, and whereby he is denominated free. Upon this occasion, I may be allowed to repeat, That our being naturally oblig'd to act in conformity to the judgments we procure by consideration, is no objection to our liberty; since this arises only in the consideration itself, which is prior to the judgment. The essence of our liberty consisting in that use of reason whereby we can occasionally turn our present determination into another channel.

In the next place the moral sense, or conscience, so universally found in our species, is a strong presumptive proof of liberty.

Every human creature has a sense of right and wrong, ought and ought not, which are evidently intended to remind him of duty and [27] obligation; and without which he could have no idea of it. It is as really a natural sense, as the external ones of sight, feeling, tasteing &c. As constitutional as the other internal ones of honor, harmony, benevolence, &c. All which where any of them are wanting, no industry or discipline can give the subject any idea of their objects, whatever the Fatalists or Moralists pretend to the contrary. It is well known that these gentlemen assert it to be generated by the occasions, although by these it is only excited into action, upon the appearance of its objects: It unfolds when the person is arrived to the use of reason, and this being its nature, it evidently implies moral laws with a capacity of obeying and refusing. Here then it is to be observ'd, that such a sense could be to no pertinent purpose, if we had not liberty. The faculty would otherwise shew great unkindness in the construction of the mind. Is it possible to believe that an infinitely wise and good Being, would have plac'd such a severe chastiser in our frame, were we really necessitated; but rather that he would have form'd us so as not wrongfully and injuriously to afflict ourselves. We should rather believe that he would have impressed mankind with an effectual bias to right conduct, or else with proper instincts for every laudable purpose. vid. Divine moral government next to be considered.

[28] The appearances of a divine moral government are presumptive of liberty.

In the general course of common providence a scheme of moral government appears. We find that right action and conduct tend to happy enjoyments; as the contrary naturally to evil effects; and this by an establishment in the nature of things. So that we are beforehand apprised of the respective general consequences, in which we find ourselves interested, and naturally accountable: Common providence having thus the nature of law and government.

As to any special providence, the Materialists would have us believe there is no such thing; but that every event is the effect of general laws without any interpositions. They are no ways concerned that observation and facts are against them, as well as the universal sense of the first ages. We find the ancients firmly persuaded of a particular and special providence, and frequently observing that good morals and religious observances, engage a kind and indulgent providence on their side. That where these and religious observances have been duly attended to, especially by their rulers, a people have been divinely smiled upon by providence; and not only so, but many times honoured with riches, power and grandeur; together with the prolonging their duration as a people; and contrariwise. This was matter of [29] their observation, an evidence of what the universal Father of his creatures expects in the moral world, viz. That all mankind, of whatever condition, or however circumstanced, should use their intelligent powers in the best manner they were capable of; by improving and disciplining themselves into virtuous, and approvable conduct; and with the use of the best religious observances they are furnished with, or can obtain. A confirmation of which we have in the beginning of St. Paul's Epistle to the Romans.

What shall we then think of the present doctrine of our sectaries, That materially good deeds are hateful to the Deity, unless in a state of grace; and that by every act of obedience, although performed with an honest intention to amend our lives, we render ourselves more abominable in the sight of God, and are further remov'd from his grace and favour, than by a course of licencious living, and total disregard of every thing praise-worthy. Do not these teachings tend to render the divine word, dispensations and grace, inconsistent and contradictory to one another, and to the harmony of the divine attributes; as well as abhorrent to any idea we can form of the divine wisdom and rectitude? But I return.

By careful examination it might evidently appear, that events are not always effects of general laws, but that at least some of them [30] are really expressive of a divine, and special administration. Cursory observers may not be sensible of this; so few of the instances being explicit enough to satisfy such persons. And yet in this very particular, they are most agreeable to that divine wisdom which would not too much interrupt our liberty. Which observations bring me to the following question;

By what rules the divine disposer governs the moral world?

And the general answer to this may be, That he does it in a manner suitable to the moral nature of mankind. Has he given man moral powers? Then surely he rules him in a moral manner, so far as those powers reach. To suppose any thing different from this, would be to charge unerring rectitude with impropriety. The most evident appearances are, that he deals with mankind as rational beings, in a state of trial and probation. Agreeable to this, if we only contemplated the system of man, with his relations to his Maker, it would naturally appear, and even prior to any perception of the fact, that there must be some sort of correspondent treatment, as by revealed will, and specialties in providence. The nature of man, and the circumstances he is placed in, absolutely require it; and the wisdom of the Deity appears concerned in it. But the mode is to treat these things with banter and ridicule; or to explain them away; or at best to give no solid reasons against them.

[31] The learned, and from them the unlearned, form to themselves, what they esteem honorary notions of the Deity. They judge of the divinity by themselves; they find care, and extensive employment, burdensome; and esteem attention to small things servile. On the contrary, that it is great and noble to have their affairs carry'd on without their own attention and looking after. This they imagine God-like. They do not advert to it, that inaction is unnatural to intelligences; and that continued, and eternal action, is essential to the Deity, the supream intelligence. From their feelings, they imagine the Deity hath surely so dispos'd the laws of nature, as to bring about all his designs without any specialties, and please themselves with their own conclusions. They indeed own there are some events which cannot be accounted for by the known laws, but they do not allow them to be specialties, or interpositions. Instead of this they tell us, there are unknown laws by which they are effected: But they do not advert to it, what such an imagination, if pursued through its

consequences, would run up into. I shall mention only one thought upon it.

Suppose then there are such unknown laws, Do we not hold that there are no confusions, contradictions, or absurdities in, or among, these laws, whether there be more or fewer, but a perfect harmony, as in the attributes of [32] their divine author? Allowing this, how shall we reason about events which require laws contrary to the known ones, and subversive of them; for such instances might be given, but for some reasons must be left to the reader's reflections to supply for himself. Such, whatever they be, must be resolv'd into a supernatural agency, an agency that does not affect matter in the manner of the laws of nature; some power interposing in the natural course of things: And for which there is always some special and moral, not natural occasion, but effected by an immediate will and agency, which it would be improper to term a law of nature, since it does not always have effect on the same occasions, and in the same circumstances. Let the matter be considered, without bias and prejudice and it will appear that there is in specialties no repugnancy to any of the natural laws, farther than a temporary suspension of their operations; or only a particular exertion of power; having the natural laws directly after to take place.

Can it imply any contradiction in the divine government, to admit such additions to common providence? I confess, that as a divine moral government of the world requires it, I can form no idea of such an administration without them: But on the contrary, that they appear most wise, and honorable to the divinity, and beneficial to the world. The [33] short question is, Hath the Divinity never interpos'd? If it be allowed that he has once done so, the argument is or ought to be given up.

It is difficult in this day of modern opinion to offer any thing in contradiction to the vogue. It is well known that there are [some] who hold the notion of visitations from the unseen world, and of various kinds: as there are others who deny them. Without asserting or denying the thing, I shall offer a few thoughts upon the supposition of it.

They who hold the doctrine of specialties, do it as the divine method of supplying events for answering the designs of infinite wisdom: This is pious and well; but may there not be some remote and future uses of them as well as the immediate intentions? for the present, supposing such events, which by the way it would be unbecoming rashly to deny, certainly the natural tendency would be to excite considerations of various kinds; particularly concerning an unseen world; the agency of a supreme cause; the being and employment of intelligences, and a divine government; by these religious reflections would naturally arise in the mind. He that form'd us knew our weakness and need of mementos; and, however the present question be determin'd has certainly [34] order'd all things in infinite wisdom. Our concern is not to injure ourselves by mistakes; but in this as in all things else, to think impartially, distinguishing well between the real, and the only apparent; and not be implicitly carry'd away by any vulgar apprehensions on one side, or modish opinions on the other: In a word, to observe well, and judge accordingly.

Mankind are creatures immers'd in sense; every instance therefore of supernal power must, and will, if realiz'd prove more or less a balance to their original sensitive propensities, which naturally impel them to undue indulgences and gratifications; it would excite ideas of their dependent state, and their obligations: Ideas of their being divinely observ'd by an all-seeing eye upon them for their good, if they conduct wisely. It may be consider'd whether they who endeavor to lessen the credibility of interpositions in providence, and the other mention'd events, are friendly to the cause of religion and virtue, and duly cautious for the supporters of revelation, the reality of which cannot be prov'd without allowing an intercourse between both worlds. Revelation was founded on miracle; and the continuance of any special agencies and visitations from the unseen world, may be ultimately design'd to prevent mankind's losing [35] all sense of the reality of it as well as of religious obligation; agreeable to what has been before observ'd, and also to what we now see, that as these specialties are denied, revelation is so too.

The Deists may tell us that natural religion would remain without any assistances of these kinds, or any other. Suppose then it did so, what effect would it have? What in any case are the benefits of it without a practical sense? alone it does not appear to be any sufficient principle of virtue. It might be shown that it is only a foundation for a superstructure; and that it is no more than a meer capacity without this. That good breeding, an impress'd habit of right decorum, with a native common honesty, are much more effectual to all the purposes of a good life than this; although it has been improv'd by its patrons, with all the helps they could obtain from revelation. Indeed the influence of the above imaginary qualifications of their natural religion have, by the Deists, been palm'd upon us as the effects of it, whereas their religion is no more than a mental sense rendering the human species capable of receiving reveal'd religion; that as far as nature goes, it might take place in belief.

[36] Opinion grounded on common providence alone, is far from answering the intentions plainly pointed out in the understanding, and moral powers of the human mind. On the contrary, the course of nature, and common providence, are, by themselves, coincident with, and every way agreeable to, the doctrines of Necessity, and Materialism.

Natural religion is founded on what is observable in the course of nature, and material objects. It is indeed own'd that these imply an intelligent author of nature; but they do not enlighten us what business we have with this cause. We see that the laws of nature affect all creatures with good or evil, according as they do, or do not, attend to them: For instance, if they approach too near the fire, it burns them; if they immerge too long under water, it drowns; and so in a thousand other mistakes, they suffer for their errors. And it is chiefly in owning the wisdom of the laws of creation, that natural religion consists; and at best, on no better principle than weak opinion, all its obligations end.

It follows as a corollary, that this natural sense of dependence on, and obligation to heaven, this native disposition to religious observance, is a proof of the design of the Maker, that man should be a religious creature, that [37] all, both good and bad, should use their utmost care to regulate their lives, and moralise their minds, by every means in their power. All powers of the creature were given with wise design, and not one of them intended to be useless, altho' some of them were designed to be regulated by the natural understanding, moral sense, and rules of life. But if this natural power of amendment is not to be used till it is superceeded by a divine and special change of heart, it was given in vain; and to be as the S. S. phrase is, wrapt in a napkin. We see, in the story of the criminal alluded to, the condemnation of a servant who neglected the use of his powers because they were small, and with the pretence, perhaps a perswasion, of his lord's being a hard master: He would not employ them according to the intention of the giver. Was he then in a converted state? certainly not; and yet his endeavors were required. To say no more, the notion is grounded on an erroneous piety, inadvertently exalting one of the divine attributes and dispensations, at the expence of the others. As to the rest, the intelligent observer will easily see how it is founded, and with what faulty arts conducted and inculcated in the present day.

After what has been said of specialties and interpositions, a Materialist may probably ask some such question as this; if specialties [38] have such a beneficial tendency, why did not the divine Being order them more frequently, and in a more determinate, and perspicuous manner? This requires an answer, and accordingly a few lines upon it will not be amiss.

All will allow, in words, at least, that there is through every part of the divine works and dispensations, the utmost consistency and agreement, no repugnancy or clashing, and nothing contradictory, redundant or deficient to be found: Whereas, was the divine conduct altered, to what the Materialists in the question requires, the case would be quite otherwise in the moral world. It would have destroy'd all Liberty, and subverted a state of probation. Man would be necessitated contrary to the divine intention. Had the divine will been to secure an uninterrupted and uniform moral conduct, no doubt the instances of specialties and interpositions would have been much more frequent, and explicit, together with immediate rewards of good, and punishment of ill deeds. The divine finger barred to mortal sight had no question astonish'd mankind into continued moral order, without any room for praise or blame. The event would have been the same as if he had impell'd mankind into right conduct, by effectual instinctive impressions, or mechanically dispos'd them to religious observance, without any capacity to the contrary. [39] But man then would not have been man. He would have been a cold unspirited lump of absurdity; such only as a Lucretian genius, or materializing projector could have had the credit of devising—No! infinite wisdom laid a nobler plan, in which the rational creature, by the use of moral powers, with Liberty, might approve himself to his maker in a suitable and determin'd degree; with attention to whose laws, providential dispensations, and by the assistances provided for him, he should obtain the happiness his nature was made capable of. I say approve himself, in the use of the talents he has given him, for it would be presumption to expect his maker should do that for him which he has given him the powers to perform; while yet in all beyond this, and what is requisite for him, he may piously expect his gracious assistance.

I shall mention but one more of these proofs of liberty, viz. that of the notions we naturally form of the Deity. As soon as we are capable of consideration, we perceive ourselves constitutionally led to negative every idea that appears to imply imperfection; and to attribute to the divine Being whatever implies the highest degrees of excellency and perfection, with the most perfect harmony of the divine attributes. And upon severe examination of the matter, we find we were right [40] in these sentiments. Whereas when we enquire into the consequences that arise from the doctrine of Necessity, we find them derogatory to them; particularly to those of divine power, wisdom, and goodness: Besides that, it unavoidably makes the perfection of holiness the author of sin; while on the contrary, the doctrine of liberty shows the origin of moral evil to be a very different thing. Thus we also find we agree with the genuine sense and meaning of S. S. I need only add, that our natural notions and common sense, have more real weight and intrinsic worth, than our Necessitarians, and Semimaterialists, of which we have a great number, will admit. But we must take care to distinguish between what is truly common sense, and the notions that arise from educated ignorance, and various misleading causes, in the course of life; together with the bias of our corporeal affections.

I shall finish what I have to say on liberty, with some very short observations on the divine fore-knowledge of events.

The Necessitarians would have us believe, that unless every action of mankind were previously decreed, (i. e.) absolutely determin'd, they could not be foreknown by the Deity. It remains therefore to examine this agreably to the foregoing theory, by which the contrary will be evident.

[41] But in order to make a right judgment concerning this weighty question, we must be suitably prepared by a competent knowledge of the nature of man, particularly the operations of his mind; how far he is necessitated and how far free; according to, or in some such manner as has been already expres'd. But especially we must have right notions of the Deity; right so far as they go, for we cannot have adequate ones. We must allow the infinite difference between his manner of knowing, and that of mankind; of him who sees the essence of matter, and all effects in their causes; to whom the past, the present, and the future are ever before him in one perfect,

and continued view. We must acknowledge the boundless immensity of that wisdom and power by which he made all Worlds; and that Omnipresence by which he is every moment of duration present to them, to every part of them, and to all, even the minutest beings in them. Then if we add to this, the dependent nature of man, whose Liberty is no more than a capacity of passing occasionally, from one necessitating motive to another, we shall be in some measure prepared to satisfy ourselves in the present question.

Admitting then the foregoing postulate, which I think will not be disrupted, we shall [42] perceive that as the Almighty sees all effects in their causes, so all the causes and changes of Motive must be accordingly foreknown by him; that he can foresee whether the subject will consider or not; whether partially or impartially; and in either case, what the event will be. For we may easily perceive, that he can as well forsee what the mental eye of the mind in consideration will discover, as what will appear to the bodily eye in the course of life; and equally what the effect will be, (i.e.) how the rational creature will determine.

It is own'd, that the determinations of the mind are greatly influenced by the different characters of persons. So that although they see the same thing, and under the same individual circumstances, they will yet judge very differently; but however perplexing this may be to mankind to determine what the party will do, it makes no difference with Omniscience. He equally sees their special peculiarities as he does any simple object; their original nature, various complications, and special influences; and in one self-same view, what particular in the whole will determine them, and exactly how. So that he cannot need an absulute decree to know what one will do.

[43] This short account of the matter, may prove sufficient for the impartial and contemplative, while the most clear and full rationale would be to no purpose for others. On this, and the foregoing way of thinking, it is evident, to me, that the Almighty could make a free agent; and that, man having liberty, his every action is yet foreknown. Such objection being remov'd, affords one more presumption of the reality of liberty, as distinguished from any absolute self-determining power; and upon the whole, that such a power is not necessary to the idea of Moral Freedom.

THE END.

[14]

JOHN TUCKER 1719–1792

An Election Sermon

BOSTON, 1771

English colonists in America began living under local government
based upon the consent of the majority before John Locke was
born, and by the time he wrote his *Second Treatise* they had evolved
most of the institutions and practices that Locke's theory implied.
Nevertheless, Locke's work had considerable impact on Americans by
the middle of the eighteenth century, probably because it nicely
justified theoretically what Americans were already doing. Locke built
his theory from rationalist assumptions, while Americans built their
institutions on biblical foundations, especially upon the notion of a
covenant. While to men in the 1770s there seemed to be no essential
conflict between what Locke and the Bible were telling them, their
synthesis of the two was in fact an American accomplishment, not a
logical necessity. John Tucker, pastor of the First Church in Newbury,
here, in the Election Day Sermon of 1771, demonstrates
how the synthesis was accomplished.

I PETER II. 13, 14, 15, 16.

> *Submit yourselves to every ordinance of man for the Lord's sake: Whether
> it be to the King as supreme, or unto Governors, as unto Governors,
> as unto them who are sent by him, for the punishment of evil-doers,
> and for the praise of them that do well.*
>
> *For so is the will of God, that with well-doing ye may put to
> silence the ignorance of foolish men: As free, and not using your liberty
> for a cloak of maliciousness, but as the servants of God.*

[158]

JOHN TUCKER 1719–1792

The great and wise Author of our being, has so formed us, that the love of liberty is natural. This passion, like all other original principles of the human mind, is, in itself [6] perfectly innocent, and designed for excellent purposes, though, like them, liable, through abuse, of becoming the cause of mischief to ourselves and others. In a civil state, the genius of whose constitution is agreeable to it, this passion, while in its full vigor, and under proper regulation, is not only the cement of the political body, but the wakeful guardian of its interests, and the great animating spring of useful and salutary operations; and then only is it unjurious to the public, or to individuals, when, thro' misapprehension of things, or by being overballanced by self-love, it takes a wrong direction.

Civil and ecclesiastical societies are, in some essential points, different. Our rights, as men, and our rights, as christians, are not, in all respects, the same. It cannot, however, be reasonably supposed, but that this useful and important principle, must, in its genuine influence and operation, be friendly to both: For although our Saviour has assured us, his kingdom is not of this world; and it be [7] manifest from the Gospel, which contains its constitution and laws, that his subjects stand in some special relation and are under some peculiar subjection to him, distinct from their relation to and connection with civil societies, yet we justly conclude, that as this divine polity, with its sacred maxims, proceeded from the wise and benevolent Author of our being, none of its injunctions can be inconsistent with that love of liberty he himself has implanted in us, nor interfere with the laws and government of human societies, whose constitution is consistent with the rights of men.

Christ came to set up a kingdom diverse, indeed, from the kingdoms of this world, but it was no part of his design to put down, or destroy government and rule among men. He came to procure liberty for his people, and to make them free in the most important sense, yet not to exempt them from subjection to civil powers, or to dissolve their obligations to one another, as members of political bodies.

[8] As to things of this nature, all ecclesiastical constitutions and laws, as coming from GOD, must leave men just as they were; because all civil societies, founded on principles of reason and equity, are, as well as the peculiar laws of Christianity, agreeable to the Deity, and

certainly, intimations from the all-perfect mind cannot be contradictory.

These things, seem not to have been rightly apprehended, and well understood by men at all times and in all places. The Jews, some of whom were early proselyted to the christian faith, had imbibed high notions of their liberty and superiority to all others, as the peculiar people of GOD; and were loth to own subjection to the Romans, as a civil state, when they were actually under their dominion. And some converts from among the Gentiles, tho' they had not these national prejudices, yet from their subjection to Jesus Christ, as their King and Ruler, and, as 'tis probable, from mistaking the meaning of some apostolic declarations asserting [9] their freedom as christians, disclaimed likewise all human authority over them.

Men of this cast, gave no small trouble both to Church and State, in the early days of the Gospel. Of such the Apostle Peter speaks where he says—*They despise government: Presumptuous are they. Self-willed, they are not afraid to speak evil of dignities.*

Such men as these, and their seditious, turbulent behaviour, I doubt not, this same Apostle had in view, when he delivered the instructions in my text, by which he endeavoured to guard christians against their evil practices.

But, as all authority, demanding submission, and all submission, due to such authority, are likely to be best understood, by having these things reduced to their first principles; by having the foundation of such authority fairly produced, and its just boundaries, which must be the measure of submission due to it, clearly marked out: And as such submission is most likely to be duly yielded, [10] by having the reasons and motives thereof plainly exhibited, so these are things which seem here aimed at by the Apostle. *Submit yourselves to every ordinance of man for the Lord's sake: whether it be to the King as supreme; or unto Governors, as unto them who are sent by him for the punishment of evil-doers, and for the praise of them that do well. For so is the will of God, that with well-doing ye may put to silence the ignorance of foolish men. As free, and not using your liberty for a cloke of maliciousness, but as the servants of God.*

In these words he gives us a compendium of civil government; representing its origin and great design; that submission, or obedience which is due to it; and the true principles from which such obedience should flow.

JOHN TUCKER 1719–1792

Upon this general view of the subject, it is obvious, that if handled with any degree of propriety, it may offer useful instructions, both to Rulers, and those under their government.—A modest attempt to do this, will not, it is hoped, be [11] disagreeable to this respectable audience, by whom I ask to be heard with patience and candor.

The first thing offered to our consideration is, the ORIGIN of civil government, from whence all authority in the state must take its rise. And this is said to be from man. *Submit yourselves to every ordinance of man,* etc. More intelligibly, perhaps, it might be rendered, "to every human institution or appointment." And this may be justly understood, as having respect to every kind of civil government, under whatever form it is administred:—It is the ordinance,—the institution or appointment of man.

This does not imply, however, that civil government is not from God; for thus it is sometimes represented, and is expressly said to be the *ordinance of God.* So St. Paul declares—*There is no power but of God. The powers that be, are ordained by God. Whoever therefore resisteth the power resisteth the ordinance of God.*‡

[12] Civil government is not, indeed, so from God, as to be expressly appointed by him in his word. Much less is any particular form of it there delineated, as a standing model for the nations of the world. Nor are any particular persons, pointed out, as having, in a lineal descent, an indefeasible right to rule over others.

But civil government may be said to be from God, as it is he who qualifies men for, and in his over-ruling providence, raises them to places of authority and rule; for by him *Kings reign:*—As he has given us, in his word, the character of Rulers, and pointed out both *their* duty, and the duty of those under their authority; which supposes, not only the existence of civil government, but that it is agreeable to his will: And especially and chiefly, as civil government is founded in the very nature of man, as a social being, and in the nature and constitution of things. It is manifestly for the good of society:—It is the dictate of nature:—It is the voice of reason, which may be said to be the voice of God.

[13] It being only thus that civil government is the ordinance of God, there is no impropriety in asserting likewise that it is the *ordinance of man.* For though it is founded in the nature of man, and

‡ Rom. XIII

in the constitution of things, which are from God, yet nothing is plainer, than that it proceeds immediately from men. It is not a matter of necessity, strictly speaking, but of choice. This is the case, as to the government in general.—This is most evidently the case, as to any particular form of government.

All men are naturally in a state of freedom, and have an equal claim to liberty. No one, by nature, nor by any special grant from the great Lord of all, has any authority over another. All right therefore in any to rule over others, must originate from those they rule over, and be granted by them. Hence, all government, consistent with that natural freedom, to which all have an equal claim, is founded in compact, or agreement between the parties;—between Rulers and their Subjects, and can be no [14] otherwise. Because Rulers, receiving their authority originally and solely from the people, can be rightfully possessed of no more, than these have consented to, and conveyed to them.

And the fundamental laws, which are the basis of government, and form the political constitution of the state,—which mark out, and fix the chief lines and boundaries between the authority of Rulers, and the liberties and privileges of the people, are, and can be no other, in a free state, than what are mutually agreed upon and consented to. Whatever authority therefore the supreme power has, to make laws, to appoint officers, etc. for the regulation and government of the state, being an authority derived from the community, and granted by them, can be justly exercised, only within certain limits, and to a certain extent, according to agreement.

To suppose otherwise, and that without a delegated power and constitutional right, Rulers may make laws, and appoint [15] officers for their execution, and force them to effect, i.e. according to their own arbitrary will and pleasure, is to defeat the great design of civil government, and utterly to abolish it. It is to make Rulers absolutely despotic, and to subject the people to a state of slavery; because it will then be in the power of Rulers, by virtue of new laws and regulations, they shall please to make, to subvert and annihilate the present constitution, and to strip the subject of every kind of privilege.

This may be briefly evidenced by a single instance.

It is essential to a free state, for without this it cannot be free, that no man shall have his property taken from him, but by his own consent, given by himself or by others deputed to act for him. Let it

JOHN TUCKER 1719–1792

be supposed then, that Rulers assume a power to act contrary to this fundamental principle, what must be the consequence? If by such usurped authority, they can demand and take a [16] penny, by the same authority they may a pound, and even the whole substance of the subject, so as to make him wholly dependent on their pleasure, having nothing that he can call his own; and what is he then but a perfect slave.*

This, at first view, is manifestly inconsistent with all just conception of freedom; and is the very essence of arbitrary and tyrannical power.

Now, all Rulers in a state, and all power and authority with which they are vested;—the very being, and form of government, with all its constitutional laws, being thus from the people, hence civil government, is called, and with great propriety, the *ordinance of man,*—an human institution.

[17] This is the case, as to the British government in particular, under which we have the happiness to live. Its constitutional laws are comprized in *Magna-Charta,* or the great charter of the nation. This contains, in general, the liberties and privileges of the people, and is, *virtually,* a compact between the King and them; the reigning Prince, explicitly engaging, by solemn oath, to govern according to these laws:—Beyond the extent of these then, or contrary to them, he can have no rightful authority at all.

If the preceding positions, and the reasonings from them are just, the following things may be noticed, as deducible therefrom, or closely connected therewith,—That it is highly requisite, for the good of the state, that both Rulers and people be well acquainted with, and keep in mind the constitutional laws of government—Rulers, that they may be directed and guided thereby, and not depart from, or counteract the design of their institution, to the injury, or disquietude [18] of the people.—And people, that knowing the bounds of

---

* Men in *society having property,* they have such a right to the goods, which by the law of the community are theirs, that nobody hath a right to take their substance, or any part of it from them, without their own consent: Without this they have no property at all; for I have truly no *property* in that, which another can by right take from me when he pleases against my consent. Hence it is a mistake to think, that the supreme or legislative power of any commonwealth, can do what it will, and dispose of the estates of the subject arbitrarily, or take any part of them at pleasure.

Lock on civil Government.

submission, and the extent of their privileges, they may be guarded against transgression, and yield a ready and full obedience.

Equally requisite it must be likewise, for the same end, that there be no mysteries in the governing plan:—That all laws and rules of government, be as plain as possible, and easy to be understood, to prevent contentious disputes between Rulers and their subjects;—to preclude the former, from tyrannical oppression, under colour of lawful authority, and the latter from rebellious disobedience, under pretence of privilege.

For, it follows from what has been said, that as all disobedience in subjects, to constitutional authority, is rebellion against government, and merits punishment adequate to the crime, so all assumed power in Rulers, not granted them by the constitution, is without just authority, and so far forth, can claim no submission. [19] "As usurpation," says the great and judicious Mr. Locke, "is the exercise of power which another hath a right to, so Tyranny is the exercise of power beyond right, which no body can have a right to." And again, "Where-ever law ends, Tyranny begins, if the law be transgressed to another's harm. And whosoever in authority exceeds the power given him by law, and makes use of the force, he has under his command, to compass that upon the subject, which the law allows not, ceases in that to be a magistrate: And acting without authority, may be opposed as any other man who by force invades the right of another."

And tho' it may not always be prudent and best, to resist such power, and submission may be yielded, yet that the people have a right to resist, is undeniable; otherwise the absurd and exploded doctrines of passive obedience, and non-resistance, must be admitted in their utmost extent, and their consequences patiently borne. And it must be granted finally, that the people as well as their [20] Rulers, are proper judges of the civil constitution they are under, and of their own rights and privileges; else, how shall they know when these are invaded;—when submission is due to authoritative requisitions, and when not?

But we are now to consider

Secondly, the great design of Civil Government, and the end for which Rulers are appointed; and that is the good of the community, or political body—*Whether it be to the King, as supreme; or unto Governors, as unto them who are sent by him, for the punishment of evil-doers, and for the praise of them that do well.*

JOHN TUCKER 1719–1792

Rulers are not appointed, indeed, for the happiness of the people, exclusive of their own, as if these things were unconnected. But, as it would be unreasonable, that some should be advanced above their brethren,—be cloathed with authority, and honorably supported meerly for the sake of their own ease, [21] dignity and grandeur, so it would be equally unreasonable, that Rulers should be slaves to the people, and watch and labour for their welfare, without sharing in it.

But the happiness of rulers and of their Subjects, are not thus exclusive of each other, but perfectly coincident. They are both parts of the same body,—their true interests are interwoven, and their happiness inseparable. Rulers, acting agreeable to their institution, and attending on that very thing, are justly entitled to esteem and reverence, and an honorable support from the people, though these are not the things they ought to have chiefly in view.

They are to consider themselves as raised above their brethren, and invested with authority, for more noble and generous purposes;— for the peace and wellfare of the Community, committed to their care: Hence it is said, of the civil Ruler, *he is the minister of God to thee for good.*†

[22] Nor can any other end be imagined, worthy of reasonable beings, why men should put themselves out of a state of natural freedom, and subject themselves to the authority and rule of others, but for their greater good;—for the securing, more effectually, their just rights, liberties and privileges.

This is the great end of their forming into society;—of their establishing certain laws, as the general measures of right and wrong, and giving power to some, to govern the whole community by such laws.

This being the design of civil government, good Rulers are justly considered as benefactors to the people. They are placed as watchmen and guardians over the state, whose special business it is, both in their legislative and executive capacity, to consult and promote its wellfare. To curb and restrain the unrighteous and factious, from acts of fraud, rapine and violence, and to protect others in the peaceable enjoyment of their rights. [23] To punish transgressors;—to relieve the oppressed, dispensing, with an equal and impartial hand, justice to all.

For, it is necessary for the support of government, and that the

† Rom. XIII. 4.

great and salutary ends of it may be answered, not only that its laws be just, but that they be enforced by proper sanctions; fitted to affect the human mind, and to engage obedience; and that Rulers have power to execute such laws, in punishment of evildoers, and for a praise,—for the support and encouragement of them that do well.

From this view of our subject, it appears of high importance, to the good of the state, that they who are vested with power to make laws for the Community, as there shall be occasion, and to appoint officers for their execution, have qualifications answerable to their high places of power and trust.—That they be men of superior knowledge and wisdom;—well acquainted with the civil constitution;—with the just boundaries between [24] the prerogative of Rulers, and the liberties of the People, that their laws may be duly framed, and adjusted to the political system.—Men able critically to examine the complection of the state;—to search out its disorders, and to apply proper remedies:—Able to judge of the natural course and tendency of things and to foresee, beyond what is common, the operation, and consequences of their own acts;—how the rights of individuals—how the common good will be affected thereby.

They should be men of great ingenuity and candor;—ready to receive light when offered,—to redress grievances, when convinced of them, and to amend, or repeal their own Acts, when found injurious, or not answering the good intentions designed. Pretences to perfect wisdom and knowledge, and inerrability of judgment, in civil, as well as ecclesiastical matters, ill become the highest mortal; and are likely to produce unhappy effects, when found in Rulers, especially if accompanied with an obstinate adherence to their own measures.

[25] They should be men of great goodness and benevolence of heart, who will naturally care for the welfare of their brethren, and treat them with condescention and kindness. Such a behaviour, corrected and managed by prudence, is perfectly consistent with their maintaining the dignity of their character, and will greatly endear them to the people. That councel of the old men, to king *Rehoboam*, was wise and good, and agreeable to the sentiments and feelings of human nature. *If thou wilt be a servant to this people this day, and wilt serve them, and answer them, and speak good words to them, then they will be thy servants forever.*†

† 1 Kings, XII. 7.

JOHN TUCKER 1719–1792

Again, RULERS should be men free from a sordid covetous temper, which has self-interest like the pole star ever in view, and endeavours to steer all things by that direction. As they are designed to act for the public good, they should be men of liberal and generous souls;—ready to prefer the common safety and happiness, to their own private emolument.

[26] They should be likewise men of great resolution and firmness of mind;—not easily dismayed and overcome by difficulties, or intimidated by threatened dangers:—Able to maintain a calmness of mind, and to guide with a steady hand, in tempestuous seasons:—Able to bear with the unpolished plainness of some honest men, and with the weaknesses and follies of others:—Not apt, in a pet, to desert the common cause, and to sacrifice the public happiness to their own passionate resentments.

And, finally. It must be a great importance, to the good order and wellfare of the state, that Rulers be men of distinguished piety and virtue, who will be likely to rule by example as well as law. It was an act of prudence, as well as piety in *Nehemiah*,—his appointing one to a place of high trust in government; *because he was a faithful man, and feared God above many.*‡ A firm belief of Revelation:—A strong impressive sense of the divine and everlasting things declared in the Gospel,—this will secure [27] the good conduct of Rulers, especially when under temptation to do wrong, above every thing else. True religion inlarges, and strengthens the mind,—fixes deep in the heart, the principles of right action, and gives steadiness and uniformity of behaviour.

Men of this character will act with fidelity and zeal in the service of the public, considering themselves as accountable to God, as well as to men. They look beyond the present state of things, and view their conduct as connected with futurities of a most interesting nature; and will aim at approving themselves, not only to the people, but to their own minds, and to God the Judge of all.

Such Rulers will best answer the great ends of their institution. They will be to the people, as the directing,—as the chearing and comforting light of the sun.—As the refreshing rain,—as the firm, unshaken pillars of the state,—the shield of its defence and safety, and the source [28] of constant blessings. Nor can they fail of engaging the esteem and love, and submission of the people.

‡ Nehem. VII. 2.

We may now in the THIRD place, consider that submission which is due to governments; and take some particular notice of the nature and extent of it. *Submit yourselves to every ordinance of man, whether it be to the King as supreme, or unto Governors,* etc. Similar to which is that of St. Paul, *Let every soul be subject to the higher powers.—Put them in mind to be subject to principalities and powers, to obey magistrates,* etc.

The duties of Rulers and Subjects are reciprocal, and mutually imply each other. If some are to govern, others are to submit to their government, and to be obedient to their authority; otherwise Rulers are but an empty name;—the constitution is dissolved, and anarchy ensues.

Nor is this submission due only to the Supreme Ruler, but to all in lawful authority [29] under him, down to the lowest officer in the state. Not only to the King, but to those who are sent by him, to carry on the various parts of the administration. Disobedience to inferior officers, while acting by lawful authority, is disobedience to the highest power, as it is by authority derived from thence, that all in subordinate places of civil trust, execute their offices. Submission is likewise due to all constitutional laws, whether they suit the present interest of individuals, or not. A man is not to disobey a just law, calculated for the public good, because, in certain circumstances, it operates against his private interest.

Unlimited submission, however, is not due to government, in a free state. There are certain boundaries, beyond which, submission cannot be justly required, nor is therefore due. These limits are marked out, and fixt, by the known, established, and fundamental laws of the state. These laws being consented to by the governing power, confine, as well as direct its operation and influence, and [30] are the connecting band between authority and obedience.

And no wise and just Ruler, we may suppose, would aim at wantonly leaping over these bounds, and acting beyond them, as this would be, not only acting without lawful authority, and injuriously robbing the people of their rights, but would tend to create unhappy jealousies, and to stir up broils and contentions in the state, which might give him much uneasiness, if no worse consequences should follow.

It was a fine expression of a Spartan Ruler, and indicated the freedom and happiness of the state, upon being asked, "Who governed at *Sparta?* answered the laws, and the magistrates *according* to these laws." The constitutional laws of the state, are, properly, the supreme power, being obligatory on the whole community,—on the highest officer, as well as the lowest subject.

[31] Here then, we have the just measure and extent of submission. It is due to all decrees and requisitions of the legislature, which are consistent with the known, and fundamental laws of the state, by which fundamental laws, the very law-making power itself is limited, and beyond which it cannot pass.

And it seems immaterial, as to the present point, whether such authority in Rulers, and submission in subjects, result directly and wholly from the original constitution and frame of government, or from subsequent compacts between them, mutually agreed to.

All such compacts, whether under the name of charter-grants, or however denominated, must be supposed agreeable to the fundamental laws of the state, and grounded thereon, i.e. Such as the ruling power has authority to make, or enter into, and the people freely accept of.

[32] Upon such agreement, a particular kind of government, in some respects new, may take place; but, so far as it is new, or variant from the original constitution, this subsequent agreement between Rulers and people, ought to be the invariable measure of adminis-tration.—This bounds the authority of Rulers, and the submission of subjects.—The people, while they owe obedience, have an undoubted right to their granted, or stipulated privileges; and may justly claim, and insist upon them, unless, by misconduct, they are forfeited.

Upon the whole therefore. Proper submission, in a free state, is a medium, between slavish subjection to arbitrary claims of Rulers, on one hand, and a lawless licence, on the other. It is obedience in subjects to all orders of government, which are consistent with their constitutional rights and privileges. So much submission is due, and to be readily yielded by every subject; and beyond this, it cannot be justly demanded, because Rulers and People are [33] equally bound, by the fundamental laws of the constitution.

The state of the world, and temper of mankind, may render these observations necessary and highly important;—important and necessary as a check upon Rulers of a despotic turn; and a restraint upon the licentious among the people; that neither, by breaking over their just bounds, may disturb the peace, and injure the happiness of the state.

For there have been Rulers, and may be such again, who look with wishful eyes on the liberties and privileges of the people. Who consider them as a prey, worthy to be seized, for the gratification of their pride and ambition,—of their cruelty or covetousness. Such, under one pretence or other, will be stretching and enlarging their power, and grasping at more and more, 'till, if not obstructed, civil government will be converted into absolute tyranny, and a free people into slaves.

A people in love with liberty, and [34] sensible to their right to it, cannot but be jealous of such Rulers; and ought to be on their guard against unjustifiable, and arbitrary claims. Tamely to submit, would be highly unworthy of them as free men and shew they deserved the yoke, under which they so readily put their necks.

On the other hand. There are found among the people, persons of a querulous and factious disposition.—Ever restless and uneasy, and prepared to raise and promote popular tumults. From the meer love of wrangling, or from ambitious views,—to rise from obscurity, to public notice, and to an important figure, they find fault with Rulers, and point out defects in the administration.—Small mistakes are magnified.—Evil designs are suggested, which, perhaps never existed, but in their own heads. They cry up liberty, and make a mighty stir to save the sinking state, when in no danger, but from themselves, and others of a like call.

There are ambitious and designing men, in the state, as well as in the [35] church; and there are fit tools to serve the purposes of both. As some make hereticks in the church, and raise an ecclesiastic posse to demolish them, chiefly with a view to render themselves distinguished, as found in the faith, so others make traitors in the state, and raise the popular cry against them, to gain to themselves the name of Patriots.

The wise and prudent will make a pause, before they inlist under such political zealots. They will judge for themselves of the faulted conduct of their Rulers. They will make reasonable allowances for human frailties, and be as ready to yield submission where it is due, as to defend their liberties where they are in danger.

We proceed now in the LAST place.—To take notice of the principles from which submission and obedience to government should flow. And these are, a sense of our duty to God, as well as to civil Authority, connected with, and animated by a sense of liberty. [36] *Submit yourselves to every ordinance of man for the Lord's sake.—As free, and not using your liberty for a cloke of maliciousness, but as the servants of God.*

True religion:—A sacred reverence of the Deity:—The love of virtue and goodness, are as necessary to make good subjects, as good Rulers: And a spirit of liberty is requisite, to render obedience true and genuine both to God and man.

Even the supreme Ruler of the world, is not a despotic, arbitrary Monarch, nor does he require obedience by meer authority. His sacred laws,—all framed agreeable to the perfect rectitude of his nature, and resulting from his infinite goodness, and righteousness, are wisely adapted to the human system, and calculated for its good.

They recommend themselves to the reason of our own minds, and manifestly tend to our happiness:—We feel our interest as well as our duty in them, and that these are closely connected.

[37] Agreeable to the nature and tendency of these divine mandates, the obedience God requires of us, is not that of slaves, to a tyrannical master, but that of children, to a wise and benevolent father. It must be *free*,—a matter of choice, and not of force, driving us on against a reluctant mind.

Like to this, is the obedience we owe to civil government. Supposing its laws founded, as they ought to be, in reason and equity, and calculated for the good of society, they demand our approbation. And being under their authority, as members of the political body, both duty and interest require our submission.

But as all earthly Rulers, as well as all human institutions, may be supposed to be imperfect; and submission may be required, inconsistent with our just rights and privileges, there is a liberty, of a somewhat different nature, respecting civil government, we have a claim to, and which should have influence on our conduct, i.e. a liberty to -hold, as well as to yield submission.

[38] For, even a christian people who, from their character, as servants of God, are bound to submit to the higher powers, and to obey Magistrates, are not, out of courtly complaisance to their Rulers, or from a mean, timorous, and slavish temper, to resign up their just rights, when imperiously demanded, or craftily sought after. Remembering they are freemen and not slaves, they should act as *free*.

They have an undoubted privilege to complain of unconstitutional measures in government, and of unlawful incroachments upon their rights, and may, while they do it, with becoming decency, do it with that noble freedom and firmness, which a sense of wrong, joined with the love of liberty, will inspire.

Even under great and manifest oppression, a prudent regard to their own, and the public safety, may forbid, indeed, violent means of resistance; but should never lead them, tamely to yield to unlawful claims.

[39] Challenging their right, and pleading for it, tho' this should not prevail to the immediate redress of grievances, yet may be of high importance, to keep alive,—to cherish and strengthen,—not a spirit of faction and discontent, but that spirit of liberty which is, as it were, the *animating soul* of a free state,—which being once gone, every thing valuable will become an easy prey, and a state of abject slavery ensue, to live in which, may be far worse, than to be *free* among the dead.

But still, on the other hand. While a people consider themselves as *free*, and are zealous to maintain their liberty, they should remember also their subjection to civil authority, and to God, the righteous Judge of all, and be careful not to carry liberty beyond its just bounds:—Not to use it for a cloke of maliciousness:—Not, under coulour and pretence of this, to refuse just obedience;—to be disorderly, factious and tumultuous. As the servants of God, and accountable to him, they should render unto all their dues, and seek [40] not only their own, but the welfare and happiness of all.

Would people, in general, possess their minds of such sentiments, and act under their direction and influence, how much would this tend to the peace and happiness of society! Many groundless and unreasonable complaints, from restless and ambitious, or from ignorant and peevish men, would be discountenanced and suppressed, and the community, by a general steady course of well-doing, would, agreeable to the will of God, put to silence the ignorance of such foolish men.

And in case of real and grievous oppression from unrighteous Rulers, such principles as these, would be likely to produce the most happy effects. They would unite the members of society, as one body.—They would guard them against rash and unlawful measures of defence;—lead them to such as are prudent and justifiable; and engage them to act with that determined resolution and firmness, resulting from reason [41] and virtue, which is most likely to hold out, and to prevail, in time, over every species of injustice and oppression.

And would both Rulers and Subjects imbibe such sentiments, and, under their direction and influence, discharge with fidelity the duties of their respective places, what a prosperous and flourishing condition might they hope for!

The springs of government, acting with vigor, and under a right direction, and the members of society, yielding correspondent and uniform submission, a general harmony and happiness must ensue.

The political state would be like a body in full health. The constitutional laws, preserved inviolate, would, like strong bones and sinews, support and steady the regular frame. Supreme and subordinate Rulers duly performing their proper functions, would be like the greater and lesser arteries, keeping up their proper tone and vibrations; and justice, fidelity, and every social virtue, [42] would, like the vital fluid, run without obstruction, and reach, refresh, and invigorate the most minute and distant parts: While the multitude of subjects, yielding, in their various places and relations, a ready and cheerful obedience, would, like the numerous, yet connected veins, convey back again the recurrent blood, to the great fountain of it, and the whole frame be vigourous, easy, and happy.

Upon that view of Civil Government we have now been taking; and while feeling in our own breaths a warm sense of liberty, and the blessings of it, can we help dropping a tear over the multitudes of our fellow creatures, who are groaning under the iron yoke of tyranny and oppression—subjected to the arbitrary will of their imperious and despotic Lords,—and to all the wretchedness, which lawless pride and ambition; which wanton cruelty and unbridled lust can inflict upon them.

How much to be pittied are such miserable objects! How ardently is it to be [43] wished that the principles of civil liberty may prevail through the earth to the breaking in pieces the power of oppressors every where, and the restoring the oppressed to freedom and happiness.

From such scenes of human wretchedness and woe, we naturally reflect, with gratitude to heaven, on our own happy condition, as subjects of the British Empire.—A constitution founded in the law of God, and of nature;—on the principles of reason and equity:—A form of government admireably contrived for the due support of authority, and the security of the rights and privileges of the people.

May this excellent constitution, formed and established by the experience and wisdom of ages, be preserved inviolate, the source of blessings to this and future generations: And his present Majesty, our most gracious Sovereign (whom may God long preserve) ever esteem it his glory, and find it his happiness, to reign over a free and loyal people.

[15]

THE PRECEPTOR

Vol. II. Social Duties of the Political Kind

BOSTON, 1772

Originally published in the May 21, 1772 issue of the *Massachusetts Spy* (Boston), this essay proceeds efficiently in laying out the basic principles of the American Whig perspective. Of special interest is the emphasis on communitarian rather than individualistic principles, and the articulation of the "politics of deference" commonly held during the colonial era, according to which the "better sort" should be deferred to in political matters, although all freemen are considered politically equal. Only quietly implied here, the grounds for breaking with England are rehearsed as a natural extension of Whig political thought.

Political Connections

The *social* principle in man is of such an expansive nature, that it cannot be confined within the circuit of a family, of friends, or a neighbourhood; it spreads into wider systems, and draws man into larger confederacies, communities and commonwealths. It is in these only, that the higher powers of our nature attain the highest improvement of which they are capable. These principles hardly find objects in the solitary state of nature. *There* the principle of action rises no higher at farthest than *natural affection* towards ones offspring. There personal or family wants entirely engross the creature's attention and labour and allow no leisure, or, if they did, no exercise for views of a more enlarged kind. In *solitude* all are employed in the same way, in providing for the animal life. And even after their utmost labour and care, single and unaided by the industry of others, they find but a sorry supply of their wants, and a feeble precarious security against wild beasts; from inclement skies and seasons; from the mistakes or petulant passions of their fellow creatures; from the preference of themselves to their neighbours; and from all the little exorbitances of self love. But in *society*, the mutual aids which men give and receive, shortens the labours of each, and the combined strength and reason of individuals, give security and protection to the whole body. There is both a variety and subordination of genius among mankind. Some are formed to lead and direct, others to contrive plans of happiness for individuals, and of government for communities, to take in a public interest, invent laws and arts, and superintend their execution, and in short to refine and civilize Human life. Others who have not such good heads, may have as honest hearts, a truly public spirit, love of liberty, hatred of corruption and tyranny, a generous submission to laws, order and public institutions, and an extensive Philanthropy. And others who have none of these capacities either of heart, or head, may be well formed for manual exercises and bodily labour. The former of these principles have no scope in solitude, where a man's thoughts and concerns do all either center on himself, or extend no farther than a family; into which circle all the duty and virtue of the solitary mortal is crouded. But society finds proper objects and exercises for every genius, and the noblest objects and exercises for the noblest geniuses, and for the highest principles in the human constitution; particularly for that warmest and most divine passion which God hath kindled in our bosoms, the inclination of doing good and reverencing our nature; which may find here both employment, and the most exquisite satisfaction. In society a man has not only more leisure, but better opportunities of applying his talents with much greater perfection and success, especially as he is supported with the joint advice and affections of his fellow creatures, who are more closely united one with the other, and sustain a common relation to the same moral system, or community. This then is an object proportioned to his most enlarged social affections, and in serving it he finds scope for the exercise and refinement of his highest intellectual and moral powers. THEREFORE *society* or *a state of civil government* rests on these two principal pillars, "that in it we find security against those evils which are unavoidable in solitude—and obtain those goods, some of which cannot be obtained at all, and others not so well in that state where men depend solely on their individual sagacity and industry."

THE PRECEPTOR

From this short detail it appears that man is a SOCIAL creature, and formed for a SOCIAL state; and that *society*, being adapted to the higher principles and destinations of his nature, must, of necessity, be his NATURAL state.

Political Duties

The duties suited to that state, and resulting from those principles and destinations, or in other words, from our social passions and social connections, or relation to a public system, are *love of our country, resignation and obedience to the laws, public spirit, love of liberty, sacrifice of life and all to the public*, and the like.

Love of One's Country

LOVE of our country is one of the noblest passions that can warm and animate the human breast. It includes all the limited and particular affections to our parents, children, friends, neighbours, fellow citizens and countrymen.

It ought to direct and limit their more confined and partial actions within their proper and natural bounds, and never let them encroach on those sacred and first regards we owe to the great public to which we belong. Were we solitary creatures, detached from the rest of mankind, and without any capacity of comprehending a *public interest*, or without affections, leading us to desire and pursue it, it would not be our duty to mind it, nor criminal to neglect it. But as we are PARTS of the *Public system*, and are capable of not only taking in large views of its interests, but with the strongest affections connected with it, and prompted to take a share of its concerns, we are under the most sacred ties to prosecute in security and welfare with the utmost ardour, especially in times of public trial. This *love of our country* does not import an attachment to any particular soil, climate, or spot of earth, where perhaps we first drew our breath, though those *natural* [attachments] are often associated with the *moral* ones; and like external signs or symbols, help to ascertain and bind them; but it imports an affection to that *moral system*, or *community* which is governed by the same laws and magistrates, and whose several parts are variously connected one with the other, and all united upon the bottom of a common interest. Perhaps indeed every member of the community cannot comprehend so large an object, especially if it extends through large provinces, and over vast tracts of land; and still less can he form such an idea if there is no *public*, i.e. if all are subjects to the caprice and unlimited will of one man; but the preference they generally shew to their native country, and concern and longing after it which they express, when they have been long absent from it; the labours they undertake and the sufferings they endure to save or serve it; and the peculiar attachment they have to their countrymen, evidently demonstrate that the passion is *natural*, and never fails to exert itself, when it is fairly disengaged from foreign clogs, and is directed to its proper object. Whenever it prevails in its genuine vigour and extent, it swallows up all sordid and selfish regard, it conquors the love of *ease, power, pleasure, and wealth*; nay when the amiable partialities of *friendship, gratitude, private affection, or regards to a family* come in competition with it, it will teach us bravely to sacrifice all, in order to maintain the rights and *promote* or *defend* the honour and happiness of our country.

Resignation and Obedience to the Laws, etc.

RESIGNATION and *obedience to the laws*, and *orders* of the society to which we belong, are *political* duties necessary to its very being and security, without which it must soon degenerate into a state of licence and anarchy. The welfare, nay, the nature of civil society requires, that there should be a subordination of order, or diversity of ranks and conditions in it; that certain men or orders of men be appointed to superintend and manage such affairs as concern the public safety and happiness; that all have their particular provinces assigned them; that such a subordination be settled among them as none of them may interfere with another; and finally that certain rules, or common *measures of actions* be agreed on, by which each is to discharge his respective duty to govern or be governed, and all may concur in securing the order, and promoting the felicity of the whole political body. Those *rules of action* are the laws of the community, and those different *orders* are the several officers, or magistrates, appointed by the public to explain them, and superintend or assist in their execution. In consequence of this settlement of things it is the duty of each individual to obey the laws enacted, to submit to the executors of them with all due deference and homage, according to their respective ranks and dignity, as to the keepers of the public peace, and the guardians of the public liberty; to maintain his own rank, and perform the functions of his own station with diligence, fidelity and incorruption. The superiority of the *higher orders*, or the authority with which the state has invested them, entitle them, especially if they employ their authority well, to the obedience and submission of the *lower*, and to a proportionable honour and respect from all. The subordination of the lower ranks claim protection, defence, and security from the higher. And the laws, being superior to all, require the obedience and submission of all, being the last resort, beyond which there is no decision or appeal. Besides these natural and stated subordinations in society, there are other accidental & artificial, the *opulent* and *indigenous*, the *great* and the *vulgar*, the *ingenious* and *prudent* & those who are less so. The *opulent* are to administer to the necessities of the indigent and the *indigent* to return the fruits of their labour to the *opulent*. The *great* ought to defend and patronize their *dependents* and *inferiors*, and *they* in their turn, return their combined strength and assistance *to* the *great*. The *prudent* should improve the ingenuities of the mind for the benefit of the *industrious* and the *industrious* lend the dexterities of their strength for the advantage of the *prudent*.

Foundation of Public Spirit, Love of Liberty, etc.

PUBLIC *spirit, heroic zeal, love of liberty*, and other *political* duties do, above all others, recommend those who practice them to the admiration and homage of mankind; because as they are the offspring of the noblest minds, so are they the parents of the greatest blessing to society. Yet exalted as they are, it is only in equal and free governments, where they can be exercised and have there due effect. For there only does a true *public* prevail, and there only is the *public good* made the standard of the civil constitution. As the end of society is the *common interest* and *welfare* of the public associated, this end must of necessity be the *supreme law* or *common standard* by which the particular rules of action of the several members of the society toward each other are to be regulated. But a *common interest* can be no other than that which is the result of the *common reason*, or *common feelings* of all. Private men, or a particular order of men, have interests and feelings peculiar to themselves, and of which they may be good judges; but these may be separate from, and often contrary to the interests and feelings of the rest of society; and therefore they can have no right to make, and much less to impose, laws on their fellow-citizens inconsistent with, and opposite to those interests and those feelings. Therefore, a *society*, a *government*, or *real public*, truly worthy of the name, and not a confederacy of banditti, a clan of lawless savages, or a band of slaves, under the whip of a master, must be such an one as consists of freemen, chusing and consenting to laws themselves; or, since it often happens that they cannot assemble and sit in a *collective* body, delegating a sufficient number of *representatives*, i.e. such a number as shall most fully comprehend, and most equally represent, their *common feelings* and *common interests*, to digest and vote laws for the conduct and controul of the whole body, the most agreeable to those common feelings and common interests.

Political Duties of Every Citizen

A society thus constituted by *common reason*, and formed on the plan of a *common interest*, becomes immediately an object of public attention, public veneration, public obedience, a public and inviolable attachment, which ought neither to be seduced by bribes, nor awed by terrors; an object, in fine, of all those extensive and important duties which arise from so glorious a confederacy. To watch over such a system; to contribute all he can to promote its good by his reason, his ingenuity, his strength, and every other ability, whether natural or acquired; to resist, and, to the utmost of his power, defeat every encroachment upon it, whether carried on by a secret corruption, or open violence; and to sacrifice his ease, his wealth, his power, nay life itself, and what is dearer still his family and friends, to defend or save it, it is the duty, the honour, the interest, and the happiness of every citizen; it will make him venerable and beloved while he lives, be lamented and honoured if he falls in so glorious a cause, and transmit his name and immortal renown to his latest posterity.

THE PRECEPTOR

Political Duties of the People

As the PEOPLE are the fountain of power and authority, the original seat of Majesty, the authors of laws, and the creators of officers to execute them; if they shall find the power they have conferred abused by their trustees, their majesty violated by tyranny, or by usurpation, their authority prostituted to support violence, or screen corruption, the laws grown pernicious through accidents unforeseen, or unavoidable, or rendered ineffectual through the infidelity and corruption of the executors of them; then it is their right and what is their right is their duty, to resume that delegated power, and call their trustees to an account; to resist the usurpation and extirpate the tyranny; to restore their sullied majesty, and prostituted authority; to suspend, alter, or abrogate those laws, and punish their unfaithful and corrupt officers. Nor is it the duty only of the united body, but every member of it ought, according to his respective rank, power, and weight in the community, to concur in advancing and supporting those glorious designs.

Political Duties of Britons

The obligation of Briton's to fulfil the political duties, receive a vast accession of strength, when he calls to mind of what a noble and well-balanced constitution of government he has the honour to partake; a constitution founded on *common reason, common consent*, and *common good*; a constitution of free and equal laws, secured against *arbitrary* will and *popular* licence, by an admirable temperament of the governing powers, controuling and controuled by one another. How must every one who has tolerable understanding to observe, or tolerable honesty to acknowledge its happy effects, venerate and love a constitution, in which the majesty of the people is, and has frequently been recognized; in which Kings are made and unmade by the choice of the people; laws enacted or annulled only by their own consent, and for their own good, in which none can be deprived of their property, abridged of their freedom, or forfeit their lives without an appeal to the laws, and the verdict of their Peers or equals; a constitution, in fine, the nurse of heroes, the parent of liberty, the patron of learning and arts, the dominion of laws, "the pride of *Britain*, the envy of her neighbours" and their Sanctuary too! How dissolute and execrable must their character and conduct be, who, instead of sacrificing their *interest* and *ambition*, will not part with the least degree of either, to preserve inviolate, and intail in full vigour to their posterity such a glorious constitution, the labour of so much blood and treasure; but would choose rather to sacrifice it, and all their independency, freedom, and dignity, to personal power, and hollow grandeur, to any little pageant of a King, who should prefer being the *master of slaves* to being the *guardian of freemen*, and consider himself as the *proprietor*, not the *father* of his people! But words cannot express the *selfishness* and *servility* of those men; and as little the public and heroic spirit of such, if any such there are as have virtue enough still left to stem the torrent of corruption, and guard our sacred constitution against the profligacy and prostitution of the corruptors and the corrupted.

[16]

A CONSTANT CUSTOMER

Extract of a Letter from a Gentleman in the Country to His Friend

BOSTON, 1773

This short piece, showing a resonance with the theory in longer essays on the same subject, is typical of much found in the newspapers of the era. It appeared in the *Massachusetts Spy* on February 18, 1773.

It gives me joy to hear something is now before the General Court concerning the emancipation of the blacks among us. It has long been a surprise to me and many others, that a people who profess to be so fond of freedom, and are taking every method to preserve the same themselves, and transmit it to their posterity, can see such numbers of their fellow men, made of the same blood, not only in bondage, but kept so even by them. Can such a conduct be reconcilable with the love of freedom? I freely confess, to one who is a stranger to the true character of this people, it has the appearance rather of temper and resentment against the rulers, than a hearty regard to that best of heaven's temporal blessings.

Men may talk and write as they please, but I must be excused from judging of any man or body of men, otherwise than by their works. The patriots in every town throughout the province, are weekly telling us how highly they value freedom, and that every temporal blessing without it is scarce worth enjoying; yet at the same time, they are stopping their ears to the cries of multitudes of their poor unhappy suffering brethren.

BOSTON, 1773

I readily grant there are difficulties which attend the freeing of them. It is no more than might justly be expected. Every community as well as every individual acting wrong, must suffer; and shall that be an excuse for not altering his or their conduct? No, they but encrease the evil by withholding the remedy; for either ruin or the remedy, which will be painful in the operation, must take place.

I pretend not to say what remedy is best to be taken by our rulers, but this one thing I may venture to say, that if a deaf ear is still turned to the complaint of those unhappy men—this people have no just reason to expect the righteous Governor of the earth, who punishes communities in this world, will afford his blessing to your endeavors to save a sinking country; but may say unto them as he did to Israel of old, "*Ye have not hearkened unto me in proclaiming liberty every one to his brother, and every man to his neighbor: Behold I will proclaim a liberty for you, saith the Lord, to the sword, to the pestilence and to the famine; and I will make you to be removed to all the kingdoms of the Earth.*"

[17]

SIMEON HOWARD 1733–1804

A Sermon Preached to the Ancient and
Honorable Artillery Company in Boston

BOSTON, 1773

Born in Massachusetts and educated at Harvard, he was regarded as only moderately bright among his classmates, but later in life Simeon Howard was said by some of his peers in the ministry to be "one of the ablest men New England ever produced." For reasons of health he chose Nova Scotia for his first preaching assignment but after two years rejected a call to a pastorate and returned to Boston for further study and occasional preaching. Soon he was invited to accept the pastorate recently vacated on the death of the great Jonathan Mayhew. Howard was widely denounced by New England Congregationalists as a heretic and suffered some ostracism because of his beliefs. He could not reconcile himself to Calvinist theology; the dogmas of predestination were repulsive to him. Hostility of surrounding congregations and harassment by British troops and American Loyalists then dominant in Boston forced Howard and his followers either to disband their church or to flee Boston. They chose to move en masse (1775) to Nova Scotia, where their pastor had enjoyed a friendly reception in his youth. Life proved to be hard in Canada, however, and learning that British forces had vacated Boston, he and his flock were back in their Massachusetts homes within a couple of years. There Howard devoted the remainder of his life to reestablishing his church, serving in various posts at Harvard University, and broadcasting his personal creed of the innate goodness of man and the infinite love of God. This sermon, preached to a Boston artillery company before the brief exile in Canada, illustrates how ideas drawn from the Bible and English Whig doctrine blended to support American experience and, rehearsed during the Stamp Act crisis, served to prepare Americans for the showdown with England they were about to face. As a consequence, when independence became a common goal, there was firmly planted and widely distributed in the population a theory that supplied a thoroughly satisfying justification of their struggle.

———————

GALATIANS V. I.

> Stand fast therefore in the liberty wherewith Christ hath made us free.

Mankind are generally averse to innovations both in religion and government. Laws and constitutions to which they have been long used, they are fond of retaining, even though better are offered in their stead. This appeared in the Jews. Their law required a burdensome and [6] expensive service: christianity set them free from this law. Nevertheless, many of them were desirous of continuing the observation of it, after they became christians; and of having the gentile converts also submit to it. Accordingly there were some Judaifing teachers who endeavoured to persuade the Galatians to this submission. The Apostle, therefore, in this epistle, particularly in the immediately foregoing chapter, asserts and proves, that christians have nothing to do with the ceremonial law of the Jews, they being freed by Christ, from this burden. And then as an inference from what he had said, and by way of admonition to the Galatians, he subjoins the exhortation in the text; stand fast therefore in the liberty wherewith Christ hath made us free.

But though the words originally refer to that freedom from the Jewish law which the gospel confers on the church of God, yet the reason of the inference holds good in the case of any other real and valuable liberty which men have a right to: So that this observation is plainly deducible from the text; vis. that it is the duty of all men to stand fast in such valuable liberty, as providence has confered upon them.

This observation I shall endeavour, by the help of God, to illustrate and improve: In order to which, I shall shew;

[7] I. What I intend by that liberty in which men ought to stand fast.

II. In what way they ought to stand fast in this liberty, or what they may and ought to do in defence of it.

III. The obligations they are under to this duty.

After which, I shall subjoin some reflections, and apply the subject to the present occasion.

I. I am to shew what is intended in this discourse by the liberty in which men ought to stand fast.

Though this word is used in various senses, I mean by it here, only that liberty which is opposed to external force and constraint, and to such force and constraint only, as we may suffer from men. Under the term liberty, taken in this sense, may naturally be comprehended all those advantages which are liable to be destroyed by the art or power of men; every thing that is opposed to temporal slavery.

This liberty has always been accounted one of the greatest natural blessings which mankind can enjoy. Accordingly, the benevolent and impartial Father of the human race, has given to all men a right, and to all naturally an equal right to this blessing.

[8] In a state of nature, or where men are under no civil government, God has given to every one liberty to pursue his own happiness in whatever way, and by whatever means he pleases, without asking the consent or consulting the inclination of any other man, provided he keeps within the bounds of the law of nature. Within these bounds, he may govern his actions, and dispose of his property and person, as he thinks proper.* Nor has any man, or any number of men, a right to restrain him in the exercise of this liberty, or punish, or call him to account for using it. This however is not a state of licentiousness, for the law of nature which bounds this liberty, forbids all injustice and wickedness, allows no man to injure another in his person or property, or to destroy his own life.

But experience soon taught that, either thro' ignorance of this law, or the influence of unruly passions, some were disposed to violate it, but encroaching upon the liberty of others; so that the *weak* were liable to be greatly injured by the superior power of bad men, without any means of security or redress. This gave birth to civil society, and

* See Locke on government.

induced a number of individuals to combine together for mutual defence and security; to give up a part of their natural liberty for the sake of enjoying the remainder in greater safety; to agree upon certain laws among themselves to regulate the social conduct of each individual, or to intrust to one or more [9] of their number, in whose wisdom and goodness they could confide, a power of making such laws, and putting them in execution.

In this state, the liberty which men have is all that natural liberty which has been mentioned, excepting what they have *expressly* given up for the good of the whole society; a liberty of pursuing their own happiness governing their actions, and disposing of their property and persons as they think fit, provided they transgress no law of nature, and keep within those restrictions which they have consented to come under.

This liberty will be different in different communities. In every state, the members will, probably, give up so much of their natural liberty, as they think will be most for the good of the whole. But different states will judge differently upon this point, some will give up more, some less, though still with the same view, the publick good. And every society have doubtless a right to act according to their own judgment and discretion in this matter, this being only an exercise of that natural liberty in which all are bound.

When a society commits to one or a few a power to govern them, the general practice is to limit this power by certain prescribed rules and restrictions. But sometimes this is omitted, and it does not appear from any act of the people, but that the power, with which they have intrusted their rulers, is unlimited. In this case [10] common sense will tell us that the power granted to rulers is to be limited by the great end and design of society and government, and he must be destitute of common sense, who does not know that this is the general good, the happiness and safety of the whole society. So that though a people should, through inadvertency, neglect to prescribe any bounds to the power of their rulers, this power would nevertheless be limited, and *they* would be at liberty to refuse submission to such restraints or laws, as were plainly inconsistent with the publick good.

There are some natural liberties or rights which no person can divest himself of, without transgressing the law of nature. A man cannot, for instance, give up the liberty of private judgment in matters of religion, or convey to others a right to determine of what religion

SIMEON HOWARD 1733–1804

he shall be, and in what way he shall worship God. A grant of this nature would destroy the foundation of all religion in the man who made it, and must therefore be a violation of the law of nature; nor would he be obliged to abide by it, if in consequence of it, he should be required to act contrary to the dictates of his conscience. Or should a man pretend to grant to others a power to order and govern all his actions that were not of a religious nature, so that in all cases he must act agreeable to their direction; this would be inconsistent with that submission which he owes to the authority of God, and his own conscience. The grant would be in itself void, and he would, notwithstanding, be at liberty to act according [11] to his own conscience, though contrary to the command of those to whom he had made so extravagant a donation.

Should therefore the legislature of a state make laws requiring the subjects to do things immoral, and which they knew to be so, such, for instance, as were apparently destructive of public happiness, though it was in consequence of an express grant of unlimited power, the subjects would be at liberty to refuse obedience, and not violate conscience or destroy their own happiness.* So that only such laws of society as are not plainly inconsistent with the end of society, or, in any other respect, inconsistent with the law of nature, the eternal rules of mortality, can restrain and limit the natural liberty of those who belong to it.

It is to be further observed here, that states or communities, as such, have naturally the same liberty which individuals have in the state of nature: but this liberty is restrained, in some measure, by what are called the laws of nations, which are certain rules, that by a tacit consent are agreed upon among all communities, at least among those who are accounted the polite and civilized part of mankind. *These,* nations are not at liberty to violate.

[12] What has been said may be sufficient to shew what that liberty is in which men ought to stand fast. In a state of nature it is all that liberty which is consistent with the law of nature; under civil government, it is all which is consistent with the law of nature, and

---

* "All conveyance of absolute power, whether to prince or a senate, with a preclusion of all rights of resistance, must be a deed originally invalid, as founded in an error about what is most essential in such transactions, the tendency of such power to the general good." Dr. Hutcheson's system of moral philosophy, Vol. 2, Page 271.

with such restrictions as they have consented to come under consistently with the law of nature and the end of society: and when we consider one independent state in reference to another, it is all that natural liberty which is consistent with the laws of nations.

And whatever share men enjoy of this liberty, we may properly say in the words of the text, that Christ has made them free with it, since after his resurrection and exaltation to the right hand of the Majesty on high, all power in heaven and in earth was committed to him, and he now sits, and is to continue at the head of God's providential government, till he hath put all enemies under his feet, after which, he shall deliver up the kingdom to God, even the Father— that God may be all in all.

II. I am in the next place to shew in what way men are to stand fast in their liberty, or what they may and ought to do in defence of it.

It is here supposed that some attempts are made to injure it. And it has been found in all ages and places that such attempts have been made by unreasonable and wicked men. The history of mankind is filled with instances [13] of this; insomuch that if from the great number of historical books that have been written, we should leave out those parts that relate to their encroachments upon one another, their injuries and injustice, most of those huge volumes would shrink to a very small size. Cain began this practice very soon after the creation: and it has been continued ever since, both among kingdoms and individuals. And the same practice is still to be expected, while human nature continues what it is.

Now for men to stand fast in their liberty means, in general, resisting the attempts that are made against it, in the best and most effectual manner they can.

When any one's liberty is attacked or threatened, he is first to try gentle methods for his safety, to reason with, and persuade the adversary to desist, if there be opportunity for it; or get out of his way, if he can; and if by such means he can prevent the injury, he is to use no other.

But the experience of all ages has shewn, that those, who are so unreasonable as to form designs of injuring others, are seldom to be diverted from their purpose by argument and persuasion alone. Notwithstanding all that can be said to shew the injustice and inhumanity of their attempt, they persist in it, till they have gratified the unruly passion which set them to work. And in this case, what is to be done by the sufferer? Is he [14] to use no other means for his safety, but remonstrance or flight, when these will not secure him? Is he patiently to take the injury and suffer himself to be robbed of his liberty or his life, if the adversary sees fit to take it? Nature certainly forbids this tame submission, and loudly calls to a more vigorous defence. Self-preservation is one of the strongest, and a universal principle of the human mind: And this principle allows of every thing necessary to self-defence, opposing force to force, and violence to violence. This is so universally allowed that I need not attempt to prove it.

But since it has been supposed by some that christianity forbids all violent resisting of evil, or defending ourselves against injuries in such a manner as will hurt, or endanger those who attack us; it may not be amiss to enquire briefly, whether defensive war be not allowed by the gospel of Christ, the Prince of peace.

And there are, if I mistake not, several passages in the new testament, which shew, that, it was not the design of this divine institution to take away from mankind the natural right of defending their liberty, even by the sword.

I will not alledge the words of John the baptist when in answer to the demand which the soldiers made; *What shall we do?*—*he said unto them, do violence to no man, neither accuse any falsely, and be content with your wages.** For [15] though they plainly imply, that, at that time, the military profession was not unlawful, and, consequently, that men might use the sword when there was occassion for it, yet it does not follow from hence, that the religion which Jesus was to institute, would allow of that profession and the use of the sword.

But there are other passages proper to be here alledged.

The first that I shall mention is our Lord's own words to Pilate, when under examination before that Governor. The chief charge bro't against Jesus was, that he was going to set up a temporal kingdom inconsistent with the sovereignty of the Roman Emperor. In answer to which he declared, that his *kingdom was not of this world;* and then offered the following argument to prove the assertion: *If my kingdom were of this world, then would my servants fight, that I should not be delivered*

* Luke 3. 14

to the Jews: But now is my kingdom not from hence.† There is an ellipsis in the latter clause; but the sense of the whole is obviously what follows. You know that those who aim at temporal dominion, endeavour to establish their authority and defend themselves, by force of arms, when it is necessary: If this had been my aim I should have taken the same method, and ordered my servants to fight against the Jews when they came to apprehend me: Wherefore, since I have made no violent resistance, but, on the contrary, "hindered [16] one of my disciples from fighting who fought to rescue me," it must now be evident to you, that the kingdom which I claim is not of this world. Our Lord here, plainly allows that it is fit and proper to temporal kingdoms to fight in defence of their liberty. His own kingdom is not, indeed, to be defended in this way, which being wholly spiritual, consisting of the obedience of men's wills and affections to the laws of God, is incapable of being directly either injured or defended by the sword, as the kingdoms of this world, and men's temporal interest may.

Cornelius, a centurion of the Italian band, was directed by an angel of God to send for Peter, who should tell him "what he ought to do."** But we do not find that the apostle directed him to quit his military profession, or intimated that it was inconsistent with the spirit of christianity; which he certainly would have done, had the character of a soldier and a good christian been incompatible.

The apostle Paul exhorts the Romans thus: *If it be possible, as much as lieth in you, live peaceably with all men.** Which words plainly imply, that notwithstanding all their endeavours to preserve peace, it might be impossible for them to live peaceably with all men, or not to contend and be at strife with some; i.e. impossible in a moral sense, improper, unlawful, for they do not require us to do all which we have a natural power to do for the sake of peace, but only [17] all that we can do consistently with higher obligations, with our duty in other respects.

Once more—let me observe that in the apocalypse of St. John, where we have a prophetic account of the future state of the church on earth, till the consummation of all things, there are several passages which intimate, that the saints of the Most High, will fight in their defence against their enemies; and that though they shall in various

† John 18. 36.
** Acts. 10.
* Chap. 12. 18.

instances be overcome, yet that they shall at length, by an amazing slaughter of their persecutors, obtain for themselves the peaceable enjoyment of that liberty, wherewith Christ hath made them free.† Now it cannot reasonably be supposed that the spirit of God would have represented his faithful servants, as thus fighting against their enemies, and being so favoured by divine providence, as finally to prevail over them, if defensive war was inconsistent with the spirit of the gospel.

It is not, however, to be denied that there are some passages in the new testament which seem to forbid all war: particularly, our Saviour's own words in his sermon on the mount. *I say unto you that ye resist not evil—love your enemies, do good to them that hate you,* etc.‡ And those of the apostle Paul; *Recompence to no man evil for evil.—Avenge not your selves:* and some others of [18] the like import. And from such passages some have supposed that christians are not allowed to defend themselves by force of arms, how violently soever they may be attacked.

Give me leave then, to offer a few remarks to take off the force of this objection.

1. When our Saviour forbids us to resist evil, he seems to have had in view only small injuries, for such are those which he mentions in the following words, as an illustration of the precept; smiting on the cheek, taking away one's coat, or compelling him to go a mile. And to such injuries it is oftentimes a point of prudence, as well as duty to submit, rather than contend. But it does not follow, that because we are forbidden to resist such slight attacks, we may not defend ourselves when the assault is of a capital kind. But,

2. Supposing our Lord's words to refer only to small injuries, they ought not to be taken in an absolute sense. Expressions of this nature frequently occur in scripture, which are universally understood with certain restrictions and limitations. For instance; *Love not the world, nor the things that are in the world.*** *Lay not up for yourselves treasure on earth.*†† *Give to him that asketh thee, and from him that would borrow of thee, turn not thou away.** Now, I believe, no body ever supposed, not even the honest *Quakers,* that these precepts were to be

† Chap. XI, ver. 7. XII. 7. XIV. 19, 20. XVII. 14. XIX. 14–21.
‡ Matthew 5. Romans 12. 17, 19
** John 2. 5.
†† Mat. 6. 19.
* Mat. 5. 42.

understood so literally, as to forbid all love of the [19] world, and all care to provide the good things of it; or to oblige us "to give to every idle fellow all he may think fit to ask, whether in charity or loan." And we have as good a right to limit the precept which forbids our resisting evil, by the nature and reason of things, as we have to limit these other indefinite expressions.

3. Defending ourselves by force of arms against injurious attacks, is a quite different thing from rendering evil for evil. The latter implies doing hurt to another, because he has done hurt to us; the former implies doing hurt to another, if he is hurt in the conflict, only because there is no other way of avoiding the mischief he endeavors to do us: the *one* proceeds from malice and revenge; the *other* merely from self-love, and a just concern for our own happiness, and argues no ill will against any man.

And therefore it is to be observed,

4. That necessary self-defence, however fatal it may prove to those who unjustly attack us, implies no principle inconsistent with that love to our enemies which Christ enjoins. For, at the same time that we are defending ourselves against their assaults, we may bear good-will towards them, wish them well, and pray God to befriend them: All which we doubtless ought to do in respect to our bitterest enemies.

Enough has been said to shew the consistency of war with the spirit of the gospel.

[20] But it is only defensive war that can be justified in the sight of God. When no injury is offered us, we have no right to molest others. And christian meekness, patience and forbearance, are duties that ought to be practiced both by kingdoms and individuals. Small injuries, that are not likely to be attended with any very pernicious consequences, are rather to be submitted to, than resisted by the sword. Both religion and humanity strongly forbid the bloody deeds of war, unless they are necessary. Even when the injury offered is great in itself, or big with fatal consequences, we should, if there be opportunity, endeavour to prevent it by remonstrance, or by offering to leave the matter in dispute to indifferent judges, if they can be had. If these endeavours are unsuccessful, it then becomes proper to use more forceable means of resistance.

A people may err by too long neglecting such means, and shamefully suffer the sword to rust in its scabberd when it ought to be employed in defending their liberty. The most grasping and oppressive power will commonly let its neighbours remain in peace, if they will submit to its unjust demands. And an incautious people may submit to these demands, one after another, till its liberty is irrecoverably gone, before they saw the danger. Injuries small in themselves, may in their consequences be fatal to those who submit to them; especially if they are persisted in. And, with respect to such injuries, we should ever act upon that ancient maxim of prudence; *obsta principiis*. The first unjust [21] demands of an encroaching power should be firmly withstood, when there appears a disposition to repeat and increase such demands. And oftentimes it may be both the right and duty of a people to engage in war, rather than give up to the *demands* of such power, what they could, without any inconveniency, spare in the way of charity. War, though a great evil, is ever preferable to such concessions, as are likely to be fatal to public liberty. And when such concessions, are required and insisted upon, as the conditions of peace, the only consideration to be attended to by the abused state, is that which our Saviour intimates common prudence will always suggest in such cases: *What king going to make war against another king, sitteth not down first and consulteth whether he be able,* etc.*

An innocent people threatened with war are not always obliged to receive the first attack. This may frequently prove fatal, or occasion an irreparable damage. When others have sufficiently manifested an injurious or hostile intention, and persist in it, notwithstanding all the admonition and remonstrance we can make, we may, in order to avoid the blow they are meditating against us, begin the assault.

After a people have been forced into war for their own security, they ought to set reasonable bounds to their resentment, or they may become as guilty as the first aggressors. They should aim at nothing more than repelling the [22] injury, obtaining reparation for damages sustained, and security against future injuries. If, after these ends are obtained, they continue the war, in order to distress their enemies, or reduce them under their power, they become offenders, and the war on their side is unjust.

Submitting the foregoing general observations to your candor, I go on to hint at some things proper to be attended to, by every

* Luke 14. 31.

people, in order to their being in a capacity to defend themselves against encroachments on their liberty.

1. They should endeavor to be united and at peace among themselves. The strength of a society, as well as its honour and happiness, depends much upon its union. Our Saviour's maxim is founded in reason, and has been confirmed by the experience of all ages: *Every kingdom divided against itself is brought to desolation.* When the body politic is divided into parties, and the members make a business of opposing each other, it is in a fair way to ruin. They are not likely to unite in measures of defence against a common enemy, and will therefore lie open to the encroachments of violence and oppression, and become an easy prey to every invader. The tyrants of the earth, sensible of this, have commonly acted upon this maxim, *divide et impera:* let us first divide the people, whom we mean to enslave, into parties, and we shall then easily bring them under our power.

[23] 2. They should endeavor to maintain among themselves a general disposition to submit to government. Society cannot subsist without government; and there can be no government without laws, and a submission to laws. If a licentious spirit prevails among a people, a general disposition to trample upon laws and despise government, they will probably make but a poor figure in defending themselves against a common enemy, for, in making this defence, there must be leaders and followers, some to command and some to obey: And, other things being equal, the more a disposition to submit to rule and order prevails among a people, the more likely will they be to defend their liberty against foreign invasions. Indeed without any enemy from abroad, the general prevalence of a licentious spirit may as effectively destroy the liberty of a people, as the most despotic government, for civil "liberty is something as really different from that licentiousness which supposeth no government, as from that slavery which supposeth tyranny: it is a freedom restrained by beneficial laws, and living and dying with public happiness."*

3. That people that would be in a capacity to defend themselves successfully against encroachments, should take care that their internal government be free and easy; allowing all that liberty to every one which is consistent with the necessary restraints of government; laying

* Bp. Hoadly.

SIMEON HOWARD 1733–1804

no burdens upon any, but what are for the good of the whole, and to which the whole society has [24] actually or virtually consented. Though the contrary evil takes its rise from the weakness or wickedness of rulers, yet in every free state it is the right and duty of all, *subjects* as well as rulers, to use their influence against it: And where the subjects have no *constitutional* right to do any thing to prevent or, remove such an evil, they are already slaves, and it may be tho't improper to talk of their defending their liberty, though they ought, doubtless, to endeavor to recover it. However, I say, it is highly necessary that this freedom from unreasonable restraints be preserved, in order to a people's retaining a spirit of liberty, and being in a capacity to defend themselves against a common enemy. It is justly observed by that great statesman, lord Verulam, that "the blessing of Judah and Issachar will never meet, that the same people or nation should be both the lion's whelp, and the ass between two burdens: neither will it be, that a people overlaid with taxes, should ever become valiant and martial."* The laying unreasonable burdens and restraints upon a people, will, if they are submitted to, debase their minds, break their spirits, enervate their courage, and sink them into cowards: if they are not submitted to, the consequence will be internal tumult, disorder, strife and contempt of government; and in either case, the defensive power of the state is greatly diminished. Behold, then the policy, or rather the madness and folly of oppressive rulers: if they are successful in their injurious measures, they are exposing themselves and their subjects [25] an helpless prey to the ravages of some ambitious neighbour: if they are not; they are raising up enemies against themselves at home, and, as it were, setting fire to their own habitations.

4. A people who would stand fast in their liberty, should furnish themselves with weapons proper for their defence, and learn the use of them.

It is indeed an hard case, that those who are happy in the blessings of providence, and disposed to live peaceably with all men, should be obliged to keep up the idea of blood and slaughter, and expend their time and treasure to acquire the arts and instruments of death. But this is a necessity which the depravity of human nature has laid upon every state. Nor was there ever a people that continued, for any

---

* Bacon's Essays, p. 113

considerable time, in the enjoyment of liberty, who were not in a capacity to defend themselves against invaders, unless they were too poor and inconsiderable to tempt an enemy.

So much depends upon the military art, in the present day, that no people can reasonably expect to defend themselves successfully without it. However numerous they may be, if they are unskilled in arms, their number will tend little more to their security, than that of a flock of sheep does to preserve them from the depredations of the world: accordingly it is looked upon as a point of wisdom, in every state, to [26] be furnished with this skill, though it is not to be obtained without great labor and expence.

In some nations the method has been to trust for defence and security to what is called a STANDING ARMY; a number of men paid by the public, to devote themselves wholly to the military profession; while the body of the people followed their peaceable employments, without paying any attention to the art of war.

But this has ever been thought, by the wise and prudent, a precarious defence.

Such armies are, as to the greater part of them, generally composed of men who have no real estate in the dominions which they are to defend; their pay is their living, and the main thing that attaches them to their employers, their manner of life tends to corrupt their morals, and, though they are naturally of the same temper with other men, they seldom continue long in this profession, before they become distinguished by their vices: So that neither their temporal interest, nor their regard to virtue can be supposed to attach them so strongly to the country that employs them, but that there will always be danger of their being tempted by the promise of larger pay to betray their trust, and turn their arms against it. No people therefore, can with safety trust intirely to a standing army, even for defence against foreign enemies.

But without any such enemy, a standing army may be fatal to the happiness and liberty [27] of a community. *They* generally propagate corruption and vice where they reside, they frequently insult and abuse the unarmed and defenceless people: When there is any difference between rulers and subjects, they will generally be on the side of the former, and ready to assist them in oppressing and enslaving the latter. For though they are really servants of the people, and paid by them; yet this is not commonly done in their name; but in the name of the supreme magistrate.* THE KING'S BREAD, and the KING'S SERVICE, are familiar expressions among soldiers, and tend to make them consider him as their only master, and prefer his personal interest to that of the people. So that an army may be the means, in the hands of a wicked and oppressive sovereign, of overturning the constitution of a country, and establishing the most intolerable despotism. It would be easy to shew from history, that this measure has been fatal to the liberties of many nations. And indeed, it has seldom been approved by the body of a people.

But rulers of an arbitrary disposition, have ever endeavored to have a standing army at their command, under a pretence indeed, of being for the safety of the state, though really with a view [28] of giving efficacy to their orders. It has sometime been pretended, that this is necessary to aid and support civil government. But whoever considers, that the design of government is the good of the people, and the great improbability there is, that a people, in general, should be against measures calculated for their good, and that *such* measures only ought to be enforced, will look upon this as the idlest pretence. For rulers to use a military power, to enforce measures of a contrary tendency, is one of the wickedest and most unjustifiable kinds of offensive war; a violation not only of the common laws of justice and humanity, but of their own sacred engagements to promote the public good. The keeping up troops sufficient to guard exposed frontier posts, may be proper; but to have an army continually stationed in the midst of a people, in time of peace, is a precarious and dangerous method of security.

A safer way, and which has always been esteemed the wisest and best, by impartial men, is to have the power of defence in the body of the people, to have a well-regulated and well-disciplined militia.† This is placing the sword in hands that will not be likely to betray their trust, and who will have the strongest motives to act their part well, in defence of their country, whenever they shall be called for.

---

* "What are we to expect, if in a future age an ambitious Prince should arise, with a dissolute and debauched army, a *flattering Clergy,* a prostitute Ministry, a bankrupt house of L——d's, a pensioned house of C——ns, and a slavish and corrupted nation?"
Trenchard's history of standing armies in England.
† Our trained bands are the trustiest and most proper strength of a free nation.
MILTON'S *Eikon.*

An army composed of men of property, who have been all their days inured to labour, will generally equal [29] the best veteran troops, in point of strength of body and firmness of mind, and when fighting in defence of their religion, their estates, their liberty, and families, will have stronger motives to exert themselves, and may, if they have been properly disciplined, be not much inferior to them in the skill of arms.

It was by a militia, by an army composed of men of property and worth of their own nation, that ancient Rome rose to be mistress of the world. The battles of *Agincourt, Poictiers* and *Cressy* are memorable proofs of the martial prowess of the ancient militia of England. Our own country will also furnish us with many instances of the bravery of a militia, both formerly and latterly.

Caution however ought to be used in constituting a militia, that it may answer the end for which it is designed, and not be liable to be made an instrument of tyranny and oppression. It should be subject to discipline and order, and somewhere in the state should be lodged a power of calling it forth to action, whenever the safety of the people required it. But this power should be so limited and restrained, as that it cannot call it unnecessarily, or oblige it to commit violence or oppression upon any of the subjects.‡ [30]

5. Once more, it is necessary for a people who would preserve their liberty, to maintain the general practice of religion and virtue. This will tend to make them courageous: The truest fortitude is ever to be found where the passions and affections are in subjection to the laws of God. Religion conciliates the favor of God, upon whom success in war essentially depends, and the hope of this favour will naturally inspire a brave and undaunted resolution. Not to mention that the unity, riches, and bodily strength of a people are greatly favoured by virtue. On the other hand, vice naturally makes men timerous, and

‡ That wise men have thought a people might be in danger from their own militia, unless great caution was used in the direction of it, appears from the following quotation: "Take away from the king the absolute power to compel men to take up arms, otherwise than in case of foreign invasion; power to compel men to go out of their counties to war, to charge men for the maintenance of wars, power to make them find arms at his pleasure, and lastly power to break the peace, or do ought that may tend thereto; certainly the power of the militia that remaineth, though never so surely settled in the king's hand, can never bite this nation."

Bacon on government, lib. 2 chap.22

fills the breast with baseness and cowardise. What is here said is agreeable to the observation of that wise King and inspired writer, who tells us, *"the wicked flee, when no man pursueth, but the righteous are bold as a lion."*

III. Let me now offer a few considerations to shew the obligations men are under to defend that liberty which providence has conferred upon them.

This is a trust committed to us by heaven: we are accountable for the use we make of it, [31] and ought therefore, to the best of our power to defend it. The servant, who hid his talent in a napkin, is condemned in our Lord's parable, and he who through inattention, indolence or cowardise, suffers it to be wrested from him, is little less criminal. Should a person, for instance, whose ability and circumstances enable him to do good in the world, to relieve his distressed brethren, and be an example of charity and other virtues, tamely yield up all his interest and become an absolute slave to some unjust and wicked oppressor, when he might by a manly resistance have secured his liberty, would he not be guilty of great unfaithfulness to God, and justly liable to his condemnation? This would in its consequences be really worse than hiding his talent in a napkin; it would be not only not improving it for the glory of the giver, but conveying it into hands which will, in all probability, employ it greatly to his dishonour. This reasoning is as applicable to a community as to an individual. A kingdom or common wealth, as such, is accountable for the improvement it makes of it's advantages: It is bound to preserve them, and employ them for the honour of God, so far as it can, to be an example of virtue to neighbouring communities, and afford them relief when they are in distress: but by yielding up their possessions and liberties to an encroaching oppressive power, they become, in a great measure, incapable of these duties, and are liable to be made the ministers of sin through the compulsion of their masters. Out of faithfulness then, to God, and in order to escape the [32] doom of slothful servants, we should endeavour to defend our rights and liberties.

Men are bound to preserve their own lives, as long as they can, consistently with their duty in other respects. Would not he, who should lose his life by neglecting to resist a wild beast, be criminal in the sight of God? And can he be innocent who loses it by neglecting to oppose the violent attacks of wicked men, oftentimes as fierce and cruel as the most savage beast?

Men are also bound, individuals and societies, to take care of their temporal happiness, and do all they lawfully can, to promote it. But what can be more inconsistent with this duty, than submitting to great encroachments upon our liberty? Such submission tends to slavery; and compleat slavery implies every evil that the malice of man and devils can inflict. Again,

The regard which we owe to the happiness of others makes this a duty.

Every man is bound both by the law of nature and revelation, to provide in the best manner he can, for the temporal happiness of his family, and he that neglects this, has, according to the declaration of an inspired apostle, *denied the faith, and is worse than an infidel.* But in what way can a man be more justly chargeable with this neglect, than by suffering himself [33] to be deprived of his life, liberty or property, when he might lawfully have preserved them?

Reason, humanity and religion, all conspire to teach us, that we ought in the best manner we can, to provide for the happiness of posterity. We are allied to them by the common tie of nature: They are not here to act their part: A concern for them is a debt which we owe for the care which our progenitors took for us: Heaven has made us their guardians, and intrusted to our care their liberty, honour, and happiness: For when they come upon the state, they will be deeply affected by the transactions of their fathers, especially by their public transactions. If the present inhabitants of a country submit to slavery, slavery is the inheritance which they will leave their children. And who that has the bowels of a father, or even the common feelings of humanity, can think without horror, of being the means of subjecting unborn millions to the iron scepter of tyranny?

But further; a regard to the happiness of mankind in general, makes it a duty to resist great injuries. Yielding to the unjust demands of bad men, not only lessens our power of doing good, but encourages them to repeat their injuries, and strengthens their hands to do mischief: It enables them to give fuller scope to their lusts, and more effectually to spread corruption, distress and misery. It is therefore an act of benevolence to oppose and destroy that power which is employed in injuring others, [34] and as much, when it is that of a tyrant, as of a wild beast.

SIMEON HOWARD 1733–1804

Once more, from a regard to religion men are obliged to defend their liberty against encroachments, though the attack should not immediately affect religion. Slavery exposes to many temptations to vice, and by debasing and weakening the mind, destroying its fortitude and magnanimity renders it less capable of resisting them, and creates a dependance upon, and subjection to wicked men, highly prejudicial to virtue. Hence it has been often observed, and is confirmed by experience that the loss of liberty is soon followed by the loss of all virtue and religion.*

Besides; the destruction of civil liberty is generally fatal to *religions*. The latter has seldom existed long in any place without the former. Nor is it to be expected that those who are wicked enough to deprive a people of *that,* should, when they have got them under their power, suffer them long to enjoy *this;* especially as tyranny has generally made these two evils subservient to each other.

But I may not enlarge: The considerations which have been suggested shew, if I mistake not, that it is not only the right but the duty of [35] men to defend that liberty, with which providence has made them free: And a duty of high obligation, as the neglect of it may be attended with consequences, the most prejudicial to human virtue and happiness, and greatly dishonorary to God.

All that now remains is to offer some reflections, and apply the subject to the present occasion.

1. What has been said may serve to caution all against invading the liberty of others;—Whoever does this, obliges others to resist him: he puts himself into a state of war with them, and is justly liable to all the evil which their necessary self-defence may bring upon him. And though he may think that his power is so great, and their's so little, that he can be in no danger from their resentment, the event may convince him of his mistake. Men, who have a just sense and value of liberty, will sometimes do wonders in its defence.

> ——"They have great odds
> Against the astonish'd sons of violence,
> Who fight with awful justice on their side."‡

---

* "The conquer'd also, and inslav'd by war shall with their freedom lost all virtue lose and fear of God.

Paradise Lost

‡ Thompson.

Oppressors may indeed for a time, be successful and overcome all opposition; yet it seldom happens that they persevere in their injurious practice, without meeting with such resistance as causes their *mischief to return upon their own heads, and their violent dealings to come down upon their own* [36] *pates:* It is an old observation, that few tyrants descend in peace to the grave. If therefore, the laws of God will not, a regard to their own safety should restrain men from invading the rights of the innocent.

2. If it be so important a duty for men to resist encroachments upon their liberty; then it cannot be improper for the christian minister, to inculcate *this* upon his hearers; to exhort them to be watchful over it, and ready to oppose all attempts against it. This is so far from being improper, that it is, I humbly conceive, his indispensible duty. Nor can I see how he could answer it to God, or his own conscience, if, when he thought his country was in danger of being enslaved, for want of a proper sense of, and opposition to the approaches of tyranny, he should neglect to point out the danger, and with

———"honest zeal
To rouse the watchmen of the public weal."†

It is readily owned, that *designedly* to spread false alarms, to fill the minds of people with groundless prejudices against their rulers, or a neighbouring state, to stir up faction and encourage opposition to *good* government, are things highly criminal, and whoever does thus, whatever character he may wear among men, is in reality a minister, not of Christ, but of the devil, the father of falsehood, confusion and rebellion. But to shew people their real danger, point out the source of it, and exhort them to such exertions [37] as are necessary to avoid it, are acts of benevolence becoming every disciple, and especially every professed minister of Christ.

3. Since the preservation of public liberty depends so much upon a people's being possessed of the art of war; those who exert themselves to encourage and promote this art, act a laudable part, and are intitled to the thanks of their brethren. Upon this account, the company, which is the occasion of this solemnity, deserves to be esteemed *honorable* though its institution were much less *ancient* than it is. And

† Pope.

SIMEON HOWARD 1733–1804

as this society has in former days furnished many brave men, who died worthily in defence of our country, so, from the spirit which at present prevails among the gentlemen who compose it, we doubt not but it will furnish others, whenever there shall be occasion for it. How far this institution, by exciting in others a spirit of imitation or emulation, has been the occasion of the present general attention to the military art among us, I pretend not to say: But whatever be the cause, it must give pleasure to every friend of public liberty, to see this people so generally engaged in military exercises. This argues a manly spirit, a sense of liberty, a just apprehension of its danger, a resolution to stand fast in it, and, as far as any thing in our power can do it, promises freedom to our country.

We are not, I hope, insensible that peace is a great blessing, and, in itself, ever to be prefered [38] to war; nor unthankful to Him who ruleth among the nations, the God of peace, for the enjoyment we have had of this blessing for a number of years past. But we have little reason to expect, however ardently we may wish, that this country will always be the habitation of peace. Ambition, avarice, and other unruly passions have a great hand in directing the conduct of most of the kingdoms of this world. British America is already become considerable among the European nations for its numbers, and their easiness of living; and is continually rising into greater importance. I will not undertake to decypher the *signs of the times,* or to say from what quarter we are most likely to be molested. But from the course of human affairs, we have the utmost reason to expect that the time will come, when we must either submit to *slavery,* or defend our liberties by our own sword. And this perhaps may be the case sooner than some imagine. No one can doubt but there are powers on the continent of Europe, that would be glad to add North-America to their dominions, and who, if they thought the thing practicable, would soon find a pretence for attempting it. The naval power of Great-Britain has been hitherto our chief security against invasions from that continent. But every thing belonging to the present state, is uncertain and fluctuating. Things may soon be in such a situation with Great-Britain, that it will be no longer proper for us to confide in her power, for the protection of our liberty. Our greatest security, under God, will be our being in a capacity to defend ourselves. Were we, [39] indeed, sure that Great-Britain would always be both *able* and *willing* to protect us in our liberty, which, from present appearances, we have little reason to expect, it would be shameful for so numerous a people as this, and a people of so much natural strength and fortitude, to be, thro' inattention to the art of war, incapable of bearing a part in their own defence. Such weakness must render them contemptible to all the world.

British America, especially the northern part of it, is by its situation calculated to be a nursery of heroes. Nothing is wanting but our own care and application to make us, with the neighbouring colonies, a formidable people. And religion, honor, patriotism, and even self-love, all unite in demanding from us this application and care. This people, it may be presumed, will never of choice, keep among them a *standing army* in time of peace: Virtue, domestic peace, the insulated walls of our State-House, and even the once crimsoned *stones of the street,* all loudly *cry out* against this measure. But every well-wisher to the public, should countenance and encourage a military spirit among our militia through the province.

Our political Fathers have it in their power to do much for this end; and we have a right to expect that, out of faithfulness to God and this people, they will not neglect it. From the countenance which his Excellency and the honorable Council shew to the military transactions of this [40] day, we would gladly hope, that, they in conjunction with the other branch of the legislature, will, in this way, as well as others, prove themselves to be God's ministers for good to the people.

It is also in the power of persons of rank and fortune, in their private capacity, greatly to promote this cause by their example and otherwise. It is highly absurd, though not uncommon, that those who have most to lose by the destruction of a state, should be least capable of bearing a part in its defence. Riches are frequently the main temptation to war. Where a people are all poor, there is little danger of their being invaded: So that there being men of affluence among a people, is often the cause of their being obliged to defend themselves by the sword. It is therefore especially *their* duty, as well as interest, to do what they can to put the people into a capacity of defence. When *they* spend their time in idleness, effeminating pleasures, or even in accumulating riches, to the total neglect of the art of war, and every measure to promote it, they act unbecoming good members of society, and set an example highly prejudicial to the community.

Whereas when gentlemen of fortune, notwithstanding the allurements of pleasure on the one hand, and the fatiguing exercise of a soldier on the other, exert themselves to acquire and promote the military art, they are an honor to their circumstances, and a blessing to the public: [41] Their example will have great influence upon others; and, other things being equal, such men will be most likely to fight valiantly in defence of their liberty, whenever it shall be necessary. By such a conduct, they shew their regard to their country, in a way that will probably be much more beneficial to it, than merely talking, writing, or preaching in favor of liberty. And it ought to be esteemed as no inconsiderable evidence, among many others, of a public, truly patriotic spirit in the honorable gentleman,* who leads his Excellency's company of Cadets, that he has so chearfully endured the fatigue of qualifying himself to be a good officer, and, by his generous exertions in conjunction with their own, rendered his company an honour to the town, to their commanders and themselves. This company in general, is indeed an example of what I was urging; of gentlemen of easy circumstances giving proper attention to the art of war, and is on that account the more respectable and important.

But we have other laudable examples of attention to arms. The Train of Artillery‡ has for a number of years past been honorably distinguished, by their military address. And the respectable appearance which the whole militia of the town made a few days ago, when called together in honor of his Majesty's birth-day, and the dexterity with which they went through their exercises, must convince all who had the [42] satisfaction of seeing them, that they are no strangers to a military spirit, and lead us to hope that by perseverance, the whole body will soon equal those, who at present excel most. May this spirit still revive and prevail through the province, till this whole people become as considerable for their skill in arms, as they are for their natural strength and courage.

The gentlemen who are engaged in acquiring this art will remember that the true end of it is only defence; that it is to be employed, not to destroy, but to protect and secure the liberty and happiness of mankind; not to infringe the rights of others, but to defend their own. While, therefore, they endeavor to resemble such men as *Alexander* and *Caesar* in military skill and valour, they will

---

* The Hon. John Hancock, Esq.
‡ A Company commanded by Major Paddock.

detest the principles from which they acted, in invading and distressing inoffensive people. For though they have been honored with the name of heroes, they were, in reality, public robbers and murderers.

They will also remember that the most desirable liberty, and which we should be ready to defend, is that of a well governed society, which is as essentially different from the licentiousness, which is without law or government, as it is from an absolute subjection to the arbitrary will of another. This is the liberty wherewith Christ has made us free; to which he has given us a right. While, therefore, these gentlemen will be always ready to stand forth in defence of true civil liberty, whenever they shall see her assaulted and be properly called upon; they will never on any consideration be prevailed [43] with, to employ their arms for the destruction of good government by aiding either tyranny on the one hand, or licentiousness on the other.

But above all they will remember, that religion is the main concern of man, and a necessary qualification for a good soldier. This, beyond any thing else, inspires with the love of liberty, with fortitude and magnanimity; and this alone can enable them to meet death with a rational composure and tranquility of mind, which is an enemy before which the bravest soldier must fall at last.

To conclude: This whole assembly will bear in mind, that there is another and more valuable kind of liberty, than that to which the foregoing discourse more immediately relates, and which, at this day, so generally employs our attention and conversation; a liberty, which consists in being free from the power and dominion of sin, through the assistance of the divine spirit, concurring with our own pious, rational and persevering endeavours. Whatever our outward circumstances may be, if we are destitute of this spiritual liberty, we are in reality slaves, how much soever we may hate the name; if we possess it we are *free indeed:* And our being free in this sense, will give us the best grounds to hope for temporal freedom, through the favour of heaven; and, at length, gain us admission into the regions of perfect and uninterrupted liberty, peace and happiness.

[18]

MASSACHUSETTENSIS

[DANIEL LEONARD 1740–1820]

To All Nations of Men

BOSTON, 1773

The several newspaper essays signed "Massachusettensis" are attributed without dispute to Daniel Leonard, a prominent Massachusetts lawyer who divided his time between the county of his birth (Bristol, adjoining Rhode Island) and Boston. Leonard was the son of well-to-do parents, attended Harvard College, and, after the customary period of reading law with a prominent attorney, set up practice in his hometown of Norton. From the beginning he exploited his political connections and before the age of thirty had been elected to the Massachusetts House of Representatives and was serving as the King's Attorney for his county. At this stage of his life he stood with the Whigs in opposition to London's policies and the governor who attempted to enforce them. As late as 1773 Leonard was serving on the Boston Committee of Correspondence, waging a campaign to alert the several colonies to British oppression and ready them for common action if grievances turned into intolerable offenses. By August of 1774 it was clear that he had been converted; he was now a staunch supporter of the newly appointed governor and no longer disposed to join in the clamor about British invasions of American rights. During the fall and winter of 1773–1774, the Massachusettensis letters appeared, and Daniel Leonard found himself irrevocably classified as a Tory. The day after the battle of Concord Bridge he signed up in the British Army, and a month after the Declaration of Independence he was in exile, an American Tory-Loyalist emigré in London. Although unusual in its discussion of Tories, this piece is typical of a large number of newspaper articles in the 1770s drawing upon Locke, Vatel, Burlamaqui, and other Whig theorists, although the notions of a state of nature, etc., were often subtly altered to bring them in line with American political principles. This essay appeared in the November 18, 1773 edition of the *Massachusetts Spy,* published in Boston.

To all Nations of Men, dwelling upon the face of the whole Earth, especially those of GREAT-BRITAIN and Ireland, more especially the Inhabitants of British North-America, and particularly those of the Massachusetts-Bay in New England.

MEN, BRETHREN and FATHERS,

It is indispensable to the well-being of civil society that every member thereof should have a sure and righteous rule of action in every occurence of life; and also that upon the observance of this rule he should be happy and secure from the molestation and disturbance of all men; municipal law, which is no more than the law of nature applied to man in society, having for its principal objects, the freedom of the person, conscience, and security of the subject in his property. And men enter into society for no other end than to place the execution of those laws in the hands of such as they esteem worthy to be entrusted with them; and to defend themselves, their laws and properties against foreign invasions. They do this in the first place to prevent that confusion and bloodshed which would inevitably take place were each individual left to judge in his own case and take by the strong hand what should appear to him satisfactory. Civil society then (to use the words of a celebrated author*) is nothing more than the union of a multitude of people who agree to live in subjection to a sovereign (i.e. any power having legislative authority) in order to find through his protection and care that happiness to which they NATURALLY ASPIRE. This is equally true whatever self governing community it is applied to, whether to the smallest principality in Germany, the weakest colony in America or the Kingdom of Great-Britain, France or Muscovy. Thus we see what forms a state and can easily perceive what are the duties both of rulers and people; viz. rulers must afford them *that protection whereby they may surely attain that felicity they naturally aspire to*—The people then should take care not to transgress the laws of society, which being formed by the wisest and best of their own body, must undoubtedly be intended at least, for the promotion and security of the public happiness.

Separate states (all self-governing communities) stand in the same relation to one another as individuals do when out of society; or to use the more common phrase, in a state of nature. And it is necessary

* Burlamaqui, Pol. Law p. 7.

says the same learned author that there should be *some law* among nations to serve as a *rule of mutual commerce*. This law can be no other than the law of nature, which is distinguished by the name of the law of nations. Mr. Hobbes says "natural law is divided into natural law of man, and natural law of states." The latter is what we call the law of nations. The laws both of nature and nations, as well as those of every free state, indeed of every lawful government under heaven are extremely watchful in ascertaining and protecting the right of private property. So great is the regard of the law for private property, that it will not authorize the least violation of it, unless applied to the detriment of the Society.—That men have a natural right to retain their justly acquired property, or dispose of it as they please without injuring others, is a proposition that has never been controverted to my knowledge: That they should lose this right by entering society is repugnant to common sense and the united voice of every writer of reputation upon the subject. All agree that no man can be justly deprived of his property without his consent in person or by his representative, unless he has forfeited it by the breach of the laws of his country to the enaction of which he consented.

All demands upon our purse, on other terms, are illegal; and put into execution robbery; if the demand be made sword in hand, the crime is till more attrocious; *"it is robbery with murderous intention!"* Can any one dispute the justice of one sentence of the above propositions? or admitting them, can they excuse the British parliament, from the violation of these most sacred bonds of human society? Have they not actually invaded the freedom of our persons pretending to bind us by laws to which our consent was never so much as asked? Have they not demanded our money at the point of the bayonet and mouth of the cannon? Have they not utterly subverted the free constitution of our state by making our extreme magistrate a mere dependent on the minister of Great Britain, and thus destroyed all confidence of the body politic in the head? Have they not further interfered with our civil policy and intruded a set of officers upon us, entirely independent of the supreme power of the province constituting that most dangerous and intolerable evil that ever was felt by a people; that source of civil discord, treasons and murders an *imperium in imperio,* which constitutes the house whose fate the breath of conscience has pronounced, viz. *"it cannot stand!"* Have they not further, to defeat all prospect of our relieving ourselves by the free course of the laws of the land, held out a bribe to our supreme executive, and doubly corrupted the council, whose duty it is to *see the commonwealth suffer no injury?* Are we not by these several most intolerable encroachments, these injurious interferences into the civil polity of our state, cut off from all hopes of relief from courts of law, and even from our high court of parliament, which the aforesaid omnipotent parliament of Great-Britain have by a late resolve, rendered, or endeavored to render as useless as a King of the Romans? For if one supreme legislative body, in which the whole continent of America have not a single voice, have power to make laws which shall be binding upon us in all cases whatsoever, rights, liberties, legislative powers, under such absolute suspending, dispensing, establishing annihilating power as this, are meer shadows, Jack o'lanterns serving only to mislead and engulph us.

There can be no doubt but it is fit, and perfectly consistent with the principle of all laws human and divine, to resist robbers, murderers and subverters of the government of free states, whether these crimes are committed by individuals or nations, or more properly a despotism endeavouring to establish itself over the most free and happy nation on the globe. The only question is, whether it be prudent to risque resistance.

To this I answer we must be sure that we have a good cause; and I think of this we are certain. We may then safely venture it with that God who loves righteousness and hates oppression; who has made it our indispensable duty to *preserve our own lives and the lives of others,* more especially our brethren of the same community. Under his protection we shall be safe while we walk in his commandments, and by his all powerful assistance one may chase a thousand, and two put ten thousand to flight.

It is highly probable our oppressors will withdraw their hand when they find our resolution, and consider how fatal it must be to themselves to drive things to extremity. Great-Britain at war with her colonies would be in the condition of a trunk deprived of its members. Besides the foundation of the dispute being an effort of her ministers to *diminish the sovereignty of so great a number of free self governing states,* and erect an absolute despotism over them, must give umbrage to every other power in Europe, this being an open violation of the law of nations, and punishable by all as Vatel B II. C. IV. [section] 53 declares in these words, "If then there is any where a nation of a restless and mischievous disposition always ready to injure others, to traverse their designs, and to raise domestic troubles; it is not to be doubted but all have a right to join in order to repress, chastise, and put it ever after out of its power to injure them." And in the next paragraph the interference with their government and dimunition of their sovereignty is declared to be capital injuries. Their schemes of oppression have heretofore been frustrated, and even now they are drove to stratagem. Their efforts to delude this people to their destruction are visible to us, and we perceive plainly the necessity to guard, not only against their brutal force, attempting to enslave us, but also against their artifice. They know we are a religious and conscientious people, but think we are ignorant of the true spirit of the laws respecting *meum* and *tuum;* therefore apprehend themselves safe in sending their *property* to America, notwithstanding that property is now constituted the *medium* of our political destruction—but they are mistaken in their men. We all know, that when even men themselves become dangerous to society, the public preservation warrant their extirpation, much less can they expect their property will be spared when in the same predicament. Men combined to subvert our civil government, to plunder and murder us, can have no right to protection in their persons or properties among us; they have by their attempts upon our liberty, *put themselves in a state of war with us,* as Mr. Locke observes, and being the agressors, if they perish, the fault is their own. "If any person in the best condition of the state, demands your purse at the muzzle of his pistol, you have no need to recur to law, you cannot give, i.e. immediate security against your adversary; and for that reason, viz. because the law cannot be applied to your relief, you make your own defence on the principles of natural law, which is now your only rule, and his life is forfeited into your hands, and you indemnified if you take it, because he is the first and a dangerous agressor." This rule applies itself to states, and to those employed by them to distress, rob or enslave other states; and shall property be secure where even life is forfeited? All wise nations think otherwise, and by every means in their power endeavour to take the forfeiture. There are many influences, wherein men lose the protection of law in their property, some, as was said before, even of their lives. I will instance a few. A ship with the plague on board, destined to any port, be she never so richly laden, or never so full of souls, may be sunk, and thereby both lives and property be lost to individuals, so the ships of a nation at peace with us, if laded with warlike stores or provisions to supply our enemies is forfeited into our hands, and in case of resistance may be sunk to the bottom.

Upon the same principle it is said a number of pole axes and scalping knives were seized by this government, (shipped by a man whose conduct has betrayed no signs of change in political sentiment since that time) when found on board a flag-of-truce bound from Boston to Louisbourgh in time of war; But of this treasonable action we have no account in Mr. Hutchinson's history of the Massachusetts Bay.

When we are reduced to the sad dilemma that we must destroy the lives of a few of our fellow men and their property or have the community destroyed by them we are not allowed to hesitate a moment; The rule here is that which is chosen by all wise men, and vindicated by the law of nature, viz. *of two evils chuse the least,* and rid society of such dangerous inmates.

These usurpers, or *foreign emissaries,* being screened from the power of the laws, by a corruption of both legislative and executive courts, have returned to a state of nature again with respect to this people, and may as justly be slain as wolves, tygers, or the private robbers and murderers above considered; and Jurors on their oaths are as much obliged to acquit the slayers in the one case as in the other. Slaying a man with a wicked intention is certainly highly criminal, but slaying him to prevent his destroying either our own lives or the constitution of the state to which we bear the most indissoluble allegiance is an act of heroism which entitled even a cobler of Messina to the just applauses of every good man who has read his story.

In former times a person *outlawed* was called Wolfshead and might be put to death by any man who met him, as that ravenous beast might, being as dangerous to society; this is to be understood of persons outlawed by due process, which might have obtained for misdemeanors much inferior to endeavours for the subversion of the state; but those who by this means break off from the society which from infancy afforded them protection, that plunder and devour their fellow men, even their best benefactors, are more execrable brutes, and may be said to be most fully ripe for exemplary destruction.

In recapitulation of the foregoing, please to attend to the few plain Propositions following, viz.

I. That men naturally have a right to life, liberty, and the possession and disposal of their property, in such wise as to injure none other.

II. That the same is true in society, with this difference that whereas in a state of nature each judged for himself, what was just or injurious, in society he submits to indifferent arbiters.

III. That all demands upon us for any part of our substance not warranted by our own consent or the judgment of our peers are robbery with murderous intention.

IV. That on these principles, the administration of Great-Britain are justly chargeable with this complicated crime.

V. That it is fit, and perfectly consistent with the principle of all laws human and divine, to resist robbers, murderers, and subverters of the constitution of our country.

VI. That both legislative and executive powers in this province being corrupted, the partizans of our oppressive plunderers and murderers are screened from public justice.

VII. That this corruption of public justice with regard to these internal enemies, and the deprivation of the people from the application of it for their own safety, naturally throws us back into a state of nature, with respect to them, whereby our natural right of self defence, and revenge returns.

VIII. That life, personal liberty, and private property, when employed to the detriment or destruction of society, where constitutional provisions cannot be applied, are forfeited into the hands of any, who have public spirit enough to take them.

IX. That Jurors who are the sole and only judges of fact and law; and at present our only security against tyranny are bound by the true interest of all law, the public security to acquit any persons who may be brought before them, for cutting off or destroying the life and property of the invaders of our liberties, from this alone consideration, viz. *That the law of the land cannot be applied to our relief.*

These are matters of the last importance, and demand the serious consideration of every man who values his freedom or his life, (the latter being but of very precarious tenure when the former is ravished) and if the foregoing propositions are founded in truth on the principles of natural justice and the security of human welfare, adopt them, and act in conformity to them; if not reject them, and substitute something better in their stead. Demonstrate that the domination of law, according to the caprice of their own arbitrary will, to the destruction of all laws, constitutions and injunctions, human and divine, is *lawful government;* and that the subject though certain to be stripped of liberty and property at pleasure; thrown into a bastile to weep out a life of anguish and distress; exposed to all the miseries of cold, hunger and confinement, may be happier than were our noble, free and generous ancestors, and none will be a more zealous and determined tory, than

MASSACHUSETTENSIS.

[19]

A PENNSYLVANIAN

[BENJAMIN RUSH 1745–1813]

*An Address to the Inhabitants of the British
Settlements in America Upon Slave-Keeping*

PHILADELPHIA, 1773

Rush was born on a farm in Pennsylvania, orphaned at age five, but supplied with a good education, including graduation from the college that later became Princeton University. He chose medicine as a career and after doing his apprenticeship in Philadelphia was able to study for three years in Edinburgh, London, and Paris. An enduring reputation as America's leading physician in the prime of his life was his reward for this commitment. But enchantment with public events and inability to resist dabbling in public affairs were competing interests that ran second to medicine and healing by no large margin. As a member of the Second Continental Congress he signed the Declaration of Independence, and as a member of the Pennsylvania Constitutional Convention of 1790, he was influential in replacing the radically democratic constitution of 1776 with a new one that comported much better with current notions of republican government. He wrote pamphlets on almost everything—slavery, capital punishment, oaths, separation of Church and State, public education, the education of women, bicameral versus unicameral legislatures, etc.
This essay is typical of his work in that it blends religious
commitment with a practical, political eye.

[1]   AN ADDRESS, &c.

So much hath been said upon the subject of Slave-Keeping, that an Apology may be required for this Address. The only one I shall offer is, that the Evil still continues. This may in part be owing to the great attachment we have to our own Interest, and in part, to the subject not being fully exhausted. The design of the following address is to sum up the leading arguments against it, several of which have not been urged by any of those Authors who have written upon it.

Without entering into the History of the facts which relate to the Slave Trade, I shall proceed to combat the principal arguments which are used to support it.

I need hardly say any thing in favour of the Intellects of the Negroes, or of their capacities for virtue and happiness, although these have been supposed, by some, to be inferior to [2] those of the inhabitants of Europe. The accounts which travellers give us of their ingenuity, humanity, and strong attachment to their parents, relations, friends and country, show us that they are equal to the Europeans, when we allow for the diversity of temper and genius which is occasioned by climate. We have many well-attested anecdotes of as sublime and disinterested virtue among them as ever adorned a Roman or a Christian character. But we are to distinguish between an African in his own country, and an African in a state of slavery in America. Slavery is so foreign to the human mind, that the moral faculties, as well as those of the understanding are debased, and rendered torpid by it. All the vices which are charged upon the Negroes in the southern colonies and the West-Indies, such as Idleness, Treachery, Theft, and the like, are the genuine offspring of slavery, and serve as an argument to prove that they were not intended for it.

Nor let it be said, in the present Age, that their black color (as it is commonly called) either [3] subjects them to, or qualifies them for slavery¶. The vulgar notion of their being descended from Cain, who was supposed to have been marked with this color, is too absurd

---

¶ Montesquieu, in his spirit of Laws, treats this argument with the ridicule it deserves.

"Were I to vindicate our right to make slaves of the Negroes, these should be my arguments.

The Europeans having extirpated the Americans, were obliged to make slaves of the Africans for clearing such vast tracts of land.

Sugar would be too dear, if the plants which produce it were cultivated by any other than slaves.

These creatures are all over black, and with such a flat nose that they can scarcely be pitied.

It is hardly to be believed that God, who is a wise being, should place a soul, especially a good soul, in such a black ugly body.

The Negroes prefer a glass necklace to that gold, which polite nations so

to need a refutation.—Without enquiring into the Cause of this blackness, I shall only add upon this subject, that so far from being a curse, it subjects the Negroes to no inconveniences, [4] but on the contrary qualifies them for that part of the Globe in which providence has placed them. The ravages of heat, diseases and time, appear less in their faces than in a white one; and when we exclude variety of color from our ideas of Beauty, they may be said to possess every thing necessary to constitute it in common with the white people.‡

It has been urged by the inhabitants of the Sugar Islands and South Carolina, that it would be impossible to carry on the manufactories of Sugar, Rice, and Indigo, without negro slaves. No manufactory can ever be of consequence enough to society to admit the least violation of the Laws of justice or humanity. But I am far from thinking the arguments used in favour of employing Negroes for the cultivation of these articles, should have any Weight.—M. Le Poivre, late envoy from the king of France, to [5] the king of Cochin-China, and now intendant of the isles of Bourbon and Mauritius, in his observations upon the manners and arts of the various nations in Africa and Asia, speaking of the culture of sugar in Cochin-China, has the following remarks.—"It is worthy observation too, that the sugar cane is there cultivated by freemen, and all the process of preparation and refining, the work of free hands. Compare then the price of the Cochin-Chinese production with the same commodity which is cultivated and prepared by the wretched slaves of our European colonies, and judge if, to procure sugar from our colonies, it was necessary to authorize by law the slavery of the unhappy Africans transported to America.§ From what I have observed at Cochin-China, I cannot entertain a doubt, but that our West-India colonies, had they been distributed, without reservation amongst a free people, would [6] have produced

---

highly value: can there be a greater proof of their wanting common sense? It is impossible to us to suppose these creatures to be men, because, allowing them to be men, a suspicion would follow, that we ourselves are not Christians."

Book IV. Chap. V.

‡ "Quamvis ille niger, quamvis tu candidus esses.   Nimium ne crede colori.
Alba Ligustra cadunt; Vaccinia nigra leguntur."

VIRGIL.

"I am black,—but comely."   SONG OF SOLOMON.

§ White sugar, of the best quality, is sold for three Dollars the Cochin China quintal, which weighs from 150 to 200 pounds French. Ninety-one pounds eight ounces French, makes one hundred pounds English.

double the quantity that is now procured from the labour of the unfortunate negroes."

"What advantage, then, has accrued to Europe, civilized as it is, and thoroughly versed in the laws of nature, and the rights of mankind, by legally authorizing in our colonies, the daily outrages against human nature, permitting them to debase man almost below the level of the beasts of the field? These slavish laws have proved as opposite to its interest, as they are to its honour, and to the laws of humanity. This remark I have often made."

"Liberty and property form the basis of abundance, and good agriculture: I never observed it to flourish where those rights of mankind were not firmly established. The earth, which multiplies her productions with a kind of profusion, under the hands of the free-born labourer, seems to shrink into barrenness under the sweat of the slave. Such is the will of the great Author of our Nature, who has created man free, and assigned to him the earth, that he might cultivate his possession with the [7] sweat of his brow; but still should enjoy his Liberty." Now if the plantations in the islands and the southern colonies were more limited, and freemen only employed in working them, the general product would be greater, although the profits to individuals would be less, —a circumstance this, which by diminishing opulence in a few, would suppress Luxury and Vice, and promote that equal distribution of property, which appears best calculated to promote the welfare of Society.—* I know it has been said by some, that none but the natives of warm climates could undergo the [8] excessive heat and labor of the West-India islands. But this argument is founded upon an error; for the reverse of this is true. I have been informed by good authority, that one European who escapes the first or second year, will do twice the work, and live twice the number of years that an ordinary Negro man will do: nor need

---

* From this account of Le Poivre's, we may learn the futility of the argument, that the number of vessels in the sugar trade, serve as a nursery for seamen, and that the Negroes consume a large quantity of the manufactures of Great Britain. If freemen only were employed in the islands, a double quantity of sugar would be made, and of course twice the number of vessels and seamen would be made use of in the trade. One freeman consumes usually four times the quantity of British goods that a Negro does. Slaves generally multiply slowly. Freemen multiply in proportion as slavery is discouraged. It is to be hoped therefore that motives of policy will at last induce Britons to give up a trade, which those of justice and humanity cannot prevail upon them to relinquish.

we be surpriz'd at this, when we hear that such is the natural fertility of soil, and so numerous the spontaneous fruits of the earth in the interior parts of Africa, that the natives live in plenty at the expence of little or no labor, which, in warm climates, has ever been found to be incompatible with long life and happiness. Future ages, therefore, when they read the accounts of the Slave Trade (—if they do not regard them as fabulous)—will be at a loss which to condemn most, our folly or our Guilt, in abetting this direct violation of the Laws of nature and Religion.

But there are some who have gone so far as to say that Slavery is not repugnant to the Genius of Christianity, and that it is not forbidden in any part of the Scripture. Natural [9] and Revealed Religion always speak the same things, although the latter delivers its precepts with a louder and more distinct voice than the former. If it could be proved that no testimony was to be found in the Bible against a practice so pregnant with evils of the most destructive tendency to society, it would be sufficient to overthrow its divine Original. We read it is true of Abraham's having slaves born in his house; and we have reason to believe, that part of the riches of the patriarchs consisted in them; but we can no more infer the lawfulness of the practice, from the short account which the Jewish historian gives us of these facts, than we can vindicate telling a lie, because Rahab is not condemned for it in the account which is given of her deceiving the king of Jericho.¶ We read that some of the same men indulged themselves in a plurality of wives, without any strictures being made upon their conduct for it; and yet no one will pretend to say, that this is not forbidden in many parts of the [10] Old Testament*. But we are told the Jews kept the Heathens in perpetual bondage‡. The Design of providence in permitting this evil, was probably to prevent the Jews from marrying amongst strangers, to which their intercourse with them upon any other footing than that of slaves, would naturally have inclined them‖. Had this taken place—their national religion would have been corrupted—they would have con-

¶ Josh. 2.
* Prov. v. 19, 12, 20.
‡ Levit. xxv. 44, 45, 46.
‖ That marriage with strangers was looked upon as a crime among the Jews, we learn from Ezra ix. 1 to 6, also from the whole of Chapter x.

traced all their vices†, and the intention of Providence in keeping them a distant people, in order to accomplish the promise made to Abraham, that "in his seed all the nations of the earth should be blessed," would have been [11] defeated; so that the descent of the Messiah from Abraham, could not have been traced, and the divine commission of the Son of God, would have wanted one of its most powerful arguments to support it. But with regard to their own countrymen, it is plain, perpetual slavery was not tolerated. Hence, at the end of seven years or in the year of the jubilee, all the Hebrew slaves were set at liberty*, and it was held unlawful to detain them in servitude longer than that time, except by their own Consent.‡ But if, in the partial Revelation which God [12] made, of his will to the Jews, we find such testimonies against slavery, what may we not expect from the Gospel, the Design of which was to abolish all distinctions of name and country. While the Jews thought they complied with the precepts of the law, in confining the love of their neighbour "to the children of their own people," Christ commands us to look upon all mankind even our Enemies§ as our neighbours and brethren, and "in all things, to do unto them whatever we would wish they should do unto us." He tells us further that his "Kingdom is not of this World," and therefore constantly avoids saying any thing that might interfere directly with the Roman or Jewish Governments: and although he does not call upon masters to emancipate their slaves,

---

† May not this be the reason why Swine's flesh was forbidden to the Jews, lest they should be tempted to eat with their Heathen neighbours, who used it in diet? This appears more probable than the opinion of Doctor MEAD, who supposes that it has a physical tendency to produce the leprosy; or that of VOLTAIRE, who asserts that the Jews learned to abstain from this Flesh from the Egyptians, who valued the Hog almost to a degree of idolatry for its great usefulness in rooting up the Ground. What makes this conjecture the more probable is, that the Jews abstained from several other kinds of flesh used by their Heathen neighbours, which have never been accused of bringing on diseases of the skin, and which were used constantly in diet by the Ægyptians. The account which Tacitus gives of the diet and customs of the Jews, is directly to our purpose—.

"Bos quoque immolantur, quem Ægyptii apin colunt," Ægyptii pleraque animalia, Essgiesque compositas veuerantur; Judaei mente sola, unumque numen intelligunt. Seperati Epulis, discreti Cubilibus, Alienarum Concubitu Abstinent."
HISTOR. LIB. V.

* Deuteronomy xxiv. 7.——
‡ Deut. xv. 12.
§ This is strongly inculcated in the story of the good Samaritan, Luke x.

A PENNSYLVANIAN

or slaves to assert that Liberty wherewith God and Nature had made them free, yet there is scarcely a parable or a sermon in the whole history of his life, but what contains the strongest arguments against Slavery. Every prohibition [13] of Covetousness—Intemperance—Pride—Uncleanness—Theft—and Murder, which he delivered,—every lesson of meekness, humility, forbearance, Charity, Self-denial, and brotherly-love, which he taught, are levelled against this evil;—for Slavery, while it includes all the former Vices, necessarily excludes the practice of all the latter Virtues, both from the Master and the Slave.—Let such, therefore, who vindicate the traffic of buying and selling Souls, seek some modern System of Religion to support it, and not presume to sanctify their crimes by attempting to reconcile it to the sublime and perfect Religion of the Great Author of Christianity.*

[14] There are some amongst us who cannot help allowing the force of our last argument, but plead as a motive for importing and

---

* The influence of Christianity in putting a stop to Slavery, appears in the first christian emperor Constantine, who commanded, under the severest penalties, all such as had Slaves, to set them at liberty. He afterwards contrived to render the manumission of them much easier than formerly, for instead of recurring to the forms prescribed by the Roman laws, which were attended with great difficulties and a considerable expence, he gave leave to masters to infranchise their slaves in the presence of a bishop, or a minister and a christian assembly.
Universal History, vol. xv. p. 574, 577.
Dr. ROBERTSON, in treating of those causes which weakened the feudal system, and finally abolished Slavery in Europe, in the 14th century, has the following Observations—
"The gentle spirit of the Christian Religion, together with the doctrines which it teaches, concerning the original equality of mankind, as well as the impartial eye with which the almighty regards men of every condition, and admits them to a participation of his benefits, are inconsistent with servitude. But in this, as in many other instances, Considerations of Interest and the Maxims of false Policy, led men to a conduct inconsistent with their principles. They were so sensible, however, of the Inconsistency, that to let their Fellow Christians at liberty from servitude was deemed an act of piety highly meritorious, and acceptable to Heaven. The humane spirit of the Christian Religion, struggled with the Maxims and Manners of the World, and contributed more than any other circumstance, to introduce the practice of manumission. The formality of manumission was executed in a church or a religious assembly.—The person to be set free, was led round the great altar, with a torch in his hand, he took hold of the horns of the altar, and there the solemn words conferring liberty, were pronounced."
CHARLES V. Historical Illustrations. Note xx.

keeping slaves, that they become acquainted with the principles of the religion of our country.—This is like justifying a highway robbery because part [15] of the money acquired in this manner was appropriated to some religious use.—Christianity will never be propagated by any other methods than those employed by Christ and his Apostles. Slavery is an engine as little fitted for that purpose as Fire or the Sword. A Christian Slave is a contradiction in terms.§ But if we enquire into the methods employed for converting the Negroes to Christianity, we shall find the means suited to the end proposed. In many places Sunday is appropriated to work for themselves, reading and writing are discouraged among them. A belief is even inculcated amongst some, that they have no Souls. In a word,—Every attempt to instruct or convert them, has [16] been constantly opposed by their masters. Nor has the example of their christian masters any tendency to prejudice them in favor of our religion. How often do they betray, in their sudden transports of anger and resentment, (against which there is no restraint provided towards their Negroes) the most violent degrees of passion and fury!—What luxury—what ingratitude to the supreme being—what impiety in their ordinary conversation do some of them discover in the presence of their slaves! I say nothing of the dissolution of marriage vows, or the entire abolition of matrimony, which the frequent sale of them introduces, and which are directly contrary to the laws of nature and the principles of christianity. Would to Heaven I could here conceal the shocking violations of chastity, which some of them are obliged to undergo without daring to complain. Husbands have been forced to prostitute their wives, and mothers their daughters to gratify the brutal lust of a master. This—all—this is practised— Blush—ye impure and hardened wretches, while I repeat it—by men who call themselves christians!

[17] But further—It has been said that we do a kindness to the

§ St Paul's letter to Philemon, in behalf of Onesimus, is said by some to contradict this assertion, but, if viewed properly, will rather support it. He desires Philemon to receive him "not as a Servant, but as a Brother beloved," "as his Son—and part of himself." In other parts of his Writings, he obliquely hints at the impossibility of uniting the duties of a Christian, with the offices of a Slave. "Ye are bought with a price, be not therefore the servants of men." I Corinth. vii 23. Had he lived to see christianity established by Law, in the countries where he preached, with what a torrent of christian eloquence may we not suppose he would have declaimed against slavery.

A PENNSYLVANIAN

Negroes by bringing them to America, as we thereby save their lives, which had been forfeited by their being conquered in war*. Let such as prefer or inflict slavery rather than Death, disown their being descended from or connected with our mother countries.—But it will be found upon enquiry, that many are stolen or seduced from their friends who have never been conquered; and it is plain, from the testimony of historians and travellers, [18] that wars were uncommon among them, until the christians who began the slave trade, stirred up the different nations to fight against each other. Sooner let them imbrue their hands in each others blood, or condemn one another to perpetual slavery, than the name of one christian, or one American, be stained by the perpetration of such enormous crimes.

Nor let it be urged that by treating slaves well, we render their situation happier in this Country, than it was in their own.—Slavery and Vice are connected together, and the latter is always a source of misery. Besides, by the greatest humanity we can show them, we only lessen, but do not remove the crime, for the injustice of it continues the same. The laws of retribution are so strongly inculcated by the moral governor of the world, that even the ox is entitled to his reward for "treading the Corn." How great then must be the amount of that injustice, which deprives so many of our fellow creatures of the Just reward of their labor.

But it will be asked here, What steps shall we take to remedy this Evil, and what shall [19] we do with those Slaves we have already

---

* "From the right of killing in case of conquest, politicians have drawn that of reducing to slavery; a consequence as ill grounded as the principle.

There is no such thing as a Right of reducing people to slavery, but when it becomes necessary for the preservation of the conquest. Preservation, but not servitude, is the end of conquest; though servitude may happen sometimes to be a necessary means of Preservation.

Even in that case it is contrary to the nature of things, that the slavery should be perpetual. The people enslaved ought to be rendered capable of becoming subjects."

Montesquie's Spirit of Law, Book x. Chap. 3.

"Servi autem ex eo appellati sunt, quod Imperatores captivos vendere, ac per hoc servare, nec Occidere solent. Servitus est Constitutio *Juris Gentium,* qua quis Dominio alie no CONTRA NATURUAM subjicitur.—

Justinian. Institut. L. i. Tit. 3.

By what right are the Children of these Captives kept in slavery?

in this Country? This is indeed a most difficult question. But let every man contrive to answer it for himself.—

The first thing I would recommend to put a stop to slavery in this country, is to leave off importing slaves. For this purpose let our assemblies unite in petitioning the king and parliament to dissolve the African committee of merchants: It is by them that the trade is chiefly carried on to America. We have the more reason to expect relief from an application at this juncture, as by a late decision in favor of a Virginia slave in Westminster-Hall, the Clamors of the whole nation are raised against them. Let such of our countrymen as engage in the slave trade, be shunned as the greatest enemies to our country, and let the vessels which bring the slaves to us, be avoided as if they bore in them the Seeds of that forbidden fruit, whose baneful taste destroyed both the natural and moral world.—As for the Negroes among us, who, from having acquired all the low vices of slavery, or who from age or [20] infirmities are unfit to be set at liberty, I would propose, for the good of society, that they should continue the property of those with whom they grew old, or from whom they contracted those vices and infirmities. But let the young Negroes be educated in the principles of virtue and religion—let them be taught to read, and write—and afterwards instructed in some business, whereby they may be able to maintain themselves. Let laws be made to limit the time of their servitude, and to entitle them to all the privileges of free-born British subjects. At any rate let Retribution be done to God and to Society.*

---

* A worthy friend of mine has favoured me with the following Extract of a letter from GRANVILLE SHARP, Esq; of London.
"I am told of some Regulations that have taken Place in the Spanish Colonies, which do the Spaniards much Honor, and are certainly worthy our Imitation, in case we should not be so happy as to obtain an entire Abolition of Slavery, and probably you wou'd find many American Subjects that wou'd be willing to promote such Regulations, tho' the same People wou'd strenuously oppose the scheme of a total Abolition of Slavery. I have never seen an Account of the Spanish Regulations in writing, but I understand that they are to the following Effect: As soon as a slave is landed, his Name, Price, &c. are register'd in a public Office, and the Master is obliged to allow him one Working Day in every Week to himself, besides Sundays, so that if the Slave chuses to work for his Master on that Day, he receives the Wages of a Freeman for it, and whatever he gains by his Labor on that Day, is so secured to him by Law, that the Master cannot deprive him of it. This is certainly a considerable Step towards the abolishing absolute Slavery. As soon as the slave is able to purchase another working Day, the master is obliged to sell it to him at a proportionable price,

[21] And now my countrymen, What shall I add more to rouse up your Indignation against Slave-keeping. Consider the many complicated crimes it involves in it. Think of the bloody Wars which are fomented by it, among the African nations, or if these are too common to affect you, [22] think of the pangs which attend the dissolution of the ties of nature in those who are stolen from their relations. Think of the many thousands who perish by sickness, melancholy, and suicide, in their voyages to America. Pursue the poor devoted victims to one of the West India islands, and see them exposed there to public sale. Hear their cries, and see their looks of tenderness at each other, upon being seperated.—Mothers are torn from their Daughters, and Brothers from Brothers, without the liberty of a parting embrace. Their master's name is now marked upon their breasts with a red hot iron. But let us pursue them into a Sugar Field: and behold a scene still more affecting than this—See! the poor wretches with what reluctance they take their instruments of labor into their hands,—Some of them, overcome with heat and sickness, seek to refresh themselves by a little rest.—But, behold an Overseer approaches them—In vain they sue for pity.—He lifts up his Whip, while streams of Blood follow every stroke. Neither age nor sex are spared.—Methinks one of them is woman far advanced in her pregnancy.—At a little distance from these [23] behold a man, who from his countenance and deportment appears as if he was descended from illustrious ancestors.—Yes.—He is the son of a Prince, and was torn by a stratagem, from an amiable wife and two young children.—Mark his sullen looks!—now he bids defiance to the tyranny of his Master, and in an instant—plunges a Knife into his Heart.—But let us return from this Scene, and see the various modes of arbitrary punishments

---

viz. I-fifth Part of his original Cost: and so likewise the remaining 4 Days at the same Rate, as soon as the Slave is able to redeem them, after which he is absolutely free. This is such an Encouragement to Industry, that even the most indolent are tempted to exert themselves. Men who have thus worked out their Freedom are inured to the Labor of the Country and are certainly the most useful Subjects that a Colony can acquire. Regulations might be formed upon the same Plan to encourage the Industry of Slaves that are already imported into the colonies, which would teach them how to maintain themselves and be as useful, as well as less expensive to the Planter. They would by such Means become Members of Society and have an Interest in the welfare of the Community, which would add greatly to the Strength and Security of each Colony; whereas, at present, many of the Planters are in continual Danger of being cut off by their Slaves.—a Fate which, they but too justly deserve!"

inflicted upon them by their masters. Behold one covered with stripes, into which melted wax is poured—another tied down to a block or a stake—a third suspended in the air by his thumbs—a fourth—I cannot relate it.—Where now is Law or Justice?—Let us fly to them to step in for their relief.—Alas!—The one is silent, and the other denounces more terrible punishment upon them. Let us attend the place appointed for inflicting the penalties of the law. See here one without a limb, whose only crime was an attempt to regain his Liberty,—another led to a Gallows for stealing a morsel of Bread, to which his labor gave him a better [24] title than his master—a third famishing on a gibbet—a fourth, in a flame of Fire! his shrieks pierce the very heavens.—O! God! where is thy Vengeance!—O! Humanity—Justice—Liberty—Religion!—Where,—where are ye fled.—

This is no exaggerated Picture. It is taken from real Life.— Before I conclude I shall take the liberty of addressing several Classes of my countrymen in behalf of our Brethren (for by that name may we now call them) who are in a state of Slavery amongst us.

In the first place let MAGISTRATES both supreme and inferior, exert the authority they are invested with, in suppressing this evil. Let them discountenance it by their example, and show a readiness to concur in every measure proposed to remedy it.

Let LEGISLATORS, reflect upon the trust reposed in them. Let their laws be made after the Spirit of Religion—Liberty—and our most excellent English Constitution. You cannot show your attachment to your King, or your love to your country better, than by suppressing an evil which endangers the dominions of the [25] former, and will in Time destroy the liberty of the latter.* Population, and the accession of strangers, in which the Riches of all countries consist, can only flourish in proportion as slavery is discouraged. Extend the privileges we enjoy, to every human creature born amongst us, and let not the

---

* "In moderate governments, it is a point of the highest importance, that there should not be a great number of slaves. The political liberty of those states adds to the value of civil liberty; and he who is deprived of the latter, is also deprived of the former. He sees the happiness of a society, of which he is not so much as a member; he sees the Security of Others fenced by laws, himself without so much as protection. He sees his master has a Soul, that can enlarge itself; while his own is constrained to submit to almost continual depression. Nothing more assimilates a Man to a Beast, than living among Freemen, himself a Slave. Such people as these are the natural enemies of a society, and their number must be dangerous."

Spirit of Laws, Book xv. Chapt. 12

[229]
A PENNSYLVANIAN

Journals of our Assemblies be disgraced with the records of laws, which allow exclusive privileges to men of one color in preference to another.¶

 Ye men of SENSE and VIRTUE—Ye ADVOCATES [26] for American Liberty, rouse up and espouse the cause of Humanity and general Liberty. Bear a testimony against a vice which degrades human nature, and dissolves that universal tie of benevolence which should connect all the children of men together in one great Family.—The plant of liberty is of so tender a Nature, that it cannot thrive long in the nieghbourhood of slavery. Remember the eyes of all Europe are fixed upon you, to preserve an asylum for freedom in this country, after the last pillars of it are fallen in every other quarter of the Globe.

 But chiefly—ye MINISTERS OF THE GOSPEL, whose dominion over the principles and actions of men is so universally acknowledged and felt,—Ye who estimate the worth of your fellow creatures by their Immortality, and therefore must look upon all mankind as equal,— let your zeal keep pace with your opportunities to put a stop to slavery. While you enforce the duties of "tithe and cummin," neglect not the weightier laws of justice and humanity. Slavery is an Hydra sin, and includes in it every violation of the precepts of the Law and the [27] Gospel. In vain will you command your flocks to offer up the incence of Faith and Charity, while they continue to mingle the Sweat and blood of Negro slaves with their sacrifices.—If the Blood of Able cried aloud for vengeance;—If, under the Jewish dispensation, Cities of refuge could not screen the deliberate murderer—if even manslaughter required sacrifices to expiate it,—and if a single murder so seldom escapes with impunity in any civilized country, what may you not say against that trade, or those manufactures—or Laws,§ which destroy the lives of so many thousands of our fellow creatures every year?—If

---

¶ The alterations in the laws in favour of Negroes, should be gradual,—'till the evil Habits they have acquired by Slavery, are eradicated. There are several privileges, however, which might be extended to them immediately, without the least risk to Society, in particular that inestimable one of Tryal by JURIES.

§ "If any Negro or other Slave under punishment by his master, or his order for running away, or any other crimes or misdemeanors towards his said master, unfortunately shall suffer in life or member, no person whatever shall be liable to any fine; But if any man shall of wantonness, or only of bloody mindedness, or cruel intention, wilfully kill a Negro, or other slave of his own, he shall deliver into the public treasury fifteen pounds sterling, and not be liable to any other punishment, or forfeiture for the same."

Laws of Barbadoes, Act 319.

in the Old Testament "God swears by his holiness, and by the excellency of Jacob, that the Earth shall tremble and every one mourn that dwelleth therein [28] for the iniquity of those who oppress the poor and crush the needy, who buy the poor with silver, and the needy with a pair of shoes,"¶ what judgments may you not denounce upon those who continue to perpetrate these crimes, after the more full discovery which God has made of the law of Equity in the New-Testament. Put them in mind of the Rod which was held over them a few years ago in the Stamp, and Revenue Acts. Remember that national crimes require national punishments, and without declaring what punishment awaits this evil, you may venture to assure them, that it cannot pass with impunity, unless God shall cease to be just or merciful.

THE END.

¶ Amos iv. 1, 2.—viii. 6. 7.

[20]

CONTINENTAL CONGRESS

Appeal to the Inhabitants of Quebec

PHILADELPHIA, 1774

As relations between Britain and her American colonies began to deteriorate, the Continental Congress assembled to represent and coordinate the efforts of the Americans, who hoped to forge in North America a solid opposition to the mother country. This appeal, written on October 26, 1774, failed to interest the Canadians, but it does provide an open window into common assumptions and principles held at the time. The text is taken from *Journals of the Continental Congress,* volume 1, pages 105–113.

Friends and fellow-subjects,
We, the Delegates of the Colonies of New-Hampshire, Massachusetts-Bay, Rhode-Island and Providence Plantations, Connecticut, New-York, New-Jersey, Pennsylvania, the Counties of Newcastle Kent and Sussex on Delaware, Maryland, Virginia, North-Carolina and South-Carolina, deputed by the inhabitants of the said Colonies, to represent them in a General Congress at Philadelphia, in the province of Pennsylvania, to consult together concerning the best methods to obtain redress of our afflicting grievances, having accordingly assembled and taken into our most serious consideration the state of public affairs on this continent, have thought proper to address your province as a member therein deeply interested.

When the fortune of war, after a gallant and glorious resistance, had incorporated you with the body of English subjects, we rejoiced in the truly valuable addition, both on our own and your account;

expecting, as courage and generosity are naturally united, our brave enemies would become our hearty friends, and that the Divine Being would bless to you the dispensations of his over-ruling providence, by securing to you and your latest posterity the inestimable advantages of a free English constitution of government, which it is the privilege of all English subjects to enjoy.

These hopes were confirmed by the King's proclamation, issued in the year 1763, plighting the public faith for your full enjoyment of those advantages.

Little did we imagine that any succeeding Ministers would so audaciously and cruelly abuse the royal authority, as to with-hold from you the fruition of the irrevocable rights to which you were thus justly entitled.

But since we have lived to see the unexpected time when Ministers of this flagitious temper have dared to violate the most sacred compacts and obligations, and as you, educated under another form of government, have artfully been kept from discovering the unspeakable worth of *that* form you are now undoubtedly entitled to, we esteem it our duty, for the weighty reasons herein after mentioned, to explain to you some of its most important branches.

"In every human society," says the celebrated Marquis *Beccaria,* "there is an *effort, continually tending* to confer on one part the heighth of power and happiness, and to reduce the other to the extreme of weakness and misery. The intent of good laws is to *oppose this effort,* and to diffuse their influence *universally* and *equally.*"

Rulers stimulated by this pernicious "effort," and subjects animated by the just "intent of opposing good laws against it," have occasioned that vast variety of events that fill the histories of so many nations. All these histories demonstrate the truth of this simple position, that to live by the will of one man, or set of men, is the production of misery to all men.

On the solid foundation of this principle, Englishmen reared up the fabrick of their constitution with such a strength as for ages to defy time, tyranny, treachery, internal and foreign wars: And, as an illustrious author of your nation, hereafter mentioned [Montesquieu] observes,—"They gave the people of their Colonies, the form of their own government, and this government carrying prosperity along with it, they have grown great nations in the forests they were sent to inhabit."

In this form, the first grand right is that of the people having a share in their own government by their representatives chosen by themselves, and, in consequence of being ruled by *laws* which they themselves approve, not by *edicts* of *men* over whom they have no controul. This is a bulwark surrounding and defending their property, which by their honest cares and labours they have acquired so that no portions of it can legally be taken from them, but with their own full and free consent, when they in their judgment deem it just and necessary to give them for public service, and precisely direct the easiest, cheapest, and most equal methods, in which they shall be collected.

The influence of this right extends still farther. If money is wanted by Rulers who have in any manner oppressed the people, they may retain it until their grievances are redressed; and thus peaceably procure relief, without trusting to despised petitions or disturbing the public tranquility.

The next great right is that of trial by jury. This provides that neither life, liberty nor property can be taken from the possessor until twelve of his unexceptionable countrymen and peers of his vicinage, who from that neighbourhood may reasonably be supposed to be acquainted with his character and the characters of the witnesses, upon a fair trial, and full enquiry, face to face in open Court before as many people as chuse to attend, shall pass their sentence upon oath against him; a sentence that cannot injure him without injuring their own reputation and probably their interest also, as the question may turn on points that in some degree concern the general welfare; and if it does not, their verdict may form a precedent that on a similar trial of their own may militate against themselves.

Another right relates merely to the liberty of the person. If a subject is seized and imprisoned, tho' by order of Government, he may by virtue of this right immediately obtain a writ termed a Habeas Corpus, from a Judge whose sworn duty it is to grant it, and thereupon procure any illegal restraint to be quickly enquired into and redressed.

A fourth right is that of holding lands by the tenure of easy rents and not by rigorous and oppressive services, frequently forcing the possessors from their families and their business to perform what ought to be done in all well regulated states by men hired for the purpose.

The last right we shall mention regards the freedom of the press. The importance of this consists, besides the advancement of truth, science, morality, and arts in general, in its diffusion of liberal sentiments on the administration of Government, its ready communication of thoughts between subjects, and its consequential promotion of union among them, whereby oppressive officers are shamed or intimidated into more honourable and just modes of conducting affairs.

These are the invaluable rights that form a considerable part of our mild system of government; that, sending its equitable energy through all ranks and classes of men, defends the poor from the rich, the weak from the powerful, the industrious from the rapacious, the peaceable from the violent, the tenants from the lords, and all from their superiors.

These are the rights without which a people cannot be free and happy, and under the protecting and encouraging influence of which these colonies have hitherto so amazingly flourished and increased. These are the rights a profligate Ministry are now striving by force of arms to ravish from us, and which we are with one mind resolved never to resign but with our lives.

These are the rights *you* are entitled to and ought at this moment in perfection to exercise. And what is offered to you by the late Act of Parliament in their place? Liberty of conscience in your religion? No. God gave it to you; and the temporal powers with which you have been and are connected, firmly stipulated for your enjoyment of it. If laws, divine and human, could secure it against the despotic caprices of wicked men, it was secured before. Are the French laws in *civil* cases restored? *It seems so.* But observe the cautious kindness of the Ministers, who pretend to be your benefactors. The words of the statute are—that those "laws shall be the rule, until they shall be *varied* or *altered* by any ordinances of the Governor and Council." Is the "certainty and lenity of the *criminal* law of England, and its benefits and advantages," commended in the said statute, and said to "have been sensibly felt by you," secured to you and your descendants? No. They too are subjected to arbitrary *"alterations"* by the Governor and Council; and a power is expressly reserved of appointing "such courts of *criminal, civil* and *ecclesiastical* jurisdiction, as shall be thought proper." Such is the precarious tenure of mere *will* by which you hold your lives and religion. The Crown and its Ministers are impowered, as far as they could be by Parliament, to establish even the *Inquisition* itself among you. Have you an Assembly composed of worthy men, elected by yourselves and in whom you can confide, to make laws for

you, to watch over your welfare, and to direct in what quantity and
in what manner your money shall be taken from you? No. The Power
of making laws for you is lodged in the governor and council, all of
them dependent upon and removeable at the *pleasure* of a Minister.
Besides, another late statute, made without your consent, has subjected
you to the impositions of *Excise,* the horror of all free states, thus
wresting your property from you by the most odious of taxes and
laying open to insolent tax-gatherers, houses, the scenes of domestic
peace and comfort and called the castles of English subjects in the
books of their law. And in the very act for altering your government,
and intended to flatter you, you are not authorized to "assess levy, or
apply any *rates* and *taxes,* but for the inferior purposes of *making roads,*
and erecting and repairing *public buildings,* or for other *local* conveniences, within your respective towns and districts." Why this degrading
distinction? Ought not the property, honestly acquired by *Canadians,*
to be held as sacred as that of *Englishmen?* Have not Canadians sense
enough to attend to any other public affairs than gathering stones
from one place and piling them up in another? Unhappy people! who
are not only injured, but insulted. Nay more! With such a superlative
contempt of your understanding and spirit has an insolent Ministry
presumed to think of you, our respectable fellow-subjects, according
to the information we have received, as firmly to persuade themselves
that your gratitude for the injuries and insults they have recently
offered to you will engage you to take up arms and render yourselves
the ridicule and detestation of the world, by becoming tools in their
hands, to assist them in taking that freedom from *us* which they have
treacherously denied to *you;* the unavoidable consequence of which
attempt, if successful, would be the extinction of all hopes of you or
your posterity being ever restored to freedom. For idiocy itself cannot
believe that, when their drudgery is performed, they will treat you
with less cruelty than they have us who are of the same blood with
themselves.

What would your countryman, the immortal *Montesquieu,* have
said to such a plan of domination as has been framed for you? Hear
his words, with an intenseness of thought suited to the importance of
the subject.—"In a free state, every man, who is supposed a free
agent, *ought to be concerned in his own government:* Therefore the *legislative*
should reside in the whole body of the *people,* or their *representatives.*"—
"The political liberty of the subject is a *tranquillity of mind,* arising

from the opinion each person has of his *safety*. In order to have this liberty, it is requisite the government be so constituted, as that one man need not be *afraid* of another. When the power of *making* laws, and the power of *executing* them, are *united* in the same person, or in the same body of Magistrates, *there can be no liberty;* because apprehensions may arise, lest the same *Monarch* or *Senate,* should *enact* tyrannical laws, to *execute* them in a tyrannical manner."

"The power of *judging* should be exercised by persons taken from the *body of the people,* at certain times of the year, and pursuant to a form and manner prescribed by law. *There is no liberty,* if the power of *judging* be not *separated* from the *legislative* and *executive* powers."

"Military men belong to a profession, which *may be* useful, but *is often* dangerous."—"The enjoyment of liberty, and even its support and preservation, consists in every man's being allowed to speak his thoughts, and lay open his sentiments."

Apply these decisive maxims, sanctified by the authority of a name which all Europe reveres, to your own state. You have a Governor, it may be urged, vested with the *executive* powers or the powers of *administration*. In him and in your Council is lodged the power of *making laws*. You have *Judges* who are to *decide* every cause affecting your lives, liberty or property. Here is, indeed, an appearance of the several powers being *separated* and *distributed* into *different* hands for checks one upon another, the only effectual mode ever invented by the wit of men to promote their freedom and prosperity. But scorning to be illuded by a tinsel'd outside, and exerting the natural sagacity of Frenchmen, *examine* the specious device and you will find it, to use an expression of holy writ, "a whited sepulchre" for burying your lives, liberty and property.

Your *Judges* and your *Legislative Council,* as it is called, are *dependant* on your Governor, and he is dependant on the servant of the Crown in Great-Britain. The *legislative, executive* and *judging* powers are *all* moved by the nods of a Minister. Privileges and immunities last no longer than his smiles. When he frowns, their feeble forms dissolve. Such a treacherous ingenuity has been exerted in drawing up the code lately offered you, that every sentence, beginning with a benevolent pretension, concludes with a destructive power; and the substance of the whole, divested of its smooth words, is—that the Crown and its Ministers shall be as absolute throughout your extended province as the despots of Asia or Africa. What can protect your property from taxing edicts and the rapacity of necessitous and cruel masters, your persons from Letters de Cachet, goals, dungeons, and oppressive services, your lives and general liberty from arbitrary and unfeeling rulers? We defy you, casting your view upon every side, to discover a single circumstance promising from any quarter the faintest hope of liberty to you or your posterity, but from an entire adoption into the union of these Colonies.

What advice would the truly great man before-mentioned, that advocate of freedom and humanity, give you, was he now living and knew that we, your numerous and powerful neighbours, animated by a just love of our invaded rights and united by the indissoluble bands of affection and interest, called upon you by every obligation of regard for yourselves and your children, as we now do, to join us in our righteous contest, to make common cause with us therein and take a noble chance for emerging from a humiliating subjection under Governors, Intendants, and Military Tyrants, into the firm rank and condition of English freemen, whose custom it is, derived from their ancestors, to make those tremble who dare to think of making them miserable?

Would not this be the purport of his address? "Seize the opportunity presented to you by Providence itself. You have been conquered into liberty, if you act as you ought. This work is not of man. You are a small people, compared to those who with open arms invite you into a fellowship. A moment's reflection should convince you which will be most for your interest and happiness, to have all the rest of North-America your unalterable friends, or your inveterate enemies. The injuries of Boston have roused and associated every colony, from Nova-Scotia to Georgia. Your province is the only link wanting, to compleat the bright and strong chain of union. Nature has joined your country to theirs. Do you join your political interests? For their own sakes, they never will desert or betray you. Be assured, that the happiness of a people inevitably depends on their liberty, and their spirit to assert it. The value and extent of the advantages tendered to you are immense. Heaven grant you may not discover them to be blessings after they have bid you an eternal adieu."

We are too well acquainted with the liberality of sentiment distinguishing your nation to imagine, that difference of religion will prejudice you against a hearty amity with us. You know that the transcendant nature of freedom elevates those who unite in her cause above all such low-minded infirmities. The Swiss Cantons furnish a memorable proof of this truth. Their union is composed of Roman Catholic and Protestant States, living in the utmost concord and peace with one another and thereby enabled, ever since they bravely vindicated their freedom, to defy and defeat every tyrant that has invaded them.

Should there be any among you, as there generally are in all societies, who prefer the favours of Ministers and their own private interests to the welfare of their country, the temper of such selfish persons will render them incredibly active in opposing all public-spirited measures from an expectation of being well rewarded for their sordid industry, by their superiors; but we doubt not you will be upon your guard against such men, and not sacrifice the liberty and happiness of the whole Canadian people and their posterity to gratify the avarice and ambition of individuals.

We do not ask you, by this address, to commence acts of hostility against the government of our common Sovereign. We only invite you to consult your own glory and welfare, and not to suffer yourselves to be inveigled or intimidated by infamous ministers so far as to become the instruments of their cruelty and despotism, but to unite with us in one social compact, formed on the generous principles of equal liberty and cemented by such an exchange of beneficial and endearing offices as to render it perpetual. In order to complete this highly desirable union, we submit it to your consideration whether it may not be expedient for you to meet together in your several towns and districts and elect Deputies, who afterwards meeting in a provincial Congress, may chuse Delegates to represent your province in the continental Congress to be held at Philadelphia on the tenth day of May, 1775.

In this present Congress, beginning on the fifth of the last month and continued to this day, it has been with universal pleasure and an unanimous vote resolved: That we should consider the violation of your rights, by the act for altering the government of your province, as a violation of our own, and that you should be invited to accede to our confederation, which has no other objects than the perfect security of the natural and civil rights of all the constituent members according to their respective circumstances, and the preservation of a happy and lasting connection with Great-Britain on the salutary and constitutional principles herein before mentioned. For effecting these purposes, we have addressed an humble and loyal petition to his Majesty praying relief of our and your grievances; and have associated to stop all importations from Great-Britain and Ireland, after the first day of December, and all exportations to those Kingdoms and the West-Indies after the tenth day of next September, unless the said grievances are redressed.

That Almighty God may incline your minds to approve our equitable and necessary measures, to add yourselves to us, to put your fate whenever you suffer injuries which you are determined to oppose not on the small influence of your single province but on the consolidated powers of North-America, and may grant to our joint exertions an event as happy as our cause is just, is the fervent prayer of us, your sincere and affectionate friends and fellow-subjects.

By order of the Congress,

Henry Middleton, *President.*

[21]

Thomas Bradbury

---

*The Ass: or, the Serpent, A Comparison
Between the Tribes of Issachar and Dan, in
Their Regard for Civil Liberty*

NEWBURYPORT, 1774

Originally published in London in 1712 and based on a sermon
given by the Reverend Bradbury on November 5 of that year,
this essay was republished in Newburyport, Massachusetts, in 1774
as being especially appropriate to the troubles then facing the colonies.
Thomas Bradbury wrote a number of essays celebrating liberty and
the Glorious Revolution of 1688, and his work is typical in that a
close textual analysis of a biblical passage is used to illustrate a political
principle or defend a political position. Readers of this pamphlet will
understand the genesis of the common revolutionary flag bearing a
serpent and the words "Don't Tread On Me." Dividing the serpent
into thirteen sections to represent the thirteen colonies completed the
efficient iconography representing thirteen republics. This reprinting
is based upon the 1774 reprinting, which in turn was based upon a
1767 reproduction of the 1712 text. The intermediate printing of
1767 included additional editing of the original, so the
version reproduced here is not precisely as
Bradbury wrote it.

GEN. XLIX. 14, 15, 16, 17, 18

> *Issachar is a strong Ass couching down between two Burdens;*
> *And he saw that Rest was good, and the Land that it was pleasant;*
> *and bowed his Shoulder to bear, and became a Servant unto Tribute.*
> *Dan shall judge his People as one of the Tribes of Israel.*

THOMAS BRADBURY

Dan shall be a Serpent in the Way, an Adder in the Path; that biteth
the Horse-heels, so that the Rider shall fall backward.
I have waited for thy Salvation, O Lord.

These Words are Part of the Prophecy that *Jacob* dealt among his Sons
when *the Days drew near that he must die;* and they let us see with what   Ch. xlvii. 29
Variety of Temper those People acted, who all grew from the same
Father: A full Argument how well the Distinction is form'd, That *all*
are not Israel, who are of Israel: Neither because they are the Seed of Abraham,   Rom. ix.
are they all Children: He here opens out *what shall befal 'em in the latter*   6, 7.
Days, and how they would carry it when they came into the promis'd   Ch. I.lix. 1.
Land; and, because some of 'em should have little or no Taste of
Liberty, and others would pursue it through all the Expence and
Danger that lay in their way, he places these Two together, that every
one who reads may do Justice upon the plain Opposition there is
between 'em.

I shall consider the Words, First, As they describe a People that
are Sluggish and Cowardly, who will venture nothing to have All, [2]
whose Souls are beneath knowing the Distinction of Bondage and
Freedom: And on the other hand, as they give us the Character of
those who admire their Liberties and will dare to seek and fetch 'em
where ever they are carried; who reckon this a Property that should
not be lost as long as it can be kept, and will scarce submit to an
Existence under Tyranny.

In these two Branches you have the Division of the Text; Here's
a Tribe of *Israel* that gives us an Example of each Temper: *Issachar* is
remembred for his neglect of that which *Dan* was resolv'd upon no
Terms to part with: And by observing what good old *Jacob* saith of
these Two that were so unlike any another, we may fix the Characters
that are due those who either despise or value the Deliverance of this
Day.

I. I shall begin with the Account that you have of *Issachar,* whose
Passive Obedience (if you'll call it so) is condemn'd to Memory by
these Words; *Issachar is a strong Ass couching down between two Burdens:*
And he saw the Rest was good, and the Land, that it was pleasant, and
bowed his Shoulder to bear, and became a Servant to Tribute: Where you
have three Things:

    1. The general Temper of this People.

2. The Subjection and Bondage they fell into. And,

3. The Reason they gave for this Stupidity.

(1) You may observe, that many of the Tribes have their History couch'd in a Resemblance that's given of 'em: They are compar'd to some Creature of that very Disposition that should obtain among 'em: Thus *Judah is a Lyons Whelp; Naphtali a Hind let loose; Joseph a fruitful Bough; and Benjamin a ravening Wolf.* Now these Allusions would convey to us such thoughts of the People as bear up to the Account we have of 'em afterwards: They are most of 'em to be understood as a Reputation; but what is said of *Issachar,* is as full of Contempt as a Metaphor can be: We are to know him by his Likeness to the [3] most heavy and stupid Animal in the Creation. Instead of having his Name from something vigorous and beautiful, his Father leaves this upon him, That he's *a strong Ass couching down between two Burdens.* The Ground of the Similitude you see is the little Relish they should have for their Liberties, the sorry and dull Surrender they would make of themselves to Tyranny; which is a Temper expos'd in this Comparison two ways.

1. It's imputed to nothing else but the Stupidity of them that submit to it; the Tribe that sinks into those Measures is resembled by an *Ass.*

2. It's condemn'd by the Insinuation that it was in their Power to have it otherways; *Issachar is a strong ass:* That very Strength that makes him couch under a Load, would be sufficient to throw it off.

1. What the Comparison leads me first to tell you, is that the Foundation of all Passive Obedience is laid in Stupidity. They that *couch down between two Burdens, who bow their Shoulders to bear, and become Servants to Tribute,* may here see what Herd they belong to.

Tho' an Ass was more us'd in those Eastern Countries than it is with us, yet the Old Testament hath accounted of it as so mean a Creature, that the Comparison is very just: It seems to be made for no higher a Design than Drudgery, bearing of Burdens no way remarkable either for its Head or its Heels, so little capable of being taught, that the Folly of our Nature is signified by it, that Man is *born as a wild Ass's Colt:* And tho' it's true in those Parts, we find the greatest Men riding on them, yet it's a Creature that the Ceremonial Law hath branded in a very peculiar way: It must, upon no Terms whatsoever, be thrown among the Offerings of the Lord: The Command

Ver. 9, 21.
22, 27.

THOMAS BRADBURY

was very general, *Thou shalt set apart unto the Lord all that opens the Matrix, and every Firstling that comes of the Beast which thou hast, the Males shall be the Lords.* This Law was laid out in that compass to put 'em often in mind of the *Messiah,* which should be *the First born of every Creature;* yet to this [4] there's one Exception, and the only Animal left out is, *every Firstling of an Ass thou shalt redeem with a Lamb; and if thou wilt not redeem it, thou shalt break its Neck.*

Exo. I xiii
12.19.

So that when *Jacob* speaks of *Issachar* under This Comparison, 'tis a viler Name than he could possibly leave him by Another; and it may intimate to us, not only the Stupidity of their Nature that run into this Crime, but a particular Unfitness for the Service of God. They seem to be the Outcast of both Worlds; they give up all that's dear to 'em in this, and shew a Dulness that can have no room in the other. The way of serving God is *without Fear, being delivered from the Wrath of Enemies, in Holiness and Righteousness all our days. The fearful and unbelieving* are in the front of *those Sinners who fill the Lake of Fire and Brimstone.* You may always observe it that an indifference to Civil Liberties goes along with a neglect of that which is Religious: A Man that throws away the Blessing of Providence, cannot have a due relish to those of Grace.

Luk. i.74,
75.
Rev. xxi.8.

Tho, submitting to the impious Will of a Monarch hath been exalted as if it was *the one thing needful,* yet it's easy to prove, both by the Rule of Scripture, and the Historys of Men, this is so far from containing the Whole of Religion, that it really possesseth no one Part of it: There can be no Faith in it, for that would both *Purifie the Heart* and *conquer the World.* It was this that made Moses *forsake Egypt, not fearing the Wrath of the King.* And there can be no *Love,* I mean to God or his People, for that would teach us to value what the One gives and the Other enjoys: And tho' this may be call'd *Patience,* yet it's a prostitution of the Name to a Temper which hath none of the Thing; for this Grace shews it self in Bearing a Burden, not in Laying it on. The overruling Hand of God we must submit to, but this will consist with all the Zeal we can use against the Tools he employs. The distinction is a good one, and as old as *David,* who knew how different his Behavior ought to be: *If the Lord hath stirred thee up against me,* saith he to *Saul, let him accept* [5] *an offering,* I have deserved it from him, and cannot answer him one of a thousand; *but if they be the Children of Men, cursed be they before the Lord.*

Heb. xi.27

I Sam.
xxvi.19.

'Tis plain that People lose their Christianity with their Liberties;

and when once an encroaching Power hath made 'em Slaves, there needs little more to make 'em Heathens. The Ministers that preach up This Doctrine, will soon understand no other: It shall drive Faith, Repentance and Holiness out of the Pulpit, and instead of feeding the Children *with Bread,* they'll give 'em a *Stone:* In a little while we shall hear of nothing else, but Obedience to the Lust of Men, as if Christ had no other Errand in laying down His Life, than to make the Kings of the Earth a compliment of Ours; that as he was a *Servant of Rulers,* we must be so too; as if no Sin could be *dangerous* but what they call Rebellion, and the Terms of *procuring to our selves Damnation* were never to be used but in one case, which is resisting of a Civil Power. We shall seldom hear a better Application of that awful Argument; tis not so warmly pleaded to make us *flee from the Wrath to come,* that *being warned of God concerning things not seen as yet, we may be moved with Fear:* They'll but seldom trouble their Heads about the Danger of Debauchery, *that Whoremongers and Adulterers God will judge:* They'll tell us but little of the Hazard such are in, who are *lovers of Pleasure more than lovers of God,* who blaspheme the whole Scheme of Religion, and use that Book to make them laugh, which makes *the Devils tremble:* who rush into the Retirements of our Worship, the Ordinances that ought to be kept clean and holy; I say, we hear little of their Danger, tho the Scripture hath given us the same dreadful Word in that case which agrees so well with them in the other: *They that eat and drink unworthily,*
I Cor. xi.29 *eat and drink to themselves Damnation.* These are the Encroachments that Slavery will make upon our Religion.

But we *have not so learned Christ.* The Apostles that went about with the Gospel, were often claiming the Privileges of the Law. For this did *Paul* argue [6] with the *Centurion* on the Stairs of the Castle, and would not let the Christian run away with the Roman; For this did he threaten to shake the Government of *Philippi,* and refuse to take his Liberty at that easy rate, of going out of the Prison; No, he was resolved to let those Magistrates know, that as the Laws of the Empire had given him a Protection so he would never lose it for want of Zeal; and tho the Jaylor, who was but converted the Night before, brought him the Message, *they have sent to let you go, now then depart in peace;* yet he useth the Advantage that Innocence gave him over
Act. xvi. Tyranny, *they have beaten us openly, and uncondemned, being Romans, and*
36, 37. *have cast us into Prison, and now do they thrust us out privily, nay verily but let 'em come themselves and fetch us out.* So tender was he of his

Privileges, that tho' he knew as much as any Man how to despise the
Pomp of the World, yet in this case he'll insist upon a Ceremony that
perhaps was never demanded before; that the Magistrates of the Town
should come to the Prison-door and beg Pardon, and bring them Out
whom through a Mistake they had put In, and desire them to *departe
from their City*. For this did he refuse to answer the Summons of *Festus*,
who would have betray'd him to his Enemies, but *appeal'd to Casar;*
and from this Principle did he deal so roundly with *Ananias, God shall
smite thee thou whited Wall, for sittest thou there to judge me according to
the Law, and commandest me to be smitten contrary to the Law.*   Ch. xxiii.3.

This is the Spirit of our Religion, it allows none of the Stupidity
that *Issachar* was run down into; for an *Ass* can no more be a *Pattern*
under the Gospel, than it could be a *Sacrifice* under the Law. But it's
enough we are told what sort of Creatures they are, by the Metaphor
in my Text; despicable to Men, and rejected by God; made for Service
and Contempt. The Comparison gives us the lowest Opinion of those
to whom it belongs. They are by this represented as a stupid servile
People, for the Word fits their Heads as well as their Shoulders.

[7] 2. The Crime of their *becoming Servants to Tribute*, is hinted
at by the further Account we have of 'em, that they lay under no
necessity of doing it: They had it in their power to do otherwise, and
might have compell'd a better Lot for themselves and their Posterity.
Had they been drain'd, and weaken'd and sunk down to an Inability,
that which was now both their Sin and Punishment, had been only
the latter. But *Issachar* was a strong *Ass,* able to Refuse a Load as well
as to Bear it.

Several Annotators give us this Note from the *Hebrew* Word, that
he was *an Ass of Bone;* which perhaps is a further Contempt of him,
to tell us his want of Spirit, as if he was only Outside, a meer Shell
and Frame of Nature: And indeed they who so tamely give up all that
can be dear, show but little Soul in that Surrender. But I shall take
the Words in the first Sense I gave you of 'em, that he is call'd *a
strong Ass;* to signifie, that he had Capacity to have done otherways,
only he wanted Heart and Courage to use it. He that *couch'd down
between two Burdens,* might easily have protected against One; *he that
bowed his Shoulder to bear,* could have cloath'd it with Armour; And
the Wealth with which he paid his *Tribute* as a *Servant,* might have
led him into the Field as a Rival.

All the instances that we have in Scripture of Submission to an unrighteous Power, represent the People as not able to do otherways. We never once find a good Man neglecting to resist an Injustice when he could reject it. *Moses* indeed fled from *Pharoah* because he had to do only with a single *Egyptian,* who was *smiting one of his Brethren,* he's no longer about it than *whilst he looks this way and that way,* and then *he kills him, and hideth him in the Sands:* And this is so far from having the Censure, that a Slave would give it, that upon That Action he was in hopes to have raised his Publick Character, and by this Justice upon the Officer, thought to have led on that of the People upon the King, as the Martyr *Stephen* tells us; for he brings in this as the Reason why *seeing one of* [8] *the Jews suffer wrong, he avenged him that was oppressed, and smote the Egyptian, because he supposed his Brethren would have understood, how that by his hand God would have delivered them, but they understood not.* If their Zeal would have come on as fast as his would have led it, they might have been saved then; but they lost 40 Years by their unbelief. *David* run away from *Saul,* when he had no Friend to stand by him, but he put himself at the Head of a little Army as soon as he could; and the only Reason why he did not give him battle was, because he had not Force enough: But when those great Numbers *came to him every day,* he makes no scruple to go out into the Field, for there fell some of *Manesseh* to *David when he came with the Philistines against Saul to Battle.*

A just and holy God may indeed deliver us over to the Will of evil Men; but to say, that he would have us deliver up ourselves, is to blaspheme his Empire; *for he hath no Fellowship with the Thrones of Iniquity, who frame Mischief by a Law.* That which held Zion in Captivity, was God's making *her Strength to fail; He had delivered her into their Hands against whom she was not able to rise up:* But when she had more strength, there's a new Exhortation to use it; *Shake thy self from the Dust, O Jerusalem; loose thy self from the Bands of thy Neck, O thou captive Daughter of Zion.*

In these two things you have the woful Temper of this People; They were stupid, and not to be imprest by a generous Argument; and tho' it's true, they had Strength and Capacity, yet it was all thrown away upon a lazy Nature, that would not use it. *Issachar is a strong Ass couching down between two Burdens.*

(2) We have the folly of their Behaviour, and are told, how soon they part with their Liberties. And here you meet with bondage in every Form and Shape. Here's Oppression in all its Weight, *he falls*

Exod. ii 11, 12.

Act. vii. 24, 25.

I Chron. xii. 19.

Ps. xciv. 20.

Iam. 1. 14.

Isa. lii. 1.

·

Thomas Bradbury

between two Burdens. Here's a Slavery to his Person, *his Shoulder is brought to bear* what they lay upon [9] him. Here's Poverty in his Concerns, *he becomes a Servant to Tribute;* and here's a Necessity for him to be Active in all this. Opression stupifies the Faculties, *he couches down beneath his Burdens,* he *bows his Shoulder,* he consents to be a *Servant:* What a *Gulph of Perdition* was this People sunk into? Whither will Tyranny lead those who have the Heart to follow it? Can we ever begin to stop too soon, when it will be so dreadful to have it too late?

    1. You observe here what weight this Opression was laid on with: 'Twas not what *Rehoboam* threatned, *the Heavines of a little Finger;* but *he couches down between two Burdens.*

    Some translate this between two Hills; and understand it of the Situation that *Issachar* had in the Land of *Canaan:* Others suppose that it referes to the Quarrels they might have with those Two Tribes that lay on each side of 'em; but the Words seem to tell us what a Load of Misery they had brought themselves under.

    Tyrants, who know no Justice, will allow no Mercy; they never think their Grandeur advanc'd high enough; they'll set no bounds to Lust of Empire, but let it rove in all the License of their own Fancy. Do not imagine that there's any dealing with an Arbitrary Government. Laws are only shackles upon you, but no Rule to 'em. *Some remove Land Marks, they violently take away Flocks and Feed thereon, they turn the Needy out of the way, the Poor of the Earth hide themselves together: Behold as the wild Asses of the Desert they go forth to Work, rising betimes for a Prey,* and it's the tame Asses of the Villages that fall into their Hands: They cause *the Naked to go without clothing, he hath no covering in the Cold; they pluck the Fatherless from the Breast and take a Pledge of the Poor; they take away the Sheaf from the Hungry: Men groan out of the City, and the Soul of the Wounded cries out.* Jeb xxiv.
2, 3,

    [10] If you would not *couch down between Two Burdens,* you must enter an effectual Protest against One: For they that submit, will, in a little Time, be brought to that pass; *Her Carriages were heavy loaden, they are a Burden to the weary Beast, they stoop, they bow down together, they could not deliver their Burden, but themselves are gone into Captivity.* Thus did the *Ammonites* with the Men of *Jabeth Gilead;* tho' the poor People would have submitted themselves unto 'em, yet they will allow of no easier Terms than *thrusting out the right Eye, and laying it as a Reproach upon all Israel.* So unlimited did *Benhadad* take himself, in the Court of a Man, who had gone too far, in saying, *My Lord, O* Isa. xlvi.
1, 2. I Sam. xi. 2.

King, I am thine, and all that I have: He does not only claim *his Silver and Gold,* but *his Wives and Children;* and would *send his Servants the next Day to take out what was pleasant in their Eyes.*

This made *David* rather chuse to *fall into the Hands of God, than into those of Man:* Not but that the former could have destroy'd him with more Expedition than the latter; but *with the Lord there was Mercy,* with Men there is none. And indeed the Process hath been very short; When once a Tyrant hath said your Laws were his, He hath soon come to affirm your Lives were so too. And therefore it's the same thing being his Vassals, and being his Cattle. All that you have *pertaining to Life and Godliness,* is thrown in as a Morsel to *Casar: They take up all of them with the Angle, they catch them with their Net, and gather them in their Drag, therefore they rejoice and are glad; They will empty continually, and not spare to slay the Nations.* And how unhappy must the Case of a People be who never know when they have done Suffering? Such a Government upon Earth resembles one of the worst Ideas that we have of Hell: where there is *no Sacrifice for Sin, but a certain* [11] *fearful looking for of more Judgment and new Indignation.*

Hab. i. ult.

2. Their Persons were made vile and contemptible, *they bow their Shoulders to bear.* There are some Usages which God always reckon'd an Indignity to Human Nature. 'Tis for this reason that he limited the Number of Stripes that were to be given to the Malefactor, *lest thy Brother seem vile to thee:* And the Statute of Murder is laid out upon this ground, That *in the Image of God made he Man.* Such an Oppression did the *Jews* live under in *Egypt;* their Burdens were very grievous in the *Brickilns,* the Task-masters oblig'd them to their whole Quantity of Work tho' they denied them *Straw,* and then punisht 'em for not doing what they knew to be impossible.

When this comes to be the Lot of such as give up their Liberties, the Justice of God calls for our Adoration; they that have *lived in Pleasure* and Vanity, are most likely to make a Sale of all that they have; they have *eaten the Bread of Idleness,* and, How righteous is it with Heaven to give 'em that of Sorrow? That they who are *brought up in Scarlet, should embrace Dunghills?* This is one Consequence of Slavery; and it fell heavily upon the Priests at *Jerusalem,* who might remember their Sin in their Punishment: They that us'd to lead the Blind, came to *wander as blind Men in the Streets,* and *so polluted with Blood, that Men could not touch their Garments: The Anger of the Lord divided 'em, and he would no more regard 'em.* An Absolute Government

Lam. iv. 14.

THOMAS BRADBURY

Swallows as fast as you can Give, and, What will this come to in time? *But the hanging up of Princes by the Hand, not honouring the Faces* Ch. v. 12, 13 *of the Elders, taking the young Men to Grind, and making the Children fall under the Wood.*

[12] 3. It runs out into Poverty. This *paying of Tribute,* must be understood of excessive Taxes; Impositions that are enough to drain a Country: Not what a People consent to for their own Defence, but what are extorted from them. And then what signifies the Goodness of the Land, when the Profits are offer'd up as a Sacrifice to the Luxury of a Stranger. Thus *hath a fruitful Land been brought into Barrenness. The Houses* of the People were *made a Dunghill;* and they that have liv'd in the midst of Plenty, *sought their Bread to relieve their Souls.* They consent to the lowest Terms meerly to enjoy what Nature had made their own: *We have given the Hand to the Assyrian to be satisfied with* Lam. v. 6. *Bread;* and, *better are they that perish by the Sword, than such as are stricken through for want of the Fruits of the Field:* It was a dreadful Article in their Judgment, *thine Enemy shall distress thee in all thy Gates.* Deut. xxviii

4. That which makes the case deporable to the last degree is, that the People themselves concur in it, either through a Necessity, or the Habit of Bondage. *They bow their own Shoulder to bear;* and, by an unaccountable mixture of Choice and Force, *become Servants to Tribute.* When a Nation hath given up their Liberties, they do not only lose the Thing, but all the Taste they us'd to have of it.

And this may be consider'd both as a growing Vice, and a Stupidity that the righteous God hath sealed 'em up under. The Misery of such a Case hath this in it, that the People are never *likely to remember from whence they are fallen or do their first Works; they sleep a perpetual sleep, and do not awake.* 'Tis not a Damage that sets them a Thinking, or warms a powerful Zeal to recover what they have lost; but by a long Course of Subjection it becomes their own Act.

[13] (3.) I'll enquire into the Reasons they give for this neglect of 'emselves, or what it is they get in exchange for their Liberties; and you find there are two things that leave 'em under the power of this Infatuation.

1. What they reckon the Favour of the Enemy, *They saw that Rest was good.*

2. The natural Advantages of their Country, *The Land it was pleasant.*

1. *They see that Rest is good;* which shews us how their judgment

is perverted, to suppose that there can be any such thing as *Rest,* while the Yoke of Tyranny hangs upon their Shoulders. Now, this Opinion hath its only Root in Cowardise and Laziness. They dread the noble Toil of War, tho' the Hazards People run that way, are far from being equal to those of a slavish Temper, you can scarce lose so much by venturing, as you give away by submitting. Whilst the *Jews* resisted *Sennacherib,* they had what we call a Chance for it; but he tells them roundly, If they *made an Agreement with him by Presents,* it must end in his *taking 'em away from their own Land. And is this the Rest wherewith they would cause the weary to lie down?* Is this all that a People get by throwing themselves upon the Mercy of a Tyrant? We may well say, Mic. ii. 10. *Arise and depart, this is not your Rest, because it's polluted.*

    2. The Benefits of their Country was another thing that soften'd 'em into this Compliance, *They saw that the Land was pleasant.* They'd no mind to be carried off, because here was enough for their own Necessity, and for the Humour of him to whom they paid Tribute. But what a poor Argument is this? If the Place was so *good,* it deserved to be fought for; If the Produce of Nature there was so great, 'tis pity that they should have All of the Profit who had None of the Pains. Neh. ix. Thus they pleaded upon their Return out of Captivity, *the Land that* 36, 37 *thou hast given to our Fathers,* [14] *to eat the Fruit thereof, and the Good thereof, behold we are Servants in it; and it yields much Increase to the Kings whom thou hast set over us because of our Sins; also they have dominion over our Bodies, and over our Cattle at their pleasure, and we are in great Distress.*

    Thus have I laid out to you the former of these Characters, and shown you how poor a Figure *Issachar* made in the World. But,

    II. We have an Account of better things in the Blessing that he pronounceth upon another Tribe. *Dan shall judge his People like one of the Tribes of Israel; Dan shall be a Serpent by the Way, and an Adder in the Path, that bites his Horse's Heels, so that his Rider falls backward; I have waited for thy Salvation, O Lord.*

    What is said of this brave People, is so plain a Reverse to the Meanness of the other, that a very little Enlargement will serve here.

    1. He begins with a new sort of Language to give us the Description of these. What they did would be worthy the Name they derived from their Father; *Dan shall judge his People like one of the Tribes of Israel.*

    2. We have the Measures that he will take in order to it; and that is, the Use both of his Policy and Courage: *He is like a Serpent by*

Thomas Bradbury

the Way, and an Adder in the Path, and, rather than not be trampled on, *he'll bite the Horses Heels;* he'll undermine the Foundations of Tyranny, *so that the Rider will fall backwards.*

3. These noble Designs are what *Jacob* recommends to the Blessing of God, in that Prophetick Rapture, *I have waited for thy Salvation, O Lord!*

(1.) We have a general Honour put upon them. *Dan shall judge his People like one of the Tribes of Israel.* What judging of his People means I [15] had occasion to show you the last Year; That it includes an Execution of their Laws, and a Defending of their Liberties from any that would oppress them. And this we find that *Sampson* did, who was of *That Tribe,* and paid less regard to an Enemy, in whose Country he lived, than any of the Judges. Now, do but consider how this is plac'd in a full Opposition to what was said of *Issachar;* and from thence you may collect, That those Rulers do not *judge their People,* who perswade 'em to *bow down under Two Burdens:* These are inconsistent with one another.

But what I would observe to you, is, the honourable Turn he gives this, That it's doing *like One of the Tribes of Israel:* As if they that Neglect it were sunk below the Name. But *Dan* kept up the Dignity of his Family, and show'd that his Descent from so many Patriarchs was not in vain. Those antient Worthies, whom God had call'd out from the rest of the World, led him the way to it. One of the most remarkable Things that *Abraham* did in a publick Manner, was the taking of *Five Kings Captive;* tho' the People, in whose Quarrel he Gen. xiii. mingled himself, are *the first Rebels* we read of: He had Armour ready for three hundred and eighteen Men, train'd up in his House. Upon his return from this Slaughter, *Melchisedek, the Priest of the most high God, meets him,* and gives him a solemn *Blessing* in His Name, who is *the Possessor of Heaven and Earth.* And tho' it's true, he refused to be *made rich* by the Spoils, yet the Right that he had to bring down and plunder so many Tyrants, appears from his paying Tythes to *Melchisedek;* for we cannot think that he would have brought *Robbery for a Burnt Offering. Jacob* recover'd a Part of the Land *with his Sword, and his Bow* out of the Hand of the Amorites; nay he had the Name of *Israel* given him in the Field of Battle, because *by his Strength he laid hold of the Angel,* [16] *and had Power both with God and Man, and prevailed:* So that Cowardice, in any of his Posterity, was a departure from that noble Spirit their Fathers had been Eminent for.

And especially, if you'll consider 'em as a People set apart to the Worship of God, they were bound to run all Hazards in defending what he gave 'em. When they were frighted with the *Anakims*, faint-hearted, and durst not go on, it was acting so far below themselves, that he will scarce own 'em to be his People; but says, That it's *a Generation that do err in their Hearts, they knew not his Ways*. Their Spirits had a wrong Turn, and he swore, *That they shall never enter into his rest;* And if they should allow an Enemy to break in upon the Land of their Possession, it was dishonourable to their Name: But *Dan* bears up the old Figure, and in *judging of his People, is like one of the Tribes of Israel.*

(2) Here are the Ways that he takes to do it. Where you may observe,

1. The Policy and Wisdom of this People: They are compar'd to *Serpents* and *Adders*.

2. Their Courage, or the Hazard they run: They'll throw themselves into the *Path*, venture being crush'ed, rather than lose their End.

3. Their Resolution to have the Blessing whatever it cost 'em: If they can't dismount a Tyrant by mere Force, they'll *bite his Horse's Heels, so that the Rider shall fall backward.*

1. They are represented as a wise and well-instructed People; *a Serpent in the Way, an Adder in the Path*. Doubtless *Issachar* thought it a good *Prudential* to humble themselves, and hold their Lives upon no other Tenure than the Will of a Prince; but *this their Way was their Folly*. *Dan* takes his Maxims as they rise from the plain Welfare of the Community: He'll neither [17] be hector'd nor wheedled out of his Privileges; he'll lose 'em neither by War nor Treaty: As he's Serpent enough to understand what's best for him; so, like *the Adder, he stops his Ears against the Voice of the Charmer, charming never so wisely*.

Job xvii. 41.   The want of such a Spirit, is the Presage of Ruin. *Thou hast hid their Hearts from Understanding, therefore thou shalt not exalt them*. Christ himself hath bid his People take to 'em the Wisdom of the Serpent; tho' here I would not have you mistake this for the mere *Wrigling* of that Creature. Fraud and Artifice, lurking Ways, and lying Words, are as much below the Wisdom that will save a Nation, as they are against the Honesty that must save a Soul. Those Men that came to *David*, and *had understanding of the Times, and knew what Israel ought to do,* found that the Wisdom of the Serpent was consistent with the Innocence of the Dove.

2. Besides a Capacity to contrive what is best, here's a Courage to execute it. This is a Tribe that *Moses* speaks well of in the Blessing that he gave 'em. *Dan is a Lyon's Whelp, and he shall leap from Bashan.* Deut. And we may observe a Character of that sort in the Verse before us, xxxiii. 22. That he'll venture himself as *a Serpent in the Way, as an Adder in the Path;* he'll run the Hazard of being trampled under foot, rather than take up with the poor and scanty Terms that an Enemy gives him. 'Tis better being crush'd at once, than condemn'd to a miserable Existence: And these are things that will deliver a People over the Voice of Fame: The good Esteem and hearty Wishes of the World will be to such as *offer themselves willingly, and jeopard their Lives in the high Places of the Field.*

3. They are determin'd to have the Blessing at any Expence: Nor will they lose Things for [18] want of meer Names and Forms; they'll endeavour to bring down a Tyrant by his own Methods, if all the rest shall fail: And, when he designs to ride over Liberty and Religion, if they cannot stop his Career, they'll break his Neck; the very *Horse's Heels,* which should have ruin'd Them, shall receive the Wound that will prove fatal to Him. And indeed when a People are thus inclin'd to *loose the Bands* of their Capacity, it's no very hard matter to humble the Wicked by the Measures they have taken. Violence and Iniquity do not so easily carry their Load, but, in a little time, their *Rider may fall backward.*

(3.) WHEN *Jacob* hath thus describ'd his Son by the brave Measures that he'll take, he commends the whole Design to the Blessing of God; *I have waited for thy Salvation, O Lord.*

Some imagine that the good old Patriarch was, at this time, almost spent upon his Deathbed with going so far as he had done; and in these Words he takes breath again: Others think there's in them the Horror of that Idolatry that he saw the Tribe of *Dan* would run into. But if you'll take 'em for a Pause, it's a Sign, that what he had said of a people getting back their Liberties, was of so much Value with him, that his Soul can rest a while upon it, before he proceeds to the other Blessings.

Or, you may understand it, as several would do, for a personal Wish, Q. D. "Let me turn aside for a Moment from telling what will happen to you, and spend one Thought upon my self. You hear what

Issachar will give up, and *Dan* retrieve; but these things belong to a World I am going from. There's something nearer me than your prosperity; *I have waited for thy Salvation, O Lord."* If [19] you take it thus, it tells us, That for good Men to know that they who come after 'em will be zealous for God, and truly concern'd for the Publick Interest, is One Cordial in a dying Hour; as *David* saith to *Solomon, I go the way of all the Earth; but be thou strong, and show thy self a Man.*

I Kings.
1, 2

But I see no reason why *the Salvation* that he *waited for,* may not be connected to the ways that *Dan* would take in *judging his People.* And then it includes in it these three things.

1. His hearty Wishes to so good a cause, Q. D. "This will be thy Temper, and my Blessing go along with it. It's what I think of with Pleasure, and in some of my last Breath commit thee to the Favour of Heaven: *The God before whom my Fathers walkt, the Angel that redeem'd me from all Evil, establish the Work of thine Hand."*

And this we have had many Examples of; tho' good People were just at the Gates of Glory, yet they could not take leave of those that stay'd behind, without a Testimony for the Cause they had been engag'd in: Which ought to be of the greatest Value with us, that such a Number of excellent Persons have died Praying for *the Peace of our Jerusalem.* They have spoke well of the Liberties of Mankind, when themselves were leaving all Things of that sort; and we cannot think that God would let 'em go out of the World, either with a Lye in their Mouths, or a Trifle in their Hearts.

2. When he adds, *I have waited for thy Salvation;* it may be understood as a Direction to those brave People, to tell 'em, they must hope for Success in a religious Way. Second Causes are employ'd; but the good old Man would let 'em know, That *their Salvation is of the* [20] Lord: And if they will conquer in earnest, they must be a People that *wait for it.*

This comprehends the Duty that they owe to him, their Dependance upon his Care, their Jealousy for his Honour. The Profane, the Unclean, the Evil-doers do not come into the Number. If they have any hopes of being deliver'd, 'tis from something else, *for God is not in all their Thoughts.* They that use his Name without Reverance, and his People without Pity, can't think that he hath any Pleasure in their Ways. But *Jacob* would have them give all their Counsels and Attempts a serious Tincture, for when *the high Praises of God are in their Mouths,* it will add a Weight to *the two edged Sword that is in their Hands.*

Is. CXLIX. 6.

THOMAS BRADBURY

3. This seems to be an Act of his Faith in the Great *Messiah;* for it's under this Name that another good old Man receiv'd him: *Lord, now lettest thou thy Servant depart in peace, for mine Eyes have seen thy Salvation.* Nor could this be thought improper to mingle with the Zeal they had for Civil Liberties: It *was* by a *Faith* in him that *the Elders obtained a good Report, in Subduing Kingdoms, working Righteousness, stopping the Mouths of Lions, waxing valiant in Fight, and turning to fight the Enemies of the Aliens.* The Believer hath in him the truest Courage. There's nothing in any one Doctrine of Christianity that will tye up the Hands of an injur'd People. One that hath *tasted that the Lord is gracious,* must have Pity to the Desolations of Mankind. He can't endure to see that Nature ruin'd by a Tyrant, that hath been honour'd by a Saviour. Luk. ii. 29, 30. Heb. xi. 33, 34.

And then, besides, as the Kingdom of a Messiah extends it self, it will *proclaim Liberty to the Captives.* It's an Institution, as well as a Prophecy, *that there shall be no hurting nor destroying in all his holy Mountain;* and he is then said to *take to himself his great Power and Reign, when he destroys them that destroy the Earth.* Rev. xi. 18.

[21] And, again, One that hath Faith in Jesus, is waiting for that time, when *Kings shall shut their Mouths at him; Princes shall see and arise,* and he'll *strike through* Monarchs *in the Day of his Wrath,* and wrinch his Glory out of their Hands, who have taken it from him.

Again, waiting for this Salvation, prepares a Man for the Day of Battle. A Christian does not fight upon those Hazards that others do, who lose two Lives at once, that which drops in the Field, and that which is eternal. The believer in these Dangers takes himself to be *fighting the good Fight, and keeping the Faith;* and if *his* Course is at an end in this Attempt, it will be *finish'd with Joy.*

And thus have I set before you the two Tempers that distinguished these Tribes. Here's *Death, and Life, and Cursing, and Blessing:* The Choice must now be your own Act. My Time hath suffer'd me to do little more than take the Words to pieces, and consider the Parts of 'em asunder; you'll easily apply what you have heard these two ways.

1. Into a full Resentment of those Doctrines that would perswade you out of your Liberties upon the same Terms that *Issachar* parted with Theirs. 'Tis pity that humane Nature it self should be so far debased; but 'tis with an Aggravation that we see the Holy Name of Christ hath been blasphem'd; that those Mysteries must be our Choice, which was the Romans Abhorrence; as the Apostle saith in another

case, it's *a Fornication not so much as nam'd among the Gentiles*. Do not take it for a small matter, for at this Gap do they throw in all the Superstitions of Worship, their *damnable Doctrines,* as well as their cruel *Measures*. 'Tis by this means they'll steal away your Religion, and fill the Nation with Darkness, and Blood.

2. This calls us up to the Praises of God, who deliver'd us from the Stupidity of *Issachar,* and inspir'd [22] us with the Temper of *Dan,* at our Revolution.

I'm sensible, this Mercy hath had all the Regards that the Children of Israel gave to the *Manna* which fell from Heaven. At first we gather'd it, we tasted it, liv'd upon it, and reckon'd it *Angels Food;* now 'tis but *light Bread,* and we want *Flesh to eat;* nay, as it is said of *Sodom,* we are *going out after strange Flesh:* And I doubt not but the Parallel would hold further, that it must come as soon *out of Our Nostrils,* as it did out of Theirs. What they desir'd in their *Lust,* they enjoy'd with a *Plague,* for *e're it was chew'd, while it was yet between their Teeth, the Wrath of God fell upon 'em.*

But I would recommend the great Things that He hath done for us, to your Value and Care; and this can be expressed in no better way, than by *walking in the Light, while we have the Light; a Conversation that becomes the Gospel;* an Aborrence of any thing that would mingle with your Religion, or defile your Practice; a Pity to the poor Protestants in *France,* upon whom *the Clouds have return'd after the Rain;* a having no *Fellowship with the unfruitful Works of Darkness.* And, whoever they are that have no Compassion for Blood, no Reverence for Leagues, *O my Soul! come not thou into their Secret, unto their Assembly, mine Honour be not thou united; for in their Anger they slew a Man, and in their Self-will they dig down a Wall: Let such Counsel of the Wicked be far from me, I have waited for thy Salvation, O Lord.*

FINIS.

[22]

NATHANIEL NILES 1741–1821

Two Discourses on Liberty

NEWBURYPORT, MASSACHUSETTS, 1774

Niles was something of a universal man in the pattern of Benjamin Franklin but without matching Franklin's productivity or acquiring his fame. Achieving little success with several inventions in his father-in-law's Connecticut factory, he headed a party that settled new land along the Connecticut River, halfway to the north end of Vermont. From that base he preached and practiced a little medicine (though licensed to do neither), served eight terms in the Vermont legislature (augmenting three terms down at Hartford before he left Connecticut), occupied a succession of other offices, including three years as a Vermont Supreme Court judge, and made money from his farm. Niles delivered this sermon at the North Church in Newburyport on June 5, 1774, only a few weeks after the British closed the port of Boston. The people of Massachusetts were not sure how much support they would receive from elsewhere in the colonies, but they knew the reprisal for radical activity would cause hardship for the people of Boston—the center of revolutionary activity. In this setting Niles begins with a careful, insightful, and dispassionate analysis of liberty. He calls upon the traditional American values of frugality and simplicity to see them through hardship. Then, in the last seven pages, Niles builds a rhetorical masterpiece that has to be one of the best examples available for conveying a sense of that time in our history. Even today it is difficult not to feel the power of the words. For both analysis and rhetorical power this sermon is at least equal to Thomas Paine's *Common Sense.* Only the first of the two discourses is reproduced here.

ADVERTISEMENT.

As what was said in public on the following subjects, was delivered, almost entirely extempore, the author finds it impossible to give an exact copy. Those things however, on account of which, he apprehends, a copy was desired, have been carefully preserved. The particular expressions could not be recollected, but the ideas are not lost. Several new thoughts on the subject are interspersed.

The author's general design is to awaken in his countrymen, proper sentiments and emotions, respecting both civil and spiritual liberty. The former, without the latter, is but a body without a soul.—As the copy is so suddenly called for, the first, rough draught, goes to the press; and the author doubts not, but many imperfections will be observed in the stile and manner; which however he trusts are less evils, than a delay at a time when every means, however imperfect, is needful, that may inspire a genuine spirit of true liberty. He feels that he wants those advantages which many others enjoy, for becoming entirely acquainted with the various branches of civil liberty.—The main ideas alone are attended to. The inquisitive mind will be able to draw a number of important consequences.

[5] SERMON I.

I. CORRINTH. Chap. VII. ver. 21.

Art thou called being *a servant? Care not for it; but if thou mayest be made free, use it rather.*

At first glance, it is certain, this text refers to a state of *personal* servitude, and extends to every instance of the same kind. It is also as clear that the Apostle exhorts the servant to prefer liberty. This proves that the inspired writer himself, prefered liberty to a state of servitude; for he would not exhort another to prefer what was not preferable in his own esteem. Now, if Paul esteemed personal liberty a valuable inheritance, he certainly esteemed the liberty of a community a far richer inheritance; for if one man's enjoyment of it was a good, the enjoyment of two must be a greater good, and so on through the whole community. From the same manner of reasoning, the slavery of a community [6] appears to be a proportionably greater evil than the slavery of an individual. Hence, we may observe from the text, that CIVIL LIBERTY IS A GREAT GOOD.

NATHANIEL NILES 1741–1821

This is the proposition to which I ask your present hour's attention, and if it should appear in the sequel to contain an important truth, you will not esteem it below the gospel preacher's duty to explain and support it in public, especially at such a time as this, a time, at the very prospect of which, our generous fore-fathers would have wept in bitterness of soul. If civil liberty is a great good, it ought to be deemed one of the blessings of Heaven; these it is the preacher's duty to illustrate, that we may feel the obligations they bring us under—that we may enquire whether we have improved them for the glory of the giver, and that we may know how to conduct toward them for the future. Be pleased then to give your candid, close, and serious attention, while I endeavour to explain the nature of civil liberty, and prove that it is a great good.

As it is much less difficult to point out the nature of true coin in general, than to determine whether any particular piece is genuine, or how far it differs from the perfect standard: So it is much easier to point out the general nature of civil liberty, than to say what degree of it enters into any particular civil constitution. [7] It is therefore most natural to enquire, in the first place, concerning the general nature of liberty; and indeed it is as necessary as natural. For until we determine this question we have no rule by which we may estimate the quantity of liberty in any particular constitution: But when once we have found the standard, we shall be prepared to examine our own constitution, or any other, at pleasure, and to determine what part of the constitution should be supported, and what may be given up with safety. An enquiry into the nature of liberty in general, is also needful on another account. Without it we cannot see the force of any evidence that may be brought to evince the value of liberty itself.

That the subject may be fairly elucidated, I will endeavour to remove some mistakes by which it has been obscured. In doing this, I observe, that liberty does not consist in persons thinking themselves free. The Jews could say we were never in bondage to any man though they wore the Roman yoke at the very same time. Again, though a certain constitution should be contended for and supported by a majority of voices; yet this would be no sure evidence that it is free: Because an hundred may as truly tyrannize over one, as one over an hundred; or otherwise, the majority may be in favour of licentiousness. What but a love of licentiousness or tyranny, or both, [8] can induce the heathen nations to approve of their several systems of government?

What but these, could induce Saul and the men of Israel to persecute David and his handful? What but one or both of these drew down the fury of Sodom on Lot—of the Jews on the prophets—on Jesus Christ—on his Apostles and their followers. What but these ever raised any one of the many terrible persecutions under which the peaceable disciples of Jesus Christ have fallen from time to time? In all these instances the majority have been unfriendly to liberty.

Civil Liberty consists, not in any inclinations of the members of a community; but in the being and due administration of such a system of laws, as effectually tends to the greatest felicity of a state. Herein consists civil liberty, and to live under such a constitution, so administered, is to be the member of a free state; and he who is free from the censure of those laws, may fully enjoy all the pleasures of civil liberty, unless he is prevented by some defect, not in the constitution, but in himself.

If liberty consists in the being and administration of a civil constitution, different from such an one as has been mentioned, I must confess, my inference from the Apostle's exhortation is not just. For certain it is, that [9] so far as a constitution doth not tend, in the highest degree, to the greatest felicity of the state, collectively considered; it is a comparitive evil and not a good.

Where there is no system of laws, not liberty, but anarchy, takes place. Some degree of liberty may, indeed, exist where neither the constitution nor the administration of it is perfect. But in order to perfect freedom, the law must extend to every member of the community alike, both in its requisitions and prohibitions. Every one must be required to do all he can that tends to the highest good of the state: For the whole of this is due to the state, from the individuals of which it is composed. Every thing, however trifling, that tends, even in the lowest degree, to disserve the interest of the state must also be forbidden.

Originally, there were no private interests.* The world and all

* The great God is the original owner of all things. He has, originally, no partner in any thing; but has been graciously pleased to invite his rational creatures, who are capable of enjoyment, to a joint participation of his possessions, according to their various capacities. Thus, antecedent to the creation of this world, whatever existed was a kind of common stock enjoyed by God and those of his creatures that could enjoy such a good. All were to exert themselves to turn every thing to the best advantage, for the whole, [10] and no one of all God's creatures, could call any thing his own, in distinction from others, except the pleasure that

things in it, were the [10] common interests of all the inhabitants,
under God the great owner. Nothing is to be esteemed [11] an interest
any farther than it tends to good or is capable of being turned to the
benefit of the possessor. But whatever has this [12] tendency, or may
be thus used, is properly termed an interest. According to this estimate,
the term *interest* includes all those various offices [13] and employments
that are capable of being improved for the good of the community.
There interests, being such as cannot be managed [14] by the whole
body collectively, are distributed among the individuals according as
they appear in the eyes of the body politic, to [15] be qualified to use
them for the good of the whole. In this way every member becomes
a servant to the state, and is a good or bad servant according to the
manner in which he discharges the trust reposed in him. This is
equally true of the King on the throne and the peasant in the field.
The laws of a free state require each individual to use the public

resulted to him from the common good. There were no private interests then.
Afterwards, God made the world, and this became an addition to the common
stock. The world itself, and all the creatures in it were enjoyed by God and his
holy Angels. At length, Adam was formed out of the dust of the earth. He was
a new addition to the common stock of wealth, and being made capable of
enjoyment, was received as a member of the grand company, and became interested
in God, Angels, Heaven and Earth, and all things in them. This world, a
particular portion of the common stock, was committed, in certain respects, to
him and his posterity to be managed by them for the grand company. I say, in
certain respects, for there are certain other respects in which it was not committed
to them; in certain respects, the Angels have the management of the world and
all things in it. Each one has his particular department assigned to him, Adam
and his posterity are to be considered both as a part of the common interest, and
as overseers. They have nothing that they can call their own, to the exclusion of
the right, either of God or his Angels. Nor was there ever any thing in the world
that any one could call his own, to the exclusion of his fellow men, *i.e.* in a state
of nature. Antecedent to compact, any one of all the individuals, had as good a
right to lay claim to the same inheritance as another. Nay, any one had as good
a right to exclude the rest from the enjoyment of every part of the whole, as
from any, even [11] the least part. Any one individual might monopolize the
whole earth by the same rule of justice, by which he could monopolize a single
acre, or inch. So that antecedent to compact, there could not possibly be any
private interest whatever, and every appearance of private interest was the effect
of violent seizure, and tenure, and not of just distribution. No man has a right
to enter on any common interest without the order of the proprietors.
    There are two modes in which earthly states were originally formed. The
one is, by the over grown influence of an individual, which put it into his power
to exercise an arbitrary government. The other is by a compact formed with a
particular design to secure and advance the private interests of those by whom

interests deposited in his hands, in every instance [16] in that very manner that shall contribute more to the good of the community, without any particular reference to Governor or subject, rich or poor, high or low. While the laws require such a continual course of conduct in every member of the community, they as critically forbid every one to take from another that part of the public property which is committed to him; or to impede him in making the best use of it for the public, unless when the community see it best to deprive an individual of his place, and authorise another to do it in their name. In this manner the laws of a free state provide security for the particular properties of each individual member, or rather for the public interest deposited in the hands of individuals, by denouncing such penalties on every offender as are exactly adequate to his offence. There must be an exact proportion between the offence and the penalty. Where there is no such proportion, or equality, liberty is infringed, because

---

the compact was made. Both of these had their rise in usurpation. As to the first there is no dispute. As to the second it may be said, that there were no private interests antecedent to compact, but such as had been taken by usurpation. It is true, that such usurpers may have appropriated such interests as they called their own, without any resistance; but this no more frees them from the charge of usurpation, than it would a tyrant, for him to say that he had obtained a state of absolute monarchy gradually, and without resistance. Stratagem, and the length of the sword are the only standards of right in either of these cases. The absolute monarch justifies himself, by saying, that he had a majority of strength in his favour, and the member of such an association, as has been named, resolved to enter on a combination, for the [12] sake of using his sword in the best manner he could for the defence of what little he had, and consented that his neighbours should hold what they had appropriated, and determined not to attempt to divest them of the public interest they have seized, lest in the scuffle he should lose what he had as unjustly monopolized. This is the maxim on which pirates and gangs of robbers live in a kind of unity. If we go on this maxim, if we suppose that is a well founded government which has its foundation in private interest, we can by no means blame the tyrant for holding absolute dominion, without condemning ourselves; nor can the tyrant blame his subjects for their rebellion, whenever they apprehend rebellion will be their greatest emolument. For, if government is first founded on private interest, it cannot be reasonably expected, that the superstructure will stand, when the foundation is removed. It matters not whether men who build their notions of government of self-interest, call themselves whigs or tories, friends to prerogative, or to the liberties of the people. Their scheme of government is the same for substance. They cannot blame their neighbour for commencing tory when it will be most conducive to his private interest. Indeed, on this scheme it is unreasonable to withstand a mob or a tyrant, or to make war on the pirates themselves, for, according to this doctrine they are none of them doing any thing but what is right. Yes, say you, they

the law is partial, as it will injure, either the public, by not giving it its due, or the offender, by inflicting a greater evil than he deserves. In this case there must be no distinctions, made by the law, between persons of different characters and stations, only as those different characters and stations may give the same criminal action different degrees of aggravation. A criminal action is more criminal in a person who fills an elevated place, than in one [17] of a more humble condition; because it has a more detrimental aspect on the state. For this reason, the offences of the great should be punished with greater indignity and severity, than the crimes of persons in low life. In a perfectly free state, friendship to the community will be as carefully noticed as an offence. Punishment will not be more exactly alloted to the transgressor, than adequate rewards to the faithful subject. The farmer, the seaman, the mechanic, the merchant, and the practitioner of such of the learned professions as belong to the state, are directed

---

infringe on my rights. I ask, what rights? None but such as you have pillaged from the community [13]—Rights in which these very persons are interested as members of the community.

The world and its inhabitants, are a common property that belongs to the whole intellectual system. They are committed to mankind to be managed for the whole. It is therefore the business of mankind collectively, to regulate and dispose of the inheritance for the emolument of the whole company. In order to this, government in its various parts is necessary; and the several offices in the government become so many parts of the common good, or stock. These, as well as the other parts of the common inheritance, are to be committed to individuals by the body of stewards, to be improved for the company of proprietors. Every individual is to have his part assigned him, and so long as he fills his place well, he is to be rewarded for his services by the community, that is, he is to have the enjoyment of such conveniences, in such a degree as shall be a sufficient recompence for his labour and care; but he is not to have any separate interest consigned to him, for this would tend to detach him from the community. Just so far as his affection is turned on private interest, he will become regardless of the common good, and when he is detached from the community in heart his services will be very precarious at best, and those will not be expected at all which imply self-denial. He is only to enjoy it at the will of the community, which is to be regulated by the interest of the whole. [14]

Some are to be rewarded for their services to the community by an exchange of commodities. Carriers, such as merchants are, are to have a certain proportion of the commodities they carry. Others are to be rewarded by a general collection from the whole. Thus each individual is to take care of the community, and the community in its turn, is to make provision for the individuals.—These observations afford us a clue to the relation that kingdoms and states, and the internal part of individual states, bear to each other. The whole world is properly, no more than a small colony of the universe. But small as it is it is too unwieldy

by the community, in effect, to reward each other by an exchange of labour, or commodities. While those servants of the state, who are employed in managing the reins of government, are rewarded by a collection from the whole, an equality to which, is returned in the happy effects of legislation and executive justice. At the same time that the laws make due provision for an equal distribution of rewards among the faithful servants of the state, both of higher and lower rank, they make as full provision for the infliction of penalties on every class alike. They render it as easy to bring a royal offender to trial,—to procure an impartial sentence against him, and to inflict deserved punishment, as in the case of the meanest subject.

In such a state, the laws extend to all the members of the society alike, by making an [18] impartial estimate of every offence, but as it is best in all communities, that some offenders should be pardoned, for special reasons, and that others should be punished; those same laws will lodge a power of determining the alternative with some one, whose capacity and integrity are equal to such a trust, so that the community may suffer no harm.

---

to be managed as one state, by reason of the feebleness of human powers. There is therefore a propriety in its being subdivided into still smaller portions called kingdoms. It is the business of these still to regard the good of the world, in subserviency to the good of the universe. Neighbouring states have no more right to rise up against each other, than neighbouring individuals. Different states are interested in the welfare of each other and ought to seek the good of each other. One has no right to devise schemes to enrich itself by impoverishing another. The case is the same with respect to different parts of the same kingdom.

This is a scheme of government perfectly consistent with the divine government, and true reason. And on this scheme we may consistently exert ourselves in favour of liberty, and punish tyrants according to their just deserts. [15]

There is much said about the prerogative of crowns. Crowned heads have a prerogative of doing good, but no prerogative for any private emolument. The true honour of a King consists in his doing good; but if he becomes an obstacle in the way of public good, he is to be removed like other common nuisances.

This scheme shews us, likewise, on what principles we are to stand ready to lay down our lives in the cause of liberty, or, which is the same thing, in vindication of good government: We, and all we have, belong to the community. Whenever therefore the common cause requires it, we should, like Paul, be ready to lay down our lives for the brethren. It is but what we owe to the community.

Our worthy forefathers, however they might greatly err in some particular instances, seem to have been inspired by this generous scheme of liberty. This was what led them to this new world, and I would hope that we their posterity have too much of that spirit, which led them to risque their lives, to suffer ourselves to be enslaved by an India herb, or English manufactures.

NATHANIEL NILES 1741–1821

A good foundation for liberty is laid in such a constitution, but its whole worth lies in due administration. Perfect liberty takes place where such a constitution is fully administered: But where the administration is imperfect, liberty is likewise imperfect. In a perfectly free state, both the constitution, and the administration of it, are full of propriety, equality, and equilibrium.

These I take to be the out-lines of genuine liberty, which, by a proper application, may assist us in our enquiries after the degree of liberty enjoyed by any particular state.

Indeed, the circumstances and occurrences, that attend human states are so numerous, extensive, and uncertain, that no one man, or body of men, can foresee and improve them all to the greatest advantage. Hence, it frequently happens, that we cannot ascertain the degree of liberty enjoyed by a community, by comparing the particular parts of a constitution, or the administration of it, with the abstract notion of liberty; [19] for we see but a small part of the whole system. Our views are very partial. This is the case not only of individual subjects, but the body of government, itself, cannot, compleatly, comprehend the whole. Some degree of partial oppression is, therefore, to be expected in every human state, even, under the wisest administration. We may, however, determine, in some instances, whether liberty is unnecessarily infringed or not. When we see the body of a community plundered for the sake of indulging individuals in pride, luxury, idleness and debauchery,—when we see thousands rewarded with pensions, for having either devised, or attempted to execute some scheme for plundering a nation, and establishing despotism, we cannot be in doubt whether some horrid attack is not made on liberty.

We may reason thus in a few particular instances; but, in general, we must form our judgments by considering the various dispositions of mankind, and by noticing their various operations and effects, in various circumstances. We must turn our attention to the facts that have already taken place; and may reasonably conclude, that the same causes will always produce the same effects, unless something special prevents. One general inference from the whole will be, that liberty is much rather to be expected in a state where a majority, first, institutes, and then varies the constitution [20] according as they apprehend circumstances require, than in any other.

Other things being equal, a majority has a more general and distinct knowledge of the circumstances, and exigencies of a state than a minority; and, of consequence, is more able to judge of what is best to be done. Add to this, that private interest is the great idol of the human mind; and, therefore, when a majority unite in any measures, it is to be supposed, they are such measures as are best calculated to secure the particular interests of the members of that majority; and, consequently, the general interests of the body are more effectually provided for, in this way, than by the security of the private interests of any minority whatever. And if the maxims adopted by the majority are general, both in their nature and extent, it is to be supposed, they will prove as salutary to the members of the minority as to those of the majority, and, consequently, to the whole body. Hence, though liberty is not necessarily, nor invariably connected with the voice of a majority; yet, it is much more likely to be found in connection with such a voice, than with that of a minority. Indeed, there is in general, no reason to expect liberty where a majority is counteracted, and, on the contrary, we may hope for some good degree of it, where a majority governs.

It is only on these maxims, that the present [21] British monarch can be exculpated from the several charges of rebellion, treachery, and usurpation, and on these, the glorious revolution in favour of the house of Hanover is perfectly justifiable.

Let us now attend a little, to a few particulars that may serve to excite in us some more adequate ideas of the worth of civil liberty. Indeed, none but an omniscient mind can fully comprehend, and exactly estimate the true worth of this blessing, in its various consequences, effects, and inseparable concomitants, as they take place on various occasions. Our views of this subject may, however, be greatly enlarged and rendered much more distinct than they generally are.

That civil liberty is of great worth, may be infered from the conduct of God towards the Jewish nation. He promised them freedom from the oppression of their enemies as a testimony of his favour in case of their obedience; and as a chastisement for their disobedience, he threatned them with a state of servitude. From this it is certain that the omniscient God himself, esteems liberty a great blessing. The Israelites were taught by him to set their hearts much on liberty, and to avoid slavery with great caution, constancy and vigour.

It was observed that liberty has its rise in [22] such a constitution as tends to the highest good of a community, and that the due administration of such a constitution affords a state of freedom. Hence, the bare idea of liberty discovers it to be an inestimable good, for whatever tends to the highest good of great numbers, must, undoubtedly, be an invaluable treasure. In this view liberty is an inexhaustable fountain, which, under God, sends forth an endless variety of such streams, as are both pleasant and salutary. I will instance in a few particulars. When we enjoy liberty, and are sure of its continuance, we feel that our persons and properties are safely guarded by her watchful eye, her impartial disposition and her powerful arm. This excites to industry, which tends to a competency of wealth. The vassal, on the other hand, having no security of his present possessions, or for those he might obtain, concludes so uncertain a prize is not worth the seeking, and therefore will do no more than barely serves to silence the clamours of necessity from day to day.

In such a situation, every bias of the human mind tends to idleness and poverty. Even generosity itself will sink into inactivity and indolence; because it loaths a connection between tyranny and wealth, and therefore refuses, will do nothing that might establish such a connection, by strengthening a tyrannical state. Liberty not only removes every obstruction [23] out of the way of industry, frugality and wealth, but rouses even indolence to action, and gives honest, laborious industry a social, sprightly, cheerful air; but in a state of slavery, sloth hangs heavily on the heels of dumb, sullen, moross melancholy. Industry and frugality spring from the same source, and are spontaneously productive of temperance. The former moderates the appetites, while the latter forbids unnecessary expence. This triple alliance is the natural parent of decent conversation and courteous behaviour. They calm the passions and urge even pride and avarice to mimic humanity, and every generous sentiment. By these and such means, they, both enable and dispose us to fulfill our contracts* with exactness, and to give us credit with our neighbours,

* Contracts are sacred things. The man that doth not feel himself bound by them, is totally incapacitated for political intercourse with mankind. Notwithstanding the depravity of human nature, we all detest the man who breaks his faith with us. One great end of civil government, in this apostate world, is to compel men to fulfill their contracts. Should the laws of a realm allow the subjects to break over their contracts at pleasure, the very constitution would contain the spirit of anarchy: And when those in the seat of government become regardless of their contracts, and break through them, in so doing, they throw the state, directly, into the depths of anarchy, and force becomes the only law:

and lay a foundation [24] for public confidence. In this manner liberty renders political virtue fashionable, and tends to diffuse public spirit. It discountenances disorder, and every narrow disposition. Thus the mind is fortified on all sides, and rendered calm, resolute, and stable. Industry and temperance give health to the body, and render it fit for the residence and operations [25] of such a soul. In a nation raised to such a pitch of vigor, firmness, health and opulence, all the natural means of defence are collected, and to such the arts of war will be an easy acquisition. These united, will prove a bulwark against every assault of lawless power, whether foreign or domestic. In such a state, a free people will enjoy composure of soul and their taste will become refined. The study of the fine arts will follow of consequence, and, after these, a long train of science. Industry, frugality, and a curious turn naturally invent and perfect the useful arts. What is more than all, liberty secures the rights of conscience, by protecting every member of the state in the free exercise of his religion, unless it be such a religion as is inconsistent with the good of the state. The first effects of liberty, on the human mind, are calmness, serenity and pleasing hope, and all the various fruits of liberty produce the same happy effects. Thus liberty, first divides itself, as it were, into various streams; which, at length, all meet together again in soothing sensations and sweet emotion of soul. The pleasure that springs from liberty is the life of every other enjoyment, and the importance of it in a single

---

For a default of one party in covenant sets the other at liberty. When Kings, therefore, infringe on chartered rights they dissolve all manner of union between themselves and their subjects. The obligation is mutual, and neither party can fail to fulfill the conditions on his part, without setting the other free. Both parts of a covenant are equally sacred, for a King, therefore, to break that which subsists between him and his people, is as criminal as for the people to renounce their allegiance to him. If this be so, it ought to be made a capital offence, for any subject to endeavour to inspire his sovereign with the notion that he is at liberty to break his faith with his subjects. It ought to be deemed the most aggravated kind of high treason; because he at once dethrones the King, and subverts the constitution of nature itself. In the British nation, every right is held by charter. When, therefore British legislators begin to talk seriously of the right of an English King to disannul his royal charters, is it not high time for the whole nation to awake? If a single charter is broken in upon, who can depend on the security of any enjoyment? Awake, Britons awake! nor suffer your King to be dethroned. Let *truce breakers* and *traitors* turn to the third chapter of the second epistle to Timothy, if they know where to find it, and read the four first verses and observe with whom they are ranked by their Maker.

instance is vastly great, too great to be conceived of, unless on a
sudden transition from a state of refined freedom, to that of the most
abject slavery. How great then must be the collective happiness that
a community derives from [26] a state of perfect freedom? I confess
liberty never has been enjoyed in perfection by any of the nations of
the earth; but this by no means affects the foregoing estimate. For,
from the small degree of liberty, with which we are acquainted, the
consequences of perfect liberty may be justly inferred. Nor is the
imperfection of liberty, as it hath taken place in the world, any
discouragment to the pursuit of it. The more we can obtain, the
greater will be our enjoyment. Each degree of liberty is a precious
pearl.

When we would learn how much any thing tends to happiness,
we must view it with reference to the taste of the person in whom
the happiness is supposed to take place. So, the happy tendency of
liberty cannot be seen, unless it be viewed as terminating on some
particular disposition in him by whom it is enjoyed. Liberty is so illy
calculated to give pleasure to either a tyrannical, or, licentious spirit,
that it proves a galling curb to both. A free spirit,—a spirit that is
consonant to a free constitution;—a spirit that seeks the highest good
of a community, in its proper place,—this, and this only, can extract
and taste all the sweets of liberty. If we would learn how great a
tendency liberty has to produce happiness, we must consider it in
such circumstances as give it an opportunity to do good.

Let us then, for once, imagine a state whose [27] members are
all of a free spirit; and then attend to the glory and pleasures of
liberty. The individuals are all of one mind. They unite in the same
grand pursuit, the highest good of the whole. Only suppose all the
members of such a state to be acquainted with the best means of
promoting their general end; and we shall see them all moving in
perfect concert. The good of the body will be their first aim. And in
subserviency to this, they will impartially regard the particular interests
of individuals. You and I shall perfectly unite in our regard for your
interest and for mine. Your interest will not be the more dear to you,
nor the less so to me, because it is yours. In these circumstances,
there would be no room for the emotions of any of the angry painful
passions; but, on the contrary, every soft and pleasing affection of
every soul, would be called forth into vigorous and harmonious
exercise. Every individual would choose to move in his proper sphere,

and that all others should move in theirs. This would at once constitute pure felicity, and exalted beauty. How *good* and how *pleasant* it is for brethren to dwell together in unity: Such a state of things, in the little community of a single family, must be productive of great good. But should it take place throughout a nation, each family would enjoy the same good from its own domestic circumstances, beside the far greater pleasure which would accrue to each individual from a consideration of the same happy condition of the whole.

[28] Should it be said, that such a scheme as has been mentioned is merely chimerical and romantic; because there never has been, nor ever will be such a general state of mind on earth; I would say, the same objection is equally strong against the worth of a state of perfect holiness. Such a state has never taken place, in perfection, in this world, nor will it hereafter; but must we therefore suppose that holiness is of no worth? The reason why we do not experience all the pleasures of liberty, that have been mentioned, is, not any defect in liberty, but the perverseness of our selfish hearts, which prevents our pursuit and enjoyments of the delights of perfect liberty. Liberty still remains a blessing too great to be compared with any other earthly good.

The thoughts that have been suggested in this discourse, open to us the nature of good government in its several branches. A legislature is denominated good, from the goodness of its laws, or, from the tendency of the laws made by it to produce the highest good of the community. In exact proportion to this tendency of the laws, is the legislature to be esteemed good:—The goodness of executive government, consists in its due administration of the laws already made. It is for the good of the community alone, that laws are either to be made or executed. So that,

Good government is not inconsistent with [29] liberty. Perfect liberty and perfect government are perfectly harmonious, while tyranny and licentiousness are inconsistent with both. Yea farther,

Good government is essential to the very being of liberty. Remove good government and you remove liberty. Abridge the former and you abridge the latter. Let good government encrease and you encrease liberty. These can never be separated in any degree. Their rise and fall is exactly uniform. Hence,

The impropriety of saying of a person, that he is a friend to government, but not to liberty; and of another, that he is a friend to liberty, but not to government, appears to be very gross. Indeed one man may be a friend to tyranny and not to liberty, but then he is as truly an enemy to government. Another may be a friend to licentiousness and not to government; but then he is as truly an enemy to liberty; and both, for this plain reason, that good government in a state, and the liberty of that state, are one and the same thing. This suggests another idea, which is, that

He who infringes on liberty rebels against good government, and ought to be treated as a rebel. It matters not what station he fills; he is a traitor; his treachery is, however, more or less aggravated in proportion to his state and condition. He that fills an elevated station [30] is proportionably more criminal in the same rebellion, than those in a lower state; and where a man proves false to confidence reposed in him, his treachery is still more base and detestable. Because his exaltation puts it into his power to do greater injury to the state than could possibly be done by an inferior.

It is equally true, that every kind and degree of opposition made against good government is an ebullition of licentiousness.* The man that rises up against good government is an enemy to liberty, a tyrant in heart, and they who are discontented and fretful under it are of the same cast.

If liberty is such a thing, and so great a blessing as it has been represented, it is, certainly, a rich tallent that Heaven has been pleased to entrust with every man, and it undoubtedly becomes all to be constantly, and thoroughly awake to a sense of their duty respecting it. We are too ready to fancy, that when once we have appointed legislators, and [31] given them charge of this inestimable treasure, we need give ourselves no farther concern about it. But this is not our whole duty. We are all stewards, to whom the God of nature has committed this talent. The design of appointing a few individuals to government, is not to free the rest from their obligations but to assist them in the discharge of their duty, in the same manner that ministers of the gospel are to assist their hearers in those duties that respect the

---

* The true spirit of a mob consists in unconstitutional violence, done with a design to bring about some private end, and therfore the term is alike applicable to armies, or navies, or a mixed multitude of madmen, minors and slaves when they are engaged in such unconstitutional violence, and they are dangerous in proportion to their elevation, influence, discernment and malice. All of them are evils and ought to be avoided.

care of their souls. Communities ought therefore to keep an impartial and watchful eye on government. They are urged to do so, by a consideration of the avaricious, and aspiring dispositions of mankind in general, and the peculiar opportunities and temptations that Governors have to indulge them. In these latter ages of the world, after it has been found by several thousands years experience, that such as have been made the guardians of liberty, have in almost every instance, where it was thought practicable, endeavoured to make themselves masters, instead of continuing stewards of the community; in these days, I say, we are more distinctly, sensible, and frequently called on to watch the conduct of government. Liberty is not an absolute right of our own, if it were, we might support, and guard, or neglect it at pleasure. It is a loan of heaven, for which we must account with the great God. It is therefore, as unreasonable for us to place an unlimited [32] confidence in any earthly ruler, as to place such a confidence in our spiritual ministers and depend wholly on them to settle our final account with the holy judge of the universe.

I do not mean that we should, as individuals, undertake to dictate to our rulers, or oppose them by force whenever we judge they act a wrong part. This would be utterly unreasonable, for surely we have at best, no better right to usurpation than they. What I mean is, that we should all endeavour to turn the attention of our fellow members of the community on the conduct of our rulers. We should notice and compare it with the standard of right and wrong ourselves; and excite others to do so likewise. We should endeavour on every alarming occasion, to collect the sentiments of the body, and vigorously pursue those measures that are thought the most salutary for the whole.

It becomes us, with united hearts, to make a firm stand against every attempt to wrest the jewel from us, either by force or fraud:— The present state of things is very alarming. In the view of the most simple common sense, we are now called on—men, women and children are called on to struggle for the preservation of those rights of mankind which are inexpressibly dear. Let us then rouse and exert ourselves to the utmost, on the present occasion. But you ask me. What shall we do? [33] Shall we renounce the authority of our gracious sovereign? Shall we take up arms against his troops? What shall we do?

I answer, By no means. Do not suffer the thought of renouncing our king's authority, so much as to turn in your mind; rather, be ready to shed your blood in defence of your rightful sovereign and his high office. Never let us think of entering on a civil war, unless the Pretender, or some other usurper should attempt to dethrone the British parent of his people. But should this be the case, then let the world see that their king is dearer to the Americans than their blood.

Though the time has been when our countrymen, but an handful, were obliged to defend themselves against thousands of the native savages; by dint of arms; yet, notwithstanding, a cloud, in some respects, much heavier than that, lowers over us at present; such is the kindness of our God, that, humanly speaking, it is in the power of America to save both herself and Great-Britain from total destruction, and that without a single hostile stroke. Nothing more than piety and oeconomy are necessary, and in these, every age and character may unite. The pious supplications of the stammering child will as effectually reach the ear of our God, and be as acceptable to him, as the most elegant address. A thousand things may intercept our petitions on their way to an earthly monarch; [34] but a combination of all our enemies in earth and hell cannot prevent a pious wish in its flight to Heaven; and let us remember, that the effectual fervent prayers of the righteous avail much. We have sought in vain for relief from our parent state—from our King. And if salvation has not come from our gracious sovereign King George, we cannot expect it from the hills. We must look still higher. Instead of railing against man let us notice and imitate the example of Michael who railed not against the devil himself. David, said, of Shimei, let him curse for the Lord hath bidden him. He saw, he had deserved so illy at God's hand, that it was no wonder, he had brought such a punishment on him. He, therefore, accepted it willingly at the hand of God; while he was not insensible to the wickedness of Shimei. It becomes us, likewise, to notice the hand of God, and settle it in our minds, that evil springs not out of the ground,—that there's no evil in the city which the Lord hath not done. Under such views, let us all, like Daniel of old, piously pour out our hearts before God, acknowledging our own sins, and those of our people. Meanwhile, let us encourage no practice, in ourselves or others, that tends to enslave our country. Let us learn to live in the plain manner of our fore-fathers. It is high time for us to reform. We have had a rich inheritance and wasted it in riotous living. Let us soon return to our father's house, least we be reduced to the want, even of husks to eat. These are the [35] only expedients that seem needful at present, But if we will risque our country for the sake of a few superfluities, posterity may curse our pride and luxury, and the present generation may find that death and carnage will terminate their folly. And should this be the case we must charge the horrid scene to our own misconduct.—If any should say, it is in vain for them as individuals to be vigilant, zealous and firm in pursuing any measures for the security of our rights, unless all would unite: I would reply.

Ages are composed of seconds, the earth of sands, and the sea of drops, too small to be seen by the naked eye. The smallest particles have their influence. Such is our state, that each individual has a proportion of influence on some neighbour at least; he, on another, and so on; as in a river, the following drop urges that which is before, and every one through the whole length of the stream has the like influence. We know not, what individuals may do. We are not at liberty to lie dormant until we can, at once, influence the whole. We must begin with the weight we have. Should the little springs neglect to flow till a general agreement should take place, the torrent that now bears down all before it, would never be formed. These mighty floods have their rise in single drops from the rocks, which, uniting, creep along till they meet with another combination so small that it might be absorbed by the travellers foot. [36] These unite, proceed, enlarge, till mountains tremble at their sound. Let us receive instruction from the streams, and, without discouragment, pursue a laudable plan. But,

Is it not to be feared, that an appetite for the leeks and onions, is the source of our difficulty? The ungenerous language of the objector seems to be, "I could wish to see my country happy, but if the fates have determined its destruction I will not forgo my share of the booty."

It is great, it is glorious, to espouse a good cause, and it is still more great and glorious in such a cause to stand alone. It is great and glorious to outbrave the reproach of the base. Should all our countrymen forsake us, perseverance would be an honour, and the honour will rise as the number of our adherents is diminished.

Let us therefore, vigorously pursue prudent measures in the present alarming state of things. Then, should it please the righteous disposer of all, to reduce us to the most abject slavery, we shall at least, have the consolation to think, that we are in no part chargeable with having riveted chains on our country, and the blessing of a clear conscience is incomparably better than the greatest temporal interest and worldly applause.

This has been a land of liberty. We have enjoyed that blessing in a great degree for a long time. It becomes us now to reflect on [37] our ingratitude to the giver. When he has wrought salvation for us, on one occasion and another, how have we expressed our thankfulness? By bonfires, illuminations, revellings, gluttony and drunkenness. Would not a stranger have thought us worshipers of the whole race of the heathen deities, rather than of that God, who is a spirit, and who seeketh such to worship him, as do it in spirit and in truth?

We have boasted of our liberty, and free spirit. A free spirit is no more inclined to enslave others than ourselves. If then it should be found upon examination that we have been of a tyrannical spirit in a free country, how base must our character appear! And how many thousands of thousands have been plunged into death and slavery by our means?

When the servant had nothing to pay, and his master had frankly forgiven him all, and he had gone and cast his fellow servant into prison, there to remain till he should pay the last farthing; the master justly punished his ingratitude and severity with the like imprisonment. Hath not our conduct very nearly resembled the conduct of that servant? God gave us liberty, and we have enslaved our fellow-men. May we not fear that the law of retaliation is about to be executed on us? What can we object against it? What excuse can we make for our conduct? What reason can we urge why our oppression shall not be repaid in [38] kind? Should the Africans see God Almighty subjecting us to all the evils we have brought on them, and should they cry to us, O daughter of America who art to be destroyed, happy shall he be that rewardeth thee as thou hast served us; happy shall he be that taketh and dasheth thy little ones against the stones; how could we object? How could we resent it? Would we enjoy liberty? Then we must grant it to others. For shame, let us either cease to enslave our fellow-men, or else let us cease to complain of those that would enslave us. Let us either wash our hands from blood, or never hope to escape the avenger.

To conclude, unless we adopt some prudent decisive measures in humble dependance on God; we have reason to fear some almost unparallelled calamity. If we do not exert ourselves: It would not be strange, should a military government be established, and popery triumph in our land. Then, perhaps those, who want fortitude to deny themselves some of the superfluities of life, may see their husbands and sons slain in battle, their daughters ravished, their wives ript up, their children dashed against the wall, and their pious parents put to the rack for the religion of Jesus. Now is the decisive moment. God sets before us life and death, good and evil, blessing and cursing, and bids us choose. Let us therefore choose the good and refuse the evil, that we may live and not die.

[23]

MONITOR

*To the New Appointed Councellors, of the
Province of Massachusetts-Bay*

BOSTON, 1774

During the colonial era there had been a struggle between the crown-appointed governors and the popularly elected legislatures in the colonies. Gradually the elected representatives had won the upper hand, but the governors continued to fight back. One tool they had was to appoint prominent colonists to a privy council or quasi-legislative body that functioned almost as an upper house. In 1774 the crown moved to make this creature of the governor function more like the House of Lords, a true second legislative body. This piece in the *Massachusetts Spy* of August 18, 1774, is typical of the response.

Gentlemen,

As most of you are new men in state affairs, and are, notwithstanding, men whom a British administration have selected to fill an important department in the government of this Province, which without ever consulting the people they have presumed to *new model.* in order, as they say, to give it a greater conformity to the constitution and government of Great-Britain, I hope to be indulged in laying down principles whose notoriety might be supposed to render their repetition disgustful; but principles which, it seems have had little weight with you in the present awful transaction wherein you have had but too great a share for your present honor or future quiet. And as I cannot presume that each individual of you either have taken, or will take the pains to revolve a great many books I shall chiefly refer you to the learned author of the commentaries on the Laws of England* for the

* Judge Blackstone

fundamentals I propose to offer for your consideration; the authority of whom I presume you will hardly be disposed to dispute.

This celebrated jurist tells you [in] vol. I p. 52. that "a *state* is a collective body, composed of a multitude of individuals united for their safety and convenience, and intending to act together as one man. If it is therefore to act as one man, it ought to act by one uniform will;" and this will once determined and declared is "understood by *law*." The form of the agreement of this multitude of individuals, wherein their particular wills are joined together in order to produce that one uniform will which is understood to be law, is commonly called the civil constitution, of the States. In the Island of Great-Britain, there have for many ages been ranks of men very different from each other in point of fortune, education, etc. which however settled down into the general divisions of Lords and Commons. The Lords having commonly a great share of property and many persons subject to their command and directions, whether as vassals, tenants, etc. and also being persons of leisure and opportunity to acquaint themselves with the relations, rights and interests of men in society; and further being but moderately numerous, and capable of sustaining the expence of attending to the conventions needful for that purpose, have chosen to retain the privilege of declaring their sense of any measure proposed to regulate the conduct of society, and have from time immemorial, had such weight in the state that their joint opposition to any such proposed measure was sufficient to prevent its passing into a law. In this body resides the aristocracy of Great Britain, wherein the superior wisdom, power and independency of the state was for many ages gloriously conspicuous. "The commons, says the same great lawyer,† consist of all such men of any property in the kingdom, as have not seats in the House of Lords; *every one* of which has a voice in parliament, either personally or by his representatives." For justly, observes he, "In a free state, every man, who is supposed a free agent, ought to be, in some measure his own governor; and therefore a branch at least of the legislative power should reside in the whole body of the people." And here is the democracy or legal power of the people of Great-Britain.

The happy Agrarian constitution of New-England, having prevented any such distinction as Lords and Commons, the cultivators

† ib. 158

being in general the Lords of the soil, the whole power of the state, besides what is stipulated to reside in the Governor, must reside in the freemen of the province.

This, gentlemen, you will find fully warranted by our charter, which entitles the grantees to all the liberties and immunities of free and natural subjects of the crown of Great-Britain to all intents, constructions, and purposes whatsoever. If you say the late act of parliament has annulled this clause of the charter, I acknowledge Lord North intended it should; but if every individual freeman ought to be so much his own governor, as that the smallest regulations of his conduct shall not pass into a law without his consent, surely a law that overthrows the whole civil constitution of his country cannot on this principle be supposed to pass into a law capable of binding him. The most ignorant among you must know that this is an absurdity of so glaring a nature, and so fatal in its consequences, that a submission to it at once gives up all that weight which the wisdom, the valour, the property, the probity of the subject in possession of his constitutional negative power has to secure him against any innovation imposed on him by the crown. And what says the great author, before quoted, of the state of a people where the equipoise of their legislative power, or sovereignty is lost? "If the supreme power were lodged in any one of the three branches separately, we must then be exposed to all the inconveniences of absolute monarchy, aristocracy, or democracy; and so want two of the three principal ingredients of good polity, either virtue, wisdom or power. If it were lodged in any two branches; for instance in the King and House of Lords, our laws might be providently made, and well executed, but might not always have the good of the people in view."‡ Now, gentlemen, please but to follow our authority to the bottom of the page quoted, and he tells you, "for if ever it should happen that the independence of any one of the three should be lost, or that it should become subservient to the views of the other two, there would soon be an end of our constitution. The legislature would be changed from that which was originally set up by the general consent and fundamental act of society": And such a change however effected, is according to Mr. Locke (he might have added Vatell and many others) at once an entire dissolution of the bonds of government; and the people are thereby reduced to a state of anarchy, with liberty

‡ ib. 41.

to constitute to themselves a new legislative power, Can you pretend that even a shadow of independence pertains to an aristocracy creable and extinguishable at mere pleasure? If abeting the dissolution of the bonds of government in the subversion of the civil constitution of your country be an evidence of piety, you have certainly a solid claim to the character. If hardly one in ten of you can boast a descent from persons above the rank of shopkeepers and mechanics, where is the lordly, the noble blood which should distinguish you from the common mass of the common people? If you can expose yourselves to the resentment of millions, as the authors of their ruin and misery, and the intailment of slavery on their innocent and numberless posterity, barely for the title of *honourable,* even admitting the addition of a trifling salary, your claim to any considerable portion of wisdom, will be disputed by some persons, if not the bulk of mankind. Your valour may indeed be put to trial, but remember, it will not be on the side the valour of those nobles was exerted, who forced from a worthless tyrant the acknowledgment of the unalienable rights of Englishmen. Your property, and I may add your personal security, will soon stand on a firm foundation, when like Agrippa the favourite general of Augustus, you have established a power which determines all questions of property, and even life itself, by a *sic volo!* Were none but you and your families concerned in the event, I would pity the latter, but with little regret behold such abettors of despotism, wringing out the dregs of the cup they had traitorously combined to mingle for their betters. Read but the history of that unfortunate man and tremble at the fate of, not only him, but thousands and tens of thousands, whom avarice and ambition have plunged them in merited and exemplary ruin; always remembering that *hostis patria est felo de se.*

MONITOR

County of Suffolk, July 12th, 1774.

[24]

GAD HITCHCOCK 1718–1803

An Election Sermon

BOSTON, 1774

B orn in western Massachusetts and educated for the ministry at Harvard, Gad Hitchcock must have been near-perfectly designed for the course in life that he pursued. Called to serve as the first pastor of a newly organized Congregational church in Pembroke, on the outskirts of Boston, Hitchcock rejected all appeals to move to larger and wealthier congregations as his fame spread throughout New England. Acclaimed for his knowledge of the Bible, history, and theological literature; for the vigor and eloquence of his sermons; for the charity inherent in the gospel he preached; for courage repeatedly displayed and a natural wit that he could not suppress—publicized among clergy and laity for these and other natural gifts and cultivated qualities,—Gad Hitchcock might have come out first in any polling to name the most loved and admired pastor of his place and his time. When the invitation came to deliver the annual election sermon selected for printing here, Hitchcock did not know that he would be addressing General Thomas Gage, newly appointed governor of Massachusetts, accompanied by shiploads of British troops and instructed to straighten out the rebellious colonials. It is doubtful that Hitchcock flinched when he got this bit of news; it is certain that he laid it on the line when the hour came to speak his mind. "The people," he declared, "are the only source of civil authority on earth." The axiom, announced early in his sermon, was elaborated with reiteration, expansion, and justification; how convincingly enunciated can be determined by a reading. The new governor and commander of the watchdog forces heard him through, but a notable number (perhaps an unprecedented number) of the audience not charged with public duties walked out. Referring later to the unexpected exodus, Hitchcock remarked that it appeared to have been a moving sermon.

BOSTON, 1774

AN
ELECTION-SERMON
PROVERBS XXIX. 2.

When the righteous are in authority, the people rejoice: but when the wicked beareth rule, the people mourn.

This is the observation of a wise ruler, relative to civil government; and the different effects of administration, according as it is placed in good or bad hands—and it having been preserved in the sacred oracles, not without providential direction, equally for the advantage [6] of succeeding rulers, and other men of every class in society; it will not be thought improper by any, who have a veneration for revelation, and the instruction of princes, to make it the subject of our present consideration—Especially as our civil rulers, in acknowledgment of a superintending Providence, have invited us into the temple this morning, to ask counsel of God in respect to the great affairs of this anniversary, and the general conduct of government.

Accordingly, I shall take occasion from it—to make a few general remarks on the nature and end of civil government—point out some of the qualifications of rulers—and then apply the subject to the design of our assembling at this time.

First, I shall make a few remarks on the nature and end of civil government.

The people mentioned are a body politic—but whether the speaker had the Jewish state more especially in view; or, as is most probable, any civil society or kingdom on earth, is a point we need not precisely determine.—On either supposition, civil government is represented as being [7] already established among them—rules framed, and consented to, for the conduct of it—proper officers appointed, and vested with authority, on this constitutional basis, to make and execute such laws, in future, as should be found necessary; the public security and welfare being their grand object.—This, at least, appears to be the most just and rational idea of government that is founded in compact; as, I suppose, all governments, notwithstanding later usurpations, originally were; and if the compact, in early ages, hath not always been expressed; yet it has been necessarily implied, and understood, both by governors, and the governed, on their entering into society.

GAD HITCHCOCK 1718–1803

To this rise of government, the Hebrew polity, so far as it related only to civil matters, is not to be considered as an exception.—For although God, a most perfect Governor, for wise reasons, and as a distinguished favor, condescended to become the political head of the Jewish state; yet he did not think proper to exercise his absolute right of government over them, without the consent of the people.

[8] And when they had foolishly and wickedly determined to give up this form of government, which was so wisely calculated for the public advantage, and substitute another in its room; their alwise and beneficent Governor did not see fit to exert his omnipotence to prevent it: Nor did he, as he justly might, abandon them for their impiety and ingratitude.

But analagous to the methods of his moral government, he went into a mode of conduct with them, adapted to their rational nature.— He treated them as free agents.—He solemnly protested against the change they were about to make in government; and, in order to disswade them from the rash attempt, he shewed them the manner of the king which should reign over them. But such paternal remonstrances proving ineffectual, and the people still persisting in their design, He not only permitted them to pursue it, but actually afforded them special aid and direction in the choice of their new king—that they might have one who should save them from their enemies—because their cry had come unto him.

[9] This instance of the uneasiness of the nation of the Jews, under the most perfect form of government, may, perhaps, be alledged by some, as an argument of the utter incapacity of a people to judge of the rectitude of administration, or of their unreasonable peevishness and discontent, when they are governed well. It ought, however, to be considered, that though God was pleased to put himself at the head of the Jewish polity, yet officers, or rulers taken from among men, were appointed to act under Him; and these might not, and in fact did not always keep the great end of their investiture in view.

This was remarkably the case in the instance before us.—The sons of Samuel, who had been appointed judges over Israel, walked not in his ways, but turned aside after lucre, and took bribes, and perverted judgment; and the evil effects of their venality, and consequent perversion of public justice being known, and felt by the people, were the immediate occasion of their general uneasiness and complaint.

In this situation of their affairs, the way, indeed, was open before them. It was [10] their indispensable duty, instead of withdrawing their allegiance, to have made their application to God their king, in a way of humble ardent prayer, for a redress of such enormities; and undoubtedly, He would have heard their petition, and returned an answer of peace, as He had before, in times of other dangers and distresses, often done.—Their sin and folly consisted in this neglect, and not in groundless suspicions, and unnecessary complaints: they had manifest cause of uneasiness—they were greatly injured, and oppressed by some of their executive officers: Bribery, which ought to be the abhorrence of all ranks, had corrupted the seats of judgment, and rendered their persons and property insecure, and without the protection of law. Of this they complained, and made it the ground of their request for a king to judge them like all the nations—And however the Israelites might be guilty of great weakness and folly, as they certainly were, in desiring, on this account, to depart from a form of government, in which God himself presided, and wherein they might have had all their grievances redressed; and to adopt one similar to that of other nations;—and how far soever God might grant [11] their desire, as a punishment of their ingratitude, yet, as it appears from Jacob's blessing on the tribe of Judah, not to mention other things, it was in the divine plan, or permission at least, that the Jews, in future time, should come under the governance of earthly kings, it is no improbable conjecture, that prevailing wickedness, and corruption among some in high station at this period, was the occasion of God's so readily complying with this request.

The passage, however, which stands at the head of our discourse, supposes the people to be judges of the good or ill effects of administration;—and as the wise king of Israel is the author, it may, perhaps, have the more weight.—"When the righteous are in authority, the people rejoice."—They are sensible of their own happiness in having men of uprightness, honor and humanity to rule over them—Men, who make a proper use of their authority—who seek the peace and welfare of the whole community, and govern according to law and equity, or the original rules of their constitution.—"But when the wicked beareth rule, the people mourn"—they are dissatisfied and grieved when [12] contrary to reasonable expectation, and the design they had in forming into civil society, it turns out, as the history of states and kingdoms authorises us to say it often does, that their rulers possess opposite qualities—are inhuman, tyrannical and wicked; and instead of guarding, violate their rights and liberties.

The great end of a ruler's exaltation is the happiness of the people over whom he presides; and his promoting it, the sole ground of their submission to him. In this rational point of view, St. Paul, that great patron of liberty, speaking of the design of magistracy, hath thought fit to place it—"he is the minister of God to thee for good"—But God's minister he cannot be, as a ruler, however he may be in another capacity, nor is subjection required, on any other principle—his making the prosperity of the state the great object of his laws, and other measures of government, is his only claim to submission: Nor will any one deny that his doing so, and attending diligently to this very thing, binds the conscience of subjects, and makes obedience their indispensible duty. But obedience on the contrary supposition, is so far [13] from being enjoined on them, that it argues meanness of spirit, and criminal servility, unless their circumstances are such as to make subjection a duty, on the foot of prudence, when it is not so in any other view.

The measures which rulers pursue, are generally good or bad, promotive of the public happiness, or the contrary, as are their moral characters. The observation of our text is grounded on the truth of this assertion, though it ought to be acknowledged, that there have been wicked rulers, such as Nero, and others of later date, who, for a while, have governed well.

Whether righteousness is to be restricted meerly to the virtue of justice, or considered as comprehensive of the entire character of piety and religion, where it is said, as in the place before us; "when the righteous are in authority, the people rejoice"; it may justly be affirmed that men of such a character are by far the fittest, other accomplishments being equal, to be entrusted with the civil interest of a community; and the people are the most likely to feel the salutary effects of government, and be happy in their administration.

[14] Religious rulers are, in every view, blessings to society; their laws are just and good—their measures mild and humane—and their example morally engaging.

Veneration for the authority of the supreme ruler of the world, prevailing in their hearts, is the most effectual security of affection to the public, which is a qualification absolutely indispensible—it inspires them with principles of equity and humanity; it begets the deepest concern in all their acts of government, to answer the great intention both of God and man, in their institution, and renders them truly benefactors to mankind.

It is, however, natural to suppose, every quality necessary to the constituting a good ruler, is comprehended in the term—righteous— the observation would not, otherwise, be without exception.—The interest of a people is not always so well served by a ruler meerly of a religious character, as it would be by the addition of other qualities.— Religion, indeed, ought ever to be esteemed as an indispensable recommendation to public trust; but other qualifications are also requisite, and must be [15] joined, to afford reasonable expectation of happiness to a community, from the exercise of authority.

There does not appear to be a like reason for supposing the want of every other qualification, as that of righteousness, in the wicked ruler, to make him incapable of governing well.—He may have many and great endowments in other respects—capacity, and address—but if he has no religion—if he is immoral and vicious, unawed by him whose kingdom ruleth over all; he is commonly unfit to have the care and direction of the public interest,—If there have been instances of good government under the conduct of rulers of vicious characters, there have been also too many of a contrary sort to make it eligible or safe, to put confidence in such. To whatever lengths natural benevolence, desire of fame, education, love of power, and the emoluments of place, may be supposed sometimes to carry men, in acting for the public advantage, it is certain, and in several, it has been sadly verified, that these are feeble motives—principles, that can give no security of lasting happiness to a people, where the superior invigorating aids of religion are wanting.

[16] The vices of a ruler pervert the due exercise of his authority, to the disadvantage of the community; and mark his public conduct with oppression and ruin. And we are not to think it strange, if the people fall into perplexity and mourning in consequence.

It is the character of one who is exalted from among his brethren, to rule over men, drawn by God himself, the Almighty guardian of the Rights of mankind—that he "must be just, ruling in the fear of God."

The safety of society greatly depends on the good disposition of rulers, and the regard they have to equity in their measures of government. If they rule in the fear of God, they will make his laws their pattern in framing and executing their own.

Administration in every mode of government, is a point of the most weighty importance to subjects.—Absolute monarchies, or such forms of government as have the powers of the state lodged in the hands of a single person, tho' generally dangerous to the Rights and Liberties of [17] mankind, and too often have proved so to recommend them to the choice of a wise people, have, notwithstanding, when the reigning Prince has supported the character of religion, been the source of great peace and security to the public.

But the effects have been different—distress and misery introduced into society, under the administration of one whose moral qualities have been of another complexion.

The same is true as to consequences, in those governments, where the whole power legislative and executive, is deposited with a few.— Good or evil ensues to the community, according as the exercise of their authority coincides with the eternal rules and laws of reason and equity, or the contrary.

In a mixed government, such as the British, public virtue and religion, in the several branches, though they may not be exactly of a mind in every measure, will be the security of order and tranquility— Corruption and venality, the certain source of confusion and misery to the state.

[18] This form of government, in the opinion of subjects and strangers, is happily calculated for the preservation of the Rights and Liberties of mankind.—Much, however, depends on union; and the concern of every part to pursue the great ends of government.

When each department centre their views in the same point, and act in their proper direction and character, as the ministers of providence, for the promotion of human happiness, things go well— the Rights of the people are secured, and they are contented—gladness fills their heart, and sparkles in their countenance!

But there may be a failure in some one or more of the governing parts, in respect to public measures, and the art of governing.—And when this happens, though it be but in one, since each part is strictly necessary to constitute the legislative body—it greatly wounds the state—embarrasses affairs—and is productive of general uneasiness and discontent.—The people soon feel inconveniences rising from jarrs and interference among their rulers—and as they have an indubitable right, they take [19] it upon them, to judge what, and how far any thing is so, and where to fix the blame.

In such a government, rulers have their distinct powers assigned them by the people, who are the only source of civil authority on earth, with the view of having them exercised for the public advantage; and in proportion as this worthy end of their investiture is kept in sight, and prosecuted, the bands of society are strengthened, and its interests promoted: But if it be overlooked, and disregarded, and another set up as the object of their pursuit; we will suppose it should be, but by one of the supreme branches, or, indeed, by a single member of any, who happens to be of leading influence and great abilities, it will go far in making a schism in the body.—Calamity and distress may be expected, in a measure, to ensue—We need not pass the limits of our own nation for sad instances of this.—Whether, or how far, it has also been exemplified in any of the American colonies, whose governments, in general, are nearly copies of the happy British original, by the operation of *ministerial* unconstitutional measures, or the public conduct of some among ourselves, is not for [20] me to determine: It is, however, certain, that the people mourn!— May God turn their mourning into joy! and comfort them, and make them rejoice from their sorrow!—

Rulers are under the most sacred ties to consult the good of society. 'Tis the only grand design of their appointment. For the promotion of this valuable end, they are ordained of God, and cloathed with authority by men.

In a state of nature men are equal, exactly on a par in regard to authority; each one is a law to himself, having the law of God, the sole rule of conduct, written on his heart.

No individual has any authority, or right to attempt to exercise any, over the rest of the human species, however he may be supposed to surpass them in wisdom and sagacity. The idea of superior wisdom giving a right to rule, can answer the purpose of power but to one; for on this plan the Wisest of all is Lord of all. Mental endowments, though excellent qualifications for rule, when men have entered into combination [21] and erected government, and previous to government, bring the possessors under moral obligation, by advice, perswasion and argument, to do good proportionate to the degrees of them; yet do not give any antecedent right to the exercise of authority. Civil authority is the production of combined society—not born with, but delegated to certain individuals for the advancement of the common benefit.

And as its origin is from the people, who have not only a right, but are bound in duty, for the preservation of the property and liberty of the whole society, to lodge it in such hands as they judge best qualified to answer its intention; so when it is misapplied to other purposes, and the public, as it always will, receives damage from the abuse, they have the same original right, grounded on the same fundamental reasons, and are equally bound in duty to resume it, and transfer it to others.—These are principles which will not be denied by any good and loyal subject of his present Majesty King George, either in Great-Britain or America—The royal right to the throne absolutely depends on the truth of them,—and the revolution, an [22] event seasonable and happy both to the mother country and these colonies, evidently supports them, and is supported by them.

But it has been objected, that the doctrine which teaches that the people are the source of civil authority, and that they may lawfully oppose those rulers, who make an ill use of it, is likely to be attended with the worst of consequences—occasion disturbance and revolutions in the state, and render the situation of rulers perpetually unsafe and dangerous.

If the rulers are of the latter character mentioned in our text, the safety of the community forbids any attempt or disposition to make their situation easy; and I trust the objection is without force in regard to those of the former.—It is altogether unreasonable to suppose a number of persons by a free and voluntary contract, should give up themselves, their families and estates so absolutely into the hands of any rulers, as not to make a reserve of the right of saving themselves from ruin—and if they should, the bargain would be void, as counteracting the will of heaven, and the [23] powerful law of self-preservation. It must be granted that the people have a right in some circumstances, or that they have not a right in any, to oppose their rulers—there is no medium—A sober and rational inquiry into the consequences of each supposition, is the best method to determine on which side the truth lies—In doing this, I shall take the liberty to adopt the sentiments and nearly the words of a writer of the first class on Government.*

* Bishop Hoadley

If it be true that no rulers can be safe, where the doctrine of resistance is taught; it must be true that no nation can be safe where the contrary is taught: If it be true that this disposeth men of turbulent spirits to oppose the best rulers; it is as true that the other disposeth princes of evil minds, to enslave and ruin the best and most submissive subjects: If it be true that this encourageth all public disturbance, and all revolutions whatsoever; it is as true that the other encourageth all tyranny, and all the most intolerable persecutions and oppressions imaginable. And on which side then will the advantage lie?—And which of the two shall we chuse, for the sake of the happy effects and consequences of it?

[24] Supposing it to be universally admitted, that if rulers contrive and attempt the ruin of the publick, it is the duty of the people to consult the common happiness, and oppose them in such a design; it must follow, I think, that the grounds of publick unhappiness would be removed, and those inconveniences, which by mistake are represented as the consequence of this doctrine, prevented; for, on this supposition, the worst of Princes would learn to do that out of interest, which the best constantly do out of a good principle and true love to their subjects—No Prince would have any persons about him, to advise and incite him to illegal or unjust actions—and if he had at any time been guilty, he would, upon the first representation, and without being forced to it, readily acknowledge his error, and set all things right again. And let who will say it, the dispositions of subjects are not so bad, nor their love to public disturbance so great, but that a Prince of such conduct may be sure of reigning in their affections, and of being obeyed out of love and gratitude; which is the securest foundation any throne can possibly be fixed on.—So far is it from being true, that the universal [25] reception of the doctrine of resistance would be the ground of public confusion and misery, that it would prevent the beginning of evil, and take away the first occasion of discontent.

It must be acknowledged, it is because this doctrine, whatever is pretended, hath not been received, that any rulers have been misled, and encouraged to take such measures, as in the end, have proved fatal to themselves. With respect therefore to rulers of evil dispositions, nothing is more necessary than that they should believe resistance, in some cases to be lawful. I intend not for a few discontented individuals who may happen to take it into their heads to resist, but for the majority of a community, either by themselves or representatives. Such rulers, indeed, cannot bear the propagation of this doctrine; but the reason why they cannot, viz. its being preventive of their pernicious designs, is an undeniable argument of its being the more necessary.

As for good rulers, they are not affected by the propagation of it, but may promote it themselves consistently with their [26] own particular interest; for it is the chief interest of princes to reign in the affections of their subjects, free from all suspicion and jealousy of evil design. Nothing can give a nation greater satisfaction that their supreme magistrate sincerely endeavors to promote their interest, or gain him more hearty love and esteem, than the admission of this doctrine; it looks open, and removed from base and unworthy purposes; but a zeal for the opposite doctrine, tends, in its nature, and has been seen, in experience, to create jealousies in the minds of subjects, to take off their affections from a prince, and to lay the foundation of their withdrawing their allegiance from him.

But supposing it to be universally received, that it is the duty of the people patiently to submit, and not oppose their rulers, tho' manifestly carrying forward the ruin of the public, nothing can be imagined to follow, but what is of the worst consequence to human society, unless we suppose rulers as angels of God, or rather, as God himself, incapable of being mistaken themselves, or misled by others. This supposition leaves no restraint on such rulers as have designs of their own, distinct from [27] the public good: Public misery and slavery will therefore ensue; and this is a state of things infinitely worse than that of public disturbance, supposing such sometimes to take place in consequence of resistance. The inconvenience of the latter will soon be felt and rectified by the people themselves; but the former, on the principle of non-resistance, is absolutely without a remedy.

When people feel the influence and blessing of a good adminis-tration, they are not, in general, disposed to complain and find fault with their rulers; it is inconsistent with their own interest, and that of their families to do so. If we will be determined on a point of such delicacy by a ruler himself, who, as absolute as he was, had wisdom and public virtue to give judgment conformable to the nature and truth of things, we shall see that it is under the influence of an evil administration the people are discontented and mourn; and that under the influence of a good, one they rejoice.

All lawful rulers are the servants of the public, exalted above their brethren not [28] for their own sakes, but the benefit of the people; and submission is yielded, not on the account of their persons considered exclusively of the authority they are clothed with, but of those laws, which in the exercise of this authority are made by them, conformably to the laws of nature and equity.

This position is so far from being unacceptable to good rulers, or thought to be derogatory of their dignity, that they esteem it as implying the highest human character, and an official resemblance of the great Saviour of mankind, who came not to be ministered unto, but to minister; and accordingly went about doing good.

The assertion that rulers are constituted by the people for the common happiness, is no denial of St. Paul's doctrine, who, speaking of magistracy, hath said—There is no power but of God; the powers that be are ordained of God:—any more than it is a denial of the blessings of husbandry, merchandize, and the mechanic arts, or, indeed any thing beneficial to society, being from God, to say, that men have invented them—They are all from God, from [29] whom cometh down every good and perfect gift; and much in the same sense, as it is his will that men should be employed in them for their own advantage: But men by their reason, which is also the gift of God, are the immediate discoverers of their utility. It is, however, necessary to observe, that as civil government holds a distinguished place among the gifts of God; and, considering the human make, the blessings of it are productive of a greater aggregate of happiness, both in a natural and moral view, than most others: Much has been said in revelation about it—the divine approbation manifested—and the qualification of rulers exactly stated.

Although government is not explicitly instituted by God, it is, nevertheless, from him; as, by the human constitution, and the circumstances men are placed in, He has signified it to be his will, that, as a security of property and liberty, and as necessary to greater improvements in virtue and happiness than could be attained in a state of nature, there should be government among them. But it is from man, as for the same end—the procuring a greater good to each individual, on the whole, than could [30] be had without it; they have, in conformity to their make and circumstances, and the dictates of reason, voluntarily instituted it. And thus government is the ordinance both of God and man. And so the new-testament writers consider it, and speak of its design as being the same in both, viz. The public happiness.

This is a striking indication to rulers, not only as to their aims in accepting any public office in a community, but as to the obligations they are under to discharge the duties of it with fidelity. They are the trustees of God, vested with authority by him, in the benevolent designs of his providence, to be employed in guarding and defending the just Rights and Liberties of mankind; and as far as they can, advancing the common welfare.

And as they are responsible to him who is no respecter of persons; they are not to expect their public conduct is to be exempted from his most strict and impartial scrutiny.

They are also the trustees of society, as their authority, under God, is derived [31] from the people, delegated to them with design it should be exercised for, and to no other purpose than, the common benefit; and this renders them justly accountable to their human constituents, whose tribunal, however some have affected to despise it, is full of dignity and majesty—Kings and emperors have trembled before it!

While meerly to possess places of dignity and eminence is sufficiently gratifying to some minds, the chief joy of rulers, mindful of the importance of their station, arises from a consciousness of such behaviour, in their public capacity, as will be approved of God, and accepted of men. For this great and valuable purpose, they will be careful to deserve the character first mentioned in the text—be just and impartial in every part of administration; and with their integrity, endeavour to join those other accomplishments which are requisite to the honorable discharge of their respective trusts.

But this brings us in the second place to point out some of the qualifications of rulers.

[32] And superior knowledge may be mentioned as one, that greatly exalts and adorns their character.

They should, therefore, be ambitious to become possessed of it, that they may be at no loss how to conduct, or which way to turn themselves in any difficult and embarrassed state of affairs; but may know what the people ought to do, and be able and ready to lead and advise them in the more boisterous and alarming, as well as in calm and temperate seasons.

Distinguished abilities and knowledge, tho' happily placed in rulers, are not indeed so absolutely necessary, in order to understand the constitution, or the general rules of any particular mode of government a people have chosen to put themselves under, as for other important matters in administration.

All fundamental laws and rules of government are, in their nature and design, and ever ought to be, plain and intelligible—such as common capacities are able to comprehend, and determine when, and how far they are, at any time, departed [33] from. Were not this the case, people's entering into society, and erecting government, could not be justified on the principle of reason, or prudence; as government instead of protecting them in the peaceable and quiet enjoyment of Liberty and property, might be made an engine of their destruction, and put it in the power of rulers of evil dispositions, under the specious pretext of pursuing constitutional measures, to introduce general misery and slavery among them.

The knowledge which the people have of the constitution, or original fundamental laws of government, whereof the plain law of self-preservation is necessarily the chief, in all forms of government, is the only adequate check on such ruinous conduct.

The people being judges of their own constitution of government, is the principle from which the British nation acted, and on the truth of which they are to be justified, when they determined, their constitution was invaded by their sovereign, and that he was carrying on designs, which if pursued, must issue in the destruction of it.

[34] But if they were no judges of such matters, if they meddled with that which did not belong to them—the revolution, and succession of an illustrious house, may have taken place without right, against law and reason, being founded in misconception and error; and the heirs of an abjured popish prince, still remain the only just, and lawful claimants to the British throne; a doctrine, which, I am sure, no American, and I hope, but few in great Britain, will ever admit. If the foundations be destroyed, what can the righteous do?

But high degrees of knowledge are requisite in rulers for other great and weighty purposes in government. If they would act with dignity and advantage in their public capacity, they should be well acquainted with human nature, and the natural rights of mankind; which are the same under every form of government: They should also be acquainted with the general rules of equity and reason, and the right application of them, as circumstances vary; with the laws of nations, their strength, manners, and views; but especially with the genius, temper, customs and religion of the people they are called [35] to govern: This will enable them to accommodate public measures to public advantage, and to frame such laws and annex such sanctions, from time to time, as may be best calculated to encourage piety and virtue, industry and frugality, and prevent immorality and vice, and every species of oppression and misery—They should moreover know, in what instances natural equity and a regard to the good of the whole require former laws to be repealed, or varied—new ones enacted, and other penalties applied, and in what way government may be the most effectually, honorably and easily supported.

Legislators, whom I have chiefly had in view, should know how to give force, and operation to their laws, that every member of the community may feel their effects, and be treated in a just and reasonable manner; and as far as may be, according to his personal circumstances and merits. This, indeed, is to be done by means of the executive part, but the executive power is strictly no other than the legislative carried forward, and of course, controulable by it.—These, and others that might be adduced, are points requiring [36] capacity and knowledge in rulers: And among other means for the attaining them, it is their indispensible duty, in imitation of a wise king, to pray for an understanding heart, that in all their acts of government, they may discern between good and bad, and lead the people in the paths of righteousness and peace.

Another qualification of rulers, is a public spirit, and a compassionate regard to mankind.

When we take into consideration the great design of civil government, no one can be thought a proper person to rule over men, who has not a prevailing regard to their interest, and a fixed determination to pursue it.

This, certainly is the great object which magistrates, as such, are under obligation to keep in their eye—as men, they have, like other men, private interest, and private views, and may as lawfully pursue them; but in their public capacity, they can, of right, have no other end, than the public advantage.

[37] And if they make use of their authority, or the influence of their rank for any different purposes—if it be their chief aim to aggrandize themselves, their posterity or friends by means thereof; if the selfish passions predominate and guide and determine their public

conduct; if they are slaves to covetousness, ambition or effeminacy; if, led by flattering prospects, they are devoted to the meer will, and arbitrary mandates of others greater and higher than themselves; if there be any thing they are more solicitous to obtain or promote than the good of the society they are connected with, and are bound to serve,—they ignominiously prostitute their trust, and basely counteract the main design of their institution.

But rulers of a patriotic spirit are actuated by better and more noble principles; they have a sincere regard to the public; their time and abilities are cheerfully employed in the promotion of its interest; this they set up as the object of their measures, and esteem it as their own good, they seek the prosperity of the people, and in the peace thereof they shall have peace—The honors and emoluments [38] of their station, though justly due and freely rendered by a sensible, obliged and grateful people, are but inferior motives with them— happy such rulers in the applauses of the multitude, happy in the approbation of their own minds!

But that which compleats the character of rulers and adds lustre to their other accomplishments, is religion.

This is the best foundation of the confidence of the people; if they fear God, it may be expected they will regard man. Vice narrows the mind and bars the exertions of a public spirit; but religion dilates and strengthens the former, and gives free course to the operations of the latter.

By religion I would be understood to intend more than a bare belief of the divine existence and perfections—The heathen world by a proper use of their reason may attain to this, because that which may be known of God is manifest in them, for God hath shewed it unto them.

But what I intend by religion is, a belief of the truth as it is in Jesus, and a temper and conduct conformable to it.

[39] It is the wisdom of christian states, to have christian magistrates, and as far as may be, such as have imbibed the spirit of the gospel, and are actuated in their high station, by the principles it inspires. If it be allowed, as to be sure it ought, that magistrates of deistick principles, may have a regard to the civil interest of mankind, and do many worthy deeds for society; it must also be allowed that they are not so likely, as those of christian principles, to be nursing fathers to the church of Christ, which, agreeable to ancient

prophecy, magistrates, under the present dispensation of the divine grace, are obliged to be.

Nor will they be so much concerned to learn from the sacred oracles, for the guidance of public measures, what is the good, and acceptable, and perfect will of God.

When a people have rulers set over them, of a religious character on the gospel plan—who own and submit to Jesus Christ as their Lord and Saviour, who are sanctified by the divine spirit and grace, and, in a good measure, purified from those corrupt principles which too often work [40] in the human heart, they have reason to expect the presence and blessing of God will be with them, and that things will go well in the state.

And on reflection, we cannot forbear the acclamation of the psalmist—happy is that people, that is in such a case!—yea, happy is that people whose God is the Lord!

The religion of rulers is a guide to their other accomplishments—it has a salutary active influence into all their measures of government, and leads them to the noblest exertions for the advancement of the common weal.

The minds of the governed are satisfied with their conduct, rejoice in their administration, and rest assured that no harm will ever happen to them, by their means, unless it be by mistake, to which all men are liable. By the blessing of the upright the city is exalted, but it is overthrown by the mouth of the wicked.

[41] We come now—thirdly—to apply the subject to ourselves, and the occasion of our present assembling.

It would be as much beyond my expectation, as, I am sure it is short of my design, to be charged with the meanness of adulation, in any thing delivered in this discourse.

But I could not obtain forgiveness of my own mind nor of the public, if I should forbear explicitly to affirm, that the two honorable branches of the legislature, we before have had, which derived their political existence more immediately from the people, have been in their general conduct and measures, but especially in the late months and years of our distress and controversy, accepted of the multitude of their brethren.

It is our ardent wish and confidence, the same vigilance, circumspection and public spirit, may distinguish the proceedings of the two houses of assembly for the current year—that which is now returned, with marks of approbation and honor, from their constituents, and the other, [42] which according to royal charter, is this day to be chosen.

This anniversary, which is so auspicious to the civil liberties of this province, fills every honest heart with joy and gladness, and I trust with the sincerest gratitude to almighty God, the great patron of liberty, and benefactor of the world.

The choice of persons from among ourselves, to sit at council board, both in a legislative capacity, and as his majesty's council to give their advice to his representative here, on all matters of government, as circumstances may require, we esteem a great security of our natural rights; and one of our most invaluable privileges—a privilege, which we never have forfeited, and we are resolved we never will, or voluntarily resign it into the hands of any of our fellowmen—though it must be acknowledged, I speak it with shame and blushing, that for the many crying sins, and enormities committed in our land, it would be righteous in the divine government, if we were deprived of this and all our mercies.

[43] The appointment of one to fill the chair, is, by royal charter, reserved to the crown. Of this we have not been much disposed to complain; for though we remember our first charter with affection, and the arbitrary despotic manner of its dissolution with abhorrence, yet we have been used to put great confidence in the paternal goodness of our gracious sovereigns; and to expect such governors to be appointed over us, as would seek the peace and welfare of this people; and however it might be thought possible for them, in any future time to receive such orders from the higher servants of the crown, as would be inconsistent with our rights and privileges, we have supposed, notwithstanding they would consider themselves as being under prior obligations to the king of kings, and obey God, rather than men.

We have been used to think they would esteem the service of his majesty within this province, and the good of the province, as being the same, and that it is as impossible for his majesty to have any good in America, separate from the good of his American subjects, as it is to have any good in Great-Britain separate from the good of his British subjects.

[44] The end of government, certainly, requires men of such dispositions and sentiments to rule over this people. Prerogative itself is not a power to do any thing it pleases, but a power to do some

things for the good of the community, in such cases as promulgated laws are not able to provide for it.

On these principles it is reasonable to expect that his Excellency who is lately appointed to the government of this province, and of whose candor and moderation we have heard with pleasure, will enter on the duties of his high station, with honor to himself and advantage to the publick, and make the happiness of this people the great object of his administration which is the surest way to conciliate their affections, and establish his own authority. We wish his Excellency much of the divine presence and guidance—the supports of religion—and the plaudit of his final Judge.

The honorable Gentlemen, who are, this day, to be concerned in the exercise of an important charter privilege, the election of his Majesty's Council; will not, [45] 'tis presumed, be unmindful of the very interesting nature of this publick transaction, nor how far its influence may extend.

Much lies at stake, honored Fathers—much depends, and will probably turn on the choice you make of Councellors, not to this province only, but to the rest of the colonies. In the present scenes of calamity and perplexity, when the contest in regard to the rights of the colonists, rises high, every colony is deeply interested in the public conduct of every other.

The happy union and similarity of sentiment and measures which take place thro' the continent in regard to our common sufferings, and which have added weight to the American cause, must be cherished by every prudent and constitutional method, and will, we trust, meet with your countenance and cultivation.

The acknowledged weight of the Council Board, in the government of this province, and its influence into the well-being of our churches, from its connection with, and inspection over a very respectable [46] seminary of learning, are not your only motives. But the united voice of America, with the solemnity of thunder and with accents piercing as the lightning awakes your attention, and demands fidelity.

The ancient advice dictated to Moses, by the priest of Midian, and approved of God, is admirably calculated, civil Fathers, for your direction on this occasion—Tis a significant compendium of the qualifications of the persons whom you ought to favor with your suffrages.—Thou shalt provide out of all the people, able men—such as fear God, men of truth, and hating covetousness, and place such over them.

The present situation of our public affairs requires good degrees of knowledge, firmness of spirit, patriotism, and the fear of God, in those who stand at helm and guide the state—they should be men able to investigate the source of our evils, point out adequate remedies, and that have resolution and public spirit to apply them.

Our danger is not visionary, but real—Our contention is not about trifles, but [47] about liberty and property; and not ours only, but those of posterity, to the latest generations. And every lover of mankind will allow that these are important objects, too inestimably precious and valuable enjoyments to be treated with neglect, and tamely surrendered:—For however some few, I speak it with regret and astonishment, even from among ourselves, appear sufficiently disposed to ridicule the rights of America, and the liberties of subjects; 'tis plain St. Paul, who was a good judge, had a very different sense of them—"He was on all occasions for standing fast, not only in the liberties with which Christ had made him free, from the Jewish law of ceremonies, but also in that liberty, with which the laws of nature, and the Roman state, had made him free from oppression and tyranny."

If I am mistaken in supposing plans are formed, and executing, subversive of our natural, and charter rights, and privileges, and incompatible with every idea of liberty, all America is mistaken with me.

Our continued complaints—Our repeated, humble, but fruitless, unregarded [48] petitions and remonstrances—and if I may be allowed the sacred allusion, our groanings, which cannot be uttered, are at once indications of our sufferings, and the feeling sense we have of them.

We think we are injured—We believe we are denied some of those privileges, enjoyed by our fellow subjects in *Great-Britain,* which have not only been insured to us by Royal Charter, but which we have a natural independent right to.

And it bears the harder on our spirits, when we recollect the deep inwrought affection we have always had for the parent state—our well known loyalty to our Sovereign, and our unremitting attachment to his illustrious house, as well as the ineffable toils, hardships and dangers which our Fathers endured, unassisted, but by

Heaven, in planting this American wilderness, and turning it into a fruitful field!

But in such circumstances, we place great confidence in the wisdom and patriotism of our civil rulers—Our eyes are fixed on them, and under the smiles of Heaven we expect a redress of our grievances [49] by their instrumentality. Or, at least, that they will not be wanting, in any thing in their power, consistent with the duties of their station, to effect it.

We sincerely hope, and trust, the elections of this day will turn on men, who shall be disposed in their proper department to restore and establish our rights—Men acquainted with the several powers vested in the honorable board, and determined, with persevering spirit, to assert and uphold them—Men, in every view, friendly to the constitution of government in this province, and resolved to maintain it, undiminished, and entire.

You will please to remember, Gentlemen, that in this weighty affair, you do not act meerly for yourselves—you act for the whole community—every member has an interest in the transaction.

But above all, suffer me to remind you, that you act for God, and under his inspection, by whose providence, this trust is committed to you—and that you must one day give an account to Him whose eyes are as a flame of fire, of the motives of your conduct.

[50] When the business of the day is finished,—the legislative body will enquire into the interior state of the province, and enter upon public concerns relative to the well ordering, and directing its affairs.

But whether circumstances require any new laws to be enacted, or new regulations, in any respect, made, we willingly refer to the superior wisdom and conduct of the guardians of our common interest— I would, however, take the liberty to say, that the public good, the peace, and prosperity of this province, ought ever to lie near your hearts, and be kept in view, as the pole star, by which all your debates, and governmental acts, are to be directed.

And if you can do any thing more effectual, than has yet been done, to prevent the too general prevalence of vice, and immortality, and promote the knowledge and practice of religion and godliness among us, you will perform great good service for the public—you will, hereby, give us the highest reason to hope, and believe, that our infinitely good and gracious God, the tenor of whose providence, hath always, from the beginning, and [51] remarkably in the days of our New-England progenitors, been favorable to his people, in times of calamity and darkness, will make bare his arm, and deliver us from our public embarrassments—Righteousness exalteth a nation—but sin is the reproach, and if continued, will be the ruin of any people.

But if you can do no more for so excellent a purpose; let us, notwithstanding, for your own sakes, and for ours, be assured of the benefit of your example.

We are easily led by the example of our superiors, whom we respect and revere, and when it is turned on the side of religion and virtue, it cannot fail of happy influence into the religion of our minds, and the morality of our lives.

Did men of exalted stations and characters, consider how much it is in their power to reform or corrupt the age,—the lower ranks and classes of mankind, we might expect a conduct from them, that would teach us to connect the ideas of greatness and religion,—at least, more nearly than we too generally have done.

[52] We are therefore, willing to think, as we sincerely wish, that from a proper zeal for the divine glory, and a generous regard to their fellow men, our civil fathers will go before us in the uniform practice of pure religion, and undefiled, before God and the Father.

Under the administration of rulers of such a character, we shall not rejoice meerly in a civil view, but in the prosperity of our souls shall we be glad; and rejoice before God, exceedingly.

Before I close, I may not omit putting the whole body of this people in mind to be subject to principalities and powers, and to obey magistrates.

This is the direction given to Titus by the same Apostle, who in another Epistle has limited the obedience of subjects, to such rulers as answer the end of their appointment; the like limitation is therefore to be understood here—To such magistrates as rule well, who are a terror, not to good works, but to the evil, which is the reason St. Paul has assigned why subjects are obliged, in point of conscience, to submit to them—to such magistrates, I say, the most [53] chearful obedience is due from the people as being the greatest blessings society can enjoy—and to withhold obedience from such, is the greatest of crimes, as it directly tends to public confusion and ruin.

As a people we have ever been remarkably tender both of our civil and religious liberties; and 'tis hoped, the fervor of our regard for them, will not cool, till the sun shall be darkened, and the moon shall not give her light.

But justice to ourselves requires us to say, that we have been as remarkable for our steady, uniform submission to those who have had the rule over us.

If it should be affirmed that no instance of general complaint and uneasiness has been known among us from the settlement of our Fathers in America, but when our liberties have been evidently struck at, I believe, impartial history would support the sentiment.

If we have complained, we have had too manifest occasion for it; and all writers on government but those of a rank, arbitrary, popish complexion, allow of complaints, and remonstrances, and even [54] opposition to measures, in free governments, which the people know to be wrong; and indeed were not this the case, there would soon be no such governments on the earth.

The people in this province, and in the other colonies, love and revere civil government—they love peace and order but they are not willing to part with any of those rights and privileges, for which they have, in many respects, paid very dear.

The soil we tread on is our own, the heritage of our Fathers, who purchased it by fair bargain of the natives, unless I must except a part, which they afterwards in their own just defence, obtained by conquest—We have therefore an exclusive right to it.

For, how far soever discovery may operate, in acquiring a right in wild uninhabited countries; every one must allow it could acquire none in this inhabited, as it was, who is not willing to grant, that the natives of America would have acquired as good a right to Great-Britain or any part of Europe, if their navigation had been able, at the same time, to have wafted them in sight of it.

[55] But while we are disposed to assert our rights, and hold our liberties sacred, let us not decline from our former temper, and despise government; but may we always be ready to esteem and support it, in its truest dignity and majesty. Let us respect and honor our civil rulers, and as much as possible lighten their burdens by a cheerful obedience to their laws, without which the great end of government, the public safety and happiness, cannot be promoted.

Under the pressing, growing weight of our public troubles and difficulties our hearts, tho' perplexed, have not fainted—We wait for the salvation of God—It is better to trust in the Lord than to put confidence in princes—Let us go on to trust in him, 'till God himself shall rise to save us—Let us not divide and crumble into parties, on little irregularities, which, however aggravated by some, are, in our circumstances, almost unavoidable. But may we have that wisdom which is profitable to direct, and distinguish between what has, and what has not, a tendency to remove our burdens and prolong our just rights and liberties; especially, let us be on our guard against a spirit of licentiousness, [56] which is the reproach of true liberty, and has been the overthrow of free governments.

And by whatever titles and characters we may be distinguished, in the limited governments of this world, let us bear it on our hearts, that we are all subjects of the divine, universal government, which is administered in righteousness; and must shortly render an account of our conduct under it to God, the judge of all.

If this important consideration was duly impressed on the minds of all ranks and orders of men, it would lead us to acquire and cultivate the spirit of the gospel, which is a spirit of love and benevolence, and beget a conduct, which while it ripens us thro' grace for immortality and glory, would be greatly promotive of the present benefit of human society.—

And when, by the efficacious influence of the blessed spirit, our rational and immortal part is established in its just supremacy—when our appetites and passions are subject to its authority, and our desires regular, modest & just—Then shall our righteousness go forth as brightness, and our salvation as a lamp that burneth,

AMEN.

[25]

LEVI HART 1738–1808

---

*Liberty Described and Recommended: in a
Sermon Preached to the Corporation of Freemen
in Farmington*

HARTFORD, 1775

Levi Hart occupied the pulpit of a Congregational church in Preston, Connecticut, for forty-six years. He appears to have commanded a high regard for eloquence and good judgment, for an unusual number of his sermons were printed for wider distribution by the members of his congregation; however, few of them dealt with political subjects. In this one, Hart echoes the preoccupation of the time—the concept of liberty. Written to raise one more voice against slavery, Hart places his recommendation in a theoretical context that carefully refines the various definitions in use for the term at that time, and nicely summarizes the basic assumptions of American political theory that underlay not only the Revolution but also the state constitutions that were shortly to be written.

Though the author of the following discourse might avail himself of the common apology for publishing Sermons, viz The importunity of friends; yet he should have been averse to this publication had it not been that the subject and occasion gave him opportunity to cast in his mite for the relief of the opressed and injured Africans, whose cause he thought himself bound to plead, and to bear his testimony against the cruel and barbarous Slave Trade. He is sensible the arguments on that subject might be treated, more at large, and to better advantage; he designed to treat the subject only in a moral and religious view, and he could only hint a few thoughts on that branch of the argument, in a short discourse in which several other things were considered.

The author pretends not to pronounce on the impropriety of the Slave Trade in a political view—this would be out of his province: but he would submit to the gentleness of the law, whether the admission of slavery in a government so democratical as that of the colony of Connecticut, doth not tend to the subversion of its happy constitution. Be this as it may, if the Slave Trade is contrary to the law of nature, which is the law of God, it is more than time it was effectually prohibited, and until that is done we are accountable to God for all the sufferings which we bring upon the unhappy Negroes; for whatever difficulties there may be in the way of freeing the slaves already among us (as there are confessedly some) these cannot be reasonably advanced, against prohibiting the importation of more. Should it be objected [vi] that preaching and printing against the slave trade will tend to encourage servants in disobedience to their masters and support them in disorder and rebellion, the author can only reply, that though he is fully convinced that there is no more reason or justice in our enslaving the Africans than there would be in their enslaving us, yet he thinks the Negro slaves among us are bound by motives of duty and interest to "be obedient to their own masters," and to "shew all good fidelity" in their service, agreeable to apostolic direction, and as the most probable method to make their yoke less, and pave the way for obtaining their freedom, or, if not their own, that of their posterity.

He would be sorry to be, even the innocent, occasion of disorders in families, but should this be the case it is no sufficient objection against asserting the truth on this subject: there is, perhaps, scarce any doctrine of christianity but what hath been made the occasion of sin, through the perversness of wicked men, especially hath this been true of the doctrine of grace. Must the doctrines of grace therefore not be preached?

[7] II. PETER ii, 19.

> While they promise them Liberty, they themselves are the servants of corruption; for of whom a man is overcome, of the same is he brought into Bondage.

To assert and maintain the cause of Liberty, is far from being peculiar to the British colonies in North-America, at the present day: our venerable Ancestors fought and found it in this western world, and at no small expense of their treasure and blood, purchased it for, and conveyed it down to us. The most distinguished and worthy characters in Great-Britain have patronized, spoke and written, and some of them even died, in defence of the sacred rights of Liberty. [8] Those ancient, renowned States of Greece and Rome, in their most flourishing condition, received their greatest stature from a set of public spirited, patriotic men whose hearts glowed with the love of liberty, who were her defenders and supporters, and whose names and writings are venerable to distant ages and nations of men, even long after those mighty empires are gone to decay, and perished through neglecting to follow the maxims of those wise men, the patrons of liberty, who pointed out the path to lasting empire and glory.

Indeed, the sacred cause of liberty ever hath been, and ever will be venerable in every part of the world where knowledge and learning flourish, and men are suffered to think and speak for themselves. Yet, it must be added, that Heaven hath appeared in the cause of liberty, and that in the most open and decisive manner. For this, the Son of God was manifest in the flesh, that he might destroy the tyranny of sin and satan, assert and maintain the equal government of his Father, redeem the guilty slaves from their more than Egyptian bondage, and cause the oppressed to go free.

The whole plan of Redemption, which is by far the greatest and most noble of all the works of God made known to us, to which they all tend and in which they cease, is comprised in procuring, preaching and bestowing liberty to the captives, and the opening of the prison to the bound. And the gospel of our salvation is principally taken up in defending that glorious liberty which is prefaced forever by the Son of God—the bondage from which he redeems us—the ransom which he paid [9] for our redemption—the way to obtain and enjoy this Liberty, and in stating and urging the most cogent and endearing arguments, and motives, to persuade us to come out of our bondage, and accept of the Liberty wherewith Christ maketh his people free. It is on this account nominated *Gospel* of *Good News;* and is to the sinner, like the jubilee trumpet to the enslaved Israelite.

But it must be remembered, that in proportion as Liberty is excellent, and to be desired on the one hand, so slavery or bondage is terrible and to be avoided on the other. These are justly esteemed the two extremes of happiness and misery in Society. It will not therefore be thought foreign to our subject, or an unsuitable attempt upon the present occasion, to enquire into the various significations of these two opposite terms, as they are used in the several kinds of society with which we are concerned, especially as they are introduced in our text as opposed to each other, and it is intimated that the most fond assertors of liberty may after all, be themselves in a state of the most abject slavery and bondage.

Liberty may be defined in general, a *power of action,* or a certain suitableness or preparedness for exertion, and a freedom from force, or hindrance from any external cause. *Liberty* when predicated of man as a moral agent, and accountable creature, is that suitableness or preparedness to be the subject of volitions, or exercises of will, with reference to moral objects; by the influence of motives, which we find belongeth to all men of common capacity, and who are come to the years of understanding.

[10] This Liberty is opposed to that want of capacity, by which there is a total ignorance of all moral objects, and so, a natural incapacity of choosing with regard to them. *Again,* the term Liberty is frequently used to denote a power of *doing as we please,* or of executing our acts of choice; this refers principally to external action, or bodily motion; and is opposed to force or opposition:—thus the prisoner who is bound in fetters, and secured with bolts and bars in a prison, is not at liberty to go out, he is deprived of this kind of liberty, and is in bondage.

Again, Liberty may be considered and defined with reference to society:—Mankind in a state of nature, or considered as individuals, antecedent to the supposition of all social connections, are not the subjects of *this freedom,* but it is absolutely necessary to the well being of society.

Human society is founded originally in compact, or mutual agreement. All the larger circles of society originate from family connection or mutual compact between husband and wife, and mutual compact necessarily implieth certain rules and obligations which neither of the parties may violate with impunity.

In the early ages of the world, before vice and wickedness had corrupted and destroyed the original natural form of civil government, as a fine writer of our own nation expresseth it,—"each patriarch sat king, priest and prophet of his growing state"* But when the wickedness of man was become exceeding [11] great, and every

LEVI HART 1738–1808

imagination of his heart evil, *the earth was filled with violence:* by the daring efforts of wicked men to subvert the original excellent form of society, and introduce despotic rule where the lives and happiness of many, even whole kingdoms should depend on the will, and be subservient to the pleasure of one man.** But as a society evidently originates from mutual compact or agreement, so it is equally evident, that the members who compose it, unite in one common interest; each individual gives up all private interest that is not consistent with the general good, and interest of the whole body: And, considered as a member of society, he hath no other interest but that of the whole body, of which he is a member: The case is similar to that of a trading company, possessed of a common stock, into which every one hath given his proportion, the interest of this common stock is now the property of the whole body, and each individual is benefited in proportion to the good of the whole, and is a good or bad member in proportion as he uniteth to, or counteracteth the interest of the body. And thus it is in the present case: civil society is formed for the good of the whole body of which it is composed. Hence the welfare and prosperity of the society is the *common good,* and every individual is to seek and find his happiness in the welfare of the whole, and every thing to be transacted in society, is to be regulated by this standard.— In particular, all the laws and rules formed in such society must tend to promote the general welfare, this is the test by which they must be tried, and by which they must stand or fall; all regulations in the body, and all rewards and punishments [12] to individuals, must be determined agreeable to this.—Those who seek and promote the public interest, are to be esteemed and rewarded; and those who counteract and oppose it, must be punished in proportion to the injury aimed or committed against the public welfare.

We may add, that as the good of the public is the end and design of all good laws and rules, established in a well regulated society, so they must be enacted by the public, i.e. by the wisest and best men in the society, appointed by the body for this purpose.—Men who best understand the public good, and have a common interest with the body, and who are above the narrow pursuits of private interest.— If Laws and rules in society are established by any man, or body of

* Mr. Pope.
** Genesis vi, 4, 5, and x. 8, 9.

men, who have not a common interest with the whole body of the members, but the contrary, it is evident at first view, they will be exposed to act in opposition to the general good.—None therefore but the representatives of the whole body, in whom as far as possible, the interest of all ranks is contained, are proper to make laws for the regulation of society. For the same reason, those who are to execute the laws, should be appointed in such a manner, and by such authority, as in the best possible way secures their attachment to the general good: And, the members of civil community who are disobedient to *such laws* and oppose the administration of *such authority* agreeable to them, deserve punishment according to the degree of their opposition, and their opportunity to promote, or counteract the general good. The crime of every private member in opposing the interest of society, is greater [13] than that of opposition to the interest of an individual, as much (other things being equal) as the interest of the society is greater and of more worth than that of an individual.

In this view of our subject, we may form some conception of the crime of a civil ruler, who sacrificeth the public interest committed to his trust by society, for the sake of his own private gain;—who betrayeth that sacred deposit, to gratify his narrow, sordid thirst of wealth or honour:—We may form *some conceptions* of his crime, but we want words to paint the horror of it.—If a private man is without excuse, and is justly doomed to die as a traitor and rebel, when he deserts his country's cause, or basely betrays it, though to save his life, what epithets of lasting infamy are black enough to draw the picture of the inhuman paricide, who basks in the glare of riches and grandeur, at the expence of the public welfare: Yea, may we not depend that heaven itself will assert the cause of liberty, defend the injured innocent, and discharge its thunderbolts on the guilty head of the oppressor, red with uncommon wrath, to blast the man that owes his greatness to his country's ruin?

From this general view of society, we are led to observe, that civil liberty doth not consist in a freedom from all law and government,—but in a freedom from unjust law and tyrannical government:—In freedom, to act for the general good, without incurring the displeasure of the ruler or censure of the law:—And civil slavery or bondage consisteth in being obliged either by a bad set of laws, or bad and tyrannical rulers, to act in opposition to the good [14] of the whole, or suffer punishment for our steady attachment to the general good.

Religious liberty is the opportunity of professing and practising *that religion* which is agreeable to our judgment and consciences, without interruption or punishment from the civil magistrate. And religious bondage or slavery, is when we may not do this without incurring the penalty of laws, and being exposed to suffer in our persons or property.—

Ecclesiastical liberty, is such a state of order and regularity in christian society, as gives every member opportunity to fill up his place in acting for the general good of that great and holy society to which the true church of Christ belongs, and of which they are a part. And *ecclesiastical slavery,* is such a state as subjects some branches of this society to the will of others, (not to the good of the whole glorious kingdom) and punisheth them with the loss of some, or all of the priviledges of ecclesiastical society, if they disobey such tyrannical will, however they may act for the good of the whole, and so, agreeable to the law of Christ.

Finally, there is another kind of liberty and bondage, which deserve particular attention in this place, only as they are especially pointed to in our text, but as being of *principle* concern to men, they may be denominated *spiritual liberty and bondage:*—This liberty is spoken of by our Lord, John viii, 32, 36. Ye shall know the truth, and the truth shall make you free,—if the Son make you *free,* ye shall be *free* indeed. And, by the Apostle, Rom. vi, 18. Being then made *free* from sin, ye became the servants of righteousness. Gallat. v. 1. Stand fast in [15] the liberty wherewith Christ has made us free. 2. Gen. iii, 18. Where the spirit of the Lord is, there is *liberty.*

Spiritual liberty then, is freedom or readiness and engagedness of soul in the love and service of God and Christ, and discharge of the various branches of christian duty.

Spiritual bondage, takes place in the dominion of sin and satan in the soul, or that state of allienation from God and Christ, to which all impenitent sinners are subject.

This brief view of the various significations of the terms *liberty* and *slavery,* might be usefully improved in many inferences and remarks. I will detain you only with those which follow. Inference first.

If civil liberty consisteth in acting freely, and without constraint, or fear of punishment, for the public good, and tyranny and slavery are the reverse of this,—it followeth, that every one who acts for the general good of society, is entitled to the approbation and assistance of the body. None can justly fall under the frowns of society, but those who prefer some private benefit to the public welfare: And every society which suffers, or even *connives at* the practice, in any of its members, of taking away the liberty or property of those who have done nothing against the public interest, connives at injustice, and is so far guilty of tyranny and oppression.

[16] Of all the enjoyments of the present life that of liberty is the most precious and valuable, and a state of slavery the most gloomy to the generous mind—to enslave men, therefore, who have not forfeited their liberty, is a most attrocious violation of one of the first laws of nature, it is utterly inconsistent with the fundamental principle and chief bond of union by which society originally was, and all free societies ever ought to be formed. I mean that of a general union for the common good, by which every individual is secure of public approbation so long as he acts for the public welfare.

Could it be thought then that such a palpable violation of the law of nature, and of the fundamental principles of society, would be practised by individuals and connived at, and tolerated by the public in British America! this land of liberty where the spirit of freedom glows with such ardour.—Did not obstinate incontestible facts compel me, I could never believe that British Americans would be guilty of such a crime.—I mean that of the *horrible slave trade,* carried on by numbers and tolerated by authority in this country. It is not my design to enter largely into the arguments on this subject; all who agree to the general principles already laid down, will join in pronouncing the African *slave trade a flagrant violation of the law of nature, of the natural rights of mankind.* What have the unhappy Africans committed against the inhabitants of the British colonies and islands in the West Indies, to authorize us to seize them, or bribe them to seize one another, and transport them a thousand leagues into a strange land, and enslave them for life? For life did I say. From generation to generation to the end of time! However the cruel bondage is somewhat lightened [17] in these northern colonies, through the kindness and lenity of the masters—kindness and lenity, I mean as far as these terms are applicable in the present case; I say, however the cruel bondage of the poor Africans is somewhat lightened among us, if we would [ask] for a just estimate of the nature of the slave trade we must be acquainted with the method of procuring the slaves—transporting them, and their treatment in the West Indies, to which, and the southern colonies a great part of them are transported, and where the nature of the slave trade is *consistently* displayed.

When the Guinea traders arrive on that coast if the trading natives are not already supplied with a proper number of slaves, they go into the back settlements and either by secret ambush, or open force, seize a sufficient number for their purpose, in accomplishing which great numbers, many times are slain, and whole towns laid in ashes. When taken they are driven like cattle to the slaughter, to the sea shore, and sold to our Guinea traders, often for a small quantity of that soul and body destroying liquor, rum, qualified however with a large proportion of water, by which the ignorant natives are imposed upon, cheated, and disappointed.—The poor slaves are bound and thrust into the filthy holds of the ship—men, women, fathers, daughters, mothers, sons, without distinction; where they are obliged to *rot together* thro' a long sea passage, which happily relieves numbers from more intolerable sufferings on the shore.—

When they are arrived at the West Indies they are again *exposed* in the markets, and sold like beasts of burden to the inhuman planters, by whose cruelty many more of them perish. It is supposed that out [18] of near an hundred thousand which are computed to be transported from Africa annually, almost one third perish on the passage and in seasoning; and those unhappy numbers whose hard lot it is to be doomed to longer slavery, wear out their wretched lives in misery which wants a name. The Egyptian bondage was a state of liberty and ease compared with the condition of these unhappy sufferers; and for a trifling offence their barbarous masters will seize and butcher them, with as little, and in many instances, perhaps less ceremony or regret than you would take away the life of one of your domestic animals. It would be an affront to your understandings to enter on a long course of reasoning to prove the injustice and cruelty of such a trade as this. Let us for once put ourselves in the place of the unhappy Negroes. Suppose a number of ships arrived from Africa at a neighbouring sea port to purchase slaves, and transport them to that distant and to us inhospitable climate and those burning sands—put the case that a prevailing party in the neighbouring towns were so lost to all sense of public welfare and to the feelings of humanity as to accept their bribes and join with them to effect the ruin of their fellow men. Let *this* be the devoted town—and even now while you are met to assert and exercise that invaluable liberty which is the distinguished glory of Englishmen, the honour and safety of Connecticut; in this destined hour while your hearts glow with the love of liberty and exult in her possession, behold this house surrounded, whole armies from the neighbouring towns rush on you, those who resist are at once overpowered by numbers and butchered, the survivors, husbands, wives, parents, children, brethren, sisters, and ardent lover and his darling fair one, all seized, bound and driven away to the neighbouring [19] sea port, where all ranged on the shore promiscuously, in a manner that pity and modesty relent to name; you are sold for a trifling sum, and see your inhuman purchasers rejoicing in their success. But the time is come for a last farewell, you are destined to different ships bound to different and far distant coasts, go husbands and wives, give and receive the last embrace; parents bid a lasting adieu to your tender offspring. What can you say? What do to comfort or advise them? Their case and yours admit not of consolation—go, mothers, weep out your sorrows on the necks of your beloved daughters whom you have nursed with so much care, and educated with such delicacy; now they must go to a distant clime, to attend the nod of an imperious mistress, covered with rags and filth (if coverd at all) they must descend to the most servile and intolerable drudgery, and every the least symptom of uneasiness at their hard usage, meet the frowns and suffer the merciless lash of a cruel master.—But why ruminate on this; behold the inhuman monsters tear you from your last embrace, bound in chains you are hurried to different vessels, crouded in their holds and transported away forever from the sight of all you love, to distant cruel lands, to live and die in slavery and bondage, without the smallest hope of ever enjoying the sweets of liberty, or revisiting your dear native country, with this only consolation, that your sons and daughters are suffering the same cruel bondage, and that from you a race of abject slaves will, probably be propagated down for hundreds of years! *Such are the sweets of this beloved slave trade!* It is the same to the unhappy sufferers now, that it would be to us if it was our own case, and the reasons against it are as strong and powerful as they would be then—in short the man that can deliberately [20] attend to this subject and not feel the emotions of pity, or indignation, or both, appears to be sunk quite below the feelings of humanity. Is it not high time for this colony to wake up and put an effectual stop to the cruel business of stealing and selling our fellow men, so far as it can be stopped by one province?

With what a very ill grace can we plead for slavery when we are the tyrants, when we are engaged in one united struggle for the enjoyment of liberty; what inconsistence and self contradiction is this! Who can count us the true friends of liberty as long as we defend, or publicly connive at slavery.—

The general assembly of the neighbouring colony have prohibited the importation of Negro slaves under a large penalty, and have enacted that such slaves shall be free as soon as they set foot on the shore within the colony. Can this Colony want motives from reason, justice, religion, or public spirit, to follow the example? When, O when shall the happy day come, that Americans shall be consistently engaged in the cause of liberty, and a final end be put to the awful slavery of our fellow men? Then may we not expect that our liberties will be established on a lasting foundation and that British America and English liberty will flourish to the latest posterity!

Inference 2. If civil liberty consisteth in acting freely and without constraint or fear of punishment for the public good, and so, agreeable to the laws formed to promote and secure it, and civil bondage or slavery is the reverse of this. We learn the importance of intrusting those, and none but those, with [21] the guardianship of our civil liberties who are themselves free, who are not under the dominion of this sordid selfishness and narrowness of soul by which they will betray their country, our dear Colony for a little private profit or honor to themselves.

Men who know the worth of public liberty, and are able and willing defenders of it, be the consequences what they may to their private interest, are the only proper persons to be rulers or representatives of this free and happy colony. In such the votes of the freemen should unite, without the least regard to party, interest, or any private views, agreeable to the nature and solemnity of their oath, and as they value their inestimable liberties, and would dread to fall a helpless prey to tyranny and oppression.

Inference 3. If it is of such importance that we enjoy and secure civil liberty, which respects only a comparatively small circle of society which must disband, at the latest, with the close of fleeting time, at what moment is it to us all, that we are the subjects of that spiritual liberty, which unites us to, and interests us in the good of the whole kingdom of God our Saviour, and which shall last forever.

It is a just way of reasoning in the present case, from the less to the greater, let me say then, with what astonishment and abhorrence should we look on a person who chuses slavery and bondage under the most cruel tyrant, with the certain prospect of a shameful, painful death, by the hand of the executioner, rather than all the sweets of English liberty!

But with what an unspeakable greater madness is he chargable who prefers the guilty slavery of sin and [22] satan, to the glorious, perfect liberty of the children of God! Yet how many make this fatal choice! How many too, who are at great expence and trouble in the cause of civil liberty and zealous assertors of it! What self-contradiction and inconsistence is here! Is not this to strain out a gnat and swallow a cammel? What is English liberty? What is American freedom? When compared with the glorious liberty of the sons of God? And what is slavery under the gauling yoke of oppression, to the hard bondage of sin and satan! Let the hitherto, willing slaves of sin and satan then *rouse up,* there is now an opportunity to escape from bondage; there is one come to preach deliverance to the captives, and the opening the prison to them who are bound. Jesus Christ the mighty king and Saviour, the scourge of tyrants, and destroyer of sin and satan, the assertor, the giver and supporter of original, perfect freedom; he sets open your prison doors, knocks off your chains, and calls you to come forth. Oh! What a prisoner who will not leap for joy at the sound of this jubilee trumpet, accept the offered pardon, embrace the given freedom,—bid adieu to slavery and bondage, and stand fast in the liberty wherewith Christ makes his subjects free. Here the most perfect liberty may be enjoyed. The exalted king seeks and secures the public interest, to this all the branches of his good government and wise administration tend, and in this they center, for this joy which was set before him, he came into our nature and world, and even endured the cross and dispised the shame.—All the subjects in this happy kingdom are united in the same honourable cause, to them there is neither Barbarian, Scythian, Greek, or Jew, bond or free, they are all one, in one cause, and pursue it animated by one spirit; they feel how good [23] and pleasant it is for brethren to dwell together in unity.— In vain shall the tyrant satan vent his impotent rage against these happy *sons of liberty:* be wise in reason then, bid adieu to the kingdom of darkness, the cause of tyranny and oppression, inlist under the Captain of the Lords host, fight under his banner, you may be sure of victory, and liberty shall be your lasting reward, for whom the son maketh *free* shall be *free indeed.*

FINIS.

[26]

[ANONYMOUS]

An English Patriot's Creed, Anno Domini, 1775

BOSTON, 1776

Newspapers contained almost every literary form imaginable, and in this instance a legalistic political statement is put in a form similar to the Apostles' Creed. It appeared in the *Massachusetts Spy* on January 19, 1776. Written the previous year when many colonists were still taking pains to show their continued loyalty as Englishmen, it enunciates a radical English Whig position that contains within the argument justification for what is to come in America.

I believe the English Government, such as it appears to have been, from the most unquestioned annals of our country, to be a free constitution of a mixed and limited form; and that its origin is to be sought for, and lies, in the consent of the people.

I believe a King of England has not a claim to absolute, uncontrouled dominion; that if the English government, in its administration, has, at some seasons, been despotic, yet its genius hath at times been free; and that the liberty of the subject, founded upon established laws, was essential to every form under which it appeared.

I believe all political power to be derived originally from, and invested in the people; which power, I believe, they may dispose of, for their own use, in what hands, and under what conditions they please.

ANONYMOUS

I believe a current of liberty has been gradually widening, as well as purifying, in proportion to the distance from its source, a feudal institution; that charters and laws have removed every scruple that might now arise about the reciprocal rights and privileges of the King and his subjects.

I believe the feudal system and absolute dominion, two things perfectly incompatible.

I believe the claim of the Norman Invader to the crown was not conquest but testamentary succession; that he renounced his conquest by a coronation oath; and before he commenced tyrant, confirmed the use of the Saxon laws.

I believe regal power to have no divine right, but to be of human or popular institution; and that the present reigning family's title to the crown, is derived only from parliamentary resolutions, to which revolutional principles alone gave birth.

I believe passive obedience was not demanded even by Elizabeth or James; nor even acknowledged, by the people, as a matter of right.

I believe legal resistance and rebellion essentially different, and that they originate from quite opposite principles. By the law of nature, every man has a right to defend himself against the abuse of power, and by the singular constitution of this kingdom, when Kings and Ministers, break through the bounds prescribed by the laws, the people's right of resistance is unquestionable.

I believe what is called the English constitution to be that system of government which was first declared by the great charter of England; and after many struggles between the crown and its subjects, was established at the glorious revolution.

I believe I am bound to maintain the Protestant succession as established by law, in the present reigning family, and also to support the Catholic Church of England, so long as it continues united with the state; and therefore I will use my utmost endeavors to oppose the designs of Papists, and every pretender to the throne, as inveterate enemies to both.

I believe a Parliament to be a legislative body, instituted by the people at large with delegated power, intended as a balance between them and the Sovereign; and elected for the sole purposes of preserving their liberties, or defending their lives and estates.

I believe it is my duty to yield an implicit obedience to the laws of my country; that these are a standard of right for both Prince and subject; and that no Englishman ought to suffer in person or property, unless by the uncontrouled judgment of his Peers.

I believe I am under an indispensable obligation to have an eye, in all my pursuits and actions, to peace, safety, and good government; I will, therefore, under God, endeavor to maintain, at all times, true loyalty to my King, and an unfeigned affection to the Magistrate; proportioned to the wisdom and integrity, with which they guard public freedom, and promote national prosperity.

I believe I ought not, on any pretence, to surrender that invaluable liberty, which has been solemnly confirmed to me, by the great transactions of former days; nor to renounce that pure religion which my ancestors sealed with their blood; I will therefore be ready, at any moment, to risque my life in their defence; and so long as I intend fairly and honestly, I trust Almighty God will bless my public and private efforts to advance his glory and my nation's welfare.

[27]

[ANONYMOUS]

The Alarm: or, an Address to the People of
Pennsylvania on the Late Resolve of Congress

PHILADELPHIA, 1776

The Americans of the founding era were a highly politicized people. Even in the midst of their most serious crisis, every action was subject to debate. The Continental Congress had passed a resolution for the separate colonies to write new constitutions commensurate with their independent statehood. It had called upon the respective state legislatures to draft the constitutions, and in this essay the author argues that constitutions should not be written by legislatures but by special conventions elected for that purpose. While that has become common practice in the United States, few of the more than two dozen state constitutions adopted by 1800 were written by special conventions. The legislature tended also to adopt the new constitutions, and only twice before 1800 did a state *both* elect a special convention and submit the document to the people for adoption, the Massachusetts Constitution of 1780 being the first.

The long continued injuries and insults, which the Continent of America hath sustained from the cruel power of the British Court, and the disadvantages, which the several provinces in the mean time labour under from the want of a permanent form of government, by which they might in a proper constitutional manner of their own, afford protection to themselves, have at length risen to such an height, as to make it appear necessary to the Honourable Continental Congress to issue a Resolve, recommending it to the several Colonies to take up and establish new governments *"on the authority of the people,"* in lieu of those old ones which were established on the authority of the Crown.

This, Fellow Countrymen, is the situation we now stand in, and the matter for your immediate consideration, is simply this: Who are, or who are not, the proper persons to be entrusted with carrying the said Resolve into execution, in what is the most eligible mode of authorizing such persons? for unless they have the full authority of the people for the *especial* purpose, any government modelled by them will not stand.

Men of interested view and dangerous designs may tell you, *The House of Assembly:* But be not deceived by the tinkling of a name, for either such an House does not now exist, or if it does exist, it is by an unconstitutional power, for as the people have not *yet,* by any public act of theirs, transferred to them any new authority necessary to qualify them agreeable to the sense and expression of Congress, which says, "on the AUTHORITY of the PEOPLE," they consequently have none other than what is either immediately derived from, or conveyed to them in consequence of, the royal charter of our enemy, and this, saith the Honourable Congress, *"should be totally suppressed".* Wherefore, in compliance with this advice and recommendation of Congress, it is proposed to enter a public protest, in order to *suppress it,* for legislative bodies of men have no more the power of suppressing the authority they sit by, than they have of creating it, otherwise every legislative body would have the power of suppressing a constitution at will; it is an act which can only be *done to them,* but cannot be done *by them.* Were the present House of Assembly to be suffered by their own *act* to suppress the *old* authority derived from the Crown, they might afterwards suppress the *new* authority received from the people, and thus by continually making and unmaking themselves at pleasure, leave the people at last no right at all. The power from which the new authority is to be derived, is the only power which can properly suppress the old one. Thus, Fellow Countrymen, you are called upon by the standing law of nature and reason, and by the sense of the Honourable Congress, to assert your natural rights, by entering your protest against the authority of the present House of Assembly, in order that a new government, founded "on the authority of the people," may be established.

Until the authority of the Crown, by which the present House of Assembly sits, be suppressed, the House is not qualified to carry

ANONYMOUS

the Resolve of Congress, respecting a new government, into execution, and after the House is suppressed, it will be again disqualified, for the want of new authority, for in that case it will be no House at all: Wherefore, both before and after suppression, the present House of Assembly cannot be adequate to the purpose of establishing a new government.

[2] Besides, if a review of the past conduct of the House of Assembly be attended to, it will appear that they are a third time disqualified, in consequence of their own resolve. The unwise and impolitic instructions which they have arbitrarily imposed on the Delegates for this province, and confirmed at their last sitting, forbidding them in the strongest and most positive terms to consent to any change of government, should such be moved for in Congress, amount to a protest against the matter itself contained in the aforesaid resolve of Congress, and have even a reasonable tendency towards disolving the happy union of the colonies, for the Delegates, conceiving themselves bound by those instructions, sat as cyphers in Congress when the loud resolve was passed, declaring that they could not vote thereon, on which ground the term "Assemblies," mentioned in the said resolve of Congress, cannot be applied, as to the purpose of forming new governments, to the Pennsylvania House of Assembly, because it withdrew from the resolve by the neutrality of its Delegates, yet, altho' the Assembly is not included within the resolve itself, as to the exercise of new powers, it is included within the *Preamble* to the resolve, which, without regard to any distinct bodies of men, recommends generally that all the old powers of government be *totally suppressed,* and that new ones be erected on the "authority of the people." And thus far, and no farther, is the Pennsylvania House of Assembly within the sense both of the preamble and the resolve of Congress.

In this situation, what is to be done? The union of the Colonies is not only our glory, but our protection, and altho' the House of Assembly hath outwitted itself, it is no reason that the Province should: Wherefore, in order to restore ourselves to our former Continental rank, which we lost in Congress by not being represented in that resolve; and in order, likewise, that the people of this province may be put into a proper capacity of carrying the said resolve of Congress into execution, we must refer to the second term mentioned therein, viz. *Conventions*, for, even admitting that the present House of Assembly was a proper body, yet, the people may choose which they please, for both are mentioned.

The House of Assembly is a fourth time disqualified by not being sufficiently *wise* for such an important trust. If the aforesaid instructions to the Delegates be examined on the principles of sound reason and policy, they give a very indifferent character of the judgment and wisdom of the House, for, experience hath now taught us, and men of discernment did, at the time of first passing them, foresee that they were unsound in their policy, and would be hurtful in their effects. They are marked with the strongest characters of mischief and ignorance. Yet, they became a precedent to such other provinces as might be induced to believe that the Pennsylvania Assembly, by its central situation for intelligence, was possessed of some secret, which afforded grounds to expect a reconciliation, and under that delusion they likewise issued instructions to the same purpose; and thus, by circulating a false hope, the hands of power were relaxed, and a poisonous prudence was produced in our councils, at a time when a direct contrary spirit ought to have taken place, for if, instead of those instructions, a motion had been made for disclaiming all allegiance to the crown of Britain; and, had proper persons been immediately dispatched to Europe, to have cleared up the character of America from the aspersions which the British court would throw on her, as a pretence for obtaining foreign assistance, and had those persons been properly authorised to have negociated and ratified a treaty of friendship and commerce therewith, there is every reason to believe that we should not only have prevented Britain from obtaining foreign mercenaries, but that we should by this time have had the goods and manufactures of such countries in our stores, and thereby relieved this country from the present scarcity, and saved the poor from the enormous expence of purchasing goods at these present high prices. Thus hath a whole winter, when no molestation could happen to us, been lost and sacrificed thro' the ill policy and ill precedent of the present House of Assembly—Therefore it is no longer worthy of our confidence.

Fifthly—The obligation which the said House of Assembly is under by oaths of allegiance to our enemy again disqualifies them fully and effectually from framing a new government. The members of the said House took those oaths, not as members of the community at large, but as members of the House particularly: Therefore they can

ANONYMOUS

only be properly discharged therefrom by ceasing to act in this official character in which, and for which, they took those oaths, besides which, as the new elected members will not now [3] take the oaths, they cannot sit in Assembly with those who have; and those who have, cannot sit as a Convention with those who have not—Therefore the present House, in its present state, has not, nor can have, either the authority of an Assembly or Convention.

Sixthly—The undue influence and partial connextions which many members of the said House are biassed by, render them unfit persons to be trusted with powers to carry the late resolve of Congress into execution; and we have very alarming apprehensions, that a government, modelled by such persons, would be calculated to transfer the good people of this province, like live stock upon a farm, to the proprietaries of the soil. Lord and landlord were never yet united since the world began, and such a government would soon reduce us and our posterity to a state even of animal slavery. The most absolute monarch is supported by revenue *only* and not by revenue and rental both.

Fellow countrymen, it must occur with the fullest force of conviction to every honest, thinking man, that the persons delegated with proper powers to form a plan of government, ought to possess the entire confidence of the people. They should be men having no false bias from old prejudices, no interest distinct or separate from the body of the people; in short, they should be a very different sort of men to what many of the present House of Assembly are. They should be men, likewise, invested with powers to form a plan of government *only*, and not to execute it after it is framed; for nothing can be a greater violation of reason and natural rights, than for men to give authority to themselves: And on this ground, likewise, the House of Assembly is again disqualified.

We have, my Fellow Countrymen, been making shift long enough. It is now high time to come to some settled point, that we may call ourselves a people; for in the present unsettled state of things we are only a decent multitude. Yet, to the honour of this province, to the honour of all America, be it told, so long as the name of America remains, that by the common consent of Citizens, the public peace was preserved inviolate, for nearly three years, *without law*. Perhaps the only instance since the world began.

We are now arrived at a period from which we are to look forward as a *legal people.* The Resolve of Congress, grounded on the justest foundation, hath recommended it to us, to establish a regular plan of *legal government,* and the means which they have recommended for that purpose, are, either by Assemblies or *Conventions.* CONVENTIONS, my Fellow Countrymen, are the only proper bodies to form a Constitution, and Assemblies are the proper bodies to make Laws agreeable to that constitution.—This is a just distinction. Let us begin right, and there is no [fear] but, under the providence of God, we shall end well. When the tyrant James the Second, king of Britain, abdicated the government, that is, ran away therefrom, or rather, was driven away by the just indignation of the people, the situation of England was like what America is *now;* and in that state a Convention was chosen, to settle the new or reformed plan of government, before any Parliament could presume to sit; and this is what is distinguished in history by the name of the REVOLUTION.—Here, my Countrymen, is our precedent: A precedent which is worthy of imitation. We need no other—we can have no better. And this precedent is more particularly striking in our situation, because it was concerted between our virtuous ancestors, and the ancestors of those German inhabitants of this and other provinces, who are now incorporated with us in one common stock. Having then a noble precedent before us, let it be our wish to imitate it. The persons who recommend this, are Fellow Citizens with yourselves. They have no private views, no interest to establish for themselves. This aim, end and wish is the happiness of the Community. He who dares say otherwise, let him step forth, and prove it, for, conscious of the purity of our intentions, we challenge the world.

Our present condition may, to many persons, seem more embarrassing than it really is; while, to those who have truly reflected thereon, it appears, that the necessary steps to be taken, in order to extricate ourselves therefrom, and to arrive at a state of legal order, are simple, easy and regular: For the purpose of which, it is proposed, that the Committees of Inspection throughout the several Counties, agreeable to the power they are already invested with, do immediately call a Convention to take charge of the affairs of the province, for we cannot conceive how the House of Assembly can any longer presume to sit, without either breaking through the resolve of Congress, or assuming to themselves arbitrary power. And we do [4] farther propose, that this Convention, when met, so issue out summonses for electing by ballot (of all the freemen throughout the province, including those

Germans, or others, who were before disqualified for not having taken oaths of allegiance to our enemy, but are now restored to their natural rights by the late resolve of Congress for suppressing the taking those oaths) a GRAND PROVINCIAL CONVENTION, consisting at least of One Hundred members, of known and established reputation, for wisdom, virtue and impartiality, without regard to country or profession of religion; whose sole business, when met, shall be to agree upon, and settle a plan of government for this province, which shall secure to every separate inhabitant thereof perfect liberty of conscience, with every civil and legal right and privilege, so that all men, rich and poor, shall be protected in the possession of their peace, property and principles.—And what more can honest men say? We mean well, and under that conscious sanction we implore God and man to help us. The die of this day will cast the fate of posterity in this province. We can no longer confide in the House of Assembly; they have, by a feeble and intimidating prudence held us up as sacrifices to a bloody-minded enemy, they have thrown cold water on the necessary military proceedings of this province and continent, and have been abettors, together with their collegues, in procrastinating the expedition to Canada, which, by that *delay only,* may probably not now succeed.

It is time, and high time, to break off from such men, and to awaken from such unmanly drowsiness: And we have no fear, that as our cause is just, our God will support us against barbarous tyrants, foreign mercenaries, and American traitors.

Having thus clearly stated the case for your consideration, we leave you to the exercise of your own reason, to determine whether the present House of Assembly, under all the disqualification, inconsistencies, prejudices and private interests herein mentioned, is a proper body to be entrusted with the extensive powers necessary for forming or reforming a government agreeable to the Resolve and Recommendation of Congress. Or whether a Convention, chosen fairly and openly for that express purpose, consisting, as has been before mentioned, of at least One Hundred members, of known reputation for wisdom, virtue and impartiality, is not a far more probable, nay the only possible, method for securing the just Rights of the people, and posterity.

[28]

A NATIVE OF THIS COLONY

[CARTER BRAXTON 1736–1797]

*An Address to the Convention of the Colony
and Ancient Dominion of Virginia on the
Subject of Government in General, and
Recommending a Particular Form
to Their Attention*

VIRGINIA, 1776

Braxton was born in Virginia and attended the College of William and Mary. His father was a well-to-do planter and sometime member of the House of Burgesses. Carter Braxton himself served in the House of Burgesses from 1761 to 1775 where he was a leader of the conservative tidewater faction. Along with George Washington, Patrick Henry, Thomas Jefferson, and Peyton Randolph, he signed the Resolutions of 1769 which argued that the right to tax Virginians lay solely in Virginia. Braxton served in the revolutionary conventions of 1774, 1775, and 1776, signed the Declaration of Independence, served in the Continental Congress and then in the Virginia Assembly from 1776 until 1785. The title of this piece by Braxton accurately sums up its contents. Virginia was in the process of writing a state constitution to replace its colonial charter. Braxton rehearses the general principles of government that should underlie a constitution suitable for his state and then outlines specific institutions based upon those principles that he feels should be included in the document proper. While only one of a number of essays written in Virginia at the time, Braxton's is noteworthy for capturing the essential Virginia perspective in relatively few pages. The essay appeared in two parts, one each in the June 8 and June 15 editions of the *Virginia Gazette.*

A NATIVE OF THIS COLONY

GENTLEMEN,

When despotism had displayed her banners, and with unremitting ardour and fury scattered her engines of oppression through this wide extended continent, the virtuous opposition of the people to its progress relaxed the tone of government in almost every colony, and occasioned in many instances a total suspension of law. These inconveniencies, however, were natural, and the mode readily submitted to, as there was then reason to hope that justice would be done to our injured country; the same laws, executed under the same authority, soon regain their former use and lustre; and peace, raised on a permanent foundation, bless this our native land.

But since these hopes have hitherto proved delusive, and time, instead of bringing us relief, daily brings forth new proofs of British tyranny, and thereby separates us further from that reconciliation we so ardently wished; does it not become the duty of your, and every other Convention, to assume the reins of government, and no longer suffer the people to live without the benefit of law, and order the protection it affords? Anarchy and riot will follow a continuance of its suspension, and render the enjoyment of our liberties and future quiet at least very precarious.

Presuming that this object will, ere long, engage your attention, and fully persuaded that when it does it will be considered with all the candour and deliberation due to its importance, I have ventured to collect my sentiments on the subject, and in a friendly manner offer them to your consideration. Should they suggest any hints that may tend to improve or embellish the fabric you are about to erect, I shall deem myself happy in having contributed my might to the benefit of a people I esteem, and a country to which I owe every obligation.

Taking for granted, therefore, the necessity of instituting a government capable of affording all the blessings of which the most cruel attempts have been made to deprive us, the first inquiry will be, which of the various forms is best adapted to our situation, and will in every respect most probably answer our purpose.

Various are the opinions of men on this subject, and different are the plans proposed for your adoption. Prudence will direct you to examine them with a jealous eye, and weigh the pretensions of each with care, as well as impartiality. Your, and your children's welfare depends upon the choice. Let it therefore neither be marked by a blind attachment to ancient prejudices on the one hand, or a restless spirit of innovation on the other.

Although all writers agree in the object of government, and admit that it was designed to promote and secure the happiness of every member of society, yet their opinions, as to the systems most productive of this general benefit, have been extremely contradictory. As all these systems are said to move on separate and distinct principles, it may not be improper to analyse them, and by that means shew the manner of their operations.

Government is generally divided into two parts, its *mode or form of constitution,* and the *principle* intended to direct it.

The simple forms of government are despotism, monarchy, aristocracy, and democracy. Out of these an infinite variety of combinations may be deduced. The absolute unlimited controul of one man describes *despotism,* whereas *monarchy* compels the Sovereign to rule agreeable to certain fundamental laws. *Aristocracy* vests the sovereignty of a state in a few nobles, and *democracy* allows it to reside in the body of the people, and is thence called a popular government.

Each of these forms are actuated by different *principles.* The subjects of an unlimited despotic Prince, whose will is their only rule of conduct, are influenced by the principle of *fear.* In a monarchy limited by laws the people are insensibly led to the pursuit of *honour,* they feel an interest in the greatness of their Princes, and, inspired by a desire of glory, rank, and promotion, unite in giving strength and energy to the whole machine. Aristocracy and democracy claim for their principle *public virtue,* or a regard for the public good independent of private interest.

Let us inquire from which of these several [   ] we should take a cion to ingraft on our wild one, see which is most congenial to our soil, and by the extent and strength of its branches best calculated to shelter the people from the rage of those tempests which often darken the political hemisphere. I will not deny, whatever others may do, that individuals have enjoyed a certain degree of happiness under all these forms. Content, and consequently happiness, depend more on the state of our minds than external circumstances, and some men are satisfied with fewer enjoyments than others. Upon these occasions the inclinations of men, which are often regulated by what they have seen and experienced, ought to be consulted. It cannot be wise to draw them further from their former institutions than obvious reasons and necessity will justify. Should a form of government directly opposite to the ancient one, under which they have been happy, be introduced and established, will they not, on the least disgust, repine at the change, and be disposed even to acts of violence in order to regain their former condition. Many examples in the history of almost every country prove the truth of this remark.

What has been the government of Virginia, and in a revolution how is its spirit to be preserved, are important questions. The better to discuss these points, we should take a view of the constitution of England, because by that model our's was constructed, and under it we have enjoyed tranquillity and security. Our ancestors, the English, after contemplating the various forms of government, and experiencing, as well as perceiving, the defects of each, wisely refused to resign their liberties either to the single man, the few, or the many. They determine to make a compound of each the foundation of their government, and of the most valuable parts of them all to build a superstructure that should surpass all others, and bid defiance to time to injure, or any thing, except national degeneracy and corruption, to demolish.

In rearing this fabric, and connecting its parts, much time, blood, and treasure were expended. By the vigilance, perseverance, and activity of innumerable martyrs, the happy edifice was at length completed under the auspices of the renowned King William in the year 1688. They wisely united the hereditary succession of the Crown with the good behaviour of the Prince; they gave respect and stability to the legislature, by the independence of the Lords, and security, as well as importance to the people, by being parties with their Sovereign in every act of legislation. Here then our ancestors rested from their long and laborious pursuit, and saw many good days in the peaceable enjoyment of the fruit of their labours. Content with having provided against the ills which had befallen them, they seemed to have forgot, that although the seeds of destruction might be excluded from their constitution, they were, nevertheless, to be found in those by whom their affairs were administered.

Time, the improver, as well as destroyer, of all things, discovered to them, that the very man who had wrought their deliverance was capable of pursuing measures leading to their destruction. Much is it to be lamented, that this magnanimous Prince, ascending a throne beset with uncertainty and war, was induced, by the force of both, to invent and practise the art of *funding* to supply his wants, and create an interest that might support him in possession of his Crown. He succeeded to his wish, and thereby established a monied interest, which was followed by levying of taxes, by a host of tax-gatherers, and a long train of dependents on the Crown. The practice grew into system, till at length the Crown found means to break down those barriers which the constitution had assigned to each branch of the legislature, and effectively destroyed the independence of both Lords and Commons. These breaches, instead of being repaired as soon as discovered, were, by the supineness of the nation permitted to widen by daily practice, till, finally, the influence of the Crown pervaded and overwhelmed the whole people, and gave birth to the many calamities which we now bewail, and for the removal of which the united efforts of America are at this time exerted.

Men are prone to condemn the whole, because a part is objectionable; but certainly it would, in the present case, be more wise to consider, whether, if the constitution was brought back to its original state, and its present imperfections remedied, it would not afford more happiness than any other. If the independence of the Commons could be secured, and the dignity of the Lords preserved, how can a government be better formed for the preservation of freedom? And is there any thing more easy than this? If placemen and pensioners were excluded a seat in either House, and elections made triennial, what danger could be apprehended for prerogative? I have the best authority for asserting, that with these improvements, added to the suppression of boroughs, and giving the people an equal and adequate representation, England would have remained a land of liberty to the latest ages.

Judge of the *principle* of this constitution by the great effects it has produced. Their code of laws, the boast of Englishmen and of freedom; the rapid progress they have made in trade, in arts and sciences; the respect they commanded from their neighbours, then gaining the empire of the sea; are all powerful arguments of the wisdom of that constitution and government, which raised the people of that island to their late degree of greatness. But though I admire their perfections, I must mourn their faults; and though I would guard against, and cast off their oppression, yet would I retain all their wise maxims, and derive advantage from their mistakes and misfortunes. The testimony of the learned Montesquieu in favour of the English constitution is very respectable. "There is (says he) one nation in the world that has for the direct end of its constitution political liberty." Again he says, "It is not my business to examine whether the English actually enjoy this liberty or not; sufficient it is for my purpose to observe, that it is established by their laws, and I inquire no further."

This constitution, and these laws, have also been those of Virginia, and let it be remembered, that under them she flourished and was happy. The same principles which led the English to greatness animates us. To that principle our laws, our customs, and our manners, are adapted, and it would be perverting all order to oblige us, by a novel government, to give up our laws, our customs, and our manners.

However necessary it may be to shake off the authority of arbitrary British dictators, we ought, nevertheless, to adopt and perfect that system, which England has suffered to be grossly abused, and the experience of ages has taught us to venerate. This, like almost every thing else, is perhaps liable to objections, and probably the difficulty of adopting a limited monarchy will be largely insisted on. Admit this objection to have weight, and that we cannot in every instance assimulate a government to that, yet no good reason can be assigned why the same *principle*, or spirit, may not in a great measure be preserved. But, honourable as this spirit is, we daily see it calumniated by advocates for popular governments, and rendered obnoxious to all whom their artifices can influence or delude. The systems recommended to the colonies seem to accord with the temper of the times, and are fraught with all the tumult and riot incident to simple democracy; systems which many think it their interest to support, and without doubt will be industriously propagated among you. The best of these systems exist only in theory, and were never confirmed by the experience, even of those who recommend them. I flatter myself, therefore, that you will not quit a substance actually enjoyed, for a shadow or phantom, by which, instead of being benefited, many have been misled and perplexed.

Let us examine the principles they assign to their government, and try its merits by the unerring standard of truth. In a late pamphlet it is thus stated: The happiness of man, as well as his dignity, consists in virtue; *if there be a form of government, then, whose principle is virtue, will not every sober man acknowledge it better calculated to promote the general happiness of society than any other form.* Virtue is the principle of a republic, therefore a republic is the best form of government.

The author, with what design I know not, seems to have

cautiously blended *private* with *public* virtue, as if for the purpose of confounding the two, and thereby recommending his plan under the amiable appearance of courting *virtue*. It is well known that *private* and *public* virtue are materially different. The happiness and dignity of man I admit consists in the practice of *private* virtues, and to this he is stimulated by the rewards promised to such conduct. In this he acts for himself, and with a view of promoting his own particular welfare. *Public* virtue, on the other hand, means a disinterested attachment to the public good, exclusive and independent of all private and selfish interest, and which, though sometimes possessed by a few individuals, never characterised the mass of the people in any state. And this is said to be the principle of democratical governments, and to influence every subject of it to pursue such measures as conduce to the prosperity of the whole. A man, therefore, to qualify himself for a member of such a community, must divest himself of all interested motives, and engage in no pursuits which do not ultimately redound to the benefit of society. He must not, through ambition, desire to be great, because it would destroy that equality on which the security of the government depends; nor ought he to be rich, lest he be tempted to indulge himself in those luxuries, which, though lawful, are not expedient, and might occasion envy and emulation. Should a person deserve the esteem of his fellow citizens, and become popular, he must be neglected, if not banished, lest his growing influence disturb the equilibrium. It is remarkable, that neither the justice of Aristides, or the bravery of Themistocles, could shield them from the darts of envy and jealousy; nor are modern times without examples of the same kind.

To this species of government every thing that looks like elegance and refinement is inimical, however necessary to the introduction of manufactures, and the cultivation of arts and sciences. Hence, in some ancient republics, flowed those numberless sumptuary laws, which restrained men to plainness and similarity in dress and diet, and all the mischiefs which attend Agrarian laws, and unjust attempts to maintain their idol equality by an equal division of property.

Schemes like these may be practicable in countries so steril by nature as to afford a scanty supply of the necessaries, and none of the conveniences, of life; but they can never meet with a favourable reception from people who inhabit a country to which Providence has been more bountiful. They will always claim a right of using and enjoying the fruits of their honest industry, unrestrained by any ideal principles of government, and will gather estates for themselves and children without regarding the whimsical impropriety of being richer than their neighbours. These are rights which freemen will never consent to relinquish, and after fighting for deliverance from one species of tyranny, it would be unreasonable to expect they should tamely acquiesce under another.

The truth is, that men will not be poor from choice or compulsion, and these governments can exist only in countries where the people are so from necessity. In all others they have ceased almost as soon as erected, and in many instances been succeeded by despotism, and the arbitrary sway of some usurper, who had before perhaps gained the confidence of the people by eulogiums on liberty, and possessing no property of his own, by most disinterestedly opposing depredations on that of his neighbours.

The most considerable state in which the shadow of democracy exists (for it is far from being purely so) is that of the united provinces of Holland, &c. Their territories are confined within narrow limits, and the exports of their own produce very inconsiderable. Trade is the support of that people, and, however said to be considerable, will not admit of luxury. With the greatest parsimony and industry, they, as a people, can but barely support themselves, although individuals among them may amass estates. I own they have exhibited to mankind an example of perseverance and magnanimity that appeared like a prodigy. By the profits of their trade they maintained large armies, and supported a navy equal to the first in their day of warfare; but their military strength, as well as the form of their government, have long since given way. Their navy has dwindled into a few ships of war, and their government into an aristocracy, as unhappy and despotic as the one of which we complain.

The state of Venice, once a republic, is now governed by one of the worst of despotisms. In short, I do not recollect a single instance of a nation who supported this form of government for any length of time, or with any degree of greatness; which convinces me, as it has many others, that the principle contended for is ideal and a mere creature of a warm imagination.

[Continuation in the next issue, June 15, 1776]

One of the first staples of our country, you know, is esteemed by many to be one of the greatest luxuries in the world, and I fancy it will be no easy matter to draw you into measures that would exclude its culture and deprive you of the wealth resulting from its exportation.

That I may not tire your patience, I will now proceed to delineate the method in which I would distribute the powers of government, so as to devise the best code of laws, engage their due execution, and secure the liberties of the people. It is agreed by most writers on this subject, that this power should be divided into three parts, each independent of, but having connection with each other. Let the people, in the first place, choose their usual number of Representatives, and let this right return to them every third year.

Let these Representatives when convened, elect a Governor, to continue in authority during his good behavior, of which the two houses of Council of State and Assembly should jointly be the Judges, and by majority of voices supply any vacancy in that office, which may happen by dismission, death, or resignation.

Let the Representatives also choose out of the Colony at large, twenty-four proper persons to constitute a Council of State, who should form a distinct or intermediate branch of the legislature, and hold their places for life, in order that they might possess all the weight, stability and dignity due to the importance of their office. Upon the death or resignation of any of the members let the Assembly appoint another to succeed him.

Let no member of either house, except the Treasurer, hold a post of profit in the government.

Let the Governor have a Privy Council of seven to advise with, tho' they should not be members of either house.

Let the Judges of the Courts of Common Law and Chancery be appointed by the Governor, with the advice of his Privy Council, to hold their offices during their good behaviour, but should be excluded a seat in either house.

Let the Treasurer, Secretary, and other great officers of state be chosen by the lower house, and proper salaries assigned to them as well as to the Judges, &c. &c.

Let all military officers be appointed by the Governor, and all other inferior civil ones.

Let the different Courts appoint their own clerks. The Justices in each county should be paid for their services, and required to meet for the dispatch of business every three months. Let five of them be authorized to form a Court to hear and determine causes, and the others impowered to keep the peace, &c. &c.

A NATIVE OF THIS COLONY

These are the out lines of a government which should, I think, preserve the principle of our constitution, and secure the freedom and happiness of the people better than any other.

The Governor will have dignity to command necessary respect and authority, to enable him to execute the laws, without being deterred by the fear of giving offence, and yet be amenable to the other branches of the legislature for every violation of the rights of the people. If this great officer was exposed to the uncertain issue of frequent elections, he would be induced to relax and abate the vigorous execution of the laws whenever such conduct would increase his popularity. Should he, by discharging his duty with impartiality give offence to men of weight and influence, he would be liable to all the opposition, threats, and insults which resentment could suggest; and which few men in such a dependent state would have sufficient resolution to neglect and dispise. Hence it would follow, that the apprehensions of losing his election would frequently induce him to court the favour of the great, at the expense of the duties of his station and the public good. For these, and a variety of other reasons, this office should be held during good behaviour.

The Council of State who are to constitute the second branch of the legislature should be for life. They ought to be well informed of the policy and laws of other states, and therefore should be induced by the permanence of their appointment to devote their time to such studies as may best qualify them for that station. They will acquire firmness from their independency, and wisdom from their reflection and experience, and appropriate both to the good of the state. Upon any disagreement between the Governor and lower house, this body will mediate and adjust such difference, will investigate the propriety of laws, and often propose such as may be of public utility for the adoption of the legislature. Being secluded from offices of profit, they will not be seduced from their duty by pecuniary considerations.

The Representatives of the people will be under no temptation to swerve from the design of their institution by bribery or corruption; all lucrative posts being denied them. And should they on any occasion be influenced by improper motives, the short period of their duration will give their constituents an opportunity of depriving them of power to do injury. The Governor and the members of the Council of State, should be restrained from intermeddling farther in the elections of Representatives, than merely by giving their votes.

The internal government and police of the Colony being thus provided for, the next object of inquiry that presents itself is, how a superintending power over the whole Continent shall be raised, and with what powers invested. Such a power is confessed on all hands to be necessary, as well for the purpose of connecting the Colonies, as for the establishment of many general regulations to which the provincial legislatures will not be competent.

Let a Congress therefore be appointed, composed of members from each Colony in proportion to their number of souls; to convene at any place that may be agreed upon, as often as occasion may require. Let them have power to adjust disputes between Colonies, regulate the affairs of trade, war, peace, alliances, &c. but they should by no means have authority to interfere with the internal police or domestic concerns of any Colony, but confined strictly to such general regulations, as tho' necessary for the good of the whole, cannot be established by any other power.

But whether you settle the affairs of government in this, or any other manner, let me recommend to your serious attention the speedy adjustment of all disputes about the boundaries of your Colony, before they rise to such a height as to threaten great uneasiness and inquietude.

The claim of the Proprietors of Indiana on one side, and that of Kantuckee, on the other, should be fairly and impartially heard and determined, and notice given to the claimants to attend, that ample justice may be done. In the mean time, would it not be proper to give notice, that none of those lands should be sold or settled, until it was known to whom they appertain. The claims of the Indiana Company are stated in a pamphlet, (sent for your perusal) and patronized by the opinions of some eminent lawyers. But this should not prevent a strict and thorough investigation of the matter. Both claims, it is certain, cannot be good. If the treaty of Stanwix should be adjudged valid and the right given up to the country of Indiana, that same treaty will confirm to the Colony on the lands on this side the Ohio from its mouth, along the river, up to the Pennsylvania lands in the direction of the place called Kittaniny in that province. In which bounds are included the lands claimed and settled by Mr. Henderson.

Our colonial right to those lands being settled, would it not be proper to sell all such as may be unappropriated for the use of the Colony, and apply the monies to the payment of the vast burden of taxes we shall have to incur by this war? The sooner you determine this, the more effectually you will frustrate the design avowed by the author of a late pamphlet, of seizing all unappropriated lands for the use of the Continent; a design, in which, I own, I see as few traces of justice, as in many other of his schemes.

Having compleated the remarks I intended to make, I hope, whatever reception they may meet with, you will impute them to my zeal for our country's welfare; the only motive that ever shall induce me to offer my opinion or advice.

 I am,

  Gentlemen,

   With the greatest regard,

    Your devoted Friend,

     A NATIVE

[29]

DEMOPHILUS

[GEORGE BRYAN?]

The Genuine Principles of the Ancient Saxon, or English [,] Constitution

PHILADELPHIA, 1776

Amerian colonists had always viewed themselves as more virtuous, more manly, than their fellow Englishmen back home, and they also viewed themselves as being freer because they possessed to a greater degree the pristine English political institutions. Put in terms of the day, Americans often viewed themselves as carrying on the Saxon yeoman tradition of self-rule by rough equals. The link with a supposed golden age of freedom before the Norman invasion was a popular theme and can be found in the piece by Richard Bland, for instance, but the connection with the supposed Saxon past is made in most full blown form in this essay by Demophilus. Several historians identify Demophilus as the radical Whig George Bryan, who, along with James Cannon and Timothy Matlack, was prominent in writing the 1776 Pennsylvania Constitution, the most radical constitution of its era. He also served in the legislature where he was a prominent figure in state politics. Regardless, this essay is a masterpiece of rhetoric. It manages to lay out a coherent and radical position and, at the same time, appeals effectively to American identification with yeoman virtues, which lends this position legitimacy.

———

Introduction.

As, by the tyranny of GEORGE the Third, the compact of allegiance and protection between him and the good people of this Colony is totally dissolved, and the whole power of government is by that means returned to the people at large; it is become absolutely necessary to

DEMOPHILUS

have this power collected and again reposed in such hands as may be judged most likely to employ it for the common good.

In most states, men have been too careless in the delegation of their governmental power; and not only disposed of it in a very improper manner, but suffered it to continue so long in the same hands, that the *deputies* have, like the King and Lords of Great-Britain, at length become possessors in their own right; and instead of *public servants,* are in fact the *masters* of the public. Our new Republics should use the utmost caution to avoid those fatal errors; and be supremely careful in placing that dangerous power of controlling the actions of individuals, in such a manner that it may not counteract the end for which it was established.

Government may be considered, a *deposite* of the power of society in certain hands, whose business it is to *restrain,* and in some cases to take off such members of the community as disturb the quiet and destroy the security of the honest and peaceable subject. *This government is founded in the nature of man, and is the obvious end of civil society;* "yet such is the thirst of power [4] in most men, that they will sacrifice heaven and earth to wrest it from its foundation; to establish a power in themselves to tyrannize over the persons and properties of others." To prevent this, let every article of the constitution or *sett of fundamental rules* by which even the supreme power of the state shall be governed, be formed by a convention of the delegates of the people, appointed for that express purpose: which constitution shall neither be added to, diminished from, nor altered in any respect by any power besides the power which first framed it. By this means an effectual bar will be opposed to those enterprizing spirits, who have told us with much assurance, that after the people had made their annual or septennial *offering,* they had no more to do with government than their cattle.

A Convention being soon to sit in PHILADELPHIA; I have thought it my duty to collect some sentiments from a certain very scarce book, entitled an Historical Essay on the English Constitution, and publish them, with whatever improving observations our different circumstances may suggest, for the perusal of the gentlemen concerned in the arduous task of framing a constitution.

"That beautiful system, formed, (as Montesquieu says,) in the German woods, was introduced into England about the year four hundred and fifty." The peculiar excellence of this system consisted in its incorporating small parcels of the people into little communities by themselves. These petty states, *held parliaments often;* for whatever concerned them in common, they met together and debated in common; and after [5] due consideration of the matter, they called a vote, and decided the question, by a majority of voices. In these councils every man had a voice, who had a residence of his own in the tithing, (or township) and paid his tax and performed his share of the public duties. This salutary institution, our honorable Conference of Committees has again revived at their late sitting.

To avoid the tumult, which always must attend the hearing and determining civil and criminal cases, by a popular tribunal, they had their executive courts in every township; and still kept the legislative and executive departments separate, in all cases whatsoever.

Among these people we find the origin of the inestimable trial by juries; and I am much mistaken if our present Justices of the Peace, may not also trace their derivation from the same salubrious source.* However that may be, one thing is certain, that "they founded their government on the common rights of mankind. They made the elective power of the people the first principle of the constitution, and delegated that power to such men as they could best confide in. But they were curiously cautious in that respect, knowing well the degenerating principles of mankind; that power makes a vast difference in the temper and behaviour of men, and often converts a good man in private life to a tyrant in office. For this reason they never gave up their natural liberty or delegated their power for making laws, to any man for a longer time than one year."

"The object upon which our elective power acts is remarkably different from that of the Romans. [6] Theirs was directed to operate in the election of their chief officers, and particularly their consuls; or those who were vested with the executive authority whom they changed annually. But the senate where the principal power in their state was lodged, was a more fixed body of men; and not subject to the elective power of the people."

"Our Saxon forefathers almost reversed this principle; for they made their wittenagemot or parliament, where the principal power was lodged, annually moveable and entirely subject to the elective power of the people; and gave a more fixed state to the executive authority. This last they continued within a certain sphere of action,

* The ancient *Conservatores,* were to all valuable purposes *Justices* of the Peace.

prescribed by law; so that it could not operate to the injury of any individual, either in his person or property; and was controllable in all acts of state, by the elective power which they vested annually in their wittenagemot, or parliament."

"The annual exercise of the elective power, was the quintessence, the life and soul of the constitution; and the basis of the whole fabric of their government, from the internal police of the minutest part of the country, to the administration of the government of the whole kingdom. This Saxon institution, formed a perfect model of government; where the natural rights of mankind were preserved, in their full exercise, pure and perfect, as far as the nature of society will admit of."

"It would be something very surprizing to find the people of England continually disputing about the principles and powers, vested in the constitutent parts of their government; did we not [7] know that at this day it consists of a mixture of the old, or first establishment, and that which took place at (and since) what is commonly called the conquest, by William the First. These two forms of government, the first founded upon the principles of liberty, and the latter upon the principles of slavery, it is no wonder they are continually at war, one with the other. For the first is grounded upon the natural rights of mankind, in the constant annual exercise of their elective power, and the latter upon the despotic rule of one man. Hence our disputants, drawing their arguments from two principles, widely different, must of course differ in their conclusions."

"Our Saxon forefathers established their government in Britain, before the transactions of mankind were recorded in writing; at least among the northern nations. They therefore handed down to posterity, the principles of their government, by the actual exercise of their rights; which became the ancient usage and custom of the people, and the law of the land. And hence it came to pass, that when this ancient custom and usage ceased to act, the remembrance of the custom ceased with it. We may add to this, that, since the conquest, our arbitrary kings and men of arbitrary principles, have endeavored to destroy the few remaining records, and historical facts that might keep in remembrance a form of government so kind, friendly and hospitable to the human species. It is for these reasons that we have such a scarcity of historical evidence, concerning the principles and manner

PHILADELPHIA, 1776

of conducting the first establishment of our mode of government in this kingdom."

[8] "However, notwithstanding these difficulties, there are many customs, forms, principles and doctrines, that have been handed down to us by tradition; which will serve as so many landmarks, to guide our steps to the foundation of this ancient structure, which, is only buried under the rubbish collected by time, and new establishments. *Whatever is of Saxon establishment is truly constitutional; but whatever is Norman, is heterogeneous to it, and partakes of a tyrannical Spirit."*

"From these sources it is, that I would endeavor to draw the outlines of this ancient model of government, established in this kingdom by our Saxon forefathers; where it continued to grow and flourish, for six hundred years; 'till it was overwhelmed and destroyed by William the First, commonly called the Conqueror, and lay buried under a load of tyranny for one hundred and forty seven years. When it arose again, like a phoenix from its own ashes in the reign of Henry the Third, by the assistance of many concurrent causes, but principally by the bravery of the English people, under the conduct and intrepidity of our ancient and immortal barons, who restored it, in part, once more to this Isle. And tho' much impaired, maimed, and disfigured, it has stood the admiration of many ages; and still remains *the most noble and ancient monument of Gothic antiquity."*

It was indeed restored in an impaired condition; as a free constitution must necessarily be, when attempted to be introduced among a people, distinguished by the odious difference of condition of Lord and Vassal.

[9]   The English Constitution

The first establishment of our CONSTITUTION, *by the* SAXONS, *to what is commonly called the* NORMAN CONQUEST, *under the* HEPTARCHY.

"The first principle of a government that is founded on the natural rights of mankind is the principle of annual election. Liberty and election are in this case synonimous terms; *for where there is no election there can be no liberty.* And therefore the preservation of this elective power, in its full extent, is the preservation of liberty in its fullest extent: and where that is restrained in any degree, liberty is restrained in just the same proportion; and where that is destroyed by any power in a state, whether military or civil, liberty is also destroyed by that power, whether it be lodged in the hands of one man, one hundred or one thousand."

"It is reported by historians that our Saxon forefathers had no kings in their own country, but lived in tribes or small communities, governed by laws of their own making, and magistrates of their own electing; and further, that a number of these communities were united together for their mutual defence and protection. But by what particular bond of union they were united, I know of no historian, that hath given us any information. There were seven tribes of Saxons, that arrived in Britain about the same [10] time, under so many different leaders; but as they had all the same intentions so far as to establish the same form of government, I shall consider them in this respect indiscriminately."

"They first divided the land into small parts, and that divided the inhabitants upon that land, and made them a distinct and separate people from any other. This division they called a tithing. Here they established a government, which was, no doubt the same as that under which they lived in their Mother-Country. They had two sorts of tithings, one called a town tithing, and the other called a rural tithing. These were governed upon the same principles, only thus distinguished; as one is expressive of a town having such a number of inhabitants as to make a tithing of itself; and the other of a tithing situated in the rural part of the kingdom. Thus they went on, as they conquered the country, to divide the land, till they had cut out the whole kingdom into tithings, and established the same form of government in each."

"In this manner they provided for the internal police of the whole country, which they vested in the respective tithings, who annually elected the magistrates that were to administer justice to them, agreeable to the laws and customs they had brought with them from their Mother-Country. And this internal police was so excellent in its nature, that it hath had the encomiums of most authors of our history."

"They had a legislative authority in every tithing, which made laws and regulations for the good government of the tithing. Besides [11] these, they had a court of law, whose jurisdiction was confined to the same limits. All which were created by the elective power of the people, who were resident inhabitants of the tithing; and the right of election, was placed in every man who paid his shot and bore his lot. From hence we may easily perceive, that, under the establishment of these tithings, by reason of their smallness, the natural rights of mankind might very well be preserved in their power by election without any confusion or inconvenience to the inhabitants."

"THE first connexion the tithings had with one another, was to form an establishment for the military defence of the country. For this end a number of these tithings were united together, so far as related to their military concerns. This union necessarily created a larger division of the land, equal to the number of tithings that were thus united; and this they called a wapentake or weapontake, and might take in as many tithings as would make a Brigade under a Brigadier General. Here likewise they established a court of council and a court of law, which last was called a wapentake court. In the court of council the chief magistrates of every tithing assembled to elect officers of the militia to their respective command, and regulate all matters relating to the militia; in which, every individual tithing was concerned. The court of law was to enforce these regulations within the jurisdiction."

"Let us now consider the third and last division, which they made of the land. This was composed of a certain number of wapentakes, [12] united together; which they called a shire or one complete share or part into which they divided the land. This division completed their system of internal police; by uniting all the tithings within the shire into one body, subject to such laws and regulations as should be made in their shiregemots or shire parliaments; for the benefit and good government of the shire."

"As this division comprehended many tithings and many people, so it had the greatest court of council in England except the high court of parliament; and the chief officer was vested with as high jurisdiction in the shire, as the king in the kingdom."

"They had likewise a court of law, called the shire court; to which, I make no doubt every man might appeal who thought himself injured by the inferior courts in the shire. These divisions in the land, are what I call the skeleton of the constitution which was animated and put in motion by all these establishments."

"We may consider each shire as a complete government; furnished with both a civil and a military power within its own jurisdiction."

"Let us now see by what mode of union, these shires became united together into a kingdom: and it will be found, I apprehend, that they pursued the same principles, which they had used in every other establishment. That is to say, wherever a combined interest was concerned and the people at large were affected by it, the immediate deputies of the people, met together to attend the respective interests of their constituents, and a majority of voices always bound the [13] whole, and determined for any measure, that was supposed to operate for the good of the whole combined body. This meeting of the deputies of the people, was called by the Saxons the wittenagemote, or assembly of the wise men of the nation; which composed their national council and legislative authority."

The English Constitution

Under the Monarchy

"I have already remarked that a number of the Saxon tribes, while in their own country, were united together for their mutual protection and defence. In like manner was our Heptarchy connected; and their mode of union became a part of the constitution, when the seven kingdoms united together under one king. The matter was simply this: one of the seven kings was always chosen generalissimo over the whole body; and they appointed him a standing council of a certain number of deputies, from each state, without whose advice and concurrence, it is probable he could not act."

"However I do not mean to make any observation upon the powers vested in this standing council; but only to point out that body of men as the origin of our house of lords. Those deputies who composed this great standing council, were appointed to their trust by the joint [14] consent of the king and parliament of the little kingdom from whence they were sent. And when Alfred the great, united the seven kingdoms into one, he undoubtedly, with the approbation of the people, incorporated this great council as a separate branch of the wittenagemote or parliament; so that they still continued to be the king's great council, and a branch of the legislative authority, which they are at this day. In confirmation of which, it is observable, that the consent of the parliament continued necessary for creating a baron of the realm about as low down as Henry the Seventh; which is the only title by which any man can obtain his seat in our House of Lords; and not as Duke, Marquis, Earl, Viscount, &c."

"It is needless to mention that after the union of the seven kingdoms under Alfred, a reduction of the members to serve in parliament became absolutely necessary, because it was then impracticable, by reason of their numbers, for the same members to attend, in one parliament, that used to attend in seven, without such anarchy and confusion as must counteract the end of their meeting."

"Nature herself has confined, or limited the number of men in all societies, that meet together to inform and be informed, by argument and debate, within the natural powers of hearing and speech. So that the question in this case must have been how to reduce the representatives of the people in parliament, to be a convenient number, to transact the business of the nation; and at the same time, to preserve the elective power of the people [15] unhurt? a question of no small difficulty to determine, considering the various interests that were affected by it." *And how was this effected?*

Our historian informs us; "they excluded from this parliament, all the representatives of the rural tithings, as being a body of men the most numerous of any, considered collectively, and yet elected by the fewest people in proportion, which, must be very evident, since the rural part of the kingdom must be more thinly inhabited than the towns. Besides the town tithings or boroughs, where a great number of inhabitants are collected together, upon a small compass of ground, were undoubtedly, the most conveniently situated, for the commodious exercise of the elective power of the people. And the towns, being few in comparison of the rural tithings, and at the same time dispersed over the whole country, were best adapted to receive the regulations they intended to make in their plan of forming the constituent parts of the new parliament."

"Tho' the barons of the realm being great freeholders, carried into parliament the greatest concern for the interest of the rural part of the kingdom; yet not being elective, they were not such a body of men as the constitution, and the safety of the inhabitants of the rural tithings required. And therefore, they constituted shire elections, for two members, to represent the shire in parliament, and those representatives were the origin of our knights of the shire."

"The barons of the realm, and the knights of the shires, I consider as two bodies of men that [16] were substituted, at the establishment of the monarchy, under Alfred the Great, in place of those representatives that used to serve under the Heptarchy for the rural tithings.

DEMOPHILUS

The alteration that was made with respect to the towns and boroughs was simply this: that all boroughs that used to send one member to the little parliament, to which they belonged, under the Heptarchy, should for the future send two to the great parliament of England."

From the above concise view of the Saxon affairs, it is plain, that in their own country, and for many years after they settled in England, they maintained that natural, wise and equal government, which has deservedly obtained the admiration of every civilized age and country. In their small republics, they often met in council upon their common concerns; and being all equally interested in every question that could be moved in their meetings, they must of course be drawn in to consider, and offer their sentiments of many occasions. It is from the prevalence of this custom among the savages, that they have been enabled to astonish our great lawyers, judges and governors, commissioned to treat with them, by displays of their sublime policy. By Alfred's constitution, all occasions for exercising these talents were cut off from the body of the people: the making and amending of laws, being in a manner entirely referred to that great deliverer and his sublime council, whose wisdom and honesty were implicitly confided in by the whole nation; and at the same time distributive justice, was so uprightly administred by his commissioners [17] of the peace, the men fell into a political stupor, and have never, to this day, thoroughly awakened, to a sense of the necessity there is, to watch over both legislative and executive departments in the state. If they have now and then opened their eyes, it is only to survey, with silent indignation, a state from whence they despair of being able to recover themselves. Fixed establishments on the one hand, rooted habits and prejudices on the other, are not easily got over. Power, like wealth, draws many admirers to its possessor: and tho' all men will confess, that, without a check, it is dangerous in any community, they often flatter themselves, that the *rising* Augustus, having smiled upon them, in his early adventures, they (*in particular*) have nothing to fear from him, and therefore will not oppose him.*

This Colony, having now but one order of freemen in it; and to the honor of Pennsylvania, but very few slaves, it will need but little argument to convince the bulk of an understanding people, that this

---

* For an example of such fatal policy, read the history of the famed Marcus Tullius Cicero.

ancient and justly admired pattern, the old Saxon form of government, will be the best model, that human wisdom, improved by experience, has left them to copy.

To effect which,

Let the first care of our approaching Convention be to incorporate every society of a convenient extent into a Township, which shall be a body politic and corporate by itself, having [18] power of electing annually by ballot a town-clerk to record all the public proceedings of the township, town council &c.—to draw up, sign, and issue warrants by order of the town-council for calling two meetings, and transact all such public business as the laws of the colony shall point out as his duty.—A town council consisting of five or seven respectable men, the major part of whom shall be a quorum, invested with full power to manage the affairs and interest of the town; and to order warrants to be issued for calling annual town meetings on such days as shall be stated for that purpose, by law, and occasionally, on the petition of ten or more freemen of the town, setting forth the cause of the requested meeting.—A town treasurer—a town sealer of weights and measures—assessors—collectors—overseers of the poor—con-stables—pound keeper—sealer of leather—surveyors of highways—fence viewers—gaugers—and all such other officers as have been or may be found necessary and shall be instituted by the present or any future convention appointed to amend the constitution of this colony.

Approaching that gulph, where all former projectors have found their systems shipwrecked, I shall, with becoming diffidence, propose a method of conducting elections, which I presume will be found a considerable improvement upon Harrington's plan.

After seating all the qualified electors in pews or squares by themselves, let them be numbered, and a box handed round to receive nomination tickets for the officers to be chosen. These [19] tickets being sorted and numbered, let the clerk enter the names of the proposed candidates; beginning with his, who has the highest number of tickets; and thus proceed 'till all are entered. Where there are ties, let one ticket of each be taken and shaken in a hat, to be drawn out in fair lot and registered. Then in this order let the name or names, being first read over distinctly, be proposed by the Moderator, and balloted for by the bean; and if the first name fails of a majority of yeas, let the next in course be put, 'till the choice is made.

To render this mode of voting as fair and convenient as possible, let beans, or balls of opposite colors, be wrapped in small pellets of the same sort of paper, and one of each sort served to every voter. By opening the paper a little, the elector sees the color; returns the paper to its former condition, and drops which he pleases in the bag, first holding it up between his thumb and finger, that the collector may see there is but one; by proceeding in this manner, a corrupt influence can hardly be exercised; which cannot be said of the common custom of balloting. Besides very little writing is needfull: and when the whole meeting is told that white is yea and black nay, every one is alike knowing in the exercise of his elective power, without having occasion to recur to any man for advice or assistance.

For the first election of a governor, deputy-governor, secretary &c. it may be well for the Convention, to send out a nomination to the respective towns or districts; as the persent urgency [20] of public affairs requires that no time be lost 'till an established government be erected.

For the future, *as all debates will undoubtedly be held in public,* the consideration of warlike matters being best managed by Committees, the body of the people will soon become acquainted with the true characters of the delegates, and will continue or withdraw their confidence accordingly.

The judges of the supreme judicatory should be nominated by the Governor and executive council, and balloted for by the Assembly.

The *Conservatores,* or justices of the peace should, according to ancient custom be again elected by the districts; and to carry the salutary practice throughout, the justices thus chosen, should, soon after their election, meet at the county town, and ballot for the judges of the county court, the clerk and *solicitor* for the peace, in the county.*

All judiciary officers should have moderate salaries; and that they might be encouraged to apply their minds to gain a thorough knowledge of their important business, they should have in their commissions, an estate for life, provided they did not forfeit it by misbehaviour.

Judges of the probate of wills, registers of conveyances, deputy-coroners, and officers of such importance to the people, should be established in every convenient district; it being a great hardship, for people in narrow circumstances, to [21] travel far, to have business of so pressing a nature performed for them.

---

* This I conceive the proper title of the officer lately called King's Attorney.

Sheriffs, coroners, county treasurers, and all such county officers, can be elected no other way, with so much convenience, as to ballot by ticket, in each district, and to send the tickets to the townsmen of the shire-town by a sworn officer, under the seals of the respective moderators, where the votes are taken. And should the tickets, when sorted and numbered, fail to afford any one name, balloted for, a clear majority of votes, that is, that one half, more by one vote, for some certain person, than all the rest; the bench of justices for the whole county being for that purpose summoned by the clerk of that township, should meet, and for that year, supply the place of the officer, thus failing of appointment, by nomination and ballot as before described.

A standing grand jury, conducing much to the peace and good order of society, twenty four members for each county should be annually chosen, in the respective districts, as the representatives; having proper regard to the proportion belonging to each district, to serve for the whole year, and watch over the behaviour of the people.

Traverse juries, should be drawn from a box, furnished annually, with the names of all nonexempt freeholders, written each fairly on a ticket, shaken together, and taken by lot.

Jurors serving one year, should be exempt the two following.

Notwithstanding it may be difficult to [22] find men properly qualified to sustain every office proposed to be established in each district; yet the electors should be supremely careful, never to heap offices or indeed confer more than one on the same person. No governor, counsellor, representative, sheriff, coroner, attorney at law, or clerk of the peace should ever be a justice of the peace. Neither, should any one in the executive departments, civil or military, have a seat in the legislature.

Salaries and fees ought to be *competent*: that able men may not be deterred from accepting them, nor covetous men conceive them a bait. The latter condition of salaries has been the evident ruin of England; while those Commonwealths who have preserved a strict economy in that respect, continue happy and flourishing.

"If we were to select the attributes of good government, we should find them to consist in *wisdom* and *justice*. And if we could divide those virtues, from all bad qualities, in men, and place such men, and such only, to rule over us, we should establish an heaven upon earth. The power of election which our government hath diffused thro' the whole nation, will always produce this happy effect, when left to operate according to its genuine principles. For by dividing the country into small parts, as our tithings were, the character of every man, that was fit to bear an office, was well known amongst his neighbours. And therefore, when the choice of an officer to preside over them was their object of election, the concurrent sentiments of an uninfluenced majority, of a multitude of people, would [23] naturally fall upon those men only, who were most eminent for their wisdom and justice."

The best constructed civil government that ever was devised, having but a poor chance for duration, unless it be defended by arms, against external force as well as internal conspiracies of bad men, it will be the next concern of the convention, to put the colony militia on the most respectable footing.

The Militia is the natural support of a government, *founded on the authority of the people only.*

And to render both the people and the government, perfectly free from any jealousy of each other, it seems proper that the associators should have the choice of all officers immediately commanding them, inclusive of their respective captains—that deputations from a convenient number of companies, consisting both of officers and privates, should ballot for their field officers, and that the legislature should appoint every general officer.

And at length, to come to that dangerous, but necessary engine of state, *a standing army*, whose operations must be conducted with all possible secrecy and dispatch; and for that reason, must be entrusted in few hands; I would propose that a committee of three gentlemen be chosen by joint ballot of the governor, council, and assembly, to be called the committee of war; and to have the conducting of all military affairs, under the direction of the governor and privy council, to whom in matters of great importance, they should always have recourse: but being competent in lesser matters, business would be less [24] subject to delay. This committee being the joint choice of the whole legislature, and by them removeable annually, or at any time, on conviction of misbehaviour, would have a sufficient confidence placed in them, and yet no power that might become dangerous to the liberty of the people.

While all kinds of governmental power reverts annually to the people, there can be little danger of their liberty. Because no maxim was ever more true than that, WHERE ANNUAL ELECTION ENDS, SLAVERY BEGINS.

Having, in as brief and particular a manner as I was able, in the very short time allotted me, deduced the general outlines of a free government from the purest fountain yet known to man; it may not be uninteresting to give a short extract of the history of

The destruction of the Saxon mode of government by a combination of the clergy with William the bastard, duke of Normandy.

Before I proceed to observe the destruction that was made in the constitution, or mode of government, by the fatal union of the church with William of Normandy, I must not forget to take notice, that I have not given the clergy a place, in the Saxon parliaments; because they were foreign to the original institution, and only grafted themselves upon it, after it was established in England. But as they afterwards obtained a considerable share, both in the legislative authority and the administration of government, it may not be amiss to give some account how they came by it.

[25] "The Roman Pontiff had already extended his plan of church power to a great degree; and the nature of the government introduced into Europe, by the northern nations, greatly contributed to his success. All history is full of the dreadful consequences, that have attended the baleful influence, which every religious hierarchy hath always had upon the bulk of mankind. And a government founded upon the elective power of the people, where their favor was the high road to riches, power and grandeur, gave a fine opportunity to such an artful designing set of men by their intrigues and influence, to procure themselves or their devotees to be elected into the chief magistracy of the country divisions. By this means they possessed themselves, in a great measure of the legislative authority; and consequently became, in proportion, the masters of the state. For whoever is master of the legislative authority in any state, is undoubtedly master of that state.

"Having thus taken possession, as it were of the mansion, they were not long before they began to plunder it. However they first established, and secured the power of the church, by a variety of laws, made in her favor; and defended them by every ecclesiastical establishment, that papal cunning could invent. So that they were now prepared to receive, in the name of the church, all the riches, honors and power, which they could by any means obtain. And what is more, they knew too how to keep them when they had obtained them. For according to their maxim, whatever was given to the church, was given to God, and therefore was never [26] afterwards subject to be taken away by any earthly power whatever."

"Thus they endeavored to provide against all revolutions in the state, that the property of the clergy might be safe, under the name of the church. Upon this ground, the clergy have grafted themselves upon every state in Europe. And as they are plants that will grow in any soil, they have taken such deep root, that scarce any state, except Holland, has been so unfriendly to their vegetation, as to exclude them from having some share in government; though they have no more business with ours, as a separate body of men, than the company of apothecaries or parish clerks."

"The church continually acquiring riches and power, and never discharging either, it must follow that the clergy would, in a short time, be the richest and most powerful body in any state where they were thus established. Such was the situation of this kingdom, at the death of Edward the confessor; when England may be said to be governed by the power, and influence of the clergy. And we shall see, presently, how these shepherds betrayed their flocks, and surrendered them to the Norman tyranny."

"Under all tyranny, whether of kings, or priests, or both, it is the people who are to be made the sacrifice; it is the people who are to be plundered of their property; it is the people who are to wear the yoke of slavery; it is they who are to be made the hewers of wood and drawers of water. But so long as the English government continued upon the original principles, [27] upon which it was founded; and the people annually exercised their elective power; so long it was out of the power, either of the king or the clergy to commit any acts of violence, with impunity."

"Indeed the clergy might recommend, and the people might consent to many things, that were wrong, and even ruinous in their consequences; yet the latter had always in their own hands, a correcting remedy for all their errors. It was this correcting power in the people, that hung, like a millstone, over the pride, and riches of the clergy; and made them apprehensive that, at some time or other, it would crush them to pieces; and put an end to all their schemes of authority riches and grandeur."

"The parliament in the reign of Edward the confessor, had given such a specimen of their correcting power, as was enough to shake the foundation of the papal chair; and that was by banishing Robert, Archbishop of Canterbury, as an incendiary and fomentor of divisions, between the king and his subjects, and appointing one Stigand, Archbishop in his room. By this they saw there was only one way to avoid the danger, and preserve and extend their tyranny over the people; and that was to destroy the elective power, and establish an arbitrary government in the state. This, they were so bold as to attempt, and so happy as to see effected by William the Bastard duke of Normandy; who in the year one thousand and sixty six, put an end to the Saxon mode of government, which [28] had subsisted six hundred years from its first establishment."

What is commonly called the conquest by William the first.

"We are now come to that period of the English history, which contaminated the purity of the English constitution, or mode of government, with a despotic spirit, which time has not been able totally to eradicate."

"After the death of Edward the confessor, there were two candidates for the crown of England, which had always been elective, and continued so to this last Saxon king. The one was Harold, an Englishman of great natural abilities, much merit, and vastly beloved by the people; who had been elected chief magistrate of three shires, Kent, Sussex and Surry, at the death of his father earl Goodwin, who before him had held the same offices."

"The other was William the bastard duke of Normandy, who was a man of a warlike genius and a very powerful prince, whose dominions being situated opposite to our coast, rendered it more convenient for him, than for any other prince, to transport an army into England, and consequently to enslave the nation. For which reason no one who was a friend to his country, would ever think of electing a man, who would be so notoriously dangerous to it's laws, liberty and constitution."

"Indeed the dangerous consequence of his election was so apparent, that, tho' the clergy had marked William for their man, yet they could not hinder the choice of Harold; and therefore [29] he was elected king of England, by the wittenagemot or parliament; and was accordingly crowned next day by the Archbishop of York."

DEMOPHILUS

"The Pope, and William, finding themselves frustrated in all their previous intrigues and secret cabals, in obtaining the crown of England, for the latter, were resolved to obtain it by open force: but the states of Normandy having refused the duke an aid of money for the undertaking, he was obliged to have recourse to some other means for assistance. The pope, therefore, was now obliged to pull off the mask, and declare openly against England, and make a crusading business of it; which, was done with a view to encourage individuals to engage in the enterprize. And that all men might see that William was the champion of the church, he first made the duke a present of a consecrated standard, with a golden *agnus dei*, and one of Saint Peter's hairs; and then solemnly excommunicated every man that should oppose him."

"The duke on his part offered the lands of England as a prize to be fought for, and to be divided amongst all those that should assist him in the conquest; by which means he engaged not only great numbers of his own subjects, but many of his neighbours to assist him. Thus the duke of Normandy was enabled to fit out a fleet and an army, with which he invaded England; and, on the 14th of October 1066, was fought the ever memorable battle of Hastings, in which the English army was routed, and king Harold slain; which flung the whole nation into confusion, [30] and soon after procured the crown of England to William."

"Morcar and Edwin, two brave officers who distinguished themselves all that day in battle, retired in the night, with the broken remains of the army to London; in hopes to recover the people from their fright and consternation, and to apply some remedy to so pressing an evil. Historians observe, that, in all probability, they would have succeeded, if the treacherous behaviour of the clergy in London had not broken all their measures, by secretly caballing amongst the people. These two officers, and some others who were zealous friends to the liberty of their country, assembled the people; and represented to them, that the first thing to be done was to come out of that state of anarchy and confusion they were in, and immediately elect some person to the chief command. That Edgar Atheling was upon the spot, and one of the family of their ancient kings; and that no man could have any just objection against his advancement to the throne. That as soon as he should be proclaimed king, he would send orders to all parts of the kingdom to levy troops, and that the duke of

Normandy should soon find to his cost, that the gaining a single battle was not sufficient to render him master of the kingdom. And to spirit up the people the more to action, they put them in mind how they had defended their country, inch by inch against the Danes, for a great many years; and had at last drove them out of the kingdom; and that there was no doubt but they would do the same by this new invader."

[31] "The clergy knew that this was the critical moment, and that if they could but keep things a little longer in confusion, their business was done, and therefore they openly opposed every proposal of resistance. The declaration of the pope in favor of William was sufficient to induce all the clergy, then in London, with the two archbishops at their head, to cabal amongst the people in order to hinder Edgar's election; which it so effectually did, that Morcar and Edwin seeing every proposal overruled, and dispairing of success, retired into the north to take their own measures."

"They were no sooner gone, than the archbishop of Canterbury, the archbishop of York, the bishop of Winchester, and the clergy about London, and some say prince Edgar himself (by their persuasion) went to the duke at Berkhamstead and swore fealty to him; as if he had been already their lawful sovereign. Hence we may justly say, that the lives, liberty, and property of the people of England, were surrendered into the hands of the Normans, by the baneful interest of the clergy. For the city of London, following the example of the clergy, surrendered, afterwards the whole kingdom, without any further resistance."

"Thus William the first obtained the crown of England by the favor of the clergy, and not by the power of the sword, as, they would seem to intimate, by his surname the conqueror. A name imposed upon him after his death, by the clergy, in order to screen the infamy of their own actions from posterity, that future generations [32] might ascribe, the miserable state of the people, to the conquest of William, and not to the dark treachery of a body of men, who had, under the mask of religion, abused every trust of the confidence reposed in them; and betrayed their flocks, bound hand and foot, like sheep to the slaughter."

"From this time, civil and religious tyranny, walked hand in hand, two monsters till then unknown in England; which are, equally, the common enemies to mankind, and have at all times, united against every principle of civil and religious liberty. This is the true origin of the alliance between church and state, so much contended for by some of our ecclesiastics; who have renounced the penances of popery, but would fain retain both its pride and its power."

And on the proceedings of Charles the first's parliament, in the expulsion of the bishops, the same author observes,

"That it was their duty, as law makers, to remove from parliament, a body of men who had, constitutionally, no right there; and who had invariably, directed their whole influence, against every principle of civil and religious liberty; and were now particularly dangerous to the state."

"It is undoubtedly the most absurd and pernicious principle, that ever was received into any society of men, to permit the clergy *of any denomination,* to have the least distant share, or influence, upon the legislative authority of any nation. And had the motives of the house of Commons, for excluding the bishops from the [33] house of Lords been as good as their motion, they would have done this kingdom a most essential piece of service; but their intent was only to pull down one nusance, in order to establish another almost as bad. Their business, as lawmakers, was to protect every man in his right of private judgment, in point of religion; and not suffer any set of men to dictate to others in a matter that merely subsists between God and a man's own soul."

——"Had they destroyed all ecclesiastical power, they had destroyed an evil in the state, and abundant matter of vexation. Had they protected all men alike, in their different modes of worshiping God, they would have taken away all just occasion of offence and established peace amongst men."

Nothing can be more evident, than the mischief that has ever followed the requisition of a declaration of faith in doctrines acknowledged to be above human comprehension, as a qualification for any civil trust.

To believe that God is, and a rewarder according to our works; is the firm foundation of natural and revealed religion; and tho' he deigned to inform Moses, I AM, we find him pleased, at that time, to make no further discovery of himself. Neither are we hitherto convinced, that any, *by searching, have found him out to greater perfection.*

What is here, faithfully quoted or modestly suggested, is intended to give no offence to any man, or body of men existing. In matters wherein all are concerned, it is the duty of all to give notice of any thing they conceive [34] might be hurtful to the public, if suffered to pass without examination. It is a time when all the sagacity and diligence, all the temper and moderation of this vast Continent, is necessary to separate the *precious* from the *vile.*

We are happy that such plain and salutary paths have been marked out before us. Whatever rubbish has been thrown into them, should be carefully removed, that, like *wisdom's ways,* they may be *pleasant,* and conduct us to a secure and virtuous PEACE.

Men entrusted with the formation of civil constitutions, should remember they are *painting for eternity:* that the smallest defect or redundancy in the system they frame may prove the destruction of millions.

Above all things, the greatest care should be taken, that the persons who grant the public money, and should of course have the power of enquiring into its disposal, should have no hand in contracts; or any connection with persons thro' whose hands the public treasure passes. A house of commons should indeed be the guardians of common right, and the interest of the public. Places, pensions and other emoluments, from the public treasury having, for near a century past, been open to British commoners, their power of bringing peculators to account, has been of no use to the oppressed people. They have indeed united with them, and formed such powerful factions as have bid defiance to the whole nation. By this means, the legislative and executive authority, which our wise and virtuous ancestors, carefully kept asunder, are become confounded [35] together, in the hands of the same men. This has principally arisen from another fatal inattention of the people to the usurpations of their deputies, when they took upon them to alter the first principle of the constitution by acts of parliament.

"Upon this foundation, they may mould it into what shape they please; and in the end make us slaves by law. The house of commons are constituted, a body of men, merely passive, with regard to their creation, duration, and dissolution; and therefore have no consent to give to their own duration, even for an hour."

"There cannot be a more dangerous doctrine adopted in a state, than to admit that the legislative authority has a right to alter the constitution."

DEMOPHILUS

This shrewd observation needs little to be said in proof of it. For as the constitution limits the authority of the legislature, if the legislature can alter the constitution, they can give themselves what bounds they please.

It is therefore, I beg leave to repeat, that after the approaching Convention has met, and settled the grand outlines of a constitution, let the legislature go on with the affairs of government, without sensible deviation from the obvious meaning of their digest; and whatever inconveniences may be found unprovided for, may be candidly advertised to the public, and amended by another Convention.

[36]   *The powers of the several parts of the* LEGISLATURE

The respective powers of the several branches of the Legislature come next into consideration. And it must be confessed, that on this question I find the greatest difference of opinion among the really wise and learned, of any pertaining to our system. Some talk of having two councils, one legislative, and the other executive: some of a small executive council only; which should have nothing to do with framing the laws. Some would have the Governor, an integral part of the legislature: others, only president of the council with a casting vote.

The latter opinion appears to me most consonant to the intentions of wise framers of Governments. The Governor should have a seat in some part of the Legislature, that he might be fully acquainted with the necessity and reasons for passing any bill into a law, and on the other hand, to prevent any one person from possessing too much, or a dangerous power, he should have no more than a casting vote when necessary.

Some are strenuous for only one legislative body namely, the house of representatives: but a council will be found necessary for the following reasons.

An Act, ever so well intended, and in appearance ever so well framed to promote the public good, will notwithstanding, throw the society into confusion, if it can be made appear that it is founded on principles which will not bear examination.

The persons selected to compose a council, [37] are of course always supposed to have a superior degree of acquaintance with the history, laws, and manners of mankind; and by that means they will be more likely to foresee the mischievous consequences, that might follow a proceeding, which at first view did not appear to have any thing dangerous in it, to many honest men, who may however, be very worthy of a seat in the house of representatives.

For on no circumstance does the public peace and prosperity more immediately depend, than on the clearness, fullness and consistency of the laws.

The Governor should be furnished with a small privy council, to afford him their advice and assistance in the executive department; but they should have no share whatever in the Legislature.

In this capacity they should take cognizance of high crimes; such as mal-administration of Judges in their offices; being the proper inquest for this purpose—The Assembly and Legislative Council, in like manner to enquire into the conduct of the Governor and privy council, and the cause of complaint being found, a regular trial by the country should determine all causes whatever.

A Council, annually eligible, will endeavor to maintain their seats by the rectitude of their conduct.

To suppose they can *inveterate* themselves, is to suppose that mankind will forget the mischiefs which have overspread the world from the days of Sylla to the present bloody period, from the same tyrannic source.

We should make all prudent provision for posterity, and indeed the most salutary provision we can possibly make for them, is to enable [38] them to provide for themselves; but we ought never to run into one extreme to avoid another.

The last important measure I would propose, is, that, whereas the heat of war in our very neighbourhood, may well be supposed to agitate the minds of the delegates in convention, and render it impossible to have every provision made for the security of our liberties, that cool and continued reflexion would suggest, after the principal parts of the constitution are established, an adjournment might be made to a convenient day; and mean while every man might be invited to give his sentiments freely and discreetly upon any part of the system he might conceive could be altered for the better.

Probably a decennial meeting of delegates, to examine the state of the constitution, and conduct of the government, would not be an imprudent provision for keeping the constitution in health and vigor, by having an opportunity to see that it did not depart from its first principles. This would be effectually holding the supreme power in its *only* safe repository *the hands of* THE PEOPLE.

CONCLUSION

[39] The last and greatest security that men can have for a permanent enjoyment of their rights, is to learn, what they are from their very elements, as they are well explained by Burlamaqui and others; and besides, to learn the art of defending them with their arms.

I, alike discommend a heedless inattention to the concerns of our country and posterity; and a despairing anxiety, grounded on a supposition, that if some particular matters are not settled in just such particular manners, that all will be lost irrecoverably.

This is a day of cool and impartial enquiry. Adversity sobers our spirits and causes us to give each other a patient hearing. We learn from our troubles that each man needs the advice and assistance of his neighbour: and perhaps this is not the most trivial lesson.

The varying circumstances of our situation, have gradually pointed out arrangements already which no man could have foreseen some months ago: those successive improvements which will thence arise, and the advantage of such a communication of sentiments as will accrue from the establishment of frequent town meetings among the people, will give such a new face to the affairs of this colony, and raise up so many able men to improve its internal police; that as arts and manufactures have already made it their peculiar, or at least principal residence, so we [40] trust in God that the principal science that ever rendered mankind happy and glorious, the science of *just* and *equal* government, will shine conspicuous in Pennsylvania.

The events which have given birth to this mighty revolution; and will vindicate the provisions that shall be wisely made against our ever again relapsing into a state of bondage and misery, cannot be better set forth than in the following Declaration of

AMERICAN INDEPENDENCE.

[41]   IN CONGRESS, JULY 4, 1776.

A DECLARATION BY THE REPRESENTATIVES OF THE UNITED
STATES OF AMERICA, IN GENERAL CONGRESS ASSEMBLED.

When in the course of human Events, it becomes necessary for one
people to dissolve the Political Bands which have connected them
with another, and to assume among the Powers of the Earth, the
separate and equal Station to which the Laws of Nature and of Nature's
God entitle them, a decent Respect to the Opinions of Mankind
requires, that they should declare the causes, which impel them to
the Separation.

    We hold these Truths to be self-evident, that all Men are created
equal, that they are endowed by their Creator with certain unalienable
Rights, that among these are Life, Liberty, and the Pursuit of
Happiness—That to secure these Rights, Governments are instituted
among Men, deriving their just Powers from the Consent of the
Governed, that whenever any Form of Government becomes destructive
of these Ends, it is the Right of the People to alter or to abolish it,
and to institute new Government, laying its foundation on such
principles, and organizing its powers in such form, as to them shall
seem most likely to effect their safety and happiness. Prudence, indeed,
will dictate that governments long established should not be changed
for light and transient causes; and accordingly all experience hath [42]
shewn, that mankind are more disposed to suffer, while evils are
sufferable, than to right themselves by abolishing the forms to which
they are accustomed. But when a long train of abuses and usurpations,
pursuing invariably the same object, evinces a design to reduce them
under absolute despotism, it is their right, it is their duty, to throw
off such government, and to provide new guards for their future
security. Such has been the patient sufferance of these colonies, and
such is now the necessity which constrains them to alter their former
systems of government. The history of the present King of Great
Britain is a history of repeated injuries and usurpations, all having in
direct object the establishment of an absolute tyranny over these states.
To prove this, let facts be submitted to a candid world.

    He has refused his assent to laws, the most wholesome and
necessary for the public good.

    He has forbidden his Governors to pass laws of immediate and pressing importance, unless suspended in their operation till his assent should be obtained; and, when so suspended, he has utterly neglected to attend to them.

He has refused to pass other laws for the accomodation of large districts of people, unless those people would relinquish the right of representation in the legislature, a right inestimable to them, and formidable to tyrants only.

He has called together legislative bodies at places unusual, uncomfortable, and distant from the depository of their public records, for the sole purpose of fatiguing them into compliance with his measures.

[43] HE has dissolved Representative Houses repeatedly, for opposing with manly firmness his invasions on the Rights of the people.

He has refused for a long time, after such dissolutions, to cause others to be elected; whereby the legislative powers, incapable of annihilation, have returned to the people at large for their exercise; the state remaining in the mean time exposed to all the dangers of invasion from without, and convulsions within.

He has endeavoured to prevent the population of these states; for that purpose obstructing the laws for naturalization of foreigners; refusing to pass others to encourage their migrations hither, and raising the conditions of new appropriations of lands.

He has obstructed the administration of justice, by refusing his assent to laws for establishing judiciary powers.

He has made Judges dependent on his will alone, for the tenure of their offices, and the amount and payment of their salaries.

He has erected a multitude of new offices, and sent hither swarms of officers to harrass our people, and eat out their substance.

He has kept among us, in times of peace, standing armies, without the consent of our legislatures.

He has affected to render the military independent of, and superior to the civil power.

He has combined with others to subject us to a jurisdiction foreign to our constitution, and unacknowledged by our laws; giving his assent to their acts of pretended legislation:

[44] For quartering large bodies of armed troops among us:

For protecting them, by a mock trial, from punishment for any murders which they should commit on the inhabitants of these states:

For cutting off our trade with all parts of the world:

For imposing taxes on us without our consent:

For depriving us, in many cases, of the benefits of trial by jury:

For transporting us beyond seas to be tried for pretended offences:

For abolishing the free system of English laws in a neighbouring province, establishing therein an arbitrary government, and enlarging its boundaries, so as to render it at once an example and fit instrument for introducing the same absolute rule into these Colonies:

For taking away our charters, abolishing our most valuable laws, and altering fundamentally the forms of our governments:

For suspending our own legislatures, and declaring themselves invested with power to legislate for us in all cases whatsoever.

He has abdicated government here, by declaring us out of his protection and waging war against us.

He has plundered our seas, ravaged our coasts, burnt our towns, and destroyed the lives of our people.

He is, at this time, transporting large armies of foreign mercenaries to compleat the works of death, desolation, and tyranny, already begun with circumstances of cruelty and perfidy scarcely [45] paralleled in the most barbarous ages, and totally unworthy the head of a civilized nation.

He has constrained our fellow Citizens taken captive on the high seas to bear arms against their country, to become the executioners of their friends and brethren, or to fall themselves by their hands.

He has excited domestic insurrections amongst us, and has endeavoured to bring on the inhabitants of our frontiers, the merciless Indian savages, whose known rule of warfare, is an undistinguished destruction, of all ages, sexes and conditions.

In every stage of these oppressions we have petitioned for redress in the most humble terms: Our repeated petitions have been answered only by repeated injury. A prince, whose character is thus marked by every act which may define a tyrant, is unfit to be the ruler of a free people.

Nor have we been wanting in attentions to our British brethren. We have warned them from time to time of attempts by their legislature to extend an unwarrantable jurisdiction over us. We have reminded them of the circumstances of our emigration and settlement here. We have appealed to their native justice and magnanimity, and we have conjured them by the ties of our common kindred to disavow

DEMOPHILUS

these usurpations, which, would inevitably interrupt our connexions and correspondence. They too have been deaf to the voice of justice and of consanguinity. We must, therefore, acquiesce in the necessity, which denounces our separation, and hold them, as we hold the rest of mankind, enemies in war, in peace, friends.

[46] We, therefore, the Representatives of the UNITED STATES OF AMERICA in GENERAL CONGRESS, assembled, appealing, to the Supreme Judge of the world for the rectitude of our intentions, do, in the name, and by authority of the good people of these colonies, solemnly publish and declare, that these United Colonies are, and of Right ought to be, FREE AND INDEPENDENT STATES; that they are absolved from all allegiance to the British Crown, and that all political connexion between them and the state of Great Britain is and ought to be totally dissolved; and that, as FREE and INDEPENDENT STATES, they have full power to levy war, conclude peace, contract alliances, establish commerce, and to do all other acts and things which INDEPENDENT STATES may of right do. And for the support of this declaration, with a firm reliance on the protection of Divine Providence, we mutually pledge to each other our lives, our fortunes, and our sacred honor.

Signed by ORDER and in behalf of the CONGRESS,

JOHN HANCOCK, President.

Attest.   CHARLES THOMPSON, Sec.

[30]

[ANONYMOUS]

Four Letters on Interesting Subjects

PHILADELPHIA, 1776

The author of these essays was probably a lawyer—or at least had considerable knowledge of legal matters—was definitely a radical republican inclined toward the use of direct consent by the people as much as possible, and was also an advanced thinker. The third and fourth letters are especially interesting for their grasp of modern constitutional theory. The author discusses why colonial charters were defective as founding documents in letter three, and in the fourth letter he lays out the distinction between a constitution and a government. The notion of a constitution as a higher law derived directly from the people and limiting the legislature is an American invention, and this author is one of the first to advance the idea.

TO THE PUBLIC

The rapid turn which Politics have taken within the course of a few days, makes it almost impossible for the Press to keep pace therewith; which will account for some few remarks in the first and second of the following Letters, if they could not appear so necessary now as at the time of writing them.

LETTER I

Every man who acts beyond the line of private life, must expect to pass through two severe examinations. First, as to his motives; secondly, as to his conduct. On the former of these depends his character for

ANONYMOUS

honesty; on the latter for wisdom. The question is, how are we to know a man's motives? I answer by tracing his conduct back to himself, as you would a firearm to the fountain-head, and comparing the measures he pursues with his own private interest and dependencies; and the conclusion will be, that if no visible connection appears between them, we are obliged, on the ground of justice and generosity, to believe that such a man acts from reason and principle; for if this criterion be taken away, there is no other general one to know men by. On the other hand, if on examining from a man's conduct back to the man himself, we find a place of an hundred or a thousand a year at the bottom, or some advantage equivalent thereto, and find likewise that all his measures have been continually and invariably directed to support the part in *every thing* which supports him in his place or office, we may, without hesitation, set that man down for an interested time-serving tool.

We used to feel a mighty indignity at hearing a king's custom-house officer, of forty or fifty pounds a year, bawling out in support of every measure of his employers; and the cause of this dislike in us was, because his motives had the appearance of selfishness; yet we have every reason to believe that the same servile principle produced the late Remonstrance, and drew together the whole tribe of Crown and Proprietary dependants to give it countenance; who, by fermenting the prejudices of some, and working on the weakness of others, endeavoured to render themselves formidable by a party. Why is it, that every governor, and almost every [2] officer under them, throughout the Continent, have uniformly trodden in the same steps? but because that ONE slavish mercenary principle has governed all. Scarcely a man amongst them have had either honesty or fortitude enough, to ask his conscience or his judgment a question. Did men reason with themselves ever so little, they would soon conclude, that the King and his Ministers could not be for *ever right,* nor the opposition, either in England or America, for *ever wrong.* Wisdom cannot be all on one side, nor ingorance all on the other; yet this levee of dependents have never dared to doubt any thing, but obeyed as implicitly as if their employers had been divine, and traveled on through thick and thin, without once enquiring into the cause, or reflecting on the consequence. The case was, that their places were at stake, and *that all commanding thought* superseded every other.

Reason and conscience form unnecessary endowments to men in

such stations; for as they use them not, they need them not, and their chiefest excellence consists in a kind of magnetical obedience, which, having no choice of its own, is governed implicitly by the influence of some other. However degrading this servile character may seem, it is nevertheless a just description of almost every man who held an office under George the Third, and the misfortune of these *"middle provinces"* has been, that the circle of duplicity was considerably enlarged therein by the addition of the Proprietary interest of that of the Crown. Did these persons see themselves in the same light which others view them in, their confidence would fail to support them in the measures they have been pursuing. The indecency of meddling and making in political matters is the same in them, as in the lowest custom-house officer under the Crown; neither does it answer their purpose, for their motives being known, their opinion passes for nothing, and their credit sinks by the very means they take to prop it up.

To the impertinence of office there have been added in this province an affectation of rank: The Proprietary party, who headed the opposers of independence, set out under the assumed distinction of "men of consequence," although it happens very unfortunately for them, that in the line of extraction [3] they are much beneath the generality of the other inhabitants. No reflection ought to be made on any man on account of birth, provided that his manners rises decently with his circumstances, and that he affects not to forget the level he came from; when he does, he ought to be led back and shewn the mortifying picture of originality. Riches in a new country are unavoidable to the descendants of the early settlers; because the lands at that time were purchased for a trifle, and rendered valuable afterwards by the addition and industry of newcomers: A capital of ten pounds well laid out in land a century ago, would, without either care or genius either in the heir or the owner, been by this time an estate; and perhaps it is owing to this accidental manner of becoming rich, that wealth does not obtain the same degree of influence here, which it does in old countries. Rank, at present, in America is derived more from qualification than property; a sound moral character amiable manners and firmness in principle constitute the first class, and will continue to do so till the origin of families be forgotten, and the proud follies of the old world over-run the simplicity of the new.

But to return. There is a more principal consequence for such

ANONYMOUS

men to contemplate than bare disappointment and disgrace. A contest for government is not to be considered as an election. The whole affair is now taking a most serious turn. The transition from Toryism to treason is nearly effected, and the rude custom of Tarring and Feathering will soon give way to the severer punishment of the gibbet. Disaffection and treachery have only received strength and encouragement from former lenity; and, until an example be made of some leading ones, the evil will continue increasing. It may perhaps be asked, what sort of people are we now to call Tories. I answer, every one who contends or argues for the supremacy of the king of England over the colonies. We have at this time but two general denominations of persons, *Independents* and *Tories,* or, if you please, *Traitors,* for to endeavour now either by words or ways to unite America to the crown and government of Britain, is the same kind of crime as it would be for a citizen of London to propose uniting England to the crown and government of France. This is plain doctrine, but it may perhaps save some man or other from the gallows, and, however to be relished by many, it is nevertheless [4] a duty due to society to shew such men their danger fully and warn them of the consequences. If, after that, they fall, their blood be upon their own head.

But the circumstance which most affects a generous mind is, that those men generally draw into their party a number of unwary, unsuspicious persons, by false and fraudulent pretences. There are men at this time who are base enough to give out that Britain wants to be reconciled—that we may make matters up if we will—and that it is our own fault if we do not—and, after painting a horrid picture of war, charge the whole guilt thereof upon the Continent. It was partly by artifices of this kind that the promoters of the Remonstrance procured signers thereto: Therefore, for the sake of such deceived persons, I'll place the case truly, and leave it to their reflection. Have not every mode for reconciliation been tried?—Have a stone been left unturned that could possibly effect it?—Have not petition after petition been sent and rejected?—Have not the petition from the Assembly of New York met with the same fate with those of the Congress?—Have not every petition of the city of London and other parts of England been indignantly discharged, and the petitioners, in some cases, accused of aiding a rebellion?—Have not every conciliatory plan, proposed by our friends in either house of parliament, failed even without a chance?—Is there now the untried method left to proceed upon, or a single hope left to stand upon?—Have not the British court amused us with Commissioners, while at the same time she was privately negociating for foreign troops?—Have she not now cut off every possibility of an accommodation by first declaring us rebels, and then declaring that rebels must be subdued before they can be treated with? Is this the case, or is it not? You that sculk into holes and corners, and exclaim against independency, can you disprove these things, or even bring the truth of them into suspicion? If you can not, the case will be, that those whom ye deceive will soon turn your accusers.

If a general review be taken of the conduct of Britain, it will confirm the suspicion which many discerning men, both on this and the other side the water, had at first, which was [5] that the British court wished from the beginning of this dispute to come to an open rupture with the Continent, that she might have a colourable pretence to possess herself of the whole. The long and scandalous list of placemen and pensioners, and the general profligacy and prodigality of the present reign, exceed the annual supplies. England is drained by taxes, and Ireland impoverished to almost the last farthing, yet the farce of state must be kept up, every thing must give way to the wants and vices of a court. America was the only remaining spot to which their oppression and extortion had not fully reached; and they considered her as a fallow field from which a large income might be drawn, if politically broken up; but the experiment of the stamp-act had taught them to know that they must not hope to effect it by taxation. It is generally believed that Mr. Grenville had nothing more in view in getting the stamp act passed than the raising a revenue in America quietly; and it is fully believed by many that the present king and ministry had no *revenue* in view in passing the tea-act; their object was a quarrel, by which they expected to accomplish the whole at once, and taxation was only the bone to quarrel about. To see America in arms is probably the very thing they wished for—the unpardonable sin which they wanted her to commit; because it furnished them with a pretence for declaring us rebels; and persons conquered under that character forfeit their all, be it where it will, or what it will, to the crown. And as Britain had no apprehension of the military strength of the Continent, nor any doubt of easily subduing it, she would, from motives of political avarice, prefer conquest to any mode of

ANONYMOUS

accomodation whatsoever; and it is on this ground only that the continued obstinacy of her conduct can be accounted for.

Some, perhaps, will object to the harshness of this supposition, and endeavour to disprove it by referring to Lord North's conciliatory plan of the 20th of February 1775, wherein the Colonies are left to tax themselves: To which I reply, that that scheme, instead of weakening, corroborates the suspicion; for, there is strong reason to believe, that the British court never wished to have even that plan, bad as it was, adopted by the Colonies; and this is presumptively proved by her beginning on hostilities between [6] the time of passing that resolve and the time of the different assemblies meeting to deliberate thereon. Had no private orders been given to General Gage, he undoubtedly would have avoided any new aggravation in the interim. He was acquainted with the resolve of the 20th of February upwards of three weeks before his famous expedition to Lexington and Concord, and knew likewise that no assembly had at that time met on the business. Truly has it been said that the tender mercies of the wicked are cruel, and when all the circumstances attending this resolve are compared, they amount to a strong presumption that it was only hung out to amuse the English while an effectual military method was taken to aggravate the Colonies to reject it, and, by driving them to hostilities, she might crush them with arms in their hands, and make them glad to compound for their lives with the surrender of their property. That *"nothing but a good battle would do"* was very common language two years ago in many companies in London; and what has happened since shews that such a scheme was in real contemplation.

A few weak or wicked men among ourselves, for the sake of keeping up a division, may talk of reconciliation, but Britain has no such thought; the amazing expence she has put herself to is a sufficient proof against it: Her aim is to get or lose the whole and repay the millions she had expended, either by laying on us a heavy yearly tribute, if she can, or by immediately seizing our property. We have now no middle line, and none but an idiot or a villain would endeavour to spread such notions. That it is the design of Britain to set up military governments throughout the provinces, if ever they come into her hands again, is doubted by no man of sense and reflection; and likewise, that we have no other mercy to expect from her but a repetition of all those savage and hellish oppressions and cruelties which she so unrelentingly inflicted on the wretched inhabitants of the East-Indies. Thank GOD! we have had a long warning given us to prepare; and, when every disadvantage which we had to encounter, from the want both of materials and experience, be considered, together with the opposition from the [7] ignorant and disaffected amid us, it is nearly a miracle that we are so well prepared.

The king and his ministers in all their speeches and harrangues have constantly held out that the Americas were aiming at independence. Pity but we could have taken the hint sooner! for all our present distresses, arising from a scarcity of goods, are owing to our not thinking of independence *soon enough*. Our non-importation agreement ought to have ceased immediately on the breaking-out of hostilities, and instead thereof we ought to have doubled or tribled our imports; and this would have been the case, had it not been for the absurd and destructive doctrine of reconciliation; because, the moment we had adopted the plan of separation we should have seen the necessity of laying in an additional stock. In short, reconciliation is a doctrine which has driven us to the edge of ruin, and the man that hereafter mentions it as a plan, ought to be considered and treated as a traitor to his country.

LETTER II

The interest of the Provinces, like that of individuals, is two-fold, public and private; for in the same rank which an individual stands in to the public, do the provinces stand in to the Continent; and he who in the present affairs looks no farther than the province he lives in, is moved thereto by the same spirit which inclines a selfish man to look no farther than himself; and in the same manner in which private interest undermines a community, does a narrow provincial spirit sap the Continental welfare: An open generous hearted man, and an open generous hearted province, are characters on the same line. A number of misers trading constantly with one another, would grow poor by their covetousness, and the same circumstance would happen with the Colonies were they to adopt a miserly provincial spirit. The happiness of individuals is secured to them by the community, and the happiness of the separate Colonies can only be secured by the Continent; and as the former yields up a part for that purpose, so must the latter. In the future regulations of [8] trade there will undoubtedly happen instances in which some one or more provinces, like some one or more individuals, may wish it were otherwise; but as the same restrictions may happen to all in their turn, the reasonableness of submitting to them will appear to all.

The more any one province may flourish, the better it will be for the rest, and it matters not where riches begin at, because the commerce carried on between the Colonies will spread it through all; and that province which receives it first, either from Europe or the West-Indies, is only in the state of the Spaniards, who first dig it. There is but very little probability that jealousy between the Colonies on account of trade can ever happen, because most of their principal articles of commerce differ from each other, and will continue to do so while the difference of soil and situation remain; and the communication being by this natural necessity always kept open, it will happen, that no one can grow rich without communicating a share of that riches to the rest, and in the like manner, no province can grow poor without communicating a part of its poverty to others; and on these grounds it is as much our interest, as it is our duty, to promote the happiness of other provinces as of our own. Were Spain, Portugal, and other nations, with whom Britain trades, to grow poor, Britain would grow poor in the same proportion; and the argument is much stronger respecting the Colonies, because they have a common national debt between them, for the payment of which they are reciprocally securities. Countries at war are obliquely benefited by each other's poverty, because inequality is equal to a defeat, but the contrary is true in commerce. In short, the number of commercial reasons, which ought to be produced to shew the advantages flowing from a perfect harmony and union of the Colonies, sufficiently proves likewise that nothing but poverty and destruction can attend their separation.

Besides, as none of the Colonies separately are able to repel the force of Great-Britain, and as it is impossible that she can make an attack on all at once, or were she to do so, her strength would be so divided as to be comparatively less than that of any single province; therefore our preservation, [9] as a people, depends upon our Union. Were Britain to attack the Continent in three places at once, each attack might be repulsed with a proportion of strength equal to four provinces; if in four places, with a force equal to three; if in six, with the force of two, exclusive of the thirteenth: And the knowledge of being thus supported and assisted by each other, is a comfortable and encouraging reflection of men under arms.

But the condition of our affairs *now* is such, that the union *must* be supported; and any Colony that should revolt therefrom, would instantly become a seat of war. The whole *must* go together, and it would be treason in any one province to act separately from the rest. Were Pennsylvania, Maryland, New York, or the Jersies, to attempt such a thing, they would instantly be invaded by the adjoining ones and perhaps the far greater part of their own inhabitants would assist in subduing the revolters. What safety would there be for this city, if the Jersey shore were possessed by the enemy? or what safety would the Jersies be in, were the Pennsylvania shore occupied in the same manner? and so on for the rest. Neither can the neutrality of any province be admitted, because it would enable Britain to bring a larger detachment against the resisting ones. A great part of our strength lies in the variety of objects which a coast so extensive as ours produces to an enemy; while she is meditating a stroke in one quarter, her attention, by some new circumstance, is called away to another. The part she has to act is likewise infinitely greater than ours: Her object is conquest, ours only to keep possession. She is conquered in not conquering us, whether we defeat her or not; and would be obliged to quit the Continent in the same principle that she quitted Boston, could we embarrass her in the same manner. While her force is small she may sculk about the coast, and pick up a living, but when her whole expedition arrives, the matter will be short with her; she must either conquer or depart; and if we can but prevent the first, the latter must follow. In short, we may conquer without a battle, but she cannot.

I shall conclude this letter with remarking, that the Tories have been exceedingly fond of impressing us with the necessity [10] of what they call a perfect union, and that we cannot hope to succeed unless we are all in one mind. For my part I am quite of a different opinion, and think that a disunion is now the thing necessary: Every province either has or must undergo a purgation; it is the lot of all. Whigs and Tories cannot unite; they must separate; and the sooner the separation takes place the better. Those who are Tories now, mean never to be otherwise; therefore it is needless to wait for them. The Proprietary party have the honour of finding out to the last; they have distinguished themselves as much by their folly as their obstinacy,

ANONYMOUS

and on our part we have this consolation, that a union with them would only have weakened us, and produced the same kind of peaceable destruction in the political constitution which opium does in the natural one.

LETTER III

The Charter, called, the Royal Charter for this province, was granted by Charles the Second, King of England, and dated at Westminster, the 4th day of March, 1681.

Interest and Time have an amazing influence over the understanding of mankind, and reconcile them to almost every species of absurdity and injustice. We have, with little or no hesitation, accustomed ourselves to look on these Crown grants as if the givers of them had really a right to do so; yet what was this right of theirs founded on? I answer, on the most villainous injustice. Had the kings of England first entered into treaty with the Indians for any part of their lands, and purchased them at ever so small a consideration, they would then have had a fair right either to have granted or disposed of them: But the case was otherwise, and the claims of the Crown was founded only on the poor pretence of sailing by, and looking at them; or, what is rather worse, because some disstressed adventurous navigator was invited on shore, and civilly treated by the gaping gazing natives. This putting foot upon land was called *"taking possession of it in the king's name;"* and is that which gives him, forsooth, a right to give away the whole country. Suppose the Indian chiefs had taken it in their heads to have disposed of England in the same manner, we [11] certainly should have laughed at their folly; but had they been able to have established their claim, we should have moved heaven and earth to have chastised their imposition: Yet the right of the one was equally as good as the other.

Any individual has a natural privilege to settle in any part of the world that suits him, and this custom all nations agree in; an Indian may settle in England, or elsewhere, purchase and occupy lands, and an European may settle in America for the same purposes, without injustice in either case: but for the kings of one country to assume a right to give away the lands in another, which they never were in possession of, either by treaty or purchase, is no better than qualified robbery, and downright arbitrary power. No man arguing from the reasonableness of things, could ever view a king's charter granting away lands which were at that time in the possession of the natives, in any other light, than as an obligation, which the Crown bound itself under, not to disturb the adventurers in whatever settlements they might make, or in whatever possessions they might afterwards acquire in America. And *William Penn,* by entering into treaty with the Indians for the sale of the lands contained within the Charter from Charles the Second, seemed by that procedure to question Charles's right to grant such a Charter, and that his own title under that Charter only was not sufficiently good; and if the groundwork be defective, it of course renders the whole so. In any case, the granting Charters with such extensive privileges to individuals is incompatible with the spirit of freedom, and would in time extinguish it; but in this case it interfered with property, by obliging the emigrants to purchase lands of *William Penn,* for his particular emolument, and at just what price he pleased to set thereon, when they might have purchased the same of the natives at three or four thousand times less price. At the time that the Proprietaries bought of the Indians at the high rate, as it was called, of *Two-pence Half-penny per Hundred acres,* they sold them again for *Fifteen pounds per Hundred acres, and one Half-penny sterling per acre quit-rent.* Perhaps no country in Europe can furnish greater instances of imposition and extortion than is to be found in the conduct of the Proprietaries of Pennsylvania.

[12] The above Charter is contained in twenty-three sections. A striking absurdity appears in the first of them; which is, that *William Penn,* one of the first and most principal of the people called Quakers, and who held even the bearing of arms to be sinful, should, nevertheless, accept from Charles the Second the grant of the province of Pennsylvania, as a reward, for a *"signal battle and victory fought and obtained by his father, under James, duke of York, against the Dutch fleet, commanded by the Heir van Opdam, in the year 1665.** To *William Penn,* therefore, this province was the price of blood. If it was, as some say, for wages due to his father as an Admiral, he is the more guilty under that excuse; because, in that case, he took the pay of a soldier, though in any case he gave, contrary to his principles, an oblique approbation of war, and exhibited a striking instance of a convenient conscience.

* First Section in the Charter.

ANONYMOUS

The first, second and third section, treat wholly of the soil, and speak of *William Penn* as proprietor *only,* no mention being made in either of them respecting the government.

By the fourth section Charles the Second hath endeavoured to grant and bestow on *William Penn* and his *Heirs* a power which no man or monarch on earth ever had or can have a right to give, viz. that of appointing him and his heirs the perpetual and absolute governors of Pennsylvania. Where there are no people, there can be no government; it is the people that constitute the government; and to give away a government is giving away the people, in the same manner that giving the proprietaryship was giving the soil. What right could Charles the Second, a deceased tyrant of the last century, have to appoint a governor for the present generation, or declare that the heirs of *William Penn* should be the Lords and Masters of persons to be born a thousand years hence? Are the inhabitants of the earth to be conveyed or transferred away, by virtue of a scrap of paper, from generation to generation, like so many head of cattle, or so many acres of land? Is such a thought, or such an act, consistent with human rights? Yet *William Penn,* regardless of every sacred privilege of freedom, carried the principle of tyranny higher than any of the Stuart family ever did; for by his Will he directed the government of Pennsylvania to be SOLD. However some may endeavour to [13] refine or explain away the sense of words I know not, but this I know, that there is no difference between selling a government and selling the people, because it is obliging them, like horses, to take for their master and rider any one who has money enough to come up to the sellers price.

"I *William Penn,* Esq., so called, Etc. give and dispose of my estate in manner following:—The GOVERNMENT of *my* province of Pennsylvania, and territories thereunto belonging, and ALL POWERS relating thereto, I give and devise to the most honourable the Earl of Oxford, and Earl Mortimer, and to William, Earl Pawlet, so called, and their heirs, upon trust, to dispose thereof to the Queen, *or to any other person,* to the best advantage and profit they can."

William Penn's last will.

Neither in this part, nor in any other part of the will, is there any exception respecting the purchaser. The only condition is, the "best advantage and profit." He might be of any denomination of religion, or of none; a man of reputation, or not; a gentleman, or a gambler; if he could but raise the money, that was all. In short, the will of William Penn is as great a violation of the rights of nature as ever appeared upon a Christian record.—When governments are put up for sale, farewell liberty: it is time, and high time, that the Being of man should be extinct, when such articles appear at public market. By what pretence the government of this province hath remained in the Proprietary family since doth not appear; whether they inherit under the Charter, or by purchase under the will: However, neither is good; the first being a nullity, and the second an infamous traffic.

The Charter of Charles the Second says, "William Penn and his heirs" generally, by which it should seem that if any of them have any right, all of them have the same: A joint heirship, male and female. Had they been a prolific family, we might have had four or five hundred governors by this time, all of them claiming under the charter; quarrelling, and perhaps fighting for superiority with each other; and CATO, like the vicar of Bray, the unprincipled chaplain of every conqueror; the purchases made by the inhabitants from [14] *one* proprietor and governor disputed by another, or invalidated by a successor, till nobody knew from whom to purchase. In fine, the evils and confusion occasioned by the obscurity of succession in the Proprietary family, would have been so great in a little time, and is even now so embarrassing, that if the present dissolution and suppression of all governments under the Crown of England had not fortunately happened, something must have been done in this province to have regulated the concerns thereof, and secured the purchasers in their possessions; otherwise we might have had heirs and lords coming from every part of Europe, "whose fathers were the Lord knows who."

William Penn, having obtained the Royal Charter, as it is called, acted very humbly under it for some little time; his first system of government is modestly entitled, "The frame of government of the province of Pennsylvania, in America, together with certain laws AGREED upon in England by the governor and divers freemen of the aforesaid province; to be farther explained and confirmed *there* by the first Provincial Council, if they see meet." By this the governor was to have three votes in passing or rejecting any bill, but not a negative upon the whole, but Mr. Penn, in less than one year, found means to get that agreement abolished, and in the forming of what he calls a Charter, managed matters so artfully, as to obtain a negative, in lieu of three votes; for which he was severely reprimanded by a future Assembly in 1704, in which they tell him, "That by a subtile contrivance and artifice of thine, laid deeper than the capacities of some could fathom, or the circumstances of many admit them since to consider of, a way was found out (by thee) to lay that aside, and introduce another Charter." "We see no just cause thou had to insist upon a negative upon bills to be passed into laws in General Assemblies." It ought to be remembered, that, according to Charles the Second's Charter, *William Penn* was only empowered to make laws with the *Consent of Freemen*. But this was not sufficiently lordly; and he soon took on himself, in imitation of his benefactor Charles, to issue out his Charter likewise, in the proud and arbitrary stile of "I do GRANT and DECLARE," etc. His piece, entitled, *"The Charter of privileges,* GRANTED, by WILLIAM [15] PENN, ESQ; *to the inhabitants of Pennsylvania and territories,"* is an insult on their understanding, it ought at least to have been entitled, "A Charter of privileges, AGREED upon and CONFIRMED between William Penn and the inhabitants of Pennsylvania." Whenever a person undertakes to grant a thing, it implies that the thing which he grants was once his own. William Penn, in this sense, might grant his lands, but that he should assume to himself the Popish power of granting liberty of conscience, and undertake to define, by a single act of his own, called a Charter, what degree of personal and political privilege we shall enjoy as freemen, is truly ridiculous. Liberty and liberty of conscience both would have a poor foundation indeed, were they to be received as privileges granted to us by William Penn. Every man who understands the true value of them will disdain to say he receives them in such a narrow line. We hold them immediately from GOD, and though it is our reciprocal duty to guarantee them to each other, we cannot be the givers of them. All Charters, which are the acts of a single man, are a species of tyranny, because they substitute the will of ONE as the law for ALL. They ought to have no Being in a free country; and no country can be free that has them. William Penn, in his Charter, called the Charter of privileges, has very arrogantly undertaken to lay down what shall be the law of this land. If this be not a species of arbitrary power, I know not what is. The people had certainly as good a right to have made a Charter for him as he for them: And it matters not what the Charter contains; the thing is, that he had no authority for that purpose, any more than he had to have granted a passport to heaven.

All constitutions should be contained in some written Charter; but *that* Charter should be the act of *all* and not of *one man*. Magna Charta was not a grant from the Crown, but only agreed or acceded to by the Crown, being first drawn up and framed by the people.

Charters, as has been already observed, when granted by individuals, are not only a species of tyranny, but of the worst kind of tyranny; because the grantors of them undertake, by an act of their own, to fix what the constitution of a country shall be; which is a higher authority than the [16] giving out temporary laws. Perhaps there was not an inhabitant of this province who would have suffered William Penn to have made a law of his own mere accord, or would have looked upon such an act of his as a law: Yet, that they should suffer him to form a Charter of his own mere accord, describing the perpetual mode of government for this province, taking to himself, and giving to them, just what proportion he pleased, was very extraordinary! But he allowed them to sit on their own adjournments.— Mighty condescention, truly! The case was, he had no right either to tell them they should, or they should not, the whole of his authority being confined to the making of "laws with the consent of the freemen," and all beyond that was arrogance and arbitrary power.

But, having assumed the prerogative of granting a Charter, he soon after assumed the right of explaining it in such manner as best suited his purpose: First, by claiming to himself the authority of proroguing and dissolving the assembly at pleasure, and summoning them by writs; and secondly, that he should have a negative on the laws passed in this province, whether he acted as governor or not, "saving always," says he in his instructions to deputy-governor Evans, "to me and my heirs, our *final assent* to all such bills as thou shall pass." But in both these he miscarried.

The contentions which have arisen between the governors of this province and the people, since the time of its first settlement, are various and numerous, and can only be attributed to that astonishing absurdity of having the proprietaryship and governorship invested in one person. The composition is as impolitic and unnatural as it would be to leave a man to determine his own wager, or sit as judge in his own cause. The interest of the proprietor and the people, being like that of buyer and seller, it was impossible but that they would sometimes disagree, and in that case, the proprietor, being likewise governor, with the power of appointing judges, disposing of all offices, and having a negative upon all laws, was quite an over-match for the people; and of this the assembly in deputy-governor Morris's administration seemed fully sensible. "If we are thus," say they, "to be driven from [17] bill to bill, without one solid reason afforded us, and can raise no money for the relief and security of our country, until we shall fortunately hit on the *only* bill the governor is allowed to pass, or till we consent to make such as the governor or proprietaries direct us to make, we see little use of assemblies in this particular; and we think we might as well leave it to the governor or proprietaries to make *for us* what laws they please, and save ourselves and the province the expence and trouble. All debates and reasonings are vain, where proprietary instructions, just or unjust, right or wrong, must inevitably be observed. We have only to find out, if we *can,* what they are, and then *submit* and *obey.*"

The Charter of privileges was accompanied with another, called *"The Charter for the* CITY *of* PHILADELPHIA,*"* from which the Corporation derives all their authority. In the preamble William Penn says, "I have, by virtue of the king's letters patent, under the great seal of England, erected the said town into a borough, and do, by these presents, erect the said town and borough into a CITY." What William Penn meant by erecting the town and burrough into a CITY, I am wholly at a loss to know, as that name particularly signifies an *Episcopal Town,* or place where the bishop's *See* is held.—*See—Seety*—or City. All towns in England are thus distinguished, and never otherwise, except Westminster, which was once a see—as, See or City of Canterbury—See or City of York—See or City of London, of Bath and Wells—of Bristol—of Salisbury, etc., etc. etc. and no place is called a City which has not a bishop's See: Wherefore William Penn's Charter, establishing a Corporation for the See or City of Philadelphia, is a sort of nullity in itself.

As to Corporations themselves, they are without exception so many badges of kingly tyranny, and tend, like every other species of useless pomp, to the oppression and impoverishment of the place, without one single advantage arising from them. They keep up a perpetual spirit of distinction and faction, engross emoluments and advantages to themselves, which ought to be employed to better purposes, and generally get [18] into quarrels and lawsuits with the other part of the inhabitants. They diminish the freedom of every place where they exist. The most flourishing towns in England, as,

Birmingham, Sheffield, Manchester, have no Corporations. A sufficient number of justices and a jury annually chosen, which shall regularly account with them successors for the monies which they may receive or pay in the year, are found to answer every *good* purpose much better.

But of all Corporations that of Philadelphia is the most obnoxious, the power resembling that of an hermaphrodite, or is at least a kind of aristocratical Corporation made hereditary by adoption.

LETTER IV.

Among the many publications which have appeared on the subject of political Constitutions, none, that I have seen, have properly defined what is meant by a *Constitution,* that word having been bandied about without any determinate sense being affirmed thereto. A Constitution, and a form of government, are frequently confounded together, and spoken of as synonomous things; whereas they are not only different, but are established for different purposes. All countries have some form of government, but few, or perhaps none, have truly a Constitution. The form of government in England is by a king, lords and commons, but if you ask an Englishman what he means when he speaks of the English Constitution, he is unable to give you any answer. The truth is, the English have no fixed Constitution. The prerogative of the crown, it is true, is under several restrictions, but the legislative power, which includes king, lords and commons, is under none; and whatever acts they pass are laws, be they ever so oppressive or arbitrary. England is likewise defective in Constitution in three other material points, viz. The crown, by virtue of a patent from itself, can increase the number of the lords (one of the legislative branches) at his pleasure. Queen Ann created six in one day, for the purpose of making a majority for carrying a bill then passing, who were afterwards distinguished by the name of the six occasional lords. Lord Bathurst, the father of the present chancellor, is the only surviving one. [19] The crown can likewise, by a patent, incorporate any town or village, small or great, and empower it to send members to the house of commons, and fix what the precise number of the electors shall be. And an act of the legislative power, that is, an act of king, lords, and commons, can again diminish the house of commons to what number they please, by disfranchising any county, city or town.

Anonymous

It is easy to perceive that individuals by agreeing to erect forms of government, (for the better security of themselves) must give up some part of their liberty for that purpose; and it is the particular business of a Constitution to make out *how much* they shall give up. In this case it is easy to see that the English have no Constitution because they have given up every thing; their legislative power being unlimited without either condition or controul, except in the single instance of trial by Juries. No country can be called *free* which is governed by an absolute power; and it matters not whether it be an absolute royal power or an absolute legislative power, as the consequences will be the same to the people. That England is governed by the latter, no man can deny, there being, as is said before, no Constitution in that country which says to the legislative powers, "Thus far shalt thou go, and no farther." There is nothing to prevent them passing a law which shall give the house of commons power to sit for life, or to fill up the vacancies by appointing others, like the Corporation of Philadelphia. In short, an act of parliament, to use a court phrase, can do any thing but make a man a woman.

A Constitution, when completed, resolves the two following questions: First, What shall the form of government be? And secondly, What shall be its power? And the last of these two is far more material than the first. The Constitution ought likewise to make provision in those cases where it does not empower the legislature to act.

The forms of government are numerous, and perhaps the simplest is the best. The notion of checking by having different houses, has but little weight with it, when inquired [20] into, and in all cases it tends to embarrass and prolong business; besides, what kind of checking is it that one house is to receive from another? or which is the house that is most to be trusted to? They may fall out about forms and precedence, and check one another's honour and tempers, and thereby produce petulances and ill-will, which a more simple form of government would have prevented. That some kind of convenience might now and then arise from having two houses, is granted, and the same may be said of twenty houses; and the question is, whether such a mode would not produce more hurt than good. The more houses the more parties; and perhaps the ill consequence to this country would be, that the landed interest would get into one house, and the commercial interest into the other; and by that means a perpetual and dangerous opposition would be kept up, and no business be got through: Whereas, were there a large, equal and annual representation in one house *only*, the different parties, by being thus banded together, would hear each others arguments, which advantage they cannot have if they sit in different houses. To say, there ought to be two houses, because there are two sorts of interest, is the very reason why there ought to be but one, and *that one* to consist of every sort. The lords and commons in England formerly made but one house; and it is evident, that by separating men you lessen the quantity of knowledge, and increase the difficulties of business. However, let the form of government be what it may, in this, or other provinces, so long as it answers the purpose of the people, and they approve it, they will be happy under it. That which suits one part of the Continent may not in every thing suit another; and when each is pleased, however variously, the matter is ended. No man is a true republican, or worthy of the name, that will not give up his single voice to that of the public; his private opinion he may retain; it is obedience only that is his duty.

The chief convenience arising from two houses is, that the second may sometimes amend small imperfections which would otherwise pass; yet, there is nearly as much chance of their making alterations for the worse as the better; and the supposition that a single house may become arbitrary, can with more reason be said of two, because their strength is [21] greater. Besides, when all the supposed advantages arising from two houses are put together, they do not appear to balance the disadvantage. A division in one house will not retard business, but serves rather to illustrate; but a difference between two houses may produce serious consequences. In queen Ann's reign a quarrel arose between the upper and lower house, which was carried to such a pitch that the nation was under very terrifying apprehensions, and the house of commons was dissolved to prevent worse mischief. A like instance was nearly happening about six years ago, when the members of each house very affrontingly turned one another by force out of doors. The two last bills in the last sessions in England were entirely lost by having two houses; the bill for encreasing liberty of conscience, by taking off the necessity of subscription to the thirty-nine articles, Athanasian creed, etc. after passing the lower house by a very great majority, was thrown out by the upper one; and at the time that the nation was starving with the high price of corn, the bill for regulating the importation and exportation of grain, after passing the lower

ANONYMOUS

house, was lost by a *difference* between the two, and when returned from the upper one was thrown on the floor by the commons, and indignantly trampled under foot.—Perhaps most of the Colonies will have two houses, and it will probably be of benefit to have some little difference in the forms of government, as those which do not like one, may reside in another, and by trying different experiments, the best form will the sooner be found out, as the preference at present rests on conjecture.

Government is generally distinguished into three parts, Executive, Legislative and Judicial; but this is more a distinction of words than things. Every king or governor in giving his assent to laws acts legislatively, and not executively: The house of lords in England is both a legislative and judicial body. In short, the distinction is perplexing, and however we may refine and define, there is no more than two powers in any government, viz. the power to make laws, and the power to execute them; for the judicial power is only a branch of the executive, the CHIEF of every country being the first magistrate.

A constitution should lay down some permanent ratio, [22] by which the representation should afterwards encrease or decrease with the number of inhabitants; for the right of representation, which is a natural one, ought not to depend upon the will and pleasure of future legislatures. And for the same reason perfect liberty of conscience, security of person against unjust imprisonments, similar to what is called the Habeas Corpus act; the mode of trial in all law and criminal cases; in short, all the great rights which man never mean, nor ever ought, to lose, should be *guaranteed*, not *granted*, by the Constitution, for at the forming a Constitution we ought to have in mind, that whatever is left to be secured by law only, may be altered by another law. That Juries ought to be judges of law, as well as fact, should be clearly described; for though in rare instances Juries may err, it is generally from tenderness, and on the right side. A man cannot be *guilty* of a *good* action, yet if the fact only is to be proved (which is Lord Mansfield's doctrine) and the Jury not empowered to determine in their own minds, whether the fact proved to be done is a crime or not, a man may hereafter be found guilty of going to church or meeting.

There is one circumstance respecting trial by Juries which seems to deserve attention; which is, whether a Jury of Twelve persons, which cannot bring in a verdict unless they are all of one mind, or appear so; or, whether a Jury of not less than Twenty-five, a majority of which shall make a verdict, is the safest to be trusted to? The objections against an Jury of Twelve are, that the necessity of being unanimous prevents the freedom of speech, and causes men sometimes to conceal their own opinions, and follow that of others; that it is a kind of terrifying men into a verdict, and that a strong hearty obstinate man who can bear starving twenty-four or forty-eight hours, will distress the rest into a compliance, that there is no difference, in effect, between hunger and the point of a bayonet, and that under such circumstances a Jury is not, nor can be free. In favour of the latter it is said, that the least majority is thirteen; and the dread of the consequences of disagreeing being removed, men will speak freer, and that justice will thereby have a fairer chance.

It is the part of a Constitution to fix the manner in which [23] the officers of government shall be chosen, and determine the principal outlines of their power, their time of duration, manner of commissioning them, etc. The line, so far as respects their election, seems easy, which is, by the representatives of the people; provincial officers can be chosen no other way, because the whole province cannot be convened, any more than the whole of the Associators could be convened for choosing by election. The mode of choosing delegates for Congress deserves consideration, as they are not officers but legislators. Positive provincial instructions have a tendency to disunion, and, if admitted, will one day or other rend the Continent of America. A continental Constitution, when fixed, will be the best boundaries of Congressional power, and in matters for the general good, they ought to be as free as assemblies. The notion, which some have, of excluding the military from the legislature is unwise, because it has a tendency to make them form a distinct party of their own. Annual elections, strengthened by some kind of periodical exclusion, seem the best guard against the encroachments of power. Suppose the exclusion was triennial, that is, that no person should be returned a member of assembly for more then three succeeding years, nor be capable of being returned again till he had been absent three years. Such a mode would greatly increase the circle of knowledge, make men cautious how they acted, and prevent the disagreeableness of giving offence, by removing some, to make room for others of equal, or perhaps superior, merit. Something of the same kind may be practised respecting Presidents or Governors, not to be eligible after a certain number of returns; and as no person, after filling that rank, can, consistent with character, descend to any other office or employment; and as it may not always happen that the most wealthy are the most capable, some decent provision therefore should be made for them in their retirement, because it is a retirement from the world. Whoever reflects on this, will see many good advantages arising from it.

Modest and decent honorary titles, so as they be neither hereditary, nor convey legislative authority, are of use in a state; they are, when properly conferred, the badges of merit. The love of the public is the chief reward which a generous [24] man seeks, and, surely, if that be an honour, the mode of conferring it must be so likewise.

Next to the forming a good Constitution, is the means of preserving it. If once the legislative power breaks in upon it, the effect will be the same as if a kingly power did it. The Constitution, in either case, will receive its death wound, and "the outward and visible sign," or mere form of government only will remain. "I wish," says Lord Camden, "that the maxim of Machiavel was followed, that of examining a Constitution, at certain periods, according to its first principles; this would correct abuses, and supply defects." The means here pointed out for preserving a Constitution are easy, and some article in the Constitution may provide, that at the expiration of every seven or any other number of years a *Provincial Jury* shall be elected, to enquire if any inroads have been made in the Constitution, and to have power to remove them; but not to make alterations, unless a clear majority of all the inhabitants shall so direct.

Farther observations were intended to have been offered in these letters, but the sudden turn of military affairs hath prevented them; I shall therefore conclude with remarking, that perfection in government, like perfection in all other earthly things, is not to be hoped for. A single house, or a duplication of them, will alike have their evils; and the defect is incurable, being founded in the nature of man, and the instability of things.

[31]

[ANONYMOUS]

The People the Best Governors: Or a Plan of Government Founded on the Just Principles of Natural Freedom

NEW HAMPSHIRE 1776

While most Americans think of the Revolution and the Declaration of Independence when they see the date 1776, that year was equally important for the state constitutions written. During the course of the war a debate of astonishing diversity and sophistication took place concerning the best form of government and how to enshrine it in the constitution. This essay is an excellent example of the outpouring of plans, ideas, and theories. In this instance emphasis is given to popular sovereignty and representation, although the broad outline of an entire constitution is efficiently presented. The state constitutions that resulted from this multivoiced conversation, eight of which were written in 1776, were the flowering of colonial experience with self-government, and formed the immediate context within which the United States Constitution was written. The author of this pamphlet, published anonymously, is thought to be a young man recently migrated to New Hampshire, hoping to become a member of the faculty of the newly created Dartmouth College. Whoever he was, he certainly deserves to be included among the nation's founding fathers.

THE PREFACE

It was observed by Sir William Temple, that none can be said to know things well, who do not know them in their beginnings. There are many very noisy about liberty, but are aiming at nothing more than personal grandeur and power. Are not many, under the delusive

ANONYMOUS

character of Guardians of their country, collecting influence and honour only for oppression? Behold Caesar! at first a patriot, a consul, and commander of the Roman army. How apparently noble his intentions, and how specious his conduct! but unbounded in his ambition, by these means he became, at length, a perpetual dictator, and an unlimited commander.

God gave mankind freedom by nature, made every man equal to his neighbour, and has virtually enjoined them, to govern themselves by their own laws. The government, which he introduced among his people, the Jews, abundantly proves it, and they might have continued in that state of liberty, had they not desired a King. The people best know their own wants and necessities, and therefore, are best able to rule themselves. Tent makers, cobblers and common tradesmen, composed the legislature at Athens. "Is not the body—(said Socrates) of the Athenian people composed of men like these."

That I might help, in some measure, to eradicate the notion of arbitrary power, heretofore drank in; and to establish the liberties of the people of this country upon a more generous footing, is the design of the following impartial work, now dedicated by the Author to the honest farmer and citizen.

[4]   THE PEOPLE the best GOVERNORS, etc.

The just power of a free people respects first the making and the executing of laws. The liberties of a people are chiefly, I may say entirely guarded, by having the controul of these branches in their own hands.

Many have been the disputes as to the best way of civil government. The Athenians boasted of their popular assemblies; the Aerolians of their representatives, whom they termed the Panaetolium; and as for the Romans, they had a more complicated plan, viz. their consuls, the senate, and plebeians.

I am not to examine into the advantages of a popular, or a representative government—in this case we are to consult the situation, and number of the inhabitants. Were the people of the different counties numerous and wealthy enough, with that degree of knowledge, which is common in many parts of the continent, every freeman might then have a hand in making laws to govern himself by, as well as in appointing the persons to execute them; but the people of these states are very unequally and thinly settled, which puts us upon seeking some mode of governing by a representative body. The freemen give up in this way just so much of their natural right as they find absolutely convenient, on account of the disadvantages in their personal action. The question now arises, how far they can with safety deposit this power of theirs into other hands? To this I answer: That where there are representatives who hold the legislature, their power ought never to extend any farther than barely the making of laws. For what matters it, whether they themselves execute the laws, or appoint persons to do it in their stead, since these very persons, being only creatures of their own appointment, will be induced by interest to act agreeable to their will and pleasure. Indeed upon this plan the greatest corruption may take place—for should there be in some important affairs very unjust decisions, where could the injury gain redress? Iniquity might be supported by the executioners [5] of it; they out of the reach of the people, from whom they do not derive their authority, and the legislative body, as they are not the immediate perpetrators, may be often skreened from just reproach.

Perhaps it will be said by some, that the people are sufficiently guarded against infringements of this nature, as their representatives are chosen only for a certain time, may be called to an account for any misconduct in their business, and withal are liable to be turned out by their constituents at any time. There is indeed something plausible in all this; but it will vanish when we consider that these representatives, while they act as such, being supreme in legislation and the appointing and supporting the executors of law, may, by these advantages, assume to themselves a lasting unlimited power. And I beg of any one to tell me what will prevent it, if they have only art, and are generally agreed among themselves.

But it seems there is another objection started by some: That the common people are not under so good advantages to choose judges, sheriffs, and other executive officers as their representatives are. This is a mere delusion, which many have taken in, and, if I may be allowed a vulgar expression, the objectors in this instance put the cart before the horse. For they say, that the people have wisdom and knowledge enough to appoint proper persons through a state to make laws, but not to execute them. It is much easier to execute, than to make & regulate the system of laws, and upon this single consideration

ANONYMOUS

the force of the objection falls: The more simple, and the more immediately dependent *(caeteris paribus)* the authority is upon the people the better, because it must be granted that they themselves are the best guardians of their own liberties.

2dly, Upon the above principles we will proceed farther, and say, that if there be a distinct negative power over those that enact the laws, it can by no means be derived from them as representatives of the people, and for these reasons: As far as there is any power over the rights of the people, so far they themselves are divested of it. Now by chusing representatives to make laws for them, they put that power out of their own hands; yet they do not deposit it into the hands of their representatives to give to others, but to exercise it in their room and stead.—Therefore, I say, for the representatives to appoint a council with a negative authority, is to give [6] away that power which they have no right to do; because they themselves derived it from the people.

Again, there is a palpable contradiction implied; for this negative power, if it cannot be called legislative, has at least, such weight in the legislature, as to be the unlimited *sine qua non.** Those therefore, who act as a council or negative body make use of a power in the room of the people, and consequently represent them so far as their power extends. In fine, to say that the legislative body can appoint them, is as absurd as to say that the representatives have a right to appoint the representatives of the people.

3rdly, It appears now that the representatives have no right to enlarge their power which they have received, nor to alter or put any incumbrance upon it, by making a negative body. The common people, and consequently their representatives, may not happen to be so learned and knowing as some others in a state; and as the latter are bound to their constituents to act by the best light they can get, they may, if they please, chuse a council, barely to give advice, and to prepare matters for their consideration; but not to negative, which is a contradiction in terms. Agreeable to this observation was the government at Athens: The council consisted of 400 persons, and in a legislative capacity, could only advise, and prepare matters for the consideration of the people.

* A restraining power

But it will be enquired, whether the inhabitants themselves through a state cannot consistently make a negativing body over those that form the laws? To this I answer, that there is no real absurdity in their taking such a step: But upon this plan those that are called representatives, have only a partial right as such; for they have a delegated power from the people to act no farther than this negative body concurs. Now this said negative body are likewise virtually the representatives of the people, and derive just so much authority from them, as will make up the defect of the others, viz. that of confirming. They have been generally named a council in our American States, though they have really acted in a legislative capacity, and seem rather to answer the idea of a *senate,* which was hereditary at Rome, but here elective.

[7] Where there is such a body of men appointed, it is best, that there should be but few in number, and chosen by the people at large through the government. At least that there should not be districts marked out, and the plan fixed, that the inhabitants in the respective counties may chose just so many, only in proportion to their present number, without any regard to the future increase of the people— rather let the same principles of an equal partition of land, settling, and settled, take place in this matter, as we shall point out under the next head, when we speak of representation.

To conclude, I do not say that it is expedient, to choose a senate, if I may so call it, with such a negative power as before mentioned; but rather propose, whether a council of advice would not answer better purposes, and that inequality be thereby prevented, which is sometimes occasioned by two destinct fountains of power.

4thly, We will next lay open the nature and right of jurisdicion more clearly, in examining, the best, by which representation may be regulated. In the first place, it is asserted by some, that representation ought to be enlarged or diminished in proportion to the amount of taxes in the different parts of the state; but such a procedure would be very unreasonable. For taxation only respects property, without regard to the liberties of a person: And, if representation should be wholly limited by that, the man, who owns six times as much as another, would consequently have six times the power, though their natural right to freedom is the same: Nature itself abhors such a system of civil government, for it will make an inequality among the

ANONYMOUS

people, and set up a number of lords over the rest. In the next place it is said, that representation should be determined entirely according to the number of inhabitants. But, to have a state represented adequately upon this plan, would puzzle the brain of a philosopher. Indeed, to effect it some townships must be cut to pieces, others tacked together—and, at best, many parts would remain defective. And, if we look into this matter critically, we shall find it still more egregious. It is an old observation, the *political bodies should be immortal*—a government is not founded for a day or a year, and, for that very reason, should be erected upon some invariable principles. Grant, for a moment, that the number of people is the only measure of representation; as often then, as the former increases or diminishes, the latter must of consequence; as often, as the inhabitants in a state vary their situation, the weight [8] of legislation changes; and, accordingly, the balance of power is subject to continual, and frequently unforseen alterations. Turn which way we will upon this plan, we shall find unsurmountable difficulties: So that those, who have adopted this measure, are either too short-sighted, to see the future interests of society, or so secret and designing, as to take the advantage of such undeterminate principles. The question now comes in, how shall we find an *invariable* free mode of representation? This I own is a delicate point; yet, if we enter into the matter, doubt not, but that we shall fix upon something useful.

Every government is necessarily confined to some extent of territory. It may happen by some peculiar circumstances, that some parts of the land in a state may be at first, much more peopled than others: Yet, in time (excepting the metropolis, and some places of trade) they become generally alike settled. We find that this was the case in the old republics of Greece, and likewise at present in Switzerland; indeed it is commonly so through the civilized kingdoms of Europe and Asia. The reasons for this are handy. The God of nature has formed the different situations of land through a government, mostly with equal advantages: Some parts are proper for agriculture, others for trade and commerce; some produce one sort of commodity, and some another. By this means it is that people have intercourse together, and are at length equally deffused within the limits of a state. We will now come nearer to the point before us. It has been said, that a government should be formed, if possible, upon so solid a foundation, as to be liable to no alterations, on account of its internal defects. A well regulated representation is the only security of our liberties: We have seen that it cannot depend upon taxation, nor the number of inhabitants solely without being subject to changes and innovations; and to have it depend on both taken together, will render it intirely capricious. Land is the most solid estate that can be taxed, and is the only permanent thing. Let that therefore be divided into equal convenient parts in a state, as is the case with our townships, and let the inhabitants possessing the said parts or townships, be severally and distinctly represented. By this means, the plan of the legislature will be fixed, and an earnest of it handed down to posterity, for whom politicians were rather made, than for those who live in their time.

[9] But, it may be objected by some, that live in a government where towns are very unequally settled, that there is no right or justice in the inhabitants having the same advantage as to representation, since those, that live in the larger towns, must not only support their own, but, also, help to support the representatives of the smaller ones. The objection is trifling. Every government is an entire body politic, and therefore, each particular member in the legislature does not represent any distinct part, but the whole of the said body. Blackstone's words are these, "For it is to be observed, that though every member is chosen by a particular county or borough, yet, as is justly observed by Lord Coke and others, when in parliament, he serves for the whole nation." The consequence is, that if every incorporate town, small as well as large, has a right to chuse a representative, he does, when chosen, represent the whole government; and therefore ought to be paid by it. Besides, the inhabitants of the smaller towns do, upon this plan, pay their proportion of representation, and a small sum may be as much for a poor man, as a large sum for a rich man, agreeable to what the scripture observes of the widow, that cast her mite into the treasury. Again, shall we sacrifice a free constitution barely to avoid the trifling expence of a free government. But is not there enough said yet, to satisfy the objectors! Then let every town support its own representative; but, in consideration of that, place the seat of government in the center of the state. This inequality will last but for a few years, the smaller towns are growing; nor does it become patriots to study their own case, at the expence of embroiling their children.

Anonymous

What has been proposed I cannot but think to be the only sure foundation to form a legislature upon—all others are wavering and uncertain.

5thly, The question now, that closes the whole, arises what it is that ought to be the qualification of a representative? In answer we observe, that fear is the principle of a despotic, honour of a kingly, and virtue is the principle of a republican government.—Social virtue and knowledge, I say then is the best, and only necessary qualification of the person before us. But it will be said, that an estate of two hundred, four hundred pounds, or some other sum is essential. So sure as we make interest necessary in this case, as sure we root out virtue, and what will then become [10] of the genuine principle of freedom? This notion of an estate has the directed tendency to set up the avaricious over the heads of the poor, though the latter are ever so virtuous. Let it not be said in future generations, that money was made by the founders of the American states, an essential qualification in the rulers of a free people. It was what never was known among the Ancients: And we find many of their best leaders in very needy circumstances. Witness the Athenians, Cimon, and Aristides; the Romans, Numa, Cato, and Regulus. Thus I have gone through what I had to say on some interesting points of government: And it is proposed with more chearfulness, as many of the sentiments oppose the present regulations of most of our states.

Now is the time for the people to be critical in establishing a plan of government: For they are now planting a seed, which will arise with boughs, either extended to shelter the liberty of succeeding ages, or only to skreen the designs of crafty usurpers.

That this short treatise may not be left imperfect, I will only propose, for the consideration of the people, a concise plan, founded on the principles that have been laid down.

It is observed then, in the first place, that the freemen of each incorporated town, through a state, shall chuse by ballot, at an annual meeting, one person respectively, whom they shall think suitable to represent them in a general assembly.

2ndly, That, if the metropolis, and some particular large places, may require an additional number of representatives, it may be granted them by the general assembly as the latter shall think proper.

3rdly, That the general assembly should meet at certain times, twice every year; and, if the state is extensive, there may be two seats of government, in which case the said assembly are to convene at them, once in their turns.

4thly, That the people chuse annually by ballot in their town meetings, a council, consisting of twelve persons, through the government at large, whose business shall be to help in preparing matters for the consideration of the assembly, to assist them with their advice: And lastly, it shall be their duty to inquire into every essential [11] defect in the regulations of government, and to give the people reasonable notice, in a public way, with their opinion respecting the matter.

5thly, That they likewise chuse annually a first executive officer, without any concern in the legislature; but it shall be his duty to transact such occasional business, as the assembly may devolve upon him: And that he be the general commander of the militia, and in these capacities the people; if they please, may stile him a governor— and, in case of his incapacity, a lieutenant, etc. may be appointed as before, to act occasionally in his stead.

6thly, This said governor, with advice of any three of the council, may, at any time, call a special assembly on extraordinary business.

7thly, That the freemen vote annually, in their town meetings respectively, for the judges of the superior court, at large through the government.

8thly, That the judges of the inferior court, attorney's general, probate judges, registrars, etc. be chosen, in manner before mentioned, by the inhabitants of each respective county: And, that the justices of the peace be also chosen by the people of each respective town, in proportion to the representatives.

9thly, That there be one general proxy day agreed upon for the people through the government, to vote for the officers as aforesaid, and that the representatives, likewise, fix upon one day of election, to be annual at which time the votes are to be brought in from the different towns and examined, and the persons for governors, a council, judges, registers, sheriffs, etc. are to be then published through the state.

10thly, That all the resolves of every assembly be conveyed from time to time, by the representatives to each respective town, and there enroled for the inhabitants to see, in order to instruct their said representatives.

11thly, That no person shall hold two public offices in a state, at the same time.

12thly, That no person shall be capable of holding any public office, except he professes a belief of one only invisible God, that governs all things; and that the bible is his revealed word; and that he be also an honest moral man.

13thly, That any freeman through the government may freely enter a complaint of defect or misdemeanour to the general assembly, against any of the executive state officers, [12] and if the assembly think there is just grounds for the said complaint, they may suspend the person so complained of in his office, appoint another for the present in his stead—but, be obliged to publish in the superior, or county courts, according as the person sustained his said office, their proceeding in that matter, with all their reasons for them; that the people, if they please, may drop the said person or persons, in their next annual election.

14thly, That the assembly may have power to negative any of their members a seat; but, should they do it, be obliged to inform the town or towns, that sent him or them, so negatived, with their reasons for such procedure, that the inhabitants may have an opportunity to chuse another or others, as soon as conveniently may be, which second choice it shall not be in power of the said assembly to negative.

15thly, That the particular town officers be chosen yearly by the inhabitants, as usual; and that each town clerk be the recorder of deeds.

16thly, That any orderly free male of ordinary capacity, and more than 21 years of age, having resided one year in a town, may be a legal voter, during his continuance; but, if he should be absent afterwards steadily more than a year that he should be divested then, of the privilege of voting in said town as if he never had resided there: Provided, he has not a real estate in the aforesaid town of at least one hundred pounds value lawful money.

17thly, That any legal voter shall be capable of holding any office, unless something that has been said to the contrary.

It is a darling principle of freedom, that those who make laws, ought not to execute them: But, notwithstanding, should it be inquired, whether there may be a proper course of appeals, in some important matters, from the superior court to the general assembly, I would answer affirmatively. The cases between man and man, together with their circumstances are so infinite in number, that it is impossible for them all to be specified by the letter of the law. The judges, therefore, in many cases, are obliged not to adhere to the letter, but to put such a construction on matters, as they think most agreeable to the spirit and reason of the law. Now, so far as they are reduced to this necessity, they assume what is in fact the prerogative of the [13] legislature, for those, that made the laws ought to give them a meaning, when they are doubtful. To make then the application: It may happen, that some very important cases may be attended with such circumstances, as are exceptions from the written law, agreeable to the old maxim, *summum jus, summa injusta, extreme right is extreme wrong*; or they may come under doubtful constructions. In either of these instances, the person, that is cast by the verdict, makes his appeal from the court to the general assembly; that they would virtually, in deciding his case, make a regulation, or rather in a legislative capacity, put a lasting construction on the written law, respecting affairs of that particular nature. Thus, by examining the principles of such appeals, we find they imply not that the legislative act in an executive capacity.

Lastly, let every government have an equal weight in the general congress and let the representatives of the respective states be chosen by the people annually by ballot, in their stated town meetings; the votes to be carried in, and published at the appointed election, as with respect to a governor, council, etc. in manner aforesaid; and the assemblies of the respective states may have power to instruct the said representatives from time to time; as they shall think proper.

It appears that the forms of government, that have hitherto been proposed since the breach with Great-Britain, by the friends of the American states, have been rather too arbitrary. The people are now contending for freedom, and would to God they might not only obtain but likewise keep it in their own hands. I own myself a friend to a popular government, have freely submitted my reasons upon it. And although the plan here proposed, might not ever been adapted as yet, nevertheless those as free, have alone secured the liberties of former ages; and a just notion of them has guarded the people against the sly insinuations and proposals of those, of more arbitrary turn, whose schemes have a tendency to deprive mankind of their natural rights.

FINIS.

[32]

JOHN ADAMS 1735–1826

Thoughts on Government

BOSTON, 1776

Revolutionary leader *par excellence,* Adams was born in Braintree, on the outskirts of Boston, where the first of his line had settled nearly a hundred years before. Educated at Harvard, he studied and practiced law in Braintree and Boston until public life pulled him away. Adams won high acclaim throughout the colonies for pamphlets, pieces in newspapers, and one extensive book that appeared as the Constitution was being drafted in Philadelphia. He represented Massachusetts in the Continental Congress from its beginning until pressed into service on a series of missions to European countries, and culminated his career with two terms as vice-president and one term as president of the United States. His greatest contributions to the conception and architecture of republican government may have been made in 1776, when he was highly influential in drafting the Declaration of Independence and the Articles of Confederation and wrote his remarkably succinct *Thoughts on Government;* and in 1780 when he was principal draftsman of the Massachusetts Constitution of that year, which is still in effect and has been widely copied.

The pamphlet *Thoughts on Government* originated as a letter written to two of North Carolina's delegates to the First Continental Congress. Adams probably wrote out three more copies with minor variations before Richard Henry Lee of Virginia put into print the version written some months before to George Wythe of Virginia. That is the version reproduced here. Lee, among others, credits Adams's "letter" with a highly determinative effect on the character of the state constitutions then being written. The editors have in this piece removed a number of commas that mar the flow of the prose.

BOSTON, 1776

My dear Sir,

If I was equal to the task of forming a plan for the government of a colony, I should be flattered with your request, and very happy to comply with it; because, as the divine science of politics is the science of social happiness, and the blessings of society depend entirely on the constitutions of government, which are generally institutions that last for many generations, there can be no employment more agreeable to a benevolent mind than a research after the best.

Pope flattered tyrants too much when he said,

> "For forms of government let fools contest,
> That which is best administered is best."

Nothing can be more fallacious than this. But poets read history to collect flowers, not fruits; they attend to fanciful images, not the effects of social institutions. Nothing is more certain, from the history of nations and nature of man, than that some forms of government are better fitted for being well administered than others.

We ought to consider what is the end of government, before we determine which is the best form. Upon this point all speculative politicians will agree, that the happiness of society is the end of government, as all divines and moral philosophers will agree that the happiness of the individual is the end of man. From this principle it will follow, that the form of government which communicates ease, comfort, security, or, in one word, happiness, to the greatest number of persons, and in the greatest degree, is the best.

All sober inquirers after truth, ancient and modern, pagan and Christian, have declared that the happiness of man, as well as his dignity, consists in virtue. Confucius, Zoroaster, Socrates, Mahomet, not to mention authorities really sacred, have agreed in this.

If there is a form of government, then, whose principle and foundation is virtue, will not every sober man acknowledge it better calculated to promote the general happiness than any other form?

Fear is the foundation of most governments; but it is so sordid and brutal a passion, and renders men in whose breasts it predominates so stupid and miserable, that Americans will not be likely to approve of any political institution which is founded on it.

Honor is truly sacred, but holds a lower rank in the scale of moral excellence than virtue. Indeed, the former is but a part of the latter, and consequently has not equal pretensions to support a frame of government productive of human happiness.

The foundation of every government is some principle or passion in the minds of the people. The noblest principles and most generous affections in our nature, then, have the fairest chance to support the noblest and most generous models of government.

A man must be indifferent to the sneers of modern Englishmen, to mention in their company the names of Sidney, Harrington, Locke, Milton, Nedham, Neville, Burnet, and Hoadly. No small fortitude is necessary to confess that one has read them. The wretched condition of this country, however, for ten or fifteen years past, has frequently reminded me of their principles and reasonings. They will convince any candid mind, that there is no good government but what is republican. That the only valuable part of the British constitution is so; because the very definition of a republic is "an empire of laws, and not of men." That, as a republic is the best of governments, so that particular arrangement of the powers of society, or, in other words, that form of government which is best contrived to secure an impartial and exact execution of the laws, is the best of republics.

Of republics there is an inexhaustible variety, because the possible combinations of the powers of society are capable of innumerable variations.

As good government is an empire of laws, how shall your laws be made? In a large society, inhabiting an extensive country, it is impossible that the whole should assemble to make laws. The first necessary step, then, is to depute power from the many to a few of the most wise and good. But by what rules shall you choose your representatives? Agree upon the number and qualifications of persons who shall have the benefit of choosing, or annex this privilege to the inhabitants of a certain extent of ground.

The principle difficulty lies, and the greatest care should be employed in constituting this representative assembly. It should be in miniature an exact portrait of the people at large. It should think, feel, reason and act like them. That it may be the interest of this assembly to do strict justice at all times, it should be an equal representation, or, in other words, equal interests among the people should have equal interests in it. Great care should be taken to effect this, and to prevent unfair, partial, and corrupt elections. Such regulations, however, may be better made in times of greater tranquillity than the present; and they will spring up themselves naturally, when all the powers of government come to be in the hands of the people's friends. At present, it will be safest to proceed in all established modes, to which the people have been familiarized by habit.

A representation of the people in one assembly being obtained, a question arises, whether all the powers of government, legislative, executive, and judicial, shall be left in this body? I think a people cannot be long free, nor ever happy, whose government is in one assembly. My reasons for this opinion are as follow:—

1. A single assembly is liable to all the vices, follies, and frailties of an individual; subject to fits of humor, starts of passion, flights of enthusiasm, partialities, or prejudice, and consequently productive of hasty results and absurd judgments. And all these errors ought to be corrected and defects supplied by some controlling power.

2. A single assembly is apt to be avaricious, and in time will not scruple to exempt itself from burdens, which it will lay, without compunction, on its constitutents.

3. A single assembly is apt to grow ambitious, and after a time will not hesitate to vote itself perpetual. This was one fault of the Long Parliament; but more remarkably of Holland, whose assembly first voted themselves from annual to septennial, then for life, and after a course of years, that all vacancies happening by death or otherwise, should be filled by themselves, without any application to constituents at all.

4. A representative assembly, although extremely well qualified, and absolutely necessary, as a branch of the legislative, is unfit to exercise the executive power, for want of two essential properties, secrecy and despatch.

5. A representative assembly is still less qualified for the judicial power, because it is too numerous, too slow, and too little skilled in the laws.

6. Because a single assembly, possessed of all the powers of government, would make arbitrary laws for their own interest, execute all laws arbitrarily for their own interest, and adjudge all controversies in their own favor.

But shall the whole power of legislation rest in one assembly? Most of the foregoing reasons apply equally to prove that the legislative power ought to be more complex; to which we may add, that if the legislative power is wholly in one assembly, and the executive in another, or in a single person, these two powers will oppose and encroach upon each other, until the contest shall end in war, and the whole power, legislative and executive, be usurped by the strongest.

The judicial power, in such case, could not mediate, or hold the balance between the two contending powers, because the legislative would undermine it. And this shows the necessity, too, of giving the executive power a negative upon the legislative, otherwise this will be continually encroaching upon that.

To avoid these dangers, let a distinct assembly be constituted, as a mediator between the two extreme branches of the legislature, that which represents the people, and that which is vested with the executive power.

Let the representative assembly then elect by ballot, from among themselves or their constituents, or both, a distinct assembly, which, for the sake of perspicuity, we will call a council. It may consist of any number you please, say twenty or thirty, and should have a free and independent exercise of its judgment, and consequently a negative voice in the legislature.

These two bodies, thus constituted, and made integral parts of the legislature, let them unite, and by joint ballot choose a governor, who, after being stripped of most of those badges of domination, called prerogatives, should have a free and independent exercise of his judgment, and be made also an integral part of the legislature. This, I know, is liable to objections; and, if you please, you may make him only president of the council, as in Connecticut. But as the governor is to be invested with the executive power, with consent of council, I think he ought to have a negative upon the legislative. If he is annually elective, as he ought to be, he will always have so much reverence and affection for the people, their representatives and counsellors, that, although you give him an independent exercise of his judgment, he will seldom use it in opposition to the two houses, except in cases the public utility of which would be conspicuous; and some such cases would happen.

In the present exigency of American affairs, when, by an act of Parliament, we are put out of the royal protection, and consequently discharged from our allegiance, and it has become necessary to assume government for our immediate security, the governor, lieutenant-governor, secretary, treasurer, commissary, attorney-general, should be chosen by joint ballot of both houses. And these and all other elections, especially of representatives and counsellors, should be annual, there not being in the whole circle of the sciences a maxim more infallible than this, "where annual elections end, there slavery begins."

These great men, in this respect, should be, once a year,

"Like bubbles on the sea of matter borne,
They rise, they break, and to that sea return."

This will teach them the great political virtues of humility, patience, and moderation, without which every man in power becomes a ravenous beast of prey.

This mode of constituting the great offices of state will answer very well for the present; but if by experiment it should be found inconvenient, the legislature may, at its leisure, devise other methods of creating them, by elections of the people at large, as in Connecticut, or it may enlarge the term for which they shall be chosen to seven years, or three years, or for life, or make any other alterations which the society shall find productive of its ease, its safety, its freedom, or, in one word, its happiness.

A rotation of all offices, as well as of representatives and counsellors, has many advocates, and is contended for with many plausible arguments. It would be attended, no doubt, with many advantages; and if the society has a sufficient number of suitable characters to supply the great number of vacancies which would be made by such a rotation, I can see no objection to it. These persons may be allowed to serve for three years, and then be excluded three years, or for any longer or shorter term.

Any seven or nine of the legislative council may be made a quorum, for doing business as a privy council, to advise the governor in the exercise of the executive branch of power, and in all acts of state.

The governor should have the command of the militia and of all your armies. The power of pardons should be with the governor and council.

Judges, justices, and all other officers, civil and military, should be nominated and appointed by the governor, with the advice and consent of council, unless you choose to have a government more popular; if you do, all officers, civil and military, may be chosen by joint ballot of both houses; or, in order to preserve the independence and importance of each house, by ballot of one house, concurred in by the other. Sheriffs should be chosen by the freeholders of counties; so should registers of deeds and clerks of counties.

All officers should have commissions, under the hand of the governor and seal of the colony.

The dignity and stability of government in all its branches, the morals of the people, and every blessing of society depend so much upon an upright and skillful administration of justice, that the judicial power ought to be distinct from both the legislative and executive, and independent upon both, that so it may be a check upon both, as both should be checks upon that. The judges, therefore, should be always men of learning and experience in the laws, of exemplary morals, great patience, calmness, coolness, and attention. Their minds should not be distracted. with jarring interests; they should not be dependent upon any man, or body of men. To these ends, they should hold estates for life in their offices; or, in other words, their commissions should be during good behavior, and their salaries ascertained and established by law. For misbehavior, the grand inquest of the colony, the house of representatives, should impeach them before the governor and council, where they should have time and opportunity to make their defence; but, if convicted, should be removed from their offices, and subjected to such other punishment as shall be proper.

A militia law, requiring all men, or with very few exceptions besides cases of conscience, to be provided with arms and ammunition, to be trained at certain seasons; and requiring counties, towns, or other small districts, to be provided with public stocks of ammunition and intrenching utensils, and with some settled plans for transporting provisions after the militia, when marched to defend their country against sudden invasions; and requiring certain districts to be provided with field-pieces, companies of matrosses, and perhaps some regiments of light-horse, is always a wise institution, and, in the present circumstances of our country, indispensable.

Laws for liberal education of youth, especially of the lower class of people, are so extremely wise and useful, that, to a humane and generous mind, no expense for this purpose would be thought extravagant.

The very mention of sumptuary laws will excite a smile. Whether our countrymen have wisdom and virtue enough to submit to them, I know not; but the happiness of the people might be greatly promoted by them, and a revenue saved sufficient to carry on this war forever. Frugality is a great revenue, besides curing us of vanities, levities, and fopperies, which are real antidotes to all great, manly, and warlike virtues.

But must not all commissions run in the name of a king? No. Why may they not as well run thus, "The colony of   to A.B. greeting," and be tested by the governor?

Why may not writs, instead of running in the name of the king, run thus, "The colony of   to the sheriff," &c., and be tested by the chief justice?

Why may not indictments conclude, "against the peace of the colony of   and the dignity of the same?"

A constitution founded on these principles introduces knowledge among the people, and inspires them with a conscious dignity becoming freemen; a general emulation takes place, which causes good humor, sociability, good manners, and good morals to be general. That elevation of sentiment inspired by such a government, makes the common people brave and enterprising. That ambition which is inspired by it makes them sober, industrious, and frugal. You will find among them some elegance, perhaps, but more solidity; a little pleasure, but a great deal of business; some politeness, but more civility. If you compare such a country with the regions of domination, whether monarchical or aristocratical, you will fancy yourself in Arcadia or Elysium.

If the colonies should assume governments separately, they should be left entirely to their own choice of the forms; and if a continental constitution should be formed, it should be a congress, containing a fair and adequate representation of the colonies, and its authority should sacredly be confined to those cases, namely, war, trade, disputes between colony and colony, the post-office, and the unappropriated lands of the crown, as they used to be called.

These colonies, under such forms of government, and in such a union, would be unconquerable by all the monarchies of Europe.

You and I, my dear friend, have been sent into life at a time when the greatest lawgivers of antiquity would have wished to live. How few of the human race have ever enjoyed an opportunity of making an election of government, more than of air, soil, or climate, for themselves or their children! When, before the present epocha, had three millions of people full power and a fair opportunity to form and establish the wisest and happiest government that human wisdom can contrive? I hope you will avail yourself and your country of that extensive learning and indefatigable industry which you possess, to assist her in the formation of the happiest governments and the best character of a great people. For myself, I must beg you to keep my name out of sight; for this feeble attempt, if it should be known to be mine, would oblige me to apply to myself those lines of the immortal John Milton, in one of his sonnets:—

"I did but prompt the age to quit their clogs
By the known rules of ancient liberty,
When straight a barbarous noise environs me
Of owls and cuckoos, asses, apes, and dogs."

[33]

SAMUEL WEST 1730–1807

On the Right to Rebel Against Governors
(Election Day Sermon)

BOSTON, 1776

Samuel West was another of New England's revered and highly influential clergymen. After completing his education at Harvard and a five-year turn at teaching, West took over the Congregational pulpit at Dartmouth, Massachusetts (later called New Bedford), and retained that post until death approached. Persistent in study, West was widely regarded to be one of the most learned men of his time, and because of his reputation, he was repeatedly sought out for advice on political matters. He was an active member of the convention that drew up the Massachusetts Constitution of 1780, but when invited to serve as a member of the Massachusetts delegation to the national convention of 1787, he declined to make the trip to Philadelphia. He was, however, a strong force for acceptance of the new Constitution in the Massachusetts ratifying convention of 1788. This particular sermon was preached before the Council and House of Representatives on the anniversary of the members' having been elected. Originally published in Boston by John Gill, the text here is based upon one edited by J.W. Thornton: *The Pulpit of the American Revolution*, pages 267–322.

PUT THEM IN MIND TO BE SUBJECT TO PRINCIPALITIES AND POWERS, TO OBEY MAGISTRATES, TO BE READY TO EVERY GOOD WORK.—Titus iii. 1.

The great Creator, having designed the human race for society, has made us dependent on one another for happiness. He has so constituted us that it becomes both our duty and interest to seek the public good; and that we may be the more firmly engaged to promote each other's welfare, the Deity has endowed us with tender and social affections, with generous and benevolent principles: hence the pain that we feel in seeing an object of distress; hence the satisfaction that arises in relieving the afflictions, and the superior pleasure which we experience in communicating happiness to the miserable. The Deity has also invested us with moral powers and faculties, by which we are enabled to discern the difference between right and wrong, truth and falsehood, good and evil: hence the approbation of mind that arises upon doing a good action, and the remorse of conscience which we experience when we counteract the moral sense and do that which is evil. This proves that, in what is commonly called a state of nature, we are the subjects of the divine law and government; that the Deity is our supreme magistrate, who has written his law in our hearts, and will reward or punish us according as we obey or disobey his commands. Had the human race uniformly persevered in a state of moral rectitude, there would have been little or no need of any other law besides that which is written in the heart,—for every one in such a state would be a law unto himself. There could be no occasion for enacting or enforcing of penal laws; for such are "not made for the righteous man, but for the lawless and disobedient, for the ungodly, and for sinners, for the unholy and profane, for murderers of fathers and murderers of mothers, for manslayers, for whoremongers, for them that defile themselves with mankind, for men-stealers, for liars, for perjured persons, and if there be any other thing that is contrary to" moral rectitude and the happiness of mankind. The necessity of forming ourselves into politic bodies, and granting to our rulers a power to enact laws for the public safety, and to enforce them by proper penalties, arises from our being in a fallen and degenerate state. The slightest view of the present state and condition of the human race is abundantly sufficient to convince any person of common sense and common honesty that civil government is absolutely necessary for the peace and safety of mankind; and, consequently, that all good magistrates, while they faithfully discharge the trust reposed in them, ought to be religiously and conscientiously obeyed. An enemy to good government is an enemy not only to his country, but to all mankind; for he plainly shows himself to be divested of those tender and social sentiments which are characteristic of a human temper, even of that generous and benevolent disposition which is the peculiar glory of a rational creature. An enemy to good government has degraded himself below the rank and dignity of a man, and deserves to be classed with the lower creation. Hence we find that wise and good men, of all nations and religions, have ever inculcated subjection to good government, and have borne their testimony against the licentious disturbers of the public peace.

Nor has Christianity been deficient in this capital point. We find our blessed Saviour directing the Jews to render to Caesar the things that were Caesar's; and the apostles and first preachers of the gospel not only exhibited a good example of subjection to the magistrate, in all things that were just and lawful, but they have also, in several places in the New Testament, strongly enjoined upon Christians the duty of submission to that government under which Providence had placed them. Hence we find that those who despise government, and are not afraid to speak evil of dignities, are, by the apostles Peter and Jude, classed among those presumptuous, self-willed sinners that are reserved to the judgment of the great day. And the apostle Paul judged submission to civil government to be a matter of such great importance, that he thought it worth his while to charge Titus to put his hearers in mind to be submissive to principalities and powers, to obey magistrates, to be ready to every good work; as much as to say, none can be ready to every good work, or be properly disposed to perform those actions that tend to promote the public good, who do not obey magistrates, and who do not become good subjects of civil government. If, then, obedience to the civil magistrates is so essential to the character of a Christian, that without it he cannot be disposed to perform those good works that are necessary for the welfare of mankind,—if the despisers of governments are those presumptuous, self-willed sinners who are reserved to the judgment of the great day,—it is certainly a matter of the utmost importance to us all to be thoroughly acquainted with the nature and extent of our duty, that we may yield the obedience required; for it is impossible that we should properly discharge a duty when we are strangers to the nature and extent of it.

In order, therefore, that we may form a right judgment of the duty enjoined in our text, I shall consider the nature and design of civil government, and shall show that the same principles which oblige us to submit to government do equally oblige us to resist tyranny; or

SAMUEL WEST 1730-1807

that tyranny and magistracy are so opposed to each other that where the one begins the other ends. I shall then apply the present discourse to the grand controversy that at this day subsists between Great Britain and the American colonies.

That we may understand the nature and design of civil government, and discover the foundation of the magistrate's authority to command, and the duty of subjects to obey, it is necessary to derive civil government from its original, in order to which we must consider what "state all men are naturally in, and that is (as Mr. Locke observes) a state of perfect freedom to order all their actions, and dispose of their possessions and persons as they think fit, within the bounds of the law of nature, without asking leave or depending upon the will of any man." It is a state wherein all are equal,—no one having a right to control another, or oppose him in what he does, unless it be in his own defence, or in the defence of those that, being injured, stand in need of his assistance.

Had men persevered in a state of moral rectitude, every one would have been disposed to follow the law of nature, and pursue the general good. In such a state, the wisest and most experienced would undoubtedly be chosen to guide and direct those of less wisdom and experience than themselves,—there being nothing else that could afford the least show or appearance of any one's having the superiority or precedency over another; for the dictates of conscience and the precepts of natural law being uniformly and regularly obeyed, men would only need to be informed what things were most fit and prudent to be done in those cases where their inexperience or want of acquaintance left their minds in doubt what was the wisest and most regular method for them to pursue. In such cases it would be necessary for them to advise with those who were wiser and more experienced than themselves. But these advisers could claim no authority to compel or to use any forcible measures to oblige any one to comply with their direction or advice. There could be no occasion for the exertion of such a power; for every man, being under the government of right reason, would immediately feel himself constrained to comply with everything that appeared reasonable or fit to be done, or that would any way tend to promote the general good. This would have been the happy state of mankind had they closely adhered to the law of nature, and persevered in their primitive state.

Thus we see that a state of nature, though it be a state of perfect freedom, yet is very far from a state of licentiousness. The law of nature gives men no right to do anything that is immoral, or contrary to the will of God, and injurious to their fellow-creatures; for a state of nature is properly a state of law and government, even a government founded upon the unchangeable nature of the Deity, and a law resulting from the eternal fitness of things. Sooner shall heaven and earth pass away, and the whole frame of nature be dissolved, than any part even the smallest iota, of this law shall ever be abrogated; it is unchangeable as the Deity himself, being a transcript of his moral perfections. A revelation, pretending to be from God, that contradicts any part of natural law, ought immediately to be rejected as an imposture; for the Deity cannot make a law contrary to the law of nature without acting contrary to himself,—a thing in the strictest sense impossible, for that which implies contradiction is not an object of the divine power. Had this subject been properly attended to and understood, the world had remained free from a multitude of absurd and pernicious principles, which have been industriously propagated by artful and designing men, both in politics and divinity. The doctrine of non-resistance and unlimited passive obedience to the worst of tyrants could never have found credit among mankind had the voice of reason been hearkened to for a guide, because such a doctrine would immediately have been discerned to be contrary to natural law.

In a state of nature we have a right to make the persons that have injured us repair the damages that they have done us; and it is just in us to inflict such punishment upon them as is necessary to restrain them from doing the like for the future,—the whole end and design of punishing being either to reclaim the individual punished, or to deter others from being guilty of similar crimes. Whenever punishment exceeds these bounds it becomes cruelty and revenge, and directly contrary to the law of nature. Our wants and necessities being such as to render it impossible in most cases to enjoy life in any tolerable degree without entering into society, and there being innumerable cases wherein we need the assistance of others, which if not afforded we should very soon perish; hence the law of nature requires that we should endeavor to help one another to the utmost of our power in all cases where our assistance is necessary. It is our duty to endeavor always to promote the general good; to do to all as we would be willing to be done by were we in their circumstances; to do justly, to love mercy, and to walk humbly before God. These

are some of the laws of nature which every man in the world is bound
to observe, and which whoever violates exposes himself to the
resentment of mankind, the lashes of his own conscience, and the
judgment of Heaven. This plainly shows that the highest state of
liberty subjects us to the law of nature and the government of God.
The most perfect freedom consists in obeying the dictates of right
reason, and submitting to natural law. When a man goes beyond or
contrary to the law of nature and reason, he becomes the slave of base
passions and vile lusts; he introduces confusion and disorder into
society, and brings misery and destruction upon himself. This,
therefore, cannot be called a state of freedom, but a state of the vilest
slavery and the most dreadful bondage. The servants of sin and
corruption are subjected to the worst kind of tyranny in the universe.
Hence we conclude that where licentiousness begins, liberty ends.

The law of nature is a perfect standard and measure of action for
beings that persevere in a state of moral rectitude; but the case is far
different with us, who are in a fallen and degenerate estate. We have
a law in our members which is continually warring against the law of
the mind, by which we often become enslaved to the basest lusts, and
are brought into bondage to the vilest passions. The strong propensities
of our animal nature often overcome the sober dictates of reason and
conscience, and betray us into actions injurious to the public and
destructive of the safety and happiness of society. Men of unbridled
lusts, were they not restrained by the power of the civil magistrate,
would spread horror and desolation all around them. This makes it
absolutely necessary that societies should form themselves into politic
bodies, that they may enact laws for the public safety, and appoint
particular penalties for the violation of their laws, and invest a suitable
number of persons with authority to put in execution and enforce the
laws of the state, in order that wicked men may be restrained from
doing mischief to their fellow-creatures, that the injured may have
their rights restored to them, that the virtuous may be encouraged in
doing good, and that every member of society may be protected and
secured in the peaceable, quiet possession and enjoyment of all those
liberties and privileges which the Deity has bestowed upon him; *i.e.,*
that he may safely enjoy and pursue whatever he chooses, that is
consistent with the public good. This shows that the end and design
of civil government cannot be to deprive men of their liberty or take

away their freedom; but, on the contrary, the true design of civil government is to protect men in the enjoyment of liberty.

From hence it follows that tyranny and arbitrary power are utterly inconsistent with and subversive of the very end and design of civil government, and directly contrary to natural law, which is the true foundation of civil government and all politic law. Consequently, the authority of a tyrant is of itself null and void; for as no man can have a right to act contrary to the law of nature, it is impossible that any individual, or even the greatest number of men, can confer a right upon another of which they themselves are not possessed; *i.e.,* no body of men can justly and lawfully authorize any person to tyrannize over and enslave his fellow-creatures, or do anything contrary to equity and goodness. As magistrates have no authority but what they derive from the people, whenever they act contrary to the public good, and pursue measures destructive of the peace and safety of the community, they forfeit their right to govern the people. Civil rulers and magistrates are properly of human creation; they are set up by the people to be the guardians of their rights, and to secure their persons from being injured or oppressed,—the safety of the public being the supreme law of the state, by which the magistrates are to be governed, and which they are to consult upon all occasions. The modes of administration may be very different, and the forms of government may vary from each other in different ages and nations; but, under every form, the end of civil government is the same, and cannot vary: it is like the laws of the Medes and Persians—it altereth not.

Though magistrates are to consider themselves as the servants of the people, seeing from them it is that they derive their power and authority, yet they may also be considered as the ministers of God ordained by him for the good of mankind; for, under him, as the Supreme Magistrate of the universe, they are to act: and it is God who has not only declared in his word what are the necessary qualifications of a ruler, but who also raises up and qualifies men for such an important station. The magistrate may also, in a more strict and proper sense, be said to be ordained of God, because *reason,* which is the voice of God, plainly requires such an order of men to be appointed for the public good. Now, whatever right reason requires as necessary to be done is as much the will and law of God as though it were enjoined us by an immediate revelation from heaven, or commanded in the sacred Scriptures.

From this account of the origin, nature, and design of civil government, we may be very easily led into a thorough knowledge of our duty; we may see the reason why we are bound to obey magistrates, viz., because they are the ministers of God for good unto the people. While, therefore, they rule in the fear of God, and while they promote the welfare of the state,—*i.e.,* while they act in the character of magistrates,—it is the indispensable duty of all to submit to them, and to oppose a turbulent, factious, and libertine spirit, whenever and wherever it discovers itself. When a people have by their free consent conferred upon a number of men a power to rule and govern them, they are bound to obey them. Hence disobedience becomes a breach of faith; it is violating a constitution of their own appointing, and breaking a compact for which they ought to have the most sacred regard. Such a conduct discovers so base and disingenuous a temper of mind, that it must expose them to contempt in the judgment of all the sober, thinking part of mankind. Subjects are bound to obey lawful magistrates by every tender tie of human nature, which disposes us to consult the public good, and to seek the good of our brethren, our wives, our children, our friends and acquaintance; for he that opposes lawful authority does really oppose the safety and happiness of his fellow-creatures. A factious, seditious person, that opposes good government, is a monster in nature; for he is an enemy to his own species, and destitute of the sentiments of humanity.

Subjects are also bound to obey magistrates, for conscience' sake, out of regard to the divine authority, and out of obedience to the will of God; for if magistrates are the ministers of God, we cannot disobey them without being disobedient to the law of God; and this extends to all men in authority, from the highest ruler to the lowest officer in the state. To oppose them when in the exercise of lawful authority is an act of disobedience to the Deity, and, as such, will be punished by him. It will, doubtless, be readily granted by every honest man that we ought cheerfully to obey the magistrate, and submit to all such regulations of government as tend to promote the public good; but as this general definition may be liable to be misconstrued, and every man may think himself at liberty to disregard any laws that do not suit his interest, humor, or fancy, I would observe that, in a multitude of cases, many of us, for want of being properly acquainted with affairs of state, may be very improper judges of particular laws, whether they are just or not. In such cases it becomes us, as good members of society, peaceably and conscientiously to submit, though we cannot see the reasonableness of every law to which we submit, and that for this plain reason: if any number of men should take it upon themselves to oppose authority for acts, which may be really necessary for the public safety, only because they do not see the reasonableness of them, the direct consequence will be introducing confusion and anarchy into the state.

It is also necessary that the minor part should submit to the major; *e.g.*, when legislators have enacted a set of laws which are highly approved by a large majority of the community as tending to promote the public good, in this case, if a small number of persons are so unhappy as to view the matter in a very different point of light from the public, though they have an undoubted right to show the reasons of their dissent from the judgment of the public, and may lawfully use all proper arguments to convince the public of what they judge to be an error, yet, if they fail in their attempt, and the majority still continue to approve of the laws that are enacted, it is the duty of those few that dissent peaceably and for conscience's sake to submit to the public judgment, unless something is required of them which they judge would be sinful for them to comply with; for in that case they ought to obey the dictates of their own consciences rather than any human authority whatever. Perhaps, also, some cases of intolerable oppression, where compliance would bring on inevitable ruin and destruction, may justly warrant the few to refuse submission to what they judge inconsistent with their peace and safety; for the law of self-preservation will always justify opposing a cruel and tyrannical imposition, except where opposition is attended with greater evils than submission, which is frequently the case where a few are oppressed by a large and powerful majority.[a] Except the above-named cases, the minor ought always to submit to the major; otherwise, there can be no peace nor harmony in society. And, besides, it is the major part of a community that have the sole right of establishing a constitution

[a] This shows the reason why the primitive Christians did not oppose the cruel persecutions that were inflicted upon them by the heathen magistrates. They were few compared with the heathen world, and for them to have attempted to resist their enemies by force would have been like a small parcel of sheep endeavoring to oppose a large number of ravening wolves and savage beasts of prey. It would, without a miracle, have brought upon them inevitable ruin and destruction. Hence the wise and prudent advice of our Saviour to them is, "When they persecute you in this city, flee ye to another."

and authorizing magistrates; and consequently it is only the major part of the community that can claim the right of altering the constitution, and displacing the magistrates; for certainly common sense will tell us that it requires as great an authority to set aside a constitution as there was at first to establish it. The collective body, not a few individuals, ought to constitute the supreme authority of the state.

The only difficulty remaining is to determine when a people may claim a right of forming themselves into a body politic, and assume the powers of legislation. In order to determine this point, we are to remember that all men being by nature equal, all the members of a community have a natural right to assemble themselves together, and act and vote for such regulations as they judge are necessary for the good of the whole. But when a community is become very numerous, it is very difficult, and in many cases impossible, for all to meet together to regulate the affairs of the state; hence comes the necessity of appointing delegates to represent the people in a general assembly. And this ought to be looked upon as a sacred and inalienable right, of which a people cannot justly divest themselves, and which no human authority can in equity ever take from them, viz., that no one be obliged to submit to any law except such as are made either by himself or by his representative.

If representation and legislation are inseparably connected, it follows, that when great numbers have emigrated into a foreign land, and are so far removed from the parent state that they neither are or can be properly represented by the government from which they have emigrated, that then nature itself points out the necessity of their assuming to themselves the powers of legislation; and they have a right to consider themselves as a separate state from the other, and, as such, to form themselves into a body politic.

In the next place, when a people find themselves cruelly oppressed by the parent state, they have an undoubted right to throw off the yoke, and to assert their liberty, if they find good reason to judge that they have sufficient power and strength to maintain their ground in defending their just rights against their oppressors; for, in this case, by the law of self-preservation, which is the first law of nature, they have not only an undoubted right, but it is their indispensable duty, if they cannot be redressed any other way, to renounce all submission to the government that has oppressed them, and set up an independent state of their own, even though they may be vastly inferior in numbers to the state that has oppressed them. When either of the aforesaid cases takes place, and more especially when both concur, no rational man, I imagine, can have any doubt in his own mind whether such a people have a right to form themselves into a body politic, and assume to themselves all the powers of a free state. For, can it be rational to suppose that a people should be subjected to the tyranny of a set of men who are perfect strangers to them, and cannot be supposed to have that fellow-feeling for them that we generally have for those with whom we are connected and acquainted; and, besides, through their unacquaintedness with the circumstances of the people over whom they claim the right of jurisdiction, are utterly unable to judge, in a multitude of cases, which is best for them?

It becomes me not to say what particular form of government is best for a community,—whether a pure democracy, aristocracy, monarchy, or a mixture of all the three simple forms. They have all their advantages and disadvantages, and when they are properly administered may, any of them, answer the design of civil government tolerably. Permit me, however, to say, that an unlimited, absolute monarchy, and an aristocracy not subject to the control of the people, are two of the most exceptionable forms of government: firstly, because in neither of them is there a proper representation of the people; and, secondly, because each of them being entirely independent of the people, they are very apt to degenerate into tyranny. However, in this imperfect state, we cannot expect to have government formed upon such a basis but that it may be perverted by bad men to evil purposes. A wise and good man would be very loth to undermine a constitution that was once fixed and established, although he might discover many imperfections in it; and nothing short of the most urgent necessity would ever induce him to consent to it; because the unhinging a people from a form of government to which they had been long accustomed might throw them into such a state of anarchy and confusion as might terminate in their destruction, or perhaps, in the end, subject them to the worst kind of tyranny.

Having thus shown the nature, end, and design of civil government, and pointed out the reasons why subjects are bound to obey magistrates,—viz., because in so doing they both consult their own happiness as individuals, and also promote the public good and the safety of the state,—I proceed, in the next place, to show that the same principles that oblige us to submit to civil government do also equally oblige us, where we have power and ability, to resist and oppose tyranny; and that where tyranny begins government ends. For, if magistrates have no authority but what they derive from the people; if they are properly of human creation; if the whole end and design of their institution is to promote the general good, and to secure to men their just rights,—it will follow, that when they act contrary to the end and design of their creation they cease being magistrates, and the people which gave them their authority have the right to take it from them again. This is a very plain dictate of common sense, which universally obtains in all similar cases; for who is there that, having employed a number of men to do a particular piece of work for him, but what would judge that he had a right to dismiss them from his service when he found that they went directly contrary to his orders, and that, instead of accomplishing the business he had set them about, they would infallibly ruin and destroy it? If, then, men, in the common affairs of life, always judge that they have a right to dismiss from their service such persons as counteract their plans and designs, though the damage will affect only a few individuals, much more must the body politic have a right to depose any persons, though appointed to the highest place of power and authority, when they find that they are unfaithful to the trust reposed in them, and that, instead of consulting the general good, they are disturbing the peace of society by making laws cruel and oppressive, and by depriving the subjects of their just rights and privileges. Whoever pretends to deny this proposition must give up all pretence of being master of that common sense and reason by which the Deity has distinguished us from the brutal herd.

As our duty of obedience to the magistrate is founded upon our obligation to promote the general good, our readiness to obey lawful authority will always arise in proportion to the love and regard that we have for the welfare of the public; and the same love and regard for the public will inspire us with as strong a zeal to oppose tyranny as we have to obey magistracy. Our obligation to promote the public good extends as much to the opposing every exertion of arbitrary power that is injurious to the state as it does to the submitting to good and wholesome laws. No man, therefore, can be a good member of the community that is not as zealous to oppose tyranny as he is ready to obey magistracy. A slavish submission to tyranny is a proof of a very sordid and base mind. Such a person cannot be under the influence of any generous human sentiments, nor have a tender regard for mankind.

Further: if magistrates are no farther ministers of God than they promote the good of the community, then obedience to them neither is nor can be unlimited; for it would imply a gross absurdity to assert that, when magistrates are ordained by the people solely for the purpose of being beneficial to the state, they must be obeyed when they are seeking to ruin and destroy it. This would imply that men were bound to act against the great law of self-preservation, and to contribute their assistance to their own ruin and destruction, in order that they may please and gratify the greatest monsters in nature, who are violating the laws of God and destroying the rights of mankind. Unlimited submission and obedience is due to none but God alone. He has an absolute right to command; he alone has an uncontrollable sovereignty over us, because he alone is unchangeably good; he never will nor can require of us, consistent with his nature and attributes, anything that is not fit and reasonable; his commands are all just and good; and to suppose that he has given to any particular set of men a power to require obedience to that which is unreasonable, cruel, and unjust, is robbing the Deity of his justice and goodness, in which consists the peculiar glory of the divine character, and it is representing him under the horrid character of a tyrant.

If magistrates are ministers of God only because the law of God and reason points out the necessity of such an institution for the good of mankind, it follows, that whenever they pursue measures directly destructive of the public good they cease being God's ministers, they forfeit their right to obedience from the subject, they become the pests of society, and the community is under the strongest obligation of duty, both to God and to its own members, to resist and oppose them, which will be so far from resisting the ordinance of God that it will be strictly obeying his commands. To suppose otherwise will imply that the Deity requires of us an obedience that is self-contradictory and absurd, and that one part of his law is directly contrary to the other; i. e., while he commands us to pursue virtue and the general good, he does at the same time require us to persecute virtue, and betray the general good, by enjoining us obedience to the wicked commands of tyrannical oppressors. Can any one not lost to the principles of humanity undertake to defend such absurd sentiments as these? As the public safety is the first and grand law of society, so no community can have a right to invest the magistrate with any power or authority that will enable him to act against the welfare of the state and the good of the whole. If men have at any time wickedly and foolishly given up their just rights into the hands of the magistrate, such acts are null and void, of course; to suppose otherwise will imply that we have a right to invest the magistrate with a power to act contrary to the law of God,—which is as much as to say that we are not the subjects of divine law and government. What has been said is, I apprehend, abundantly sufficient to show that tyrants are no magistrates, or that whenever magistrates abuse their power and authority to the subverting the public happiness, their authority immediately ceases, and that it not only becomes lawful, but an indispensable duty to oppose them; that the principle of self-preservation, the affection and duty that we owe to our country, and the obedience we owe the Deity, do all require us to oppose tyranny.

If it be asked, Who are the proper judges to determine when rulers are guilty of tyranny and oppression? I answer, the public. Not a few disaffected individuals, but the collective body of the state, must decide this question; for, as it is the collective body that invests rulers with their power and authority, so it is the collective body that has the sole right of judging whether rulers act up to the end of their institution or not. Great regard ought always to be paid to the judgment of the public. It is true the public may be imposed upon by a misrepresentation of facts; but this may be said of the public, which cannot always be said of individuals, viz., that the public is always willing to be rightly informed, and when it has proper matter of conviction laid before it its judgment is always right.

This account of the nature and design of civil government, which is so clearly suggested to us by the plain principles of common sense and reason, is abundantly confirmed by the sacred Scriptures, even by those very texts which have been brought by men of slavish principles to establish the absurd doctrine of unlimited passive obedience and non-resistance, as will abundantly appear by examining the two most noted texts that are commonly brought to support the strange doctrine of passive obedience. The first that I shall cite is in 1 Peter ii. 13, 14: "Submit yourselves to every ordinance of man,"—or, rather, as the words ought to be rendered from the Greek, submit yourselves to every human creation, or human constitution,—"for the Lord's sake, whether it be to the king as supreme, or unto governors, as unto them that are sent by him for the punishment of evil-doers, and for the praise of them that do well." Here we see that the apostle asserts that magistracy is of human creation or appointment; that is, that magistrates have no power or authority but what they derive from the people; that this power they are to exert for the punishment of evil-doers, and for the praise of them that do well; *i. e.,* the end and design of the appointment of magistrates is to restrain wicked men, by proper penalties, from injuring society, and to encourage and honor the virtuous and obedient. Upon this account Christians are to submit to them for the Lord's sake; which is as if he had said, Though magistrates are of mere human appointment, and can claim no power or authority but what they derive from the people, yet, as they are ordained by men to promote the general good by punishing evil-doers and by rewarding and encouraging the virtuous and obedient, you ought to submit to them out of a sacred regard to the divine authority; for as they, in the faithful discharge of their office, do fulfill the will of God, so ye, by submitting to them, do fulfil the divine command. If the only reason assigned by the apostle why magistrates should be obeyed out of a regard to the divine authority is because they punish the wicked and encourage the good, it follows, that when they punish the virtuous and encourage the vicious we have a right to refuse yielding any submission or obedience to them; *i. e.,* whenever they act contrary to the end and design of their institution, they forfeit their authority to govern the people, and the reason for submitting to them, out of regard to the divine authority, immediately ceases; and they being only of human appointment, the authority which the people gave them the public have a right to take from them, and to confer it upon those who are more worthy. So far is this text from favoring arbitrary principles, that there is nothing in it but what is consistent with and favorable to the highest liberty that any man can wish to enjoy; for this text requires us to submit to the magistrate no further than he is the encourager and protector of virtue and the punisher of vice; and this is consistent with all that liberty which the Deity has bestowed upon us.

The other text which I shall mention, and which has been made use of by the favorers of arbitrary government as their great sheet-anchor and main support, is in Rom. xiii., the first six verses: "Let every soul be subject to the higher powers; for there is no power but of God. The powers that be are ordained of God. Whosoever therefore resisteth the power, resisteth the ordinance of God; and they that resist shall receive to themselves damnation; for rulers are not a terror to good works, but to the evil. Wilt thou then not be afraid of the power? Do that which is good, and thou shalt have praise of the same: for he is the minister of God to thee for good. But if thou do that which is evil, be afraid; for he beareth not the sword in vain: for he is the minister of God, a revenger to execute wrath upon him that doth evil. Wherefore ye must needs be subject not only for wrath, but also for conscience' sake. For, for this cause pay you tribute also; for they are God's ministers, attending continually upon this very thing." A very little attention, I apprehend, will be sufficient to show that this text is so far from favoring arbitrary government, that, on the contrary, it strongly holds forth the principles of true liberty. Subjection to the higher powers is enjoined by the apostle because there is no power but of God; the powers that be are ordained of God; consequently, to resist the power is to resist the ordinance of God: and he repeatedly declares that the ruler is the minister of God. Now, before we can say whether this text makes for or against the doctrine of unlimited passive obedience, we must find out in what sense the apostle affirms that magistracy is the ordinance of God, and what he intends when he calls the ruler the minister of God.

I can think but of three possible senses in which magistracy can with any propriety be called God's ordinance, or in which rulers can be said to be ordained of God as his ministers. The first is a plain declaration from the word of God that such a one and his descendants are, and shall be, the only true and lawful magistrates: thus we find in Scripture the kingdom of Judah to be settled by divine appointment in the family of David. Or,

Secondly, By an immediate commission from God, ordering and appointing such a one by name to be the ruler over the people: thus Saul and David were immediately appointed by God to be kings over Israel. Or,

Thirdly, Magistracy may be called the ordinance of God, and rulers may be called the ministers of God, because the nature and reason of things, which is the law of God, requires such an institution for the preservation and safety of civil society. In the two first senses the apostle cannot be supposed to affirm that magistracy is God's ordinance, for neither he nor any of the sacred writers have entailed the magistracy to any one particular family under the gospel dispensation. Neither does he nor any of the inspired writers give us the least hint that any person should ever be immediately commissioned from God to bear rule over the people. The third sense, then, is the only sense in which the apostle can be supposed to affirm that the magistrate is the minister of God, and that magistracy is the ordinance of God; viz., that the nature and reason of things require such an institution for the preservation and safety of mankind. Now, if this be the only sense in which the apostle affirms that magistrates are ordained of God as his ministers, resistance must be criminal only so far forth as they are the ministers of God, *i. e.,* while they act up to the end of their institution, and ceases being criminal when they cease being the ministers of God, *i. e.,* when they act contrary to the general good, and seek to destroy the liberties of the people.

That we have gotten the apostle's sense of magistracy being the ordinance of God, will plainly appear from the text itself; for, after having asserted that to resist the power is to resist the ordinance of God, and they that resist shall receive to themselves damnation, he immediately adds as the reason of this assertion, "For rulers are not a terror to good works, but to the evil. Wilt thou then not be afraid of the power? Do that which is good, and thou shalt have praise of the same: for he is the minister of God to thee for good. But if thou do that which is evil, be afraid; for he beareth not the sword in vain: for he is the minister of God, a revenger to execute wrath upon him that doth evil." Here is a plain declaration of the sense in which he asserts that the authority of the magistrate is ordained of God, viz., because rulers are not a terror to good works, but to the evil; therefore we ought to dread offending them, for we cannot offend them but by doing evil; and if we do evil we have just reason to fear their power; for they bear not the sword in vain, but in this case the magistrate is a revenger to execute wrath upon him that doeth evil: but if we are found doers of that which is good, we have no reason to fear the authority of the magistrate; for in this case, instead of being punished, we shall be protected and encouraged. The reason why the magistrate is called the minister of God is because he is to protect, encourage, and honor them that do well, and to punish them that do evil; therefore it is our duty to submit to them, not merely for fear of being punished by them, but out of regard to the divine authority, under which they are deputed to execute judgement and to do justice. For this reason, according to the apostle, tribute is to be paid them, because, as the ministers of God, their whole business is to protect every man in the enjoyment of his just rights and privileges, and to punish every evil-doer.

If the apostle, then, asserts that rulers are ordained of God only because they are a terror to evil works and a praise to them that do well; if they are ministers of God only because they encourage virtue and punish vice; if for this reason only they are to be obeyed for conscience' sake; if the sole reason why they have a right to tribute is because they devote themselves wholly to the business of securing to men their just rights, and to the punishing of evil-doers,—it follows, by undeniable consequence, that when they become the pests of human society, when they promote and encourage evil-doers, and become a terror to good works, they then cease being the ordinance of God; they are no longer rulers nor ministers of God; they are so far from being the powers that are ordained of God that they become the ministers of the powers of darkness, and it is so far from being a crime to resist them, that in many cases it may be highly criminal in the sight of Heaven to refuse resisting and opposing them to the utmost of our power; or, in other words, that the same reasons that require us to obey the ordinance of God, do equally oblige us, when we have power and opportunity, to oppose and resist the ordinance of Satan.

Hence we see that the apostle Paul, instead of being a friend to tyranny and arbitrary government, turns out to be a strong advocate for the just rights of mankind, and is for our enjoying all that liberty with which God has invested us; for no power (according to the apostle) is ordained of God but what is an encourager of every good and virtuous action,—"Do that which is good, and thou shalt have praise of the same." No man need to be afraid of this power which is ordained of God who does nothing but what is agreeable to the law of God; for this power will not restrain us from exercising any liberty which the Deity has granted us; for the minister of God is to restrain us from nothing but the doing of that which is evil, and to this we have no right. To practise evil is not liberty, but licentiousness. Can we conceive of a more perfect, equitable, and generous plan of government than this which the apostle has laid down, viz., to have rulers appointed over us to encourage us to every good and virtuous action, to defend and protect us in our just rights and privileges, and to grant us everything that can tend to promote our true interest and happiness; to restrain every licentious action, and to punish every one that would injure or harm us; to become a terror of evil-doers; to make and execute such just and righteous laws as shall effectually deter and hinder men from the commission of evil, and to attend continually upon this very thing; to make it their constant care and study, day and night, to promote the good and welfare of the community, and to oppose all evil practices? Deservedly may such rulers be called the ministers of God for good. They carry on the same benevolent design towards the community which the great Governor of the universe does towards his whole creation. 'Tis the indispensable duty of a people to pay tribute, and to afford an easy and comfortable subsistence to such rulers, because they are the ministers of God, who are continually laboring and employing their time for the good of the community. He that resists such magistrates does, in a very emphatical sense, resist the ordinance of God; he is an enemy to mankind, odious to God, and justly incurs the sentence of condemnation from the great Judge of quick and dead. Obedience to such magistrates is yielding obedience to the will of God, and, therefore, ought to be performed from a sacred regard to the divine authority.

For any one from hence to infer that the apostle enjoins in this text unlimited obedience to the worst of tyrants, and that he pronounces damnation upon those that resist the arbitrary measures of such pests of society, is just as good sense as if one should affirm, that because the Scripture enjoins us obedience to the laws of God, therefore we may not oppose the power of darkness; or because we are commanded to submit to the ordinance of God, therefore we may not resist the ministers of Satan. Such wild work must be made with the apostle before he can be brought to speak the language of oppression! It is as plain, I think, as words can make it, that, according to this text, no tyrant can be a ruler; for the apostle's definition of a ruler is, that he is not a terror to good works, but to the evil; and that he is one who is to praise and encourage those that do well. Whenever, then, the ruler encourages them that do evil, and is a terror to those that do well,—*i. e.,* as soon as he becomes a tyrant,—he forfeits his authority to govern, and becomes the minister of Satan, and, as such, ought to be opposed.

I know it is said that the magistrates were, at the time when the apostle wrote, heathens, and that Nero, that monster of tyranny, was then Emperor of Rome; that therefore the apostle, by enjoining submission to the powers that then were, does require unlimited obedience to be yielded to the worst of tyrants. Now, not to insist upon what has been often observed, viz., that this epistle was written most probably about the beginning of Nero's reign, at which time he was a very humane and merciful prince, did everything that was generous and benevolent to the public, and showed every act of mercy and tenderness to particulars, and therefore might at that time justly deserve the character of the minister of God for good to the people,— I say, waiving this, we will suppose that this epistle was written after that Nero was become a monster of tyranny and wickedness; it will by no means follow from thence that the apostle meant to enjoin unlimited subjection to such an authority, or that he intended to affirm that such a cruel, despotic authority was the ordinance of God. The plain, obvious sense of his words, as we have already seen, forbids such a construction to be put upon them, for they plainly imply a strong abhorrence and disapprobation of such a character, and clearly prove that Nero, so far forth as he was a tyrant, could not be the minister of God, nor have a right to claim submission from the people; so that this ought, perhaps, rather to be viewed as a severe satire upon Nero, than as enjoining any submission to him.

It is also worthy to be observed that the apostle prudently waived mentioning any particular persons that were then in power, as it might have been construed in an invidious light, and exposed the primitive Christians to the severe resentments of the men that were then in power. He only in general requires submission to the higher powers, because the powers that be are ordained of God. Now, though the emperor might at that time be such a tyrant that he could with no propriety be said to be ordained of God, yet it would be somewhat strange if there were no men in power among the Romans that acted up to the character of good magistrates, and that deserved to be esteemed as the ministers of God for good unto the people. If there were any such, notwithstanding the tyranny of Nero, the apostle might with great propriety enjoin submission to those powers that were ordained of God, and by so particularly pointing out the end and design of magistrates, and giving his definition of a ruler, he might design to show that neither Nero, nor any other tyrant, ought to be esteemed as the minister of God. Or, rather,—which appears to me to be the true sense,—the apostle meant to speak of magistracy in general, without any reference to the emperor, or any other person in power, that was then at Rome; and the meaning of this passage is as if he had said, It is the duty of every Christian to be a good subject of civil government, for the power and authority of the civil magistrate are from God; for the powers that be are ordained of God; *i. e.,* the authority of the magistrates that are now either at Rome or elsewhere is ordained of the Deity. Wherever you find any lawful magistrates, remember, they are of divine ordination. But that you may understand what I mean when I say that magistrates are of divine ordination, I will show you how you may discern who are lawful magistrates, and ordained of God, from those who are not. Those only are to be esteemed lawful magistrates, and ordained of God, who pursue the public good by honoring and encouraging those that do well and punishing all that do evil. Such, and such only, wherever they are to be found, are the ministers of God for good: to resist such is resisting the ordinance of God, and exposing yourselves to the divine wrath and condemnation.

In either of these senses the text cannot make anything in favor of arbitrary government. Nor could he with any propriety tell them that they need not be afraid of the power so long as they did that which was good, if he meant to recommend an unlimited submission to a tyrannical Nero; for the best characters were the likeliest to fall a sacrifice to his malice. And, besides, such an injunction would be directly contrary to his own practice, and the practice of the primitive Christians, who refused to comply with the sinful commands of men in power; their answer in such cases being this, We ought to obey God rather than men. Hence the apostle Paul himself suffered many cruel persecutions because he would not renounce Christianity, but persisted in opposing the idolatrous worship of the pagan world.

This text, being rescued from the absurd interpretations which the favorers of arbitrary government have put upon it, turns out to be a noble confirmation of that free and generous plan of government which the law of nature and reason points out to us. Nor can we desire a more equitable plan of government than what the apostle has here laid down; for, if we consult our happiness and real good, we can never wish for an unreasonable liberty, viz., a freedom to do evil, which, according to the apostle, is the only thing that the magistrate is to refrain us from. To have a liberty to do whatever is fit, reasonable, or good, is the highest degree of freedom that rational beings can possess. And how honorable a station are those men placed in, by the providence of God, whose business it is to secure to men this rational liberty, and to promote the happiness and welfare of society, by suppressing vice and immorality, and by honoring and encouraging everything that is honorable, virtuous, and praiseworthy! Such magistrates ought to be honored and obeyed as the ministers of God and the servants of the King of Heaven. Can we conceive of a larger and more generous plan of government than this of the apostle? Or can we find words more plainly expressive of a disapprobation of an arbitrary and tyrannical government? I never read this text without admiring the beauty and nervousness of it; and I can hardly conceive how he could express more ideas in so few words than he has done. We see here, in one view, the honor that belongs to the magistrate, because he is ordained of God for the public good. We have his duty pointed out, viz., to honor and encourage the virtuous, to promote the real good of the community, and to punish all wicked and injurious persons. We are taught the duty of the subject, viz., to obey the magistrate for conscience' sake, because he is ordained of God; and that rulers, being continually employed under God for our good, are to be generously maintained by the paying them tribute; and that disobedience to rulers is highly criminal, and will expose us to the divine wrath. The liberty of the subject is also clearly asserted, viz., that subjects are to be allowed to do everything that is in itself just and right, and are only to be restrained from being guilty of wrong actions. It is also strongly implied, that when rulers become oppressive to the subject and injurious to the state, their authority, their respect, their maintenance, and the duty of submitting to them, must immediately cease; they are then to be considered as the ministers of Satan, and, as such, it becomes our indispensable duty to resist and oppose them.

Thus we see that both reason and revelation perfectly agree in pointing out the nature, end, and design of government, viz., that it is to promote the welfare and happiness of the community; and that subjects have a right to do everything that is good, praiseworthy, and consistent with the good of the community, and are only to be restrained when they do evil and are injurious either to individuals or the whole community; and that they ought to submit to every law that is beneficial to the community for conscience' sake, although it may in some measure interfere with their private interest; for every good man will be ready to forego his private interest for the sake of being beneficial to the public. Reason and revelation, we see, do both teach us that our obedience to rulers is not unlimited, but that resistance is not only allowable, but an indispensable duty in the case of intolerable tyranny and oppression. From both reason and revelation we learn that, as the public safety is the supreme law of the state,— being the true standard and measure by which we are to judge whether any law or body of laws are just or not,—so legislatures have a right to make, and require subjection to, any set of laws that have a tendency to promote the good of the community.

Our governors have a right to take every proper method to form the minds of their subjects so that they may become good members of society. The great difference that we may observe among the several classes of mankind arises chiefly from their education and their laws: hence men become virtuous or vicious, good commonwealthsmen or the contrary, generous, noble, and courageous, or base, mean-spirited, and cowardly, according to the impression that they have received from the government that they are under, together with their education and the methods that have been practised by their leaders to form their minds in early life. Hence the necessity of good laws to encourage every noble and virtuous sentiment, to suppress vice and immorality, to promote industry, and to punish idleness, that parent of innumerable evils; to promote arts and sciences, and to banish ignorance from among mankind.

And as nothing tends like religion and the fear of God to make men good members of the commonwealth, it is the duty of magistrates to become the patrons and promoters of religion and piety, and to make suitable laws for the maintaining public worship, and decently supporting the teachers of religion. Such laws, I apprehend, are absolutely necessary for the well-being of civil society. Such laws may be made, consistent with all that liberty of conscience which every good member of society ought to be possessed of; for, as there are few, if any, religious societies among us but what profess to believe and practise all the great duties of religion and morality that are necessary for the well-being of society and the safety of the state, let every one be allowed to attend worship in his own society, or in that way that he judges most agreeable to the will of God, and let him be obliged to contribute his assistance to the supporting and defraying the necessary charges of his own meeting. In this case no one can have any right to complain that he is deprived of liberty of conscience, seeing that he has a right to choose and freely attend that worship that appears to him to be most agreeable to the will of God; and it must be very unreasonable for him to object against being obliged to contribute his part towards the support of that worship which he has chosen. Whether some such method as this might not tend, in a very eminent manner, to promote the peace and welfare of society, I must leave to the wisdom of our legislators to determine; be sure it would take off some of the most popular objections against being obliged by law to support public worship while the law restricts that support only to one denomination.

But for the civil authority to pretend to establish particular modes of faith and forms of worship, and to punish all that deviate from the standard which our superiors have set up, is attended with the most pernicious consequences to society. It cramps all free and rational inquiry, fills the world with hypocrits and superstitious bigots—nay, with infidels and skeptics; it exposes men of religion and conscience to the rage and malice of fiery, blind zealots, and dissolves every tender tie of human nature; in short, it introduces confusion and every evil work. And I cannot but look upon it as a peculiar blessing of Heaven that we live in a land where every one can freely deliver his sentiments upon religious subjects, and have the privilege of worshipping God according to the dictates of his own conscience without any molestation or disturbance,—a privilege which I hope we shall ever keep up and strenuously maintain. No principles ought ever to be discountenanced by civil authority but such as tend to the subversion of the state. So long as a man is a good member of society, he is accountable to God alone for his religious sentiments; but when men are found disturbers of the public peace, stirring up sedition, or practising against the state, no pretence of religion or conscience ought to screen them from being brought to condign punishment. But then, as the end and design of punishment is either to make restitution to the injured or to restrain men from committing the like crimes for the future, so, when these important ends are answered, the punishment ought to cease; for whatever is inflicted upon a man under the notion of punishment after these important ends are answered, is not a just and lawful punishment, but is properly cruelty and base revenge.

From this account of civil government we learn that the business of magistrates is weighty and important. It requires both wisdom and integrity. When either are wanting, government will be poorly administered; more especially if our governors are men of loose morals and abandoned principles; for if a man is not faithful to God and his own soul, how can we expect that he will be faithful to the public? There was a great deal of propriety in the advice that Jethro gave to Moses to provide able men,—men of truth, that feared God, and that hated covetousness,—and to appoint them for rulers over the people. For it certainly implies a very gross absurdity to suppose that those who are ordained of God for the public good should have no regard to the laws of God, or that the ministers of God should be despisers of the divine commands. David, the man after God's own heart, makes piety a necessary qualification in a ruler: "He that ruleth over men (says he) must be just, ruling in the fear of God." It is necessary it should be so, for the welfare and happiness of the state; for, to say nothing of the venality and corruption, of the tyranny and oppression, that will take place under unjust rulers, barely their vicious and irregular lives will have a most pernicious effect upon the lives and manners of their subjects: their authority becomes despicable in the opinion of discerning men. And, besides, with what face can they make or execute laws against vices which they practise with greediness? A people that have a right of choosing their magistrates are criminally guilty in the sight of Heaven when they are governed by caprice and humor, or are influenced by bribery to choose magistrates that are irreligious men, who are devoid of sentiment, and of bad morals and base lives. Men cannot be sufficiently sensible what a curse they may bring upon themselves and their posterity by foolishly and wickedly choosing men of abandoned characters and profligate lives for their magistrates and rulers.

We have already seen that magistrates who rule in the fear of God ought not only to be obeyed as the ministers of God, but that they ought also to be handsomely supported, that they may cheerfully and freely attend upon the duties of their station; for it is a great shame and disgrace to society to see men that serve the public laboring under indigent and needy circumstances; and, besides, it is a maxim of eternal truth that the laborer is worthy of his reward.

It is also a great duty incumbent on people to treat those in authority with all becoming honor and respect,—to be very careful of casting any aspersion upon their characters. To despise government, and to speak evil of dignities, is represented in Scripture as one of the worst of characters; and it was an injunction of Moses, "Thou shalt not speak evil of the ruler of thy people." Great mischief may ensue upon reviling the character of good rulers; for the unthinking herd of mankind are very apt to give ear to scandal, and when it falls upon men in power, it brings their authority into contempt, lessens their influence, and disheartens them from doing that service to the community of which they are capable; whereas, when they are properly honored, and treated with that respect which is due to their station, it inspires them with courage and a noble ardor to serve the public: their influence among the people is strengthened, and their authority becomes firmly established. We ought to remember that they are men like to ourselves, liable to the same imperfections and infirmities with the rest of us, and therefore, so long as they aim at the public good, their mistakes, misapprehensions, and infirmities, ought to be treated with the utmost humanity and tenderness.

But though I would recommend to all Christians, as a part of the duty that they owe to magistrates, to treat them with proper honor and respect, none can reasonably suppose that I mean that they ought to be flattered in their vices, or honored and caressed while they are seeking to undermine and ruin the state; for this would be wickedly betraying our just rights, and we should be guilty of our own destruction. We ought ever to persevere with firmness and fortitude in maintaining and contending for all that liberty that the Deity has granted us. It is our duty to be ever watchful over our just rights, and not suffer them to be wrested out of our hands by any of the artifices of tyrannical oppressors. But there is a wide difference between being jealous of our rights, when we have the strongest reason to conclude that they are invaded by our rulers, and being unreasonably suspicious of men that are zealously endeavoring to support the constitution, only because we do not thoroughly comprehend all their designs. The first argues a noble and generous mind; the other, a low and base spirit.

Thus have I considered the nature of the duty enjoined in the text, and have endeavored to show that the same principles that require obedience to lawful magistrates do also require us to resist tyrants; this I have confirmed from reason and Scripture.

It was with a particular view to the present unhappy controversy that subsists between us and Great Britain that I chose to discourse upon the nature and design of government, and the rights and duties both of governors and governed, that so, justly understanding our rights and privileges, we may stand firm in our opposition to ministerial tyranny, while at the same time we pay all proper obedience and submission to our lawful magistrates; and that, while we are contending for liberty, we may avoid running into licentiousness; and that we may preserve the due medium between submitting to tyranny and running into anarchy. I acknowledge that I have undertaken a difficult task; but, as it appeared to me, the present state of affairs loudly called for such a discourse; and, therefore, I hope the wise, the generous, and the good, will candidly receive my good intentions to serve the public. I shall now apply this discourse to the grand controversy that at this day subsists between Great Britain and the American colonies.

And here, in the first place, I cannot but take notice how wonderfully Providence has smiled upon us by causing the several colonies to unite so firmly together against the tyranny of Great Britain, though differing from each other in their particular interest, forms of government, modes of worship, and particular customs and manners, besides several animosities that had subsisted among them. That, under these circumstances, such a union should take place as we now behold, was a thing that might rather have been wished than hoped for.

And, in the next place, who could have thought that, when our charter was vacated, when we became destitute of any legislative authority, and when our courts of justice in many parts of the country were stopped, so that we could neither make nor execute laws upon offenders,—who, I say, would have thought, that in such a situation the people should behave so peaceably, and maintain such good order and harmony among themselves? This is a plain proof that they, having not the civil law to regulate themselves by, became a law unto themselves; and by their conduct they have shown that they were regulated by the law of God written in their hearts. This is the Lord's doing, and it ought to be marvellous in our eyes.

From what has been said in this discourse, it will appear that we are in the way of our duty in opposing the tyranny of Great Britain; for, if unlimited submission is not due to any human power, if we have an undoubted right to oppose and resist a set of tyrants that are subverting our just rights and privileges, there cannot remain a doubt in any man, that will calmly attend to reason, whether we have a right to resist and oppose the arbitrary measures of the King and

Parliament; for it is plain to demonstration, nay, it is in a manner self-evident, that they have been and are endeavoring to deprive us not only of the privileges of Englishmen, and our charter rights, but they have endeavored to deprive us of what is much more sacred, viz., the privileges of men and Christians;[a] *i. e.,* they are robbing us of the inalienable rights that the God of nature has given us as men and rational beings, and has confirmed to us in his written word as Christians and disciples of that Jesus who came to redeem us from the bondage of sin and the tyranny of Satan, and to grant us the most perfect freedom, even the glorious liberty of the sons and children of God; that here they have endeavored to deprive us of the sacred charter of the King of Heaven. But we have this for our consolation: the Lord reigneth; he governs the world in righteousness, and will avenge the cause of the oppressed when they cry unto him. We have made our appeal to Heaven, and we cannot doubt but that the Judge of all the earth will do right.

Need I upon this occasion descend to particulars? Can any one be ignorant what the things are of which we complain? Does not every one know that the King and Parliament have assumed the right to tax us without our consent? And can any one be so lost to the principles of humanity and common sense as not to view their conduct in this affair as a very grievous imposition? Reason and equity require that no one be obliged to pay a tax that he has never consented to, either by himself or by his representative. But, as Divine Providence has placed us at so great a distance from Great Britain that we neither are nor can be properly represented in the British Parliament, it is a plain proof that the Deity designed that we should have the powers of legislation and taxation among ourselves; for can any suppose it to be reasonable that a set of men that are perfect strangers to us should have the uncontrollable right to lay the most heavy and grievous burdens upon us that they please, purely to gratify their unbounded avarice and luxury? Must we be obliged to perish with cold and hunger to maintain them in idleness, in all kinds of debauchery and dissipation? But if they have the right to take our property from us without our

---

[a] The meaning is not that they have attempted to deprive us of liberty of conscience, but that they have attempted to take away those rights which God has invested us with as his creatures and confirmed in his gospel, by which believers have a covenant right to the good things of this present life and world.

consent, we must be wholly at their mercy for our food and raiment, and we know by sad experience that their tender mercies are cruel.

But because we were not willing to submit to such an unrighteous and cruel decree,—though we modestly complained and humbly petitioned for a redress of our grievances,—instead of hearing our complaints, and granting our requests, they have gone on to add iniquity to transgression, by making several cruel and unrighteous acts. Who can forget the cruel act to block up the harbor of Boston, whereby thousands of innocent persons must have been inevitably ruined had they not been supported by the continent? Who can forget the act for vacating our charter, together with many other cruel acts which it is needless to mention? But, not being able to accomplish their wicked purposes by mere acts of Parliament, they have proceeded to commence open hostilities against us, and have endeavored to destroy us by fire and sword. Our towns they have burnt, our brethren they have slain, our vessels they have taken, and our goods they have spoiled. And, after all this wanton exertion of arbitrary power, is there the man that has any of the feeling of humanity left who is not fired with a noble indignation against such merciless tyrants, who have not only brought upon us all the horrors of a civil war, but have also added a piece of barbarity unknown to Turks and Mohammedan infidels, yea, such as would be abhorred and detested by the savages of the wilderness,—I mean their cruelly forcing our brethren whom they have taken prisoners, without any distinction of whig or tory, to serve on board their ships of war, thereby obliging them to take up arms against their own countrymen, and to fight against their brethren, their wives, and their children, and to assist in plundering their own estates! This, my brethren, is done by men who call themselves Christians, against their Christian brethren,—against men who till now gloried in the name of Englishmen, and who were ever ready to spend their lives and fortunes in the defence of British rights. Tell it not in Gath, publish it not in the streets of Askelon, lest it cause our enemies to rejoice and our adversaries to triumph! Such a conduct as this brings a great reproach upon the profession of Christianity; nay, it is a great scandal even to human nature itself.

It would be highly criminal not to feel a due resentment against such tyrannical monsters. It is an indispensable duty, my brethren, which we owe to God and our country, to rouse up and bestir ourselves, and, being animated with a noble zeal for the sacred cause of liberty, to defend our lives and fortunes, even to the shedding the last drop of blood. The love of our country, the tender affection that we have for our wives and children, the regard we ought to have for unborn posterity, yea, everything that is dear and sacred, do now loudly call upon us to use our best endeavors to save our country. We must beat our ploughshares into swords, and our pruning-hooks into spears, and learn the art of self-defence against our enemies. To be careless and remiss, or to neglect the cause of our country through the base motives of avarice and self-interest, will expose us not only to the resentments of our fellow-creatures, but to the displeasure of God Almighty; for to such base wretches, in such a time as this, we may apply with the utmost propriety that passage in Jeremiah xlviii. 10: "Cursed be he that doth the work of the Lord deceitfully, and cursed be he that keepeth back his sword from blood." To save our country from the hands of our oppressors ought to be dearer to us even than our own lives, and, next the eternal salvation of our own souls, is the thing of the greatest importance,—a duty so sacred that it cannot justly be dispensed with for the sake of our secular concerns. Doubtless for this reason God has been pleased to manifest his anger against those who have refused to assist their country against its cruel oppressors. Hence, in a case similar to ours, when the Israelites were struggling to deliver themselves from the tyranny of Jabin, the King of Canaan, we find a most bitter curse denounced against those who refused to grant their assistance in the common cause; see Judges v. 23: "Curse ye Meroz, said the angel of the Lord, curse ye bitterly the inhabitants thereof; because they came not to the help of the Lord, to the help of the Lord against the mighty."

Now, if such a bitter curse is denounced against those who refused to assist their country against its oppressors, what a dreadful doom are those exposed to who have not only refused to assist their country in this time of distress, but have, through motives of interest or ambition, shown themselves enemies to their country by opposing us in the measures that we have taken, and by openly favoring the British Parliament! He that is so lost to humanity as to be willing to sacrifice his country for the sake of avarice or ambition, has arrived to the highest stage of wickedness that human nature is capable of, and deserves a much worse name than I at present care to give him. But I think I may with propriety say that such a person has forfeited his right to human society, and that he ought to take up his abode, not among the savage men, but among the savage beasts of the wilderness.

Nor can I wholly excuse from blame those timid persons who, through their own cowardice, have been induced to favor our enemies, and have refused to act in defence of their country; for a due sense of the ruin and destruction that our enemies are bringing upon us is enough to raise such a resentment in the human breast that would, I should think, be sufficient to banish fear from the most timid male. And, besides, to indulge cowardice in such a cause argues a want of faith in God; for can he that firmly believes and relies upon the providence of God doubt whether he will avenge the cause of the injured when they apply to him for help? For my own part, when I consider the dispensations of Providence towards this land ever since our fathers first settled in Plymouth, I find abundant reason to conclude that the great Sovereign of the universe has planted a vine in this American wilderness which he has caused to take deep root, and it has filled the land, and that he will never suffer it to be plucked up or destroyed.

Our fathers fled from the rage of prelatical tyranny and persecution, and came into this land in order to enjoy liberty of conscience, and they have increased to a great people. Many have been the interpositions of Divine Providence on our behalf, both in our fathers' days and ours; and, though we are now engaged in a war with Great Britain, yet we have been prospered in a most wonderful manner. And can we think that he who has thus far helped us will give us up into the hands of our enemies? Certainly he that has begun to deliver us will continue to show his mercy towards us, in saving us from the hands of our enemies: he will not forsake us if we do not foresake him. Our cause is so just and good that nothing can prevent our success but only our sins. Could I see a spirit of repentance and reformation prevail through the land, I should not have the least apprehension or fear of being brought under the iron rod of slavery, even though all the powers of the globe were combined against us. And though I confess that the irreligion and profaneness which are so common among us gives something of a damp to my spirits, yet I cannot help hoping, and even believing, that Providence has designed this continent for to be the asylum of liberty and true religion; for can we suppose that the God who created us free agents, and designed that we should glorify and serve him in this world that we might enjoy him forever hereafter, will suffer liberty and true religion to be banished from off the face of the earth? But do we not find that both religion and liberty seem to be expiring and gasping for life in the other continent?—where, then, can they find a harbor or place of refuge but in this?

There are some who pretend that it is against their consciences to take up arms in defence of their country; but can any rational being suppose that the Deity can require us to contradict the law of nature which he has written in our hearts, a part of which I am sure is the principle of self-defence, which strongly prompts us all to oppose any power that would take away our lives, or the lives of our friends? Now, for men to take pains to destroy the tender feelings of human nature, and to eradicate the principles of self-preservation, and then to persuade themselves that in so doing they submit to and obey the will of God, is a plain proof how easily men may be led to pervert the very first and plainest principles of reason and common sense, and argues a gross corruption of the human mind. We find such persons are very inconsistent with themselves; for no men are more zealous to defend their property, and to secure their estates from the encroachments of others, while they refuse to defend their persons, their wives, their children, and their country, against the assaults of the enemy. We see to what unaccountable lengths men will run when once they leave the plain road of common sense, and violate the law which God has written in the heart. Thus some have thought they did God service when they unmercifully butchered and destroyed the lives of the servants of God; while others, upon the contrary extreme, believe that they please God while they sit still and quietly behold their friends and brethren killed by their unmerciful enemies, without endeavoring to defend or rescue them. The one is a sin of omission, and the other is a sin of commission, and it may perhaps be difficult to say, under certain circumstances, which is the most criminal in the sight of Heaven. Of this I am sure, that they are, both of them, great violations of the law of God.

Having thus endeavored to show the lawfulness and necessity of defending ourselves against the tyranny of Great Britain, I would observe that Providence seems plainly to point to us the expediency, and even necessity, of our considering ourselves as an independent state. For, not to consider the absurdity implied in making war against a power to which we profess to own subjection, to pass by the impracticability of our ever coming under subjection to Great Britain upon fair and equitable terms, we may observe that the British Parliament has virtually declared us an independent state by authorizing their ships of war to seize all American property, wherever they can find it, without making any distinction between the friends of administration and those that have appeared in opposition to the acts of Parliament. This is making us a distinct nation from themselves. They can have no right any longer to style us rebels; for rebellion implies a particular faction risen up in opposition to lawful authority, and, as such, the factious party ought to be punished, while those that remain loyal are to be protected. But when war is declared against a whole community without distinction, and the property of each party is declared to be seizable, this, if anything can be, is treating us as an independent state. Now, if they are pleased to consider us as in a state of independency, who can object against our considering ourselves so too?

But while we are nobly opposing with our lives and estates the tyranny of the British Parliament, let us not forget the duty which we owe to our lawful magistrates; let us never mistake licentiousness for liberty. The more we understand the principles of liberty, the more readily shall we yield obedience to lawful authority; for no man can oppose good government but he that is a stranger to true liberty. Let us ever check and restrain the factious disturbers of the peace; whenever we meet with persons that are loth to submit to lawful authority, let us treat them with the contempt which they deserve, and even esteem them as the enemies of their country and the pests of society. It is with peculiar pleasure that I reflect upon the peaceable behavior of my countrymen at a time when the courts of justice were stopped and the execution of laws suspended. It will certainly be expected of a people that could behave so well when they had nothing to restrain them but the laws written in their hearts, that they will yield all ready and cheerful obedience to lawful authority. There is at present the utmost need of guarding ourselves against a seditious and factious temper; for when we are engaged with so powerful an enemy from without, our political salvation, under God, does, in an eminent manner, depend upon our being firmly united together in the bonds of love to one another, and of due submission to lawful authority. I hope we shall never give any just occasion to our adversaries to reproach us as being men of turbulent dispositions and licentious principles, that cannot bear to be restrained by good and wholesome laws, even though they are of our own making, nor submit to rulers of our own choosing. But I have reason to hope much better things of my countrymen, though I thus speak. However, in this time of difficulty and distress, we cannot be too much guarded against the least approaches to discord and faction. Let us, while we are jealous of our rights, take heed of unreasonable suspicions and evil surmises which have no proper foundation; let us take heed lest we hurt the cause of liberty by speaking evil of the ruler of the people.

Let us treat our rulers with all that honor and respect which the dignity of their station requires; but let it be such an honor and respect as is worthy of the sons of freedom to give. Let us ever abhor the base arts that are used by fawning parasites and cringing courtiers, who by their low artifices and base flatteries obtain offices and posts which they are unqualified to sustain, and honors of which they are unworthy, and oftentimes have a greater number of places assigned them than any one person of the greatest abilities can ever properly fill, by means of which the community becomes greatly injured, for this reason, that many an important trust remains undischarged, and many an honest and worthy member of society is deprived of those honors and privileges to which he has a just right, whilst the most despicable, worthless courtier is loaded with honorable and profitable commissions. In order to avoid this evil, I hope our legislators will always despise flattery as something below the dignity of a rational mind, and that they will ever scorn the man that will be corrupted or take a bribe. And let us all resolve with ourselves that no motives of interest, nor hopes of preferment shall ever induce us to act the part of fawning courtiers towards men in power. Let the honor and respect which we show our superiors be true and genuine, flowing from a sincere and upright heart.

The honors that have been paid to arbitrary princes have often been very hypocritical and insincere. Tyrants have been flattered in their vices, and have often had an idolatrous reverence paid them. The worst princes have been the most flattered and adored; and many such, in the pagan world, assumed the title of gods, and had divine honors paid them. This idolatrous reverence has ever been the inseparable concomitant of arbitrary power and tyrannical government; for even Christian princes, if they have not been adored under the character of gods, yet the titles given them strongly savor of blasphemy, and the reverence paid them is really idolatrous. What right has a poor sinful worm of the dust to claim the title of his most sacred Majesty? Most sacred certainly belongs only to God alone,—for there is none holy as the Lord,—yet how common is it to see this title given to kings! And how often have we been told that the king can do no wrong! Even though he should be so foolish and wicked as hardly to be capable of ever being in the right, yet still it must be asserted and maintained that it is impossible for him to do wrong!

The cruel, savage disposition of tyrants, and the idolatrous reverence that is paid them, are both most beautifully exhibited to view by the apostle John in the Revelation, thirteenth chapter, from the first to the tenth verse, where the apostle gives a description of a horrible wild beast[a] which he saw rise out of the sea, having seven

---

[a] Wild beast. By the beast with seven heads and ten horns I understand the tyranny of arbitrary princes, viz., the emperors and kings of the Eastern and Western Roman Empire, and not the tyranny of the Pope and clergy; for the description of every part of this beast will answer better to be understood of political than of ecclesiastical tyrants. Thus the seven heads are generally interpreted to denote the several forms of Roman government; the ten horns are understood of the ten kingdoms that were set up in the Western Empire; and by the body of the beast it seems most natural to understand the Eastern, or Greek Empire, for it is said to be like a leopard. This image is taken from Daniel vii. 6, where the third beast is said to be like a leopard. Now, by the third beast in Daniel is understood, by the best interpreters, the Grecian Monarchy. It is well known that John frequently borrows his images from Daniel, and I believe it will be found, upon a critical examination of the matter, that whenever he does so he means the same thing with Daniel; if this be true (as I am fully persuaded it is), then, by the body of this beast being like a leopard in the Revelation of John, is to be understood the Eastern, or Greek Empire, which was that part of the old Roman Empire that remained whole for several ages after the Western Empire was broken into ten kingdoms. Further: after the beast was risen it is said that the dragon gave him his seat. Now, by the dragon is meant the devil, who is represented as presiding over the Roman Empire in its pagan state; but the seat of the Roman Empire in its pagan state was Rome. Here, then, is a prophecy that the emperor of the East should become possessed of Rome, which exactly agrees with what we know from history to be fact; for the Emperor Justinian's generals having expelled the Goths out of Italy, Rome was brought into subjection to the emperor of the East, and was for a long time governed by the emperor's lieutenant, who resided at Ravenna. These considerations convince me that the Greek Empire, and not the Pope and his clergy, is to be understood by the body of the beast, which was like a leopard. And what further confirms me in this belief is, that it appears to me that the Pope and the papal clergy are to be understood by the second beast which we read of in Revelation xiii. 11–17, for of him it is said that "he had two horns like a lamb." A lamb, we know, is the figure by which Jesus Christ is signified in the Revelation and many other parts of the New Testament. The Pope claims both a temporal and spiritual sovereignty,

heads and ten horns, and upon his heads the names of blasphemy. By heads are to be understood forms of government, and by blasphemy, idolatry; so that it seems implied that there will be a degree of idolatry in every form of tyrannical government. This beast is represented as having the body of a leopard, the feet of a bear, and the mouth of a lion; *i. e.,* a horrible monster, possessed of the rage and fury of the lion, the fierceness of the bear, and the swiftness of the leopard to seize and devour its prey. Can words more strongly point out, or exhibit in more lively colors, the exceeding rage, fury, and impetuosity of tyrants, in their destroying and making havoc of mankind? To this beast we find the dragon gave his power, seat, and great authority; *i. e.,* the devil constituted him to be his vicegerent on earth; this is to denote that tyrants are the ministers of Satan, ordained by him for the destruction of mankind.

Such a horrible monster, we should have thought, would have been abhorred and detested of all mankind, and that all nations would have joined their powers and forces together to oppose and utterly destroy him from off the face of the earth; but, so far are they from doing this, that, on the contrary, they are represented as worshipping him (verse 8): "And all that dwell on the earth shall worship him," viz., all those "whose names are not written in the Lamb's book of life;" *i. e.,* the wicked world shall pay him an idolatrous reverence, and worship him with a godlike adoration. What can in a more lively manner show the gross stupidity and wickedness of mankind, in thus tamely giving up their just rights into the hands of tyrannical monsters, and in so readily paying them such an unlimited obedience as is due to God alone?

We may observe, further, that these men are said (verse 4) to "worship the dragon;"—not that it is to be supposed that they, in direct terms, paid divine homage to Satan, but that the adoration paid to the beast, who was Satan's vicegerent, did ultimately centre in

---

denoted by the two horns, under the character of the vicar of Jesus Christ, and yet, under this high pretence of being the vicar of Jesus Christ, he speaks like a dragon; *i. e.,* he promotes idolatry in the Christian Church, in like manner as the dragon did in the heathen world. To distinguish him from the first beast, he is called (Revelation xix.) "the false prophet that wrought miracles;" *i. e.,* like Mahomet, he pretends to be a lawgiver, and claims infallibility, and his emissaries endeavor to confirm this doctrine by pretended miracles. How wonderfully do all these characters agree to the Pope! Wherefore I conclude that the second, and not the first beast, denotes the tyranny of the Pope and his clergy.

him. Hence we learn that those who pay an undue and sinful veneration to tyrants are properly the servants of the devil; they are worshippers of the prince of darkness, for in him all that undue homage and adoration centres that is given to his ministers. Hence that terrible denunciation of divine wrath against the worshippers of the beast and his image: "If any man worship the beast and his image, and receive his mark in his forehead, or in his hand, the same shall drink of the wine of the wrath of God which is poured out without mixture into the cup of his indignation, and he shall be tormented with fire and brimstone in the presence of the holy angels, and in the presence of the Lamb; and the smoke of their torment ascendeth for ever and ever: and they have no rest day nor night, who worship the beast and his image, and who receive the mark of his name."[a] We have here set forth in the clearest manner, by the inspired apostle, God's abhorrence of tyranny and tyrants, together with the idolatrous reverence that their wretched subjects are wont to pay them, and the awful denunciation of divine wrath against those who are guilty of this undue obedience to tyrants.

Does it not, then, highly concern us all to stand fast in the liberty wherewith Heaven hath made us free, and to strive to get the victory over the beast and his image—over every species of tyranny? Let us look upon a freedom from the power of tyrants as a blessing that cannot be purchased too dear, and let us bless God that he has so far delivered us from that idolatrous reverence which men are so very apt to pay to arbitrary tyrants; and let us pray that he would be pleased graciously to perfect the mercy he has begun to show us by confounding the devices of our enemies and bringing their counsels to nought, and by establishing our just rights and privileges upon such a firm and lasting basis that the powers of earth and hell shall not prevail against it.

Under God, every person in the community ought to contribute his assistance to the bringing about so glorious and important an event; but in a more eminent manner does this important business belong to the gentlemen that are chosen to represent the people in this General Assembly, including those that have been appointed members of the Honorable Council Board.

Honored fathers, we look up to you, in this day of calamity and

[a] Rev. xiv. 9, 10.

SAMUEL WEST 1730–1807

distress, as the guardians of our invaded rights, and the defenders of our liberties against British tyranny. You are called, in Providence, to save your country from ruin. A trust is reposed in you of the highest importance to the community that can be conceived of, its business the most noble and grand, and a task the most arduous and difficult to accomplish that ever engaged the human mind—I mean as to things of the present life. But as you are engaged in the defence of a just and righteous cause, you may with firmness of mind commit your cause to God, and depend on his kind providence for direction and assistance. You will have the fervent wishes and prayers of all good men that God would crown all your labors with success, and direct you into such measures as shall tend to promote the welfare and happiness of the community, and afford you all that wisdom and prudence which is necessary to regulate the affairs of state at this critical period.

Honored fathers of the House of Representatives: We trust to your wisdom and goodness that you will be led to appoint such men to be in council whom you know to be men of real principle, and who are of unblemished lives; that have shown themselves zealous and hearty friends to the liberties of America; and men that have the fear of God before their eyes; for such only are men that can be depended upon uniformly to pursue the general good.

My reverend fathers and brethren in the ministry will remember that, according to our text, it is part of the work and business of a gospel minister to teach his hearers the duty they owe to magistrates. Let us, then, endeavor to explain the nature of their duty faithfully, and show them the difference between liberty and licentiousness; and, while we are animating them to oppose tyranny and arbitrary power, let us inculcate upon them the duty of yielding due obedience to lawful authority. In order to the right and faithful discharge of this part of our ministry, it is necessary that we should thoroughly study the law of nature, the rights of mankind, and the reciprocal duties of governors and governed. By this means we shall be able to guard them against the extremes of slavish submission to tyrants on one hand, and of sedition and licentiousness on the other. We may, I apprehend, attain a thorough acquaintance with the law of nature and the rights of mankind, while we remain ignorant of many technical terms of law, and are utterly unacquainted with the obscure and barbarous Latin that was so much used in the ages of popish darkness and superstition.

BOSTON, 1776

To conclude: While we are fighting for liberty, and striving against tyranny, let us remember to fight the good fight of faith, and earnestly seek to be delivered from that bondage of corruption which we are brought into by sin, and that we may be made partakers of the glorious liberty of the sons and children of God: which may the Father of Mercies grant us all, through Jesus Christ. AMEN.

[34]

WORCESTRIENSIS

Number IV

BOSTON, 1776

Contrary to our working principle today, during the eighteenth century the notion of separation of Church and State did not mean a prohibition on their mutual support, but simply that there should not be one denomination established as the official religion of the state. As long as there was toleration of all denominations that did not as an article of faith attempt to undermine the established civil order, the encouragement of religion by the state, especially the Calvinist Christian denominations, was considered good for both religion and the state. This article, which appeared in the September 4, 1776 issue of the *Massachusetts Spy* (Boston), outlines the basic position held by Americans of the founding era that predominated until late in the century when a more modern doctrine of separation rose to challenge this view.

To the Hon. LEGISLATURE of the STATE of MASSACHUSETTS-BAY

The subject of this disquisition (begun in my last) which is humbly offered to your consideration, is the promotion and establishment of religion in the State. In the course of the reasoning, it was suggested that a toleration of all religious principles (in other words, of all professions, modes & forms of worship) which do not sap the foundation of good government, is consistent with equity and the soundest policy. To establish this, as well as the general doctrine is my present design.

We live in [an] age of the world, in which the knowledge of the arts and sciences, calm and dispassionate enquiries and sound reasoning have been carried to surprising lengths, much to the honor of mankind. The rights of men and things, as well in an intellectual as a civil view, have by able writers, friends of human nature, been ascertained with great degrees of precision. Therefore it now becomes us in all our words and action to do nothing ungenerous, nothing unworthy the dignity of our *rational nature.*

In a well regulated state, it will be the business of the Legislature to prevent sectaries of different denominations from molesting and disturbing each other; to ordain that no part of the community shall be permitted to perplex and harrass the other for any supposed heresy, but that each individual shall be allowed to have and enjoy, profess and maintain his own system of religion, provided it does not issue in *overt acts* of treason against the state undermining the peace and good order of society.

To allow one part of a society to lord it over the faith and consciences of the other, in religious matters is the ready way to set the whole community together by the ears. It is laying a foundation for persecution in the abstract; for (as the judicious MONTESQUIEU observes) "it is a principle that every religion which is persecuted, becomes itself persecuting; for as soon as by some accidental turn it arises from persecution, it attacks the religion that persecuted it; not as a religion but as a tyranny."

It is necessary then that the laws require from the several religions, not only that they shall not embroil the State, but that they shall not raise disturbances among themselves. A citizen does not fulfill the laws by not disturbing the government; it is requisite that he should not trouble any citizen whomever.

Compulsion, instead of making men religious, generally has a contrary tendency, it works not conviction, but most naturally leads them into hypocrisy. If they are honest enquirers after truth; if their articles of belief differ from the creed of their *civil* superiors, compulsion will bring them into a sad *dilemma.* If they are conformists to what they do not believe, great uneasiness of mind must continuously perplex them. If they stand out and persist in nonconformity, they subject themselves to pains and penalties. There is further this ill consequence resulting from the establishment of religious dominion, viz. That an endeavor to suppress nonconformists, will increase, rather than diminish their number: For, however strange it may appear, yet indubitable facts prove that mankind [is] naturally compassionate [toward] those who are subjected to pains and hardships for the sake of their religion, and very frequently join with them and espouse their cause, raise sedition and faction, and endanger the public peace.

Whoever will read the history of Germany (not to mention the mother of harlots) will find this exemplified, in a manner and degree sufficient to shock any one who is not destitute of every spark of humanity. Calvinists and remonstrants made the religious divisions of the people: sometimes one party then the other was superior in their bloody disputes.

The fire first began among and between the congregations of different persuasions (calvinistic and arminian) the women and children came to blows and women pulled each others caps and hair as they passed and repassed the streets after (what they called divine) service was over in the several congregations, and the children gave each other bloody noses. This brought on civil dissention and altercation, until at length, rivers of blood in quarrels about things entirely immaterial and useless, relative either to this world or the other were shed; the nearest kindred embrued their hands in each others blood, subjects withdrew their allegiance and tumbled their rulers from their seats.

This is a true representation of facts, and is sufficient to deter any legislature from enacting laws requiring conformity to any particular mode or profession of religion, under pains of persecution in case of refusal.

This is not suggested because a *persecuting spirit* has of late years been conspicuous among the inhabitants of this state. On the contrary, a candid, catholic, and benevolent disposition has increased and prevailed. The principle reason why this is exhibited is, that as the GOOD PEOPLE of this and its sister states had just cause to alter and amend their civil constitution, so also, it is probable, the legislature of this State will take into consideration the eclesiastical discipline and government, and make such alterations and amendments in the constitution of the churches, as by them, in their wisdom shall be thought proper. We would therefore guard against everything that might be construed to have the least colour of a persecuting tendency, that so the law, relative to religion, may be the most candid, catholic and rational, that the nature of human society will admit of.

Perhaps some sticklers for establishments, requiring conformity to the prevailing religion, may now enquire whether, upon the principles above laid down, any legal establishment at all can take place? and if any, what? In answer to such querists, I would say that if by an establishment they intend the enacting and ordaining laws obliging dissenters from any certain religion to conform thereto, and, in case of nonconformity, subjecting them to pains, penalties and disabilities, in this sense there can and ought to be none. The establishment contended for in this disquisition, is of a different kind, and must result from a different legal Procedure.

It must proceed only from the benign frames of the legislature from an encouragement of the GENERAL PRINCIPLES of religion and morality, recommending free inquiry and examination of the doctrines said to be divine; using all possible and lawful means to enable its subjects to discover the truth, and to entertain good and rational sentiments, and taking mild and parental measures to bring about the design; these are the most probable means to bring about that establishment of religion which is recommended, and a settlement on an immoveable BASIS. It is lawful for the directors of a state to give preference to that profession of religion which they take to be true, and they have right to inflict penalties on those who notoriously violate the laws of natural religion, and thereby disturb the public peace. The openly profane come within their penal jurisdiction. There is no stronger cement of society than a sacred regard to OATHS; nothing binds stronger to the observation of the laws, therefore the public safety, and the *honor* of the SUPREME BEING require that public *profaneness,* should bring down the public vengeance upon those who dare hurl profanities at the throne of OMNIPOTENCE, and thereby *lessen* the reverence of the people for oaths, and solemn appeals to almighty God, and so shaking the foundation of good order and security in society. The same may be said of all Profaneness, and also of debauchery, which strike a fatal blow at the root of good regulation, and the well-being of the state.

And now with regard to the positive interposition of civil magistracy in behalf of religion, I would say, that what has been above suggested with respect to *toleration,* will not disprove the right of the legislature to exert themselves in favor of one religious profession rather than another, they have a right of private judgment as well as others, and are BOUND to do their *utmost* to propagate *that* which they esteem to be true. This they are to do by providing *able* and *learned* TEACHERS, to instruct the people in the knowledge of what they deem the truth, maintaining them by the public money, though at the same time they have no right in the least degree to endeavor the depression of professions of any religious denomination. Nor let it be said (in order to a perfect toleration) that all religious denominations have an equal right to public countenance, for this would be an evident infringement on the right of private judgment in the members of the legislature.

If the greatest part of the people, coincide with the public authority of the State in giving the prefference to any one religious system and creed, the dissenting few, though they cannot conscientiously conform to the prevailing religion, yet ought to acquiesce and rest satisfied that their religious Liberty is not *diminished*.

This suggestion starts a question, which has caused much debate among persons of different religious sentiments, viz. Whether a minor part of a parish or other corporation, are, or can be consistently obliged to contribute to the maintenance and support of a minister to them disagreeable, who is approved by the majority.

This is answered by a very able writer in the following manner, viz. "that this will stand upon the same footing with their contributing towards the expence of a war, which they think not necessary or prudent. If no such power were admitted, covetousness would drive many into dissenting parties in order to save their money.

So that none can reasonably blame a government for requiring such a *general Contribution,* and in this case it seems fit it should be yielded to, as the determination of those to whose guardianship the minority have committed themselves and their possessions.

We hope and trust that you, Hon. directors of this State, will exert yourselves in the cultivation and promotion of pure and RATIONAL RELIGION among your constituents. If there were no arguments to be drawn from the consideration of a *future* world, yet those drawn from the great influence of religion upon the LAWS and the *observance* of them, must, and ought to prevail."

I would add, that our Legislature of the last year have declared that "a Government so popular can be supported only by universal Knowledge and VIRTUE, in the body of the people."

In addition to this, I shall produce the opinion of the above cited *Montesquieu* (a great *authority!*) and so conclude this number.

"Religion may support a state, when the laws themselves are incapable of doing it.

"Thus when a kingdom is frequently agitated by civil wars,

religion may do much by obliging one part of the state to remain always quiet.

"A prince who loves and fears religion, is a lion, who stoops to the hand that strokes or to the voice that appeases him. He who fears and hates religion, is like the savage beast, that growls and bites the chain which prevents his flying on the passenger. He who has no religion at all, is that terrible animal; who perceives his liberty only when he tears in pieces, and when he devours."

WORCESTRIENSIS

[35]

[ANONYMOUS AND WILLIAM WHITING]

Berkshire's Grievances

PITTSFIELD, 1778

One consequence of the spreading demand for independence from England was the insistence of many people in western Massachusetts that the courts no longer had jurisdiction over them. This was the case, they felt, because the courts derived their existence and authority from British law, and the judges held their appointments from a governor who had been appointed by the Crown. Within a short time after the Declaration of Independence courts were effectively out of business in western Massachusetts and remained so for about four years. In June, 1777, a constitutional convention convened, and in the following March it submitted a proposed constitution for ratification by the people assembled in town meetings. The constitution was rejected during the next few weeks, with the consequence that the government which derived its authority from the colonial charter continued to function. In the fall of 1778 the Massachusetts legislature sent a committee to Pittsfield, in Berkshire County, to hear and investigate complaints. The first of these two documents makes the case for closing the courts. The second document is the response of William Whiting for the investigating committee. The first document is as printed in Oscar Handlin and Mary Handlin (editors), *The Popular Sources of Political Authority: Documents on the Massachusetts Constitution of 1780,* pages 374–379.

Statement of Berkshire County Representatives,
November 17, 1778

To the Honorable Committee from the General Court of Massachusetts Bay now convened at Pittsfield—

Mr. Chairman, Sir

We whose Names are underwritten indulging some Apprehensions of the Importance of Civil and religious Liberty, the destructive Nature of Tyranny and lawless power, and the absolute necessity of legal Government, to prevent Anarchy and Confusion; have taken this method to indulge our own Feelings and Sentiments respecting the important matters that have for some Time been the Subject of debate in this present Meeting—Political Disquisitions, if managed with Decency, Moderation and Candor are a good preservative against Ignorance and Servility and such a state of perfect Quietude as would endanger the Rights of Mankind united in the Bands of Society. We wish to preserve this Character in what we have now to offer in the Defence of our Constituents in opposing, in times past, the executive Courts of Justice in this County.

We wish with the least Delay to come to the Merits of the cause, and shall now proceed to make those observations on the Nature of Government which are necessary to bring into view the Apprehensions we indulge respecting the present Condition of this state, whether we have a fundamental Constitution or not; and how far we have Government duly organized and how far not: In free States the people are to be considered as the fountain of power. And the social Tie as founded in Compact. The people at large are endowed with alienable and unalienable Rights. Those which are unalienable, are those which belong to Conscience respecting the worship of God and the practice of the Christian Religion, and that of being determined or governed by the Majority in the Institution or formation of Government. The alienable are those which may be delegated for the Common good, or those which are for the common good to be parted with. It is of the unalienable Rights, particularly that of being determined or governed by the Majority on the Institution or formation of Government of which something further is necessary to be considered at this Time. That the Majority should be governed by the Minority on the first Institution of Government is not only contrary to the common apprehensions of Mankind in general, but it contradicts the common Law of Justice and benevolence.

Mankind being in a state of nature equal, the larger Number (Caeteris paribus) is of more worth than the lesser, and the common happiness is to be preferred to that of Individuals. When Men form the social Compact, for the Majority to consent to be governed by the

ANONYMOUS

Minority is down right popery in politicks, as submission to him who
claims Infallibility, and of being the only Judge of Right and wrong,
is popery in Religion. In all free Governments duly organized there
is an essential Distinction to be observed between the fundamental
Constitution, and Legislation. The fundamental Constitution is the
Basis and ground work of Legislation, and ascertains the Rights
Franchises, Immunities and Liberties of the people, How and how
often officers Civil and military shall be elected by the people, and
circumscribing and defining the powers of the Rulers, and so affoarding
a sacred Barrier against Tyranny and Despotism. This in antient and
corrupt Kingdoms when they have woke out of Slavery to some happy
dawnings of Liberty, has been called a Bill of Rights, Magna Charta
etc. which must be considered as imperfect Emblems of the Securities
of the present grand period. Legislators stand on this foundation, and
enact Laws agreeably to it. They cannot give Life to the Constitution:
it is the approbation of the Majority of the people at large that gives
Life and being to it. This is the foundation of Legislation that is
agreeable to true Liberty, it is above the whole Legislature of a free
state, it being the foundation upon which the Legislature stands. A
Representative Body may form but cannot impose said Constitution
upon a free people. The giving Existence to the fundamental Constitution of a free state is a Trust that cannot be delegated. For any
rational person to give his vote for another person to aid and assist in
forming said Constitution with a view of imposing it on the people
without reserving to himself a Right of Inspection Approbation
rejection or Amendment, imports, if not impiety, yet real popery in
politicks. We could bring many Vouchers for this Doctrine sufficient
for our present purpose is the following Extracts from a Noted Writer.
In answer to that assertion of another respectable writer that 'The bare
Idea of a State without a power some where vested to alter every part
of its Laws is the height of political Absurdity.' [Introduction to
Blackstone's *Commentaries*, p. 97; note by the editor of *Acts and Resolves*]
He remarks upon it, 'A position, which I apprehend, ought to be, in
some Measure limited and explained. For if it refers to those particular
Regulations, which take place in Consequence of Immemorial Custom,
or are enacted by positive Statute, and at the same Time, are subordinate
to the fundamental Constitution from which the Legislature itself
derives its Authority; it is admitted to be within the power or Trust
vested in the Legislature to alter these, pro, Re nata, as the good of

Society may require. But this power of Authority of the Legislature to make Alterations cannot be supposed to extend to the Infringement of those essentials Rights and previleges, which are reserved to the Members of a free state at large, as their undoubted Birthright and unalienable property. I say, in every free State there are some Liberties and previleges, which the Society has not given out of their own Hands to their Governors, not even to the Legislature: and to suppose the contrary would be the height of political absurdity; for it is saying that a state is free and not free at the same Time; or which is the same thing, that its Members are possessed of Liberties, of all which they may be divested at the will of the Legislature; that is, they enjoy them during pleasure, but can claim no property in them.

In a word nothing is more certain than that Government in the general nature of it is a Trust in behalf of the people. And there cannot be a Maxim, in my opinion, more ill grounded, than that there must be an arbitrary power lodged somewhere in every Government. If this were true, the different kinds of Government in the world would be more alike, and on a level, than they are generally supposed to be. In our own Government in particular, tho' no one thinks with more respect of the powers which the Constitution hath vested in every branch of the Legislature; yet I must be excused in saying what is strictly true, that the whole Legislature is so far from having an absolute power, that it hath not power in several Cases that might be mentioned. For instance, their Authority does not extend to making the house of Commons perpetual, or giving that house a power to fill up their own vacancies: the house of Commons being the representatives of all the Commons of England and in that Capassity only a branch of the Legislature; and if they concur in destroying the foundation on which they themselves stand; and if they annihilate the Rights of their Constituents and claim a share in the Legislature upon any other footing than that upon which the Constitution hath given it to them; they subvert the very Trust under which alone they act, and thereby forfeit all their Authority. In short they cannot dispence with any of those essential Rights of the people which it ought to be the great object of Government as it is our Constitution in particular to preserve.'—

These reasonings tend abundantly to evince, that the whole Legislature of any state is insufficient to give Life to the fundamental Constitution of such state, it being the foundation on which they themselves stand and from which alone the Legislature derives its Authority—

May it be considered, further, that to suppose the Representative Body capable of forming and imposing this Compact or Constitution without the Inspection and Approbation Rejection or Amendment of the people at large would involve in it the greatest Absurdity. This would make them greater than the people who send them, this supposes them their own Creators, formers of the foundation upon which they themselves stand. This imparts uncontroulable Dominion over their Constituents for what should hinder them from making such a Constitution as invests them and their successors in office with unlimited Authority, if it be admitted that the Representatives are the people as to forming and imposing the fundamental Constitution of the state upon them without their Approbation and perhaps in opposition to their united sense—In this the very essence of true Liberty consists, viz in every free state the Constitution is adopted by the Majority.

It is needful to be observed that we are not to Judge of true Liberty by other Nations of the Earth, darkness has overspread the Earth, Tyranny Triumphs thro' the world. The Day light of Liberty, only begins to dawn upon these Ends of the Earth. To measure the freedom, the Rights and privileges of the American Empire by those enjoyed by other Nations would be folly.

It is now both easy and natural to apply these reasonings to the present State of Massachusetts Bay. We think it undeniably follows from the preceeding Reasonings that the Compact in this state is not yet formed: when did the Majority of the people at large assent to such Constitution, and what is it? if the Majority of the people of this state have adopted any such fundamental Constitution it is unknown to us and we shall submit to it as we always mean to be governed by the Majority—

Nor will any of those consequences follow on this supposition, that we have no Law, or that the Honorable Council and House of Representatives are Usurpers and Tyrants. Far from it. We consider our case as very Extraordinary. We do not consider this state in all Respects as in a state of Nature tho' destitute of such fundamental Constitution. When the powers of Government were totally dissolved in this state, we esteemed the State Congress as a necessary and useful body of Men suited to our Exigencies and sufficiently authorized to levy Taxes, raise an Army and do what was necessary for our common defence and it is Sir in this Light that we view our present Honorable Court and for these and other reasons *have inculcated* a careful Adherence to their orders. Time will not permit to argue this Matter any longer, for your Honors patience must have been tryed already. These have been some of the reasons we have indulged, and Sentiments we have cultivated respecting a Constitution, and for these Reasons we have been looking forward towards a new Constitution—But we must further add

That a fear of being finally deprived of a Constitution and of being thrown into confusion and divisions by delaying the formation of a new Constitution, has caused our Constituents so early and invariably to oppose the executive Courts—We have feared, we now realize those fears, that upon our submission we shall sink down into a dead Calm and never transmit to posterity a single Right nor leave them the least Knowledge of so fair an Inheritance, as we may now convey to them.—

We and our Constituents have also indulged some fears respecting some of the particular persons appointed for our Rulers least in the future Execution of Law they should execute their own private Resentments, we are willing to hope the best—

We have been ready to consider some of them as indulging an unnatural temper in vilifying and reproaching their own County but we hope they will do better for the future, and that we shall do better, and we wish to give them our confidence.—We are determined to cultivate a spirit of meekness forbearance and Love and to study the Things that shall make for peace and order.

It has appeared to us and those we are appointed to represent that in an early opposition to the executive Courts, such opposition would become general thro' the state, which in our opinion would bring on a new Constitution without Delay. Our hope of which is now very much weakened, and such are the Dissentions of this state that we are now ready to fear we shall never obtain any other than what is called our present Constitution our Apprehensions of which have been already explained—

It is with Gratitude we reflect on the Appointment of this Honorable Committee by the General Court for the purpose of peace Reconciliation and order thro' this County, and their impartial and faithful Execution of their Commission. We are persuaded by the

WILLIAM WHITING

Temper and Moderation exhibited that they will not embibe any prejudices against this County, by what they have seen and heared, and that they will make a Just Representation of our state to the General Court.—

To evince to your Honors our Love of peace Reconciliation and legal Government, and that we have been actuated not by personal Prejudices or Motives of Ambition, notwithstanding the powerful Reasons we have had for a Suspension of the Executive Courts we are willing to forego our own opinions and if it shall be thought best by our Constituents to submit to the establishment of the Executive Courts in this Country—

Pittsfield   Valentine Rathbone
Josiah Wright
James Noble

We the Subscribers Delagates from the Several Towns in the County of Berksheir Approveing of and consenting to the foregoing letter have hereunto Set our hands
Town
Hancock   Reuben Ely
Asa Douglas
New Providence   Joab Stafford

Lanesborough   James Barker
Partridgefield   Ebenr. Peirce
Daniel Kinne
Windsor   Arnold Lewes
Washington   Esebius Bushnell
Jonathan Smith

WILLIAM WHITING
*An Address to the Inhabitants of Berkshire
County, Mass. (1778)*

My Dear Friends and Fellow Countrymen,
Impelled by the most ardent solicitude for your real felicity, prosperity and peace, I beg leave to present you with a few thoughts on the present unhappy situation of our public affairs; ernestly beseeching

that you would consider them with all that candor and dispassionate attention which is absolutely necessary, when called to act on matters of the most serious importance, and which may naturally be expected from a people, who have displayed such heroic fortitude and firmness in the glorious cause of liberty, and acquired immortal honors in the field of battle.

Every sincere friend to the inhabitants of the county of Berkshire, must certainly feel the most poignant regret at the prospect of seeing all that glory which they have acquired by their noble exertions and warlike achievements, most shamefully tarnished by occasion being given for this base reflection, That their struggle has not been for the establishment of a free and equal government on the ruins of tyranny, but rather, that they might introduce a state of total anarchy and licentiousness, on the ruins of all government whatever.

The inhabitants of the county, my brethren, have already given too great occasion for this reflection. Let us now weigh the advantages and disadvantages on each side the question, in an even balance; and everyone whose mind is not debased even below that of the most uncultivated savage, must surely prefer a free and equal government to a state of anarchy and confusion. For a civilized people to live, for any considerable time, under a suspension of government, is intollerable: Nothing, therefore, short of the most weighty and important reasons, can justify the people of this county in their present opposition to law and government.

Let us therefore now chiefly attend to those arguments and objections that are urged against the due execution of law, and the powers of government; and if, on the most impartial inquiry, it shall appear dangerous to the just liberties of the people of this county to submit thereto, before a new constitution is formed, I will venture to engage, that the advocates for the immediate execution of law, shall, to a man, join its opposers in their opposition. But should those arguments and objections appear to be insufficient to justify this opposition, we have a right to expect that those persons, on their part, will immediately lay aside their opposition; or, at least, that they will not complain, should the supreme authority of the state take speedy and effectual measures to establish a due course of law in the county.

But alas! my friends, to what purpose will it be to reason with you, while you suffer yourselves to be governed entirely by passion and prejudice? In many of our public meetings and conventions, for

WILLIAM WHITING

discussing political matters, to me, it has afforded a melancholy prospect, to see so many of the people appear to pay a much greater regard to the person speaking, than to the arguments he offers. If he be of their party, they implicitly receive all that he says, for truth and sound reason, when it too often appears to be destitute of both. This, my brethren, more than the want of a new constitution, endangers your liberties, and renders you the dupes and tools of knaves and imposters. These ambitious and designing men, knowing their influence over you to be originally founded, and the continuance of it to depend, on blasting your reason, by blowing up your passions and prejudices into a continual flame; they suffer none of your old prejudices to subside, but constantly endeavor to excite new ones in your breasts, without any foundation: for they very well know, that should they give you time for serious reflection, the enchantment would be back, and all the mighty bug-bears they have raised in your minds against law and government, would vanish into mere phantoms and their influence over you, and importance in your esteem, evaporate into smoke and, "like the baseless fabrick of a vision, leave not a wreck behind."

In this address, I pretend not to offer you any new, and cunningly devised arguments to convince you, that your present opposition against government is groundless, disreputable, and highly injurious to the peace and safety of the county. Can I only be so happy as to persuade you calmly and dispassionately to reflect on the matter, your own good sense and feelings will suggest sufficient arguments to convince you, and I shall think my labour well bestowed. But, if you are determined to rush on headlong in anarchy and licentiousness, till the arm of power shall stop your career and bring you to reflection, I shall still have the satisfaction to reflect, that I have attempted from motives of pure benevolence, to save you from misery and disgrace.

Before the present contest began, the greater part of you, my brethren, of this county, were necessarily employed in cultivating new farms; and altho' there may not, perhaps, be a set of people in the world, who are blessed with better natural geniuses than you are; yet your particular callings and circumstances in life, did not admit of your paying that attention to matters of a political nature, which might enable you accurately to distinguish the principles of a free and equal government, from those of despotism and tyranny. While you were thus honestly employed in cultivating your new farms, you were under a necessity of contracting debts. Innumberable lawsuits were soon commenced, heavy bills of cost were taxed upon you, larger, in many instances, than the original debt: And thus you came to be cruelly oppressed, even by that law which was designed to determine and secure the rights and properties of the people. From hence originated your violent prejudices against law.

When the tyrant of Britain sent over his tools and vessels for the purpose of binding the freeborn sons of America in chains of perpetual slavery, you, my brethren, the brave sons of freedom in the county of Berkshire, fired with the most ardent zeal for liberty, left your ploughs, your farms, your families, and all that was dear at home, and bravely flew to arms. And, to your honor, it must be acknowledged, that no set of people on the continent, of equal numbers, have contributed more, in a military way, towards defeating the vile and sanguinary purposes of the British tyrant, than the inhabitants of the county of Berkshire.

When you came to have leisure to consider, who was on this side, and who on that, of the important question; you unluckily found the greater number of those gentlemen, whom you had been wont to revere as the makers of law, the judges of law, the pleaders of law, and the executors of law, were, contrary to the law of nature, reason and humanity, taking party with the tyrant, and endeavoring to fix his hateful chains upon you. This circumstance, in addition to your former prejudice against law, excited an undue jealousy and hatred against all those men who have since been appointed to administer, or have attempted to introduce, law into the county.

This gave birth to a new set of politicians who started up among you. You now withdrew your confidence from all those men of parts and learning who were, at that time, or had before been invested with any kind of civil office, and you placed it in a set of men who had nothing more to recommend them to your esteem, than their high pretentions to zeal in the cause of liberty: These men, being sensible where their great strength lay, were constantly endeavoring to keep you in a kind of ferment, and to chain you down under the most fatal prejudices against law and government. They never once informed you of this fundamental and eternal truth, that there is no other way given under heaven among men, whereby you can enjoy, and have secured to you, the inestimable blessings of liberty, peace and safety, but by resigning your alienable natural rights into the hands of the community, and submitting to be governed by such laws and rules as may be prescribed by the free representatives of the people—They have never told you that the oppressions you have heretofore suffered from the unnecessary and vexatious lawsuits that have been commenced against you, were not occasioned by any essential defect in the constitution of government you were then under, but, that they arose entirely from the advantages which a certain set of men took of the particular circumstances, in which many of the honest inhabitants of the county then were: They have not told you, that instead of applying that fatal remedy, far worse than the defeate itself, renouncing all law and government, it would have been wise and prudent for you to have inquired from what defect of law such cruel oppression might originate, and effectually to have removed[;] that they have not told you that, as experience has taught you that those men who were heretofore set over you in the law, have endeavored to enslave you, you ought to hast[en] to the arbitrary will of no set of men whatever; and that your only security herein is, to introduce, and firmly to establish, just and equal laws; laws made by yourselves, or which is the same, by your representatives; laws, by which your judges, your justices, and all your civil officers are bound, equally with yourselves, they being no other than the servants of the public. But instead of this, do they not move you to erect arbitrary despotic governments in your towns—to invest your committees, (who are bound by no laws, and have no other rule of conduct than their own arbitrary will) with unlimited power. Permit me my dear friends, in the most solemn manner, to warn you of the danger of these proceedings. Let me assure you of what everyone who is tolerably versed in the history of foreign nations, knows to be a fact; that the most tyrannical and despotic governments now on the face of the earth, have originated from almost exactly the same measures which you have adopted. And your infatuation has risen to that degree, that, unless prevented by the exertions of those friends to law and government which you now detest as your greatest enemies, it is greatly to be feared that you yourselves, or at least, your posterity, will be reduced to as abject a state of slavery as the most miserable in Turkey now are.

Let us now, my brethren, return from this long (tho I trust not altogether impertinent) digression and consider those mighty objections which are so zealously urged against the introduction of law into this county. And I think they may be substantially comprehended in these few words, viz. "We have no constitution of government. And how can we have government without a constitution, or a foundation for it to stand upon?"

Here let me call up your best and most careful attention, while we take a short view of what is termed a state of nature, and afterwards that of civil society.

In a state of nature, each individual has a right, not only to dispose of, order, and direct, his property, his person, and all his own actions, within the bounds of the law of nature, as he thinks fit, but he also has a right in himself, not only to defend, but to judge and to punish the person who shall make any assault or encroachment, either upon his person or property, without asking leave, or depending on the will of any other man, or any set of men whatever.

Now when any number of men enter into a state of society with each other, they resign into the hands of the society, the right they had in a state of nature, of disposing, directing and ordering their own persons and properties, so far as the good of the whole may require it. And as to the right of judging and punishing injuries done to any of the individuals, that is to be wholly given up to the society. Hence, it is obvious, there can be no medium between being in a state of nature, and in a state of civil society.

Again, in all societies of men, united together for mutual aid, support and defense, there exists one supreme, absolute, and rightful judge over the whole; one, who has a right, at all times, to order, direct, and dispose of the persons, actions and properties of the individuals of the community, so far as the good of the community shall require it; and this judge is no other than the majority of the whole.

The great Mr. Locke tells us, "That when men enter into a community, they must give up all the powers necessary for the purposes for which they entered into society, to the majority of the community, and this is done barely by agreeing to enter into political society; which is all the compact there is, or need be, between the individuals to make up a commonwealth. And this is that, and that only, which gives beginning to any lawful government in the world."

Here let it be carefully observed, that when men emerge from a state of nature, and unite in society, in order to form a political government; the first step necessary is, for each individual to give up his alienable natural rights and privileges, to be ordered, directed, and disposed of, as the major part of the community shall think fit;

so far as shall be necessary for the good of the whole, of which the majority must be the judges. And this must necessarily take place previous to the community's forming any particular constitution, mode, or form of government whatever: For, to be in a state of society, so far as to be under obligation to obey the rules, and orders prescribed by the major part of the society, is one thing; and for that society to be under any particular constitution or form of government, is another. The latter is necessarily subsequent to the former, and must depend entirely on the pleasure of the supreme judge; that is, the major part of the community, who have an undoubted right to enter upon, or postpone that matter, when, and so long as they see fit; and no individual can, on that account, be justified in withdrawing their allegiance, or refusing to submit to the rules and orders of the society.

Here my brethren, let me call upon you to consider, what an absurd and ridiculous figure those men cut, who cry out vehemently for a *new Constitution,* while, at the same time, by refusing to make that resignation of their alienable rights which is the necessary condition on which men enter into civil society, they positively declare, that they do not even belong to the political society of the State of Massachusetts Bay.

I know some will object, that on the declaration of Independence, all civil government was annihilated; consequently, that we are under no obligation to submit to government, till we have a constitution that we approve of. To which I answer, That even admitting the declaration of Independence did actually annihilate the *Constitution* of the province of the Massachusetts Bay; yet it did not annihilate or materially affect, the union or compact existing among the people: For, as I have already showed, that for a people to be in a state of political society, as to be under indispensable obligation to obey the rules and orders prescribed by the major part of the society, and to be under any particular constitution or form of government, are things entirely distinct, and, that the latter is subsequent to, and wholly dependent on, the former. This, being the case, it follows, that no revolution in, or dissolution of, particular constitutions or forms of government, can absolve the members of the society from their allegiance to the major part of the community. And I can hardly conceive how it is possible for such a society to be dissolved, unless by their being dispersed abroad as the Jews are, so that the will of the major part cannot be, either known or obeyed, or by the usurpation and deadly breath of an absolute tyrant.

It is true, when the majority of a society do not act, or when their will and orders cannot be known to the members; during such suspension, the natural right of defending and protecting himself, reverts back to each individual; and on this principle only, can those salutary mobs, and necessary exertions of the people in the beginning of the present contest, be justified. But after congress and assemblies, composed of the free representatives of the people, had prescribed rules for ordering and conducting the public affairs of the community, whatever has taken place of that sort since, has generally, if not universally, been unnecessary, unwarrantable and seditious.

But should we admit for once, that on the declaration of independence, not only all modes and forms of government were dissolved, but also, that civil society was annihilated at the same time: Yet, as it plainly appears from what has been said, that previous, and in order to the forming of a constitution or mode of government, it is essentially necessary that the people enter into society, and give up their alienable natural rights, and submit to be governed by the major part of the community, I ask, with what face you can pretend to the least colour of right to give your voices in, or to say anything about, a constitution, while you utterly refuse to comply with the necessary preliminaries? This is really no less preposterous than it would be for the savages of the wilderness to run together, and take upon them, in hideous yells, to frame, and enact, a constitution and form of government for the state of Massachusetts Bay.

It is a fact which needs no proof, that whatever state the inhabitants of the Massachusetts Bay might be in at the time independence was declared, they are now in a state of civil society, and (the county of Berkshire excepted) enjoy the blessings of a free and equal government.

And now my brethren, let me ask you this very plain, tho' pertinent and important question, Are you members of the political society of the state of Massachusetts Bay? Or are you not? If you answer in the affirmative; then let me ask you again, why do you refuse to submit to those rules which the community have prescribed? And not only this, but why, by threats and violence, do you deter the servants of the community, in this county, from redressing injuries and insults offered to others, and like the fable of the dog in the manger, neither enjoy the blessings of government yourselves, nor suffer others to enjoy them? Or how will you exculpate yourselves from the charge of being in a state of rebellion against the community?

But should you say that you do not belong to the community, that you do not mean to give up any of your natural rights till you know what constitution you are to be governed by: Then let me tell you, that you must be considered, as being, at best, in a state of nature, and that you can have no right to join, or give your voice in forming a constitution of government.

But perhaps you will say, that you do not act, in this affair, as individuals, but, as a community: For, when the minds of the inhabitants of the county were lately taken upon the expedience or inexpediency of setting up courts, there appeared to be a very great majority against it. Here let me repeat a former question: Are the inhabitants of the county of *Berkshire*, members of the political society of the Massachusetts Bay? Or, are they not? Your conduct, in sending members to the general court, answers this question in the affirmative. A majority of the inhabitants of the county therefore, can be of no more real avail in this matter, than a majority of any particular town, or, than even a majority of any particular family in any particular town in the county. For, it is only a major part of the community that have a right to determine matters of this kind, and they have ordered that courts of sessions be held in this county. The friends of government therefore cannot consider themselves as being, in any measure, included in this vote of the county. The truth of the fact is, that should ninety nine out of an hundred thro the county, vote against law, yet, that hundredth part would, as loyal subjects of the community, have a right to enjoy the benefits of government, and the major part of the community are under absolute obligation, therein to protect and support them. Otherwise the community could have no right to punish them, should they even commit treason against the state: For, no maxim can stand on firmer ground than this, *That protection and allegiance are reciprocal:* and that, *where protection is wanting, allegiance is not due.* Let me entreat you, my brethren, seriously to consider, how shockingly unreasonable, as well as grossly immoral your conduct is, while by threats and violence, you deprive the peaceable and loyal inhabitants of this county, of that inestimable previlege of having their grevances redressed in that ancient and equal way, of tryal by jurors, as well as of all other benefits of a free and lawful government. And all this, upon the most frivolous pretences, as I have already showed, and shall further evince in the course of these observations.

You loudly proclaim yourselves to be *sons of liberty*. Pray, what kind of liberty is it you contend for, against Great Britain? Does not your conduct testify against you, that you contend to the same thing, for which all tyrants contend with each other; viz: that each one may monopolize the whole empire of tyranny to himself? But lest, ere I am aware, I should catch the epidemic disease myself, and a flame of passion, begin to rage in my own breast, I will dismiss this head, and proceed to notice some other objections that are made against the introduction of law into this county.

It is said, and, no doubt has great weight with many of you, my brethren, that a set of designing men are now artfully endeavouring to bring in the old British constitution again, and thereby to reduce you to the same state of servitude which you have lavished so much blood and treasure to extricate yourselves from. This is so groundless an objection, and is fraught with such glaring absurdity and nonsense, that to attempt to confute it (as Doctor Tillotson observes in another case) is "like proving that an egg 'is not an eliphant, or that a musket ball is not a pike staff'".

The plain truth of the case is in fact no other than this,—The inhabitants of the state of Massachusetts Bay, are now in a state of some measure familiar to that which every community must pass through, while they are emerging from a state of nature to that of a free and equal government. They are, at least in a state of civil society, by virtue of a compact or agreement among the people, wherein, as hath been said, every individual hath given up into the hands of the major part of the community, his alienable natural rights, and submitted to be governed by them.

There cannot indeed with propriety, be said to be now, any constitution of government existing in this state, which is designed to be permanent, and to remain for generations to come; but we are now in a proper condition to form one, whenever the major part of the community shall think proper to enter upon so important an undertaking: And then, every individual must submit to such a constitution as the majority shall agree to; though, the larger that majority, the happier it will be.

Now, let me ask, what similarity is there between our present government, and that under the old British constitution while it was in force in its original latitude? In that, the king of Great Britain held the reins of government fast in his iron hand,—he appointed our governor, lieutenant governor, and secretary: The governor appointed all our military, and had the greatest share in appointing our civil officers: He always took care to appoint such as were friends, not to the people, but to the prerogative: He had a negative on all our laws and other acts of the general court; and as his dependence was upon the crown, and not the people, his constant endeavour was to please the king by enslaving the people. At present, the community annually choose a house of representatives, the house choose a council, and these two branches exercise the powers of government.

Now, should we grant the utmost that even prejudice and envy can suggest,—That there are men in the state, wicked and safe enough to enslave the people, if they had it in their power; I defy anyone to show how it is possible for them, in our present circumstances, to effect it,—But oh! not quite so fast: The British charter here falls in our way, over which, it seems, we are like to brake our shins.

Alas! what a surprising piece of sacred old parchment; for which we have heretofore had so great anxiety, lest it should be curtailed or disannulled; but now, like the manna in the wilderness, by being kept too long, it breeds worms and stinks!

It is true, we have solemnly declared ourselves independent of the king and parliament of Great Britain, and renounced their authority forever. We have, long since passed a fatal rolling bill, which has gone through the state, and crushed every officer who held his commission, by virtue of the British charter, to nothing. As we annually choose a house of representatives, and they, a council; they are sufficiently apprized that if they do not choose the most fit and proper men to that important trust, they will not be elected themselves again. When a council are thus chosen, there is now no governor to negative the choice. Before they are admitted to their seats, they all take a solemn oath, to be true to the people of the state, and to support and defend them against George the third, king of Great Britain, and all his emissaries. This council and house of representatives, make all our laws, appoint all our public officers, and transact all our important publick business. And I must confess, I cannot conceive how it is possible to have a legislative body more entirely dependent on the people, or further removed, even from a possibility of enslaving them.

But still, we must be in danger of being enslaved by the old British constitution. This vile charter still lurks at the bottom; and our general assembly meet, and the council are chose on the same day that the charter directs, and in many other important matters of a like nature, the charter is still conformed to, & etc. & etc. & etc. But indeed, I am quite out of breath in reciting these insignificant scarecrows.

The truth of the matter is this: On the declaration of independence, the inhabitants of this state, although they considered themselves as being entirely absolved from their allegiance to the powers of Great Britain, and from being any further held by the old constitution than they chose to adopt it; yet they did not think themselves absolved from that mutual compact or union they were in with each other as a civil society, but still considered themselves as being under the government and direction of the major part of the community. Now, in order that society might exercise that degree of government which the peace and safety of the community required, it was also necessary that some particular rule, or form of government should be adopted. Whatever modes and forms therefore, they had been accustomed to from the old charter, and still found would be useful and expedient for a free and independent society, they surely would not be so childish as to deny themselves the benefit of, merely because they were contained in the British charter. And here, my bretheren, will you be so kind as seriously to consider, for once, what strange inconsistencies you suffer your prejudices to drive you into? Most of you who are now so terribly alarmed at the apparition of our old defunct charter, are, at the same time, charmed with the constitution of Connecticut, and long to be under it; notwithstanding their government is built upon, and invariably conformed to, a British charter; a charter, too, that was drawn up under the auspice of that impious tyrant, Charles the second, whilst our monster of a thing, which, though dead, yet belcheth forth the most dreadful terrors was formed by those amiable royal characters, William and Mary, who drove out that bigotted popish tyrant, James the second, and restored liberty to the then respectable kingdom, of Great Britain. But dust to dust, earth to earth, ashes to ashes, without either hope or fear of its resurrection; let us dismiss this frightful corpse of a charter.

WILLIAM WHITING

But I must not yet close my address; for the din of a new constitution continually rings in my ears.

For myself, I most heartily wish that we had now such a constitution of government and bill of rights firmly established, as would secure to us and our posterity, all the benefits of a free and equal government, forever: And I will pledge myself that the small abilities and influence I possess, shall be exerted to procure them as soon as possible. At the same time I am fully persuaded that our violent opposition to a due execution of law in this county, is not only groundless, unjust, and exceedingly detrimental to the peace, safety, and welfare of the county; but, will prove the greatest impediment to our ever obtaining such a constitution as we shall be pleased with; for, we hereby lose our influence in the state. We are now considered by the greater part of the people in the state, as being in a kind of political delirium; accordingly they pay but little regard to us. Besides, as hath been observed, we cannot, in justice, claim any right to a share in forming a constitution, so long as, by refusing to submit to the majority, we deny that we belong to the civil community.

Neither do I apprehend it will at all expedite the business of a constitution to threaten the people of this state with a revolt, in case they do not immediately set about a new constitution. Suppose the state to which we apply for their protecting wing, should ask us, why we desire to forsake our parent state and join with strangers? Must not our answer be, because the ancient and extensive state of the Massachusetts Bay are so arbitrary and tyranical, that they will not submit to be governed agreeable to the capricious humor of the county of Berkshire. And will they, knowing our political character, be fond of taking us into their bosoms? Will they not rather reject our suit, under these circumstances, from a just apprehension that we may prove to their community, like the dead fly in the apothecaries precious ointment?

But the word constitution, *like great is Diana,* still sounds in my head. Here, therefore, I must observe, that most of the people are so carried away with this word, as though some magick was contained in it, and under sanction thereof, oppose all law and government are, at the same time, totally ignorant of what is meant by the term, *constitution:* They have affixed an idea to the word, which it by no means admits of. Here then, let us briefly inquire what is meant by a *bill of rights,* and *constitution of government?*

And first, negatively. A bill of rights and constitution of government have no immediate connexion with, or influence in, altering or amending any laws, usages, customs, or modes of proceeding in the general distribution of law among the people as, for instance,— altering laws for the collection of debts, fee bills, regulating the recording of deeds, or transfering the business from county registers to town clerks & c. There is the same door open now for the redress of grievances of this kind (if any such you have) which there will be after the establishment of a new constitution; for these are matters, with which that has nothing to do.

Again, a new constitution will not in the least alter the present mode of proceeding in the different courts of law that are now held in the state. For these are all matters that have no immediate connexion, with a constitution of government.

In order therefore, to a better understanding of this matter, let it be observed, that all mankind are born equally free, and that, by nature, no one is above another;—that when men enter into civil society, they give up, into the hands of the society, many of their natural rights and liberties, to be ordered and directed by the will of the society, which, in a state of nature, could be controlled only by their own wills. Men also possess other natural rights which they cannot divest themselves of, nor give the controul of to any power under heaven. These are called the *unalienable rights of mankind;* and are chiefly the rights of conscience, right of protection & c. Now the design of a bill of rights is to ascertain and clearly describe the rights of conscience, and that security of person and property which the supreme power of the state is bound to protect every individual in the enjoyment of.

A *constitution of government* is that which points out and determines the several branches of authority that shall exist in the state, as, legislative, judicial, and executive, in what manner they shall be appointed,—the kind, and degree of power each branch shall be vested with, and how far they shall be dependent, or independent on each other: It also includes the establishment of general rules for the government of the militia and navy departments; and the whole to be *fixed* and *unalterable,* (unless by the same power which first gave it being) for preventing usurpations, and for the security of future

generations; and, as I said before, without any immediate respect to
the distribution of law and justice among the people, any otherwise,
than as from a tree that grows on a good root, we naturally look for
good fruit.

I am sensible that the discription here given of a bill of rights,
and constitution of government, is general and concise. All I design
by it, is to show that if we had such a bill of rights, and constitution
of government now established, this would not remove any of those
supposed grievances which I have yet heard complained of in the
country of Berkshire; unless the present mode of appointing civil
officers be considered as a grievance. And I confess, I see no reason
why the inhabitants of this county should be more grieved at this,
than the inhabitants of any other part of the state. Should it be
thought best to establish some other mode of appointing these officers,
this will, doubtless, be duly attended to, whenever the matter of
forming a new constitution is taken up. In the meantime, how
unbecoming, and arrogant is it, for the inhabitants of this single
infant county, to proclaim, as they do by their conduct, that unless
the state will immediately comply with their disposition, and form,
and content to such a constitution, in all respects, as they approve of,
they will continue their revolt from the community? Pray, my brethren,
attend seriously to this matter. The business of forming a constitution,
is a most weighty and important undertaking and ought not to be
gone into by men whose minds are fired with passion, or influenced
by prejudice. In a matter of such moment, and in a state so extensive
as this, there will necessarily be a great variety of sentiment and
opinions: And every particular town and county in the state who differ
in sentiment in this important matter, will have, one, as good a right
as another, to insist on all the other parts of the community conforming
to their plan of government, and to refuse submission to the laws of
the state, unless their dispositions are immediately complied with.

And now, my brethren, only consider, how shocking would be
the consequences, should your example be followed by all the towns
and counties in this state, and through the continent! Instead of being
the *United States of America* we should be (I had almost said) the *infinite
number of jarring, disunited factions of America!* Our different towns and
counties would soon become fields of blood, and exhibit the most
dreadful scenes of tumult, violence, and destruction! and our common

enemy would have little more to do, than to march through the country and seize on their prey!

Again; is not this the language of our conduct, that the state of Massachusetts Bay is composed of a set of knaves, on the one hand, who are leading the people into slavery, and of fools on the other, who (the county of Berkshire excepted) are suffering themselves to be led by the nose into their snare? And can it be expected that the other counties in the state will feel themselves very much obliged by such a compliment?

As I said before, so say I now again, no person more ardently desires a constitution that shall be acceptable to this county, and to the state in general, than myself: And it grieves me to my heart to meet with such fatal obsticles in the way of it as have now been mentioned. For, as hath been observed, there are, in the state, a great variety of opinions respecting the form of a constitution for this state, as well as to the most proper time for taking up this important business. We shall therefore, never be able to obtain a form of government, till we bring ourselves to such a disposition, that after comparing all those different opinions together, we shall be willing to submit to one that shall be a kind of medium between the whole, and conformable (as near as possible) to the sentiments of the whole. And it is too apparent, that there is not, at present, such a disposition in the inhabitants of this county.

And now, my brethren, from the foregoing observations, I think it evident to a demonstration, that the common cry in this county, *that we have no foundation of government,* is altogether groundless. For, even admitting that we have no particular constitution yet, it hath been shown, that such a constitution is not so essential to government, that there can be no foundation of government without it; but, on the contrary, that a compact or union among the people, by which they agree to submit themselves to be governed by the major part of the community, is itself, a sufficient and substantial foundation of government. And this being the case, how surprising is your conduct, that while you protest to belong to the community, by joining with it in making all the laws and rules for the government thereof, by your representatives, you, at the same time, refuse to submit to those very laws and rules; because, say you, we have no foundation of government. Although the great Mr. Locke tells you, and common sense tells you the same, that this, and this only, is that which can lay a foundation for any lawful government in the world.

I have shown, that the common cry of danger of being enslaved, and again brought under the British yoke of bondage, by introducing (for present convenience) the old constitution, as now practiced upon, is perfectly idle and ridiculous. I have shown that our conduct, in refusing to submit to law, till we have a new form of government established, instead of bringing forward, will have a direct and powerful tendency to retard and embarrass, that desirable and important object.—I have shown, that the people of this county, who at present oppose the due execution of law, have entirely mistook the true meaning and import of the words, *constitution* and form of government. I have shown, that for a people to give up their alienable natural rights, and to agree to be directed by the major part of the society, so far as the good of the whole shall require it, is the only foundation of lawful government; and that this is absolutely necessary, previous to their forming any particular mode of government; and therefore, that as the people of this county refuse to comply with these preliminaries, they do thereby exclude themselves from all just rights to give their voices in forming a constitution.

Notwithstanding the pains I have taken to set these matters in a just point of view, it will be to no good purpose, so long as the people are determined that they will retain all the rights of a state of nature. Let me tell you, my brethren, you cannot retain these rights, and at the same time enjoy the protection of society. It is therefore high time to away with these shocking inconsistencies, in which you have gone on for several years past—pretending to belong to the community of Massachusetts Bay by sending representatives, or rather spies, to the general court, and, at the same time, refusing to obey those laws and rules which they prescribe, unless in some particular instances, wherein they happen to coincide with your fancies! And here I can't but take notice, how shamefully that ancient maxim, *vox populi est vox Dei* (the voice of the people is the voice of God) has been prostituted in this county. When the major part of a free and independent community, by their representatives, declare to the individual members, and the world, their acts and resolutions, this being considered as the greatest power on earth, nothing can more fitly resemble *the voice of God*. But when a small number of individuals, who ought to be members of the society, inflamed with passion (if not with strong drink) collect together for the avowed purpose of opposing the true *vox populi,* let any one say whether their voice is not rather that of blasphemy and treason, than god like.

I shall close my address by repeating my most serious advice to you to act a part more consistent. And as you are now erecting little democracies in several of your towns, you ought to withdraw your representatives from the general assembly of the Massachusetts Bay; for it is highly unreasonable they should sit there as spies. You ought to send them as ambassadors, or commissioners plenipotentiary, and in that character they ought to be received, if received at all, and not as representatives. You ought to send the like officers to the American Congress, and to have your independence confirmed by that august body, before you proceed further in the exercise of your novel governments; otherwise, it is more than possible you may meet with difficulty: For, should you compel anyone to submit to your assumed authority, he will have a right to demand satisfaction, and the state is bound to see him redressed. And you may be assured that the supreme authority of the state will not be easily convinced that those trifling objections against law, which are so easily confused, are sufficient to justify you in setting up independent governments in your several towns, unless you can obtain a ratification of your independence from Congress, which, I dare say, in your most extravagant excursions of fancy, you never once thought of.

And now, my brethren, before I take my leave of you; permit me, in the most serious manner, to assure you, that I wish for nothing more ardently, than for the liberty, peace and safety of this county, and that these blessings may be secured to you and your posterity, on the most permanent foundation, even such as the gates of hell shall never be able to prevail against. If anything has occurred in the course of the foregoing observations which may favor too much of harshness and severity, for this I ask your pardon, and assure you, I meant no reflection. I can truly say, I have had nothing more in view, in writing this address than the good of the county.

As to those people who are so violently attached to their licentious principles, as to fly into a rage with every one who, by rational arguments, attempts their reformation, I must consider them in the same light with my other unhappy patients, who, labouring under phrensys and deliriums, will often strike at the friendly hand which holds out to them the specific medicine which is designed for their cure.

I am, gentlemen, notwithstanding I have been so long despised and rejected by you, your sincere friend,

IMPARTIAL REASON.

[36]

[THEOPHILUS PARSONS]

The Essex Result

NEWBURYPORT, MASSACHUSETTS, 1778

In 1777 the Massachusetts General Court (the state's legislative body) decided that in its next session it should draw up a constitution for the state, which document should then be submitted to the people for approval or disapproval in their town meetings. Accordingly, the people of the state were advised to consider suitability for making a constitution in their choice of legislators in the coming election. The newly elected legislature did submit a document (the proposed Constitution of 1778), but it failed to get the required vote for adoption in the town meetings, in part because of its content (what it provided and what it failed to provide), but also because there was strong feeling that constitutions ought always be drawn up in a convention of men chosen for that sole purpose. The legislature then provided for popular election of delegates whose sole job would be the presentation of a constitution; those delegates met and proposed a document that was approved in the town meetings and became the Massachusetts Constitution of 1780. The item presented here relates to the acceptability of the constitution submitted in the spring of 1778. As a first step, prior to decision in the town meetings, a number of the towns in Essex County (the northeast corner of Massachusetts) elected to send delegates to a convention where they should thoroughly debate the merits and defects of the proposed document and report back to the several towns the common sentiments of those who attended the proceedings. Twelve of the twenty-one towns in Essex county appear to have sent delegations. The cumulative judgment of the assemblage was summarized and subjected to remarkably incisive analysis in the famed *Essex Result,* here presented in its entirety. The composition of the *Result,* read to the convention and accepted by it, is credited to Theophilus Parsons, a lawyer of Newburyport and then a young man of twenty-eight years. Parsons was later to have a distinguished career as attorney-at-law before Massachusetts courts and to serve for seven years as Chief Justice of the Supreme Judicial Court of Massachusetts. Source: Oscar Handlin and Mary Handlin, eds., *The Popular Sources of Authority: Documents on the Massachusetts Constitution of 1780*, pp. 324–65.

Result of the Convention of Delegates Holden at Ipswich in the County of Essex, Who Were Deputed to Take into Consideration the Constitution and Form of Government, Proposed by the Convention of the State of Massachusetts-Bay

In Convention of Delegates from the several towns of Lynn, Salem, Danvers, Wenham, Manchester, Gloucester, Ipswich, Newbury-Port, Salisbury, Methuen, Boxford, and Topsfield, holden by adjournment at Ipswich, on the twenty-ninth day of April, one thousand seven hundred and seventy-eight.

PETER COFFIN Esq; in the Chair.

The Constitution and form of Government framed by the Convention of this State, was read paragraph by paragraph, and after debate, the following votes were passed.

1. That the present situation of this State renders it best, that the framing of a Constitution therefor, should be postponed 'till the public affairs are in a more peaceable and settled condition.

2. That a bill of rights, clearly ascertaining and defining the rights of conscience, and that security of person and property, which every member in the State hath a right to expect from the supreme power thereof, ought to be settled and established, previous to the ratification of any constitution for the State.

3. That the executive power in any State, ought not to have any share or voice in the legislative power in framing the laws, and therefore, that the second article of the Constitution is liable to exception.

4. That any man who is chosen Governor, ought to be properly qualified in point of property—that the qualification therefor, mentioned in the third article of the Constitution, is not sufficient—nor is the same qualification directed to be ascertained on fixed principles,

as it ought to be, on account of the fluctuation of the nominal value of money, and of property.

5. That in every free Republican Government, where the legislative power is rested in an house or houses of representatives, all the members of the State ought to be equally represented.

6. That the mode of representation proposed in the sixth article of the constitution, is not so equal a representation as can reasonably be devised.

7. That therefore the mode of representation in said sixth article is exceptionable.

8. That the representation proposed in said article is also exceptionable, as it will produce an unwieldy assembly.

9. That the mode of election of Senators pointed out in the Constitution is exceptionable.

10. That the rights of conscience, and the security of person and property each member of the State is entitled to, are not ascertained and defined in the Constitution, with a precision sufficient to limit the legislative power—and therefore, that the thirteenth article of the constitution is exceptionable.

11. That the fifteenth article is exceptionable, because the numbers that constitute a quorum in the House of Representatives and Senate, are too small.

12. That the seventeenth article of the constitution is exceptionable, because the supreme executive officer is not vested with proper authority—and because an independence between the executive and legislative body is not preserved.

13. That the nineteenth article is exceptionable, because a due independence is not kept up between the supreme legislative, judicial, and executive powers, nor between any two of them.

14. That the twentieth article is exceptionable, because the supreme executive officer hath a voice, and must be present in that Court, which alone hath authority to try impeachments.

15. That the twenty second article is exceptionable, because the supreme executive power is not preserved distinct from, and independent of, the supreme legislative power.

16. That the twenty third article is exceptionable, because the power of granting pardons is not solely vested in the supreme executive power of the State.

17. That the twenty eighth article is exceptionable, because the

THEOPHILUS PARSONS

delegates for the Continental Congress may be elected by the House of Representatives, when all the Senators may vote against the election of those who are delegated.

18. That the thirty fourth article is exceptionable, because the rights of conscience are not therein clearly defined and ascertained; and further, because the free exercise and enjoyment of religious worship is there said to be *allowed* to all the protestants in the State, when in fact, that free exercise and enjoyment is the natural and uncontroulable right of every member of the State.

A committee was then appointed to attempt the ascertaining of the true principles of government, applicable to the territory of the Massachusetts-Bay; to state the non-conformity of the constitution proposed by the Convention of this State to those principles, and to delineate the general outlines of a constitution conformable thereto; and to report the same to this Body.

This Convention was then adjourned to the twelfth day of May next, to be holden at Ipswich.

The Convention met pursuant to adjournment, and their committee presented the following report.

The committee appointed by this Convention at their last adjournment, have proceeded upon the service assigned them. With diffidence have they undertaken the several parts of their duty, and the manner in which they have executed them, they submit to the candor of this Body. When they considered of what vast consequence, the forming of a Constitution is to the members of this State, the length of time that is necessary to canvass and digest any proposed plan of government, before the establishment of it, and the consummate coolness, and solemn deliberation which should attend, not only those gentlemen who have, reposed in them, the important trust of delineating the several lines in which the various powers of government are to move, but also all those, who are to form an opinion of the execution of that trust, your committee must be excused when they express a surprise and regret, that so short a time is allowed the freemen inhabiting the territory of the Massachusetts-Bay, to revise and comprehend the form of government proposed to them by the convention of this State, to compare it with those principles on which every free government ought to be founded, and to ascertain it's conformity or non-conformity thereto. All this is necessary to be done, before a true opinion of it's merit or demerit can be formed. This opinion is to be certified within a time which, in our apprehension, is much too short for this purpose, and to be certified by a people, who, during that time, have had and will have their minds perplexed and oppressed with a variety of public cares. The committee also beg leave to observe, that the constitution proposed for public approbation, was formed by gentlemen, who, at the same time, had a large share in conducting an important war, and who were employed in carrying into execution almost all the various powers of government.

The committee however proceeded in attempting the task assigned them, and the success of that attempt is now reported.

The reason and understanding of mankind, as well as the experience of all ages, confirm the truth of this proposition, that the benefits resulting to individuals from a free government, conduce much more to their happiness, than the retaining of all their natural rights in a state of nature. These benefits are greater or less, as the form of government, and the mode of exercising the supreme power of the State, are more or less conformable to those principles of equal impartial liberty, which is the property of all men from their birth as the gift of their Creator, compared with the manners and genius of the people, their occupations, customs, modes of thinking, situation, extent of country, and numbers. If the constitution and form of government are wholly repugnant to those principles, wretched are the subjects of that State. They have surrendered a portion of their natural rights, the enjoyment of which was in some degree a blessing, and the consequence is, they find themselves stripped of the remainder. As an anodyne to compose the spirits of these slaves, and to lull them into a passively obedient state, they are told, that tyranny is preferable to no government at all; a proposition which is to be doubted, unless considered under some limitation. Surely a state of nature is more excellent than that, in which men are meanly submissive to the haughty will of an imperious tyrant, whose savage passions are not bounded by the laws of reason, religion, honor, or a regard to his subjects, and the point to which all his movements center, is the gratification of a brutal appetite. As in a state of nature much happiness cannot be enjoyed by individuals, so it has been conformable to the inclinations of almost all men, to enter into a political society so constituted, as to remove the inconveniences they were obliged to submit to in their former state, and, at the same time, to retain all those natural rights, the enjoyment of which would be consistent with

[485]
Theophilus Parsons

the nature of a free government, and the necessary subordination to the supreme power of the state.

To determine what form of government, in any given case, will produce the greatest possible happiness to the subject, is an arduous task, not to be compassed perhaps by any human powers. Some of the greatest geniuses and most learned philosophers of all ages, impelled by their sollicitude to promote the happiness of mankind, have nobly dared to attempt it: and their labours have crowned them with immortality. A Solon, a Lycurgus of Greece, a Numa of Rome are remembered with honor, when the wide extended empires of succeeding tyrants, are hardly important enough to be faintly sketched out on the map, while their superb thrones have long since crumbled into dust. The man who alone undertakes to form a constitution, ought to be an unimpassioned being; one enlightened mind; biassed neither by the lust of power, the allurements of pleasure, nor the glitter of wealth; perfectly acquainted with all the alienable and unalienable rights of mankind; possessed of this grand truth, that all men are born equally free, and that no man ought to surrender any part of his natural rights, without receiving the greatest possible equivalent; and influenced by the impartial principles of rectitude and justice, without partiality for, or prejudice against the interest or professions of any individuals or class of men. He ought also to be master of the histories of all the empires and states which are now existing, and all those which have figured in antiquity, and thereby able to collect and blend their respective excellencies, and avoid those defects which experience hath pointed out. Rousseau, a learned foreigner, a citizen of Geneva, sensible of the importance and difficulty of the subject, thought it impossible for any body of people, to form a free and equal constitution for themselves, in which, every individual should have equal justice done him, and be permitted to enjoy a share of power in the state, equal to what should be enjoyed by any other. Each individual, said he, will struggle, not only to retain all his own natural rights, but to acquire a controul over those of others. Fraud, circumvention, and an union of interest of some classes of people, combined with an inattention to the rights of posterity, will prevail over the principles of equity, justice, and good policy. The Genevans, perhaps the most virtuous republicans now existing, thought like Rousseau. They called the celebrated Calvin to their assistance. He came, and, by their gratitude, have they embalmed his memory.

The freemen inhabiting the territory of the Massachusetts-Bay are now forming a political society for themselves. Perhaps their situation is more favorable in some respects, for erecting a free government, than any other people were ever favored with. That attachment to old forms, which usually embarrasses, has not place amongst them. They have the history and experience of all States before them. Mankind have been toiling through ages for their information; and the philosophers and learned men of antiquity have trimmed their midnight lamps, to transmit to them instruction. We live also in an age, when the principles of political liberty, and the foundation of governments, have been freely canvassed, and fairly settled. Yet some difficulties we have to encounter. Not content with removing our attachment to the old government, perhaps we have contracted a prejudice against some part of it without foundation. The idea of liberty has been held up in so dazzling colours, that some of us may not be willing to submit to that subordination necessary in the freest States. Perhaps we may say further, that we do not consider ourselves united as brothers, with an united interest, but have fancied a clashing of interests amongst the various classes of men, and have acquired a thirst of power, and a wish of domination, over some of the community. We are contending for freedom—Let us all be equally free—It is possible, and it is just. Our interests when candidly considered are one. Let us have a constitution founded, not upon party or prejudice—not one for to-day or to-morrow—but for posterity. Let *Esto perpetua* be it's motto. If it is founded in good policy; it will be founded in justice and honesty. Let all ambitious and interested views be discarded, and let regard be had only to the good of the whole, in which the situation and rights of posterity must be considered: and let equal justice be done to all the members of the community; and we thereby imitate our common father, who at our births, dispensed his favors, not only with a liberal, but with an equal hand.

Was it asked, what is the best form of government for the people of the Massachusetts-Bay? we confess it would be a question of infinite importance: and the man who could truly answer it, would merit a statue of gold to his memory, and his fame would be recorded in the annals of late posterity, with unrivalled lustre. The question, however, must be answered, and let it have the best answer we can possibly give it. Was a man to mention a despotic government, his life would be a just forfeit to the resentments of an affronted people. Was he to hint monarchy, he would deservedly be hissed off the stage, and consigned to infamy. A republican form is the only one consonant to the feelings of the generous and brave Americans. Let us now attend to those principles, upon which all republican governments, who boast any degree of political liberty, are founded, and which must enter into the spirit of a FREE republican constitution. For all republics are not FREE.

All men are born equally free. The rights they possess at their births are equal, and of the same kind. Some of those rights are alienable, and may be parted with for an equivalent. Others are unalienable and inherent, and of that importance, that no equivalent can be received in exchange. Sometimes we shall mention the surrendering of a power to controul our natural rights, which perhaps is speaking with more precision, than when we use the expression of parting with natural rights—but the same thing is intended. Those rights which are unalienable, and of that importance, are called the rights of conscience. We have duties, for the discharge of which we are accountable to our Creator and benefactor, which no human power can cancel. What those duties are, is determinable by right reason, which may be, and is called, a well informed conscience. What this conscience dictates as our duty, is so; and that power which assumes a controul over it, is an usurper; for no consent can be pleaded to justify the controul, as any consent in this case is void. The alienation of some rights, in themselves alienable, may be also void, if the bargain is of that nature, that no equivalent can be received. Thus, if a man surrender all his alienable rights, without reserving a controul over the supreme power, or a right to resume in certain cases, the surrender is void, for he becomes a slave; and a slave can receive no equivalent. Common equity would set aside this bargain.

When men form themselves into society, and erect a body politic or State, they are to be considered as one moral whole, which is in possession of the supreme power of the State. This supreme power is composed of the powers of each individual collected together, and VOLUNTARILY parted with by him. No individual, in this case, parts with his unalienable rights, the supreme power therefore cannot controul them. Each individual also surrenders the power of controuling his natural alienable rights, ONLY WHEN THE GOOD OF THE WHOLE REQUIRES it. The supreme power therefore can do nothing but what is for the good of the whole; and when it goes beyond this line, it is

a power usurped. If the individual receives an equivalent for the right
of controul he has parted with, the surrender of that right is valid; if
he receives no equivalent, the surrender is void, and the supreme
power as it respects him is an usurper. If the supreme power is so
directed and executed that he does not enjoy political liberty, it is an
illegal power, and he is not bound to obey. Political liberty is by
some defined, a liberty of doing whatever is not prohibited by law.
The definition is erroneous. A tyrant may govern by laws. The
republics of Venice and Holland govern by laws, yet those republics
have degenerated into insupportable tyrannies. Let it be thus defined;
political liberty is the right every man in the state has, to do whatever
is not prohibited by laws, TO WHICH HE HAS GIVEN HIS CONSENT.
This definition is in unison with the feelings of a free people. But to
return—If a fundamental principle on which each individual enters
into society is, that he shall be bound by no laws but those to which
he has consented, he cannot be considered as consenting to any law
enacted by a minority: for he parts with the power of controuling his
natural rights, only when the good of the whole requires it; and of
this there can be but one absolute judge in the State. If the minority
can assume the right of judging, there may then be two judges; for
however large the minority may be, there must be another body still
larger, who have the same claim, if not a better, to the right of
absolute determination. If therefore the supreme power should be so
modelled and exerted, that a law may be enacted by a minority, the
inforcing of that law upon an individual who is opposed to it, is an
act of tyranny. Further, as every individual, in entering into the
society, parted with a power of controuling his natural rights equal
to that parted with by any other, or in other words, as all the members
of the society contributed an equal portion of their natural rights,
towards the forming of the supreme power, so every member ought
to receive equal benefit from, have equal influence in forming, and
retain an equal controul over, the supreme power.

It has been observed, that each individual parts with the power
of controuling his natural alienable rights, only when the good of the
whole requires it, he therefore has remaining, after entering into
political society, all his unalienable natural rights, and a part also of
his alienable natural rights, provided the good of the whole does not
require the sacrifice of them. Over the class of unalienable rights the
supreme power hath no controul, and they ought to be clearly defined

THEOPHILUS PARSONS

and ascertained in a BILL OF RIGHTS, previous to the ratification of any constitution. The bill of rights should also contain the equivalent every man receives, as a consideration for the rights he has surrendered. This equivalent consists principally in the security of his person and property, and is also unassailable by the supreme power: for if the equivalent is taken back, those natural rights which were parted with to purchase it, return to the original proprietor, as nothing is more true, than that ALLEGIANCE AND PROTECTION ARE RECIPROCAL.

The committee also proceeded to consider upon what principles, and in what manner, the supreme power of the state thus composed of the powers of the several individuals thereof, may be formed, modelled, and exerted in a republic, so that every member of the state may enjoy political liberty. This is called by some, *the ascertaining of the political law of the state.* Let it now be called *the forming of a constitution.*

The reason why the supreme governor of the world is a rightful and just governor, and entitled to the allegiance of the universe is, because he is infinitely good, wise, and powerful. His goodness prompts him to the best measures, his wisdom qualifies him to discern them, and his power to effect them. In a state likewise, the supreme power is best disposed of, when it is so modelled and balanced, and rested in such hands, that it has the greatest share of goodness, wisdom, and power, which is consistent with the lot of humanity.

That state, (other things being equal) which has reposed the supreme power in the hands of one or a small number of persons, is the most powerful state. An union, expedition, secrecy and dispatch are to be found only here. Where power is to be executed by a large number, there will not probably be either of the requisites just mentioned. Many men have various opinions: and each one will be tenacious of his own, as he thinks it preferable to any other; for when he thinks otherwise, it will cease to be his opinion. From this diversity of opinions results disunion; from disunion, a want of expedition and dispatch. And the larger the number to whom a secret is entrusted, the greater is the probability of it's disclosure. This inconvenience more fully strikes us when we consider that want of secrecy may prevent the successful execution of any measures, however excellently formed and digested.

But from a single person, or a very small number, we are not to expect that political honesty, and upright regard to the interest of the body of the people, and the civil rights of each individual, which are essential to a good and free constitution. For these qualities we are to go to the body of the people. The voice of the people is said to be the voice of God. No man will be so hardy and presumptuous, as to affirm the truth of that proposition in it's fullest extent. But if this is considered as the intent of it, that the people have always a disposition to promote their own happiness, and that when they have time to be informed, and the necessary means of information given them, they will be able to determine upon the necessary measures therefor, no man, of a tolerable acquaintance with mankind, will deny the truth of it. The inconvenience and difficulty in forming any free permanent constitution are, that such is the lot of humanity, the bulk of the people, whose happiness is principally to be consulted in forming a constitution, and in legislation, (as they include the majority) are so situated in life, and such are their laudable occupations, that they cannot have time for, nor the means of furnishing themselves with proper information, but must be indebted to some of their fellow subjects for the communication. Happy is the man, and blessings will attend his memory, who shall improve his leisure, and those abilities which heaven has indulged him with, in communicating that true information, and impartial knowledge, to his fellow subjects, which will insure their happiness. But the artful demagogue, who to gratify his ambition or avarice, shall, with the gloss of false patriotism, mislead his countrymen, and meanly snatch from them the golden glorious opportunity of forming a system of political and civil liberty, fraught with blessings for themselves, and remote posterity, what language can paint his demerit? The execrations of ages will be a punishment inadequate; and his name, though ever blackening as it rolls down the stream of time, will not catch its proper hue.

Yet, when we are forming a Constitution, by deductions that follow from established principles, (which is the only good method of forming one for futurity,) we are to look further than to the bulk of the people, for the greatest wisdom, firmness, consistency, and perseverance. These qualities will most probably be found amongst men of education and fortune. From such men we are to expect genius cultivated by reading, and all the various advantages and assistances, which art, and a liberal education aided by wealth, can furnish. From these result learning, a thorough knowledge of the interests of their country, when considered abstractedly, when compared with the

THEOPHILUS PARSONS

neighbouring States, and when with those more remote, and an acquaintance with it's produce and manufacture, and it's exports and imports. All these are necessary to be known, in order to determine what is the true interest of any state; and without that interest is ascertained, impossible will it be to discover, whether a variety of certain laws may be beneficial or hurtful. From gentlemen whose private affairs compel them to take care of their own household, and deprive them of leisure, these qualifications are not to be generally expected, whatever class of men they are enrolled in.

Let all their respective excellencies be united. Let the supreme power be so disposed and ballanced, that the laws may have in view the interest of the whole; let them be wisely and consistently framed for that end, and firmly adhered to; and let them be executed with vigour and dispatch.

Before we proceed further, it must be again considered, and kept always in view, that we are not attempting to form a temporary constitution, one adjusted only to our present circumstances. We wish for one founded upon such principles as will secure to us freedom and happiness, however our circumstances may vary. One that will smile amidst the declensions of European and Asiatic empires, and survive the rude storms of time. It is not therefore to be understood, that all the men of fortune of the present day, are men of wisdom and learning, or that they are not. Nor that the bulk of the people, the farmers, the merchants, the tradesmen, and labourers, are all honest and upright, with single views to the public good, or that they are not. In each of the classes there are undoubtedly exceptions, as the rules laid down are general. The proposition is only this. That among gentlemen of education, fortune and leisure, we shall find the largest number of men, possessed of wisdom, learning, and a firmness and consistency of character. That among the bulk of the people, we shall find the greatest share of political honesty, probity, and a regard to the interest of the whole, of which they compose the majority. That wisdom and firmness are not sufficient without good intentions, nor the latter without the former. The conclusion is, let the legislative body unite them all. The former are called the excellencies that result from an aristocracy; the latter, those that result from a democracy.

The supreme power is considered as including the legislative, judicial, and executive powers. The nature and employment of these several powers deserve a distinct attention.

The legislative power is employed in making laws, or prescribing such rules of action to every individual in the state, as the good of the whole requires, to be conformed to by him in his conduct to the governors and governed, with respect both to their persons and property, according to the several relations he stands in. What rules of action the good of the whole requires, can be ascertained only by the majority, for a reason formerly mentioned. Therefore the legislative power must be so formed and exerted, that in prescribing any rule of action, or, in other words, enacting any law, the majority must consent. This may be more evident, when the fundamental condition on which every man enters into society, is considered. No man consented that his natural alienable rights should be wantonly controuled; they were controulable, only when that controul should be subservient to the good of the whole; and that subserviency, from the very nature of government, can be determined but by one absolute judge. The minority cannot be that judge, because then there may be two judges opposed to each other, so that this subserviency remains undetermined. Now the enacting of a law, is only the exercise of this controul over the natural alienable rights of each member of the state; and therefore this law must have the consent of the majority, or be invalid, as being contrary to the fundamental condition of the original social contract. In a state of nature, every man had the sovereign controul over his own person. He might also have, in that state, a qualified property. Whatever lands or chattels he had acquired the peaceable possession of, were exclusively his, by right of occupancy or possession. For while they were unpossessed he had a right to them equally with any other man, and therefore could not be disturbed in his possession, without being injured; for no man could lawfully dispossess him, without having a better right, which no man had. Over this qualified property every man in a state of nature had also a sovereign controul. And in entering into political society, he surrendered this right of controul over his person and property, (with an exception to the rights of conscience) to the supreme legislative power, to be exercised by the power, *when the good of the whole demanded it.* This was all the right he could surrender, being all the alienable right of which he was possessed. The only objects of legislation therefore, are the person and property of the individuals which compose the state. If the law affects only the persons of the members, the consent of a majority of any members is sufficient. If the law affects the

THEOPHILUS PARSONS

property only, the consent of those who hold a majority of the property is enough. If it affects, (as it will very frequently, if not always,) both the person and property, the consent of a majority of the members, and of those members also, who hold a majority of the property is necessary. If the consent of the latter is not obtained, their interest is taken from them against their consent, and their boasted security of property is vanished. Those who make the law, in this case give and grant what is not theirs. The law, in it's principles, becomes a second stamp act. Lord Chatham very finely ridiculed the British house of commons upon that principle. "You can give and grant, said he, only your own. Here you give and grant, what? The property of the Americans." The people of the Massachusetts-Bay then thought his Lordship's ridicule well pointed. And would they be willing to merit the same? Certainly they will agree in the principle, should they mistake the application. The laws of the province of Massachusetts-Bay adopted the same principle, and very happily applied it. As the votes of proprietors of common and undivided lands in their meetings, can affect only their property, therefore it is enacted, that in ascertaining the majority, the votes shall be collected according to the respective interests of the proprietors. If each member, without regard to his property, has equal influence in legislation with any other, it follows, that some members enjoy greater benefits and powers in legislation than others, when these benefits and powers are compared with the rights parted with to purchase them. For the property-holder parts with the controul over his person, as well as he who hath no property, and the former also parts with the controul over his property, of which the latter is destitute. Therefore to constitute a perfect law in a free state, affecting the persons and property of the members, it is necessary that the law be for the good of the whole, which is to be determined by a majority of the members, and that majority should include those, who possess a major part of the property in the state.

The judicial power follows next after the legislative power; for it cannot act, until after laws are prescribed. Every wise legislator annexes a sanction to his laws, which is most commonly penal, (that is) a punishment either corporal or pecuniary, to be inflicted on the member who shall infringe them. It is the part of the judicial power (which in this territory has always been, and always ought to be, a court and jury) to ascertain the member who hath broken the law. Every man is to be presumed innocent, until the judicial power hath determined him guilty. When that decision is known, the law annexes the punishment, and the offender is turned over to the executive arm, by whom it is inflicted on him. The judicial power hath also to determine what legal contracts have been broken, and what member hath been injured by a violation of the law, to consider the damages that have been sustained, and to ascertain the recompense. The executive power takes care that this recompense is paid.

The executive power is sometimes divided into the external executive, and internal executive. The former comprehends war, peace, the sending and receiving ambassadors, and whatever concerns the transactions of the state with any other independent state. The confederation of the United States of America hath lopped off this branch of the executive, and placed it in Congress. We have therefore only to consider the internal executive power, which is employed in the peace, security and protection of the subject and his property, and in the defence of the state. The executive power is to marshal and command her militia and armies for her defence, to enforce the law, and to carry into execution all the others of the legislative powers.

A little attention to the subject will convince us, that these three powers ought to be in different hands, and independent of one another, and so ballanced, and each having that check upon the other, that their independence shall be preserved—If the three powers are united, the government will be absolute, *whether these powers are in the hands of one or a large number.* The same party will be the legislator, accuser, judge and executioner; and what probability will an accused person have of an acquittal, however innocent he may be, when his judge will be also a party.

If the legislative and judicial powers are united, the maker of the law will also interpret it; and the law may then speak a language, dictated by the whims, the caprice, or the prejudice of the judge, with impunity to him—And what people are so unhappy as those, whose laws are uncertain. It will also be in the breast of the judge, when grasping after his prey, to make a retrospective law, which shall bring the unhappy offender within it; and this also he can do with impunity—The subject can have no peaceable remedy—The judge will try himself, and an acquittal is the certain consequence. He has it also in his power to enact any law, which may shelter him from deserved vengeance.

Should the executive and legislative powers be united, mischiefs

THEOPHILUS PARSONS

the most terrible would follow. The executive would enact those laws it pleased to execute, and no others—The judicial power would be set aside as inconvenient and tardy—The security and protection of the subject would be a shadow—The executive power would make itself absolute, and the government end in a tyranny—Lewis the eleventh of France, by cunning and treachery compleated the union of the executive and legislative powers of that kingdom, and upon that union established a system of tyranny. France was formerly under a free government.

The assembly or representatives of the united states of Holland, exercise the executive and legislative powers, and the government there is absolute.

Should the executive and judicial powers be united, the subject would then have no permanent security of his person and property. The executive power would interpret the laws and bend them to his will; and, as he is the judge, he may leap over them by artful constructions, and gratify, with impunity, the most rapacious passions. Perhaps no cause in any state has contributed more to promote internal convulsions, and to stain the scaffold with it's best blood, than this unhappy union. And it is an union which the executive power in all states, hath attempted to form: if that could not be compassed, to make the judicial power dependent upon it. Indeed the dependence of any of these powers upon either of the others, which in all states has always been attempted by one or the other of them, has so often been productive of such calamities, and of the shedding of such oceans of blood, that the page of history seems to be one continued tale of human wretchedness.

The following principles now seem to be established.

1. That the supreme power is limited, and cannot controul the unalienable rights of mankind, nor resume the equivalent (that is, the security of person and property) which each individual receives, as a consideration for the alienable rights he parted with in entering into political society.

2. That these unalienable rights, and this equivalent, are to be clearly defined and ascertained in a BILL OF RIGHTS, previous to the ratification of any constitution.

3. That the supreme power should be so formed and modelled, as to exert the greatest possible power, wisdom, and goodness.

4. That the legislative, judicial, and executive powers, are to be

lodged in different hands, that each branch is to be independent, and further, to be so ballanced, and be able to exert such checks upon the others, as will preserve it from a dependence on, or an union with them.

5. That government can exert the greatest power when it's supreme authority is vested in the hands of one or a few.

6. That the laws will be made with the greatest wisdom, and best intentions, when men, of all the several classes in the state concur in the enacting of them.

7. That a government which is so constituted, that it cannot afford a degree of political liberty nearly equal to all it's members, is not founded upon principles of freedom and justice, and where any member enjoys no degree of political liberty, the government, so far as it respects him, is a tyranny, for he is controuled by laws to which he has never consented.

8. That the legislative power of a state hath no authority to controul the natural rights of any of it's members, unless the good of the whole requires it.

9. That a majority of the state is the only judge when the general good does require it.

10. That where the legislative power of the state is so formed, that a law may be enacted by the minority, each member of the state does not enjoy political liberty. And

11. That in a free government, a law affecting the person and property of it's members, is not valid, unless it has the consent of a majority of the members, which majority should include those, who hold a major part of the property in the state.

It may be necessary to proceed further, and notice some particular principles, which should be attended to in forming the three several powers in a free republican government.

The first important branch that comes under our consideration, is the legislative body. Was the number of the people so small, that the whole could meet together without inconvenience, the opinion of the majority would be more easily known. But, besides the inconvenience of assembling such numbers, no great advantages could follow. Sixty thousand people could not discuss with candor, and determine with deliberation. Tumults, riots, and murder would be the result. But the impracticability of forming such an assembly, renders it needless to make any further observations. The opinions and consent of the majority must be collected from persons, delegated by every freeman of the state for that purpose. Every freeman, who hath sufficient discretion, should have a voice in the election of his legislators. To speak with precision, in every free state where the power of legislation is lodged in the hands of one or more bodies of representatives elected for that purpose, the person of every member of the state, and all the property in it, ought to be represented, because they are objects of legislation. All the members of the state are qualified to make the election, unless they have not sufficient discretion, or are so situated as to have no wills of their own. Persons not twenty one years old are deemed of the former class, from their want of years and experience. The municipal law of this country will not trust them with the disposition of their lands, and consigns them to the care of their parents or guardians. Women what age soever they are of, are also considered as not having a sufficient acquired discretion; not from a deficiency in their mental powers, but from the natural tenderness and delicacy of their minds, their retired mode of life, and various domestic duties. These concurring, prevent that promiscuous intercourse with the world, which is necessary to qualify them for electors. Slaves are of the latter class and have no wills. But are slaves members of a free government? We feel the absurdity, and would to God, the situation of America and the tempers of it's inhabitants were such, that the slave-holder could not be found in the land.

The rights of representation should be so equally and impartially distributed, that the representatives should have the same views, and interests with the people at large. They should think, feel, and act like them, and in fine, should be an exact miniature of their constituents. They should be (if we may use the expression) the whole body politic, with all it's property, rights, and privileges, reduced to a small scale, every part being diminished in just proportion. To pursue the metaphor. If in adjusting the representation of freeman, any ten are reduced into one, all the other tens should be alike reduced: or if any hundred should be reduced to one, all the other hundreds should have just the same reduction. The representation ought also to be adjusted, that it should be the interest of the representatives at all times, to do justice, therefore equal interest among the people, should have equal interest among the body of representatives. The majority of the representatives should also represent a majority of the people, and the legislative body should be so constructed, that every law affecting property, should have the consent of those who hold a majority of the property. The law would then be determined to be for the good of the whole by the proper judge, the majority, and the necessary consent thereto would be obtained: and all the members of the State would enjoy political liberty, and an equal degree of it. If the scale to which the body politic is to be reduced, is but a little smaller than the original, or, in other words, if a small number of freemen should be reduced to one, that is, send one representative, the number of representatives would be too large for the public good. The expences of government would be enormous. The body would be too unwieldy to deliberate with candor and coolness. The variety of opinions and oppositions would irritate the passions. Parties would be formed and factions engendered. The members would list under the banners of their respective leaders: address and intrigue would conduct the debates, and the result would tend only to promote the ambition or interest of a particular part. Such has always been in some degree, the course and event of debates instituted and managed by a large multitude.

For these reasons, some foreign politicians have laid it down as a rule, that no body of men larger than an hundred, would transact business well: and Lord Chesterfield called the British house of commons a mere mob, because of the number of men which composed it.

Elections ought also to be free. No bribery, corruption, or undue influence should have place. They stifle the free voice of the people, corrupt their morals, and introduce a degeneracy of manners, a supineness of temper, and an inattention to their liberties, which pave the road for the approach of tyranny, in all it's frightful forms.

The man who buys an elector by his bribes, will sell him again, and reap a profit from the bargain; and he thereby becomes a dangerous member of society. The legislative body will hold the purse strings, and men will struggle for a place in that body to acquire a share of the public wealth. It has always been the case. Bribery will be attempted, and the laws will not prevent it. All states have enacted severe laws against it, and they have been ineffectual. The defect was in their forms of government. They were not so contrived, as to prevent the practicability of it. If a small corporation can place a man in the legislative body, to bribe will be easy and cheap. To bribe a large corporation would be difficult and expensive, if practicable. In Great-Britain, the representatives of their counties and great cities are freely elected. To bribe the electors there, is impracticable: and their representatives are the most upright and able statesmen in parliament. The small boroughs are bought by the ministry and opulent men; and their representatives are the mere tools of administration or faction. Let us take warning.

A further check upon bribery is, when the corrupter of a people knows not the electors. If delegates were first appointed by a number of corporations, who at a short day were to elect their representatives, these bloodhounds in a state would be at fault. They would not scent their game. Besides, the representatives would probably be much better men—they would be double refined.

But it may be said, the virtuous American would blast with indignation the man, who should proffer him a bribe. Let it now be admitted as a fact. We ask, will that always be the case? The most virtuous states have become vicious. The morals of all people, in all ages, have been shockingly corrupted. The rigidly virtuous Spartans, who banished the use of gold and silver, who gloried in their poverty for centuries, at last fell a prey to luxury and corruption. The Romans, whose intense love to their country, astonishes a modern patriot, who fought the battles of the republic for three hundred years without pay, and who, as volunteers, extended her empire over Italy, were at last dissolved in luxury, courted the hand of bribery, and finally sold themselves as slaves, and prostrated their country to tyrants the most ignominious and brutal. Shall we alone boast an exemption from the general fate of mankind? Are our private and political virtues to be transmitted untainted from generation to generation, through a course of ages? Have we not already degenerated from the pure morals and disinterested patriotism of our ancestors? And are not our manners becoming soft and luxurious, and have not our vices begun to shoot? Would one venture to prophecy, that in a century from this period, we shall be a corrupt luxurious people, perhaps the close of that century would stamp this prophecy with the title of history.

The rights of representation should also be held sacred and inviolable, and for this purpose, representation should be fixed upon known and easy principles; and the constitution should make provision, that recourse should constantly be had to those principles within a very small period of years, to rectify the errors that will creep in through lapse of time, or alteration of situations. The want of fixed principles of government, and a stated regular recourse to them, have produced the dissolution of all states, whose constitutions have been transmitted to us by history.

But the legislative power must not be trusted with one assembly. A single assembly is frequently influenced by the vices, follies, passions, and prejudices of an individual. It is liable to be avaricious, and to exempt itself from the burdens it lays upon it's constituents. It is subject to ambition, and after a series of years, will be prompted to vote itself perpetual. The long parliament in England voted itself perpetual, and thereby, for a time, destroyed the political liberty of the subject. Holland was governed by one representative assembly annually elected. They afterwards voted themselves from annual to septennial; then for life; and finally exerted the power of filling up all vacancies, without application to their constituents. The government of Holland is now a tyranny *though a republic.*

The result of a single assembly will be hasty and indigested, and their judgments frequently absurd and inconsistent. There must be a second body to revise with coolness and wisdom, and to controul with firmness, independent upon the first, either for their creation, or existence. Yet the first must retain a right to a similar revision and controul over the second.

Let us now ascertain some particular principles which should be attended to, in forming the executive power.

When we recollect the nature and employment of this power, we find that it ought to be conducted with vigour and dispatch. It should be able to execute the laws without opposition, and to controul all the turbulent spirits in the state, who should infringe them. If the laws are not obeyed, the legislative power is vain, and the judicial is mere pageantry. As these laws, with their several sanctions, are the only securities of person and property, the members of the state can confide in, if they lay dormant through failure of execution, violence and oppression will erect their heads, and stalk unmolested through the land. The judicial power ought to discriminate the offender, as soon after the commission of the offence, as an impartial trial will admit; and the executive arm to inflict the punishment immediately after the criminal is ascertained. This would have an happy tendency to prevent crimes, as the commission of them would awaken the attendant idea of punishment; and the hope of an escape, which is often an inducement, would be cut off. The executive power ought therefore in these cases, to be exerted with union, vigour, and dispatch.

Another duty of that power is to arrest offenders, to bring them to trial. This cannot often be done, unless secrecy and expedition are used. The want of these two requisites, will be more especially inconvenient in repressing treasons, and those more enormous offences which strike at the happiness, if not existence of the whole. Offenders of these classes do not act alone. Some number is necessary to the compleating of the crime. Cabals are formed with art, and secrecy presides over their councils; while measures the most fatal are the result, to be executed by desperation. On these men the thunder of the state should be hurled with rapidity; for if they hear it roll at a distance, their danger is over. When they gain intelligence of the process, they abscond, and wait a more favourable opportunity. If that is attended with difficulty, they destroy all the evidence of their guilt, brave government, and deride the justice and power of the state.

It has been observed likewise, that the executive power is to act as Captain-General, to marshal the militia and armies of the state, and, for her defence, to lead them on to battle. These armies should always be composed of the militia or body of the people. Standing armies are a tremendous curse to a state. In all periods in which they have existed, they have been the scourge of mankind. In this department, union, vigour, secrecy, and dispatch are more peculiarly necessary. Was one to propose a body of militia, over which two Generals, with equal authority, should have the command, he would be laughed at. Should one pretend, that the General should have no controul over his subordinate officers, either to remove them or to supply their posts, he would be pitied for his ignorance of the subject he was discussing. It is obviously necessary, that the man who calls the militia to action, and assumes the military control over them in the field, should previously know the number of his men, their equipments and residence, and the talents and tempers of the several ranks of officers, and their respective departments in the state, that he may wisely determine to whom the necessary orders are to be issued. Regular and particular returns of these requisites should be frequently made. Let it be enquired, are these returns to be made only to the legislative body, or a branch of it, which necessarily moves slow?—Is the General to go to them for information? intreat them to remove an improper officer, and give him another they shall chuse? and in fine is he to supplicate his orders from them, and constantly walk where their leading-strings shall direct his steps? If so, where are the power and force of the militia—where the union—where the dispatch and profound secrecy? Or shall these returns be made to him?—when he may see with his own eyes—be his own judge of the merit, or demerit of his officers—discern their various talents and qualifications, and employ them as the service and defense of his country demand. Besides, the legislative body or a branch of it is local—they cannot therefore personally inform themselves of these facts, but must judge upon trust. The General's opinion will be founded upon his own observations—the officers and privates of the militia will act under his eye: and, if he has it in his power immediately to promote or disgrace them, they will be induced to noble exertions. It may further be observed here, that if the subordinate civil or military executive officers are appointed by the legislative body or a branch of it, the former will become dependent upon the latter, and the necessary independence of either the legislative or executive powers upon the other is wanting. The legislative power will have that undue influence over the executive which will amount to a controul, for the latter will be their creatures, and will fear their creators.

One further observation may be pertinent. Such is the temper of mankind, that each man will be too liable to introduce his own friends and connexions into office, without regarding the public interest. If one man or a small number appoint, their connexions will probably be introduced. If a large number appoint, all their connexions will receive the same favour. The smaller the number appointing, the more contracted are their connexions, and for that reason, there will be a greater probability of better officers, as the connexions of one man or a very small number can fill but a very few of the offices. When a small number of men have the power of appointment, or the management in any particular department, their conduct is accurately noticed. On any miscarriage or imprudence the public resentment lies with weight. All the eyes of the people are converted to a point, and produce that attention to their censure, and that fear of misbehaviour, which are the greatest security the state can have, of the wisdom and prudence of its servants. This observation will strike us, when we recollect that many a man will zealously promote an affair in a public assembly, of which he is but one of a large number, yet, at the same time, he would blush to be thought the sole author of it. For all these reasons, the supreme executive power should be rested in the hands of one or of a small number, who should have the appointment of all subordinate executive officers. Should the supreme executive officer be elected by the legislative body, there would be a dependence of the executive power upon the legislative. Should he be elected by the judicial body, there also would be a dependence. The people at large must therefore designate the person, to whom they will delegate this power. And upon the people, there ought to be a dependence of all the powers in government, for all the officers in the state are but the servants of the people.

We have not noticed the navy-department. The conducting of that department is indisputably in the supreme executive power: and we suppose, that all the observations respecting the Captain-General, apply to the Admiral.

We are next to fix upon some general rules which should govern us in forming the judicial power. This power is to be independent upon the executive and legislative. The judicial power should be a court and jury, or as they are commonly called, the Judges and the jury. The jury are the peers or equals of every man, and are to try all facts. The province of the Judges is to preside in and regulate all trials, and ascertain the law. We shall only consider the appointment of the Judges. The same power which appoints them, ought not to have the power of removing them, not even for misbehavior. That conduct only would then be deemed misbehavior which was opposed to the will of the power removing. A removal in this case for proper reasons, would not be often attainable: for to remove a man from an office, because he is not properly qualified to discharge the duties of it, is a severe censure upon that man or body of men who appointed him—and mankind do not love to censure themselves. Whoever appoints the judges, they ought not to be removable at pleasure, for they will then feel a dependence upon that man or body of men who hath the power of removal. Nor ought they to be dependent upon either the executive or legislative power for their sallaries; for if they are, that power on whom they are thus dependent, can starve them into a compliance. One of these two powers should appoint, and the other remove. The legislative will not probably appoint so good men as the executive, for reasons formerly mentioned. The former are composed of a large body of men who have a numerous train of friends and connexions, and they do not hazard their reputations, which the executive will. It has often been mentioned that where a large body of men are responsible for any measures, a regard to their reputations, and to the public opinion, will not prompt them to use that care and precaution, which such regard will prompt one or a few to make use of. Let one more observation be now introduced to confirm it. Every man has some friends and dependents who will endeavor to snatch him from the public hatred. One man has but a few comparatively, they are not numerous enough to protect him, and he falls a victim to his own misconduct. When measures are conducted by a large number, their friends and connexions are numerous and noisy—they are dispersed through the State—their clamors stifle the execrations of the people, whose groans cannot even be heard. But to resume, neither will the executive body be the most proper judge when to remove. If this body is judge, it must also be the accuser, or the legislative body, or a branch of it, must be—If the executive body complains, it will be both accuser and judge—If the complaint is preferred by the legislative body, or a branch of it, when the judges are appointed by the legislative body, then a body of men who were concerned in the appointment, must in most cases complain of the impropriety of their own appointment. Let therefore the judges be appointed by the executive body—let their salaries be independent—and let them hold their places during good behaviour—Let their misbehaviour be determinable by the legislative body—Let one branch thereof impeach, and the other judge. Upon these principles the judicial body will be independent so long as they behave well and a proper court is appointed to ascertain their mal-conduct.

The Committee afterwards proceeded to consider the Constitution framed by the Convention of this State. They have examined that Constitution with all the care the shortness of the time would admit. And they are compelled, though reluctantly to say, that some of the principles upon which it is founded, appeared to them inconsonant, not only to the natural rights of mankind, but to the fundamental condition of the original social contract, and the principles of a free republican government. In that form of government the governor appears to be the supreme executive officer, and the legislative power is in an house of representatives and senate. It may be necessary to descend to a more particular consideration of the several articles of that constitution.

The second article thereof appears exceptionable upon the principles we have already attempted to establish, because the supreme executive officer hath a seat and voice in one branch of the legislative

THEOPHILUS PARSONS

body, and is assisting in originating and framing the laws, the Governor being entitled to a seat and voice in the Senate, and to preside in it, and may thereby have that influence in the legislative body, which the supreme executive officer ought not to have.

The third article among other things, ascertains the qualifications of the Governor, Lieutenant Governor, Senators and Representatives respecting property—The estate sufficient to qualify a man for Governor is so small, it is hardly any qualification at all. Further, the method of ascertaining the value of the estates of the officers aforesaid is vague and uncertain as it depends upon the nature and quantity of the currency, and the encrease of property, and not upon any fixed principles. This article therefore appears to be exceptionable.

The sixth article regulates the election of representatives. So many objections present themselves to this article, we are at a loss which first to mention. The representation is grossly unequal, and it is flagrantly unjust. It violates the fundamental principle of the original social contract, and introduces an unwieldy and expensive house. Representation ought to be equal upon the principles formerly mentioned. By this article any corporation, however small, may send one representative, while no corporation can send more than one, unless it has three hundred freemen. Twenty corporations (of three hundred freemen in each) containing in the whole six thousand freemen, may send forty representatives, when one corporation, which shall contain six thousand two hundred and twenty, can send but nineteen. One third of the state may send a majority of the representatives, and all the laws may be enacted by a minority—Do all the members of the state then, enjoy political liberty? Will they not be controuled by laws enacted against their consent? When we go further and find, that sixty members make an house, and that the concurrence of thirty one (which is about one twelfth of what may be the present number of representatives) is sufficient to bind the persons and properties of the members of the State, we stand amazed, and are sorry that any well disposed Americans were so inattentive to the consequences of such an arrangement.

The number of representatives is too large to debate with coolness and deliberation, the public business will be protracted to an undue length and the pay of the house is enormous. As the number of freemen in the State encreases, these inconveniences will encrease; and in a century, the house of representatives will, from their numbers, be a mere mob. Observations upon this article croud upon us, but we will dismiss it, with wishing that the mode of representation there proposed, may be candidly compared with the principles which have been already mentioned in the course of our observations upon the legislative power, and upon representation in a free republic.

The ninth article regulates the election of Senators, which we think exceptionable. As the Senators for each district will be elected by all the freemen in the state properly qualified, a trust is reposed in the people which they are unequal to. The freemen in the late province of Main, are to give in their votes for senators in the western district, and so, on the contrary. Is it supposeable that the freemen in the county of Lincoln can judge of the political merits of a senator in Berkshire? Must not the several corporations in the state, in a great measure depend upon their representatives for information? And will not the house of representatives in fact chuse the senators? That independence of the senate upon the house, which the constitution seems to have intended, is visionary, and the benefits which were expected to result from a senate, as one distinct branch of the legislative body, will not be discoverable.

The tenth article prescribes the method in which the Governor is to be elected. This method is open to, and will introduce bribery and corruption, and also originate parties and factions in the state. The Governor of Rhode Island was formerly elected in this manner, and we all know how long a late Governor there, procured his re-election by methods the most unjustifiable. Bribery was attempted in an open and flagrant manner.

The thirteenth article ascertains the authority of the general court, and by that article we find their power is limited only by the several articles of the constitution. We do not find that the rights of conscience are ascertained and defined, unless they may be thought to be in the thirty fourth article. That article we conceive to be expressed in very loose and uncertain terms. What is a *religious* profession and worship of God, has been disputed for sixteen hundred years, and the various sects of christians have not yet settled the dispute. What is a free exercise and enjoyment of religious worship has been, and still is, a subject of much altercation. And this free exercise and enjoyment is said to be *allowed* to the protestants of this state by the constitution, when we suppose it to be an unalienable right of all mankind, which no human power can wrest from them. We do not find any bill of

THEOPHILUS PARSONS

rights either accompanying the constitution, or interwoven with it, and no attempt is made to define and secure that protection of the person and property of the members of the state, which the legislative and executive bodies cannot withhold, unless the general words *of confirming the right to trial by jury*, should be considered as such definition and security. We think a bill of rights ascertaining and clearly describing the rights of conscience, and that security of person and property, the supreme power of the state is bound to afford to all the members thereof, ought to be fully ratified, before, or at the same time with, the establishment of any constitution.

The fifteenth article fixes the number which shall constitute a quorum in the senate and house of representatives—We think these numbers much too small—This constitution will immediately introduce about three hundred and sixty mumbers into the house. If sixty make a quorum, the house may totally change its members six different times; and it probably will very often in the course of a long session, be composed of such a variety of members, as will retard the public business, and introduce confusion in the debates, and inconsistency in the result. Besides the number of members, whose concurrence is necessary to enact a law, is so small, that the subjects of the state will have no security, that the laws which are to control their natural rights, have the consent of a majority of the freemen. The same reasoning applies to the senate, though not so strikingly, as a quorum of that body must consist of nearly a third of the senators.

The eighteenth article describes the several powers of the Governor or the supreme executive officer. We find in comparing the several articles of the constitution, that the senate are the only court to try impeachments. We also conceive that every officer in the state ought to be amenable to such court. We think therefore that the members of that court ought never to be advisory to any officer in the state. If their advice is the result of inattention or corruption, they cannot be brought to punishment by impeachment, as they will be their own judges. Neither will the officer who pursues their advice be often, if ever, punishable, for a similar reason. To condemn this officer will be to reprobate their own advice—consequently a proper body is not formed to advise the Governor, when a sudden emergency may render advice expedient: for the senate advise, and are the court to try impeachments. We would now make one further observation, that we cannot discover in this article or in any part of the constitution that the executive power is entrusted with a check upon the legislative power, sufficient to prevent the encroachment of the latter upon the former—Without this check the legislative power will exercise the executive, and in a series of years the government will be as absolute as that of Holland.

The nineteenth article regulates the appointment of the several classes of officers. And we find that almost all the officers are appointed by the Governor and Senate. An objection formerly made occurs here. The Senate with the Governor are the court to remove these officers for misbehaviour. Those officers, in general, who are guilty of male-conduct in the execution of their office, were improper men to be appointed. Sufficient care was not taken in ascertaining their political military or moral qualifications. Will the senators therefore if they appoint, be a proper court to remove. Will not a regard to their own characters have an undue bias upon them. This objection will grow stronger, if we may suppose that the time will come when a man may procure his appointment to office by bribery. The members of that court therefore who alone can remove for misbehaviour, should not be concerned in the appointment. Besides, if one branch of the legislative body appoint the executive officers, and the same branch alone can remove them, the legislative power will acquire an undue influence over the executive.

The twenty second article describes the authority the Governor shall have in all business to be transacted by him and the Senate. The Governor by this article must be present in conducting an impeachment. He has it therefore in his power to rescue a favourite from impeachment, so long as he is Governor, by absenting himself from the Senate, whenever the impeachment is to be brought forwards.

We cannot conceive upon what principles the twenty third article ascertains the speaker of the house to be one of the three, the majority of whom have the power of granting pardons. The speaker is an officer of one branch of the legislative body, and hourly depends upon them for his existence in that character—he therefore would not probably be disposed to offend any leading party in the house, by consenting to, or denying a pardon. An undue influence might prevail and the power of pardoning be improperly exercised.—When the speaker is guilty of this improper exercise, he cannot be punished but by impeachment, and as he is commonly a favourite of a considerable party in the house, it will be difficult to procure the accusation; for his party will support him.

The judges by the twenty fourth article are to hold their places during good behaviour, but we do not find that their salaries are any where directed to be fixed. The house of representatives may therefore starve them into a state of dependence.

The twenty-eighth article determines the mode of electing and removing the delegates for Congress. It is by joint ballot of the house and Senate. These delegates should be some of the best men in the State. Their abilities and characters should be thoroughly investigated. This will be more effectually done, if they are elected by the legislative body, each branch having a right to originate or negative the choice, and removal. And we cannot conceive why they should not be elected in this manner, as well as all officers who are annually appointed with annual grants of their sallaries, as is directed in the nineteenth article. By the mode of election now excepted against, the house may choose their delegates, altho' every Senator should vote against their choice.

The thirty-fourth article respecting liberty of conscience, we think exceptionable, but the observations necessary to be made thereon, were introduced in animadverting upon the thirteenth article.

The Committee have purposely been as concise as possible in their observations upon the Constitution proposed by the Convention of this State—Where they thought it was nonconformable to the principles of a free republican government, they have ventured to point out the nonconformity—Where they thought it was repugnant to the original social contract, they have taken the liberty to suggest that repugnance—And where they were persuaded it was founded in political injustice, they have dared to assert it.

The Committee, in obedience to the direction of this body, afterwards proceeded to delineate the general outlines of a Constitution, conformable to what have been already reported by them, as the principles of a free republican government, and as the natural rights of mankind.

They first attempted to delineate the legislative body. It has already been premised, that the legislative power is to be lodged in two bodies, composed of the representatives of the people. That representation ought to be equal. And that no law affecting the person and property of the members of the state ought to be enacted, without the consent of a majority of the members, and of those also who hold a major part of the property.

In forming the first body of legislators, let regard be had only to the representation of persons, not of property. This body we call the house of representatives. Ascertain the number of representatives. It ought not to be so large as will induce an enormous expence to government, nor too unwieldy to deliberate with coolness and attention; nor so small as to be unacquainted with the situation and circumstances of the state. One hundred will be large enough, and perhaps it may be too large. We are persuaded that any number of men exceeding that, cannot do business with such expedition and propriety a smaller number could. However let that at present be considered as the number. Let us have the number of freemen in the several counties in the state; and let these representatives be apportioned among the respective counties, in proportion to their number of freemen. The representation yet remains equal. Let the representatives for the several counties be elected in this manner. Let the several towns in the respective counties, the first wednesday in May annually, choose delegates to meet in county convention on the thursday next after the second wednesday in May annually, and there elect the representatives for the county—Let the number of delegates each town shall send to the county convention be regulated in this manner. Ascertain that town which hath the smallest number of freemen; and let that town send one. Suppose the smallest town contains fifty. All the other towns shall then send as many members as they have fifties. If after the fifties are deducted, there remain an odd number, and that number is twenty five, or more, let them send another, if less, let no notice be taken of it. We have taken a certain for an uncertain number. Here the representation is as equal as the situation of a large political society will admit. No qualification should be necessary for a representative, except residence in the county the two years preceeding his election, and the payment of taxes those years. Any freeman may be an elector who hath resided in the county the year preceeding. The same qualification is requisite for a delegate, that is required of a representative. The representatives are designed to represent the persons of the members, and therefore we do not consider a qualification in point of property necessary for them.

These represenatives shall be returned from the several parts of the county in this manner—Each county convention shall divide the county into as many districts as they send representatives, by the following rule—As we have the number of freemen in the county, and the number of county representatives, by dividing the greater by the less we have the number of freemen entitled to send one representative. Then add as many adjoining towns together as contain that number of freemen, or as near as may be, and let those towns form one district, and proceed in this manner through the county. Let a representative be chosen out of each district, and let all the representatives be elected out of the members who compose the county convention. In this house we find a proportionate representation of persons. If a law passes this house it hath the consent of a majority of the freemen; and here we may look for political honesty, probity and upright intentions to the good of the whole. Let this house therefore originate money-bills, as they will not have that inducement to extravagant liberality which an house composed of opulent men would, as the former would feel more sensibly the consequences. This county convention hath other business to do, which shall be mentioned hereafter. We shall now only observe, that this convention, upon a proper summons, is to meet again, to supply all vacancies in it's representation, by electing other representatives out of the district in which the vacancy falls. The formation of the second body of legislators next came under consideration, which may be called the senate. In electing the members for this body, let the representation of property be attended to. The senators may be chosen most easily in a county convention, which may be called the senatorial convention. Ascertain the number of senators. Perhaps thirty three will be neither too large nor too small. Let seven more be added to the thirty three which will make forty—these seven will be wanted for another purpose to be mentioned hereafter—Apportion the whole number upon the several counties, in proportion to the state tax each county pays. Each freeman of the state, who is possessed of a certain quantity of property, may be an elector of the senators. To ascertain the value of a man's estate by a valuation is exceedingly difficult if possible, unless he voluntarily returns a valuation—To ascertain it by oath would be laying snares for a man's conscience, and would be a needless multiplication of oaths if another method could be devised—To fix his property at any certain sum, would be vague and uncertain, such is the fluctuation of even the best currency, and such the continual alteration of the nominal value of property—Let the state-tax assessed on each freeman's estate decide it—That tax will generally bear a very just proportion to the nominal value of a currency, and of property. Let every freeman whose estate pays such a proportion of the state-tax that had been last assessed previous to his electing, as three pounds is to an hundred thousand pounds, be an elector—The senatorial convention may be composed of delegates from the several towns elected in this manner. Ascertain the town which contains the smallest number of freemen whose estates pay such tax, and ascertain that number. Suppose it to be thirty. Let that town send one, and let all the other towns in the county send as many delegates as they have thirties. If after the thirties are deducted, there remains an odd number, and that number is fifteen, or more, let them send another, if it is less than fifteen let no notice be taken of it. Let the delegates for the senatorial convention be chosen at the same time with the county delegates, and meet in convention the second wednesday in May annually, which is the day before the county convention is to meet—and let no county delegate be a senatorial delegate the same year—We have here a senate (deducting seven in the manner and for the purpose hereafter to be mentioned) which more peculiarly represents the property of the state; and no act will pass both branches of the legislative body, without having the consent of those members who hold a major part of the property of the state. In electing the senate in this manner, the representation will be as equal as the fluctuation of property will admit of, and it is an equal representation of property so far as the number of senators are proportioned among the several counties. Such is the distribution of intestate estates in this country, the inequality between the estates of the bulk of the property holders is so inconsiderable, and the tax necessary to qualify a man to be an elector of a senator is so moderate, it may be demonstrated, that a law which passes both branches will have the consent of those persons who hold a majority of the property in the state. No freeman should be a delegate for the senatorial convention unless his estate pays the same tax which was necessary to qualify him to elect delegates for that convention; and no freeman shall be an elector of a delegate for that convention, nor a delegate therefor, unless he has been an inhabitant of the county for the two years next preceeding. No person shall be capable of an election into the senate unless he has been an inhabitant of the county for three years next preceeding his election—His qualification in point of estate is also to be considered. Let the state tax which was assessed upon his estate for the three years next preceeding his election be upon an average, at the rate of six pounds in an hundred thousand annually.

This will be all the duty of the senatorial convention unless there should be a vacancy in the senate when it will be again convened to fill up the vacancy. These two bodies will have the execution of the legislative power; and they are composed of the necessary members to make a just proportion of taxes among the several counties. This is all the discretionary power they will have in apportioning the taxes.

Once in five years at least, the legislative body shall make a valuation for the several counties in the State, and at the same time each county shall make a county valuation, by a county convention chosen for that purpose only, by the same rules which the legislative body observed in making the State valuation—and whenever a State valuation is made, let the several county valuations be also made. The legislative body after they have proportioned the State tax among the several counties, shall also proportion the tax among the several plantations and towns, agreeably to the county valuation, to be filed in the records of the General Court for that purpose. It may be observed that this county valuation will be taken and adjusted in county convention, in which persons only are to be equally represented; and it may also be objected that property ought also to be represented for this purpose. It is answered that each man in the county will pay at least a poll tax, and therefore ought to be represented in this convention—that it is impracticable in one convention to have persons and property both represented with any degree of equality, without great intricacy—and that, where both cannot be represented without great intricacy, the representation of property should yield the preference to that of persons. The counties ought not to be compelled to pay their own representatives—if so, the counties remote from the seat of government would be at a greater charge than the other counties, which would be unjust—for they have only an equal influence in legislation with the other counties, yet they cannot use that influence but at a greater expense—They therefore labor under greater disadvantages in the enjoyment of their political liberties, than the other counties. If the remote counties enjoyed a larger proportional influence in legislation than the other counties, it would be just they should pay their own members, for the enhanced expence would tend to check this inequality of representation.

All the representatives should attend the house, if possible, and all the senators the senate. A change of faces in the course of a session retards and perplexes the public business. No man should accept of a seat in the legislative body without he intends a constant attendance upon his duty. Unavoidable accidents, necessary private business, sickness and death may, and will prevent a general attendance: but the numbers requisite to constitute a quorum of the house and senate should be so large as to admit of the absence of members, only for the reasons aforesaid. If members declined to attend their duty they should be expelled, and others chosen who would do better. Let seventy five constitute a quorum of the house, and twenty four of the senate. However no law ought to be enacted at any time, unless it has the concurrence of fifty one representatives, and seventeen senators.

We have now the legislative body (deducting seven of the senators.) Each branch hath a negative upon the other—and either branch may originate any bill or propose any amendment, except a money bill, which should be concurred or nonconcurred by the senate in the whole. The legislative body is so formed and ballanced that the laws will be made with the greatest wisdom and the best intentions; and the proper consent thereto is obtained. Each man enjoys political liberty, and his civil rights will be taken care of. And all orders of men are interested in government, will put confidence in it, and struggle for it's support. As the county and senatorial delegates are chosen the same day throughout the State, as all the county conventions are held at the same time, and all the senatorial conventions on one day, and as these delegates are formed into conventions on a short day after their election, elections will be free, bribery will be impracticable, and party and factions will not be formed. As the senatorial conventions are held the day before the county conventions, the latter will have notice of the persons elected senators, and will not return them as representatives—the senatorial convention should after it's first election of senators be adjourned without day, but not dissolved, and to be occasionally called together by the supreme executive officer to keep the senate full, should a senator elected decline the office, or afterwards resign, be expelled, or die. The county conventions in the same way are to keep the representation full, and also supply all vacancies in the offices they will be authorised to appoint to and elect as will be presently mentioned. By making provision in the constitution that recourse be had to these principles of representation every twenty years, by taking new lists of the freemen for that purpose, and by a new distribution of the number of representatives agreeably thereto, and of the senators in proportion to the State tax, representation will be always free and equal. These principles easily accommodate themselves to the erection of new counties and towns. Crude and hasty determinations of the house will be revised or controuled by the senate; and those views of the senate which may arise from ambition or a disregard to civil liberty will be frustrated. Government will acquire a dignity and firmness, which is the greatest security of the subject: while the people look on, and observe the conduct of their servants, and continue or withdraw their favour annually, according to their merit or demerit.

The forming of the executive power came next in course. Every freeman in the State should have a voice in this formation; for as the executive power hath no controul over property, but in pursuance of established laws, the consent of the property-holders need not be considered as necessary. Let the head of the executive power be a Governor (or in his absence, or on his death, a Lieutenant Governor) and let him be elected in the several county conventions by ballot, on the same day the representatives are chosen. Let a return be made by each man fixed upon by the several conventions, and the man who is returned by any county shall be considered as having as many votes, as that county sends representatives. Therefore the whole number of votes will be one hundred. He who hath fifty one or more votes is Governor. Let the Lieutenant-Governor be designated in the same way. This head of the supreme executive power should have a privy council, or a small select number (suppose seven) to advise with. Let him not chuse them himself—for he might then, if wickedly disposed, elect no persons who had integrity enough to controul him by their advice. Let the legislative body elect them in this manner. The house shall chuse by ballot seven out of the senate. These shall be a privy council, four of whom shall constitute a quorum. Let the Governor alone marshal the militia, and regulate the same, together with the navy, and appoint all their officers, and remove them at pleasure. The temper, use, and end of a militia and navy require it. He should likewise command the navy and militia, and have power to march the latter any where within the state. Was this territory so situated, that the militia could not be marched out of it, without entering an enemy's country, he should have no power to march them out of the state. But the late province of Main militia must march through New-

Hampshire to enter Massachusetts, and so, on the contrary. The neighbouring states are all friends and allies, united by a perpetual confederacy. Should Providence or Portsmouth be attacked suddenly, a day's delay might be of most pernicious consequence. Was the consent of the legislative body, or a branch of it, necessary, a longer delay would be unavoidable. Still the Governor should be under a controul. Let him march the militia without the state with the advice of his privy council, and his authority be continued for ten days and no longer, unless the legislative body in the mean time prolong it. In these ten days he may convene the legislative body, and take their opinion. If his authority is not continued, the legislative body may controul him, and order the militia back. If his conduct is disapproved, his reputation, and that of his advisers is ruined. He will never venture on the measure, unless the general good requires it, and then he will be applauded. Remember the election of Governor and council is annual. But the legislative body must have a check upon the Captain General. He is best qualified to appoint his subordinate officers, but he may appoint improper ones—He has the sword, and may wish to form cabals amongst his officers to perpetuate his power—The legislative body should therefore have a power of removing any militia officer at pleasure—Each branch should have this power. The Captain General will then be effectually controuled. The Governor with his privy council may also appoint the following executive officers, viz The attorney General and the justices of the peace, who shall hold their places during good behaviour—This misbehaviour shall be determined by the senate on impeachment of the house. On this scheme a mutual check is thus far preserved in both the powers. The supreme executive officer as he is annually removeable by the people, will for that, and the other reasons formerly mentioned, probably appoint the best officers: and when he does otherwise the legislative power will remove them. The militia officers which are solely appointed, and removeable at pleasure, by the Governor, are removeable at pleasure by either branch of the legislative. Those executive officers which are removeable only for misbehaviour, the consent of the privy council, chosen by the legislative body, is first necessary to their appointment, and afterwards they are removeable by the senate, on impeachment of the house. We now want only to give the executive power a check upon the legislative, to prevent the latter from encroaching on the former, and stripping it of all it's rights. The legislative in all states hath attempted it where this check was wanting, and have prevailed, and the freedom of the state was thereby destroyed. This attempt hath resulted from that lust of domination, which in some degree influences all men, and all bodies of men. The Governor therefore with the consent of the privy council, may negative any law, proposed to be enacted by the legislative body. The advantages which will attend the due use of this negative are, that thereby the executive power will be preserved entire—the encroachments of the legislative will be repelled, and the powers of both be properly balanced. All the business of the legislative body will be brought into one point, and subject to an impartial consideration on a regular consistent plan. As the Governor will have it in charge to state the situation of the government to the legislative body at the opening of every session, as far as his information will qualify him therefor, he will now know officially, all that has been done, with what design the laws were enacted, how far they have answered the proposed end, and what still remains to compleat the intention of the legislative body. The reasons why he will not make an improper use of his negative are—his annual election—the annual election of the privy council, by and out of the legislative body—His political character and honour are at stake—If he makes a proper use of his negative by preserving the executive powers entire, by pointing out any mistake in the laws which may escape any body of men through inattention, he will have the smiles of the people. If on the contrary, he makes an improper use of his negative, and wantonly opposes a law that is for the public good, his reputation, and that of his privy council are forfeited, and they are disgracefully tumbled from their seats. This Governor is not appointed by a King, or his ministry, nor does he receive instructions from a party of men, who are pursuing an interest diametrically opposite to the good of the state. His interest is the same with that of every man in the state; and he knows he must soon return, and sink to a level with the rest of the community.

The danger is, he will be too cautious of using his negative for the interest of the state. His fear of offending may prompt him, if he is a timid man, to yield up some parts of the executive power. The Governor should be thus qualified for his office—He shall have been an inhabitant of the state for four years next preceeding his election, and paid public taxes those years—Let the state tax assessed upon his estate those years be, upon an average, at the rate of sixteen pounds in an hundred thousand annually.

The Lieutenant Governor should have the same qualifications that are required from the Governor. In the absence out of the state of the Governor and Lieutenant Governor, or on their deaths, or while an impeachment is pending against them, or in case neither should be chosen at the annual election, let the executive power devolve upon the privy council until the office is again filled. By ascertaining in this way the qualification required from the Governor in point of property, and from the other servants of the state of whom a qualification in point of property is required, that ambition which prompts a man to aspire to any of these offices or places will benefit the state as the public tax he pays will be one criterion of his qualification. By electing the Governor in this manner, he hath the major voice of the people, and bribery or undue influence is impracticable. The privy council have also the major voice of the people, as they are chosen by a majority of the representatives: they are also selected from the senate, which it is to be presumed, will be composed of some of the best men in the state. As a further security against any inconveniency resulting from the length of time a Governor may hold the chair, no man ought to be a Governor more than three years in any six. There ought also, as soon as the circumstances of the state will admit of it, to be a gradation of officers, to qualify men for their respective departments— a rotation also of the senators will prevent any undue influence a man may acquire, by the long possession of an important office. After a period of six years let the following rules be observed. Let no man be eligible as Governor, (or Lieutenant Governor) unless he has had a seat in the senate or privy council for two years, or hath formerly been Governor or Lieutenant Governor. Let no man be eligible as senator, unless he had a seat in the house, senate, or privy council, the preceeding year—And let one fourth of the senate (which for this purpose is to include the privy council) be annually made ineligible to that rank, for two years; and let this fourth part be ascertained by lot. This lot, together with the provisions just mentioned, will introduce a rotation in the chair, privy council, senate and house: and the state will have a sufficient number of it's members qualified for these important offices, by the gradation established. These servants of the state should have competent and honourable stipends; not so large, as will enable them to raise a fortune at the expence of the industrious classes of the people; nor so small, that a man must injure his estate by serving the public. An inadequate salary would exclude from service, all but the vainly ambitious; and the ambitious man will endeavour to repay himself by attempting measures which will hazard the constitution. These stipends should be paid out of the public treasury, and the Governor's should be made certain upon fixed principles, otherwise the legislative body could starve him into a state of dependence.

There still remain some other officers to be elected—Let the legislative body choose the delegates for Congress, and the Receiver General and Commissary General, and let each branch have a right to originate or negative the choice.

Let the following officers, who may be considered as county officers, be thus elected—Let each county convention every three years choose the Sheriff, Coroners, and county Registers; and let that convention annually choose a county Treasurer, and a deputy Attorney General, to prosecute on behalf of the state at the court of sessions, in the absence of the Attorney General.

Let us also consider in whose hands the power of pardoning should be lodged. If the legislative body or a branch of it are entrusted with it, the same body which made or were concerned in making the law, will excuse the breach of it. This body is so numerous that most offenders will have some relation or connexion with some of it's members, undue influence for that reason may take place, and if a pardon should be issued improperly, the public blame will fall upon such members, it would not have the weight of a feather; and no conviction upon an impeachment could follow—The house would not impeach themselves, and the senators would not condemn the senate. If this power of pardoning is lodged with the Governor and privy council, the number is so small, that all can personally inform themselves of the facts, and misinformation will be detected. Their own reputation would guard them against undue influence, for the censure of the people will hang on their necks with the weight of a mill-stone—And impeachments will stare them in the face, and conviction strike them with terror. Let the power of pardoning be therefore lodged with the Governor and privy council.

The right of convening, adjourning, proroguing, and dissolving the legislative body deserves consideration. The constitution will make provision for their convention on the last wednesday in May annually.

Let each branch of the legislative, have power to adjourn itself for two days—Let the legislative body have power to adjourn or prorogue itself to any time within the year. Let the Governor and privy council have authority to convene them at pleasure, when the public business calls for it, for the assembling of the legislative body may often be necessary, previous to the day to which that body had adjourned or prorogued itself, as the legislative body when dispersed cannot assemble itself. And to prevent any attempts of their voting a continuance of their political existence, let the constitution make provision, that some time in every year, on or before the wednesday preceeding the last wednesday in May, the Governor shall dissolve them. Before that day, he shall not have power to do it, without their consent.

As the principles which should govern in forming the judicial power have been already mentioned, a few observations only, are necessary to apply those principles.

Let the judges of the common law courts, of the admiralty, and probate, and the register of probate, be appointed by the Governor and privy council; let the stipends of these judges be fixed; and let all those officers be removeable only for misbehaviour. Let the senate be the judge of that misbehaviour, on impeachment of the house.

The committee have now compleated the general out lines of a constitution, which they suppose may be conformable to the principles of a free republican government—They have not attempted the description of the less important parts of a constitution, as they naturally and obviously are determinable by attention to those principles—Neither do they exhibit these general out lines, as the only ones which can be consonant to the natural rights of mankind, to the fundamental terms of the original social contract, and to the principles of political justice; for they do not assume to themselves infallibility. To compleat the task assigned them by this body, this constitution is held up in a general view, to convince us of the practicability of enjoying a free republican government, in which our natural rights are attended to, in which the original social contract is observed, and in which political justice governs; and also to justify us in our objections to the constitution proposed by the convention of this state, which we have taken the liberty to say is, in our apprehension, in some degree deficient in those respects.

To balance a large society on republican or general laws, is a work of so great difficulty, that no human genius, however comprehensive, is perhaps able, by the mere dint of reason and reflection, to effect it. The penetrating and dispassionate judgments of many must unite in this work: experience must guide their labour: time must bring it to perfection: and the feeling of inconveniencies must correct the mistakes which they will probably fall into, in their first trials and experiments.

The plan which the preceeding observations were intended to exhibit in a general view, is now compleated. The principles of a free republican form of government have been attempted, some reasons in support of them have been mentioned, the out lines of a constitution have been delineated in conformity to them, and the objections to the form of government proposed by the general convention have been stated.

This was at least the task enjoined upon the committee, and whether it has been successfully executed, they presume not to determine. They aimed at modelling the three branches of the supreme power in such a manner, that the government might act with the greatest vigour and wisdom, and with the best intentions—They aimed that each of those branches should retain a check upon the others, sufficient to preserve it's independence—They aimed that no member of the state should be controuled by any law, or be deprived of his property, against his consent—They aimed that all the members of the state should enjoy political liberty, and that their civil liberties should have equal care taken of them—and in fine, that they should be a free and an happy people—The committee are sensible, that the spirit of a free republican constitution, or the moving power which should give it action, ought to be political virtue, patriotism, and a just regard to the natural rights of mankind. This spirit, if wanting, can be obtained only from that Being, who infused the breath of Life into our first parent.

The committee have only further to report, that the inhabitants of the several towns who deputed delegates for this convention, be seriously advised, and solemnly exhorted, as they value the political freedom and happiness of themselves and of their posterity, to convene all the freemen of their several towns in town meeting, for this purpose regularly notified, and that they do unanimously vote their disapprobation of the constitution and form of government, framed by the convention of this state; that a regular return of the same be made to the secretary's office, that it may there remain a grateful monument

[522]

NEWBURYPORT, MASSACHUSETTS, 1778

to our posterity of that consistent, impartial and persevering attachment to political, religious, and civil liberty, which actuated their fathers, and in defence of which, they bravely fought, chearfully bled, and gloriously died.

The above report being read was accepted.

Attest,   PETER COFFIN, *Chairman.*

[37]

PHILLIPS PAYSON

A Sermon

BOSTON, 1778

Samuel Phillips Payson was a Congregationalist minister at Chelsea, Massachusetts. A graduate of Harvard, a member of the American Academy of Sciences, and a scholar in natural philosophy and astronomy, the Reverend Mr. Payson was also renowned for leading a group of irregulars in combat during the Revolution. This essay is the Massachusetts Election Sermon of 1778 printed in Boston by John Gill, the printer to the General Assembly. The sermon could well have been subtitled "On the virtues essential for popular self-government." The text is reprinted from J. W. Thornton (editor), *The Pulpit of the American Revolution*.

BUT JERUSALEM, WHICH IS ABOVE, IS FREE, WHICH IS THE MOTHER OF US ALL. SO THEN, BRETHREN, WE ARE NOT CHILDREN OF THE BOND WOMAN, BUT OF THE FREE.—Gal. iv. 26, 31.

It is common for the inspired writers to speak of the gospel dispensation in terms applicable to the heavenly world, especially when they view it in comparison with the law of Moses. In this light they consider the church of God, and good men upon earth, as members of the church and family of God above, and liken the liberty of Christians to that of the citizens of the heavenly Zion. We doubt not but the Jerusalem above, the heavenly society, possesses the noblest liberty to a degree of perfection of which the human mind can have no adequate conception in the present state. The want of that knowledge and rectitude they are endowed with above renders liberty and government so imperfect here below.

Next to the liberty of heaven is that which the sons of God, the heirs of glory, possess in this life, in which they are freed from the bondage of corruption, the tyranny of evil lusts and passions, described by the apostle "by being made free from sin, and becoming the servants of God." These kinds of liberty are so nearly related, that the latter is considered as a sure pledge of the former; and therefore all good men, all true believers, in a special sense are children of the free woman, heirs of the promise. This religious or spiritual liberty must be accounted the greatest happiness of man, considered in a private capacity. But considering ourselves here as connected in civil society, and members one of another, we must in this view esteem civil liberty as the greatest of all human blessings. This admits of different degrees, nearly proportioned to the morals, capacity, and principles of a people, and the mode of government they adopt; for, like the enjoyment of other blessings, it supposes an aptitude or taste in the possessor. Hence a people formed upon the morals amd principles of the gospel are capacitated to enjoy the highest degree of civil liberty, and will enjoy it, unless prevented by force or fraud.

Much depends upon the mode and administration of civil government to complete the blessings of liberty; for although the best possible plan of government never can give an ignorant and vicious people the true enjoyment of liberty, yet a state may be enslaved though its inhabitants in general may be knowing, virtuous, and heroic. The voice of reason and the voice of God both teach us that the great object or end of government is the public good. Nor is there less certainty in determining that a free and righteous government originates from the people, and is under their direction and control; and therefore a free, popular model of government—of the republican kind—may be judged the most friendly to the rights and liberties of the people, and the most conducive to the public welfare.

On account of the infinite diversity of opinions and interests, as well as for the other weighty reasons, a government altogether popular, so as to have the decision of cases by assemblies of the body of the people, cannot be thought so eligible; nor yet that a people should delegate their power and authority to one single man, or to one body of men, or, indeed, to any hands whatever, excepting for a short term of time. A form of government may be so constructed as to have useful checks in the legislature, and yet capable of acting with union, vigor, and despatch, with a representation equally proportioned, preserving the legislative and executive branches distinct, and the great essentials of liberty be preserved and secured. To adjust such a model[a] is acknowledged to be a nice and difficult matter; and, when adjusted, to render it respectable, permanent, and quiet, the circumstances of the state, and the capacities and morals both of rulers and people, are not only of high importance, but of absolute necessity.

It by no means becomes me to assume the airs of a dictator, by delineating a model of government; but I shall ask the candid attention of this assembly to some things respecting a state, its rulers and inhabitants, of high importance, and necessary to the being and continuance of such a free and righteous government as we wish for ourselves and posterity, and hope, by the blessing of God, to have ere long established.

In this view, it is obvious to observe that a spirit of liberty should in general prevail among a people; their minds should be possessed with a sense of its worth and nature. Facts and observation abundantly teach us that the minds of a community, as well as of individuals, are subject to different and various casts and impressions. The inhabitants of large and opulent empires and kingdoms are often entirely lost to a sense of liberty, in which case they become an easy prey to usurpers and tyrants. Where the spirit of liberty is found in its genuine vigor it produces its genuine effects; urging to the greatest vigilance and exertions, it will surmount great difficulties; [so] that it is no easy matter to deceive or conquer a people determined to be free. The exertions and effects of this great spirit in our land have already been such as may well astonish the world; and so long as it generally prevails it will be quiet with no species of government but what befriends and protects it. Its jealousy for its safety may sometimes appear as if verging to faction; but it means well, and can never endanger a state unless its root and source is corrupted.

Free republican governments have been objected to, as if exposed

---

[a] The form or constitution of government that has been submitted to the people of this state so amply secures the essentials of liberty, places and keeps the power so entirely in the hands of the people, is so concise and explicit, and makes such an easy step from the old to the new form, that it may justly be considered as a high evidence of the abilities of its compilers; and if it should not be complied with, it is very probable we never shall obtain a better.

to factions from an excess of liberty. The Grecian states are mentioned for a proof, and it is allowed that the history of some of those commonwealths is little else but a narration of factions; but it is justly denied that the true spirit of liberty produced these effects. Violent and opposing parties, shaking the pillars of the state, may arise under the best forms of government. A government, from various causes, may be thrown into convulsions, like the Roman state in its latter periods, and, like that, may die of the malady. But the evils which happen in a state are not always to be charged upon its government, much less upon one of the noblest principles that can dwell in the human breast. There are diseases in government, like some on the human body, that lie undiscovered till they become wholly incurable.

The baneful effects of exorbitant wealth, the lust of power, and other evil passions, are so inimical to a free, righteous government, and find such an easy access to the human mind, that it is difficult, if possible, to keep up the spirit of good government, unless the spirit of liberty prevails in the state. This spirit, like other generous growths of nature, flourishes best in its native soil. It has been engrafted, at one time and another, in various countries: in America it shoots up and grows as in its natural soil. Recollecting our pious ancestors, the first settlers of the country,—nor shall we look for ancestry beyond that period,—and we may say, in the most literal sense, we are children, not of the bond woman, but of the free. It may hence well be expected that the exertions and effects of American liberty should be more vigorous and complete. It has the most to fear from ignorance and avarice; for it is no uncommon thing for a people to lose sight of their liberty in the eager pursuit of wealth, as the states of Holland have done; and it will always be as easy to rob an ignorant people of their liberty as to pick the pockets of a blind man.

The slavery of a people is generally founded in ignorance of some kind or another; and there are not wanting such facts as abundantly prove the human mind may be so sunk and debased, through ignorance and its natural effects, as even to adore its enslaver, and kiss its chains. Hence knowledge and learning may well be considered as most essentially requisite to a free, righteous government. A republican government and science mutually promote and support each other. Great literary acquirements are indeed the lot of but few, because but few in a community have ability and opportunity to pursue the paths of science; but a certain degree of knowledge is absolutely necessary to be diffused through a state for the preservation of its liberties and the quiet of government.

Every kind of useful knowledge will be carefully encouraged and promoted by the rulers of a free state, unless they should happen to be men of ignorance themselves; in which case they and the community will be in danger of sharing the fate of blind guides and their followers. The education of youth, by instructors properly qualified,[a] the establishment of societies for useful arts and sciences, the encouragement of persons of superior abilities, will always command the attention of wise rulers.

The late times of our glorious struggle have not indeed been favorable to the cause of education in general, though much useful knowledge of the geography of our country, of the science of arms, of our abilities and strength, and of our natural rights and liberties, has been acquired; great improvements have also been made in several kinds of manufactory. But our security and the public welfare require yet greater exertions to promote education and useful knowledge. Most of the internal difficulties of a state commonly arise from ignorance, that general source of error. The growls of avarice and curses of clowns will generally be heard when the public liberty and safety call for more generous and costly exertions. Indeed, we may never expect to find the marks of public virtue, the efforts of heroism, or any kind of nobleness, in a man who has no idea of nobleness and excellency but what he hoards up in his barn or ties up in his purse.

It is readily allowed there have not been wanting statesmen and heroes of the generous growth of nature, though instances of this sort are not so common. But if these had been favored with the improvements of art, they would have appeared to much greater advantage, and with brighter lustre. Nothing within the compass of human ability is of that real weight and importance as the education of youth—the

[a] The want of proper instructors, and a proper method of instructing, are the reason that what we call common education, or school-learning, is generally so imperfect among us. Youth should always be taught by strict rule in reading, writing, and speaking, and so in all parts of their education. By this means the advantages of their education will commonly increase with their age, that by a little application in their riper years persons may raise a useful superstructure from a small foundation that was well laid at school in their earlier days. It would be of eminent service if instructors would more generally endeavor to fix in the minds of their scholars the rules of reading, of spelling, of writing, or of whatever branch of knowledge they teach.

propagation of knowledge. Despotism and tyranny want nothing but wealth and force, but liberty and order are supported by knowledge and virtue.

I shall also mention the love of our country, or public virtue, as another essential support of good government and the public liberties. No model of government whatever can equal the importance of this principle, nor afford proper safety and security without it. Its object being the approbation of conscience, and its motive to exertion being the public welfare, hence it can only dwell in superior minds, elevated above private interest and selfish views. It does that for the public which domestic affection does among real friends; but, like other excellences, is more frequently pretended to than possessed.

In the ancient Roman republic it was the life and soul of the state which raised it to all its glory, being always awake to the public defence and good; and in every state it must, under Providence, be the support of government, the guardian of liberty, or no human wisdom or policy can support and preserve them. Civil society cannot be maintained without justice, benevolence, and the social virtues. Even the government of the Jerusalem above could not render a vicious and abandoned people quiet and happy. The children of the bond woman, slaves to vice, can never be free. If the reason of the mind, man's immediate rule of conduct, is in bondage to corruption, he is verily the worst of slaves. Public spirit, through human imperfection, is in danger of degenerating to selfish passion, which has a malignant influence on public measures. This danger is the greater because the corruption is not commonly owned, nor soon discerned. Such as are the most diseased with it are apt to be the most insensible to their error.

The exorbitant wealth of individuals has a most baneful influence on public virtue, and therefore should be carefully guarded against. It is, however, acknowledged to be a difficult matter to secure a state from evils and mischiefs from this quarter; because, as the world goes, and is like to go, wealth and riches will have their commanding influence. The public interest being a remoter object than that of self, hence persons in power are so generally disposed to turn it to their own advantage. A wicked rich man, we see, soon corrupts a whole neighborhood, and a few of them will poison the morals of a whole community. This sovereign power of interest seems to have been much the source of modern politics abroad, and has given birth to such maxims of policy as these, viz., that "the wealth of a people is their truest honor," that "every man has his price," that "the longest purse, and not the longest sword, will finally be victorious." But we trust and hope that American virtue will be sufficient to convince the world that such maxims are base, are ill-founded, and altogether unfit and improper to influence and lead in government. In the infancy of states there is not commonly so much danger of these mischiefs, because the love of liberty and public virtue are then more general and vigorous; but the danger is apt to increase with the wealth of individuals. These observations are founded upon such well-known facts, that the rulers of a free state have sufficient warning to guard against the evils. The general diffusion of knowledge is the best preservative against them, and the likeliest method to beget and increase that public virtue, which, under God, will prove, like the promises of the gospel, an impregnable bulwark to the state.

I must not forget to mention religion, both in rulers and people, as of the highest importance to the public. This is the most sacred principle that can dwell in the human breast. It is of the highest importance to men,—the most perfective of the human soul. The truths of the gospel are the most pure, its motives the most noble and animating, and its comforts the most supporting to the mind. The importance of religion to civil society and government is great indeed, as it keeps alive the best sense of moral obligation, a matter of such extensive utility, especially in respect to an oath, which is one of the principal instruments of government. The fear and reverence of God, and the terrors of eternity, are the most powerful restraints upon the minds of men; and hence it is of special importance in a free government, the spirit of which being always friendly to the sacred rights of conscience, it will hold up the gospel as the great rule of faith and practice. Established modes and usages in religion, more especially the stated public worship of God, so generally form the principles and manners of a people, that changes or alterations in these, especially when nearly conformed to the spirit and simplicity of the gospel, may well be esteemed very dangerous experiments in government. For this, and other reasons, the thoughtful and wise among us trust that our civil fathers, from a regard to gospel worship and the constitution of these churches, will carefully preserve them, and at all times guard against every innovation that might tend to overset the public worship of God, though such innovations may be urged from the most foaming zeal. Persons of a gloomy, ghostly, and mystic cast, absorbed in visionary scenes, deserve but little notice in matters either of religion or government. Let the restraints of religion once be broken down, as they infallibly would be by leaving the subject of public worship to the humors of the multitude, and we might well defy all human wisdom and power to support and preserve order and government in the state. Human conduct and character can never be better formed than upon the principles of our holy religion; they give the justest sense, the most adequate views, of the duties between rulers and people, and are the best principles in the world to carry the ruler through the duties of his station; and in case a series of faithful services should be followed with popular censure, as may be the case, yet the religious ruler will find the approbation of his conscience a noble reward.

Many other things might be mentioned as circumstances much in favor of a free government and public liberty, as where the inhabitants of a state can, in general, give their suffrages in person, and men of abilities are dispersed in the several parts of a state capable of public office and station; especially if there is a general distribution of property, and the landed interest not engrossed by a few, but possessed by the inhabitants in general through the state. Things of this nature wear a kind aspect. But, for the preservation and permanence of the state, it is of still higher importance that its internal strength be supported upon the great pillars of capacity, defence, and union. The full liberty of the press—that eminent instrument of promoting knowledge, and great palladium of the public liberty—being enjoyed, the learned professions directed to the public good, the great principles of legislation and government, the great examples and truths of history, the maxims of generous and upright policy, and the severer truths of philosophy investigated and apprehended by a general application to books, and by observation and experiment,—are means by which the capacity of a state will be strong and respectable, and the number of superior minds will be daily increasing. Strength, courage, and military discipline being, under God, the great defence of a state, as these are cultivated and improved the public defence will increase; and if there is added to these a general union, a spirit of harmony, the internal strength and beauty of the state will be great indeed. The variety and freedom of opinion is apt to check the union of a free state; and in case the union be interrupted merely from the freedom of opinion,

PHILLIPS PAYSON

contesting for real rights and privileges, the state and its government may still be strong and secure, as was, in fact, the case in ancient Rome, in the more disinterested periods of that republic. But if parties and factions, arising from false ambition, avarice, or revenge, run high, they endanger the state, which was the case in the latter periods of the republic of Rome. Hence the parties in a free state, if aimed at the public liberty and welfare, are salutary; but if selfish interest and views are their source, they are both dangerous and destructive.

The language of just complaint, the voice of real grievance, in most cases may easily be distinguished from the mere clamor of selfish, turbulent, and disappointed men. The ear of a righteous government will always be open to the former; its hand with wisdom and prudence will suppress the latter. And, since passion is as natural to men as reason, much discretion should be used to calm and quiet disaffected minds. Coërcives in government should always be held as very dangerous political physic: such as have gone into the practice have commonly either killed or lost their patients.

A spirit of union is certainly a most happy omen in a state, and, upon righteous principles, should be cultivated and improved with diligence. It greatly strengthens public measures, and gives them vigor and dispatch; so that but small states, when united, have done wonders in defending their liberties against powerful monarchs. Of this we have a memorable example in the little state of Athens, which destroyed the fleet of Xerxes, consisting of a thousand ships, and drove Darius with his army of three hundred thousand men out of Greece.

It must not be forgotten that much, very much, depends upon rulers to render a free government quiet, permanent, and respectful; they ought therefore, in an eminent degree, to possess those virtues and abilities which are the source and support of such a government. The modern maxims of policy abroad, the base arts of bribery and corruption, of intrigue and dissimulation, will soon be productive of evils and mischiefs in the state; and, since a corruption of manners almost necessarily follows a corruption of policy, the rulers of a free state ought to be influenced by the most generous and righteous principles and views. Ignorant and designing men should be kept from public offices in the state, as the former will be dupes to the ambitious, and the latter will be likely to prove the instruments of discord. Men, upon their first promotion, commonly act and speak with an air of meekness and diffidence, which however may consist with firmness and resolution. The practice of power is apt to dissipate these humble airs; for this and other reasons it may generally be best not to continue persons a long time in places of honor and emolument.

The qualities of a good ruler may be estimated from the nature of a free government. Power being a delegation, and all delegated power being in its nature subordinate and limited, hence rulers are but trustees, and government a trust; therefore fidelity is a prime qualification in a ruler; this, joined with good natural and acquired abilities, goes far to complete the character. Natural disposition that is benevolent and kind, embellished with the graceful modes of address, agreeably strike the mind, and hence, in preference to greater real abilities, will commonly carry the votes of a people. It is, however, a truth in fact, that persons of this cast are subject to a degree of indolence, from which arises an aversion to those studies which form the great and active patriot. It is also a temper liable to that flexibility which may prove prejudicial to the state. A good acquaintance with mankind, a knowledge of the leading passions and principles of the human mind, is of high importance in the character before us; for common and well-known truths and real facts ought to determine us in human matters. We should take mankind as they are, and not as they ought to be or would be if they were perfect in wisdom and virtue. So, in our searches for truth and knowledge, and in our labors for improvement, we should keep within the ken or compass of the human mind. The welfare of the public being the great object of the ruler's views, they ought, of consequence, to be discerning in the times—always awake and watchful to the public danger and defence. And in order that government may support a proper air of dignity, and command respect, the ruler should engage in public matters, and perform the duties of his office, with gravity and solemnity of spirit. With wisdom he will deliberate upon public measures; and, tenacious of a well-formed purpose and design, he will pursue it with an inflexible stability. Political knowledge, a sense of honor, an open and generous mind, it is confessed, will direct and urge a ruler to actions and exertions beneficial to the state; and if, added to these, he has a principle of religion and the fear of God, it will in the best manner fit him for the whole course of allotted duty. The greatest restraints, the noblest motives, and the best supports arise from our holy religion. The pious ruler is by far the most likely to promote the public good.

PHILLIPS PAYSON

His example will have the most happy influence; his public devotions will not only be acts of worship and homage to God, but also a charity to men. Superior to base passions and little resentments, undismayed by danger, not awed by threatenings, he guides the helm in storm and tempest, and is ready, if called in providence, to sacrifice his life for his country's good. Most of all concerned to approve himself to his God, he avoids the subtle arts of chicanery, which are productive of so much mischief in a state; exercising a conscience void of offence, he has food to eat which the world knows not of, and in the hour of his death—that solemn period—has a hope and confidence in God, which is better than a thousand worlds.

A state and its inhabitants thus circumstanced in respect to government, principle, morals, capacity, union, and rulers, make up the most striking portrait, the liveliest emblem of the Jerusalem that is above, that this world can afford. That this may be the condition of these free, independent, and sovereign states of America, we have the wishes and prayers of all good men. Indulgent Heaven seems to invite and urge us to accept the blessing. A kind and wonderful Providence has conducted us, by astonishing steps, as it were, within sight of the promised land. We stand this day upon Pisgah's top, the children of the free woman, the descendants of a pious race, who, from the love of liberty and the fear of God, spent their treasure and spilt their blood. Animated by the same great spirit of liberty, and determined, under God, to be free, these states have made one of the noblest stands against despotism and tyranny that can be met with in the annals of history, either ancient or modern. One common cause, one common danger, and one common interest, has united and urged us to the most vigorous exertions. From small beginnings, from great weakness,—impelled from necessity and the tyrant's rod, but following the guidance of Heaven,—we have gone through a course of noble and heroic actions, with minds superior to the most virulent menaces, and to all the horrors of war; for we trusted in the God of our forefathers. We have been all along the scorn and derision of our enemies, but the care of Heaven, the charge of God; and hence our cause and union, like the rising sun, have shone brighter and brighter. Thanks be to God! we this day behold in the fulness of our spirit the great object of our wishes, of our toils and wars, brightening in our view. The battles we have already fought, the victories[a] we have won, the pride of tyranny that must needs have been humbled, mark the characters of the freemen of America with distinguished honor, and will be read with astonishment by generations yet unborn.

The lust of dominion is a base and detested principle, the desire of revenge is an infernal one; and the former, if opposed, commonly produces the latter. From these our enemies seem to have taken their measures, and hence have treated us with the greatest indignities, reproaches, insults, and cruelties that were ever heaped upon a people when struggling for their all. The remembrance of these things can never be lost. And although, under God, American wisdom and valor have hitherto opposed and baffled both their force and fraud, and we trust ever will, yet justice to our cause, to ourselves, and to our posterity, as well as a most righteous resentment, absolutely forbid that anything should pacify our minds short of a full and perfect independence. This, supported by the wisdom, virtue, and strength of the continent, must be our great charter of liberty. Nature has given us the claim, and the God of nature appears to be helping us to assert and maintain it. I am led to speak upon this point with the greatest confidence, from the late measures and resolves of that august assembly, the American Congress, which were so circumstanced and timed as must, with their general conduct, raise a monument to their fame that will bid defiance even to the devouring hand of time itself.

We must be infidels, the worst of infidels, to disown or disregard the hand that has raised us up such benevolent and powerful assistants in times of great distress. How wonderful that God, who in ancient times "girded Cyrus with his might," should dispose his most Christian Majesty the king of France to enter into the most open and generous alliance with these independent states!—an event in providence which, like the beams of the morning, cheers and enlivens this great continent. We must cherish the feelings of gratitude to such friends in our distress; we must hold our treaties sacred and binding.

Is it possible for us to behold the ashes, the ruins, of large and

---

[a] The memorable and complete victory obtained over General Burgoyne and his whole army will not only immortalize the character of the brave General Gates and the officers and troops under his command, but, considering the immense expense Britain would be at in replacing such an army in America, together with other reasons, renders it highly probable it may prove one of the capital events that decides the war and establishes the independency of these states.

opulent towns that have been burnt in the most wanton manner, to view the graves of our dear countrymen whose blood has been most cruelly spilt, to hear the cries and screeches of our ravished matrons and virgins that had the misfortune to fall into the enemies' hands, and think of returning to that cruel and bloody power which has done all these things? No! We are not to suppose such a thought can dwell in the mind of a free, sensible American. The same feelings in nature that led a Peruvian prince to choose *the other place,* must also teach us to prefer connections with any people on the globe rather than with those from whom we have experienced such unrighteous severities and unparalleled cruelties.

It seems as if a little more labor and exertion will bring us to reap the harvest of all our toils; and certainly we must esteem the freedom and independency of these states a most ample reward for all our sufferings. In preference to all human affairs our cause still merits, and ever has done, the most firm and manly support. In this, the greatest of all human causes, numbers of the virtuous Americans have lost their all. I recall my words—they have not lost it; no, but, from the purest principles, have offered it up in sacrifice upon the golden altar of liberty. The sweet perfumes have ascended to heaven, and shall be had in everlasting remembrance.

In this stage of our struggle we are by no means to indulge to a supine and dilatory spirit, which might yet be fatal, nor have we to take our resolutions from despair. Far from this, we have the noblest motives, the highest encouragements. I know the ardor of the human mind is apt in time to abate, though the subject be ever so important; but surely the blood of our friends and countrymen, still crying in our ears, like the souls of the martyrs under the altar, must arouse and fire every nobler passion of the mind. Moreover, to anticipate the future glory of America from our present hopes and prospects is ravishing and transporting to the mind. In this light we behold our country, beyond the reach of all oppressors, under the great charter of independence, enjoying the purest liberty; beautiful and strong in its union; the envy of tyrants and devils, but the delight of God and all good men; a refuge to the oppressed; the joy of the earth; each state happy in a wise model of government, and abounding with wise men, patriots, and heroes; the strength and abilities of the whole continent, collected in a grave and venerable council, at the head of all, seeking and promoting the good of the present and future generations. Hail, my happy country, saved of the Lord! Happy land, emerged from the deluges of the Old World, drowned in luxury and lewd excess! Hail, happy posterity, that shall reap the peaceful fruits of our suffering, fatigues, and wars! With such prospects, such transporting views, it is difficult to keep the passions or the tongue within the bounds of Christian moderation. But far be it from us to indulge vain-glory, or return railing for railing, or to insult our foes; we cultivate better principles of humanity and bravery, and would much rather cherish the feelings of pity, especially to those of our enemies of better minds, whose names, with the baser, may appear in the pages of impartial history with indelible blemish. We wish, from the infatuation, and wickedness, and fate of our enemies, the world would learn lessons in wisdom and virtue; that princes would learn never to oppress their subjects; that the vaunting generals of Britian would learn never more to despise and contemn their enemy, nor prove blasphemers of God and religion. We wish the whole world may learn the worth of liberty. And may the inhabitants of these states, when their independence and freedom shall be completed, bless God for ever and ever; for thine, O Lord, is the power, and the glory, and the victory.

But, under our raised expectations of seeing the good of God's chosen, let us think soberly, let us act wisely. The public still calls aloud for the united efforts both of rulers and people; nor have we as yet put off the harness. We have many things amiss among ourselves that need to be reformed,—many internal diseases to cure, and secret internal enemies to watch against, who may aim a fatal blow while making the highest pretensions to our cause; for plausible pretenses are common covers to the blackest designs. We wish we had more public virtue, and that people would not be so greedy of cheating themselves and their neighbors. We wish for much greater exertions to promote education, and knowledge, and virtue, and piety. But in all states there will be such as want no learning, no government, no religion at all.

For the cure of our internal political diseases, and to promote the health and vigor, the defence and safety, of the state, our eyes, under God, are directed to our rulers; and, from that wisdom and prudence with which they have conducted our public affairs in the most trying times, we have the highest encouragement to look to them.

As a token of unfeigned respect, the honorable gentlemen of both

PHILLIPS PAYSON

Houses of Assembly present will permit me, by way of address, to observe, that the freemen of this state, by delegating their powers to you, my civil fathers, have reposed the greatest trust and confidence in you, from whence, we doubt not but you are sensible, arises the most sacred obligation to fidelity. Preserving a constant sense of this, and keeping the public welfare as your great object in view, we trust you will never be wanting in your best endeavors and most vigorous exertions to defend and deliver your country. The matters of the war will undoubtedly, at present, claim your first and principal attention,— always esteeming its great object, the liberty of your country, of more inestimable value than all the treasure of the world; and therefore, to obtain and secure it, no necessary charges or costs are to be spared. The internal matters of the state that claim your attention, though they may pass a severe scrutiny, will be noticed with all justice and impartiality; and in the choice of a Council,—that important branch of our Legislature from which we have experienced such eminent services—of which branch, or one nearly similar, we hope this state will never be destitute,—in this choice, persons of known ability, of public virtue and religion, and possessed of the spirit of liberty, will have the preference.

The burdens of your station are always great, and in these times are much increased; but you have the best of motives for exertion,— you have the consolation which arises from the fullest assurance of the justice of our cause; you have the unceasing prayers of good men; more than all these, you have the countenance and smiles of Heaven: with unceasing ardor, therefore, you will strive to be laborers together with God.

As nothing will be omitted that the good of the state calls for, we expect to see greater exertions in promoting the means of education and knowledge[a] than ever have yet been made among us. You will especially allow me, my fathers, to recommend our college, so much the glory of our land, to your special attention and most generous

[a] In matters of science we have a most ample field open for improvement. To complete the geography of our country, to improve in the arts of agriculture and manufacture, and of physic, and other branches of science, are great objects that demand our special attention, and to obtain which an uninterrupted course of observation and experiment ought to be kept up. And if our General Assembly would form, and establish upon generous principles, a Society of Arts and Sciences in this state, they would most certainly do great honor to themselves, and most eminent service to the public.

encouragements; for everything that is excellent and good that we hope and wish for in future, in a most important and essential sense, is connected with and depends upon exertions and endeavors of this kind. I need not observe, the leaders and rulers in our glorious cause have a fair opportunity of transmitting their names to posterity with characters of immortal honor. With my whole soul, I wish you the blessing of God, and the presence and guidance of his Holy Spirit.

My hearers, let us all harken to the calls of our country, to the calls of God, and learn those lessons in wisdom which are so forcibly inculcated upon us in these times, and by such wonderful measures in Providence. From a sacred regard both to the goodness and severity of God, let us follow the guidance of his providence, and in the way of duty leave ourselves and all events with God. Remembering that Jerusalem which is above is the mother of us all, that we are children "not of the bond woman, but of the free," let us stand fast in the liberty where-with Christ hath made us free, and be not entangled again with the yoke of bondage. Imitating the virtue, the piety, the love of liberty, so conspicuous in our pious ancestors, like them let us exert ourselves for the good of posterity. With diligence let us cultivate the spirit of liberty, of public virtue, of union and religion, and thus strengthen the hands of government and the great pillars of the state. Our own consciences will reproach us, and the world condemn us, if we do not properly respect, and obey, and reverence the government of our own choosing. The eyes of the whole world are upon us in these critical times, and, what is yet more, the eyes of Almighty God. Let us act worthy of our professed principles, of our glorious cause, that in some good measure we may answer the expectations of God and of men. Let us cultivate the heavenly temper, and sacredly regard the great motive of the world to come. And God of his mercy grant the blessings of peace may soon succeed to the horrors of war, and that from the enjoyment of the sweets of liberty here we may in our turn and order go to the full enjoyment of the nobler liberties above, in that New Jerusalem, that city of the living God, that is enlightened by the glory of God and of the Lamb. AMEN.

[38]

ZABDIEL ADAMS 1739–1801

An Election Sermon

BOSTON, 1782

Zabdiel Adams was a first cousin of John Adams, the second president of the United States, and, like the latter, a second or third cousin of Samuel Adams, revolutionary leader who was three times elected governor of Massachusetts. (John, Samuel, and Zabdiel had a great-grandfather in common.) Like the two more-famous members of his family, Zabdiel demonstrated a deep, persistent interest in the struggle for independence and the establishment of republican government. Unlike them, he showed no disposition to assume roles of agitator, organizer, and public leader. His duties as a minister held first claim to his time and energy; an occasional sermon and an active correspondence satisfied his need for expression of his political views. In this election day sermon, delivered while pastor of the Congregational church in Lunenburg, the Reverend Zabdiel provides a comprehensive view of American political principles. This is a mainstream analysis for the day and provides much of the reasoning underlying the design of state constitutions in the north, at least of many of them. The essay has the additional strength of showing awareness that, when it comes to defining a political culture, what men actually do in the realm of politics is as important as what constitutions say they should do.

ECCLESIASTES, 8th Chap. 4th Verse.

> Where the Word of a King is, there is Power; and who may say unto him what doest thou?

Lest it should be thought, by any of this assembly, that the preacher has stumbled at the threshold in chusing a text contrary to the genius of our present constitution, it may not be amiss to observe, that according to the language of scripture, the word king signifies any kind of governor, or the ruling power of any state. Accordingly Moses is called king in the 33rd chapter of Deuteronomy; the [6] Judges have the same appellation, Judges xvii; to the four great Monarchies, the government of some of which was democratic, viz. *Greece* and *Rome,* the same title is given; and in the new testament, the seven kings, mentioned Rev. xvii. 10, are, by some of the latest and best expositions, understood of seven particular emperors of *Rome.* So that by king in the text, without putting any force upon the words, may be understood the ruling power of any nation; be it called in modern language by what name soever. Were this not the truth of fact; it would be necessary for us, as we have changed our form of government, to omit a considerable part of the scripture as inapplicable to our condition. But interpreted in the manner above suggested, these *passages* are as proper to be used by us, as by any people under heaven. The truth of the case seems to be this. At the time the text was penned, kingly rule was the most prevalent. Those who were called by this name, were vested with different degrees of power. *Some* governed by standing laws; and *others* conducted the great affairs of states and kingdoms according to their own arbitrary pleasure. Amongst the Jews, the king was only the [7] supreme executive magistrate. He had little or nothing to do with matters of legislation. Their code of laws was previously settled by God himself, and given to Moses for the rule of their conduct, in all the subsequent stages of their political existence. In the times of the *Judges* the administration of their government was in the hands of God; and hence, by the learned it is frequently called *theocracy:* But the Jews, tired with having Jehovah for their supreme ruler, and perceiving that the nations around them had a mortal man to stand in this place, desired, as is too common at the present day, to be in the fashion, and to have a king like others. The request, as being to their own disadvantage, was displeasing to the God of heaven. But, as he would not rule them in a manner contrary to their own inclination, he consented to their petition, after pointing out to them the oppressive manner of the king. Their kings of several generations ruled in righteousness, and made the institutes of Moses the measure of their administration. Concerning such, Solomon pronounces as in our text, *where the word of a king is, there is power.* Whilst they keep within constitutional [8] limits they cannot be resisted with impunity. Disobedience to such, exposes both to temporal and eternal punishments. To temporal, as the king is vested with great authority, and may do whatever he pleases for the preservation of order and the advancement of the public happiness: To eternal also; as government is of divine institution; and it is the will of heaven that we should obey not only for *wrath,* but also for *conscience sake,* provided the ruling power *be the minister of God for good.*

There is no necessity of supposing the declaration of Solomon true only of kingly government, properly so called. It is, or ought to be true of all kinds of government; and if there be *any* concerning which the assertion of the wise man may not, with truth, be made, it is evidently defective, and ought immediately to be amended, or totally changed. Three different modes of civil rule have been prevalent among the nations of the earth, a *monarchy, aristocracy,* and *democracy;* and indeed *some* have a combination or mixture of all three, as England. This has been esteemed by enlightened foreigners to be [9] the happiest of any other, and infinite ecomiums have been passed upon it. Under such a form the people were free for many centuries. Corruption has at length taken place, and deprived the community at large of many of the blessings which they formerly enjoyed.* Hence we learn that something else is necessary towards making a people free and happy, besides a good constitution.

Amidst the different forms, it has often been enquired, which is the best? To such a question it may truly be answered, that no *particular one* for the *same people always.* [10] As the tempers and manners of nations change, a change in their government becomes necessary. The Jews, at first, lived under a free commonwealth. Advancing in vice, they chose a different one; and being indulged, they descended at last, namely, before their Babylonish captivity to a

---

* There was formerly a proper balance of power between the three constituent branches of the British constitution; and at that time it was a noble one. It had the strength and dispatch of Monarchy; the dignity and wisdom of Aristocracy, and the freedom of Democracy all combined in one. But this happy equipoise of power was destroyed, when the Commons granted to the King certain duties and customs, in lieu of personal service due to the Lord paramount, by the feudal system, together with the disposal of all the lucrative places that become necessary for the collection of those customs. This gave the king an undue influence, and enabled him to carry any point in Parliament. He is now vertually, though not nominally, an absolute monarch; especially as the people are very venal and corrupt. Innovations in government are dangerous.

mode of civil rule, similar to that of the eastern nations, at the present day, where one man, by birth or conquest, takes the sole command, and rules according to his despotic will.—The Romans underwent many changes in this regard. Formed at first of a set of outlaws and insolvent debtors, they instituted kingly rule. This continued for a few generations, till their kings, intoxicated with power, broke over all wholesome restraints, and committed *personally,* and by their *sons,* crimes intolerable to a free and virtuous people. *Brutus,* teaching the evil of a certain nefarious deed, and seconded by his worthy citizens, banished the royal family from Rome. After this, they set up a government of the popular kind, under which they enjoyed their liberties in great perfection, till falling under the burden of their own vices, and descending to a thousand factions, *Julius Caesar,* at the head of [11] a well-disciplined body of troops, taking the advantage of this distracted state of the republic, retired from *Gaul,* and thundering with his legions at the gates of *Rome,* struck terror into the inhabitants, and fighting a battle with *Pompey,* one of a wicked triumvirate, obtained a complete victory over him, and was, in consequence, declared by the senate perpetual Dictator, a title similar to that of absolute Monarch. Now, it may well be questioned, whether *this,* for that people, under their present temper, was not the best government they could possibly have. *Holland* was once governed by a monarch who bid defiance to all former laws. They groaned under his jurisdiction; they refused his edicts; and, though they suffered much, they, at last, obtained a compleat independency, and remain to this day free in *constitution,* though some have pretended to affirm that they are slaves in *reality.*

From this view of the matter, it is apparent, that the character of a people is to be taken into account, in order to pronounce what mode of civil policy is best for them. This may, on the whole, be affirmed, that no people can be said to [12] enjoy freedom, who have not the choice of their rulers, either *mediately* or *immediately,* in their own power. A different doctrine, I am sensible, has frequently been preached. *Time-serving priests* and *fawning sycophants* have sometimes flattered kings that they enjoyed their places *jure divino;* and scripture has been quoted in defence of the absurd tenet. Thus St. Paul has been supposed to patronize the doctrine, when he tells us, *that the powers which be are ordained of God.* But as this cannot intend that rulers are elevated to their places by the immediate agency of heaven; so neither does it mean that *Peter, Richard, John, Charles, Henry* or *George* are particularly designated to office. From *that passage* we learn *only,* that government is of divine appointment, and that rulers have no other qualifications for their places, but what God, in the course of his providence, has given them. King Solomon has been produced as an advocate for the doctrine of passive obedience and non-resistance, the divine hereditary right of rulers. My text has been quoted in support of this opinion by men, from whose genius and learning we might have expected more sober and [13] rational sentiments. But, is it possible that a book written by divine guidance should teach the doctrine of unreserved obedience! The second verse of my context plainly demonstrates the contrary. Hear what the wise man says; *I counsel thee to keep the king's commandment, and that in regard of the oath of God.* Now, can we suppose it is the pleasure of heaven that we should obey the unrighteous and oppressive commands of those in power, and *that,* not merely for *wrath,* but *for conscience sake.* What! Does the command of heaven make it necessary that we should take an oath of fealty and allegiance to all kinds of authority; and that, by virtue of it, we are obliged to obey even those magistrates who command us to practise idolatry, or any other evil work? The case is too evident to need many words. All that Solomon, therefore, meant was, that it is impious and dangerous to resist the authority of those who rule for God, and consult the common good.

My following discourse will be to shew how the supreme authority of any state should be appointed and conduct, in order [14] to its coming with power in its several edicts and commands; and then, secondly, show what is the proper application of this power.

1st. The ruling power of every state or kingdom should be elected by the body of the people. As no man is born a ruler, so there is no possible way for him to get regularly into office, but by the election of his fellow-citizens. Dominion by *conquest,* by *artifice,* by *saintship,* or *grace,* is justly to be reprobated. It is our duty to resist such usurpers whenever we are able. Under God, the original source of all power, mankind enjoy, or ought to do so, the liberty of governing themselves. The powers of government are vested in the body of the people, and they may exercise them as they please, either personally, or by representatives. Their local situation and numbers make it inconvenient to do the former; hence the latter mode usually prevails.

Government by deputation does not consist with that plenitude of liberty in the people that they might enjoy, could they give their suffrages personally. [15] However, when our representatives are regularly chosen, are amenable to our tribunals, and their election is not of long duration, then we may be said to be as free as the state of the world will commonly admit. To be deprived of the power of chusing our rulers, is to be deprived of self dominion. If *they* are appointed over us, by those over whom we have no controul, we are in a state of slavery. There is no difference, in this respect, between such a people, and the horses they ride on; neither are governed by their own will, in which the essence of all freedoms consists. Indeed, it is generally allowed at the present day, by men of the first character, that the choice of the people is the only source of power; and that *republican government looks best on paper,* but that it is not sufficiently energetic and decisive to answer the necessities of the state. There has been, it must be confessed, too much reason for the above observation. Very popular governments have sometimes been found too weak to prevent tumults, insurrections and factions. A wise people, therefore, in the organization and establishment of a constitution, will take all possible care to guard against such a defect. [16] But how shall this be done? Shall they recur to the long since exploded doctrine of the divine right of rulers; and labor to possess the body of the people with an opinion that damnation will be the inevitable consequence of opposing tyrants? Shall they give up the claim of election, and assert that magistrates are sent immediately from heaven, and govern independently of them? *This would be speaking wickedly for God.* There is no necessity of recurring to any such paltry expedients. To give energy to governments erected with our own hands nothing more is necessary than a union of all the most enlightened and virtuous people in support of them. And if our elections are made in wisdom, if we *choose out able men, who fear God and hate covetousness,* then among such a people, obedience will be chearful and prompt. All laws bind by consent. The *majority can,* and *does always govern.* It is their consent and concurrence; their countenance and support that give energy and power; and in order to obtain this, nothing more is necessary, than to have the whole government administered for the public good. This makes it the interest of the people in general to obey. Individuals [17] having a different interest may be disposed to resist and even to call others into their vortex; but their feeble efforts may be easily overcome by the contrary exertions of the more numerous, the more virtuous and more rational part of their fellow citizens.

Republican governments are said not only to be destitute of energy, but to be *slow* and *unperforming*. This defect may be removed by allowing such prerogatives to a *single person* as are necessary to the vigor and dispatch of public measures. However, in large assemblies, where there is a diversity of interests and opinions, matters of importance will never be speedily discussed. This is an inconvenience to which we must submit, and it is the price we pay for our liberties. It ought to be remembered there is *safety,* tho' there is *expence* in these slow and tedious discussions; and if we allow it a defect, we certainly can find no form of government, but what is chargeable with as great or greater.

In all free states the people have a right, not only to say who shall be their rulers, but also by what *tenure* they shall hold their offices, and the *steps* by which they shall arrive at them. [18]

In order to avoid the feuds and factions that the election of a chief magistrate would occasion in some large nations, the constitution provides, that certain families should rule by hereditary right. Though this establishment avoids some, it is exposed perhaps to greater inconveniences. By means hereof, they may oftentimes have for their first ruler, tho' not a compleat ideot, yet perhaps one separated therefrom, only by a thin partition. Further, when children are born heirs apparent to some high and important station in government, their education is commonly such, as to fill them with ideas of superiority, unfriendly to the rights of mankind. To govern well, with justice, clemency and mercy, we ought to be acquainted with human nature in the lowest walks of life.

In elective kingdoms, the election for the most part, is either for life or for a considerable number of years. The better way is to chuse our rulers frequently. The term ought to be known and ascertained; at the expiration of which we may omit them if we please. This is true if they conduct ever so well; and there is great reason for it, if they have been [19] guilty of mal-administration. But tho' frequent elections may be proper, yet it must be highly imprudent, frequently to change those who are qualified for their trust and disposed to do the duties of it. This observation is true of any officer, but more especially of those who are high in command. There may be reasons for electing the chief magistrate annually; but if a new person is yearly chosen, it will lessen the influence of authority, weaken the sinews of government, crumble the people into parties, and establish habits inconsistent with the spirit of submission which is highly necessary to the good of society. A *monopoly* of office should never be permitted; a *rotation* indeed excludes it; and changes at proper intervals, excite people to a laudable application to business and books, that they may become qualified for polls of eminence and distinction. But on the contrary, if the man who holds the first place in the government, knows that he shall enjoy it but a short space, let his deportment be ever so unexceptionable, he will hardly be warm in his office, get but a miserable acquaintance with his duty, acquire no facility in the performance of it, and lose a grand *stimulus* to excel. Unless therefore we were [20] born *governors, legislators,* etc. it must be wise in a people to elect their principal officers for a succession of years, provided they answer the end of their elevation. In this way, we shall secure to ourselves more of the beneficial influences of government, than it is possible for us in the contrary practice.

As the choice of the people is the only rational source of power, so it makes obedience the most rational act. *Slaves* fear the rod, but *freemen* are kept in the line of duty by more ingenuous principles. That society who will not be governed but by brutal force, is unworthy any degree of freedom, and will not long enjoy it. If we will not govern ourselves, we must be ruled by those over whom we have no controul.

The nation of America is remote from such a calamitous event. The whole series of our conduct, the unexampled patience with which we have waded thro' a sea of trouble, in order to gain the present separate and independent station among the nations of the earth; the blood we have [   ] spilt in this unhappy contest, and the present determined spirit of [21] by far the greater part of the community, will not admit the most distant thought of ever returning to a foreign jurisdiction, thro' want of alacrity in obedience to those whom we have by our free, unbiassed suffrages constituted our rulers. But it is not to every kind of injunction they will readily submit. Several things are necessary to procure chearful obedience to laws, besides their being enacted by men in our own election. Particularly, first, they should be agreeable to the *genius* of the people, and the *spirit* of the *constitution.* The *constitution* contains the fundamental principles of the state in which we live. It is the *civil compact* and points out the manner in which we chuse to be governed, the *privileges* of the people, and the *prerogatives* of the governing body. These powers are ceded to others, not for the sake of aggrandizing any class of men; not for the purpose of keeping up the vain distinction among those who by nature are equal; not that *some* may *riot* in *plenty,* whilst *others* are indigent and distressed; but only that they may use them for the public good. As the rivers empty their waters into the sea, that common receptacle, in order to receive them again, that their sources may not be dried up, that they may [22] wash their banks, spread over and fertilize the adjacent plains; so the people delegate a part of their inherent power to those whom they constitute their rulers, that it may be used in defence of their properties, their remaining liberties and their lives.— For this purpose *some* are cloathed with those extensive powers, which by the *constitution* reside in the first magistrate of the Commonwealth— He is the "mirror of the people's majesty, and the right hand of their power." If he were more limited in his prerogatives, he would be incapacitated to answer the exigencies of the state, and be only an empty pageant, an image of tinsel, or of gold, unworthy the confidence of the people.—The same may be said of the emoluments of his office,—poverty and power are incompatible. The poor man's authority as well as wisdom is despised. Wealth gives influence. A splendid exterior does much towards commanding respect. Such is the nature of mankind, that with huge reluctance they obey those, on whom furtune does not smile.—Besides, his stipend is granted, partly, in order to support the dignity of the Commonwealth. He is the representative of the people's *wealth* as well as *power.* To him foreigners of distinction [23] resort, by him they are accommodated in a manner suited to their condition, and in him they view the ability of the state, as in him all their scattered rays of opulence are reduced to one common focal point. Further, it ought to be observed, that he who bears the burden, should reap the benefit. Rulers of exalted station have a painful service. A great weight lays upon them; *they bear the cumbrance of all the people.* It is therefore certainly reasonable, that they who exhaust their strength, and spend their wakeful hours in the service of the public, should reap in some measure, the fruit of their toil and vigilance. At the same time no worthy magistrate would chuse to become opulent from the profits of his office, especially at a time of general distress. Good *Nehemiah* was so far from this, that when his countrymen were poor and aflicted, he would not so much as eat the bread of the governor.—In conquered countries, where governors have been sent, they have frequently robbed the people of their dear earned wealth, and returned to the land which gave them birth, after a few years absence, with their coffers filled with the issues of oppression. Witness some of the *pro consals* of Rome. But with us, where our governors are at [24] our own election, who are natives of the country, there is no fear of this. The probability rather is, that they will spend their own inheritance in order to keep up the dignity of the government.

The *legislative* body is superior in power to the *executive*. They hold the reins of government in their hands; but as in *this,* and all free countries, they constitute a numerous assembly, it is not to be expected that at the public expence, each individual should be supported in affluence. They ought however, certainly to be supported. Many of their *High Mightinesses,* the members of the *States General,* make no great personal appearance; the splendor of majesty resides in the *Stadtholder.* But tho' the individuals who compose this body, may not all of them be personally very respectable, yet as a part of one great whole, they are, when acting constitutionally, an assembly with whom resides a power, which no separate parties may resist. But if this assembly stretch their prerogatives beyond constitutional bounds, they may lawfully be opposed. Power is extremely apt to dilate, or spread itself abroad. Hence there is need of vigilancy on the side of the people. They who [25] guard the golden alter of liberty, should be possessed of eagle-eyes. This sacred depositum cannot be watched with too great attention. But then there is a wide difference between *reasonable care* and *capricious jealousy.* Allowances are ever to be made for the *involuntary failings of rulers, but none for their designed faults.* There are, and ever will be, in all free states, a number of restless spirits, who under the specious cloak of liberty, are perpetually raising a clamour against those in authority. We need no such prompters. A gross infraction of the constitution and oppressive measures, will be immediately perceived by an intelligent people. Public incendiaries are baneful. To be called into combinations, under the notion of supporting liberty, is always a dangerous measure, and ought never to be complied with, except in some extreme cases. A government within a government is a monster in politicks. It is attended with the most unhappy consequences. The best organized constitution in the world, may be subverted by the frequent meetings of such *demagogues.* Of combinations there can be no need, where our rulers are so immediately under our controul, where they are elected once a year, and where every [26] corporate body may meet as often as they please, to give instructions to those whom they have deputed from their number. But tho' such proceedings as I have now mentioned are justly to be dispised; yet a ready obedience is not to be expected to resolves and edicts that generally appear to sensible people to be *unwise* and *hurtful*. It concerns rulers therefore to keep within the boundaries established by common consent. A departure therefrom will bring their measures into contempt. In this case they may "resolve and resolve and dye the same." What signified the mandatory letters of Philip the second, to the people of the United States, when the design of them was to deprive that people of the unalienable rights of men and christians? Equally unavailing were the laws of the British parliament, at the beginning of these times, when their manifest purpose was to despoil us of our *chartered rights,* and bring us into a state of bondage. Such acts are as little regarded as the *bulls* and *thunders* of the Vatican, at this enlightened period of christianity.

Further, in order to have the word, or laws of rulers come with power, it is necessary to make frequent appeals to their [27] constituents, and inform them of the necessity of their measures. This among an intelligent people has a weighty tendency to procure respect, and a ready obedience. Indeed this cannot always be done with safety. There is a maxim often mentioned of late, that there should be no mysteries in government. If this be understood of the theoretick principles, it is just; but if of the administration thereof, it is not always true. The necessities of the state sometimes require great secrecy. The most important *expedition* or *negociation* might otherwise fail. But where secrecy is not essential, there the *authority* ought to make known the necessity of their measures. As rulers should be *just,* so they should remember that they *rule over men,* who are intelligent beings, and who are commonly governed by reason. To set before them, therefore, the necessity of their proceedings especially when they are burdensome, as is always the case in time of war, is the directest way to have a cheerful compliance. If taxes are heavy, and people know not to what uses they are applied; if they are left to vain conjectures, and finally conclude that they are swallowed up in a manner not beneficial to the public, no wonder there is a reluctance [28] in paying them. Frequent settlements with those who are intrusted with public monies, and a proper account of the expenditure of them, laid before the community, will silence all murmerings among a people, where reason is more prevalent than passion, and where every noble principle is not under the controul of avarice.

Again, if rulers would speak with power, they must *speak* in the language of justice. All their *laws, resolves* and *taxes* must be agreeable to the eternal rules of right. To do impartial justice to all; to preside with an even hand, and carry the balance in *equilibrio,* is certainly their indispensible duty. There is often times a jealousy between the different parts of a nation or commonwealth; a struggle and competition between the *landed* and *mercantile interest.* It is the business of rulers to lay all such jealousies asleep, and by their public determinations demonstrate that they are not so friends to the *one* or the *other party,* but that they are greater friends to *truth* and *equity.* The same rule is to be observed in the proportion of taxes, that are laid upon the different states in the continental confederacy. This should not only be invariably maintained, but reasonable evidence of it communicated [29] to the constituents. Nothing gives life and spirit to any corporate body; nothing induces them to submit to burdens with greater alacrity than to find they are necessary and levied in equal proportions.

Further, those measures that are evidently calculated to promote the welfare and prosperity of the republick, are ever attended with energy and power. Government was instituted for the happiness of the community at large. Rulers are ministers of the people; they should be *ministers of God for good,* and where they are evidently so, there is but little danger of their commands being resisted. If the people oppose such power, thus benevolently exercised, it is an evidence they have fallen into a most distempered state, and are *nigh unto cursing.*

Again, in this view much depends on the conduct of the *executive power.* In the administration of justice and execution of the laws, much firmness, impartiality and mercy are requisite. The supreme ruler of heaven and earth has required this. He will not allow one rule of administration for the poor man, and another for the rich. He says to the Judges, *take heed* [30] *what you do; for you judge not for man but for the Lord who is with you in the judgment: Wherefore let the fear of the Lord be upon you; for there is no iniquity with the Lord, nor respect of persons, nor taking of gifts.* 2 Chro. 19. 6. 7. As on the one hand, they should not take bribes and favour the rich; so on the other, an idle compassion should not lead them to befriend the poor, and indulge them in measures iniquitous, to the exclusion of a worthy part of the community from their just demands. The obstructing the course of *commutative* justice even in a small degree, tho' it may be done under the notion of mercy, is, however, a very pernicious precedent, and in the issue will be found to be extremely detrimental. It discourages the most industrious part of the community, and puts it out of their power to support the burdens of government, on whose shoulders they principally fall. If any thing further can be done to prevent litigation, and the exhorbitant expences of *suits* instituted for the recovery of property, it certainly demands the attention of those in power.

The *Judges* of the supreme judicial court have deserved well of the public in these [31] distracted times. With an even hand, with a resolute courage, and with a proper mixture of compassion have they distributed justice in their circuitous course; and much to them are we indebted for that *peace* and *order* which have been conspicuous at a time when the sinews of government have been much relaxed.

Lastly, if those in authority would have their world come with power, they must themselves be an example to others. *To lay heavy burdens grievous to be borne, which they will not so much as touch with one of their fingers,* is what a rational people will not suffer in those that preside over them. Hence we see the reason why the measures of Britain with regard to this country were so *very* disgusting. Living at ease, and rioting in luxury, they wanted assistance to support them in this course. In this state they cast a wishful look upon America: From us they proposed to draw a revenue sufficient to uphold their prodigality, and enable them to live in splendor and pleasure. Her Parliaments accordingly assumed a right of taxation, and of making laws to bind us in all cases whatever. Feeling none of the burden, and under the influence of the most rapacious desires, [32] they would soon have brought us into the most unhappy situation, and imposed burdens upon us, which neither *our fathers nor we were able to bear.* But *now* that our rulers feel themselves a proportionable part of the burden, what rational body of men can with propriety complain? Are taxes at any time heavy, and do we under the burden begin to entertain hard thoughts? It is enough to repress the rising emotion, when we remember, that the same persons who lay them, bear an equal proportion of the whole, and are taxed according to their estates. As self-interest has so predominant a sway among all orders of men, it cannot be thought, without doing violence to nature, that such taxes are laid with ill design. *Imposts* and *duties* of the same denomination with those formerly laid upon us by Britain, which were *then* objected against, may be reasonable *now*, as the objection was not against the duties themselves, but the *appropriation* of the *monies* thence arising, and the *authority* by which they were imposed.

As it is the business of those in power to see justice done between man and man, and to keep the law open for that purpose, so example loudly calls upon them, as a [33] public body, to do justice both to individuals and to other states. In short, I mean, it is of high importance, that *public credit* be maintained; as a failure of it is attended with a thousand difficulties.

The matter of example is to be extended still further. Rulers should not only be exemplary in matters that relate to the duties of their particular station; but in all the virtues of life, they should go before us in a shining example, if they would have their measures properly respected. Those who live at the upper end of the world are greatly observed. Their manners are contagious. They do as much to support *order* by their behaviour as by their laws, nay more. As every government makes laws to punish offenders, proportioned to the nature and degree of their crimes, so they ought to adopt a code of regulations which tend to prevent the commission of evil. This is the most essential and benevolent part of government. Now, laws of this kind can never be better enforced than by the examples of men in authority. The examples of men in places of eminence and distinction, have such an influence on their constituents, that the matter may be aptly illustrated [34] by Ezekiel's vision of the living creatures and the wheels; *when the living creatures went, the wheels went by them; and when the living creatures were lift up from the earth, the wheels were lift up. When these stood, those stood; for the spirit of the living creatures was in the wheels.*

Thus I have mentioned some of the principle things that have a tendency to give weight and influence to the public measures of *authority*. After all, it is not to be supposed, that *every one* will be contented. A few dark designing knaves, a busy plotting crew love to make distracted times. But this is certain, where a government is constituted and administered in the manner above mentioned, the body of the people; a goodly majority will always be in favour of it. For what should make them oppose it? Do they think it unnecessary? Let them try; let them live without government if they can? A few enthusiasts in former, and at the present times, thought it a useless and burdensome institution. But they are grossly mistaken. Indeed, were all men righteous there would be no need of human laws. *The law was not made for the righteous* [35] man. But as there are multitudes who *fear not God,* and are not much influenced by future considerations; hence the restraints of human laws are necessary to keep the world in order. Without these, *murder, adultery, rapine,* and *every evil work* would frequently happen. In vain would it be for individuals to have distinct interests, were they not preserved in the enjoyment of them, by the combined power of the whole. Dreadful must be the state of the world, when every man does what is right in his own eyes; *when there is no king in Israel,* and when every person gives an unbounded licence to a spirit of *avarice, revenge* and *lust.* What scenes of misery would hence ensue? Altho' a state of nature may have some attendant advantages; yet the inconveniences of it are a thousand times greater— It is a state of war. The passions of mankind being left to an uncontrouled rage, would multiply numerous spectacles of distress. *Implacable revenge,* under the *impulse of keen resentment,* would hunt the real or supposed offender, and in order to meet him, stretch the length of a spacious continent, traverse prominent mountains, wade through eternal snows, penetrate almost inaccessible woods, and when [36] it overtakes him, inflict a punishment greatly superior to the nature of his crime. But why do I multiply words in so plain a case. Without government societies cannot live in any security.

Again, as this is necessary to the public order and happiness, so it is an *appointment* of heaven, the *ordination of God, who is a God of order and not of confusion. By him kings reign and princes decree justice. The powers that be are ordained of God; therefore let every soul be subject to the higher powers. Whoso resisteth the power, resisteth the ordinance of God, and they that resist shall receive to themselves damnation: For rulers are not a terror to good works, but to the evil. Wilt thou then not be afraid of the power? do that which is good, and thou shalt have praise of the same; for he is the minister of God to thee for good; but if thou do that which is evil be afraid; for he beareth not the sword in vain; for he is the minister of God, a revenger to execute wrath upon him that doth evil; wherefore ye must needs be subject, not only for wrath, but also for conscience sake. For this cause pay ye tribute also; for they are God's minister's attending continually on this very* [37] thing.—These are the words of St. Paul. And in perfect harmony therewith, says St. Peter; *submit yourselves to every ordinance of man for the Lord's sake, whether it be to the king as supreme, or unto governors as unto them that are sent by him, for the punishment of evil doers, and for the praise of them that do well.* From those passages it appears, not only that government is an ordinance of heaven, but also that obedience to it is a duty enjoined under the highest penalty. Upon the whole, therefore, I may be allowed to conclude that those rulers who are introduced into office by the choice of the people, and are *upright* and *faithful* in their stations, *ought* to be regarded as much as the Dictator, when he marched thro' the streets of Rome, preceeded by *Lictors,* bearing *axes* and *rods.*

We cannot resist such government without subverting the order, and interrupting the happiness of society. Oppugnation to it is opposition to the Deity himself; it exposes to many troubles here, and to damnation in the future world. *Rebellion* against such authority is *as the sin of witchcraft, and stubbornness as the iniquity of idolatry.* [38]

I shall say a few things concerning the application of this power, and have done.

It should be put forth to make the people industrious. *Industry* is the life of all states. It is this that supports the world. When any are idle there must be a deficiency somewhere. The *Chinese* have a maxim, that the earth produces no more than is sufficient to maintain very industrious persons. Perhaps it is from a conviction of the truth of this observation, that the Emperor of *China* goes forth once a year, in solemn pomp, and sowes a quantity of seed with his own hand, in the view of numerous spectators. This industry is a matter of importance at all times, but more especially so at the present day, when demands are great for the various products of the earth. The best rulers have heretofore been called from the plow. *Cincinnatus* was twice taken from thence, and made *dictator.* Tho' we do not desire to have all our rulers in this way employed, yet we could wish to have them industrious in their proper stations, and thereby set an example of diligence to others, who should be farther excited thereto by *premiums,* and [39] other methods within the limits of the magistrate's power.

Frugality is another important object of the rulers attention. This, both as it relates to *dress* and *food* is a matter of moment. Millions since the present war commenced might have been saved in this way. *Sumptuary laws* have often times been made; why they should be improper *now* it is difficult to say? At least the regulation of *licenced houses* and a discouragement to the too copious consumption of *spirituous liquors,* is a matter on which the welfare of society much depends.

The promotion of learning demands the attention of the civil authority. It is never expected that all should be philosophers. The state of the world, the necessities of mankind demand a different improvement of their time and talents. All, however, ought to be taught the rudiments of science. *Schools* should be maintained, at the public expense, for this purpose; otherwise, in a few years, we shall not know the *nature* or the *value* of that liberty, for which we are now *so justly* contending. An ignorant people will never long live under a free government. [40] They will soon become slaves, or run into anarchy. This, therefore teaches the infinite necessity of diffusing intelligence among the body of the people. Several valuable *literary institutions* have lately been founded by government; and the establishment adds a brilliancy to their character. These societies are still in their infancy. Much is wanting to their perfections; to make them the glory and ornament of the land. When by a series of *observation* and *experiment,* by diving into the *arcana* of nature, and investigating the *occult qualities* of things, they shall have made considerable accessions to the heep of science, then their benign influence will be felt. *Speculative knowledge* may please the possessor, but *that* which is practical is only beneficial to mankind. What can be more so than the science and art of medicine. Health is one of the noblest blessings. To have for the conservators of it, men of *genius, penetration* and *study,* who understand the human *constitution,* the connections, dependence and subservience of the particular parts of it, the diseases to which it is obnoxious, and the most effectual means of cure, how happy the attainment? The *Medical Society,* if properly encouraged, [41] will in a few years, give us a plenty of enlightened Physicians, before whom all *empiricks,* all pretenders to *nostrums* and *catholicons* will hide their diminished heads.—Our *University,* which has for a long time supplied both state and church with men of eminence and renown, now stands with uplifted hands imploring the aid of government. Let not our *academies,* erected by patriotick persons, cast our *alma mater* into obscurity, or in any degree supersede its utility. May not the former, tho' noble foundations, acquire such credit in the view of the authority as to put them on a par with the society which was early instituted, which is richly furnished with a *library,* and an *apparatus* in natural philosophy, and at the head of which there are men of eminent abilities.

Again; religion and morality among the people, are an object of the magistrate's attention. As to religion, they have no farther call to interpose than is necessary to give a general encouragement to it. Matters of conscience are to be left to God and our own soul. *Modes* and *forms* of religion; sentiments concerning doctrines, etc. people should be indulged in, without molestation. If coercion would bring mankind [42] to a uniformity of sentiment, no advantage would result therefrom. It is on the contrary best to have different facts and denominations live in the same societies. They are a mutual *check* and *spy* upon each other, and become more attentive to their principles and practice. Hence it has been observed that where *Papists* and *Protestants* live intermingled together, it serves to meliorate them both. The same may be observed of any other sects. It is however greatly to be lamented that there is not a more catholick and comprehensive spirit among different denominations of christians. Bigotry and censoriousness sour the temper and interrupt the happiness of society. The diffusion of light lessens this unhappy temper; and among people of knowledge, though of different communions, a harmonious intercourse commonly takes place. With madmen and enthusiasts there can be no agreement, except among people as distracted as themselves. But even such, where they put on a religious guise, and do not interrupt the peace of society, are not to be disturbed by the civil arm. *Render to Caesar the things that are Caesar's, and to God the things that are God's. To their own master they stand or fall.* But that part of [43] religion which has an immediate aspect on the good of the community falls under the cognizance of the ruler. Every thing that tends to promote the fear of God and reverence for an oath, to advance the interests of virtue and morality in the world, should be encouraged and enjoined by those in power; for where there is not the fear of God and reverence for an oath, it will be *extremely* difficult to keep the world in order. The *young* should not only be instructed at schools in matters of science, but also in the principles of morality; and *they* together with the *adult* should attend those places where they may hear the sacred obligations of religion pointed out and inculcated. To compel them to attend any *particular society* in preference to *any,* or *all others,* would be an infringement on the rights of conscience. But to oblige them to attend somewhere, is what the authority have an undoubted right to, and it is moreover a most benevolent exercise of power: for should publick instructions in religion and morality be laid aside, *profaneness, barbarism,* and every evil work, would become triumphant. *Righteousness exalteth a nation;* it gives dignity, strength and firmness to every body politick. Whilst the Romans reverenced [44] the Gods, and were nice in their notions of *honour, truth* and *temperance,* they conquered the neighbouring nations, spread themselves far and wide, and were possessed of all worldly felicity. But when they lost their virtue, they were weakened by feuds and factions; they were straightened and brought low; tyrants ruled over them; till at length, being greatly enervated by voluptuousness and effeminacy, they were overran and totally subdued by the hardy sons of the North. *Sin is a reproach* or debasement *to any people.* It is especially detrimental to free states. Statesmen may plan and speculate for liberty, but it is religion and morality alone which can establish the principles upon which freedom can securely stand. The only foundation of a free constitution is pure virtue; and if this cannot be inspired into the people at large, in a greater measure than we have reason to think they possess it now, they may change their rulers and the forms of their government, but they will not obtain a lasting liberty; they will only exchange *tyrants* and *tyrannies.* So fully was *Lycurgus,* the *Spartan* king, persuaded of this truth, that he took particular care of the youth, and had them educated in a manner suited to the genius of their government. [45]

Lastly; The power of rulers is to be exerted in the management of the great affairs of war. We have reason to be thankful that wars do not always rage; yet so frequent are they, that they should be studied as a science, and prosecuted by the rules of art. Britain, a haughty and high-spirited nation, have been at war near half their time for some centuries past. It is lamentable to think what desolations they have made in the earth. What judgment is there greater than this? How are the civil establishments of former times subverted by war, and confusion introduced in the world? The blood of our citizens is spilt; the bands which tye together the dearest connexions are frequently in the most painful manner dissolved; the pensive widow and the prattling babe being deprived of those on whom, under God, was their main dependence. What benevolent heart can contemplate the ravages of war without pain? There are none but the *fierce* and *savage* who can delight in scenes of carnage. But, though the horrors of *war* are great; yet, when we come to contrast them with *slavery*, we find the darkness of the night-piece immediately lessens! Where slavery reigns, nothing good or [46] great can possibly take place. Look into despotick governments, and you find no ebullitions of genius, no strokes of the sublime; but on the contrary, poverty of spirit; a depressed temper marks the character of the enslaved nation. "What a high value ought we then to set upon liberty, since without it, nothing great, or suitable to the dignity of human nature can possibly be produced? Slavery is the fetter of the tongue, the chain of the mind as well as the body.—*Reason* and *Freedom* are our own, and given to continue so. We are to use, but cannot resign them, without rebelling against him who gave them. The invaders of *either* ought to be resisted by the united force of all men, since they encroach on the privileges we receive from God, and traverse the designs of infinite goodness." Where, therefore, there is no other alternative but *war* or *slavery*, there should be no kind of hesitancy. Being in this situation, we were compelled, more than seven years ago, to take up the sword and make our solemn appeal to Heaven, who has remarkably owned our cause and succeeded our military enterprizes. So wonderful were the interpositions of God's providence, in many instances, in our favour, that we may, [47] without presumption, adopt the words of the Psalmist and say, *the Lord of hosts is with us, the God of Jacob our refuge.* How did the Almighty *ride on the heavens for our help,* and *in his excellency on the skies,* in the capture of two famous generals, with their powerful forces.* Such events rarely take place, and are to be ascribed to *the Lord of hosts, the God of armies. They are the Lord's doings, and are marvellous in our eyes.*

If slavery still clanks her iron chains, we must resolutely persevere in a measure which has been hitherto so very successful. To arms, America, to arms! Let the former experience you have had of God's gracious assistance, induce you to put your trust in him for the future, and say with the Apostle, *he that hath delivered, and doth deliver, will still deliver.* But hark! Rumours of accommodation are circulating through the air. Great-Britain, it is said, holds out the olive-branch, and makes overtures of peace. If the terms are not insidious; if our *independency* can be secured; and treaties formerly made with our illustrious Ally, the King of *France,* kept sacred, then it must be the

---

* Burgoyne and Cornwallis.

wish of every good man in [48] America to have the horrors of war speedily closed by such a peace. But of this our rulers in Congress must be the judges in the *dernier* resort. With them it lays to make peace or prolong the war; and in them we should confide. But, in order to a rational confidence in them, they should be men of wisdom, penetration, knowledge of mankind, their arts and intrigues; men of known probity, who are above the influence of venality and corruption; men of steadiness and courage; incapable of being either *terrified* or *flattered* into measures *dishonourable,* or *incompatible* with the publick weal. Of such men, there is a plenty, even at these times. It is the duty of the electors to give their suffrages for them, and to act with caution in the choice of all our officers. A neglect in this regard, will be the source of the most formidable evils. The direction of Moses is, to chuse out *able men, men of truth, who fear God* and hate *covetousness,* and constitute such to be rulers. Now, if instead of regarding this direction, people are inattentive to the qualifications of those men whom they chuse into office; if they will suffer themselves to be influenced in this matter by private piques, or favour, by party views, [49] or sinister motives; or, if they should become generally indifferent about the election, and not attend assemblies called for that purpose; then our pleasing prospects from our republican governments will "vanish like the baseless fabrick of a vision."

It is a matter of great importance to have wise men at helm at all times, but more especially so in times of difficulty and danger. Abler pilots are wanted in a storm, when the waves run high, and the wind is boisterous, than in a calm when the sea is smooth and placid. *Now* is a tempestuous time, and with difficulty is the political ship kept from rocks and quicksands, from shipwreck or foundering. How necessary then is it for the people at large to have at the helm, men who may with propriety be called Gods, for the superior qualifications of their minds and hearts? If we are favoured with such, we should treat them with peculiar *reverence* and *honor.* This honoring rulers, implies that we esteem them highly for their *office* and *works* sake. I know of no men more deserving of esteem and honor than good magistrates. He that has a suitable idea of the necessity of civil government, can [50] not easily prevail upon himself to reproach, defame, malign those in power; because such conduct tends to weaken their hands. To honor *government,* is impossible, according to the apprehensions of mankind in general. We testify our respect to the *office,* by our respectful treatment of the *officer.* As speaking evil of dignities has a powerful tendency to weaken their hands and lessen their power to do good; hence God has forbidden us to speak evil of them; and *those, who despise government, and are not afraid to speak evil of dignities,* are ranked amongst those presumptuous and self-willed persons who are *reserved to the judgment of the great day.* From a conviction of the truth of the above observations, all *virtuous considerate* persons will bear their testimony against those discontented men who are continually raising a cry against those in power, and in this way keeping society in confusion. On the contrary, they will endeavour in all proper ways to *strengthen their hands and encourage their hearts,* that their united exertions may come with power; and *that under their wise and equitable rule, we may lead peaceable and quiet lives in all godliness and honesty.* [51]

Such has been the wisdom of our elections in time past, that we may place a rational confidence in (I would charitably hope) all; but certainly in those who have been some time in station, and possess some of the most important places in government. We have had experience of their *firmness, fidelity, love of liberty, patriotism, uniformity of conduct, and talents for command.* His Excellency, the third time chosen the first magistrate of the Commonwealth, will excuse me in saying, that the suffrages of his countrymen are an attestation to his merit, greatly surpassing the encommons of an individual; and that his love of mankind, his generous soul, large as the sands of the seashore, his princely munificence, his voluntary sacrifice of ease and fortune, for the sake of placing his country beyond the reach of despotism, have set his virtues so on high, that the tongue of malevolence and slander has not been able to throw them into the shade.—May God take his *Excellency,* his *Honor,* the Council, and both branches of the *Legislature* under his protection and guidance, bless them and make them blessings to the people. My honored Sirs, you have taken the lead at the time of great distress, when burdens are heavy, when [52] jealousies are strong, when clamours are rife; and when it requires the wisdom and prudence of Angels to avoid the censures of petulant and licentious tongues. It is yours faithfully to discharge the duties of your trust. In doing these you will have the approbation of your own minds, and, I dare say, the concurrence, the good wishes and support of by far the greater part of the community.

The late measures of the British Parliament and king, will

embarrass your proceedings and make your path of duty more difficult than it was before. The total change of the ministry, and the introduction of those who were heretofore deemed our friends, will probably bring on a negotiation delicate in its nature and difficult in its settlement, for those before whom it properly comes.

Some seem to be confident we shall have a speedy peace; but what honorable and lasting peace can we expect when the luxury and pride, the profaneness and debauchery, the dissipation and intemperance of the people are so great? To pave the way for so desirable a blessing, rulers and people should exert themselves to bring about a reformation. [53] No wonder the *times are perilous, when men are lovers of themselves, covetous, proud, blasphemers, false accusers, incontinent, dispisers of those that are good, lovers of pleasure more than lovers of God.* When we discern a different spirit, we may rationally hope for better times. *Then will our peace be as a river, when our righteousness is as the waves of the sea.* Much may be done by you, civil fathers, towards bringing the people to an outward reformation. The *enacting* and *carrying* into execution wholesome laws, tending to the better observation of the sabbath; requiring persons under suitable penalties to attend, where they may hear their duty, and be reminded of the awful consequences of neglecting it; where a future world may be brought into view, and the moral character of the Deity, as governor of the universe, is unfolded, will tend much to this. Laws of this kind properly executed, would very soon put a new face upon things; especially if at the same time suitable care was taken to regulate some other matters of internal policy. I am sensible. I speak the sentiments of *very many,* when I assert, that serious people long to see a system of *preventive jurisprudence* better established, more attended to, and more [54] generally carried into execution. This would make government easy, prevent a multitude of crimes, conciliate reverance to the persons of those that are in command, recreate the hearts of the pious, and contribute to the peace and pleasure of society.—Whilst people are fighting against the burdens of despotic rule, some of the blessings of free government should be tasted by them, least they become discouraged, and ready to say, *the former times were better than these.* And tho' the war will take up much of the attention of our civil rulers, yet we hope they will find leisure to prosecute measures for bettering the morals of the people. As this may be in part effected by proclamation, by law, and advancing none to places of trust, but men of virtue; so perhaps more effectually by the shining examples of those in power. If you will tread the paths of piety, probity, truth and honor, multitudes will follow you with a resolute and persevering pace, through the whole steep ascent of duty.

You have, it must be confessed, a difficult station, a laborious task. Some perhaps may seek the place thro' a love of power or *lust* of domination. But the [55] better instructed know that there is no *good* in *power,* but the *power* of doing *good.* You have great opportunities for this. Your influence is large. If it be properly directed, you are *Gods* to the world; his vice regants of earth. As you have this title given to you by the great Jehovah himself, so it becomes you to imitate him in his perfections of justice and righteousness, of wisdom and truth, of patience and compassion, and especially, of benevolence and diffusive goodness.—How extensive a blessing is a good magistrate? *He is a father to the poor, and the cause which he knows not, he searches out. He breaks the jaws of the wicked, and plucks the spoil out of his mouth. He delivers the poor that cries, and the fatherless and him that hath none to help him: He is eyes to the blind and feet to the lame. The blessing of him that is ready to perish comes upon him; and he causes the widows heart to sing for joy. He puts on righteousness, and it cloaths him; his judgment is a robe and diadem. Such an one is as the light of the morning, when the sun risest, even a morning without clouds, as the tender grass springing out of the earth, by clear shining after rain.* This should not only reconcile those in power to the [56] arduous and multiplied labours of their places, but also animate them to the faithful discharge thereof. This will embalm their memory, and procure them juster praise than ever was bestowed on Alexander or Caesar. Good magistrates are excited to fidelity by *other* and *nobler considerations* than those of going off the stage with the applause of their fellow men. They labour to approve themselves to the heart searching, and omniscient Jehovah. They know that though they are *called God's,* yet they *must die like* other *men,* and appear *before the bar of Christ,* to answer for the improvement of their time and talents. Keeping this solemn event in view, they endeavour to approve themselves to their divine master, that so when they are called to account, they may receive this blessed *euge* from his lips, *well done good and faithful servants, enter ye into the joy of your Lord.*—If you, my honored Sirs, act under the impression and influence of this solemn thought, I am persuaded the elections of this day, and all the transactions of the ensuing year, will be such as to meet the approbation of the wise and virtuous, and bid defiance to the impotent attacks of disappointed ambition, or the unhallowed clamors of the licentious. [57]

Finally, may the people at large see the importance of supporting government, and the necessity of carrying on the war with vigor. We are now in sight of the promised land. How humiliating would it be to have our independence, just brought to the birth, fail for want of strength to be delivered? To encourage us to persevere, let us anticipate the rising glory of America. Behold her seas whitened with commerce; her capitals filled with inhabitants, and resounding with the din of industry. See her rising to independence and glory. Contemplate the respectable figure that she will one day make among the nations of the earth; behold her venerable for wisdom, for counsel and for might; flourishing in science, in agriculture and navigation, and in all the arts of peace. Figure to yourselves that this your native country will ere long become the permanent seat of Liberty, the retreat of philosophers, the asylum of the oppressed, the umpire of contending nations, and, we would hope, the *glory* of *Christ,* by a strict attachment to his gospel, and divine institutions. What though the present generation may not live to see the completion and fulfilment of these grand events? If [58] we have laid the foundation of them, and can die in expectation that our children will taste the happy fruits of our toil, it will give to benevolent parents the most heartfelt joy; and children possessing the effects of their fathers sacrifice, *will rise up and call them blessed.*—But if there be *any* on whom these noble considerations will make no impression, I would beg leave just to turn their attention to those scenes of distress and carnage, which will certainly take place, provided we fail in our present enterprize, and are brought, by artifice or power, to submit to the dominion of the British king. May the United States of America therefore bow down their shoulders to bear all the future burdens that may be devolved upon them, in the progression of this tedious and expensive conflict. A few more campaigns will determine the event of the present struggle, and doubtless land us on the rock of independence, security and peace. *Expence* is not to be regarded in a contest of such magnitude. What can possibly be a compensation for our liberties? It is better to be *free among the dead,* than slaves among the living. The ghosts of our friends, slain in war; the spirits of our [59] illustrious ancestors, long since gone to rest, who transmitted our fair inheritance to us; a regard to children still unborn, all call upon us to make greater exertions; and will rise up in judgment against us, if, through cowardice, we desert the noble cause, in which, for many years past, we have been engaged. From these considerations, therefore, let us persevere till we have obtained the completion of our wishes, and have placed our country beyond the reach of over-bearing foes.—But let us remember that we are engaged in a higher warfare; and that, if we overcome our spiritual enemies, we shall, at last, be put in possession of that kingdom where perpetual peace will reign, and liberty, the most exalted and refined, shall be obtained. *Be thou faithful unto death, and I will give thee a crown of life.*

AMEN.

[39]

[ANONYMOUS]

Rudiments of Law and Government Deduced from the Law of Nature

CHARLESTON, 1783

Between 1776 and 1789 there was a tremendous outpouring of essays on constitutionalism, often with specific designs for state constitutions attached. This is one of the better efforts, both in terms of the breadth of discussion and in terms of the careful thinking and precise expression. The author begins by listing and discussing the basis for the various human rights, and uses this as the context within which to lay out the principles and design for a state constitution. Although he often cites men like Beccaria, Montesquieu, Blackstone, Trenchard and Gordon, Puffendorf, Virgil, and Cicero, the anonymous author writes in the tradition of Aristotle—matching the form of government to the virtues, abilities, and circumstances of the people. The resulting essay is somewhat disorganized, but a good example of how Americans during the founding era always used political theory with a clear-eyed sense of the realities of their situation.

Deduced from the Law of Nature

ADDRESS
To the People of South-Carolina

The following composition is as brief as it could be, for two reasons; because in its present state, it is sufficient to assist the views of such as wish well to their Country; and because the Author would avoid the indelicacy of prescribing more than necessary on a subject which may possibly employ the publick attention.

As to the doctrine and facts, it is founded on incontrovertible truth; and the author will undertake to defend it against all opponents.

Let not its simplicity be an objection to it. Government is not such a mysterious business as the World are apt to suppose. Intricacy is often but a convenient word for embarrassment: For an original error creates occasion for an endless series of expedients, to obviate its ill effects, which still, instead of being overcome, multiply by opposition.*

The common sense given to mankind, is great enough to direct them in all necessary affairs, then they are not bewildered by pernicious tenets and examples. And, on all occasions in life, good hearts and common understandings are preferable to superior abilities when accompanied with ambition.

When this Revolution was yet incompleat, it was a common practice to revert to Grecian, Roman and British customs,** for precedents and models, whereby [iv] to build our political edifice. Is there a necessity for our being always a dependent people? And when our bodies and property are rescued from the controul of others, must our minds shew submission still? Arouse, my friends, and consider yourselves as what you are, of judgement equal to the rest of mankind, with the advantage of their experience. Exert your talents and improve upon the efforts of others. And be it your endeavor to establish a system, which may, by the same act, benefit yourselves and latent posterity, and excite the applauses of admiring nations.

On the present crisis, depends your fate. If you make use of your opportunity, you secure the good of many generations: But, if you neglect it, you may be doomed to drudge in your own fertile fields, and, what would be otherwise a blessing, will be a snare and a misfortune to you.

* Ce qui ne vaut rien dans son principe, ne peut pas devenir bon dans la suite.
ELEMENTS DE LONGIONE

** In truth government is a thing not so much as known in by far the greatest part of the earth. Government supports on one side a just execution of rational standing laws made by the consent of society; and on the other side a rational subjection to those laws. But what has arbitrary will, wanton and outrageous lust, cruelty and oppression to do with government, but to destroy it?
CATO'S LETTERS by *Gordon* and *Trenchard*

ANONYMOUS

A good Constitution established; only one evil is left to fear. A degree of inconstancy is too apparent in our public acts, which however justifiable by necessity, shews there is a defect somewhere. A system of Government, once approved of, should be abided by invariably. A relaxation in one point, is a precedent in another, and if we admit of a non-execution in any, we shall annul the whole in time. I would wish to have it inculcated that default of operation of our laws, is the greatest evil that can betide us; because it will prove the generative source of all others.

It is fatally prejudicial to accustom yourselves to consider the interests of society and the rights of individuals as distinct. The body politic, like the human [v] frame, is liable to corrupt and mortify on whatever side assailed by distempers: If the hands or feet are first attacked, the noble parts will in time be invaded. It is incumbent on you to take care that each part remains unhurt, and to remember that, as disorders first appear in the weaker parts of our bodies, so, every assault on the Constitution will probably be made on the most defenseless members.

Let it be your firm determination to guard your Rights; and let no inducement whatever incline you to recede from this resolution.* All motives of policy that can be urged, are deceptious and futile. And if the effect was likely to be good, yet the remedy would be worse than the evil. Three-fourths of the irregularities in the world originate from unequal and inadequate government. Remove the cause, and the effect will cease. At least it is the safest and justest cure practicable by you.

Objections have been made to popular governments, because most of such have been oligarchies; and men have argued from the abuse against the use. Few, if any, have ever had our opportunities. And our situation is unparallelled, if we comprehend our political and local advantages.

O Jupiter, serva, obsecro, haec nobis bona!

TERENT.

---

* Let us therefore lay down as a maxim that whenever the Public Good happens to be the matter in question, it is never for the advantage of the public to deprive an individual of his property, or even to retrench the least part of it by a law or political regulation—The civil law should, with the eyes of a mother, regard every individual as the whole community.

MONTESQUIEU

[vi]   INTRODUCTION

Writers on jurisprudence and government, in their first induction of
arguments, have pretended to commence their enquiries concerning
mankind with a history of the subordination of some single family.
Taking their conceptions from animals of prey, which are always
proportionately few in number, and are consequently solitary, distrib-
uting themselves at a distance, and concealing themselves in holes and
corners: They suppose, that prior to national connections, there was a
period when persons in general, or at least families, kept themselves
distinct and aloof from each other.

The fact is otherwise. Man is a gregarious animal, always united
in societies, however unengaged by formal political compacts; his
passions such, that society is to his mental, what the air is to his
corporal, system, elementary, necessary, natural.

There are but two occasions, whereon the condition of men is
different: When the sterility of the country obliges them to keep at
due distances from each other; and when general mistrust and defiance
have taken place, and safety is obtained only by privacy, stratagem or
force. Both of these are, with respect to the majority, *involuntary
conditions*.

Vestiges of natural society are still to be perceived in most villages
of civilized nations, and in whole tribes of uncivilized. But what
evinces its quondam existence, is that it is a *natural law* provided for
it, the law of the heart and the law of necessity or self-defence.

The first is a monitor in every breast, which at once warns and
pains us in case of injustice done by ourselves; which prompts and
delights us to do good; which [vii] urges us to condemn or applaud
the behaviour of others; and which leaves a consciousness of a similar
sense of things in the rest of mankind, *and makes our satisfaction or
discontent depend on the general estimation of our morals.**

The monitor instructs us to entertain a charitable construction
of the intention of others; to bear patiently with the petulance of
others; and to forbear long shewing resentment. But, when nothing
else will do, the law of self defence, and a common sense of common
danger, suggest the necessity, on particular occasions, of the many
uniting to restrain the destructive proceedings of a few.

* It is from the latter circumstances, that the liberty of the press becomes so
essential to freedom.

ANONYMOUS

This natural law is not yet effaced, but in despite of capricious customs, oppression and written laws still maintain a considerable sway over the actions of mankind.

Let us enquire how it became so far superseded. Written or oral laws had two different origins: In cases of tyranny, they were intended to restrict; in cases of increased population and equal government, to extend; the benefits of natural law. From these contradictory motives, arose the motley appearance of modern jurisprudence. For in time, the few of evil intentions, by plotting together, proved that unanimity and wickedness, that stuck at nothing, were superior to numbers without design; and one or two overcame the many [viii] by open force, by corruption of others, or by abuse of the confidence* placed in them.

When tyranny was once established, it behoved every other society of men to be on their guard; for there are no bounds to ambition. Unanimity was necessary for their defence, unanimity concentered their authority somewhere.** A power to do much good, too constantly included a power to do equal mischief. And these in their turn fell a sacrifice to their own credulity, and were imposed on by those they confided most in.

(A few perhaps dwelling in least temperate climes, secured by

---

* Men of the best and brightest characters have often done most mischief, and by well serving their country, have been enabled to destroy it: Numberless instances might be advanced of this.

> As when the sea breaks oer it's bounds,
> And overflows the level grounds.
> Those banks and dams, that like a screen,
> Did keep it out, now keep it in.
>
> HUDIBRAY

** In every human society, there is an effort continually tending to confer on one part the height of power and happiness, and to reduce the other to the extream of weakness and misery. The intent of good laws is to oppose this effort, and to diffuse their influence universally and equally. But men generally abandon the care of their most important concerns to the uncertain prudence and discretion of those, whose interest it is to reject the best and wisest institutions.

> BECCARIA.

Human society has often had no enemies so great as their own magistrates; who wherever they were trusted with too much power, always abused it, and grew mischievous to those who made them what they were.

CATO'S *Letters*

what they deemed their greatest evils, a dreary habitation and unenvied poverty, retained for a long time, with the blessing of health, uncorrupted manners*** and primeaval liberty.)

Riches and power were now to be secured to the new monarchs. And their adherents were to be gratified, to make them persevere in taking part against what was otherwise their own interest. *And this was to be done, only by diminishing the property and liberty of the multitude.*

[ix] In these circumstances, commences a capital deviation from the law of nature. And in the refinement in the other instance, sometimes the original intention was forgot, and passion and fancy, in the spirit of law-making, dictated instead of reason.

In general, the force of equal natural law was suspended. Those in authority monopolized the dominion, and also the fruits of the earth, the emoluments of others labour; and left to the rest, the toil of culture and the scanty gleanings of the fields, themselves had tilled.

In this situation, only two choices were left; to resist by open force, or to oppose artifice and cunning to the undue methods taken by men in power. The latter was found most likely to succeed, attended with least risk, and almost universally adopted, and a new species of warfare ensued. *Iraeque, insidiaeque, et crimina noxia cardi.* Virgil. *The Great passed laws to perpetuate in themselves and families, their vast estates, which they pretended was a principle view of uniting in society. And the Little watched their opportunities of unlimited trusts, unguarded statutes, and** civil dissensions, to enrich themselves and dispossess their pretended betters.

In this course of things, statutes upon statutes were enacted to prevent a further retaliation of injuries. What the ingenuity of man

*** Extrema per illes
    Justitia excedens terris, vestigia secit.
    Ultima Caelestum terras astrea reliquit.
                                                    VIRGIL.
                                                    OVID MET.
    Poets are not always philosophers, but they often convey the sense of mankind; and here is concurrent testimony.
* And they give the name of peace to this general effort of all against all.
** The grievous forest laws of England fell into disuse during the revolution in 1688.
                                                    BLACKSTONE
    The restoration of Charles 2d. occasioned other advantages.

[571]
ANONYMOUS

could not achieve, was resigned over to severity.*** And death was
made [x] the result of a breach of law, both in important and in most
mean cases. The reproachable conduct of a few, to be sure, countenanced
the authors of such proceedings in some instances. But no discrimination
was made; and the man who acted from some sense of right*, and the
atrocious infringer of all justice, have been alike brought to shameful
punishment.

By such means as these, the calamity became aggravated; and
liberty, property, and independence, were in a great measure subverted.

Now and then, to be sure, the contentions of the prince** and
magnates made each reduce in part the condition of the other, and
thus intentionally serve the interests of the people. And at other times,
the supreme authority, to keep up appearances, to facilitate interested
designs, to serve all alike in matters wherein their interests were
mutual, or from an intrusive impulse of benignity and natural justice,
have taken into their consideration, and ordained laws of general
welfare.

Some partial conveniences were necessary to palliate great hardships, and appearances of attention to qualify violent injustice. But
even salutary acts have been only deliberately consented to, that advantage might recur to the law-makers in the end. And the poor****

*** It is a melancholy truth, that among the variety of actions which men are
daily liable to commit, no less than one hundred and sixty have been declared
by act of Parliament, to be felonies without benefit of clergy.

BLACKSTONE

* Whatever laws deviate from the principles of justice, will always meet with a
resistance, which will frustrate them in the end.

BECCARIA

** Lewis the Gross, in order to create some power that might counterbalance
those potent vassals who controlled or gave law to the Crown, first adopted the
plan of conferring new privileges on towns.

ROBERTSON'S *Charles Vth*

The usurpations of the nobles were become unbounded and intolerable. They
had reduced the great body of the people into a state of actual servitude.

Ibid

**** Tyrants reduce mankind to the condition of brutes, and make that reason
which God gave them, useless to them. They deprive them even of the blessings
of nature; starve them in the midst of plenty, and frustrate the natural bounty
of earth to men. The very hands of men given them by nature for their support,
are turned by tyrants into instruments of their misery, to gratify the lust and
vanity of their execrable lords.

CATO'S *Letters*

subject [xi] (which is a name implying a conquered slave) stript of natural rights, is forced to serve the most ignoble purposes; to bear arms and fight in quarrels not his own; to perpetrate murder, and help to desolate provinces; and thus to uphold in his tyranny, the common foe of mankind.

If the consequences of such oppressive acts were not well known, would not any deem such a condition insupportable? But immemorial custom has taken away the sense*** of injury, and disposed the people, instead of repining at what they have lost, to rejoice that some little matter of priviledge, useless perhaps to their oppressors, still remains to comfort them.

Completely humbled and no longer tenacious of their *positive* natural rights, they now solace themselves with ideas of comparative advantages over their neighbours; and are taught by a strange perversion of reason to deduce proofs of their own liberty from the higher approaches to slavery in others, and actually to *glory* in their present condition.

This was all that was wanting to complete the catastrophe of human dignity.

Sophistry comes necessarily in aid of fallacy; and bold assertions in the form of comparisons, and flights [xii] of fancy, are received as proofs of the fitness and even superiority of their monstrous constitution. At one time, a certain triform condition is like a pyramid* composed of base, summit and mediate space, each necessary for the support or completion of the rest.** At another, the three estates are formed to clash and jar with each other, and then good institutions are only to be fabricated by an opposition and collision of interests.

*** Under all these distressing circumstances, it was impossible that they could retain vigour or generosity of mind. The independent spirit which had distinguished their ancestors, became extinct among all the people subjected to the Roman yoke; they lost not only the habit but even the capacity of deciding for themselves, or of acting from the impulse of their own minds; and the dominion of the Romans, like that of all great empires, degraded and debased the human species.

ROBERTSON'S *history Charles Vth*

* Sir William Temple, Sir William Blackstone.

** Many have inclined to compliment a prince with a power which made all men, and themselves among the rest, depend for their life and property upon his breath; for no other reason than that it made many others depend at the same time upon theirs.

CATO'S *Letters*

ANONYMOUS

It is the property of prejudice to maintain all causes espoused, right or wrong; and when people are in this mood, if a constitution defends in some, unnecessary riches and power, it is notwithstanding a good one; if all tenures are best foedal, and may be with-holden from the innocent heir for a felony committed by the present possessor, it is a good one; if a poor sailor or even a labourer is liable to be taken away from his family and home without his consent, it is a good one; if its laws are replete with cruelty, inconsistency, injustice, ambiguity and fiction, it is a good one; if bribery is the avowed rule of practice, and the majority of senators are placemen, it is a good one; and lastly, if the order of things is inverted*, and the people are made to serve the king, and not the king the people, it is a good one still.

I am not going to detect the inconsistencies of all ancient and modern political fabrics, nor to criticize more than necessary on the British. I even acknowledge [xiii] some comparative advantages of the latter; but from our former prejudices in favour of it, and from the idea, almost become universal, of its perfection; it is requisite to shew that the best form of government extant, is a tyranny, a jumble of contradictions, and an incongruity with the law of nature.

To reconcile right and wrong with each other, and assimilate opposites into the same system, may require greater exertions of skill and logical talents than only to delineate the simple course which nature points out to us. And I grant that the compound of English jurisprudence is ingenious enough.

The ingenuity however, conveys no idea of goodness. And, abstracted from the intentions of the actors, a separation of the offices of king and judge, does not make the power, still retained by the king, justifiable; the privilege of decision by jury, does not vindicate the dilatoriness and changeableness of other law proceedings; nor is a habeas corpus act, a satisfaction for unequal property and the endless infringements of liberty by the combination of the Great and by undue influence.

Relief from oppression, no doubt, affords a rational ground for rejoicing. But such pleasures are the feelings of slaves, not of freemen. And it has been the peculiar felicity of America to have been always

* The order of things is always inverted, when any man or set of men, instead of preventing wrong from being done, arrogate to themselves the power of doing wrong.

in a great measure out of reach, or out of the power of arbitrary tyrants; and it is now to be so altogether.

It is therefore our business, without confining ourselves to imitate such wretched exemplars, to recur immediately to that great Law of Nature; concerning which, those who follow it least, acknowledge, "That no human laws are of any validity if contrary to it, and that such of them as are valid, derive all their force and authority mediately or immediately from this original." BLACKSTONE

[15] THE RIGHTS of individuals from society by Natural Law, are, SAFETY, LIBERTY, KINDNESS, and DUE PORTIONS of COMMON Property, of POLITICAL CONSEQUENCE, and of SOCIAL EMOLUMENTS.

As the senses are the foundation of our knowledge of matters of fact, so are the innate feelings, which suggest these rights, the basis of duty and justice: And *from these principles all enquiries of natural law must commence.*

The INTENT of special SOCIETY, is, by justice, sympathy, wisdom and joint means of self-defence, to render the enjoyment of those rights permanent and certain.

PERSONAL SAFETY

Both humanity and policy dictate that the members of society should be protected in* life, limb, organ and feature.

[16] These no resentment should affect, no policy invade. Nothing but indispensable necessity in self-defence, can warrant the effusion of

* By the laws of Arragon, the ricos homres were not subject to capital punishment.
ROBERTSON'S *history Charles Vth*
Nor was a citizen, by the laws of Rome.
The punishment of death is the war of a whole nation against an individual.
BECCARIA
The countries and times most notorious for severity of punishments, were always those in which the most bloody and inhuman actions and the most atrocious crimes were committed; for the hand of the legislator and the assassin were directed by the same spirit of ferocity.
Ibid.
A man or set of men have no more power over lives of others than they have over their own lives, nor by one degree so much.
BLACKSTONE.

another's blood. There is a choice of expedients to shun this horrid custom in criminal cases, as will be shewn hereafter.

To deduce the propriety of capital punishments from the power of individuals, is to argue from the abuse for the right.

The reputation of a man, ought also to be inviolate: In many cases, his safety is dependant on it; his peace of mind and happiness always.

PERSONAL LIBERTY

LIBERTY of THOUGHT has been said to be uncontrolable, but it is not so altogether. Fear and affection will insensibly sway it: In matters of political concern, such conduct requires censure.*

LIBERTY of SPEECH and of the PRESS should be free, except where manifest injury** is [17] done by it; and then censure should pass on it. When reproach is merited, it is natural punishment, and must be borne with.

LIBERTY of ACTION ought not to be abridged by political compacts. In some cases it is directed not restrained. Freedom is not to be construed a liberty to do evil or detriment, even to the persons themselves. In free governments and equal representations, the levy of taxes, or other State transactions do not imply compulsion; for how can that be compulsion, which reason has suggested, his delegates advised, and his self permitted.

The fundamentals of a Constitution, inferred, and once determined on, from natural law and local circumstances, should like the laws of

* The Julian law de ambitu indicted fines and infamy on all who were guilty of indirect methods of corruption in cases that regarded public concerns.
** Laws whether made with or without our consent, if they regulate and constrain our conduct in matters of mere indifference; are laws destructive of liberty.
BLACKSTONE
The liberty of the press is the palladium of all civil, political and religious rights.
JUNIOUS'S *Letters*
Negligere quid de se quisque sentiat: con suium arrogantis est sed etiam omnino dissoluti.
Cic. de Off.

the Medes and Persians, be unalterable and irrevocable*: The people in this case have the power, but ought not to have the will, to revoke; therefore have not the liberty.

LIBERTY of LOCO-MOTION should likewise be unrestrained, except only in cases of atrocious misdemeanours. Let measures of government [18] be as equal and mild as they can, there is no reason for compelling any to remain involuntary members of it.

OF KINDNESS

Benevolence is due from one to another, not as a return of advantage received, but as an essential mark of humanity, demanded of our conscience by our Creator. And the omission to indifferent persons, is reproachable; to relations, allies and friends, infamous.

Kindness, necessity, unalienable right, entitle every one to the means of subsistence, in whosesoever hands those means may be; but to prevent irregularity and disquietude, when any are in distress and without natural friends, it is the part of Government to undertake the care of them.

Hospitality also is due unto strangers; that is, charity, decent behaviour, and protection from cruelty and addition of evil, while with us. To think of including an equal care of all mankind, would be to *disclaim a national union;* which implies a necessary, distinct, interest, benefited often, warrantably, by the imprudencies of others.

OF PROPERTY

Natural property consists of land, spontaneous produce, game, and the elements.

This property is *common,* in the sense of a patrimony; of which, until a division, the inhabitants are co-heirs. The title to all, is, the

---

* Constancy and uniformity of design are necessary to cause duration. "Since the world" says Montesquieu "subsists through so long a succession of ages, it must certainly be directed by invariable laws."

When the best plans possible are designed and adopted, there is neither room nor occasion for alterations.

Analysis of Man

equal gift of the Creator; and the intention of the gift, [19] is deducible from the indicative utility and equal want.

Where there are no laws to make distributions, occupancy *in due degree* becomes valid, as the necessary personal act of each individual: But it is a requisite condition, that it be confined within the limits of *necessity* or *equality;* for, whatever may be said to the contrary, the consent implied or exprest of others is considered, or the possession militates against the very essence of natural law.

Artificial property acquired by honest industry; such as the product of the earth by tillage, or as manufacturers, ought to be *particular.*

This is natural law; but local circumstances and the condition of settlements by migration from other countries, occasion some necessary variation. Natural law imparts an *equality of property;* which however is liable to alteration from the difference of acquisition by different talents and industry. Settlements by migration are not practicable without the assistance of the rich, who will require encouragement proportioned to their own possessions.

From some fortunate circumstances, however, America has not yet departed far from the rule of right, which ought as much as possible to be observed, not only as the law of God pointed out to us, but as a just law, and as productive of happiness and safety.

*Its efficiency with respect to the last consideration [20] may be evinced from the following observations:

> Men in moderate circumstances, are most virtuous.
> An equality of estate, will give an equality of power; and equality of power is a natural commonwealth.
>
> <div align="right">CATO'S <i>Letters.</i></div>
> The first seeds of anarchy are produced from hence, that

---

* Men will ever govern or influence those whom they employ, pay, feed and clothe, and who cannot get the same necessary means of subsistance upon as advantageous terms elsewhere. *This is natural power.*

CATO'S Letters

Arguments deduced from the nature of mankind, are literally ad hominem, within the ken of all possessed of common sense; and when just, demonstrative beyond a possibility of doubt. Republics end with luxury, monarchies with poverty.

MONTESQUIEU

The effect of wealth is to inspire every heart with ambition; that of poverty is to give birth to despair.

Ibid.

some are ungovernably rich, and many more are miserably poor; that is, some are masters of all means of oppression and others want all the means of self-defence. *Ibid.*

The eagerness to obtain large fortunes, arises frequently from emulation. Equality may be borne with; but superiority from incidental circumstances, not annexed to merit, is galling and insufferable.

* Equality, or submission only to magistrates, age and superior knowledge and wisdom, should be the prevailing disposition, and compose the spirit that pervades the whole state system. When, [21] with the extent of property permitted, every just honour is attainable; the mind must be warped indeed, that is still dissatisfied. Let such be allowed to retire to countries, where liberty is less cherished. It is a happiness to be rid of them. With a less ambitious bias, the man, who was already as rich as he could be, would turn his endeavours towards distinguishing himself by works of elegance and taste, would foster the arts of painting and sculpture, encourage the faithful historian to relate how one State only of the whole distracted world, formed itself on a generous benevolent footing; or perhaps cause stately domes to arise for his own gratification, or cut useful canals from one river to another for the benefit of his country.

But how is this balance to be moderately maintained? By ceasing to be unjust.

Instead of the natural right as before stated; designing men have pretended, that what was common property, was not equally the property of each person, but the property of the government or king; to dispose of ad libitum, and in some cases to resume; And the same men who have the effrontery to assert that their king never dies, because the kingship or office endures have insisted that there is no natural right which continues the possession of parents in the children.**

It is the business of those men, qui iras et verba locant, to maintain fictions and deny facts. In [22] the eye of reason, children are an enlargement or continuation of those they sprung from; they participate in their rights, and represent them.

* The good sense and happiness of individuals depend greatly on the mediocrity of their abilities and fortunes.

L'Esprit des Leix.

** Nothing but the very excess and rage of despotic power ordained that the father's disgrace should drag after it that of the wife and children.

MONTESQUIEU

ANONYMOUS

Where else in case of demise of their parents, are they to obtain a modicum of property? A conviction of this inherent right formerly occasioned the laws of England to restrict parents from bequeathing away more than a *certain part of their possessions*. So the laws of Rome allowed sisters and brothers to succeed equally to land; and the reason of ordaining title by primogeniture, or to men in preference to women, arose solely from the intent of feudal tenures: When the reason of which ceased, the law and usage should.**

A just and equal succession will diffuse property in portions not greatly dissimilar. But should this measure not have all the effect desired, real estates might be made unalienable, without particular permission. And if this won't do, further increase of property must be positively restricted.

There were two reasons why in England real estates were made alienable. When the Norman Barons possessed the dominion and the land was tenanted by vassals, conveyance by sale was permitted, that, by extravagance, by cruzades, or other ways, the land holders might be induced to transfer to others their property, (which would thereby become more generally possest) and to accede to a reduction of their own exorbitant power. The other reason was, to promote the security and encouragement of trade.

[23] If, when property was monopolized by a few, transfers were permitted to diffuse the civil right to it; does it not follow, when it is as moderately divided as we can expect it ever will be, that they should be prohibited to prevent a contrary alteration?

The reason with respect to trade, ought not to have the least weight here. In countries less favored by Heaven, they are forced to recur to a thousand shifts to supply, by industry and ingenuity, the deficiencies of a bleak or barren climate. But it is far otherwise with us; lands annually renewed and a vertical sun, furnish us with staple commodities that cannot fail to procure immediately or by purchase every convenience or even luxury of life without such adventitious assistance; as will be shewn more largely hereafter.

Right of property consists in the free use and possession of it without control or diminution, but does not necessarily imply a power of cession or divestment to the detriment of heirs, who certainly ought in some measure to be accounted joint owners.

** Cessante ratione legis unica et adequata, cossat ipsalex.

From what has been already said, this right appears so indefeasable, that it ought not to be subject to forfeiture in case of crimes, or be made to escheat on failure of regular succession, but rather left to delapse to collaterals, allies or even friends.

Nothing herein is meant to restrain the disposal of personal estate.

OF POLITICAL CONSEQUENCE

*Every man feels himself entitled to an equal [24] degree of consideration with others, allowing for the difference of abilities; and the partial custom of an accorded choice in election of representatives, confirms the claim.

This right however has been greatly restricted. In some countries, freeholders are not allowed even the privilege of chusing whom they will be governed by. In others, they are obliged to vote openly and not by ballot in the election of representatives. And in the best, unless men of large estate, they are confined to a choice of others, and are not eligible theirselves.

The argument urged in behalf of such practice, is that men who are indigent and low in circumstances, are more liable to yield to temptations and bribes, and therefore more likely to betray the public trust. But experience proves, that none are more insatiable than the rich; perhaps the truth is, that those of moderate estates are least to be corrupted. But there are men of virtue in all stations of life: And shall we, on account of the unequal distributions of fortune, exclude such from exerting themselves to their own credit and the service of others?

Some standard ought to be affixed, by which the right of a citizen may be ascertained, such as a modicum of possessions, long sojournment with means of maintenance, or an act of naturalization; [25] nor should we admit every adventurer to assume consequence among us: But, this matter settled, the people must be left to elect, without the interference of others, the parish and county officers and magistrates.

* Every act of authority of one man over another, for which there is not an absolute necessity, is tyrannical.

BECCARIA

ANONYMOUS

To annex privileges and immunities to men of certain fortunes, is to allow of different ranks and different interests among us; which is the subversion of a free system. Liberty depends on a unity of interest. And if we prize, as we ought, the rare, inestimable blessing; we must sacrifice former prejudices and habits to its security. Ex virtute nobilitas coepit. And as with virtue, nobility begins, so it ought to end. As there can be no inheritance of good deeds, there ought to be none of honors. Whatever politics set aside the observance of this maxim, are destructive of liberty; because none can be made great in the sense of powerful without a proportionate debasement of the rest.

*According to the encouragement given, will be our efforts. And who that thinks aright would not rather wish to see his son virtuous than great? But when glory and renown are to be the sure concomitants of virtue, every desire becomes gratified. Those indeed who would govern only by fear, are but shallow politicians. A perfect government should not only punish for crimes, but reward for a contrary [26] conduct. Let humanity, public spirit and knowledge, be distinguished by particular honors.

***The ill effect of superfluous riches has been already taken notice of: To maintain a mediocrity and equipoise, not only some must be prevented from soaring too high, but others must be encouraged to elevate their ideas, and not be permitted to consider themselves as a grovelling, distinct species, uninterested in the general welfare.

For the latter defect, education** is the natural remedy. With this view schools should be established in every parish or petty district,

---

* The best security of a Governour, is the affections of the people, which he may always gain by making their interest his own. They will then, as they love themselves, love him, and defend him who defend them. *This is the natural basis of superiority and distinction.*

CATO'S *Letters*

*** It is a custom destructive of right, to permit men in public capacities, to arrogate to themselves judgement concerning those privileges. The error is of boundless consequence that invests fallible men with what are called sacred characters, or that imparts excessive authority to any.

One of the evils civil government was intended to remedy, is to prevent men from being judges in their own causes.

BLACKSTONE

** The most certain method of preventing crimes, is to perfect the system of education.

MARQ. OF BECCARIA

to initiate children in learning. And, in some healthy situation, a college should be built and liberally endowed; where their further studies may be prosecuted; where every science useful and amusing may be taught, but particularly ethicks or the duty of man towards God, himself, his connections and country. This study will necessarily comprehend a knowledge of himself and of his relationship to other things: And this is so essential a part of learning that the perfection of it ought to be the ultimate view with which we acquire other branches. To content ourselves with making science barely ornamental, is to pursue a shadow and neglect the substance. [27] The least fault indeed resulting from it, is pedantry or foppery: for without some direction, learning often serves only to make men eminently mischievous and hurtful.

By means of such seminaries of learning, many will emerge from obscurity and become shining members of the community, who would otherwise, from confinements to occupations not suited to their capacities, be lost to their country and themselves; all who please will be made acquainted with the bright ornaments of other countries and times, and some be induced to follow their example; some again will incline to contemplate the overbearing tyranny of other constitutions, and will discern with heart-felt satisfaction the equal, parental, benign, influence of their own.

Many are the advantages both of honor and profit that will accrue from these institutions. Our country will be enriched; our manners will be polished; our minds will be illumined; and the liberty of the press will be valued and preserved: Whilst other nations, defected by their declining affairs, discouraged by oppression, and blinded by superstition, embrace the contrary tenets; wrangle about unmeaning words; degenerate by degrees into breakers of all faith and order; and finish their career in anarchy, barbarity and ignorance.

OF SOCIAL EMOLUMENTS

It is absolutely requisite that all ranks of men should enjoy equally, if duly qualified, the posts of honour and profit (which are on the same footing as common property). To confine these to a particular

[28] set, or to those* who are too rich and great already, is to infringe the natural terms of alliance. It is therefore necessary to make the appointments of short duration; to select officers from as many different parts of the State as we can; and to prevent a re-election of any to the same office.

However just this recommendation is, many difficulties will oppose its acceptation: Party, interest, friendship, combat against it. And perhaps nothing but rigid, precise laws will render it efficacious.

Such ought to be the equal participaton between acknowledged citizens. But, whilst the world continues as it is, in a state of hostility or indifference between one nation and another; none other has a right to expect, a kindness they do not shew; and, whatever hospitality may be extended to an individual, no foreigner can be entitled to the privileges of a proper member, but must content himself with such terms as he acceded to on his arrival, until the lenity or prudence of the State relieve his condition.

In the state of defiance before alluded to, the nature of man is, to consider not only what one nation *has done* to another, but what it probably *would do* if it had more in its power; and to pursue a conduct accordingly. In cases of this kind, injuries which proceed from reciprocal ill intentions, cease to be acts of injustice: and we only take that advantage of others, which, when opportunity [29] served would be taken of us. I acknowledge that there is no kindness in this, but it is common conduct, and situated as the world is, it is necessary and just. Not to benefit by these opportunities, would be inconsistent. To rescue men of another color from the condition of slaves, by purchasing them from less considerate owners. To put them on the footing of servants, by constraining their masters under peril of fines and disgrace, to cloathe and feed them well, to be moderate in exaction of labour, to allow them one day in seven for rest, and to be temperate in punishment. This is not the occupation of rigid task masters, but of men who accommodate themselves to the world, who avail themselves of advantages that arise a thousand ways from the superiority of their own, and inferiority of other constitutions, and who protect, and alleviate the condition of all within their power, as far as compatible with their own internal union and engagement.

* Cato the younger said, he considered the Public, as the proper object of his care, zeal and attendance; and not as a bank for his private wealth, or a source of personal honours.

The danger of contaminating ourselves by a gradual mixture of manumised or fugitive blacks, is an evil little noticed because yet in embrio, but of a nature that requires our most serious attention. This disorder, I fear, creeps on us and gains ground imperceptibly.

> *Utque malum late solet immedicabile cancer*
> *Serpere, et illaesas vitiatis addere partes*
> *Ovid. Met.*

But what would be the case, if a general emancipation should take place.

Let every spark of honest pride concur to save us from the infamy of such a mongrel coalition! [30] Let honour forbid its being said, that we were thus degraded willingly and intentionally! And let prudence avert that so foul a stain should be affixed on us from want of vigilance and forethought!

If the inconsiderate debaucheries of youth; if the indelicacy of the poor and negligent, have made some approaches towards this jumble of colors; it is the business of the steady and discreet, to prevent the contagious mischief from spreading, by assigning impassable bounds, which may still keep the different species apart, and preserve their ancient conditions and distinctions invariably.

If this is now a difficult task, what would it be on an addition of numbers? I would advise all seriously to consider the various consequences of an unlimited importation.

OF GOVERNMENT

The preservation and maintenance of these rights, is the final cause of association; and all constitutions are just, in degree as they conform to these views; and weak and tyrannical as they deviate from them.

The *regulations of government must owe their form to the efficience of

* That government so easy, where the people find or fancy they find, their own happiness in their submission.

CATO'S *Letters.*

There are but two ways to govern a nation: One is, by their own consent; the other by force: One gains their hearts, the other holds their hands. The first is always chosen by those who design to govern for the people's interest, the other, by those who design to oppress them from their own.

Ibid.

these purposes. And the DISTRIBUTION of AUTHORITY, the BODY of LAWS, the ADMINISTRATION of JUSTICE and the GENERAL POLICY of the Republic, must breathe no other intention.

[31]   OF THE DISTRIBUTION OF AUTHORITY

The community are naturally judges of our conduct, to approve or condemn, and, in case of depredation, insult or assault, to restrain in self-defence. This, every man feels for and of himself. There is however a certain stage of life, necessary to acquire experience of things and even a knowledge of language under which period, persons must be deemed incompetent judges. In regard to difference of abilities; every man is capable of feeling what is right, and the dullest ought not to be excluded from giving his vote and opinion. For laws and regulations seeming inconsistent, and not of self-evident utility to the meanest capacity; cannot be consonant to nature.

The community are also sole judges in matters of common concern, and, however represented, ought to remain the supreme authority and ultimate judicature.

No sufficient reason can be assigned, why the representatives of a country should not be restricted in their power. It ought to be a maxim that their authority* extends not to doing wrong. In momentous cases, highly essential to the whole, the whole** should be consulted maturely; and they alone should fix the decree. In *them* that plenary power rests and abides which all agree should rest somewhere; and which, sycophants and designing men would deceive us into an opinion, should be vested in kings or parliaments exclusively of the people.

[32] For, the welfare of the community, once confided to the

---

* Whoever desires only to protect the people, will covet no useless power to injure them.

Ibid.

** The supposition of the law is that neither the king nor either House of Parliament, collectively taken, is capable of doing any wrong,—Since in such cases, the law feels itself incapable of furnishing an adequate remedy.

Shall not our prudence supply a remedy?

BLACKSTONE

uncontrolled discretion of one person or of a* set of men encourages
a propensity to improper indulgence in those to whom the opportunity
is given. (There is a vis inertiae in human nature, which inclines men,
already distinguished by, and from, the public, to make others
subservient to their purposes, rather than to labor to obtain the same
things by their own efforts). It causes a separation of interests; and
sets the wills of most in opposition to each other.

The principle of self-preservation was implanted in mankind with
peculiar inducements of both a positive and negative kind for each
and all to take upon them the care of themselves: Nor can this case
be imparted with propriety to others, except by way of mediation in
disputed points: A situation which can not happen to the rights of
mankind, as they are clear to every capacity, and ought to be unalienable
even by the parties themselves. This is a natural trust and cannot be
resigned without a base relinquishment of the charge committed to
them.

[33] The office of denouncing their minds, may be delegated to
a chosen few, that of determining a right never should.

**Whatever difficulty there may be in convening and taking the

---

* Constant experience shews that every man invested with power is apt to abuse
it, and to carry his authority as far as it will go.

MONTESQUIEU

It is not to be expected from human nature, that the few should be always
attentive to the interests and good of the many.

BLACKSTONE

We have every thing to fear from those, who hold a power inconsistent with
liberty.

CATO'S Letters

No wise nation ever trusted to the sole management, mere mercy, and
absolute discretion of its own magistrate, when it could help doing it. In truth,
where magistrates are most limited, it has been often as much as a whole people
could do to restrain them to their trusts, and to keep them from violence.

Ibid.

Not to provide against these sinister events (which if they are not always
certain consequences, most certainly may and will be consequences sometimes) is
madness or stupidity.

Ne offeramus nos periculis fine causa: quo nihil potest esse stultius.

In tranquillo temestatem adversam optare, dementis est.

Cic.

** The Legislative power, when the territories of a State are small, and its
inhabitants easily known should be exercised by the people, in their aggregate
or collective capacity, as was wisely ordained by the petty republic of Greece and
the first rudiments of the Roman State.

BLACKSTONE

sense of all the members of a society at once; there is none in assembling parishes separately. In which way, matters of constitutional concern, suggested by men of prudence and discernment, should be duly deliberated on and fairly submitted to vote, and a final issue may be taken in General Assembly on a certain majority of vouched and recorded parochial decisions.

The assembly or Representatives should either consist of one house of men of mature years (which perhaps is the best) or of two of young, and old; Juniors and Senate; (The division of old and young being natural and just, the world consisting of such, and experience approving the distinction) who are to be the guardians of the people*, to receive the reports of the executive officers; to communicate to their constituents, to be restricted to a punctual observance of the will of their parishioners and of the constitution; to perform the routine of business within the limits prescribed by the people; and to nominate all officers of State; themselves not eligible.** Their authority should hereto be positively [34] confined. Like the faculties of the mind, they must be content with perception and circumscribed volition; and must altogether leave the active part to executive members.

Which executive branch of government is best formed of a small body with one superior. The executive only to perform, (without a will of their own), what the constitution and representation enacts.*** The executive to nominate pro tempore to offices in case of demise during a recess of parliament.

Whenever both powers are united in one, the temptation to ambition is too great for human frailty; and the danger to liberty imminent. And such is the facility of mankind to forget themselves;

* The power of reviewing the proceedings of all inferior courts, the privilege of inspecting every department of administration, and the right of redressing all grievances, belonged to the courts of Ariaten—Nor did those who conceived themselves to be aggrieved address the Cortes in the humble tone of supplicants, and petition for redress; they demanded it as the birthright of freemen.
ROBERTSON'S *Hist. Chs. Vth*
** It would be a matter of indifference from what part of the Republic the Legislative body was taken; if, after election, the members are free to act of their own accord, instead of abiding by the direction of their constituents. What nation in their senses ever sent ambassadors to another without limiting them by instructions.
*** A good government is not that, where the well or ill being of the subjects depends on the virtues or the vices of the rulers; but when the well or ill being of the rulers necessarily follows or depends on the well or ill being of the subjects.
Memoirs of Holland

that it is incumbent to limit the duration of these confined honors, as well as just to afford a chance of them to all: Besides the consideration, that not to limit, would be not to entrust, but to aliene.

Where natural law is *not sufficiently explicit;* reason must supply its place, by adopting regulations which tend best to preserve and pursue those points where *it is.* If it does not intimate to us exactly such appointments, as are here advised; it at least informs us of the propriety of employing men of talents who are upright, and in cases either of trouble or profit, of a rotatory change of men. Where a convention of all would be inconvenient, it certainly suggests a deputation. But [35] with respect to determination of numbers, as a point without consequence, it leaves the different parties to suit themselves.

OF LAWS

It is said, to leave the decision of causes to discretion, would be to relinquish the power of judicature to fancy, avarice, resentment, and ambition; that a new practice would be established on every fresh occasion, and that we should for ever fluctuate in uncertainty and litigation.

But this perhaps should be understood with allowance. When there is a contrariety between law and reason; the judges *must be* embarrassed. When there is not justice on either side, there *can be no* rule of decision, but practice. When judges are not permitted to appeal to their own sober feelings, but are liable to be harrassed and distracted by the fraudulent insinuations of others, their judgments *cannot* be consistent and methodical.

On the other hand, no number of statutes will comprehend every particular case; so indefinite is the variety from changes of circumstances: And one insurmountable difficulty is formed from the attempt; for every new law, where such is the practice, acts as rubbish, under which we bury the former. To endeavour to compose a compleat system, is in reality the amusement of speculative casuists; not the employment of the guardians of the people.* Law, to be just, should

* Would you prevent crimes? Let the laws be clear and simple; and let the laws be feared, and the laws only.

BECCARIA

ANONYMOUS

be simple, clear, and intelligible to the meanest capacity, in the same degree in which it operates.

**And why else was a sense of right and wrong imparted [36] to mankind, if not to enable them to decide concerning it in some measure? For the mind is as competent to a moral decision, ex aequo et bono, as to a knowledge of facts, secundum quinque femus. Besides this is certainly natural law, and ought not to be departed from.

What then is to be done? Is no middle course pervious, which may enable us to shun the principal difficulties of either extreme? Let principles of law be defined, and axioms be described. If we cannot comprize the species; let us effectuate ut rerum genera complecigrentur. When perhaps we shall do more, than if we attempted more.

And thus much is necessary. Salus populi suprema lex esto (let the good of the community be the chief rule of conduct) is not always a sufficient direction to magistrates, *and some laws are necessary to shew how far their authority does not extend.* Local circumstances and proportions too, require adjustments and regulations, which ought to be constant and uniform. But at all events, the code* of laws should not be too

---

Every member of society should know when he is criminal and when innocent.

Ibid.

Happy the nation where the knowledge of the law is not a [   ].

Ibid.

** It is much easier to feel a moral certainty of proofs than to define it exactly, and safer to judge from our feelings than by opinion of a knowledge of the law.

BECCARIA

Men feel with sensibility and describe with force, when they have made but little progress in investigation or reasoning.

ROBERTSON'S *Chas. Vth.*

* Non tamen plura legibus civilibus sancienda sunt, quam ad bonum civitatis et civium conducunt. Nam cum de eo, quod facere vel non facere debent, foepius per rationem naturalem, quam perscientiam legum homines deliberate solent; ubi plures leges sunt quam ut facile memoria comprehendi queant; et per eas prohibeantur ea quae ratio per se non prohibet, necessae est, ut per ignorantiam sine uila prava inentione incidant in leges, tanquam in laqueos.

PUFFENDORF

Qui leges et officium alicui injungit, efficere solet et debet, ut in notitiam subjecti illae pervenient. Et ad subjecti captum leges ae regulae officii attemperari solent et debent: circa quas conoscendas et retinendas quemlibet solicitum esse oportet. *Unde qui est causa ignorantiae, respondere etiam tenebitur de iis actionibus quae ex ille ignorantis promanant.*

Nullam esse legem, quae aliquam rem [   ], aut iniquam, fieri velit.

Cic de Invent.

large for the attainment of moderate capacities: The knowledge of it should not need the study of a whole life, but be attainable with ease at leisure.

[37] Law from precedent should be altogether exploded. Either there is no exercise of justice in the case, or the law is deficient. And it is not a single evil that results fostering law courts to become legislative. What people in their senses would make the judges, who are fallible men, depositaries of the law; when the easy, reasonable method of printing, at once secures its perpetuity, and divulges it to those who ought in justice to be made acquainted with it.

OF THE ADMINISTRATION OF JUSTICE

Whatever choice there may be of measures conducive to these purposes; the best only should be chosen and abided by. In this particular, things and methods differ. In the former may be a difference of substance and sameness of quality. In the latter; the difference is of good, bad, and indifferent: And perfect resemblance becomes co-incidence.

It cannot be therefore good, to have one method [38] of trial* by king or governor, another by a judge, and a third by jury.

Taking it for granted that particular defects in one mode are avoided in another; this does not afford a choice of remedies, but of inconveniences, or at best it is creating difficulties to have the trouble of removing them.

Let then our justiciary proceedings be uniform and unical.

Onmes leges ad commodium reipub. referre oportet; et eas ex utilitate communi, non scriptione, quae in literis est, interpretari, *Ibid.*

Alteram etiam legum conditionem addere oportet, seilicet, ut nihil in se contineant superiori alicui legi contrarium, alter non obligant.

JOHNSON AND PUFFENDORF.

Laws not sufficiently promulgated, like laws ex post facto, are acts of tyranny, not of reason.

BLACKSTONE

* The appeals admitted in *courts of chancery* from day to day and from court to court upon questions merely of fact, are a perpetual source of obstinate chicane, delay, and expensive litigation.

BLACKSTONE

ANONYMOUS

*Trial by jury is certainly best, because natural, equitable, expeditius, and least liable to influence. The jury should be literally peers of the vicinage. A grand jury should find or reject the bills of indictment. Parties should plead their own cause. The office of the judge should be to enforce order in court, to expound the law, to sum up the evidence. The decision should be according to law, evidence and justice. And the verdict of the jury should be determined by a majority: For it is preposterous to expect unanimity at all times.

The award should be according to the enormity, to utility from sufferance, and to degree of proof: which degree must be ascertained by the proportionate majority of the convicting jury.

[39] Utility from the sufferance of criminals is either negative or positive. Negative, from an incapacitation to do further harm; as in case of exile, which is a species of punishment perhaps best adapted to offenders not satisfactorily convicted. Positive; as in cases of award of damages to individuals, and, in atrocious malpractices, servitude and even hard labor in public service for a term or for life.

From these methods, advantage will accrue to the community, but none from death**. And as to banishment of criminals, what right have we to turn loose upon others nations, such ungovernable spirits as no consideration could restrain? And might not others in their turn cast forth their outlaws upon us? The same objection does not present itself on the occasion recommended. To remove a person of dubious character, is right with respect to ourselves, from the consideration that security is better than danger; and where the character of the person is suspected, is not absolutely forfeited, he is laid under a necessity of behaving with more prudence in another

---

* It is an admirable law which ordains that every man shall be tried by his peers; for when life, liberty, and property are in question, the sentiments which a difference of rank and fortune inspire, should be silent.

BECCARIA

The sole balance of the faedal times which the people had against the nobility, was the trial by jury: As it will always prove the best defence on every other occasion.

BLACKSTONE

Trial by jury was the bulwark of Gothic liberty.

Ibid.

** It is a kind of quackery in government and argues a want of skill to apply the same universal remedy, the ultimum supplicium to every case of difficulty. It is, it must be owned, much easier to extirpate mankind than to amend them.

BLACKSTONE

society, lest he should again be subjected to the inconvenience of a removal or to a less mild punishment.

It is an erroneous maxim that cases made difficult by obscure laws, should be left to the decision of a Judge (arbitrio boni vire): An unintelligible law is on the [40] footing of a blank, and ought not to have any weight.

**As there is no propriety in punishing the assumption of private vindication and vengeance, where the law has not provided a remedy; it is incumbent to institute courts of enquiry as in military matters, of responsible members of society, wherein acquital or disapprobation may be given, and to make their judgement a foundation for bills of indictment against accusants; and this not only in the case of moral defects but of constitutional; the latter of which, when irremediable, are painful enough without the addition of sarcasm.

In a system aiming at perfection, it seems requisite to stigmatize flagrant ingratitude; and to dignify those, who have distinguished themselves by useful exertions of sympathy.

The discouragement shewn to actions of slander not meerly litigious, appears of evil tendency. People of weak capacities will be induced to estimate less a good character, in proportion as their complaints of detraction are discountenanced.

All cases should be bailable except for disfranchising offences. Imprisonment should not be permitted for debt, but seizure of personals only allowed: Whoever gives credit, consents to run the risk of another's fortune.*

Of the GENERAL POLICY of the Republic

This head comprizes a variety of subjects; MEANS of MAINTE-NANCE, COMMUNICATION, OPULENCE, POPULATION, HABITATION, PEACE and WAR, NATIONAL CHARACTER, FINANCIERING, and MODES OF DEFENCE.

These subjects duly digested; a plan of action may be instituted; according to which all our councils must be directed and our intentions

---

** The punishment of a crime cannot be just, that is necessary, if the laws have not endeavored to prevent that crime by the best means which times and circumstances would allow.

M. OF BECCARIA

* Great is the superiority which a creditor has over a debtor in having money to lend.

MONTESQUIEU

must [41] conform: For without such deliberate operative preparation; we shall be in the condition of individuals, governed by contingency and caprice, doing to repent, and involving our selves and posterity in needless difficulties.

OF MEANS OF MAINTENANCE

These are in every country, real or artificial. Artificial means with prudence and industry, are better than real without: But artificial means are insecure; being at best but comparatively good, and succeeding from the inattention and omission of others. Artificial means indeed are but a substitute for natural: For who would think of seeking by trade or commerce with others, advantages which he holds already in possession; when the principles of commerce are to improve on favourable events, and to pursue such methods as promise greatest profit. Real advantages too do not preclude artificial, but render them unnecessary. And we ought to remember that natural advantages do not become means of maintenance unless made use of. An insight into what there are, is absolutely necessary; lest our inhabitants, admiring the ingenious performances of nations differently circumstanced, should emulate them, and neglect their own more fortunate opportunities.

What then are our natural advantages? Swamps, of inexhaustible fertility, full of cypresses and cedars, fit to produce rice, indigo, tobacco, madder, hemp, flax and corn; vast tracts of land covered with useful pines; and the barrenest sand-hills covered with durable oaks; rivers intersecting the whole country; and the earth itself replete in most places with clay for brick-making and in many with iron serviceable on almost every occasion in life.

Does not then the very face of things recommend agriculture as the means of supporting ourselves and raising of *staples* for commerce, and ship-building as the means of disposing of them at an easy cost?

[42] *Those* can scarce conceive the superiority of our own lands, who have not visited other countries nor seen the endless labor and expence necessary to excite fertility there. Here climate and soil co-operate to the sure acquest of gain and to the exclusion almost of a possibility of that distressful evil, a famine.

Abundance of grain and fodder, and the tender herbage vegetating with such celerity in cultivated lands, are beneficial to stock, and are the means of amply supplying our tables, and of furnishing us with leather, with wool, and with other ingredients sufficient to answer our necessary wants.

Do not these circumstances indicate to us that we ought to confine our views to the product of our lands, and to the manufacture for home consumption of articles, of which the materials are provided to our hands. In which case, we shall only need from others, ornamental conveniences of such things as in time of interupted commerce we can dispense with use of.

It ought early to be considered, what stores we are possessed of, and whether we have more of some articles (timber in particular) than may be requisite for our own uses; that a prohibition to vend or destroy, may take place before a scarcity.

OF COMMUNICATION

Communication with every part of the country, by making and regulating of roads, and by forming canals between one river and another to encrease our inland navigation, is a task at once practicable with ease and necessary for our convenience as well as profit.

We have neither rocks to perforate or eject, nor many hills to level or surmount, but in general a soft and not unfirm sandy soil; that leaves no trouble to make a high way but that of removing the trees therefrom or of sinking small drains to prevent water from stagnating on it; and respecting canals, the natural curves in our rivers, evidently point out to us the places [43] where we may benefit by our labor: The ease of water carriage, and the expence of land transportation, will not bear a moment's comparision. The Creator of the world has formed large reservoirs of water on higher land, and has given us hands and ingenuity to avail ourselves of it, if we are willing. And this is all the aid he in general affords or we have right to expect. The quality of fertility in the earth, is not in a greater degree beneficial to us, until industry adds application to fitness and converts it into use.

ANONYMOUS

OF OPULENCE

True opulence consists in the possession of, or means of obtaining, in abundance the real necessaries of life and also such articles of taste as serve to render our existence not only satisfactory but happy. When our possessions once exceed the limits of amusement and become objects of fastidious emulation, glare, and trouble; they cease to be desirable, and change* their power of gratification for qualities pestiferous and baleful. When therefore, if ever, such an inundation of riches flows in upon us, it is incumbent by taxes on importation or exportation of the lucrative articles to divert part of the current into the public funds for the necessary purpose of fortifications or ship building or the assumed one of elegant buildings for public use. But half the *extravagance* in living is owing to the vile invention of *credit,* the expedient of men and countries who, not having real possessions, wished to assume the name and appearance of having; or at best to profit by the use of what was not their own. When real expences are incurred on ideal profits and ideal funds; irregular indulgences, false appearances, and discouragements of industry, [44] are the consequences. Abolish this pernicious custom; and at least half the evil of excess is averted.

The same glowing sun which quickens the vegetable creation so instantly into life, also induces us to relax from our labor; and performing by its rays the office of invigorating the plant, saves us the degree of toil necessary in other climes, and invites us to indulge in the enjoyment of what we have already gained, and not to persevere in an eager and useless pursuit of riches.

Gold and silver from universal assent are become necessary as mediums of commerce. In a certain degree therefore they are desirable. Beyond that proportion, we should consider that we are paying more for them than is their intrinsic value. Whenever we decline the slave trade, the Southern States of America will drain Europe of these metals as much as the Indies did before. We shall then have occasion to guard against an excess instead of a scarcity.

Before I finish this chapter, I must say a few words on the subject

* Ubi divitiae clarae habentar, ibi omnia bona vilia sunt, fides probites, pudor, pudicitia. Nam ad virtutem una et ardua via est; ad pecuniam, qua ciuque lubet, nititur; et malis et bonis rebus creatur.

SALLUST

of interest or the premium for the use of money. According to the value of money is the denomination-value of every thing else in an inverse ratio. And the value of money is in proportion to the lawful interest. It has been the custom of countries supported by artificial means to reduce the interest as much as they can. Perhaps on consideration the practice will be found detrimental to landed property. Men who have views of selling their property and removing to other countries may find an advantage in raising the denomination-value here of estates. But it is our business to keep it rather below the par of others: because it retains the rich inhabitants among us; because the real value computed from utility is the same, or rather is greater according to the use made of it; because the comparatively low price attracts the industrious of other countries to settle among us; and because it enables our own people in articles wherein we vie [45] with others, to manufacture cheaper, or oblige others to sell us at a lower rate.

Where profit is easy to acquire, the premium for the use of money, which is the medium of commerce, ought to be high: And this circumstance must and will fix the value and rate; and not, as generally believed, the *quantity* of the metals, which intrinsically are less estimable than cheaper forms. Even paper money prudently issued, will support a credit.

OF POPULATION

This is a subject which has been as little considered as it well could be. In arbitrary governments, the common policy has esteemed an encrease of numbers, as an extension of authority. And the conduct of kings informs us, disguise it how they will, that each aspires after universal monarchy. But the business of ingenuous men, is to seek the general happiness of their own society, and to pursue it by whatever steps it is best attainable. The happiness of those who at the time compose the society, is the object in view. And an addition of numbers is no further advisable than as contributary to the advantage of the former inhabitants.*

* There are countries where a man is worth nothing; there are others where he is worth less than nothing—With the enjoyment of a small territory and great happiness, it is easy for the number of citizens to increase to such a degree as to become burdensome.

MONTESQUIEU

A constitution so equitable and uncommon, will excite the discontented of other countries to swarm in upon us, except some inhibitory measures are taken on our part; and the consequence will be the minority in their own country. The truth is, that such an admission will be prudent as shall proportionate the inhabitants to the extent of land, *in such a manner* that a decent maintenance may remain to each and that all may not be obliged to jostle one an other. But under such [46] inviting circumstances, we ought not to incline indifferently to receive every particular that offers, but to select those, whose reception will be not only consequentially but immediately advantageous to the Republic, as well as to themselves.*

Natural boundaries, such as mountains and rivers, between us and other States, are desirable, because permanent and serving to obviate contentions. But extension of empire is destructive of peace and enjoyment, and tends only to involve us in inextricable difficulties. Single marriages, because natural from the attachment of the sexes, and necessary for the maintenance and care of children; ought to be enforced. To prevent clandestine amours and to countenance unions formed by passion instead of interest; marriages should be encouraged at an early age. Restraints within certain degrees of affinity are just and political: For without these, we should degenerate into a number of petty distinct tribes, instead of forming one family from the whole nation taken together.

OF HABITATION

Habitation regards the propriety of a general dispersion of the inhabitants over the country or of collecting them together into villages and towns.

To consult conveniently, is the duty of men who undertake the guardianship of others. And however early we may be in our attention,

* In Holland and West Friezeland, letters of naturalization do not render a person qualified to hold places either of honor or profit but only communicate protection and the benefits of the law.

Resolution prise parles etats. 25th Sept. 1670.

"Mais pour ceux qui sont nez en Hollande, c'est leur naissance, qui les fait Hollandois, & l'on ne pent leur donner l'exclusion des charges. C'est la le Droit commun a toutes les nations, qui donne aux enfans pour patrie, la terre ou ils sont nez."

Dissertation sur las Naturilization

now is the time, by purchasing at the confluence natural or artificial of rivers and other suitable places to make public property of [47] parts which will hereafter become the seite of towns: This purchase is necessary, lest individuals should hereafter derive all the advantage from a measure which ought to be equally beneficial to the community in general. However unfit we may be at present for the speculative amusements which attract mankind to assemble and dwell together; the time is perhaps not far distant when hamlets for either pleasure or profit will be formed in most parishes in the State: And it will be much better to use circumspection in our choice of situations than to leave the event to whim and accident.

In the dispositions and plans of towns; it is requisite to reserve large squares for public structures, walks and gardens; to make the streets airy and convenient, by forming them wide and regular; and to place the cemeteries or burying places without the towns.

OF PEACE AND WAR

Peace is the blessing that crowns every other enjoyment; and without it, the most desirable event is imperfect and unsatisfactory. Even the unthinking wretch that apparently delights in war, is tempted thereto by a fancied superiority that confers security, which is of the nature of peace, and by hopes to enjoy hereafter in quiet his ill-gotten plunder.

In short where the distinctions of right and wrong, of just and fraudulent, are weighed and perceived; peace should be maintained inviolate by every consideration of prudence, conscience, and honor.

Nor is it an impracticable undertaking to prevent its infraction; a candid, upright, conduct will equally escape all danger of civil dissentions and foreign contests. The only precaution requisite for nations as well as for individuals, is for each to pursue his own true interest. Machiavelian politics are never necessary, except to carry into effect unjust designs. And the refinements of Statesmen are no ways proofs of genius; but indications of little minds, and of dishonest inclinations.

[48] To secure peace at home, we must preserve a union of interests, and the real good of the Republic must ever be considered

and pursued. To secure it abroad, the confederacy*** with our sister States, must be religiously adhered to: And with respect to foreign nations, we must be just *towards them,* by punishing our own people who wantonly give offence; and *towards ourselves,* by abstaining from offensive alliances with any. But, I repeat, the confederacy of the States and the convention in Congress ought to be our chief dependence. To make the benefit of it however perfect and lasting; matters of common public concern only, should be cognizable by Congress, and the bounds of authority should be marked with certain precision. To avoid mistrust and jealousy in the nation, the passions should be transferred from the people to the laws. Undefined authority is indicatory of tyranny. And any maxim that the nature of certain relatives is too delicate for inspection, like the idea of a wound that will not bear probing, shews there is a caries at bottom.

In respect to acquisitions by conquest, the *hazard* of waging war with other nations is great; and the *injustice,* let the advantages be what they might, an insuperable objection. But exclusive of the consideration of its being unjust, it is* *unwise.* The booty to be obtained by war, is uncertain as to acquisition; it is dissipated with as little care as it is gained; it subjects [49] the parties to the extremes of abundance and indigence and of consequence to the feelings of tumultuous passions, and leads to rapacity, vicious indulgencies, stupid indolence, and slavery; it destroys the equality among mankind, and instead of the just distinctions of industrious and idle, wise and foolish, old and young, substitutes the factitious of lords and vassals.** And

---

*** A Republic of this kind able to withstand an external force, may support itself *without any internal corruption:* The form of this society prevents all manner of inconvenience.

MONTESQUIEU

* The long duration of the Republic of Sparta was owing to her having continued in the same extent of territory after all her wars.

MONTESQUIEU

The spirit of monarchy is war and enlargement of dominion: Peace and moderation is the spirit of a Republic.

Ibid.

A conquering Republic can hardly communicate her government and rule the conquered State according to her own constitution.

Ibid.

** War is comprehensive of most if not all the mischiefs which do or ever can afflict men. It depreciates nations; lays waste the finest countries, destroys arts, sciences, and learning: butchers innocents; ruins the best men and advances the

as to a doubtful or unsuccessful war, no pen can describe the horrors
of it. From woeful experience we can form some judgment concerning
it. But however we have suffered already; it is nothing to what we on
a future occasion may. Mercenary armies are always unfeeling and
unjust: But the fury of such as we have already had among us, has
been often restrained by the compunctions of conscience and by the
fancied necessity of preserving appearances.

OF A NATIONAL CHARACTER

An unsullied character is perhaps as serviceable to collective bodies as
to individuals. Let a state be remarkable for a pious observance of
treaties, and a greater confidence will be placed in them by others.
By such means, one advantage at least is gained, the prevention of
aggression by others from an apprehended infraction of treaties by us.

To merit a good public name, we must lay the foundation by
first establishing the quality of private characters. Laws wisely ordained
and vigorously enforced must suffer no sinister purposes to interfere
with public designs; and no ill-placed confidence or imaginary
convenience must be allowed to sap the constitution by dispensing for
a moment with its operation.

So much of Religion ought to be the care of Government [50]
as regards attendance at places of worship on stated days, where
resignation should be declared, and prayers offered, to our universal
creator; and where the incontested doctrine of his supremacy and
omniscience, and the advantages of morality, should be preached. A
general toleration of course should be allowed, for right judgment is
not to be expected from every man, and the intention of the superstitious
and mistaken is to act right if they can.

OF FINANCIERING

Able Financiers in their mode of taxation, will sometimes bring money
into the treasury by the same step by which they benefit the people;
at other times they will raise a fund by measures the least burdensome
that may be, and at worst, by ways equally burdensome to all.

worst; and introduces confusion, anarchy, and all kinds of corruption.

ANONYMOUS

Under an independent government, expences will be necessary; nor ought we to expect to contribute at the same moderate rate as before. To make the burden as little grievous as may be, judgment must be exerted in the determination of peace; and the original levies must be as little as possible reduced by useless offices and collectors appointed for private ends, or from a complication of ways in many respects hurtful to a country.

Duties on importation and exportation should be imposed from political motives, and never for the sake of supplies only.

Perhaps an opportunity occurs at present to establish funds for Government expenses on a durable lay. Large tracts of land lie yet ungranted, which may as well be disposed of in short leases as given or sold: Or at least they might be exchanged for others convenient for building of towns, the houses or areas of which might be leased for the same purpose.

We all know the mutual benefit derived in other countries from the postage of letters. Public carriages [51] and stage conveniences might perhaps be made equally useful. Artificial canals for inland navigation offer another constant income: And at worst our own custom, a little methodized, of a tax ad valorem is equitable and unexceptionable.

To limit the expenses of Government as much as we can, appointments should be rather honorary than profitable. There will be more propriety in this, if the nomination is in some degree rotatory. A government, must be fundamentally weak that cannot shake off a set of leaches who manifestly prey on its vitals. And it would be a very faulty beginning that sets out as others end. Our decision on this occasion will probably fix a criterion of our destiny. And we shall soon be enabled to conclude whether we yet stand on firm ground, or have another revolution to expect to fix and settle us.

ON MODES OF DEFENCE

There are three ways of defending ourselves from an enemy; by a naval armament, by a standing army, and by militia.

A navy is not to be formed on a sudden, nor are mariners to be obtained without extensive commerce and successful navigation. Unluckily for us, most of our trade hitherto has been carried on in British bottoms, manned with British seamen. It is incumbent on us to establish some academy wherein children may receive the necessary instructions to fit them for the sea service; by means of which surfery, *natives of the country* may be found to navigate our vessels: For such alone will be ready when occasion calls, and will be proper to rely upon.

An encreasing commerce almost without limits must when well regulated, create mariners. Most certainly every requisite to compose a navy, is within our compass: I know not any article of ship's stores except canvas, which has not been produced here already, and of that we have the rough ingredients.

[52] A conclusive reason in favor of a naval armament, is, that we have nothing to fear except from seawards; and that a navy is never dangerous to the liberties of their country. And is it not possible to build and maintain a navy almost without expense? Where is the impropriety of using our vessels of war as freighters during peace and of the Public becoming the carriers of our produce? Would not such a conduct always command seamen and *fairly* surmount a difficulty which forces others to recur to the odious practice of impressing?

*But what shall I say of a standing army? Under the best discipline they are a nuisance to society; and serve to introduce a system of laws repugnant to civil liberty. Are they not rendered useless by a navy? Are they not a doubtful good, which may either establish or overturn the constitution of the country?

Use, which reconciles us to a homely visage, has enured us to consider this as well as many other ** innovations of very modern times, without aversion; but this does not render the measure less

* The supreme power in every country is possest by those who have arms in their hands.

ROBERTSON'S *Charles Vth*

That government is certainly and necessarily a military government, where the army is the strongest power in the country.

CATO'S *Letters*

** Mercenary troops were now introduced into all the considerable kingdoms on the continent. They gradually became the only military force. It has long been the chief object of policy to increase and to support them, and the great aim of princes or ministers to discredit and to annihilate all other means of national activity or defence . . . Efforts made on these occasions gave the people of Europe the first idea of the expence which accompanies great and continued operations, and accustomed them to the burden of those impositions which are necessary for supporting them.

ROBERTSON'S *Ch.s. Vth*

ANONYMOUS

deformed and irregular. I acknowledge that standing armies have been maintained in ancient times, but it was only during the decline of liberty. Why will we persist in the pernicious examples of others? Measures to be suitable, [53] should grow out of the occasion, and be independant of usage. Standing armies were introduced by ambitious men, and intended not as means of defence but of offence. A well regulated militia*** will answer every purpose even of garrison duty; and what they are deficient in, a navy should supply.

It is not the interest of any power on earth to be on unfriendly terms with us, and with God's favor and our own endeavors, we may become necessary to most. It is nevertheless our duty to be on our guard. And the greatest degree of safety arises from annihilating the danger.

Money has been called the sinews of war, but the best provision is, the articles which money is wanted to procure; and such are certainly more valuable in the outset. We should therefore be well provided with warlike stores.

The teloque animus praestantior omni, preferred by Lord Bacon, in his essays, to money, is the natural consequence of a free system. But so far is money from being the sovereign good, that the absence of it has been the salvation of these United Republics. I speak to men who know the world. Had we been possest of money, many reasons would have determined the different States to levy mercenary troops instead of depending on militia.

I will shew what would have been the consequence. Want of abilities and experience and the inevitable confusion of the times have occasioned many irregularities. If I am asked what these are, I reply. Unlimited* trusts that have left the private citizen without the benefit of [54] a habeas corpus; acts of Assembly assuming at one time the power of forming constitutions, at another of setting aside trial by jury and the right** of defence; and the odious prerogatives of

*** The Roman Legions who conquered so considerable a part of the world, were draughted citizens or militia.
* They wanted to make the laws reign in conjunction with despotic power; but whatever is joined to the latter loses all its force.
MONTESQUIEU
** Closarius made a law that no one should be condemned without being heard; which shews that a contrary custom had prevailed in some particular case or among some barbarous people.
Ibid.

purveyance and pre-emption allowed to both military and civil establishments.

A State under such circumstances like a body under fermentation, is laboring for a change. The dissatisfaction and impatience inseparable from the people in such conditions, have a natural tendency to make them indifferent*** concerning what it may be. Nor were bad men ever wanting in any country to excite unjust undertakings.

That no such undertaking has been formed; you owe to the virtue of some individuals and to a numerous warlike militia. And that militia you owe to the want of money.

[55]   OF THE LAWS OF NATURE AND NATIONS

In the preceding part of this essay, a sufficient detail is given of the law of kindness, which is properly the law of perfect nature.

It may not be improper to expatiate a little concerning the laws of necessity, which, from the condition of humanity, all have been obliged to recur to in the best of times in some degree or other. These consist of the Law of Interest, of the Law of Retaliation, and of the Law of Self-Defence.

The LAW of INTEREST imposes on every individual a care of himself, and impels mankind from their experience and sensibility reluctantly to consider those, who are not well-affected towards them, as disaffected from the following axiom: Whoever does not confine his views of advantage to kindness and equality, expects to be bounded only by inclination and opportunity.

This is no way irreconcileable with the law of kindness, which is only with held from action, not extinguished, hereby: For he who under such circumstances, does not help himself when he has it in his power, neglects the sole chance that can be presented to him.

This is therefore the necessary condition of men, where the law of kindness does not intimately unite them. More or less of this law intrudes itself into and sows dissention in every government in proportion to the degree of imperfection in its policy; but as the

*** It was not affection for the Stuart family or preference of kingly government, but love of regularity and ease that occasioned the restoration of Charles the second.

interests of people of the same community are necessarily mutual in some particulars, the law of interest at such time gives way to the law of kindess or assumes its appearance.

The next stage of necessity is the LAW of RETALIATION or REPRISAL, when the mischief done is not confined to acts of advantage to ourselves, but is governed by the affront received and by the principle of aspiration asserting our independancy and due consequence. Kindness is by no means inconsistent with [56] this proceeding: And, the person retaliating often wounds his own feelings by the same act by which he afflicts others.

The last resort of necessity is when the inveteracy and malice of enemies compel others in *Self-Defence* to oppose or even to destroy those whose safety is incompatible with their own. Their destruction however is warrantable only when every other expedient would prove incompetent.

The LAW of KINDNESS with as small an alloy as possible of those of necessity, is the natural law of civil society.

The LAW of INTEREST is the LAW of POLICY or LAW of NATIONS in a tranquil state; which law of nations admits of a portion of the law of kindness, when engaged thereto by articles of alliance between separate States; and of the law of defence when urged thereto by the violence of others.

Here then the line should be drawn as the limits appear.

Ques ultra citraque nequit confutere rectum.

All unprovoked assaults therefore which are pernicious to others and not profitable to the assailants themselves, even supposing no breach of positive agreements, cannot be vindicated by the laws of God or man, but are contrary to all maxims of prudence, justice and honor.

In case of positive agreements, whether implied or exprest; if equitable, each person is obliged to observe them by every consideration of duty and justice, and to be guilty of a breach of them, is to incur disgrace and infamy; but if unequitable, the obligation is the force and the danger of withstanding it.

FINIS.

[40]
PHILODEMUS
[THOMAS TUDOR TUCKER 1745–1828]

Conciliatory Hints, Attempting, by a Fair
State of Matters, to Remove Party Prejudice

CHARLESTON, 1784

Born in Port Royal, Bermuda, Tucker studied medicine at the University of Edinburgh, Scotland, practiced medicine in South Carolina, and served as a surgeon in the revolutionary war. His political career included service in the Continental Congress in 1787 and 1788, two terms in the United States House of Representatives (1789–1793), and appointment as United States treasurer from 1801 until his death. In this piece Tucker begins with a discussion of how to treat returned Tories, but moves quickly to outlining the basics of creating a government according to principles of republican government as it was understood at the time. He was quite advanced in his thinking, however, and clearly draws the distinction between a constitution as fundamental law versus simple legislative law.

In a Government where Despotism and Tyranny are established, it is both dangerous and useless for a private Citizen to meddle with Politics or to complain of Grievances. Men habituated to Slavery become patient of the Yoke, and cannot be roused to throw it off but by the Weight of some new and intolerable Oppression. Reason pleads in vain. The People are deaf to her Voice, blind to their own Claims and Interest, and cannot be made to understand that they hold their Privileges or Lives from any higher Power than the Will of their proud and arbitrary Rulers. It is scarcely possible to persuade them that they are of the same Class of Beings, that they are made of the same

Materials. Or that they are equally the Objects of the Divine Care and Protection. Such is the fatal Influence of Slavery on the human Mind, that it almost wholly effaces from it even the boasted Characteristic of Rationality.

[6] In a state that is blest with freedom, or a near approach to it, the case is greatly reversed. Every man may freely and securely exercise the privilege of giving his sentiments on all subjects of public concern: and they will generally be well received, provided they are offered with a decent regard to the opinions of his fellow-citizens, not with the authoritative tone of a dictator: It becomes the watchful spirit of patriotism to investigate the sources of every political mischief, and to point out the most easy, peaceable and effectual remedies: It is the duty of all to contribute their endeavours to establish freedom and good order in the community. The writer of the following observations feels himself to be sincerely interested in behalf of the natural and equal claims of mankind to political freedom, and would deem it the highest honor to be able to call himself a member of the most free commonwealth that ever existed. His thoughts will be found to be neither methodically arranged nor compactly expressed, owing in some measure to a want of leisure to bestow due attention on the subject. If, however, they shall be so far happily set forth as to meet with approbation, he will rejoice in the good fortune of having successfully performed the duty of a citizen. Should his well meant endeavours be frustrated by the feebleness of his abilities, yet the intention at least must always stand approved in his own breast.

The disturbances which not long ago interrupted the peace of this City, and the alarming length to which the heat and rage of party were carried, suggested the idea of endeavouring to lay before the public a fair state of matters, with a view to promote the restoration of that tranquility and harmony so necessary to the freedom as well as to the happiness of the community. What good purposes the disorderly proceedings alluded to could have been intended to answer, must perhaps for ever remain a secret in the minds of those by whom they were instigated. Nor is it easy to say what just cause of complaint could be urged in vindication of them. If the re-admission of proscribed persons was considered as a grievance, it [7] certainly was a grievance which might have been prevented. The inhabitants of every District were long apprized of the petition proffered to the Legislature, and they had an unquestionable right to instruct their respective Delegates on that or any other subject. It is to be presumed that no member of either house would have thought himself at liberty to disregard the instruction of a majority of his constituents. But if no instructions at all were given, then was every man left to the guidance of his own reason and discretion; and if he acted conscientiously, he could not be chargeable with blame even tho' it should be proved that he had committed an error. There appears to be no good reason for supposing that the members of the Legislature acted a dishonest part; for it is difficult to comprehend why the admission of the Tories should have been more interesting to them than to the rest of the citizens. If they were more connected with them by the ties of consanguinity, friendship or interest, it was surely a misfortune and next to a miracle that the people should have concurred so generally in such a choice. But if it be true that the Representatives in both Houses stood nearly or exactly in the same relation to the tory party that others did, it affords a presumption that their decision was, in its principle at least, not very different from what would have been made by the general voice of the people. This opinion will receive farther support from the consideration that petitions in behalf of some of the most obnoxious delinquents were presented from people of their own neighbourhood, who had been most exposed to injurious treatment from them, and that some of the members were actually instructed by their constituents to shew them all possible lenity. It does not appear that any instructions were given to treat them with severity. There was, I think, but one petition sent in against any of them, and this not accompanied with substantial evidence. In the joint committee appointed to the consideration of these matters, there was free access to every person who chose to give his deposition, yet it is notorious that much was alleged in favor of the most atrocious offenders, whilst the heavy charges exhibited against them without doors, however well [8] founded, were in few instances properly or at all supported. Many were forward to vindicate, none, or but very few, inclined to accuse. Under these circumstances, could it rationally be supposed that it was the general will of the people that the Legislature should without evidence, or rather against evidence, confirm the severe penalities of the Jacksonborough law? a law passed at a time when men's minds were inflamed by the sense of recent injuries and the pressure of present distress, and when it was perhaps deemed good policy to act with spirit and vigor even bordering on violence, with a view of recalling to their duty by threats such men as were incapable of being influenced by any other arguments than what were addressed to their fears or their private interest. It is not here meant to justify the severity of that act even at the time of passing it; but we may venture to contend, that although it should have been proper then, yet it does not follow that there was an impropriety in mitigating the rigor of it afterwards. And from what has been said, it seems reasonable to conclude that such was really the sense of a majority of the citizens of the State. If it be alleged that this should have extended only to certain instances, the answer is, that it was impossible to make a proper discrimination, as those characters, which were painted in the darkest colours by common report, had generally the greatest number of evidences to gloss over the baseness of their conduct. Without allowing any thing to the feelings of compassion, it is a rule of justice in doubtful cases to incline to the merciful side. But if we consider that in the present instance the decision involved in it the happiness or misery of hundreds of helpless women and children, it is hard to suppose that the hearts of men could be so steeled as to be unmoved by the supplicating voice of distress, or that they could obstinately determine on refusing that comfort and relief which they conceived themselves to be left at liberty to administer. It will scarcely be denied that some of the characters admitted were truly base and detestable; and this must certainly have been the opinion of every member of the Legislature: but circumstances with respect to each were so various, and the evidences so imperfect, that it was impossible by any scale to fix [9] the just proportion of crimes and penalties. That this was not satisfactorily done by the Jacksonborough Assembly, appears from the great complaints made, that some persons scarcely chargeable with a fault were treated with the utmost rigor, whilst others highly criminal were suffered to pass without penalty or censure. This unequal distribution of justice, or rather unjust distribution of punishments, was the inevitable effect of the method that was adopted; and an attempt to remedy it would have been only to multiply errors and confusion. The intricacy of the case seemed only to admit of the following alternative; either to leave the Jacksonborough law, however partial, to operate in its full force, or to shew a general disposition to lend an ear of mercy to the prayers of the petitioners. The last appeared to accord most with the sentiments of the people at large, and it was most consonant to humanity; I mean a compassionate regard, not to the offenders themselves, where the delinquency was great, but to their distressed and innocent families.

The measure was pardonable, even if it should prove to be an error against sound policy. But it is the lenient principle only, not the method of proceeding that I mean to justify.—I have dwelt the longer on this subject because it was made the chief pretext for the disturbances that have happened.

But this is not the only complaint that has been exhibited against the Legislature. They have been accused of an attempt to fix their own privileges too high, to stretch their authority too far, and to establish in the State an aristocratical plea of government. I am sorry, on this occasion, to revive the remembrance of an affair that made much noise during the last sitting of the Assembly:—the dispute betwixt two citizens, one of whom was of the House of Representatives. It is neither necessary nor agreeable to enter into the merits of the dispute, as it is not a matter of public concern which of the parties was first or most in fault. The question was brought before the House, and they thought proper to pronounce the insult or threat offered to one of their body to be a breach of privilege. Certain concessions were required of the offending party, which not being [10] complied with, he was committed to jail. This was agreeable to parliamentary usage in England, and it is alleged that less rigor was exercised on this, than what is common on like occasions. But I am afraid we are too apt to derive our notions of government from the British constitution, which certainly is not in any one of its parts built on principles of true freedom. Our own constitution (if such it may be called) does perhaps warrant the measure, as it expressly gives to the Legislature every power formerly exercised or claimed under a monarchical government. But who gave them this power? Not the people, but the Legislature themselves, who, without leave of the people, took upon them to frame a constitution to their own mind. Whether intentional or not, it is a great error, and leaves them by far too much latitude in judging of their own privileges. The mysterious doctrine of undefinable privileges, transcendent power, and political omnipotence, so pompously ascribed to the British parliament, may do very well in a government where all authority is founded in usurpation, but ought certainly to be for ever banished from a country that would prefer the freedom of a commonwealth. We can not be too cautious of admitting the political language of other countries. The language of slavery must ever be either the offspring or the parent of slavery.

But although it is improper that the Legislature should have unlimited or very extensive privileges, yet it seems necessary that some respectability should be annexed to the character of every servant of the public, and that personal protection should be afforded to a member during the sitting of the Legislature, otherwise his constituents might be injured in one of their first rights, that of voting in all cases where themselves are to be bound. Whether or not, in the present instance, the House of Representatives carried their ideas of privilege too far, I will not pretend to decide. I believe they did not mean to stretch their power beyond the true meaning of the constitution, tho' possibly the habit of considering themselves on the same footing with the British Commons, might have led them into an error. [11] Certainly they ought to have no privilege but what is demonstrably essential to the freedom and welfare of their constituents. The State is not made to dignify its officers, but the officers to serve the State. The dignity of the commonwealth does not consist in the elevation of one or a few, but in the equal freedom of the whole. The privileges of the legislative branches ought to be defined by the constitution, and should be fixed as low as it is consistent with the public welfare. Nor does it appear reasonable that they should be judges in their own cause, further than to give security to their members. If this be true, it shews the impropriety of blending, as we do, the legislative, judiciary, and executive powers of government in the same individuals. Other States have wisely thought it necessary to keep them entirely distinct.

There is a clear reason to be assigned why the privileges and powers of the British Parliament are undefinable, which will by no means properly apply to our Legislature. Their constitution is established only on precedents or compulsory concessions, betwixt parties at variance. These can be no longer binding than whilst the parties respectively possess the means of enforcing their observance. Of course it is, and always has been, a government of contention, in which the opposite parties have been for a length of time by chance so nearly balanced as not yet to have destroyed each other. How long this will last, it is difficult to say: but it may be affirmed that there is nothing of stability in their constitution, and that almost every new case of importance introduces some innovation in it. This is evident from their history, and will appear particularly so from a perusal of Judge Blackstone's ingenious explanation of the right of succession to the crown; where it may be seen how every fresh incident has given occasion to a different modification of this right. The several powers of governmment are limited though in an uncertain way, with respect to each other; but the three together are without any check in the constitution, although neither can be properly called the Representatives of the people. It is for this reason that this transcendent power or [12] omnipotence is ascribed to the Parliament. What stretch of authority they have usurped and exercised with impunity, is considered as their established privilege; for they hold it as a maxim, that whatever they have once done (however improperly) they have a right to do again. What farther powers they may safely assume, experiment only can teach. Their privileges are undefinable, because it is impossible to say, how far they may be extended without rousing the people to a tumultuous opposition or civil war; for with them there is no other remedy against tyranny and oppression. Where there is a standing army, even this remedy, dreadful as it is, is scarcely to be had. With a few troops, it is easy to prevent the unarmed multitude from concerting measures for the security or recovery of their freedom. It must be some flagrant and heavy oppression that can at the same moment excite so general a resentment as to kindle the flame of war. And when this is done, and attended with success, it is again a thousand to one that the leaders of the opposition grasp at the very power they had condemned in others, and establish themselves more arbitrary tyrants than those they had contributed to overthrow. Witness the Decemviri in Rome, Cromwell in England, and, in short, examples from the records of all nations.

The difference betwixt a true commonwealth or democracy and other forms of government we shall here endeavour to point out.

In a true commonwealth or democratic government, all authority is derived from the people at large, held only during their pleasure, and exercised only for their benefit. The constitution is a social covenant entered into by express consent of the people, upon a footing of the most perfect equality with respect to every civil liberty. No man has any privilege above his fellow-citizens, except whilst in office, and even then, none but what they have thought proper to vest in him, solely for the purpose of supporting him in the effectual performance of his duty to the public. No man has surrendered any portion [13] of his natural freedom, except the liberty of refusing to contribute his equal share of personal and pecuniary service for the common benefit. This he gives up in exchange for the valuable consideration of receiving protection both in person and property against the evil disposed part of his fellow citizens or a foreign enemy, and of partaking the advantages of all civil regulations. In an uncivilized State he has a right to consider himself or his family as independent of all the world, and to refuse entering into any compact or contributing his share of service for any general good. But in this case, it is evident that he is not intitled to the assistance or protection of his neighbours under any circumstances whatever, and therefore must be exposed to every injury which the malevolence or avarice of wicked men may prompt them to commit. There cannot be a moment secure of property, liberty or life. Still less is he intitled to share in the advantages of any useful regulations or works executed by general contribution.—As to the power of injuring one's neighbour, it is not a matter of right even in an uncivilized State, and therefore the restraint a man suffers in that respect in society is not to be considered as any abridgement of his natural freedom. It is no restraint upon him as a good man, but only as a wicked man. All the difference is, that in exercising the power of doing injuries in an uncivilized State, he only makes war against the persons injured; in a State of society he declares war against a whole nation, who are mutually bound to make it a common cause and to defend each other against all invaders of their just rights. The primary end of social institutions is, or ought to be, to impose, by force or the fear of punishment, that restraint on the actions of wicked men, which good men voluntarily impose on their own. The other considerations before hinted at, are also of great weight, namely, the doing for general convenience, by joint exertions, many things which no individual could possibly effect or separately enjoy. But these are secondary matters, and their utility springs chiefly from a state of society previously established. And as every citizen does, either directly or indirectly, receive from every regulation, or, at least, [14] from all together, advantages more than equivalent to his proportion of labor or expence, he is content, when he enters into a social compact, to subject himself to be called upon for his quota of service on all occasions where the public good is supposed to be interested, which is to be judged of by a majority of voices collected individually throughout the State, or (which is infinitely more convenient) through the means of representatives freely chosen and, as nearly as possible, proportioned to the number of persons represented in the several Districts. These representatives are invested with such certain powers as the constituents think proper to intrust them with, and none other, and those for such time only as is judged safe and expedient. Whilst they confine themselves within the limits prescribed, their act is the act of the people. But when they exceed their bounds and violate the conditions of their appointment, their acts are no longer binding, and they are accountable to their constituents for a traiterous abuse of trust. But the terms of the compact or constitution should be so contrived, as to provide a remedy, in all such cases, without outrage, noise or tumult. If tumultuous measures are necessary to procure redress, in any case of grievance whatever, it is owing to a fault in the original compact. If turbulent men are allowed with impunity to violate the rights of their fellow-citizens, under pretence of obtaining redress of grievances, or any other pretence whatever, it is an evil that may likewise be traced to the same source.—This is a short and imperfect sketch of a free or democratic constitution. It is the only form that can possibly consist with the common and unalienable rights of mankind.

In every other form of government authority is acquired more by usurpation than by appointment of the people; it serves to give dignity and grandeur to a few, and to degrade the rest; and it is exercised more for the benefit of the rulers than of the nation. The constitution as established upon a compromise of differences betwixt two or more contending parties, each according to the means it possesses, extorting from the others every concession that can possibly be obtained, without the [15] smallest regard to justice or the common rights of mankind. It is a truce, by which the people are always compelled to surrender some, and generally a very large portion of their freedom, and of course they have a right to reclaim it whenever more favorable circumstances put it in their power.—If the Prince at the head of an armed force, reduces them to unconditional submission, he becomes a despotic Monarch and the people are in the most deplorable state of slavery. They have no longer the presumption to imagine themselves created for any other purpose than to be subservient to his will, and to administer to his pleasures and ambition. They even think it an honor to be made the base instruments of his tyranny. They look up to him with a reverential awe surpassing what they feel for the Almighty Parent of the Universe. Such is the servility of man degraded by oppression.

If the people retain still some resources which may render the issue of the contest doubtful, the Prince, for his own safety, most humanely grants them some privileges, and is then a limited Monarch. They are often deluded into an opinion, that what liberties they enjoy are intirely derived from his bounty; and taught to consider themselves as the happiest of mankind in having a sovereign who graciously condescends to allow them the possession of what happily he had not the power to wrest out of their hands.

In the first of these cases the government has a chance to be lasting. The Prince having obtained every thing has nothing more to wish for; the people having lost every thing can scarcely feel any new grievance to stir up their resentment. The former is possessed of the means of supporting his usurpation; the latter, being totally disarmed, lose all spirit of resistance.—In the other case, that of a limited monarchy, the government is likely to be fluctuating. An ambitious Prince makes farther encroachments on the people's liberties; a weak Prince loses a part of the authority he inherited. The opposite powers being in a manner balanced, now one now the other [16] prevails, according to the spirit and judgment of their respective exertions. It is, in short, a state of nature as a state of war; but the same may with equal truth be affirmed likewise of the state of society, in every instance except in the case of a true Democracy, if fortunately such should exist. When the Prince is despotic, the people may be considered as prisoners at discretion, their lives, liberties, and property being all at his mercy. If his power is limited, occasional truces are made for reciprocal convenience, and broken by the party that first finds its interest in their violation. The same is true of all mixt governments, the component of balancing powers being ever at variance.

Often it happens that the contest for power is betwixt the Prince and Nobles, the people having been previously enslaved. In this case the form of government is variable so far as relates to the Prince and Nobility, but the slavery of the people is lasting. This happens in all feudal governments.

Sometimes the dispute is betwixt the bulk of the people and a few leading men, who having been honored with the confidence of their fellow-citizens, betray their trust, grasp at power, and endeavour to establish themselves in permanent superiority. Their success constitutes an Aristocracy, which is generally a most oppressive government, although often, for the sake of blinding the people, it is dignified with the name of a Republic. Indeed every constitution that has hitherto existed under that name has partaken more or less of the nature of an Aristocracy: and it is this aristocratic leaven that has generally occasioned disorders and tumults in every republican government, and has so far brought the name into disrepute, that it is become a received opinion, that a Commonwealth, in proportion as it approaches to Democracy, wants those springs of efficacious authority which are necessary to the production of regularity and good order, and degenerates into anarchy and confusion. This is commonly imputed to the capricious humour of the people, [17] who are said to run riot with too much liberty, to be always unreasonable in their demands, and never satisfied but when ruled with a rod of iron.

These are the common place arguments against a democratic constitution. They are the pleas of ambition to introduce Aristocracy, Monarchy, and every species of tyranny and oppression. Unfortunate indeed for the liberties of mankind, if it be true, that, to render them orderly, it is necessary to render them slaves. However generally this position may have been admitted, we may venture to deny that it is an inference fairly drawn from experience. Without better proof than has yet been adduced, we cannot justly grant that the people at large are capricious or unreasonable, or that a true Democracy will be productive of disorder or tumult. On the contrary, I am inclined to believe, that in general the people are pretty easily satisfied when no injustice is intended towards them; and if it be allowed to reason a priori in such case, I conclude that a real Democracy, as it is the only equitable constitution, so it would be of all the most happy, and perhaps of all the most quiet and orderly.

What is here advanced I shall undertake to maintain upon the principles I have already endeavoured to establish.

A despotic government is often both quiet and durable, because the tyrant, having an army at command, is thereby enabled to keep the people always in awe and subjection, and to deprive them of all opportunity of communicating their complaints, or deliberating on the means of relief. Conspiracies happen often among the troops, the reigning Prince is murdered or dethroned, but another tyrant takes his place, and the nation remains in peaceable servitude, scarcely sensible of the revolution.—When the government is less despotic, the people have more both of power and inclination to resist oppression. They are not so thoroughly stript of the means of defence, they have more opportunity of concerting their measures, and their [18] mental faculties retain more of their natural activity. Such a government must generally be contentious and changeable. The rules cannot be long satisfied with a limitation of prerogative, or the people with the abridgement of their privileges. The blame is generally laid on the people, but it is easy to see that the change is unjust. So far from being unreasonable in their demands, there is perhaps no one instance in history, where they have ventured at once to push their claims to the full extent of reason, and to make an ample demand of justice. They rarely complain at once of more than one or a few grievances. When these are removed, they become sensible of others. In proportion as they acquire more freedom, they gain more strength of mind and independence of spirit. They see farther into the nature and extent of their own rights, and call louder for the restoration of them. This is called turbulence and caprice, but is in reality only a requisition of justice; which being always refused, or but partially and unwillingly granted, it is to the oppressors, and not the oppressed, that the mischief is to be imputed.

It is thus, I apprehend, and no otherwise, that a government approaching to Democracy, is apt to be disorderly. The people have a right to complain, so long as they are robbed of any portion of their freedom, and if their complaints are not heard, they have a right to use any method of enfranchising themselves. They have a just claim to perfect political equality, and it is ungenerous and base to deny them justice, and at the same time load them with reproaches.

It is true indeed, that they sometimes mistake the object they are in pursuit of, and still more frequently, the proper means of obtaining it. Deceived and misled by the artifices of factious men asuming the mask of patriotism, they wander from the path that leads to freedom and happiness, and precipitately rush into a wilderness of confusion, terminating in irretrievable ruin. Although they are at all times intitled to demand an ample redress of grievances yet it is not by violent means [19] that this is properly or effectually to be sought. Violence can only be justifiable where it is the only resource. This is commonly the case in countries where a standing force is kept up, which may hinder the peaceable deliberations of the people, and render it impossible for any matter to be quietly determined by a majority of voices. We have already observed, that even in those cases, it is a very uncertain resource, and often productive of infinitely more mischief than good. In this State we are happily in no need of having recourse to such an expedient. Nothing could possibly excuse the absurdity of adopting it, as it would certainly be the most effectual method that could be devised of bringing on us the very evil we would prevent. The authors or instigators of such measures ought to be held in the utmost detestation, unless it should first evidently appear that it was the only remedy. Nor are secret combinations better authorized, or less dishonorable to the characters of the promoters. They are to be regarded in no other light than as insidious and treacherous attempts of a minority to rule a majority; which is the very definition of an aristocratical government, so loudly and so justly condemned. In vain shall any man pretend to patriotism, who encourages a violation of the laws and of the rights of his fellow citizens. In vain shall he call himself a friend to freedom, who daringly sets himself up as a dictator and tyrant over his neighbours. No one can be a well-wisher to the rights of mankind, who would by secret practices, or actual violence, take the advantage of the unsuspecting security of others, to deprive them of the free and effectual exercise of those rights. An honest man, and a real lover of freedom, will fairly and openly declare what he has to propose, and leave to a majority to judge of it, to adopt or reject it. He is free to support his opinion by every possible argument, but he must finally allow others the liberty of having an opinion too. It is a strange way that some men have of vindicating the cause of freedom, by denying others even the freedom of thinking. Whoever acts in this manner is a tyrant at heart, and should he, under the cloak of patriotism, gain influence with the people, he will be no longer their friend than [20] whilst he stands in need of their countenance and support. Whenever he can securely do it, he will shew himself the bitter enemy of all who stand in the way of his ambition.

It is from a perfect conviction of their fatal consequences, that I warn my fellow-citizens against irregularities and civil dissention. But I mean not to inculcate the fallacious and dangerous opinion of security. On the contrary, I would wish it to be understood, that, without our most earnest and vigilant exertions, we shall never be firmly established in that glorious condition of freedom, which was the object of our late bloody contest. But let us charitably hope that the danger does not spring from any sinister views of any who have lately been intrusted with the powers of government. Let us generously allow, until we have more conclusive evidence of the contrary, that in general they have done their duty to the best of their judgment, and have not been desirous of exercising any greater powers than what they conceived to be delegated to them by the constitution. But although we may be honest men, we were, at the commencement of the late war, but novices in politics; and it is to be wise that we may not now be too indolent to correct our mistakes. Bred up in the erroneous notion of the freedom and excellence of the British constitution, we have unthinkingly adopted many of its faults. After lopping off the monarchical part, we vainly imagined that we had arrived at perfection, and that freedom was established on the broadest and most solid basis that could possibly consist with any social institution. That we have in some points been mistaken, is too evident to be denied. But error is the inheritance of human nature, and, when it is not intentional, it must ever be excused. It is the part of prudence to guard against its evil consequences; but to impute it always to motives of dishonesty, is neither generous nor just. Ambitious rulers will indeed be found in all countries;—a few, who, to aggrandize themselves, will not scruple to invade the rights of their fellow-citizens. If such there be amongst us, let them be held in merited contempt; let them be accounted unworthy of any public trust; and, if the laws are adequate, [21] let them be punished with severity. But, of all things, let us avoid the rock of dissention and violence. Let us consider, that in our present situation, tumultuous proceedings are as unnecessary as they would be improper and ineffectual. Other means are in our hands, as much preferable as good order is to confusion, as peace to discord, as efficacy and security to disappointment and ruin. However faulty our constitution may be, it has fixed no set of men so firmly in power as to enable them to set themselves up against the general voice of the people. The sovereignty of the State (except so much as has been imparted to the United States in Congress) is still in the hands of the latter. They have made no formal surrender of any portion of their liberty, nor is there any standing force in the State to deprive them of the exercise of it.

Our present Constitution was framed in a time of distress and confusion, and is perhaps fully as good as might have been expected under such circumstances. It is not founded on proper authority, being only an act of the legislature; but the people have hitherto acquiesced in it, and it must serve, and ought to be supported, as the rule of government, until some regular method is adopted of amending, and fixing it on a more solid basis. If it is the sense of a majority of the citizens that this ought to be done, it is entirely in their power to effect it without the smallest disturbance.

The constituents of every District have an undoubted right (however speciously it may have been lately denied) to instruct their representatives in both Houses. Without entering into arguments upon the subject, we may confidently affirm, that the right is as certain, and founded in the same principle of freedom as the right of any State to instruct its delegates in Congress. We may also be bold to assert that if the people ever suffer a contrary doctrine to be established, they will have yielded up the distinguishing privilege of free citizens. It must indeed be very rare that the exercise of this right can be either [22] necessary or prudent. The frequent exercise of it must be productive of infinite embarrassment to the representatives, who ought certainly to have the liberty of retiring whenever they receive instructions which their own feelings cannot approve. But the right is inherent in the people, and the acknowledgment of it ought to make a clause of the constitution.

Let the inhabitants of every District, at the next meeting of the Assembly, authorize and require their representatives in both Houses to appoint a time for choosing delegates to meet in convention, for the express purpose (and no other) of revising and amending the Constitution, rendering it more conformable to the true principles of equal freedom, and fixing it on the firm and proper foundation of the express consent of the people, unalterable by the legislative, or any other authority but that by which it is to be framed. Nor should this be done hastily. The members elected should, before they meet, be allowed at least six months to consider of the important business to which they are appointed, that they may not enter upon it unprepared. The convention should, after the most mature deliberation, publish the articles of the new constitution, and adjourn for at least six months, that the people at large may also have an opportunity to consider the matter duly, and to give, if they think proper, fresh instructions with respect to any or every article. The whole being again debated in convention, must at length be determined by a majority of voices, and notice given when the new form is to have effect. Thus may every real grievance be removed, and peace, freedom and happiness lastingly established in the Commonwealth. I am sanguine enough to flatter myself, that, by pursuing these measures, the most free and happy constitution would be established that ever existed in any part of the globe; and being founded in undeniable authority, it would have the most promising chance of stability. Whatever aristocratical principles have, through inexperience, inadvertence or design, been admitted into our present system, might, by these means, be totally done away. It is [23] in no wise surprizing, that, accustomed as we were to a monarchical government, we should not have been able to divest ourselves of inculcated prejudices, and immediately arrive at pure republican principles; especially as there is perhaps not a single precedent in the annals of mankind that would serve as a proper guide, every government that has yet been denominated republican, at least all of modern date, partaking (as we have before observed) more or less of the aristocratical form. It is rather to be admitted that the several States came so near as they did to the true nature of a commonwealth. In this, however, some of our sister States have certainly excelled us; although imperfections have been discovered in the constitutions of them all.

The matter of a convention was proposed at the last sitting of the Assembly, and passed in the House of Representatives, though not without very powerful opposition. In the Senate it was rejected unanimously, or by a great majority; which was by some supposed to arise from an apprehension that this branch of the legislature would be thrown out by the new constitution. Were the minds of men always free to decide without prejudice or partiality, two branches would be entirely useless in the legislature. But, subject as we all are to be influenced by interest, by passion, and by the sentiments of a few leading men, the division of the legislative power seems necessary to furnish a proper check to our too hasty proceedings. Two separate bodies of men do not so readily, without good reason, come into each other's opinions, as the same men collected together in one general meeting. It is therefore probable, that such an innovation in the constitution would not be judged necessary, or proper.

The opposition made to a convention, in the House of Represen-tatives, was founded chiefly on the following reasoning:

1st. That there must be a total dissolution of our present [24] constitution, and that of course the country must be thrown into a state of anarchy and confusion, before a new one could be established.

2d. That the powers of government being annihilated, every person in the land would have an equal right to become a party in

the new compact, and to give his vote as such; the consequences of which might be fatal to republican freedom.

3d. That the new constitution, being framed in compliance with an act of the legislature, could not possibly be of more validity or stability than the present, which rests on the same authority.

4th. That the people at large having never applied for or directed any alteration of the present constitution, was to be considered as a tacit acknowledgement that they are satisfied with it as it now stands.

5th and lastly, That the convention being under no control with respect to the form they were to establish, might fix on a monarchy, or any other form injurious to the rights of the people.

With regard to the first and second of these objections it may be observed, that a State is only a large society of men connected together under certain regulations, to which the assent of all has either been expressly given, or implied by silent acquiescence. The actual citizens only are the members of this society, and the general consent, or the concurrence of a majority, may, just as in a society of twenty or fifty, alter the rules of their establishment, either wholly or in any degree they choose, without throwing it into any confusion, and without admitting to a vote a single person who is not already intitled to the full privilege of a member. Aliens therefore can have no claim of interest in the business, nor will there be occasion [25] for a moment's interval betwixt the abolition of the present and the giving force to the new constitution. This latter difficulty was never thought of, when the legislature, in the year 1778, undertook, by their own authority, to abolish the first constitution of the State, and substituted the present in its place.

The third objection would be conclusive against the method proposed in the legislature, of passing an act to order a convention, and to dictate to them their business. If it had passed, it should have been in form of a recommendation to the people, not of an order. What is done by order of the legislature, is the act of the legislature, and nothing more. But what is done by advice of the legislature, is the free act of the people, as much as if the proposal originated with them.—But this objection does not apply against the plan being proposed. The authority of the people at large being the true sovereign authority, and superior to the legislative, a constitution framed by their express order, and not made of force without first having the sanction of their approbation, would be superior to the legislative power, and therefore not alterable by it. It is a vain and weak argument, that, the legislature being the representatives of the people, the act of the former is therefore always to be considered as the act of the latter. They are the representatives of the people for certain purposes only, not to all intents and purposes whatever. In a free state, every officer, from the Governor to the constable, is, so far as the powers of his office extend, as truly the representative of the people, as a member of the legislature; and his act, within the appointed limitation, is the act of the people; for he is their agent, and derives his authority from them. I say, in a free state; for in other governments the officers are more properly the representatives of the prince, or of others who have usurped the sovereign power. With us it would be an absurd surrender of liberty, to delegate full powers to any set of men whatever, unless in cases of the most urgent necessity; such a necessity as rarely exists in any country. Delegates may be sent to a convention with powers, under certain [26] restriction, to frame a constitution. Delegates are sent to the General Assembly with powers, under certain restrictions prescribed, or supposed to be so, by a previously established compact or constitution, to make salutary laws. But if either one or the other should exceed the powers vested in them, their act is no longer the act of their constituents.—Whatever is done by the particular injunctions of the people, can never be lawfully repeated or altered but by their express consent. Such would be a constitution made on proper conventional authority, as here proposed. Whatever is done without their instructions or express consent may at any time be repealed without consulting them. Such are most acts of the legislature, it being rarely either necessary or possible to receive instructions in such case; and such also particularly is our present constitution founded in such an act, passed at a time when it was impossible to consult the people, and therefore alterable or repealable at pleasure by the same authority. There is indeed a clause prohibiting a repeal or alteration under certain conditions; but this is trifling and unavailing; for no legislature can, by any clause in an act, prevent a future legislature from repealing it, either wholly or partially, as they please. Besides, were these conditions to be inviolably observed, they are not sufficiently restrictive to secure the public freedom.

As to the 4th objection, it may be said, that if the people think proper to come into the plan here proposed, the objection will be removed, for it will then be evident, that they see the insufficiency of the present constitution, and wish for one contrived upon a more solid and permanent establishment, and also (if it may be done) upon principles of more perfect political equality. But should the people really determine to be silent in so important a business, then indeed will this objection have all the weight that was intended. If they are resolved not to adopt those regular and peaceable means, which are in their power, of obtaining, an alteration, it will appear that they are actually satisfied, or what amounts to the same thing, too indolent to concern themselves about the matter, and in this case [27] the present constitution, with all its faults, must still be the rule of government; and it will be the duty of every citizen to acquiesce in it as the act of a majority, since a majority cannot be prevailed on to determine on its alteration. If our constitution is ever so defective, it does not follow that it is not to be regarded. Until altered, it must be considered as the voice of the people, and he that infringes it is an enemy to the State. A defective constitution is infinitely preferable to anarchy, confusion, and a toleration of the licentious proceedings of turbulent and violent men, who have no better way of evincing their regard for liberty than by an outrageous invasion of the liberties of others.—But it is to be hoped that the people at large will not be so careless of their own interests as to neglect paying the most serious attention to a permanent establishment of freedom, whilst it is yet in their power. At the present time they may quietly carry into execution any thing they think proper. Their hands are not yet tied, though there is danger that they may be so at a future day.

The last objection above stated is obviated by the terms of the instructions here proposed, requiring that the constitution should be framed on principles of equal freedom, and therefore precluding all power of establishing any but a republican form.

In order to shew how easily this business may be performed, we shall here point out more particularly the method which seems to be advisable, and which being uniformly pursued cannot fail to be effectual.—In each district, let any set of men, or any individual (for any one has a right to do it), put up advertisements in the most frequented places, to the following effects:

ADVERTISEMENT

The inhabitants of the district (or parish) of _____ properly qualified to vote at elections, who wish to have the constitution amended and fixed on an authority that may [28] secure permanent freedom to the community, are requested to meet at ———— on the *tenth day of December, in order to instruct their Representatives in both Houses to appoint a convention for the above purpose. And that no person may imagine that this invitation is intended to draw him into a blind concurrence in disorderly or unwarrantable measures, the following is offered in the form of the instructions proposed to be signed; which will remain, from the above appointed day until the meeting of the Assembly, in the bounds of A. B., in said place, for the convenience of those who would choose to put their names to it, but do not find it suits them to attend the meeting.

A. B. Senator, and C. D. Member of the House of Representatives for the district of (or parish) ————

We whose names are undersigned, free citizens and electors of the district of ———— do recommend to you, and if it shall appear that we are a majority of the electors of this district, we do hereby authorize and require you in the respective houses in which you represent us, to move for and endeavor to get passed a resolve for appointing a day to elect delegates to the several districts and parishes throughout the State (the number in each, to prevent disputes about the proportion, to be the same as the number of representatives in both Houses) to meet in convention six months or thereabouts after [29] their election, for the express purpose (and no other) of revising and amending the constitution, rendering it more conformable to the true principles of equal freedom, and fixing it on the firm and proper foundation of the free and express consent of the people, unalterable by the legislative or any other authority but that by which it is to be framed, namely the free voice of the citizens at large, to be occasionally collected in such manner as shall be therein appointed. And the said convention shall be obliged, after drawing up the articles of the said constitution and before making it of force, to have the same printed

* Any other day may be appointed, but the earlier the better, as it is in contemplation with some to alter the constitution by legislative authority at the next meeting of the Assembly. Should this practice go on (however good the intention) it is evident that the Constitution can be nothing more than the will of the legislature, always changing without the consent of the people, and perhaps always for the worse: at least this will be the case whenever men of influence in the legislature shall happen to be actuated by motives of ambition and self-interest. Another reason why this is the proper time is, that at future elections we may possibly have many foreigners qualified to vote, who may care very little about a form of government to which they have not been accustomed.

at the public expense, and a sufficient number of copies distributed throughout the State for the inspection and consideration of the people. And the said convention shall afterwards adjourn for six months or thereabouts and then meet again to pass the said constitution and carry it into effect, either wholly or with such alterations as may be agreed to by the majority of voices, the Delegates from each District or Parish being bound to obey any instructions they may receive relative thereto from a majority of their respective constituents, if any they should think proper to give. But that no Delegate may be compelled to vote contrary to his own feelings and ideas of rectitude any who shall disapprove his instructions shall be at liberty to resign in favor of another to be elected in his place.

Signed
A. B.
C. D. &c.

Such an instruction or recommendation, although it should not be signed by a majority, ought to have considerable weight with the Representatives, unless they should receive a counter instruction or recommendation from a dissenting party.—If the above form should seem sufficient and not liable to exceptions, it would be best to adopt it for the sake of conducting the business upon one uniform plan. Measures that might happen, in some particulars, to be contradictory, would be apt to defeat the main intention.

[30] It has been observed that the present constitution appears to be in many respects faulty, but the compass of this publication does not permit the author to enter into a detail of its defects. Nor does he think himself at all competent to so arduous an undertaking. Should the measures be approved which have been above proposed, a few remarks on some necessary alterations might possibly furnish the subject of another paper. It would be the duty of every citizen to contribute what useful hints his reflection and reading might suggest. And it would behove the people at large to be particularly careful, on so important an occasion, to elect as Delegates none but men of the most liberal and disinterested sentiments—men disposed, in real sincerity of heart, to lay the foundation of equal and permanent freedom.

Although we decline expatiating here on the imperfections of our present constitution, yet it will not be amiss, by way of urging the expediency of our plan, to repeat that one great and sufficient objection to it, if no other could be found, is that it has not the sanction of that authority which is absolutely necessary to give it a chance of stability. It is established on no higher authority than that of the Legislature, and it is ridiculous to suppose that any body of men can make a law to limit their own power; for such a law can only be of force during the pleasure of those who made it. If the law itself is allowed to be valid, the repeal of it must be so likewise.—The constitution should be the avowed act of the people at large. It should be the first and fundamental law of the State, and should prescribe the limits of all delegated power. It should be declared to be paramount to all acts of the Legislature, and irrepealable and unalterable by any authority but the express consent of a majority of the citizens collected by such regular mode as may be therein provided. Who can say that the laws of this State are now, and will at all times be, strictly conformable to the words of the constitution? And if they are not, who can deny that they are nevertheless of force, and do therefore operate as a partial repeal of it? What security then can there possibly be for its duration? Clearly none at all.

[31] That a constitution should be established on conventional authority and expressly superior to the legislative power will be more fully evinced by an affair which happened in one of our sister states.— A law was inadvertently passed which militated against the constitution. A case in point occured, on which depended the lives of several citizens. The question was learnedly argued by the first lawyers before the Supreme Court of Appeals, and the Judges, who were deemed equal in ability to any on the continent, were much embarrassed and delivered the most opposite opinions on the matter. The constitution of that state was formed by authority of a convention, but it did not expressly declare that no act of the legislature contravening it should be of force.—The Judges were sworn to judge according to law.— Some of them vainly endeavoured, by a forced construction to reconcile the act with the constitution.—Others were of opinion, that an act of the legislature infringing the constitution was *ab initio* void, and not to be regarded as a law.—Others, in short, held themselves to be bound by their oath to judge according to law, and not competent to pronounce that to be no law which was really an act of the legislature.— Thus was their constitution, although founded on better authority than ours, in danger of being infringed by the inadvertence of the

General Assembly. How much greater is the danger with us?—especially if we should ever be so unfortunate as to have in appointment a set of men capable of using their authority to sinister purposes. A thousand evils may arise from the want of that stamp of conventional authority to our constitution which is so intirely necessary to give it stability. It is also necessary to give energy and effect to the powers of government. The legislature having their limits prescribed will be less liable to give cause of jealousy to the people, and both their laws and their persons will be more respected. The Magistrates deriving their powers from the proper source of all power, will do their duty with that confidence and spirit, which naturally flow from a consciousness of acting on authority lawfully conferred, not unjustly assumed. They will be sensible that they are truly the servants of the public, and that any opposition made to [32] them in the due discharge of their respective offices, must be considered and treated as a violation of the sacred rights of the people at large, for whose benefit, and by whose undeniable authority, they are empowered to officiate. They will be convinced that it cannot but be the intention and wish of the community, that they should be vested with such powers as are necessary for the primary purposes of social institutions, powers sufficient to enable them to preserve the peace of the commonwealth, and to protect every member of it both in person and property. Without powers adequate to these purposes, we may as well be without Magistrates, without Laws, without a constitution, for no man can be said to enjoy even the shadow of freedom in a state whose laws and police do not protect him from insult and injury. Licentiousness is a tyranny as inconsistent with freedom and as destructive of the common rights of mankind, as is the arbitrary sway of an enthroned despot. And those, who wish to call themselves truly free, have to guard, with equal vigilance, against the one and the other. It will be of little use to have the means of preventing oppression from men of our own appointment, if we are obliged to bear it from those who, in opposition to the voice of the people, choose to appoint themselves rulers and dictators of the state. The Magistrates should have ample power to preserve the peace, by requiring the assistance of citizens, not by employing a military force, of which happily, we have none at present in the state; and happy it would be for us, that we should never have occasion for any. Officers of government acting in the best of their judgment for the good of the community in all emergencies, have a claim to the support and approbation of all good citizens. In such a state of freedom as we have described, it is to be hoped that this support will always be at hand, but very seldom wanted. In such a state it would be fairly tried (and certainly the object is worth the pains of an experiment) whether a constitution founded on the just and generous principles of perfect political equality is really productive of riots and commotions, or whether, on the contrary, it would not prove to be the most quiet, as it certainly is the only equitable system [33] that can be devised. Surely no just inference can be drawn against it, until one fair trial at least shall have been made; and hitherto we know of none. It has been too common with us to search the records of other nations, to find precedents that may give a sanction to our own errors, and lead us unwarily into confusion and ruin. It is our business to consult their histories not with a view to tread, right or wrong, in their steps, but in order to investigate the real sources of the mischiefs that have befallen them, and to endeavor to escape the rocks which they have all unfortunately split upon. It is paying ourselves but a poor compliment, to say that we are incapable of profiting by the misfortunes of others, and that with all the information which is to be derived from their fatal experience, it is so rash for us to attempt to excell them. If with all those advantages, together with the peculiar happiness of our present free, uncontrolled, and, as it were unconnected situation (such as no nation before us ever did, and probably none after us ever can enjoy); if with all these, I say, we are incapable of surpassing our predecessors, we must be a degenerate race indeed, and quite unworthy of those singular bounties of Heaven, which we are so unskilled or undesirous to turn to our benefit. The superiority of our condition over that of other nations is truly amazing. It seems as if the Almighty had intended the various revolutions and misfortunes of all other states for our particular instruction, and then placed us in the only possible situation in which we could practically profit by it. Before us, no people were ever so intirely relieved from the control of hereditary rulers and arbitrary force. Before, as none have ever been so free to associate upon terms of equality. And could it have been their lot to be ever thus circumstanced, still would it have availed them nothing. All before us, have been surrounded with neighbours who would have been ready to support the first usurper that should seize upon the reins of government. In order to render such a condition of real utility to the people, it was necessary to provide for them a new world, out of reach of the interference of the rest of mankind. It is on us, and us only, that the great Ruler [34] of the Universe has bestowed this great and wonderful blessing. To shew our grateful sense of his benificence, we should improve these happy circumstances to our own and the welfare of our posterity. We should set an example of prudence, justice, and generosity, becoming the characters of men who have made the noblest struggle in the cause of freedom.

Having thus finished (though very incorrectly) the intention of this little publication, the author most cheerfully submits it to the consideration and judgment of his fellow citizens.—Abhorring equally the pride of aristocracy and the turbulence of faction, he has endeavoured to pursue the middle road of candid and impartial discussion.—If what he has suggested shall be deemed worthy of the public attention, and shall contribute to promote in the commonwealth the permanent establishment of harmony, freedom, and happiness, he will have attained the important objects of his sanguine wishes.

FINIS.

[41]

[JAMES MADISON (1749–1836) et al.]

Memorial and Remonstrance Against Religious Assessments

VIRGINIA, 1785

Fortunately, James Madison needs little introduction. Like those of John Adams and Benjamin Franklin, his contributions to the founding of the American Republic were prodigious. Best known for his notes on the debates in the Philadelphia Convention and for joint authorship of *The Federalist,* which proved that he had no superior if he had an equal, in fixing the content of the Constitution and securing its adoption, he continued his role as founding father by directing, in the United States House of Representatives, the legislation that fleshed out the government ordained by the new Constitution. His sponsorship of the Bill of Rights incorporated in the first ten amendments of the United States Constitution provided early evidence of his opposition to a state church and his distrust of governmental intrusion into religious faith and clerical affairs. The Virginia Memorial and Remonstrance, now to be read, owes it composition to several hands, but James Madison is known to have been a main contributor to its language and to have been prominent in the fight against the legislation that the Memorial protests. The bill referred to in this document was introduced in the Virginia legislature during the session of 1784–85 but never came to a vote. It would have levied a tax upon property holders generally, and the proceeds would have been used "to restore and propagate the holy Christian religion." Apparently, use of the fund would not have been restricted to support of teachers of religion, as the title suggests, but instead would have paid salaries of clergymen and met other costs of the Protestant Episcopal Church. This piece, with modernization of punctuation and some other editing, is as printed in *The Writings of James Madison,* edited by Gaillard Hunt, volume 2, pages 183–191.

We, the subscribers, citizens of the said Commonwealth, having taken into serious consideration, a Bill printed by order of the last Session of General Assembly, entitled "A Bill establishing a provision for Teachers of the Christian Religion," and conceiving that the same, if finally armed with the sanctions of a law, will be a dangerous abuse of power, are bound as faithful members of a free State, to remonstrate against it, and to declare the reasons by which we are determined. We remonstrate against the said Bill,

1. Because we hold it for a fundamental and undeniable truth, "that religion or the duty which we owe to our Creator and the manner of discharging it, can be directed only by reason and conviction, not by force or violence." The religion then of every man must be left to the conviction and conscience of every man, and it is the right of every man to exercise it as these may dictate. This right is in its nature an unalienable right. It is unalienable because the opinions of men, depending only on the evidence contemplated by their own minds, cannot follow the dictates of other men. It is unalienable also because what is here a right towards men, is a duty towards the Creator. It is the duty of every man to render to the Creator such homage, and such only, as he believes to be acceptable to him. This duty is precedent, both in order of time and degree of obligation, to the claims of Civil Society. Before any man can be considered as a member of Civil Society, he must be considered as a subject of the Governor of the Universe. And if a member of Civil Society, who enters into any subordinate association, must always do it with a reservation of his duty to the general authority, much more must every man who becomes a member of any particular Civil Society do it with a saving of his allegiance to the Universal Sovereign. We maintain therefore that in matters of religion no man's right is abridged by the institution of Civil Society, and that religion is wholly exempt from its cognizance. True it is that no other rule exists, by which any question which may divide a society can be ultimately determined, but the will of the majority; but it is also true, that the majority may trespass on the rights of the minority.

2. Because if religion be exempt from the authority of the society at large, still less can it be subject to that of the Legislative Body. The latter are but the creatures and vicegerents of the former. Their jurisdiction is both derivative and limited. It is limited with regard to the co-ordinate departments; more necessarily is it limited with

JAMES MADISON (1749–1836) ET AL.

regard to the constituents. The preservation of a free government requires not merely that the metes and bounds which separate each department of power may be invariably maintained, but more especially that neither of them be suffered to overleap the great barrier which defends the rights of the people. The rulers who are guilty of such an encroachment, exceed the commission from which they derive their authority, and are tyrants. The People who submit to it are governed by laws made neither by themselves nor by an authority derived from them, and are slaves.

3. Because it is proper to take alarm at the first experiment on our liberties. We hold this prudent jealousy to be the first duty of citizens, and one of [the] noblest characteristics of the late Revolution. The freemen of America did not wait till usurped power had strengthened itself by exercise and entangled the question in precedents. They saw all the consequences in the principle, and they avoided the consequences by denying the principle. We revere this lesson too much, soon to forget it. Who does not see that the same authority which can establish Christianity in exclusion of all other religions, may establish with the same ease any particular sect of Christians in exclusion of all other sects? That the same authority which can force a citizen to contribute three pence only of his property for the support of any one establishment, may force him to conform to any other establishment in all cases whatsoever?

4. Because the bill violates that equality which ought to be the basis of every law. . . . If "all men are by nature equally free and independent," [then] all men are to be considered as entering into Society on equal conditions, as relinquishing no more and therefore retaining no less, one than another, of their natural rights. Above all are they to be considered as retaining an *"equal* title to the free exercise of religion according to the dictates of conscience." Whilst we assert for ourselves a freedom to embrace, to profess, and to observe the religion which we believe to be of divine origin, we cannot deny an equal freedom to those whose minds have not yielded to the evidence which has convinced us. If this freedom be abused, it is an offence against God, not against man. To God therefore, not to men, must an account of it be rendered. As the Bill violates equality by subjecting some to peculiar burdens, so it violates the same principle by granting to other peculiar exemptions. Are the Quakers and Menonists [to whom exemptions are granted] the only sects who think a compulsive

support of their religions unnecessary and unwarantable? Can their piety alone be intrusted with the care of public worship? Ought their religions to be endowed above all others with extraordinary privileges by which proselytes may be enticed from all others? We think too favorably of the justice and good sense of these denominations to believe that they either covet pre-eminencies over their fellow citizens, or that they will be seduced by them from the common opposition to the measure.

5. Because the bill implies either that the Civil Magistrate is a competent judge of religious truth, or that he may employ religion as an engine of civil policy. The first is an arrogant pretension falsified by the contradictory opinions of rulers in all ages and throughout the world; the second an unhallowed perversion of the means of salvation.

6. Because the establishment proposed by the Bill is not requisite for the support of the Christian religion. To say that it is, is a contradiction to the Christian religion itself; for every page of it disavows a dependence on the powers of this world. It is a contradiction to fact, for it is known that this religion both existed and flourished, not only without the support of human laws, but in spite of every opposition from them; and not only during the period of miraculous aid, but long after it had been left to its own evidence and the ordinary care of Providence. Nay, it is a contradiction in terms, for a religion not invented by human policy must have pre-existed and been supported before it was established by human policy. It is moreover to weaken in those who profess this religion a pious confidence in its innate excellence and the patronage of its Author and to foster in those who still reject it, a suspicion that its friends are too conscious of its fallacies to trust it to its own merits.

7. Because experience witnesseth that ecclesiastical establishments, instead of maintaining the purity and efficacy or religion, have had a contrary operation. During almost fifteen centuries has the legal establishment of Christianity been on trial. What have been its fruits? More or less in all places, pride and indolence in the Clergy [and] ignorance and servility in the laity; in both, superstition, bigotry, and persecution. Enquire of the teachers of Christianity for the ages in which it appeared in its greatest lustre; those of every sect point to the ages prior to its incorporation with Civil policy. Propose a restoration of this primitive state in which its teachers depended on the voluntary rewards of their flocks; many of them predict its downfall.

On which side ought their testimony to have greatest weight, when for or when against their interest?

8. Because the establishment in question is not necessary for the support of Civil Government. If it be urged as necessary for the support of Civil Government only as it is a means of supporting religion, and it be not necessary for the latter purpose, it cannot be necessary for the former. If religion be not within [the] cognizance of Civil Government, how can its legal establishment be said to be necessary to civil Government? What influence in fact have ecclesiastical establishments had on Civil Society? In some instances they have been seen to erect a spiritual tyranny on the ruins of Civil authority; in many instances they have been seen upholding the thrones of political tyranny; in no instance have they been seen the guardians of the liberties of the people. Rulers who wished to subvert the public liberty may have found an established clergy convenient auxiliaries. A just government, instituted to secure and perpetuate it, needs them not. Such a government will be best supported by protecting every citizen in the enjoyment of his religion with the same equal hand which protects his person and his property; by neither invading the equal rights of any Sect nor suffering any Sect to invade those of another.

9. Because the proposed establishment is a departure from that generous policy which, offering an asylum to the persecuted and oppressed of every nation and religion, promised a lustre to our country and an accession to the number of its citizens. What a melancholy mark is the Bill of sudden degeneracy? Instead of holding forth an asylum to the persecuted, it is itself a signal of persecution. It degrades from the equal rank of citizens all those whose opinions in religion do not bend to those of the legislative authority. Distant as it may be, in its present form, from the Inquisition it differs from it only in degree. The one is the first step, the other the last in the career of intolerance. The magnanimous sufferer under the cruel scourge in foreign regions, must view the Bill as a beacon on our coast, warning him to seek some other haven where liberty and philanthropy in their due extent may offer a more certain repose from his troubles.

10. Because it will have a like tendency to banish our citizens. The allurements presented by other situations are every day thinning their number. To superadd a fresh motive to emigration, by revoking the liberty which they now enjoy, would be the same species of folly which has dishonoured and depopulated flourishing kingdoms.

11. Because it will destroy that moderation and harmony which the forbearance of our laws to intermeddle with religion has produced amongst its several sects. Torrents of blood have been spilt in the old world by vain attempts of the secular arm to extinguish religious discord by proscribing all difference in religious opinions. Time has at length revealed the true remedy. Every relaxation of narrow and rigorous policy, wherever it has been tried, has been found to assuage the disease. The American theatre has exhibited proofs that equal and complete liberty, if it does not wholly eradicate it, sufficiently destroys its malignant influence on the health and prosperity of the State. If, with the salutary effects of this system under our own eyes, we begin to contract the bonds of religious freedom, we know no name that will too severely reproach our folly. At least let warning be taken at the first fruits of the threatened innovation. The very appearance of the Bill has transformed that "Christian forbearance, love and charity," which of late mutually prevailed, into animosities and jealousies which may not soon be appeased. What mischiefs may not be dreaded should this enemy to the public quiet be armed with the force of a law?

12. Because the policy of the bill is adverse to the diffusion of the light of Christianity. The first wish of those who enjoy this precious gift ought to be that it may be imparted to the whole race of mankind. Compare the number of those who have as yet received it with the number still remaining under the dominion of false religions, and how small is the former! Does the policy of the Bill tend to lessen the disproportion? No; it at once discourages those who are strangers to the light of [revelation] from coming into the region of it; and [it] countenances, by example, the nations who continue in darkness in shutting out those who might convey it to them. . . .

13. Because attempts to enforce, by legal sanctions, acts obnoxious to so great a proportion of Citizens tend to enervate the laws in general and to slacken the bands of Society. If it be difficult to execute any law which is not generally deemed necessary or salutary, what must be the case where [the law] is deemed invalid and dangerous? And what may be the effect of so striking an example of impotency in the Government, on its general authority.

14. Because a measure of such singular magnitude and delicacy ought not to be imposed, without the clearest evidence that it is called for by a majority of citizens; and no satisfactory method is yet proposed by which the voice of the majority in this case may be determined,

JAMES MADISON (1749–1836) ET AL.

or its influence secured. "The people of the respective countries are indeed requested to signify their opinion respecting the adoption of the Bill to the next Session of Assembly." But the representation must be made equal before the voice either of the Representatives or of the Counties, will be that of the people. Our hope is that neither of the former will, after due consideration, espouse the dangerous principle of the Bill. Should the event disappoint us, it will still leave us in full confidence that a fair appeal to the latter will reverse the sentence against our liberties.

15. Because, finally, "the equal right of every citizen to the free exercise of his Religion according to the dictates of conscience" is held by the same tenure with all our other rights. If we recur to its origin, it is equally the gift of nature. If we weigh its importance, it cannot be less dear to us. If we consult the Declaration of those rights which pertain to the good people of Virginia as the "basis and foundation of Government," it is enumerated with equal solemnity, or rather studied emphasis. Either, then, we must say that the will of the Legislature is the only measure of their authority, and that in the plenitude of this authority, they may sweep away all our fundamental rights; or, that they are bound to leave this particular right untouched and sacred. Either we must say that they may controul the freedom of the press, may abolish the trial by jury, may swallow up the Executive and Judiciary powers of the State—nay that they may despoil us of our very right of suffrage and erect themselves into an independent and hereditary assembly—or we must say that they have no authority to enact into law the Bill under consideration. We the subscribers say, that the General Assembly of this Commonwealth have no such authority. And that no effort may be omitted on our part against so dangerous an usurpation, we oppose to it this remonstrance, earnestly praying, as we are in duty bound, that the Supreme Lawgiver of the Universe, by illuminating those to whom it is addressed, may on the one hand turn their councils from every act which would affront his holy prerogative or violate the trust committed to them, and on the other, guide them into every measure which may be worthy of his [blessing, may re] dound to their own praise, and may establish more firmly the liberties, the prosperity, and the happiness of the Commonwealth.

[42]

[AMICUS REPUBLICAE]

Address to the Public, Containing Some Remarks on the Present Political State of the American Republicks, etc.

EXETER, 1786

Published anonymously in Exeter, New Hampshire, as a response both to growing civil unrest and to attacks on the state constitutions, this essay defends the state constitutions from both radicals and Federalists. Admitting the need for some alterations in state political systems, the author advises against complacency on the one hand, and needless change on the other. In addition to presenting a balanced view, the essay lays out the basics of the Whig perspective on politics. In this last regard, the essay is one of the best we have for illustrating how American Whigs approached political problems and how they used language in political discourse.

Friends and Fellow Citizens,

Nothing but the critical situation of our governments could have induced me to become an author upon this subject. For some considerable time, I have been in expectation of seeing some able pen employed in pointing out our dangerous situation; and in enlightening the minds of the people into that which is absolutely necessary for our existence and happiness as an independent nation. Something of this nature appears to be very necessary at this critical period; for although there may be some persons in our republicks, who are so politically corrupt, that they will [4] not receive instruction, yet there are many, whose minds are unstable and in doubts, for want of information and direction; and who have sufficient regard to public virtue to pursue it, when they can understand in what it does consist.

I shall therefore attempt to make some remarks on this subject, leaving my deficiencies to be supplied hereafter, by more able writers.

The important end of government is the good of the whole. And in order to the forming and establishing of any government, it is necessary for individuals to give up, by a civil compact, some of their natural rights, for securing to themselves others which they would retain. And all those, who enter voluntarily into such civil compacts with one another, are as to matters of government free and independent, so long as government is administered agreeable to the principles of this their political constitution. But it is directly incompatible with the end of government, and every civil constitution, for subjects to claim the exercise of those natural rights which they have given up by their civil compact, in any mode but such as their constitution shall warrant and point out;—for then, had they such a [5] right, all ideas of civil government would be exploded, and they would be, in the most strict sense, in a *state of nature*. A state of nature, and a state of civil government, are in the nature of things repugnant the one to the other.—The states of America have respectively, by civil compacts voluntarily and solemnly entered into covenant for the defence of liberty, life and property. The subjects in each state have, voluntarily, given up some of their natural rights, that they might be secured in the enjoyment of those, that they would retain: and the public interest and welfare being the end of this civil combination, those that have entered into covenant, have solemnly engaged to be governed by the voice of the major part, in all administrations of government corresponding with their several compacts.—The several states having thus adopted and established civil constitutions, they organized their governments, by filling every department, with rulers and officers, for the due administration of justice, agreeably to the principles of their governmental establishment. And each state, in order to secure to themselves, the blessings of their independent governments against intestine feuds and foreign invasions, have entered into solemn covenant with each other according to the federal constitution.—Thus the wisdom and [6] power of all these states are united for the support and defence of every part. And in order further to secure the tranquility and happiness of these republicks, our Foederal Council or Congress have entered into treaties of alliance with foreign governments, upon principles of mutual advantage:—They have also entered into treaties of peace and commerce, in the capacity of the Supreme Executive Council of the United States.

Thus there is a most important connection in our governments, beginning in our distinct governmental compacts, running through every branch of civil administration; reaching up to our national confederation; and extending to all our national treaties of alliance, peace and commerce, and all our national engagements. This connection ought ever to be attended to, by every subject, by all our governments, and by our confederate power, in order to secure the good of the whole, and of every part. It is then, of the greatest importance, that each State in the Union should exert themselves, both rulers and people, to support their civil constitutions, and the administrations of government.—The respective constitutions of the states are in general doubtless well adapted to secure the great end of government. [7] The several states have formed and adopted such civil compact, as they supposed was best adapted to their situation, and ability; and such as they presumed would best secure their liberties, property and life.—They have summoned their united wisdom in this great undertaking; and have had the wisdom and experience of many ages past to improve upon, and to guard them against mistakes:—nor is it supposeable, that there is any constitution of government, or any mode of administration, in any kingdom or state on the earth, that is better adapted to render the subjects happy than the constitutions and administrations of government in these states, were they strictly adhered to and supported.

But then, we are not to suppose, that these constitutions are perfect, or without such errors, as may in some instances, operate to the injury of some individuals. It is not in the power of the most enlightened politicians always to foresee the operations of all principles of government and modes of administration, so as to prevent the evils that may arise from them. It is ever the wisdom of all men to fix their governments upon an establishment, that will come as nigh perfection as possible: But the most perfect civil governments will ever come far short [8] of this. There is not, nor can there be, any government absolutely perfect in its constitution and adminstration in every respect, but only the moral government of God. But then after any people have adopted, and voluntarily established, a civil compact, which is the result of their united wisdom, they ought to adhere to, and endeavor to support it; and in this case alterations and innovations may be dangerous, and without any beneficial effects. If all men would conform to the virtue, or the moral government of God, civil government would be unnecessary. They might then all continue secure in a state of nature; and might enjoy their natural rights without giving up any of them, for the security of those that remained in their hands. But the human mind, is not yet formed to such a state of moral improvement, as to admit of this. The necessity of having civil governments arises from the moral corruptions of mankind. But it is difficult for any man to determine, otherwise than by experience, how much power must be lodged in any government, to secure the subjects from the vices of one another, and render them the most happy.

But, it has been generally observed from experience, that republican governments have not in [9] their operation, answered this important end, so effectually as some other mode, and constitution. All the republics that have existed, through many ages, have been convulsed by their vices; and they have generally come to dissolution, for want of consistency and energy: And it has been supposed by many wise politicians in Europe, as well as feared by many in America, that these States would prove, that they were incapable of governing themselves upon republican principles. The States, however, we trust, will not coincide with such a supposition. Well might we presume and hope at the period of the revolution, that the Americans were possessed of wisdom and virtue, to enable them to form and support a republic with consistency and energy. —Though we had the follies, the vices and ill success of all preceeding republicks to check our hopes, yet we presumed that the wisdom and virtue of the people of this country would carry civil improvements higher than all that had gone before them; and enable them to support the honor and dignity of an independent, and powerful republic. They are now making the experiment. And it is now, doubtless, in the power of the states, under God, to become great and happy. But in order to this, they must be possessed of public virtue [10] sufficient to enable them to support their governments. The very existence of republican governments, depends upon public virtue. By public virtue I would be understood to mean, such an attachment to the interest of the public as shall excite the subjects of government voluntarily to support the constitution and laws, even though it should in some instances be much to their present injury. Nothing short of this will be sufficient to support a government, that devolves into the hands of the people annually, or in short periods. There must be in the minds of the people a disposition to support the constitution, the laws and the various officers of government in the exercise of constitutional powers, or all government must cease. Under despotic governments, public virtue, in the major part of the people, is not so necessary for the support of government. In this case, a supreme uncontroulable power will compel the subjects to obedience; nor is resistance in this case practicable without the greatest hazard and difficulty. In the beginning of the contest with Great-Britain, the people of the States, in general, seemed disposed to run the greatest hazards, to expend even half their property, and to expose their lives at the point of the sword, in order to extricate themselves from the oppressions of [11] tyranny; and they entered into a civil compact by mutual consent, that life and property might be more secure. They fought and obtained all their desires. At the conclusion of the war they were full of expectation. They looked back and viewed the difficulties they had passed through, and the dangers to which they had been exposed: They looked forward, and contemplated their rising greatness. Both Europe and America echoed honor to our arms. And it seems as though a view of these important transactions, and our noble prospects, would carry the states above all future difficulties. The states were then masters of an extensive country, perhaps equal, in a complex view, to any upon the globe. They had conquered, and were in possession of a free and independent government. Nations viewed them in a light of great importance; and several of the potentates of Europe recognized their independence, and entered into treaties of alliance with them. This was the political situation of the states, when they obtained peace with the government of Britain. And they are yet in possession of these excellent liberties and advantages. But the spirit, that carried them through former difficulties, seems to be declining, and threatens the introduction [12] of consequences of the most serious nature. Many that were most active in effecting our governmental revolution, seem to be inimical to, and are endeavoring to overturn our republics. This is a matter really paradoxical, as there can be no visible prospect of the least advantage finally from such an attempt, even to the insurgents themselves.—If the people of the states cannot be happy under, and will not support the governments they have already established, it is evident they will never voluntarily support, nor will they be happy under any constitution of government whatever. They have voluntarily entered into civil compacts, and such as they presumed were most free from errors and defects. They retain a right of annually electing their Legislators and Supreme Executive Magistrates; and the right of these elections devolving into their hands annually gives them an effectual check upon the exercise of all unconstitutional power. In case of any mal-administration in the officers of government, they are liable to impeachment and trial by their equals, and to be removed from office. The interest of those, who have the power of legislation, being one with the interest of their subjects, has a tendency to induce them to consult the interest of the people in their legislations. And [13] should the subjects ever presume, that they labour under any grievances, they have the right of remonstrating and petitioning in an orderly manner as distinct corporations for redress. Thus whilst the governments are vested with sufficient power to secure the great end of government among a virtuous people, there are in the several constitutions, sufficient checks provided against all exorbitant power; and the subjects that would subvert such a constitution of government as this, must be actuated not by their virtues, but their vices.—And if they cannot bear up under the restrictions, laws and orders of such a government, surely they would not find in themselves public virtue sufficient for supporting any government, in which less extensive powers were vested; but they would be restless and dissatisfied under every government, and would return to a state of nature, unless their wills were bent by some irresistible force.

If such a general disaffection should prevail against our governments as to issue in a civil war, many weary weighty evils would be the result, without one single general benefit or advantage. Life and property would be then more insecure than they would be in a state of nature. Every man's word would [14] be turned against his fellow; and mutual jealousy, resentment and malice, would operate in acts of the greatest cruelty. Our republics would become one general scene of plunder and slaughter. Thus vexation would harrass the mind; and by our own crimes we should be reduced to a condition of extreme poverty. Our national debts would be continually accumulating, whilst we were rendering ourselves less and less able to discharge them; all these civil commotions, instead of placing us under a government, which would render us more happy than we might be under our present governments, would leave us in a state of nature, or would probably introduce a government that was absolute; for if by experience it was evident that our governments were overturned for want of energy, necessity would lead us to establish a government vested with more extensive power. Anarchy has a direct tendency to the introduction of tyranny. This is abundantly evident from the experience of ages. The States of America will not long continue without a government that has energy, though they should be unable to retain their different civil constitutions. Some power or other will rise up and give them law. So long as there are powerful nations in Europe, America will be viewed as an object worth their attention. And should our [15] republicks be overthrown, and should we not be able to govern ourselves, some power or powers in Europe will interpose, and fix a chain upon our necks which will cause us to couch under the burden.

But it is highly supposeable, should the states be involved in civil war, that Great-Britain or some other power, would so interfere, as to prevent our determining whether we should have been able again to establish our governments. In this case we could have no great prospect of any thing, but subjection to foreign matters.—Britain would eagerly grasp such an opportunity to retrieve her losses, and spend her resentment upon a people who had formerly bid defiance to her power. And, although France has been, and still continues to be our magnanimous ally, yet if our governments were convulsed or overthrown, she would be justified, upon the best national principles, in interfering to secure the demands she has upon us. Thus the states being convulsed and rent in sunder by intestine contentions, and foreign invasions, would present a picture of the greatest calamities; and demonstrate the impossibility of any republic long existing, in this state of moral imperfection.

[16] Are these, my fellow-citizens, observations that have the support of reason, or not? Consider and examine for yourselves: Consider well the nature, the necessity and operations of governments: Consider well the danger of dissaffection to your own governments, and the distressing consequences of anarchy and civil wars.

Look around you: view your present political situation, and your political connections with nations in Europe. You have, by your late achievements, obtained honor with nations of the world; and you ought to strive to retain it.—Let us not by our vices tarnish all our glory, and plunge ourselves into a state of national ruin. Our situation is critical and dangerous; and our national vices are the only cause:

but it is not yet too late to reform, and to become and continue to
be happy as a nation. Our civil constitutions and administrations must
be supported, or we can reasonably expect nothing but national ruin.
Nor is it in the power of the wisest statesman to draw and support
our civil compacts, and honor and support the authority of the officers
of government. Those that are in administration doubtless endeavor
to [17] manage the affairs of government in general with fidelity. But
it is not a matter of astonishment if there be some ill designing men
in office, or places of administration. This, it is probable, may be the
case in all governments. But our civil rulers, as a body at least, deserve
our confidence and support. But should those in administration commit
an error, this ought not to disaffect us to our governments. Their
business as legislators is complicated and difficult; and it would be
beyond the wisdom of any politicians on the earth to manage, at all
times, the weighty affairs of government in our present situation,
without incurring censures from some in the community. Or should
individuals in government, be detected in criminal proceedings, our
civil constitution directs us how to proceed. Such persons are liable
to impeachment, and upon conviction of mal-conduct they shall be
displaced. What more could we desire for a guard, in this case, of our
liberties? can it be prudent and constitutional—can it be doing justice
to the public interest, to clamour against government, and attempt
to subvert it, on account of the misconduct of some particular persons
in administration, while at the same time our civil compact points us
to an easy remedy, that can be attended with no fatal consequences?
or should [18] the general administration of government be unconstitutional and subject us to grievances, we have a constitutional mode
for obtaining redress. We are authorized to assemble as towns, in an
orderly manner, to remonstrate and petition for redress of grievances:
and in this case our rulers will doubtless retract, and afford us relief,
upon their being convinced of their mistakes and deviations. They are
chosen from amongst ourselves; and their interest is involved on the
welfare of the public; and they must necessarily bear a portion of the
common burden, and feel our common calamities.

But should we not be able, in this way, to obtain redress, we
surely may do it within the period of one year. Their powers of
administration are taken from their hands annually by the constitution;
and we have then a constitutional right to another election of the
officers of government; we may elect such persons as we think will

best promote the public interest. Surely then it must be very impolitic to throw the public into convulsions, and attempt to overturn our governments to relieve ourselves from an unconstitutional administration, since we may have it in our power to effect it, without injury to the public.—It can never be justifiable to throw the states into a civil war which perhaps could continue [19] years to obtain redress of grievances, when it might be effected within one year constitutionally, and without any dangerous or injurious consequences. Were the people in the states groaning under the burdens of an absolute and tyrannical government, which could not be thrown off or rectified, without their rising to arms, the case would be altogether different from our present situation. Then seven years war might be compensated perhaps, by an hundred years enjoyment of liberty and its consequent blessings. When we revolted from the British government and flew to arms, it was the only possible method by which we supposed we should be able to recover and enjoy the liberties and blessings of a free government: the supreme executive power of government was not lodged in our hands, or in a person of our appointment.—But under our present governments, all our rulers and officers are of our own creating, and are amendable to us according to certain modes pointed out in our civil compacts. Let us then look about us, and be wise, and make a judicious improvement of our national liberties; and let us resolve to exert all our power in supporting our excellent governments.

I am far from supposing that the number is at present very considerable in the states, that are inimical [20] to our civil governments. The most substantial, and indeed a very large majority of the people are determined to abide by, and endeavor to support the governments: and I hope and trust that they will stand up and defend them against all opposition. But there are clamours and insurrections by so large a number of people in some of the states, that they afford a melancholy aspect, and indicate the danger of their terminating in serious consequences.—And it is of great importance, that those who wish for the support of our civil constitutions, exert themselves to strengthen the hands of government: to remove errors and mistakes from the minds of those that are misinformed; and guard themselves against being misled, and overcome by wickedly designing men, that wish to see our states sink into a state of anarchy and ruin,—Nothing is now necessary under the providence of God, for our becoming great and happy, but a close attachment to our governments, and prudence, fidelity and honesty in our proceedings and engagements. It is true, however, that the states labour under great embarassments in their commerce, and their finances; and they are burthened with a very considerable national debt. But diligence, oeconomy, patience, honesty and perseverance, in pursuing the great object of government, [21] will carry them above all their difficulties and embarrassments. A very considerable part of our national burdens originated from our own vices, from our dishonesty and luxury, and from an uneasy and discontented disposition of some particular classes of subjects, who have supposed that their civil liberties and independence might be enjoyed without expence, and would enable them to throw off every burden, without their contributing any thing as an adequate compensation. This is an idea incompatible with a state of civil society. No government can be established, defended and exercised without considerable expence; and the reward of this expence is the protection and defence of our remaining natural rights, and the defence of life, and of that property which is guaranteed to the subject by the civil compact. Many of the people in the states made great mistakes immediately after the conclusion of the war, and have persisted in them 'till absolute necessity has obliged them in some measure to desist. The exorbitant importation of foreign luxuries has introduced most pernicious consequences. It has encouraged idleness and every species of extravagance; and has in a great measure, robbed us of a circulating medium of trade and business.—The specie that has been exported from this [22] country in payment for foreign luxuries, might have been sufficient to pay the one quarter or one half of our national debt, had we prudently kept it amongst us. We have imprudently expended our monies in luxuries; and now we begin to feel the consequence, and groan under burdens for want of a circulating medium. But our past errors ought to excite us to a reformation, and to different practices in future. We have not yet tried the experiment of thoroughly retrenching in our unnecessary expenditures. And should we pursue this object, so far as we might do, and yet live comfortably, we should make a prodigious saving, which would enable us to diminish our burdens very considerably. There are but few necessaries of life, but what we might obtain from our own soil, and manufactories. The one half perhaps of what we now expend of foreign commodities and manufactures, may be classed among our superfluities. The gauzes, ribbons, silks, feathers, flowers &c. for which we export our monies

to Europe, are moths to our purses and rob us of that cash, which
ought to be advanced for the payment of our debts. Rum and tea are
other superfluities in general; and there is ten times so much of them
consumed in the states as is beneficial: and the revenue that might
arise from denying ourselves those [23] superfluities, would pay every
farthing annually of the demands our governments have upon us. But
we will not in general retrench in the use of them; we are prodigal
and extravagant, and then complain of the burdens of governments.
We ought first to retrench, be frugal, be industrious, and then we
shall know our wealth and ability. But we have but very trifling
reasons for complaints of the burdens of a good government, 'till we
throw aside our superfluities and luxuries.

It is true our national debt accumulated by the war is very
considerable: Nor could we rationally presume it would be otherwise.
At the time that we commenced war with Great Britain, we had not
monies in fund to enable us to carry it on. We were without warlike
resources; and could devise no method to defend our liberties, but by
involving ourselves in debt to individuals amongst ourselves, and to
nations in Europe. The people of the state well knew that this was
the only method, by which we could maintain our independence; and
they consented to these debts being contracted by their legislatures,
their agents and ambassadors. And doubtless they were as sparing in
borrowing monies, and in entering into engagements, as the necessity
of our [24] circumstances would admit of. And doubtless the monies
were expended with all possible oeconomy and prudence. And instead
of our national debt being so large as it is, we may wonder it is not
larger, considering our situation, and the long period of the war. The
expenditures of Great Britain within the period of one year were nearly
as much as the whole of our present national debt contracted through
the whole of the war. The whole of our national debt amounts to
about *ten millions three hundred thousand pounds,* our lawful money. This
is collectively a large sum for the states to pay. But when it is divided
equally to the citizens of the states, according to their ability, it is
not a demand that they are beyond the possibility of discharging. The
proportion of the debt, that will fall to a citizen to pay that is worth
six hundred pounds, will not exceed *one hundred dollars.* And surely a
man of such an estate may, if frugal and diligent, be able to discharge
this in the term of five or ten years, without diminishing his real
estate, or capital. And can it be wise and prudent to injure or

overthrown the governments of the states to obtain a freedom from discharging such a demand? But this measure would only bring us more and more into debt and increase our calamities. Were not our liberties worth purchasing [25] at so moderate a price. Was it not much better to pay six or ten or even twenty percent upon our estates, than to lose all our liberties, to become slaves to foreign masters, and to have all our property insecure?

Let us judge like men of reason, be honest and speak our minds.—It must however be allowed, that we must at present find it very difficult to discharge this debt speedily for want of a larger circulation of coin. But we may now perhaps, annually, so exert ourselves as to discharge the interest arising: and this may suffice, if we are honest, and exert ourselves so far as possible.—If we are really honest, and disposed to do the best we can to pay our foreign creditors, they may consider our situation, and wait with patience 'till we can command specie to pay the principal. But the way to acquire this ability, is to vest Congress with ample powers to enter into treaties of commerce, to be diligent and frugal, and to bring the balance of trade in our favour, so that we can receive cash in return for our own productions. We must for this purpose also be so honest as to endeavor to discharge our private debts, and renounce all ideas of introducing paper money and tender acts, to the injury of creditors. All this is necessary, in order to call [26] forth the specie that is accumulated and retained by men of affluence. But it is surely for our interest to exert ourselves to the utmost, to diminish and pay our national debt; for it must be effected sooner or later, or we shall bring upon us the resentments and power of European creditors. It is a thing absolutely impossible for the states to avoid paying their foreign creditors. Should the subjects of the states attempt a subversion of their governments for this purpose, it would sink them into a state of ruin. Or should the governments refuse to make payment, they would lose all their national honor and credit, and would bring the power of their creditors upon them, to obtain satisfaction. In this case our soil must be given up to discharge a debt, we might have paid with our monies, without diminishing our capital. And if America should prove so base, so dishonorable, and so dishonest as this, her vices would give her a shock, from which she would not perhaps speedily if ever recover. The states would become a reproach, a hissing and a bye word among the nations. And should they ever recover from their state of ruin, they would not find it easy to form alliances with nations for their safety and defence. Foreign kingdoms would be jealous of their honor and fidelity. Nor would the states in this situation find their credit to be sufficient to borrow monies [27] on loan, to enable them to defend their liberties and property in case of an invasion. Thus they would be deserted perhaps by all the world, as unfit for any national alliances or connections; and they would become liable to the attack of other kingdoms, whilst they would obtain no foreign aid.

Thus every person of honesty and common sense may see, that our national debt must be discharged sooner or later, or our national ruin will inevitably ensue.—We ought then to be patient under our national burdens and diminish our debt as fast as we possibly can.— There seem to be some persons in our republics that are oppressed from some cause, and wish to relieve themselves, by one bold stroke, in subverting our governments; and the method they would pursue, will only add ten fold weight to their burdens. Some of their burdens that they cast upon the government, originate from their own vices, and they must relinquish them, before they can expect rationally to throw off their embarrassments. Others of their burdens originate from the imperfections of the present state, and the imperfections connected with a state of civil society, which are unavoidable. But yet such a state is far preferable to a state of nature. It is entirely unreasonable for subjects to ascribe all their sufferings to the mal-administrations [28] of government, whilst they originate principally from other causes.

It is of importance that such unreasonable restless minds should be brought to a better understanding of the nature and importance of government, and that they be taught due obedience to the constitution and laws. An attempt to subvert the constitution of government, or to obstruct the administration of justice, is generally under all governments, accounted and made high treason; and the offence is of the most enormous size, and the highest kind that can be committed against men.—It is an offence that is capital, being an attempt upon the life of every subject in the community. The safety and life of all the subjects depend upon the civil compact and the due administration of justice; and the person, who would destroy either aims at the destruction of all the community, in a rational and legal sense of explication. High treason is then intentional murder and robbery, and by all civilized states is wisely made a capital offence.—This is a matter that the subjects of all governments ought to consider and understand, and to govern themselves accordingly.

There are some persons that would pretend to [29] make matter of conscience of all their actions, but those that relate to matters of government. They pretend to much religion, and to be much more sanctified than others. But they lose their consciences, when they act as subjects of civil government; and they will pretend it is not morally wrong to rise up against a civil constitution or the laws of a state, if they are not in all things agreeable to the humours and taste. But in this case they really violate the most solemn compact or agreement. If they were dissatisfied with the civil constitution, they were at liberty to elope, and put themselves under some other government. But if they continued under the constitution they consented and implicitly engaged to abide by the principles of it, and to conform to the orders of a constitutional administration. This is the case by just explication, whether they did actually give their vote or not for the constitution. Therefore by their rising against the constitution or the just administrations of government, they violate a solemn covenant or compact. And in doing this, they must sin against their own consciences, if they have any, and they sin against God. It is as criminal, and it is a more heinous offence, to violate a public contract, than a private or individual one, because the consequences may be much more extensive. Every man and especially those who [30] make any pretentions of religion and honesty, ought to consider this. All governmental compacts are formed and established by the majority of the people; and must be considered as binding upon all the community, so long as such a compact continues, and all opposition to it by the minority or individuals is a violation of a covenant, is high treason and rebellion.

But we may further observe that it is not only of importance to support the constitutions of our respective governments, and a constitutional administration; but it is of importance to support our federal union. By this union the wisdom and power of all the states become united, in the direction and support of the republics. Had not the states entered into this combination, they must respectively depend on their own strength to defend themselves from intestine feuds and foreign invasions: and in this case they might become an easy prey to their enemies. Without this, they could not have recovered their liberties, nor can they long support their independence. The states severally are not known to the nations of Europe as sovereign and independent. They are known only in the capacity of one united republic, represented by Congress. Annihilate, then our confederation and Congress, and all our [31] national alliances, treaties and connections with the sovereignties of Europe will cease; and we shall no longer be considered as an united and independent republic. And in this case, we should become the sport of the jealosy and various interests of the respective states, and might be convulsed and rent in sunder, by the powers of our governments being opposed to each other. It is then of importance that we support the union upon the principles of the confederation; and conform, as distinct governments, to all the constitutional recommendations and ordinances of Congress.—And we ought to honor that respectable body, and enable them to support the honor and dignity of their station. In order to this, we ought as far as possible to enable them, by payment of our taxes, to fulfill their public engagements. By the confederation they are authorised to borrow monies and engage payment, in the name and in behalf of the states. And their situation must be very disagreeable, when pressed for payment, not to have it in their power to do it, not even the interest of the debt. And when their credit is injured, the credit of the states is equally affected, as they are the representative body of all our governments. We ought, then, by every safe and constitutional method, to enable them to collect and establish a sufficient continental fund to answer the demands of our nation, government and [32] creditors. In order to this, we should do well to give them an exclusive power, for a term of years, to levy and collect a duty of impost according to their request, upon the importations of the several states. Had this been done at the commencement of the peace, our national finances would now have been on a respectable establishment, and our national debt would have been diminished.—The states in general have acceded to the requisition or desires of Congress; and it is to be hoped that all the states will speedily grant full powers for the purpose. The states ought also to support Congress in all their national engagements, alliances and treaties. All this is of great importance in order to our national happiness.

But it is much more easy to prescribe what ought to be done, than it is to persuade the people in general to practice accordingly. Never was there a people upon the face of the earth that had it more in their power to become happy, as a nation, than the people of this country. They have been exalted to heaven in point of privilege both civil and religious. But a wise improvement of them, only, will render them honorable, wealthy and powerful, and ensure them peace and happiness. They ought then to be jealous of themselves, lest they misapply [33] and abuse their liberties. Could the people of the states in general, obtain just conceptions of the people in other kingdoms of the world, groaning under their lords and task-masters, and compelled to obedience by arbitrary power, they would prize and hold fast their dear bought liberties; and would shudder at the idea of being either under an absolute government, or in a state of anarchy, as both are attended with most weighty calamities. They would then be likely to prize their civil constitutions, and honor and support the civil magistracy. But what the future political condition of this country will be is not in the power of the most extensive human sagacity to foresee. If we could foresee how the people would in future periods conduct in a political view, we could form a judgment of their future condition. If they should by their contentions and convulsions overturn their governments, they will be plunged into a state of the greatest calamities. Should they in future, exercise public virtue sufficient to support their republics, they will become wealthy, honorable, powerful and happy. But every judicious and honest mind must, when it considers the present licentious disposition of many persons, be depressed, and elated alternately by hope and fear. These states are now the only free and independent [34] republics of any importance, that are upon the globe. The states of Greece and Rome were overturned by their licentious abuse of liberty.—The states of Holland were obliged to deviate from republican principles, in order to prevent the dissolution of their government. We ought, then, to take warning from the misconduct of the other republics in the abuse of liberty, and avoid similar practices. Our virtues or vices will, through every period of our republics determine our condition. We cannot reasonably depend on the support of the providence of the great ruler of the world, if we pursue practices that tend to our national ruin. But, we shall be suffered to plunge into a state of ruin, and feel all the consequences of our crimes.

The happiness of the states depends under God upon their own wisdom and virtue. And they have every inducement to pursue practices that tend to the support of these republics. They have purchased their inheritance and liberties at a great price. With much labour, and many difficulties, they obtained possession of, and defended their country against the savages. And they have defended their rights against the encroachments of British tyranny. This has cost them the blood of thousands of their fathers and brethren, and a vast consumption of property. This has called forth their wisdom and united exertions for more than eight years in a war with Great Britain. From small beginnings their numbers have become great, and their landed improvements, [35] extensive. A large field is now opened before them for enterprize. From these beginnings and improvements, they have it in their power to become wise, great, powerful and happy. They, by their political virtues and conduct, may fix the worldly conditions of millions yet unborn. If by their vices they subvert their governments, anarchy, a state of nature, or absolute tyranny will be the condition of future generations. The political actions of this generation may have an influence on the actions and political situation of generations for centuries to come. If the people of these states now support and establish their governments, and cultivate the virtues that tend to national happiness, future generations may from hence derive wisdom, liberty and blessings, which may descend through centuries, and raise this young empire to a state of greatness far exceeding our present conceptions. These are considerations, that will be to all minds of sensibility, as weighty as mountains, and stimulate them to the most noble political actions. These are considerations that will overbalance every spark of ambition for honor or interest, at the expence of our governments, or the good of the public. These are ideas that will induce every honest mind to resolve to support our civil constitution, and our confederation; and fulfil all national alliances, treaties and engagements, though difficult to be accomplished. Let us then, my fellow citizens, prove, that we think and act upon a generous and extensive scale in our political conduct. Let us demonstrate that we love not only ourselves, but also our country, and wish well to those millions who will act upon the stage in our places after our names are enrolled amongst the dead. Let us demonstrate that we not only [36] wish to be free, but also that we are determined to be honest, to be virtuous, and can surmount burdens and difficulties in the way to national glory. Let us stand up to our social compacts, be patient under unavoidable burdens, be frugal and industrious, and retrench in our unnecessary expenditures. Let us not suffer the unhallowed hands of licentiousness, vain ambition or covetousness, to touch our liberties, or break in upon our constitutional rights. Let us elect to public offices and places of government, from time to time, men that we have reason to presume are the wisest, the most honest, and such as have the good of their country at heart; and let us acquiesce in, and endeavor to support, all their good administrations. Unreasonable clamours against government let us discountenance and despise. Tumults and insurrections against the constitutions, the laws and administrations of government, let us endeavor to suppress and discourage.—These are evils that spread their influence like witchcraft, and lead on to the most ruinous consequences. The convulsions of a political nature, in several of our states, have probably, before this period, spread through most of the courts and kingdoms of Europe.— Some doubtless lament our licentious folly: Others rejoice in our confusion. Shall we demonstrate to all the world, that we fought for liberty only to abuse it? and shall we prove that we cannot govern ourselves, but must submit to some tyrant amongst ourselves, or to foreign task-masters?—Let us then resolve to be virtuous: We shall then support our governments, we shall be FREE, INDEPENDENT and HAPPY.

N———b-H———n, December 4, 1786

[43]

DEAN SWIFT

*Causes of a Country's Growing Rich
and Flourishing*

WORCESTER, 1786

A content analysis by Richard Merrit showed that around 1765 the
colonists began referring to themselves in the newspapers more
frequently as Americans than as Englishmen. A content analysis of
the press in the 1780s would undoubtedly show the rise of Federalist
commercial influence. This short piece is an efficient expositor of this
growing theory of political economy and illustrative of how it was
usually presented—in short, pithy statements rather than in lengthy
essays, as is perhaps more typical of those commercially oriented rather
than theoretically oriented. Note how some of the public virtues are
now hitched to economic development and prosperity rather than to
political liberty. Compare, for example, with the piece by The
Tribune in 1766. Swift's article appears in the issue of the *Worcester
Magazine* (Massachusetts) published during the last week in
June, 1786.

I. The first cause of a kingdom's flourishing is, the fruitfulness
of the soil to produce the necessaries and conveniences of life, not only
sufficient for the inhabitants but for exportation into other countries.

II. The second cause is, the industry of the people in working
up all their native commodities to the last degree of manufacture.

III. The third is, the conveniency of safe ports, and havens, to
carry out their own goods as much manufactured, and bring in those

of others as little manufactured as the nature of mutual commerce will allow.

IV. The fourth is, that the natives should as much as possible, export and import their goods in vessels of their own timber, and made in their own country.

V. The fifth is, a free trade with all sovereign countries which will permit them, except those who are at war with their own Prince or State.

VI. The sixth is, by being governed by laws made with their own consent, for otherwise they are not a free people.—And therefore all appeals for justice, or applications for favour or preferment to another country, are so many grievious impoverishments.

VII. The seventh is, by improvement of land, encouragement of agriculture, and thereby increasing the number of people, without which any country, however blessed by nature, must continue poor.

VIII. The eighth is, the residence of the Prince or chief administer of the civil power.

IX. The ninth is, the concourse of foreigners for education, curiosity, or pleasure, or as to a general mart of trade.

X. The tenth is, by disposing of all offices of honour, profit, or trust, only to natives, or at least with very few exceptions, where strangers have long inhabited the country, and are supposed to understand and regard the interest of it as their own.

XI. The eleventh is, when the rents of lands and profits of employment are spent in the country which produced them, and not in another, the former of which will certainly happen where the love of our native country prevails.

XII. The twelfth is, by the publick revenues being all spent and employed at home except on the occasion of a foreign war.

XIII. The thirteenth is, where the people are not obliged, unless they find it for their own interest or conveniency to receive any monies except of their own coinage, by a publick mint, after the manner of all civilized nations.

XIV. The fourteenth is, a disposition of the people of a country to wear their own manufactures, and import as few incitements to luxury, either in cloths, furniture, food or drink, as they can live conveniently without.

[44]

JOSEPH LATHROP 1731–1820

A *Miscellaneous Collection of Original Pieces*
(Selections)

SPRINGFIELD, 1786

The first Lathrop arrived at Massachusetts Bay Colony in 1634, but the family moved west, and Joseph was born in Norwich, Connecticut. Immediately after graduating from Yale he was ordained as pastor of the Congregational Church in West Springfield, Massachusetts, a post that he held for more than sixty years. He became one of the most widely known and highly respected ministers of the gospel in New England. A seven-volume collection of his sermons was published near the end of his career, but many other sermons and essays are found only as separate pamphlets. Reproduced here are three pieces published under the name Censor and five published under The Reformer. Industry, frugality, virtue, religion, and their relation to government were typical topics for Lathrop. Reading Lathrop back to back with the pieces by John Leland, a Baptist, that appear later in this collection will dramatize the split during the founding era on the relationship of religion to politics. Leland defends a position most comfortable to the Federalists, while Lathrop here assumes a relationship between religion and politics congruent with the position held by the Whigs dominant before the advent of the Federalists.

JOSEPH LATHROP 1731–1820

The CENSOR.
NUMBER II.
GOVERNMENT.
Quid tristes querimoniae,
Si non supplicio culpa reciditur?
Quid leges sine moribus
Vanae proficiunt————?

The natural passions of mankind lead them, and their natural wants impel [42] them to society; for neither can their desires be gratified, nor their miseries relieved in a state of solitude. In society there must be government. Not only the vices, but the natural imperfections of the human race require it. Were men ever so virtuous, yet unless they were also perfectly wise, a diversity of interest, opinion, humour and inclination would call for some superintending and controuling power. In the prophetick descriptions of the happiest period, that mankind are ever to enjoy below the skies, government makes an essential part; nor is it omitted in the inspired representations of celestial bliss. In a society as virtuous as may be supposed, government would have little more to do, than direct the common prudentials; but so much, at least, must be done. A virtuous society cannot be happy without government; a vicious one cannot subsist without it. Peccant humours prevailing to a certain degree destroy the natural body; and there is a certain pitch of vice that dissolves society; government must restrain the latter, as medicine checks the former. In proportion as society is more extensive and populous; more civilized and refined, more opulent and commercial, and is farther removed from the simplicity of nature, government necessarily [43] becomes more complex and difficult; and as vice more prevails, government must be more severe. Various forms have taken place among the nations of the earth. Which form is most eligible, has been much controverted among politicians: but as well may physicians dispute, what is the best remedy for diseases. In both cases, the condition of the subject is to be considered. Medicine will not make a patient healthy without a proper regimen, nor government render a people happy without virtue. The preference of one form to another is perhaps more in speculation than reality. A virtuous people under any form well administered will be happy; a people deep sunk in vice and corruption will be miserable under the best form. A people will usually run sooner or later into such a kind of government as is most suitable to their manners and habits. Among a virtuous people there is always a love of liberty, and their government, whatever be the form, will be administered in such a manner as to gratify this passion. A people that have lost their virtue, soon lose their passion for liberty, and of course lose the object. Their government, however liberal in its principles, becomes rigorous in its administration; and they can subsist [44] under no other. Virtue will be free; vice must be enslaved. A people that would be happy must support the honour and dignity of government; and, that they may enjoy the greatest possible freedom under it, they must zealously cultivate and generously encourage knowledge and virtue. The main body of a people cannot be politicians. They have not leisure to attend to, opportunity to be informed of, nor ability to understand all that variety of matters, which concern the community. Many things they must leave with implicit confidence to the wisdom and integrity of their rulers. But they all understand the nature and obligations of virtue. There is therefore no way, in which they can so effectually promote their own and the general freedom and happiness, as by maintaining virtue in private practice, and encouraging it in society. No man is so inconsiderable, but he may render important services to mankind in this way. He that practises every virtue in private life, and trains up a family in virtuous principles and manners, is no useless or unimportant member of society. In elective governments the people may encourage and promote virtue by a wise and judicious choice of rulers. They should always esteem it unsafe to commit their interests [45] into the hands of men who are themselves void of those virtues on which the happiness of society depends. Virtue exemplified in government will diffuse its salutary influence through the society. The foundation of all social virtue is a belief in the existence and government of a Deity. A regard to the Deity cannot be maintained without some publick exercises of religion. Social worship is therefore necessary to the happiness of society, and to the easy administration of government, and in this view worthy the attention of every legislature, while in a higher view it deserves the regard of the individual.

JOSEPH LATHROP 1731–1820

The CENSOR.
NUMBER III.
INDUSTRY.
——Labor omnia vincit
Improbus, et duris urgens in rebus egestas.

Most of the evils, which are matters of complaint at the present day, are such as it is in our own power to remedy. If we would be as virtuous as a people may [46] be, we should be as happy as a people need to be. Virtue would remove many of our grievances, and enable us to bear the rest. It will be replied, 'Virtue generally prevailing might do great things, but this is not to be expected.' Will you then look for happiness in some other way? You cannot succeed, unless the course of nature, and the plan of the supreme government should be reversed. 'But will it avail for me singly to be virtuous, when I cannot expect the generality will be so?' Make the experiment: Perhaps others will be as wise as you: Your example may possibly have some influence; at least you may relieve your own mind, and lighten your own burthens. If general virtue helps society, private virtue will help the individual: And then how do you know, but there is another world where your virtue will turn to your account, though it should do you but little good here? 'But what are the virtues of immediate use to society, and of chief importance at the present day?' *Industry* is undoubtedly one. This is a country which affords all the means not only of subsistence, but of wealth. But means must be applied or the end is not attained. Greater industry may be necessary here, than in some other climes; but this is no unhappiness. [47] A people that grow rich suddenly and without much labour, soon become luxurious and effeminate. They presently sink again into poverty, or their wealth is confined to a few. They lose their strength and vigour and the spirit of liberty, and fall an easy prey to the first powerful invader or ambitious usurper. A habit of industry is first acquired by necessity, and, once acquired, it may continue for a while, after the necessity abates, unless their circumstances alter too suddenly. It strengthens the body, braces the mind, aids other virtues; it gives patience in adversity, courage in danger, and perseverance in difficulty. No people ever maintained their liberty long, after they ceased to be industrious, and became dissolute and luxurious. Agriculture ought to be one main object of industry in such a country, and at such a time as this. Our lands are our chief source of wealth; but lands uncultivated are like gold sleeping in the mines. It is culture only that makes them useful. Too great attention to commerce will soon introduce idleness and luxury; and though it may enrich a few particular persons, it will impoverish the country.

Our husbandry ought to be directed into such a channel, that after supplying our [48] own necessary consumption, the surplus may bring us not merely luxuries, but such foreign articles as will be really useful, and a sufficiency of silver and gold for a medium. Grain of various kinds, flax, sheep, pork, beef, butter, and cheese are commodities that may be turned to much better advantage, than those cargoes of horses and lumber, which are shipped for the West-Indies, only to bring in upon us a flood of ardent spirits, to drown our vitals and our morals.

To agriculture we must join the necessary arts of life, and the more useful and important branches of manufacture. We may purchase many articles cheaper, than we can manufacture them: but if we purchase them, they must be paid for: if we make them they are our own. Manufactures will promote industry, and industry contributes to health, virtue, riches and population. If we purchase our cloathing one half of our women must be idle, or only trifling: how then will those young women who depend on their labour, procure the next suit when they have worn out the present? If we manufacture, our men will be employed in procuring and preparing the materials; and our women will not be under a necessity of spending five afternoons in a week in giving and receiving visits, and [49] chatting round the tea-table. What they do is so much added to the wealth of the country. When industry becomes reputable among ladies in higher life, it will of course take place among all ranks. And the rosy cheek, the ruby lip, and the sparkling eye will then be deemed more beautiful, than the pale, sickly countenance. Vivacity, strength and activity will not then be thought too indelicate, coarse and masculine for a fine lady, nor will affected timidity, artificial faintings and laboured shrieks and startings be supposed to have charms.

JOSEPH LATHROP 1731–1820

The CENSOR.
NUMBER IV.
FRUGALITY.

Vivitur parvo bene, cui paternum
Splendet in mensa tenui falinum:
Nec leves somnos timor aut cupido
Serdidus aufert.

Industry and *frugality* are kindred virtues and similar in their principles and effects. They ought always to accompany [50] each other and go hand in hand, for neither without the other can be a virtue, or answer any valuable purpose to the individual or to society. He that is laborious only that he may have the means of extravagance and profuseness; and he that is parsimonious only that he may live in laziness and indolence, are alike remote from virtue. Each is governed by his strongest passion, and enslaved to his predominant vice. To live sparingly for the sake of amassing a useless heap, is not *frugality*, but *sordidness*. To live within the bonds of nature, that we may enjoy better health and may be more free from wordly embarrassments, is *prudence*. To live frugally, that we may be just to all men; may do more good to the indigent, and may be more useful to society is *virtuous*. *Decency* and *propriety* ordinarily require, that we live according to our rank and ability. But there are times, when *patriotism* calls upon those in affluence and high life, to fall a little below the usual mark, that their example may encourage moderation among others. As private oeconomy enriches the individual, so the prevalence of it would enrich the community. A country so deeply in debt, and subjected to so great expences, as [51] this country now is, should consider frugality as a cardinal virtue. Let it begin with particular persons and spread through the community; let it take place in families, nor be over looked in government; let it not be confined to the poorest, or the middle ranks; but appear among the rich and great. While the poor are frugal from *necessity*, and the common farmers and mechanics are frugal from *prudence*, let the opulent be frugal from *patriotism:* and if they would make their patriotism a still more excellent virtue, let the savings of extraordinary frugality be applied to some charitable purpose. For the rich no certain rules can be prescribed; their frugality must be voluntary and discretionary. People of moderate fortunes, and moderate incomes should aim at a regular conduct. Excuse a few hints, even though they may appear too trifling to be observed. If they appear worthy of notice, let them be carried into practice.

Spend not your money before you have earned it, nor promise it before you are sure of it. Promises made on other men's credit, or on mere contingencies are liable to fail. If you disappoint your neighbour often, you lose your credit, and his confidence, [52] and perhaps provoke a suit, which breaks friendship, disturbs your peace, augments your expence, and throws your money into the hands of those, whom you chiefly envy. Estimate your probable incomes, making some allowance for disappointments, and let your expences fall so much short, that something may be left at the year's end. He that daily consumes the fruits of daily labour is unprepared for the day of misfortune. Most men, if they will live within the bounds of nature, may by moderate industry, provide for themselves and their families. It is always reputable to live moderately, when we have not the means of living splendidly. Compute the needless consumption of ardent spirits for one year, and will it not make a sum worth saving? The example of others is not the standard by which we are to judge of extravagance, but our own circumstances and abilities. That may be extravagance in one, that would be parsimony in another. Enter not into too close connections with those of superior fortunes, if they are disposed to live faster, than you can follow. Never make a vain ostentation of wealth, which you don't possess, nor live at other men's expence, so long as you can live at your own. Waste not in indulgence, that time which you owe [53] to the duties of life, the culture of your mind, and the support and education of your family. Consume not in luxury the money, which you owe to your creditor or to the publick, or by which you might relieve your family from distress. When you see another grow rich, or *seem* to grow rich in any calling, conclude not that you could do the same, nor quit your own profession for one which you don't understand and have not the means of pursuing. Many have fallen by reaching at things too high for them. Lay out for yourself business to fill up your time, but not more than you can manage well. Be not in too great haste to be rich: The moderate profits of your own proper business are the surest, and the honest gains of industry and frugality are the most sweet, reputable and durable.

JOSEPH LATHROP 1731–1820

[143]   *The* REFORMER.
                         NUMBER I.

              Virtue the happiness of a people.

Men often complain of those evils, which are wholly of their own
procuring, and which it is in their own power to remove, whenever
they please. There is nothing more evident from reason, revelation
and common experience, than the tendency of virtue to the happiness,
and the tendency of vice to the misery of mankind, both in private
and social life; but while this is generally acknowledged in speculation,
it is much disregarded in practice. All expedients to relieve the
burthens and distresses of the day, without a general reform of manners,
will be but *palliatives:* [144] *This* will effect a RADICAL cure.

Let rulers, influenced by the fear of God, and by love to mankind
use all their power and authority to encourage righteousness, protect
innocence, redress wrongs and banish iniquity; let laws be made with
a single design to advance the general interest, and be executed with
diligence and fidelity; let people, in all ranks, conscientiously discharge
the duties of their respective stations; let justice and integrity take
place in all private intercourse; let benevolence operate in all exigencies
to excite mutual aid and succour, so that no man shall be miserable,
while it is in his neighbour's power to relieve him; in all controversies
between man and man or in society, let condescension immediately
step in to adjust the difference; let every man, in his private capacity,
maintain sobriety, purity, temperance, industry and self-government,
and attend more to the culture of his mind, the improvement of his
virtue, and the regulation of the manners of his domesticks, than to
the indulgence of pleasure or the accumulation of wealth; let this be
the general spirit and conduct of mankind, and what will be wanting
to make them as happy as the condition of mortals will permit, or as
beings in a state [145] of probation can reasonably desire?

But if, on the contrary, pride, selfishness, and the love of pleasure
reign among all ranks: if injustice, fraud, idleness, luxury, oppression
and other vices generally prevail, there is no need of special judgements
to make them miserable, and no need of a spirit of prophesy to foresee
their destruction. Every man therefore, as he regards his own and the
general happiness, is bound to practice virtue himself, and promote

it among others. This obligation immediately results from his present condition as a man, and from his relation to society, abstractly from the consideration of those more grand and solemn motives which religion proposes.

We have seen the time, when the people of this country, alarmed at the dangers which threatened them from a usurping and invading power, could unite in arms for the common defence. They thought no expence too great to be incurred, no sacrifice too dear to be made, that they might rescue their trembling liberties from the devouring jaws of oppression. Our social happiness is now in danger from another quarter, from the prevalence of vice and impiety, from our increasing luxury, extravagance, [146] selfishness and injustice: let us exert ourselves, with the same united ardour, to extirpate this internal enemy, as we have to repel a foreign enemy, and we may hope for equal success; and success in this attempt will give our liberties a firmer establishment and a more permanent security than all the successes of war.

The REFORMER.
NUMBER II.

Piety the basis of Virtue.

The necessity of virtue to the happiness of society, was shewn in a former number. It is no less evident that a belief of, and regard to the government of a Diety, is the only sure foundation of virtue. What motive can there be sufficient to engage men in the general practice of sobriety, justice, integrity and beneficence, and to restrain them from the contrary vices, if they can once disbelieve the doctrines of a divine government and a future retribution? The beauty and reasonablness of virtue, and its tendency to the happiness [147] of mankind in private and social life, though an argument of real truth and importance, yet is, in some respects, too refined to be clearly perceived, and in other respects, too disinterested to be strongly felt by men not used to such speculations, or not already formed to a benevolent temper. But the consideration of an ever present Deity, who exercises a righteous government in the world, and will bring

JOSEPH LATHROP 1731–1820

his rational subjects to a solemn judgment, and distribute his rewards and punishments in the most equitable manner, according to their real characters, is an argument of awful weight, and level to the lowest capacity. To talk of virtue independent of piety, is as absurd in morals, as it is, in nature, to talk of an animal that lives without breath. But how shall a sense of the Deity, his perfections and providence, and a future state, be generally diffused and maintained among a people, so as to become a principle prompting them to virtue, without some publick forms of social worship? No means can be imagined so conducive to this end, as that divine institution, which requires us, at stated times, to intermit the common labours and amusements of life, and unite in acknowledging the supreme governour of [148] the universe, in paying our devout adorations to him, and in hearing our duty to him and to one another inculcated upon us. The sabbath is an institution co-eval with man's creation; revived in the time of Moses, numbered with and placed on the same foot as the most important moral precepts, and constantly observed by the great founder of the christian dispensation and by his servants, whom he immediately authorized to disseminate his religion in the world. The observance of a sabbath and of social worship, is of such importance to the preservation of religion, and to the happiness of a people, that God enjoins it as a grand condition of his favour, and second only to a belief of his existence. 'Ye shall make no idols—I am the Lord your God. Ye shall keep my sabbaths and reverence my sanctuary; I am the Lord. If ye shall walk in my statutes, then will I give you rain in due season, and the land shall yield her increase; ye shall dwell therein safely. I will set my tabernacle among you, and my soul shall not abhor you.' If sabbaths, social worship and publick instructions should be discontinued, ignorance, vice and savageness of manners would soon ensue; virtue and even civility would, in a great measure, be lost; government [149] would either be subverted, or changed into downright tyranny; society must either disband, or be held together by absolute force. For as there can be no piety without the worship of the Deity, nor real virtue without piety; so there can be no voluntary union nor mutual confidence in society without virtue, and consequently no government but that which is of the most arbitrary kind consisting in mere force and violence.

SPRINGFIELD, 1786

The REFORMER.
NUMBER III.

Religion patronized by Government.

From the foregoing reasonings it follows, that the civil government of a people ought to provide for the encouragement of divine worship, because, without *this,* no people can long subsist in a state of freedom and happiness. It is sometimes asked, Why should government have any thing to do with religion? But the answer is obvious; Because religion has much to [150] do with government. If any imagine, that rulers should never interpose in matters that relate to religion, let them consider, what would be the consequence, if all laws against injustice, fraud, perjury, profaneness, theft, and drunkenness, were abolished and men were left to pursue without controul the dictates of their own lusts. Could society subsist? They will at once say: 'This is carrying liberty too far. There must be laws against vice. But why should rulers enjoin men to observe a sabbath, or support and attend publick worship?' The reason is plain; If publick worship is a proper means of preventing vice and promoting virtue, there is the same reason why they should make laws in favour of *that,* as why they should make laws for the punishment of vice. This is to secure the existence and happiness of society, in a way much more consistent with the dignity of human nature and the liberty of mankind, than to do every thing by whips, prisons and cords.

No free government was ever maintained without some form of religion. No religion is so perfect and rational, so intelligible in its doctrines, pure in its precepts, powerful in its sanctions and benovolent in its design as the christian religion. It must [151] then be the wisdom of any government to protect and encourage it, because this is to provide for the preservation of itself.

The law of Christ expressly requires, that divine worship be publickly maintained, and that all christians, according to their abilities, contribute their aid to this purpose. But it has not particularly pointed out the *manner* in which they shall do it. *This* is left to human prudence. All that government does in the case, is to prescribe the mode of doing that, which the law of Christ requires, and which every christian owns must be done in some mode or other. And there can be nothing unjust in this, more than in pointing out certain ways for

JOSEPH LATHROP 1731–1820

the relief of the poor, which the gospel requires us to relieve in some way or other; or in procuring schools for the education of youth, whom reason and religion require us to educate in knowledge and virtue by some means or other, or in annexing penalties to certain dangerous vices, which religion obliges us to bear testimony against in some form or other.

The great end of divine worship is the salvation of men's souls. When we consider it *only* in this view, we think it absurd, that government should concern itself in the matter; for what has government to do, [152] to direct me, how I shall be saved? Must I not judge for myself what is the way of salvation? Yes by all means. But though this is the principal end of publick worship, yet there is another end which it in fact serves, the present peace and happiness of mankind; and considered in this view, it as properly falls under the patronage of government, as learning or virtue, or any thing else, with which the happiness of society is essentially connected. The latter bear as real and as important a relation to men's future hopes, and on this principle might as reasonably be wrested out of the hands of government, as the former. But government encourages learning and virtue, not on the foot of their connection with futurity, but on account of their tendency to the present happiness of society: and on the same principle it patronizes the worship of the Deity.

It would be absurd to prescribe certain forms of worship and compel men to conform to *these* and to these *only;* for every man must be at liberty to judge what is truth, and what is the most acceptable way of serving his Maker, and to conduct himself accordingly, provided his conduct no way interferes with the peace and safety of others. But to require an abstinence from [153] the common labours of life one day in seven, and an attendance on the worship of God in some form or other, is no more an invasion on the rights of conscience, than a prohibition of vice or an injunction to maintain the poor and support schools, is an invasion on the rights of conscience; for though men may conscientiously differ as to the particular forms of worship, yet christians, and almost all mankind are agreed, that God is to be worshipped in some mode or other; and he that is allowed to choose his own mode of doing that, which he owns himself obliged and professes himself willing to do, very absurdly complains of oppression.

Men may, if they please, traduce religion under the name of *tradition,* or government under the name of *tyranny;* but to call things by ill names alters not their nature. Truth ceases not to be truth, nor does a usage good in itself, become evil, because the one has been believed, and the other practised by our fathers, or even by *Jews*. If our faith and practice are *founded* only in human authority, or human custom, they are essentially defective in a religious view; but to make the practice of others the mark of evil is as absurd, as to make it the standard of right. If we must reject every [154] thing in the gross as wrong, which was adopted by our fathers religion must of course change its nature every generation.

The observance of fasts, sabbaths, and publick worship has lately been reproached as mere tradition. But however well the writer may mean, he reasons very ill. Instead of shewing it to be of evil tendency with respect to the morals, or the happiness of mankind, contrary to reason or revelation, his only argument is, that it is mere *tradition* or *judaism;* that is, it is doing as others have done; and therefore should be done no more: and it was enjoined on *Jews,* and therefore ought to be abhorred by *Christians.* But this rule would lead us as much to discard the virtues as the vices of our fathers; and to reject the whole decalogue as the fourth commandment. His arguments to prove that there ought to be no laws in favour of religion, operate alike against all laws in support of learning, virtue and good manners, that is, they operate not at all, unless it be in the minds of the thoughtless and the undiscerning.

[155]   *The* REFORMER.
                       NUMBER IV.

                Submission to Civil Government.

Mankind cannot subsist without society, nor society without government. If there were no way to controul the selfishness, check the passions and restrain the vices of men, they would soon become so intolerable to one another, that they must disperse, and, being dispersed, must perish or be miserable. Government is a combination of the whole community against the vices of each particular member. The design of it is not merely to provide for the general defense against foreign power, but to exercise a controul over each member, to restrain him from wrong and compel him to right, so far as common safety requires. Mankind, by entering into society and coming under government, put the protection of their rights and the redress of their wrongs out of their own hands, and instead of defending or recovering their rights by private force, they agree to submit to the more impartial decision of the society, or of those whom the society has constituted judges.

That a people may be free and happy under [156] government, they must be wise and virtuous. A well framed constitution may be some security; the wisdom and virtue of the people is a greater. A virtuous people may subsist under a mild government; a corrupt and vicious people must be ruled with rigour. They who are governed by rational principles of their own, need but little other government; they who are wholly destitute of such principles must be governed by external force and terrour. 'The law is not made for a righteous man, but for the lawless.'

We have, by force, repelled a foreign encroachment on our liberties, and established a government of our own. Whether we shall be safe and happy now, depends much more on our own conduct, than on the form of government, which we have adopted, or any other that can be devised.

We should always be careful to commit the powers of government into the hands of wise and virtuous men; for it is manifestly absurd to trust the common safety with those, whose ability and integrity would not entitle them to our confidence in private life.

We should contribute our aid to carry into execution the wholesome laws of the community, especially those which immediately [157] relate to the virtue and morals of the people.

We should educate our children in rational notions of civil liberty, but, at the same time, in just sentiments of subordination and submission to authority, and instill into their minds such principles of honour, benevolence, integrity, piety and universal virtue, that they may have little occasion for the restraints of publick laws.

A wise people will inspect the conduct of their rulers, and guard their rights from every invasion. But they will not indulge an excessive jealousy, nor complain of measures which they understand not, or which could not be avoided.

When a people are greatly burthened, they may justly demand the severest œconomy in the application of publick treasures but they should be careful, that they impute not to prodigality those expenses, which arise from necessity.

If rulers are profuse, we may prefer men of more frugality, but let us, in private life, exercise the same frugality, which we expect of them in their publick station. The man that wastes his own substance, would not be very sparing of publick money, if it was committed to his disposal, [158] and such a man complains of extravagance with a very ill grace.

If the general character of a people is frugal, such of course will be the prevailing disposition of rulers because men of this character will be chosen to places of publick trust, and their conduct will be much influenced by the prevailing taste and manners of the people.

We commonly say, Rulers ought to be our examples. And so they ought. And why ought not we also to be theirs? In absolute governments, where the people are dependent on the will of their rulers, the publick examples very much govern private manners. In popular and elective governments, like ours, the case is, in some measure, the reverse. Rulers are here chosen by, and dependent on the people, and it may naturally be expected, that they will be good or bad, frugal or profuse, very much according to the prevailing character of their constituents.

If we would have the government reformed, we must reform ourselves. The more virtue there is among private persons, the more there will be among rulers, and the more easy it will be for government to carry into execution laws for the suppression of vice and the encouragement of virtue. [159] The best laws are impotent things, when the general disposition is to violate them. They are but cobwebs, which may happen now and then to entangle some feeble insect, while the strong will break through and escape. But good laws carry force and terrour, when the main body of the people approve them, and are resolved to obey and support them.

The REFORMER.
NUMBER V.

The mischiefs of Idleness.

The Creator has so framed the world and the condition of mankind in it, that industry is necessary to the support of human life. 'He becometh

JOSEPH LATHROP 1731–1820

poor' says the wise king of Israel, 'that dealeth with a slack hand, but the hand of the diligent maketh rich. The hand of the diligent shall bear rule, but the slothful shall be under tribute. Slothfulness casteth into a deep sleep, and the idle soul shall suffer hunger. The sluggard will not [160] plow by reason of the cold, therefore shall he beg in harvest and have nothing.'—These observations are often verified in experience. It is rare that we see a prudent and industrious man reduced to real want, or a slothful, indolent creature prosperous.

Industry is not only necessary to the subsistence, but conducive to the *health* of the body. *This* can no more be preserved without action, than the salubrity of the air can be preserved without winds, or the purity of waters without motion. Dead puddles soon become foul and putrid, so the indolent and inactive soon contract diseases. The fluids of the human body, like other fluids, purge off their peccant humours by motion.

The idle are not only useless, but mischievous members of society. An Apostle describes them 'as strolling about from house to house, meddling with other peoples matters, tatling and speaking things which they ought not.' Soloman gives a similar description of them. 'They are wise in their own conceit; apt to meddle with strife which belongs not to them; they deceive their neighbours in sport, as a madman casts about firebrands; they serve as talebearers to reveal secrets and hand round mischievous reports, [161] which separate nearest friends. As coals, to burning coals, and as wood to fire, so are such contentious people to kindle strifes.'

The idle are they who make the most disturbance in neighbourhoods and societies. They are usually very conceited and self-important, and imagine themselves much wiser than their neighbours. As they have no business of their own, they are at leisure to find fault with every body else. The times are always bad for them, and they are extremely apt to complain, that times are so bad. They always ascribe to other people the grievances which they bring on themselves by their own laziness. If by indolence and negligence they are reduced to poverty, then the government is severe, the laws are unreasonable, their neighbours are inhuman and their creditors cruelly oppressive. They justify themselves and curse the times, and look for relief by exciting disquietudes.

Idleness is not a solitary vice. Intemperance is one of its usual companions; gaming is frequently an attendant, and it is soon joined with a perverseness of temper, tormenting to itself and vexatious to all around. The day of calamity and distress is [162] at hand; sickness or age is coming on, when they, who once were idle from habit or inclination, will become inactive through necessity. Then they must live on the labours of others, or live no longer. They have made no provision for such a day, and *can* make none now. One would think the consideration of future impotence might be a sufficient motive with every man to improve the healthful and vigorous part of life in some honest and useful labours, that, in the day of infirmity and affliction, he may relieve his unavoidable wants by the fruits of former industry, and soothe the distresses of his body by some agreeable reflections of mind. If any are incapable of being influenced by such considerations, they should be called upon in a way more efficacious.

Christianity instructs us to 'work with our hands the thing that is good, that we may have to give to him that needeth.' He that needeth constant supplies from the hand of charity is not the person able to work with his hands, for he is directed to work that he may give. The apostolick church was ordered to exclude not only from her communion, but from her charitable support, such as refused to contribute to their own maintenance by honest industry. [163] The same rule should be still observed by those societies which are charged with the care of the poor. They should cheerfully relieve those who are really needy; but that they may not be overburthened, they should exercise their benevolence, in a different way, towards such members as are spending their time and substance in vain.

[45]

BENJAMIN RUSH 1745–1813

*A Plan for the Establishment of Public Schools
and the Diffusion of Knowledge in
Pennsylvania; to Which Are Added, Thoughts
upon the Mode of Education, Proper
in a Republic.*

PHILADELPHIA, 1786

The compleat revolutionary, Benjamin Rush divided his time between his medical practice and thinking about how the American revolution could be brought to a complete and permanent conclusion. Far from viewing the struggle as simply independence from Britain, Rush hoped to foster the social conditions appropriate to, and supportive of, republican government. He viewed education as the key element in this process, and this essay nicely summarizes his views. Always a man of action as well as one of contemplation, he taught for a number of years at the College of Philadelphia (later called the University of Pennsylvania) and helped to found Dickinson College.

PLAN FOR THE ESTABLISHMENT OF PUBLIC SCHOOLS

Before I proceed to suggest a plan for the establishment of public schools in Pennsylvania, I shall point out, in a few words, the influence and advantages of learning upon mankind.

I. It is friendly to religion, inasmuch as it assists in removing prejudice, superstition, and enthusiasm, in promoting just notions of the Deity, and in enlarging our knowledge of his works.

II. It is favorable to liberty. A free government can only exist in an equal diffusion of literature. Without learning, men become savages or barbarians, and where learning is confined to a *few* people, we [4] always find monarchy, aristocracy, and slavery.

III. It promotes just ideas of laws and government. "When the clouds of ignorance are dispelled," says the Marquis of Beccaria, "by the radiance of knowledge, power trembles but the authority of laws remains immovable."

IV. It is friendly to manners. Learning in all countries promotes civilization and the pleasures of society and conversation.

V. It promotes agriculture, the great basis of national wealth and happiness. Agriculture is as much a science as hydraulics or optics and has been equally indebted to the experiments and researches of learned men. The highly cultivated state and the immense profits of the farms in England are derived wholly from the patronage which agriculture has received in that country from learned men and learned societies.

VI. Manufactures of all kinds owe their perfection chiefly to learning—hence the nations of Europe advance in manufactures and commerce only in proportion as they cultivate the arts and sciences.

For the purpose of diffusing knowledge through every part of the state, I beg leave to propose the following simple plan:

I. Let there be one university in the state, and let this be established in the capital. [5] Let law, physic, divinity, the law of nature and nations, economy, etc. be taught in it by public lectures in the winter season, after the manner of the European universities, and let the professors receive such salaries from the state as will enable them to deliver their lectures at a moderate price.

II. Let there be four colleges. One in Philadelphia; one at Carlisle; a third, for the benefit of our German fellow citizens, at Manheim; and a fourth, some years hence, at Pittsburgh. In these colleges let young men be instructed in mathematics and in the higher branches of science, in the same manner that they are now taught in our American colleges. After they have taken a degree in one of these colleges, let them, if they can afford it, complete their studies by spending a season or two in attending the lectures in the university. I prefer four colleges in the state to one or two, for there is a certain size of colleges, as there is of towns and armies, that is most favorable to morals and good government. Oxford and Cambridge in England are the seats of dissipation, while the more numerous and less crowded universities and colleges in Scotland are remarkable for the order, diligence, and decent behavior of their students.

III. Let there be an academy established in each county for the purpose of instructing [6] youth in the learned languages and thereby preparing them to enter college.

IV. Let there be free schools established in every township or in districts consisting of one hundred families. In these schools, let children be taught to read and write the English and German languages and the use of figures. Such of them as have parents that can afford to send them from home and are disposed to extend their educations may remove their children from the free school to the county academy.

By this plan the whole state will be tied together by one system of education. The university will in time furnish masters for the colleges, and the colleges will furnish masters for the academies and free schools, while the free schools, in their turn, will supply the academies, the colleges, and the university with scholars, students, and pupils. The same systems of grammar, oratory, and philosophy will be taught in every part of the state, and the literary features of Pennsylvania will thus designate one great and equally enlightened family.

A question now rises, and that is, How shall this plan be carried into execution? I answer—

The funds of the University of Pennsylvania (if the English and other schools were separated from it) are nearly equal to the [7] purpose of supporting able professors in all the arts and sciences that are taught in the European universities.

A small addition to the funds of Dickinson College will enable it to exist without any further aid from government.

Twenty thousand acres of good land in the late Indian purchase will probably afford a revenue large enough to support a college at Manheim and another on the banks of the Ohio in the course of twenty years.

PHILADELPHIA, 1786

Five thousand acres of land, appropriated to each county academy, will probably afford a revenue sufficient to support them in twenty years. In the meanwhile let a tax from £200 to £400 a year be laid on each county for that purpose, according to the number and wealth of its inhabitants.

Let sixty thousand acres of land be set apart to be divided twenty years hence among the free schools. In the meanwhile let a tax from £30 to £60 a year be levied upon each district of one hundred families for the support of the schoolmaster, and to prompt him to industry in increasing his school, let each scholar pay him from 1s6 to 2s6 every quarter.

But, how shall we bear the expense of these literary institutions under the present weight of our taxes? I answer—These institutions [8] are designed to *lessen* our taxes. They will enlighten us in the great business of finance. They will teach us to increase the ability of the state to support government by increasing the profits of agriculture and by promoting manufactures. They will teach us all the modern improvements and advantages of inland navigation. They will defend us from hasty and expensive experiments in government by unfolding to us the experience and folly of past ages, and thus, instead of adding to our taxes and debts, they will furnish us with the true secret of lessening and discharging both of them.

But, shall the estates of orphans, bachelors, and persons who have no children be taxed to pay for the support of schools from which they can derive no benefit? I answer in the affirmative to the first part of the objection, and I deny the truth of the latter part of it. Every member of the community is interested in the propagation of virtue and knowledge in the state. But I will go further and add {that} it will be true economy in individuals to support public schools. The bachelor will in time save his tax for this purpose by being able to sleep with fewer bolts and locks to his doors, the estates of orphans will in time be benefited by being protected from the ravages of unprincipled and idle boys, and the children of wealthy parents [9] will be less tempted, by bad company, to extravagance. Fewer pillories and whipping posts and smaller jails, with their usual expenses and taxes, will be necessary when our youth are properly educated than at present. I believe it could be proved that the expenses of confining, trying, and executing criminals amount every year, in most of the counties, to more money than would be sufficient to maintain all the schools that would be necessary in each county. The confessions of these criminals generally show us that their vices and punishments are the fatal consequences of the want of a proper education in early life.

I submit these detached hints to the consideration of the legislature and of the citizens of Pennsylvania. The plan for the free schools is taken chiefly from the plans which have long been used with success in Scotland and in the eastern states* of America, where the influence of learning in promoting religion, morals, manners, government, [10] etc. has never been exceeded in any country.

The manner in which these academies and schools should be supported and governed, the modes of determining the characters and qualifications of schoolmasters, and the arrangement of families in each district, so that children of the same religious sect and nation may be educated as much as possible together, will form a proper part of a LAW for the establishment of schools and, therefore, does not come within the limits of this plan.

I shall conclude this part of the plan by submitting it to the wisdom of the legislature whether in granting charters for colleges in future they should not confine them to giving degrees only in the *arts,* especially while they teach neither law, physic, nor divinity. It is a folly peculiar to our American colleges to confer literary honors in professions that are not taught by them and which, if not speedily checked, will render degrees so cheap that they will cease to be the honorable badges of industry and learning.

I have said nothing of the utility of public libraries in each college, academy, and free school. Upon this subject I shall only remark that they will tend to diffuse knowledge more generally if the farmers and tradesmen [11] in the neighborhood of them (upon paying a moderate sum yearly) are permited to have access to them.

The establishment of newspapers in a few of the most populous county towns will contribute very much to diffuse knowledge of all kinds through the state. To accomplish this, the means of conveying the papers should be made easy, by the assistance of the legislature.

---

* There are 600 of these schools in the small state of Connecticut, which at this time, have in them 25,000 scholars. Only two natives of this state have been executed in the course of the last 25 years. The German Lutherans in Pennsylvania take uncommon pains in the education of their youth. Not one of this society has submitted to the ignomiy of a legal punishment, of any kind, in the course of the last 17 years.

The effects of a newspaper upon the state of knowledge and opinions appear already in several of the counties beyond the Susquehanna. The passion for this useful species of instruction is strongly marked in Pennsylvania by the great encouragement this paper has received in those counties. In the space of eight months the number of subscribers to the *Carlisle Gazette* have amounted to above 700.

Henry the IVth of France used to say he hoped to live to see the time when every peasant in his kingdom would dine on a turkey every Sunday. I have not a wish for the extension of literature in the state that would not be gratified by living to see a weekly newspaper in every farmhouse in Pennsylvania. Part of the effects of this universal diffusion of knowledge would probably be to produce turkies and poultry of all kinds on the tables of our farmers, not only on Sundays, but on every day of the week.

[12] By multiplying villages and county towns, we increase the means of diffusing knowledge. Villages are favorable to schools and public worship, and county towns, besides possessing these two advantages, are favorable to the propagation of political and legal information. The public officers of the county, by being obliged to maintain a connection with the capital of the government, often become repositories and vehicles of news and useful publications, while the judges and lawyers who attend the courts that are held in these towns seldom fail of leaving a large portion of knowledge behind them.

[13]   THOUGHTS UPON THE MODE OF EDUCATION
PROPER IN A REPUBLIC

The business of education has acquired a new complexion by the independence of our country. The form of government we have assumed has created a new class of duties to every American. It becomes us, therefore, to examine our former habits upon this subject, and in laying the foundations for nurseries of wise and good men, to adapt our modes of teaching to the peculiar form of our government.

The first remark that I shall make upon this subject is that an education in our own is to be preferred to an education in a foreign country. The principle of patriotism stands in need of the reinforcement of *prejudice,* and it is well known that our strongest prejudices in favor of our country are formed [14] in the first one and twenty years of our lives. The policy of the Lacedamonians is well worthy of our imitation. When Antipater demanded fifty of their children as hostages for the fulfillment of a distant engagement, those wise republicans refused to comply with his demand but readily offered him double the number of their adult citizens, whose habits and prejudices could not be shaken by residing in a foreign country. Passing by, in this place, the advantages to the community from the early attachment of youth to the laws and constitution of their country, I shall only remark that young men who have trodden the paths of science together, or have joined in the same sports, whether of swimming, skating, fishing, or hunting, generally feel, through life, such ties to each other as add greatly to the obligations of mutual benevolence.

I conceive the education of our youth in this country to be peculiarly necessary in Pennsylvania while our citizens are composed of the natives of so many different kingdoms in Europe. Our schools of learning, by producing one general and uniform system of education, will render the mass of the people more homogeneous and thereby fit them more easily for uniform and peaceable government.

[15] I proceed, in the next place, to inquire what mode of education we shall adopt so as to secure to the state all the advantages that are to be derived from the proper instruction of youth; and here I beg leave to remark that the only foundation for a useful education in a republic is to be laid in RELIGION. Without this, there can be no virtue, and without virtue there can be no liberty, and liberty is the object and life of all republican governments.

Such is my veneration for every religion that reveals the attributes of the Deity, or a future state of rewards and punishments, that I had rather see the opinions of Confucius or Mohammed inculcated upon our youth than see them grow up wholly devoid of a system of religious principles. But the religion I mean to recommend in this place is the religion of JESUS CHRIST.

It is foreign to my purpose to hint at the arguments which establish the truth of the Christian revelation. My only business is to declare that all its doctrines and precepts are calculated to promote the happiness of society and the safety and well-being of civil government. A Christian cannot fail of being a republican. The history of the creation of man and of the relation of our species to each other by birth, which is recorded in the Old Testament, is the best [16] refutation that can be given to the divine right of kings and the strongest argument that can be used in favor of the original and natural equality of all mankind. A Christian, I say again, cannot fail of being a republican, for every precept of the Gospel inculcates those degrees of humility, self-denial, and brotherly kindness which are directly opposed to the pride of monarchy and the pageantry of a court. A Christian cannot fail of being useful to the republic, for his religion teacheth him that no man "liveth to himself." And lastly, a Christian cannot fail of being wholly inoffensive, for his religion teacheth him in all things to do to others what he would wish, in like circumstances, they should do to him.

I am aware that I dissent from one of those paradoxical opinions with which modern times abound: that it is improper to fill the minds of youth with religious prejudices of any kind and that they should be left to choose their own principles after they have arrived at an age in which they are capable of judging for themselves. Could we preserve the mind in childhood and youth a perfect blank, this plan of education would have more to recommend it, but this we know to be impossible. The human mind runs as naturally into principles as it does [17] after facts. It submits with difficulty to those restraints or partial discoveries which are imposed upon it in the infancy of reason. Hence the impatience of children to be informed upon all subjects that relate to the invisible world. But I beg leave to ask, Why should we pursue a different plan of education with respect to religion from that which we pursue in teaching the arts and sciences? Do we leave our youth to acquire systems of geography, philosophy, or politics till they have arrived at an age in which they are capable of judging for themselves? We do not. I claim no more, then, for religion than for the other sciences, and I add further that if our youth are disposed after they are of age to think for themselves, a knowledge of *one* system will be the best means of conducting them in a free inquiry into other systems of religion, just as an acquaintance with one system of philosophy is the best introduction to the study of all the other systems in the world.

I must beg leave upon this subject to go one step further. In order more effectually to secure to our youth the advantages of a religious education, it is necessary to impose upon them the doctrines and discipline of a particular church. Man is naturally an ungovernable animal, and observations on particular societies and countries will teach us [18] that when we add the restraints of ecclesiastical to those of domestic and civil government, we produce in him the highest degrees of order and virtue. That fashionable liberality which refuses to associate with any one sect of Christians is seldom useful to itself or to society and may fitly be compared to the unprofitable bravery of a soldier who wastes his valor in solitary enterprises without the aid or effect of military associations. Far be it from me to recommend the doctrines or modes of worship of any one denomination of Christians. I only recommend to the persons entrusted with the education of youth to inculcate upon them a strict conformity to that mode of worship which is most agreeable to their consciences or the inclinations of their parents.

Under this head, I must be excused in not agreeing with those modern writers who have opposed the use of the Bible as a schoolbook. The only objection I know to it is its division into chapters and verses and its improper punctuation which render it a more difficult book to read *well* than many others, but these defects may easily be corrected, and the disadvantages of them are not to be mentioned with the immense advantages of making children early and intimately acquainted with the means of acquiring happiness both here and hereafter. [19] How great is the difference between making young people acquainted with the interesting and entertaining truths contained in the Bible, and the fables of Moore and Croxall, or the doubtful histories of antiquity! I maintain that there is no book of its size in the whole world that contains half so much useful knowledge for the government of states or the direction of the affairs of individuals as the Bible. To object to the practice of having it read in schools because it tends to destroy our veneration for it is an argument that applies with equal force against the frequency of public worship and all other religious exercises.

The first impressions upon the mind are the most durable. They survive the wreck of the memory and exist in old age after the ideas acquired in middle life have been obliterated. Of how much consequence then must it be to the human mind in the evening of life to be able to recall those ideas which are most essential to its happiness, and these are to be found chiefly in the Bible. The great delight which old people take in reading the Bible, I am persuaded, is derived chiefly from its histories and precepts being *associated* with the events of childhood and youth, the recollection of which forms a material part of their pleasures.

[20] I do not mean to exclude books of history, poetry, or even fables from our schools. They may and should be read frequently by our young people, but if the Bible is made to give way to them altogether, I foresee that it will be read in a short time only in churches and in a few years will probably be found only in the offices of magistrates and in courts of justice.†

NEXT to the duty which young men owe to their Creator, I wish to see a SUPREME REGARD TO THEIR COUNTRY inculcated upon them. When the Duke of Sully became prime minister to Henry the IVth of France, the first thing he did, he tells us, "was to subdue and forget his own heart." The same duty is incumbent upon every citizen of a republic. Our country includes family, friends, and property, and should be preferred to them all. Let our pupil be taught that he does not belong to himself, but that he is public property. Let him be taught to love his family, but let him be [21] taught at the same time that he must forsake and even forget them when the welfare of his country requires it.

He must watch for the state as if its liberties depended upon his vigilance alone, but he must do this in such a manner as not to defraud his creditors or neglect his family. He must love private life, but he must decline no station, however public or responsible it may be, when called to it by the suffrages of his fellow citizens. He must love popularity, but he must despise it when set in competition with the dictates of his judgment or the real interest of his country. He must love character and have a due sense of injuries, but he must be taught to appeal only to the laws of the state, to defend the one and punish the other. He must love family honor, but he must be taught that neither the rank nor antiquity of his ancestors can command respect without personal merit. He must avoid neutrality in all questions that divide the state, but he must shun the rage and acrimony of party spirit. He must be taught to love his fellow creatures in every

---

† In a republic where all votes for public officers are given by *ballot,* should not a knowledge of reading and writing be considered as essential qualifications for an elector? And when a man who is of a doubtful character offers his vote, would it not be more consistent with sound policy and wise government to oblige him to read a few verses in the Bible to prove his qualifications than simply to compel him to kiss the *outside* of it?

part of the world, but he must cherish with a more intense and peculiar affection the citizens of Pennsylvania and of the United States.

I do not wish to see our youth educated with a single prejudice against any nation or country, but we impose a task upon human nature repugnant alike to reason, [22] revelation, and the ordinary dimensions of the human heart when we require him to embrace with equal affection the whole family of mankind. He must be taught to amass wealth, but it must be only to increase his power of contributing to the wants and demands of the state. He must be indulged occasionally in amusements, but he must be taught that study and business should be his principal pursuits in life. Above all he must love life and endeavor to acquire as many of its conveniences as possible by industry and economy, but he must be taught that this life "is not his own" when the safety of his country requires it. These are practicable lessons, and the history of the commonwealths of Greece and Rome show that human nature, without the aids of Christianity, has attained these degrees of perfection.

While we inculcate these republican duties upon our pupil, we must not neglect at the same time to inspire him with republican principles. He must be taught that there can be no durable liberty but in a republic and that government, like all other sciences, is of a progressive nature. The chains which have bound this science in Europe are happily unloosed in America. *Here* it is open to investigation and improvement. While philosophy has protected us by its discoveries [23] from a thousand natural evils, government has unhappily followed with an unequal pace. It would be to dishonor human genius only to name the many defects which still exist in the best systems of legislation. We daily see matter of a perishable nature rendered durable by certain chemical operations. In like manner, I conceive that it is possible to analyze and combine power in such a manner as not only to increase the happiness but to promote the duration of republican forms of government far beyond the terms limited for them by history or the common opinions of mankind.

To assist in rendering religious, moral, and political instruction more effectual upon the minds of our youth, it will be necessary to subject their bodies to physical discipline. To obviate the inconveniences of their studious and sedentary mode of life, they should live upon a temperate diet, consisting chiefly of broths, milk, and vegetables. The black broth of Sparta and the barley broth of Scotland have been alike celebrated for their beneficial effects upon the minds of young people. They should avoid tasting spirituous liquors. They should also be accustomed occasionally to work with their hands in the intervals of study and in the busy seasons of the year in the country. Moderate sleep, silence, occasional solitude, [24] and cleanliness should be inculcated upon them, and the utmost advantage should be taken of a proper direction of those great principles of human conduct—sensibility, habit, imitation, and association.

The influence [of] these physical causes will be powerful upon the intellects as well as upon the principles and morals of young people.

To those who have studied human nature, it will not appear paradoxical to recommend in this essay a particular attention to vocal music. Its mechanical effects in civilizing the mind and thereby preparing it for the influence of religion and government have been so often felt and recorded that it will be unnecessary to mention facts in favor of its usefulness in order to excite a proper attention to it.

In the education of youth, let the authority of our masters be as *absolute* as possible. The government of schools like the government of private families should be *arbitrary,* that it may not be *severe.* By this mode of education, we prepare our youth for the subordination of laws and thereby qualify them for becoming good citizens of the republic. I am satisfied that the most useful citizens have been formed from those youth who have never known or felt their own wills till they were one and twenty years of age, and I have often thought that society owes a great deal [25] of its order and happiness to the deficiencies of parental government being supplied by those habits of obedience and subordination which are contracted at schools.

I cannot help bearing a testimony, in this place, against the custom which prevails in some parts of America (but which is daily falling into disuse in Europe) of crowding boys together under one roof for the purpose of education. The practice is the gloomy remains of monkish ignorance and is as unfavorable to the improvements of the mind in useful learning as monasteries are to the spirit of religion. I grant this mode of secluding boys from the intercourse of private families has a tendency to make them scholars, but our business is to make them men, citizens, and Christians. The vices of young people are generally learned from each other. The vices of adults seldom infect them. By separating them from each other, therefore, in their hours of relaxation from study, we secure their morals from a principal source of corruption, while we improve their manners by subjecting them to those restraints which the difference of age and sex naturally produce in private families.

I have hitherto said nothing of the AMUSEMENTS that are proper for young people in a republic. Those which promote health and [26] good humor will have a happy effect upon morals and government. To increase this influence, let the persons who direct these amusements be admitted into good company and subjected by that means to restraints in behavior and moral conduct. Taverns, which in most countries are exposed to riot and vice, in Connecticut are places of business and innocent pleasure because the tavernkeepers in that country are generally men of sober and respectable characters.

The theater will never be perfectly reformed till players are treated with the same respect as persons of other ornamental professions. It is to no purpose to attempt to write or preach down an amusement which seizes so forcibly upon all the powers of the mind. Let ministers preach *to* players instead of *against* them; let them open their churches and the ordinances of religion to them and their families, and, I am persuaded, we shall soon see such a reformation in the theater as can never be effected by all the means that have hitherto been employed for that purpose. It is possible to render the stage, by these means, subsurvient to the purposes of virtue and even religion. Why should the minister of the gospel exclude the player from his visits or from his public or private instructions? The Author of Christianity knew no difference in the occupations of men. He [27] ate and drank daily with the publicans and sinners.

From the observations that have been made it is plain that I consider it as possible to convert men into republican machines. This must be done if we expect them to perform their parts properly in the great machine of the government of the state. That republic is sophisticated with monarchy or aristocracy that does not revolve upon the wills of the people, and these must be fitted to each other by means of education before they can be made to produce regularity and unison in government.

Having pointed out those general principles which should be inculcated alike in all the schools of the state, I proceed now to make a few remarks upon the method of conducting what is commonly called a liberal or learned education in a republic.

PHILADELPHIA, 1786

I shall begin this part of my subject by bearing a testimony against the common practice of attempting to teach boys the learned languages and the arts and sciences too early in life. The first twelve years of life are barely sufficient to instruct a boy in reading, writing, and arithmetic. With these, he may be taught those modern languages which are necessary for him to *speak*. The state of the memory, in early life, is favorable to the acquisition of languages, especially [28] when they are conveyed to the mind through the ear. It is, moreover, in early life only that the organs of speech yield in such a manner as to favor the just pronunciation of foreign languages.

I do not wish the LEARNED OR DEAD LANGUAGES, as they are commonly called, to be reduced below their present just rank in the universities of Europe, especially as I consider an acquaintance with them as the best foundation for a correct and extensive knowledge of the language of our country. Too much pains cannot be taken to teach our youth to read and write our American language with propriety and elegance. The study of the Greek language constituted a material part of the literature of the Athenians, hence the sublimity, purity, and immortality of so many of their writings. The advantages of a perfect knowledge of our language to young men intended for the professions of law, physic, or divinity are too obvious to be mentioned, but in a state which boasts of the first commercial city in America, I wish to see it cultivated by young men who are intended for the counting house, for many such, I hope, will be educated in our colleges. The time is past when an academical education was thought to be unnecessary to qualify a young man for merchandise. I [29] conceive no profession is capable of receiving more embellishments from it.

Connected with the study of our language is the study of ELOQUENCE. It is well known how great a part it constituted of the Roman education. It is the first accomplishment in a republic and often sets the whole machine of government in motion. Let our youth, therefore, be instructed in this art. We do not extol it too highly when we attribute as much to the power of eloquence as to the sword in bringing about the American Revolution.

With the usual arts and sciences that are taught in our American colleges, I wish to see a regular course of lectures given upon HISTORY and CHRONOLOGY. The science of government, whether it relates to constitutions or laws, can only be advanced by a careful selection of facts, and these are to be found chiefly in history. Above all, let our youth be instructed in the history of the ancient republics and the progress of liberty and tyranny in the different states of Europe.

I wish likewise to see the numerous facts that relate to the origin and present state of COMMERCE, together with the nature and principles of MONEY, reduced to such a system as to be intelligible and agreeable to a young man. If we consider the commerce of our metropolis only as the avenue of the wealth [30] of the state, the study of it merits a place in a young man's education, but, I consider commerce in a much higher light when I recommend the study of it in republican seminaries. I view it as the best security against the influence of hereditary monopolies of land, and, therefore, the surest protection against aristocracy. I consider its effects as next to those of religion in humanizing mankind, and, lastly, I view it as the means of uniting the different nations of the world together by the ties of mutual wants and obligations.

CHEMISTRY, by unfolding to us the effects of heat and mixture, enlarges our acquaintance with the wonders of nature and the mysteries of art; hence it has become in most of the universities of Europe a necessary branch of a gentleman's education. In a young country, where improvements in agriculture and manufactures are so much to be desired, the cultivation of this science, which explains the principles of both of them, should be considered as an object of the utmost importance.

In a state where every citizen is liable to be a soldier and a legislator, it will be necessary to have some regular instruction given upon the ART OF WAR and upon PRACTICAL LEGISLATION. These branches of knowledge are of too much importance in a republic [31] to be trusted to solitary study or to a fortuitous acquaintance with books. Let mathematical learning, therefore, be carefully applied in our colleges to gunnery and fortification, and let philosophy be applied to the history of those compositions which have been made use of for the terrible purposes of destroying human life. These branches of knowledge will be indispensably necessary in our republic, if unfortunately war should continue hereafter to be the unchristian mode of arbitrating disputes between Christian nations.

Again, let our youth be instructed in all the means of promoting national prosperity and independence, whether they relate to improvements in agriculture, manufactures, or inland navigation. Let him be instructed further in the general principles of legislation, whether they relate to revenue or to the preservation of life, liberty, or property. Let him be directed frequently to attend the courts of justice, where he will have the best opportunities of acquiring habits of arranging and comparing his ideas by observing the secretion of truth in the examination of witnesses and where he will hear the laws of the state explained, with all the advantages of that species of eloquence which belongs to the bar. Of so much importance do I conceive it to be to a young man to attend occasionally to the [32] decisions of our courts of law that I wish to see our colleges and academies established only in county towns.

But further, considering the nature of our connection with the United States, it will be necessary to make our pupil acquainted with all the prerogatives of the federal government. He must be instructed in the nature and variety of treaties. He must know the difference in the powers and duties of the several species of ambassadors. He must be taught wherein the obligations of individuals and of states are the same and wherein they differ. In short, he must acquire a general knowledge of all those laws and forms which unite the sovereigns of the earth or separate them from each other.

I have only to add that it will be to no purpose to adopt this or any other mode of education unless we make choice of suitable masters to carry our plans into execution. Let our teachers be distinguished for their abilities and knowledge. Let them be grave in their manners, gentle in their tempers, exemplary in their morals, and of sound principles in religion and government. Let us not leave their support to the precarious resources to be derived from their pupils, but let such funds be provided for our schools and colleges as will enable us to allow them liberal salaries.

By these means we shall [33] render the chairs—the professorships and rectorships of our colleges and academies—objects of competition among learned men. By conferring upon our masters that independence which is the companion of competency, we shall, moreover, strengthen their authority over the youth committed to their care. Let us remember that a great part of the divines, lawyers, physicians, legislators, soldiers, generals, delegates, counselors, and governors of the state will probably hereafter pass through their hands. How great then should be the wisdom, how honorable the rank, and how generous the reward of those men who are to form these necessary and leading members of the republic!

I beg pardon for having delayed so long, to say anything of the separate and peculiar mode of education proper for WOMEN in a republic. I am sensible that they must concur in all our plans of education for young men, or no laws will ever render them effectual. To qualify our women for this purpose, they should not only be instructed in the usual branches of female education but they should be instructed in the principles of liberty and government, and the obligations of patriotism should be inculcated upon them. The opinions and conduct of men are often regulated by the women in the [34] most arduous enterprises of life, and their approbation is frequently the principal reward of the hero's dangers and the patriot's toils. Besides, the *first* impressions upon the minds of children are generally derived from the women. Of how much consequence, therefore, is it in a republic that they should think justly upon the great subjects of liberty and government!

The complaints that have been made against religion, liberty, and learning have been made against each of them in a *separate* state. Perhaps like certain liquors they should only be used in a state of mixture. They mutually assist in correcting the abuses and in improving the good effects of each other. From the combined and reciprocal influence of religion, liberty, and learning upon the morals, manners, and knowledge of individuals, of these upon government, and of government upon individuals, it is impossible to measure the degrees of happiness and perfection to which mankind may be raised. For my part, I can form no ideas of the golden age, so much celebrated by the poets, more delightful than the contemplation of that happiness which it is now in the power of the legislature of Pennsylvania to confer upon her citizens by establishing proper modes and places of education in every part of the state.

[35] The *present time* is peculiarly favorable to the establishment of these benevolent and necessary institutions in Pennsylvania. The minds of our people have not as yet lost the yielding texture they acquired by the heat of the late Revolution. They will *now* receive more readily than five or even three years hence new impressions and habits of all kinds. The spirit of liberty *now* pervades every part of the state. The influence of error and deception are *now* of short duration. Seven years hence the affairs of our state may assume a new complexion.

We may be riveted to a criminal indifference for the safety and happiness of ourselves and our posterity. An aristocratic or democratic junto may arise that shall find its despotic views connected with the prevalence of ignorance and vice in the state, or a few artful pedagogues who consider learning as useful only in proportion as it favors their pride or avarice may prevent all new literary establishments from taking place by raising a hue and cry against them, as the offspring of improper rivalship or the nurseries of party spirit.

But in vain shall we lavish pains and expense in establishing nurseries of virtue and knowledge in every part of the state, in vain shall we attempt to give the minds of our citizens a virtuous and uniform bias in [36] early life, while the arms of our state are opened alike to receive into its bosom and to confer equal privileges upon the virtuous emigrant and the annual refuse of the jails of Britain, Ireland, and our sister states. Of the many criminals that have been executed within these seven years, four out of five of them have been foreigners who have arrived here during the war and since the peace. We are yet, perhaps, to see and deplore the tracks of the enormous vices and crimes these men have left behind them. Legislators of Pennsylvania!— Stewards of the justice and virtue of heaven!—Fathers of children who may be corrupted and disgraced by bad examples, say—can nothing be done to preserve our morals, manners, and government from the infection of European vices?

{ 46 }

THEOPHRASTUS

A Short History of the Trial by Jury

WORCESTER, MASSACHUSETTS, 1787

"Remind the people of their greatest privilege."
Chatham's Speech

This essay on the trial by jury and the dangers of excluding citizens from jury lists was published in the *Worcester Magazine* during the second week of October, 1787.

"The most usual method of trial among the Saxons, was by juries, as at this day, that is, by twelve of the *pares curia*. The invention of these is attributed by the English lawyers to Alfred, and greatly do they exult over the laws of other countries, in the excellency of this method; but had they been acquainted with the ancient laws of the continent, they would have found the trial by *pares* common to all the northern nations, though since wore out by the introduction of the civil law— not so common indeed any where else as in England, where every age has gained ground, and wore out the other. Alfred's merit was therefore in fixing the *number,* and determining the *quality* of jurors, rather than in the invention." Sullivan's lectures, p. 251

By this as well as by other learned and judicious writers, we are informed, that the trial by jury is older than the British constitution itself; that it existed among all the northern nations, until the tyranny of the Roman empire had subverted it, by establishing the civil law; that it is considered as the only bulwark of the freedom of the people of England; and also that much has been done to give a permanent qualification to jurors, in order to prevent their being made the tools of tyranny, rather than the guardians of liberty.

The qualification of jurors, was expressed in Magna Charta in these words, "liberas et legales homines," good and lawful freemen. What good and lawful freemen were, was settled by a number of subsequent statutes; those who had been stigmatized, or whipt upon lawful trial, or outlawed by lawful process, were incapable at common law to serve as jurors. By a statute of the 13th of Edward the first, the age of seventy years excused. By the same statute, none were to serve unless they could *dispend* twenty shillings a year; but as money grew worse, the qualification was altered to keep up the dignity of the order, but was not carried so high as to deprive those who in its origin would have had it from the *privilege* and *honour* of serving. A statute made in the reign of Elizabeth, declared that the juror must have an income annually of four pounds a year, from his own freehold estate; a variety of statutes were made restoring the institution, when time or accident had altered it from its ancient standing; and finally, in the reign of George the second, the qualification of jurors was fixed at a freehold estate of twenty pounds a year, over and above the rent reserved; from that time money has remained nearly the same, and no alteration has been necessary to be done, in order to keep jurors upon their ancient constitutional footing.

Thus, amidst all the revolutions which have happened in the empire of Britain, the trial by jury, according to ancient method, has been handed down entire; indeed, as it is coeval with their freedom, it cannot be survived by their liberty.

The institution was brought into this country by the first settlers, who claimed all the rights of Englishmen; in the year 1641 they established county courts, and made provision for a trial by jury. From that time to the year 1759 the inhabitants in town meeting, holding a certain quantity of property, chose jurors of men of like conditions with themselves.

By the charter granted the province in 1692, every person seized in his own right of a freehold estate of the yearly income of forty shillings, or possessed of personal estate of the value of sixty pounds sterling, was capable of being elected a representative, and of voting in town meeting for members of the General Court. By a law made in 1694 jurors were to have the same quantity of estate as voters for representatives. In the year 1759, an act was passed, providing that the selectmen in each town, sometime before the month of December in that year, should take a list of persons liable by law, and which they should judge able and qualified to serve as jurors, and lay the same before their *towns,* and that the *towns* should select one quarter part for the Superiour, and the residue should remain for the Inferiour

Court; and the names of those persons were to be put into separate boxes, and locked up, and the key to be delivered the town clerk, and those were to be drawn in future to serve on the jury. But even this drawing was not intrusted to the selectmen, nor were they the judges of the qualifications, but the whole was to be done by the *people,* assembled in town meeting.

Thus from the first rise of juries to the twenty sixth day of February last, a certain quantity of property was a qualification for jurors, both in England and here, and in this country their appointment was in their fellow citizens. But the crown of Great Britain, while we were a part of that empire, despairing to reduce us to slavery, while this privilege remained with us, in the year 1773 procured an act of parliament, providing "that jurors should not hereafter be elected, nominated, or appointed by the freeholders of the several towns, but should be returned and summoned by the sheriffs;" this act of parliament may be seen at large in the record of the Secretary's office, recited in Ramsay's history of the war, and complained of in the declaration of independence. It was treated by the Americans as an engine of despotism, and disregarded accordingly.

Previous to the present form of government, and in the year 1777, a law was made, describing the crime of treason, and for regulating the trial thereof. This was done as a permanent law, but was called forth at the time as a check upon the enemies of the revolution, who then remained in the state, and were considered as dangerous and traitorous enemies. By this act it is provided, that any person indicted for treason, shall have the name of the jury two days at least before the day of trial, and shall have the privilege of challenging twenty without cause. No alteration was attempted in the mode of appointment of jurors, or in their qualifications, for however necessary it might appear to *withdraw* from the box those who favoured the British invasion, yet their advocates were too numerous, too learned, and too powerful, to let such a dangerous innovation take place; indeed all the people were so fully jealous of this darling privilege, while they were spilling their blood to defend it, that no such system could be rendered practicable for a day.

When the present constitution was made, a committee was appointed to revise the laws, and to report such acts as should render them consonant to the present constitution. By the constitution the qualification of electors of representatives was altered from what it used to be under the royal charter, and a law was made in 1784 continuing the mode of appointing jurors, only altering the pecuniary qualification to be the same as that of voters for senators and representatives. Still the people held the right of electing jurors for the boxes; for the declaration of rights established that the General Court should not make any law to deprive any one "of life, liberty or immunities, without trial by jury, unless for the government of the army or the navy." And here, unless the word *jury* had a certain and fixed meaning, no privilege was secured by this article; but the word jury has been long established to mean twelve men, appointed in a particular mode, and holding a certain quantity of property, which gives them the right of voting for legislators. To suppose that a power any where exists, to alter or annul this foundation principle of civil liberty, is supposing that there is no constitutional security in the government. The privilege of serving as a juror is a noble privilege, which can never be justly estimated until there is an attempt to deprive us of it, and should there ever be a good federal government established, this will be the only security which will remain, for the freedom of the citizens of the separate states; upon this the freedom of posterity depends.

By the law made in 1784, the selectmen are to lay a list of persons qualified to vote for senators and representatives before their respective towns once in every three years at the least, and the *town* is to vote one quarter part for the box of the Supreme Judicial Court, and the residue for the other Courts. And that if any person, whose name is put into the box, shall be convicted of any infamous crime, or be guilty of any gross immorality, his name shall not be restored again *by vote of the town.*

A few remarks upon this act may not be amiss. 1st. The being put into the box is a privilege, which every citizen must be injured in being deprived of.

2. The distinguishing qualification, both in England and here, arises from a certain quantity of estate.

3. We have the privilege by the suffrage of our fellow citizens, and warranted by the constitution.

4. *The selectmen cannot deprive a citizen of this privilege without the vote of the town, nor restore it but by that same authority.*

5. The town cannot do it but upon the conviction of an infamous crime, or upon acts of gross immorality; should they do it unjustly,

the subject can procure a trial by jury, and have a *mandamus* to restore him to his privilege.

6. That this act does by no means alter the ancient institution, but guards it more strongly against fraud and corruption.

Thus, in this Commonwealth, trial by jury stood until the twenty sixth of February 1787, when an act was passed, providing "that it shall be the duty of the selectmen of the several towns, to which a *venire facias* shall be issued for jurors, to leave at the Supreme Judicial Court, &c. *at any time within one year from the passsing of this act,* and such selectmen are hereby required to withdraw from the jury boxes the names of all such persons, AS THEY SHALL JUDGE to have been *guilty of favouring the present rebellion,* [Shays' Rebellion] *or giving aid or support thereto, prior to drawing out the names of the jurors,* that may be called for by the *ventie facias."*

Another clause in the same act provides that the judges, "where there is provable grounds for a suggestion, that any person called to serve as a juror has been guilty of favouring the rebellion, they shall set him aside as disqualified."

A few remarks on this act may be pertinent.

1. That though the election of jurors had been in the people, from the first settlement of the country to the twenty sixth of February 1787, and had been confirmed by the constitution, yet by this act the *selectmen, independent of the people,* are to withdraw from the box such men as THEY SHALL JUDGE *to have been guilty of favouring the rebellion,* which establishes a precedent for depriving the people at large of the privilege of choosing jurors.

2. The laws before had guarded this important privilege against the corruption of selectmen, as well as that of other officers; but by this act a jury may be completely packed; the judges may send their *venire facias* to such towns as have selectmen to their own liking, and they may withdraw the names of such persons as they please.

3. Though this is only a measure for one year, yet if it can be done now, it can be done again; if it can be done by a good government, it can be done by a bad one—if it can be done while we have upright judges, it may be done when we have not such.

4. The act was passed when divers persons were in prison, under charge for crimes, and the selectmen had thereby an opportunity to draw jurors which would acquit, or condemn, according to the taste of the selectmen, upon the causes then under protest.

5. The constitution provides, that we shall be governed by fixed and standing laws, but this is a measure calculated for a particular purpose, and for one year only; surely if any right ought to be settled by permanent laws, it should be the mode of returning jurors.

6. Should any person suffer for murder, &c. in consequence of a verdict found by jurors returned upon this law, and the law is unconstitutional, it would be sealing the violation of the people's rights with their own blood.

7. It is not material to the present question whether the persons condemned are guilty; for however guilty they may be, they are not to suffer without a fair and constitutional trial; because from such a precedent an innocent man may suffer in the same way.

But it may be asked, what is to be done? Shall we have rebels to try rebels? the answer is, state the case as strong as you can, the constitutional rights of the people never ought to be violated, for if this can be done in a green tree, what cannot be done in a day? unless this act is repealed as unconstitutional, it being passed at so early a period after the constitution was made, it will be hereafter considered as part of it.

Some quotations from Judge Blackstone shall close this essay.

"Every man's property, his liberty, and his life, depends upon maintaining in its legal force, the *constitutional* trial by jury." *Vol. 3d. Page 351.* "If the administration of justice was entirely entrusted to the majistracy, or a select body of men, and those generally appointed by the prince, or such as enjoy the highest offices in the state, their decisions, inspite of their own natural integrity, will have frequently an involuntary bias towards those of their own rank and dignity." *Same 379.* "This therefore preserves in the hands of the people their share, which they ought to have, in the administration of justice, and prevents the encroachments of the more powerful and wealthy citizens." *Same 380.*

[47]

THE WORCESTER SPECULATOR

No. VI

WORCESTER, MASSACHUSETTS, 1787

Written by a Federalist in Massachusetts, most of the sentiments contained in this short piece could be supported by the Whigs, or Anti-Federalists, as well. Matching the government to the virtues of the people, enhancing public virtue through education made widely available—these are ideas generally accepted by Americans of all persuasions. The emphasis upon "literature" rather than the Bible would identify this anonymous author as a Federalist, however, even if other numbers by The Worcester Speculator did not certify such.

This piece appeared in the issue of the *Worcester Magazine* that appeared during the last week in October, 1787.

———

There is no circumstance which so unfavorably proclaims the imperfections of human nature, as the necessity of transferring our natural liberty to some foreign power, thereby to create an additional obligation to perform our duties, as moral and social beings. That government is made necessary by the constitution of human nature, is a truth, highly evident to every rational member of social society.

However agreeable in speculation, yet there is not a greater inconsistency in the moral world, than a particular form of government which can operate equally, or even be maintained, under the protective stages of civilization. Hence moral necessity, or civil policy, has introduced as many forms, as there are gradations from the highest stages of refinement down to the rude state of barbarity. A government calculated to controul the turbulent passions of the uncultivated sons of nature, could but with wretched policy be transferred to the inhabitants of a civilized age. It is not, therefore, the enquiry of politicians, what mode of government may best be established as a general standard—but what form will best conduce to the happiness of society in any particular stage of civilization.

Whoever frames to himself an idea of perfect republican government, must necessarily consider the inhabitants in the highest stages of refinement, possessing the moral and social virtues in the highest perfection. The farther any nation recedes from this standard, the nearer it approaches to slavery. For a proof of this, we need take but a slight survey of the European nations. There we trace the various stages from slavery to freedom. From these observations we deduce the following political truth—that the more enlightened any people are, the more perfect and equitable is their government.

Whoever can trace the connexion between cause and effect, will be convinced, that if the people are corrupt, the government will of necessity be so. If the spark of emulation is extinct, if their sentiments are servile, they are the fit subjects of an absolute monarch. In old and established nations, we may invariably determine the form of government from the temper and manners of the people; and with the same degree of certainty we trace the genius of the people in their constitution and government. But in new formed governments this rule becomes defective—witness the present situation of Massachusetts. Was our character reflected from our constitutions, we might cease to deplore the frailties of human nature—instead of being stigmatized for our want of private as well as public virtue, we should be esteemed as a race of superiour rank, sent to polish and refine the world.

That our constitution is not suited to the disposition of the people, has of late been sufficiently proved. Before half the determined period of its existence is accomplished, we find it attacked by the lawless hands of faction.

Perhaps there is not a people on earth better instructed than the inhabitants of this state: But our stage of refinement is the most unfavourable to political tranquillity—did we know *more,* we might govern ourselves—did we know *less,* we should be governed by others. If America would flourish as a republick, she need only attend to the education of her youth. Learning is the *paladium* of her rights—as this flourishes her greatness will encrease.

It is true, those who are busied in the humbler walks of life need not the aid of literature to become proficients in their occupations: But in a republican government, learning ought to be universally diffused. Here every citizen has an equal right of election to the chief offices of state. I would not insinuate that every man ought to aspire at the chief magistracy—this would throw a community into great confusion. But every one, whether in office or not, ought to become acquainted with the principles of civil liberty, the constitution of his country, and the rights of mankind in general. Where learning prevails in a community, liberality of sentiment, and zeal for the publick good, are the grand characteristicks of the people.

The members of a republick are mutual guards upon each other's conduct: Should a few, from ambitious motives, endeavour to subvert the constitution, or aggrandize themselves at the publick expense, the community at large would take the alarm, and with united efforts frustrate their designs. While learning expands the heart, and is the sure basis of a republican government, ignorance by an opposite tendency, is the only foundation of a monarchical. Let us for a moment examine the state of those nations where monarchy presides; there we find the common people but little superiour to the untutored herd. It is the interest of this kind of government to keep them in total ignorance of their natural rights, to cramp their minds, and bend them to servitude.

France is pointed out as the residence of despotism: There ignorance pervades the populace, who, never having enjoyed the genial rays of liberty, endure its extinction with slavish insensibility. From their infancy they are so accustomed to dependence, that the heavenly spark, which nature has implanted into the breast of every man, fires them not to noble actions, but soon becomes extinct.

If we would maintain our dear bought rights inviolate, let us diffuse the spirit of literature: Then will self interest, the governing principle of a savage heart, expand and be transferred into patriotism: Then will each member of the community consider himself as belonging to one common family, whose happiness he will ever be zealous to promote. But, should we neglect the education of our children— should we transmit to them our rights and possessions, without teaching them their value, they would soon become a prey to internal usurpers, or invite the attention of some foreign power.

> "Fair Education bends the pliant mind;
> She bids it traverse regions unconfin'd.
> From this pure source our choicest blessings flow:
> This makes us angels while we're here below."

[48]

BOSTONIANS

Serious Questions Proposed to All Friends to
The Rights of Mankind, With Suitable
Answers

BOSTON, 1787

T he catechism-like question and answer format of this piece
efficiently conveys the American Whig view of a proper constitution. Published as an implied rebuke to the proposed Federal
Constitution in the November 19, 1787 *Boston Gazette,* the piece does
effectively summarize some of the basic changes in view on constitutions
between 1776, when the radical Whigs were in ascendance,
and 1787, when the Federalists were on the rise.

――――――

As much has been said in favour of the proposed New Constitution,—and as
little is allowed to be said against it,—I now send you, for the information
and consideration *of your readers, the ideas the people had of a Constitution*
in the year 1776, contained in a number of serious questions and answers,
published in the Pennsylvania Evening Post, at a time when the whole people
were contending with a powerful nation for the security of their Liberties and
a free Constitution, with a determined resolution to transmit the same to
succeeding generations. And as we are now about to establish the free
Constitution which they then fought and bled for, shall we not be allowed to
examine it?—shall we not be allowed to give our sentiments upon it, with
the same manly freedom with which they were inspired while the bayonet was
held at their breasts? WE WILL.

BOSTONIANS

BOSTONIANS

Serious QUESTIONS proposed to all friends to the rights of mankind, with suitable ANSWERS.

Q. What is government?

A. Certain powers vested by society in public persons for the security, peace and happiness of its members.

Q. What ought a society to do to secure a good government?

A. Any thing. The happiness of man, as an inhabitant of this world, depends entirely upon it.

Q. When ought a new government to be established?

A. When the old becomes impracticable, or dangerous to the rights of the people.

Q. Who ought to form a new constitution of government?

A. The people.

Q. From whom ought public persons to derive their authority to govern?

A. From the people whom they are to govern.

Q. What ought to be the object of government?

A. The welfare of the governed.

Q. How is such a government to be obtained?

A. By forming a constitution which regards men more than things, by framing it in such a manner that the interest of the governours and governed shall ever be the same; and by delegating the powers of government so that the people may always have it in their power to resume them, when abused, without tumult or confusion, and to deliver them to persons more worthy of trust.

Q. Should the officers of the old constitution be entrusted with the power of making a new one when it becomes necessary?

A. No. Bodies of men have the same selfish attachments as individuals, and they will be claiming powers and prerogatives inconsistent with the liberties of the people. Aristocracies will by this means be established, and we shall exchange a bad constitution for a worse, or the tyranny of one for the tyranny of many.

Q. Who ought to have such a trust conferred upon them, as it is the highest and most important which men can delegate?

A. First, Men of the greatest wisdom and integrity, who have as much, if not more, natural than acquired sense and understanding. Secondly, Men who can be under no temptations to frame political distinctions in favour of any class or set of men. Thirdly, Men who the moment the constitution is framed, must descend into the common paths of life, and have as great a chance to feel every defect in the constitution as any man. And lastly, Men who regard not the person of the rich, nor despise the state of the poor, but who prefer justice and equity to all things, and would go any lengths to establish the common rights of mankind on the firmest foundation.

Q. Ought the constitution which a proper number of such persons agree upon to be immediately adopted?

A. No. After agreeing upon a constitution, or form of government, they ought to adjourn for six or nine months, publish the plan, request every man to examine it with the utmost seriousness and attention, make remarks upon it, point out any defects which may appear in it, and offer amendments. Then let the same body of men who framed it, joined by an additional number of new members, meet at the time fixed in their adjournment, canvass the whole again, take the defects pointed out into consideration, and finally agree.—N. B. This frame of government, when agreed upon, should be intituled the SOCIAL COMPACT of the People of ———, &c. and should be unalterable in every point, except by a delegation of the same kind of that which originally framed it, appointed for that purpose.

Q. What should be done after this compact is finally agreed upon?

A. The same, or another body of men, should be appointed to draw up what I shall call *a charter of delegation,* being a clear and full description of the quantity and degree of power and authority, with which the society, vests the persons instructed with the power of the society, whether civil or military, legislative, executive or judicial.